BIOGRAPHY AND THE QUESTION OF LITERATURE IN FRANCE

Biography and the Question of Literature in France

ANN JEFFERSON

OXFORD

UNIVERSITY PRESS

OXFORD
UNIVERSITY PRESS

Great Clarendon Street, Oxford OX2 6DP

Oxford University Press is a department of the University of Oxford.
It furthers the University's objective of excellence in research, scholarship,
and education by publishing worldwide in

Oxford New York

Auckland Cape Town Dar es Salaam Hong Kong Karachi
Kuala Lumpur Madrid Melbourne Mexico City Nairobi
New Delhi Shanghai Taipei Toronto

With offices in

Argentina Austria Brazil Chile Czech Republic France Greece
Guatemala Hungary Italy Japan Poland Portugal Singapore
South Korea Switzerland Thailand Turkey Ukraine Vietnam

Oxford is a registered trade mark of Oxford University Press
in the UK and in certain other countries

Published in the United States
by Oxford University Press Inc., New York

© Ann Jefferson 2007

The moral rights of the author have been asserted
Database right Oxford University Press (maker)

First published 2007

British Library Cataloguing in Publication Data
Data available

Library of Congress Cataloging in Publication Data
Data available

Typeset by Laserwords Private Limited, Chennai, India
Printed in Great Britain
on acid-free paper by
Biddles Ltd, King's Lynn, Norfolk

ISBN 978–0–19–927084–2

1 3 5 7 9 10 8 6 4 2

for Mike

Acknowledgements

Without the generosity of the Leverhulme Foundation, which granted me a Major Research Fellowship for the three years between 2001 and 2004 during which most of the work for this book was undertaken, the project would never have been anything more than a pipe dream; I wish, therefore, to record my thanks to the Foundation for this unparalleled opportunity for reading, research, and writing. I am also deeply grateful to the Faculty of Modern Languages at the University of Oxford and to New College for allowing me to take up the Fellowship and for providing such congenial circumstances in which to carry it out. The library staff at the Taylor Institution Library in Oxford have contributed in no small measure to those circumstances, and I should also like to record my gratitude to the Bibliothèque nationale de France, where I spent a number of fruitful months.

My bibliography is a record of debts, delights, and indispensable discoveries made possible by three uninterrupted years of leave. What follows in this book takes its starting point from the work of others and could not have been conceived in any other context.

The project is nevertheless and to a considerable degree the fruit of three decades of teaching (and originally studying) the paper known in the Faculty of Modern Languages at Oxford as 'Paper 8, the Modern Period of Literature, 1715–Present'. Had I not lived for so long with the constant demands of this pedagogical requirement it is doubtful that I should have dared to imagine anything quite as ambitious as the history I have chosen to outline in this book. Over and above the bald requirements set out in the Examination Statutes of the University of Oxford, I am deeply indebted to the generations of students with whom I have explored and discussed many of the authors and issues that were the springboard for some of the thoughts I have pursued in the rather particular framework I have chosen to address here.

I am grateful to the organizers and audiences of the various conferences, colloquia, and seminar series that gave me the opportunity to present and discuss some of the material that found its way into this book: 'Conférences du mardi', French Department, Birkbeck College, University of London; Research Seminar, French Department, University of Edinburgh; 'Littérature française actuelle à Oxford', Maison française d'Oxford; Early Modern French Research Seminar, University of Oxford; Society for French Studies; Modern French Research Seminar, University of Cambridge; French Research Seminar, University of Kent; Modern French Research Seminar, University of Oxford; École doctorale Lettres, langues, spectacles, Université de Paris X-Nanterre; Journée d'étude, 'Pierre Michon et l'histoire', Groupe de recherches interdisciplinaires sur l'histoire du littéraire, Université de la Sorbonne Nouvelle, Paris III; French Department Research Seminar, University of Nottingham; 'Fictions biographiques XIXe–XXIe siècles', Université Stendhal, Grenoble 3; 'Life-Forms and the Languages of Life-Writing', Maison française d'Oxford. Particular thanks are due to the British Academy, which funded this last project; its rolling seminar has provided the stimulus that came from exchange and engagement with the work of Dominique Rabaté at the Université Michel de Montaigne, Bordeaux 3, and Michael Sheringham at the University of Oxford.

Earlier versions of parts of Chapters 6, 15, and 17 have appeared in *Mapping Lives: The Uses of Biography*, edited by Peter France and William St Clair (Oxford: Oxford University Press for the British Academy, 2002); *Sartre Studies International*, 11/1-2 (2005); and *Fictions biographiques*, ed. Geneviève Chignard et al. (Collection Cribles; Presses Universitaires de Toulouse Le Mirail, 2006). Permission to reuse this material is gratefully acknowledged.

I have also benefited in incalculable ways from information, conversations, suggestions, questions, encouragement, and comments that have come from many others, not all of whom may be aware of how much they have contributed. In particular I should like to thank Carole Allamand, Malcolm Bowie, Katherine Clarke, David Constantine, Peter France, Alexandre Gefen, Monique Gosselin, Eddie Greenwood, Miranda Griffin, George Holmes, Christina Howells, Tony Hunt, Katherine Ibbett, Andrew Leak, Hermione Lee, Katherine MacDonald, Tony Nuttall, Tony Phelan, Siegbert Prawer, Eric Southworth, Jean-Yves Tadié, Adrianne Tooke, and Dominique Viart.

Terence Cave, Miranda Gill, Mike Holland, Wojciech Jajdelski, Marie-Chantal Killeen, Katherine Lunn-Rockliffe, Wes Williams, and Toril Moi deserve special mention for their willingness to read and comment on drafts of parts of what follows and for proving once again that a book is always part of a dialogue. Wes Williams was a constant source of reminder about the pre-modern dimension of my subject, as well as an exemplary colleague alongside Karen Leeder and Catriona Kelly who with Marie-Chantal Killeen all covered—and without a moment's complaint—for my absence during the three years of the Leverhulme Fellowship. Oliver Davis and Jake Wadham provided invaluable editorial and bibliographical help with tracking down and transcribing English translations. Michael Wood performed a miracle with the manuscript, making it a cleaner, but above all a much clearer piece of writing than it would otherwise have been. My greatest debt is to Mike Holland, for the breadth of his knowledge, his judicious comments, and for his continuing support of all that this book has entailed.

A.J.

Contents

V. INWARDNESS, EXPERIENCE, AND THE TURN TO FICTION

VI. ACTS OF LITERATURE: THE SACRED AND THE WRITER'S LIFE

Note on Translations

ALL translations are my own unless otherwise indicated in the form of a page reference in square brackets to the published English translation of the relevant text as cited in the Bibliography. Any alteration to the published translation is signalled by an asterisk after the page number.

Introduction

'What is literature?' is an infantile [question], but one that a whole lifetime
can be spent evading.

(Jean Paulhan, *Les Fleurs de Tarbes*)

The issue of the relation between literature and biography is one which has
elicited surprisingly decided views from the many people who have chosen to
express them, whether with respect to a particular writer or work, or as a matter
of general theoretical principle. Discussion of this relation, which was sustained
with considerable passion over the course of more than two centuries, has almost
always focused on the extent to which literature might be considered to be
dependent on biography, and especially on the degree to which the appreciation
of a work of literature might be thought to depend on a knowledge of the life of
its author. If passions nowadays tend to run a little less high, it is perhaps as much
as anything because the dependency is perceived to be mutual, with literature
becoming necessary to biography as the basis for its new-found credentials as a
genre in its own right. In what follows I shall not be attempting to reinject fervour
into a debate whose capacity to excite is no doubt on the wane, neither shall I
be seeking to defend any theoretical position on the matter. Instead, I shall start
with the simple historical fact that in French, as in all the other major European
languages, the terms 'literature' and 'biography' share a common birthdate in the
eighteenth century. That these terms, despite the fact that they seem to refer to
phenomena extending much further back in time, turn out to be of such recent
provenance may be a matter of some surprise—as indeed it was to me. But their
relative novelty should serve as a reminder that, whatever arguments might be
mobilized in the debates they give rise to, the terms themselves cannot be treated
as self-evident and should rather be viewed as the product of a particular cultural
history to which they have also powerfully contributed. The basic premise of
the discussion in this book derives, therefore, from the impossibility of taking
these terms for granted. The result is a history much more than a theory or
even a specific critical interpretation, being a history of the two terms and
of the many and various relations between them. More precisely, I shall be
arguing that the historically relative concept of literature has existed largely as a
question to itself about its own definition, and I shall be proposing, further, that

throughout the brief existence of this concept, that question has been repeatedly and regularly fuelled by interventions from the equally time-bound form of writing that is biography. The issue is not one of biography's status *as* literature, nor of its necessity for the existence or intelligibility of a literary text; rather, it is that of the nature of literature itself and of the part that biography might play in exploring and contesting its definition. (The terms of this discussion are going to require a fairly lengthy exposition and I advise readers that they have ahead of them longer than average Introduction where I shall attempt to prepare the ground for what follows in the rest of the book.)

In making biography so central to the idea of literature, I am going against the grain of much of the thinking about literature that dominated the twentieth century where biographical perspectives were repeatedly condemned as inimical to the essential literariness of literature, and where authorial personality and circumstance appeared as an obstacle to what was considered to be most interesting and valuable in literature, namely, the thing that makes it literary. Writers and theorists were equally vehement on this matter. T. S. Eliot observed that literature demands 'a continual extinction of the personality'; Proust condemned the biographical preoccupation with the 'moi social' (social self) as an irrelevance to the 'moi profond', where the true roots of creation lie; Valéry declared that 'biographical facts are nothing'; Sartre claimed that biographies falsified the nature of the writer's creative project; Blanchot defined the work of literature as entailing 'a dissolving of [the writer], his disappearance, his defection and, to put it more brutally, his death', an assertion subsequently echoed in the title of Barthes's famous essay 'The Death of the Author', all of which would seem to make any idea of biography entirely otiose for an understanding of specifically literary issues. In more modestly stated terms, the critic Gérard Genette has described 'l'homme et l'œuvre'—the man and the work, or, as the English prefer, the life and works—as 'the two caryatids' of an outmoded study of literature.[1]

The fascinated preoccupation with the nature of literature that is evident in so much twentieth-century thought seems almost always to preclude biography and biographical reference—if not authorship itself—in face of the question: 'What is literature?' This expunging of any concern with the lives of authors is presented as necessary both for a proper understanding of how literature is produced, and for an appropriate reception of literary texts: reading literature as more or less

---

[1] I am referring here to the following: T. S. Eliot, 'Tradition and the Individual Talent', in *The Sacred Wood* (London: Methuen, 1960), reproduced in Seán Burke (ed.), *Authorship: From Plato to the Postmodern: A Reader* (Edinburgh: Edinburgh University Press, 1995), pp. 73–80 (p. 76); Paul Valéry, *Cahiers* [1929], quoted in Jean Marie Goulemot and Daniel Oster, *Gens de lettres, écrivains et bohèmes: l'imaginaire littéraire, 1630–1900* (Paris: Minerve, 1992), p. 185; Jean-Paul Sartre, *Qu'est-ce que la littérature? Situations II* (Paris: Gallimard, 1947); Maurice Blanchot, *Après-coup, précédé par Le Ressassement éternel* (Paris: Éditions du Minuit, 1983), p. 86; Gérard Genette, 'Stendhal', in id., *Figures II* (Paris: Éditions du Seuil, 1969), pp. 155–93 (p. 156).

disguised biography is not to read it as literature. Some of the most energetic arguments for separating life and work have come not just from critics but frequently from writers themselves and were already being voiced in the nineteenth century. Flaubert was one of the first and most adamant in asserting the need to separate biographical concerns from literary ones. Much of his correspondence with Louise Colet, his mistress and a fellow writer, deals with this issue, and his conviction that art should be kept separate from the personal life is expressed in such remarks as 'I do not believe that the pen has the same instincts as the heart'.[2] The biographer may be interested in the personal life of the artist, but for Flaubert this has nothing to do with his art. More seriously, he clearly thought that Louise Colet's own work was marred by her inability to keep these two instincts apart, and that she put too much of her life into her art, with detrimental results for her work. He concludes this particular letter with the rather portentous statement that 'Art has no truck with the artist!', a claim designed to put paid to the presuppositions of any would-be biographer.

If this remark was intended chiefly as an admonition to a writer who supposedly allowed the personal preoccupations of her heart to override her pen, its minatory force applied as much to the readers of literature as to its practitioners or prospective biographers. So that when Mallarmé, thinking broadly on the same lines as Flaubert, writes to his friend Cazalis, 'I am now impersonal and no longer the Stéphane you once knew',[3] his comment is not advice on how to write, or even primarily a report on his current state of mind, so much as an indication of how his new poetic practice might best be read by the few friends he thought capable of doing so. His poetry is no longer to be understood as the product of personal expression, but of a literarizing force within language itself. Proust adopted a more aggressively anti-biographical stance, and expressed his exasperation with biographical anecdote, which he saw as the basis of Sainte-Beuve's critical 'method', when he asked: 'In what way does the fact of having been Stendhal's friend make one a better judge of him?'[4] In the particular case of Stendhal, Proust goes on to suggest, the critic's acquaintance with the man, and the second-hand information about him that he had sought from some of the novelist's friends and contemporaries actually contributed to a gross misjudgement on Sainte-Beuve's part when he concluded that Stendhal's novels were 'frankly detestable'. In short, says Proust, biography is a profoundly misleading basis for the reading of literature, let alone for the appreciation of its literariness.

[2] Letter of 27 July 1852, in Gustave Flaubert, *Préface à la vie d'écrivain: extraits de la correspondance*, ed. Geneviève Bollème (Paris: Éditions du Seuil, 1963), pp. 83–4.
[3] Stéphane Mallarmé, *Correspondance, 1862–1871*, ed. Henri Mondor (Bibliothèque de la Pléiade; Paris: Gallimard, 1959), p. 242.
[4] Marcel Proust, 'La Méthode de Sainte-Beuve', in id., *Contre Sainte-Beuve*, ed. Pierre Clarac and Yves Sandre (Bibliothèque de la Pléiade; Paris: Gallimard, 1971), pp. 219–32 (p. 222).

BIOGRAPHICAL APPROACHES TO LITERATURE
AND LITERARY APPROACHES TO BIOGRAPHY

Yet, the twentieth century also saw a huge proliferation of biographical writing, and this served to associate literature with biography in a number of different and often very compelling ways: literary biography has become a hugely respected practice, particularly in Britain; much literary criticism has been productively informed by biographical assumptions; and, finally, biography itself has become a mode of literary writing in its own right. It is these factors that are likely to be in the mind of any reader of this book, and, because I am taking a somewhat different tack, it would seem worth making explicit the nature of these various connections, if only to distinguish my own concerns from them. (Anyone wishing to cut to the chase of my own argumentation might wish to skip this section, whose purpose is principally to clear the ground for what is to follow.)

I would suggest that there are four main categories of assumption that inform the relations between lives and literature as they are commonly perceived. The first is contained in the current notion of 'literary biography', and raises the question of the structure and style of biographical practice. Although there are, of course, biographies of many figures other than writers, so-called literary biographies, which recount the lives of writers, seem to have acquired a certain prestige as models of the genre, perhaps because the contact with literary texts through the portrayal of their authors leads biographers to a sharpened awareness of the structural and stylistic features of their own writing. A large number of books—often edited volumes of essays by divers hands who have themselves practised biography—testify to this tendency.[5] The importance of proper attention to the forms of biography is plaintively stated by Thomas Carlyle in an essay dating from 1827, where he writes: 'the truth is, that, rich as we are in Biography, a well-written Life is almost as rare as a well-spent one; and there are certainly many more men whose history deserves to be recorded than persons willing and able to record it.' In another essay, still deploring the poor quality of biographies in his day, he claims that 'in England we have simply one good Biography', Boswell's *Life of Johnson*, suggesting that the well-written biography requires either its author or its subject (or both) to be professionally

---

[5] For discussion of some of these issues see Richard Ellmann, *Literary Biography: An Inaugural Lecture Delivered before the University of Oxford on 4 May 1971* (Oxford: Clarendon Press, 1971); John Batchelor (ed.), *The Art of Literary Biography* (Oxford: Clarendon Press, 1995); Dale Salwak (ed.), *The Literary Biography: Problems and Solutions* (Iowa City: University of Iowa Press; Basingstoke: Macmillan, 1996); Warwick Gould and Thomas F. Staley (eds.), *Writing the Lives of Writers* (Basingstoke: Macmillan/Centre for English Studies, School of Advanced Study, University of London, 1998).

involved with literature.[6] In short, literary biography is often viewed as a kind of paragon of a broader biographical genre.

Within literary biography there can be two approaches to the writer: either the author is seen as having had a life interesting enough to be worth recounting in its own right; or else the life is presented as justifying recall for the light it casts on the work—though the two are, of course, not mutually exclusive. This illuminating character generally presupposes some kind of equivalence between the life and the work, one kind being broadly mimetic (the life is represented in the work), and the other expressive (the life leaves its mark in the work even where it is not directly portrayed). These two forms of equivalence constitute the second and the third of my four categories of assumption about the relations between biography and literature. According to the mimetic relation, the work is seen as depicting the life, albeit transformed and enhanced by the process of composition. Richard Ellmann adduces this principle as the one behind his life of James Joyce when he writes: 'This book enters Joyce's life to reflect his complex incessant joining of event and composition.'[7] This preoccupation with the relation between lived event and compositional shaping is not just that of the biographer; the principles of a certain kind of literary criticism are based on the presumption of just such a possibility, whose ideal, expressed by Gustave Lanson in the preface to his edition of Lamartine's *Méditations poétiques*, would be the discovery for each sentence of 'the fact, the text, or the remark that triggered the thought-processes or the imagination of the author'.[8] The task of the critic here is to track the implied biographical reference in each and every line of the poet's work on the assumption that the key moments of the life are in some way reflected in the writing.

My third category, the expressive equivalence that the biographical perspective discerns in the work, serves to illuminate the author's project, whether understood in terms of a global perspective on the world, or defined in a narrower emotional or philosophical application. While it suspends the question of whether every element in a literary text might have had a real-life counterpart, this approach offers a framework for the text that can be decisive in determining its interpretation as the expression of an outlook whose determinants lie in the circumstances of the writer's life. Broadly speaking, this is the Romantic attitude, which presumed that, as a critic of the period put it, 'a work of art can be original and true, only when it is an intimate part of the man who created it and when it

---

[6] Thomas Carlyle, 'Jean-Paul Richter', in id., *Critical and Miscellaneous Essays*, 3rd edn., 4 vols. (London: Chapman and Hall, 1847), vol. i, pp. 1–24 (p. 1), and 'Biography', ibid., vol. iii, pp. 1–17 (p. 17).

[7] Quoted by Jon Stallworthy, 'A Life for a Life', in Batchelor, *Literary Biography*, pp. 27–42 (p. 37).

[8] Quoted by Antoine Compagnon, 'Histoire de la littérature ou histoire des auteurs?', in Brigitte Louichon and Jérôme Roger (eds.), *L'Auteur entre biographie et mythographie* (Modernités, 18; Bordeaux: Presses Universitaires de Bordeaux, 2002), pp. 29–36 (p. 30).

bears the imprint of his personality'.[9] The work of art is viewed as the repository of the 'secret emotions', the 'tears', and the 'soul' of its creator; it can be seen as a biographical record in its own right of the author's life and character, but it also presupposes the possibility of reconstructing that life as a free-standing biographical narrative in order to cast further light on the author's emotional or metaphysical outlook.

This wider sense of the authorial project is not necessarily as precise as the much-maligned authorial intention,[10] and Borges's fable 'Pierre Menard, Author of the *Quixote*' illustrates how differently the same text—in this instance 'the ninth and the thirty-eighth chapters of the first part of *Don Quixote* and a fragment of chapter twenty-two'—will be read, depending on its authorial attribution and implied biographical origin. Dated at the beginning of the seventeenth century and read as the work of Cervantes, the text is one thing; but taken as the work of Pierre Menard, a French writer from the turn of the twentieth century, its general purport, its argument, and even its style are totally transformed, even though the words on the page remain the same.[11] The change of author, and of historical, geographical, and cultural context produces an entirely different conception of the undertaking that is assumed to inform the work. In short, read as the expression of an authorial attitude, the work must be treated as a quite different entity according to its biographical attribution and ceases to be a single, self-identical object.

The fourth and final category of the commonly recognized forms of relation between literature and biography is that in which a biographical text is read as literature. I shall excluding fictional biography from consideration, for reasons that I shall explain in due course, but there are many non-fictional biographical texts that are read as literature for reasons of style, or for what Gérard Genette calls 'diction'.[12] Unlike the case of the literary biography, these biographical subjects are not predominantly literary figures. In France, Chateaubriand's posthumously published *Vie de Rancé* (1849) is read as part of its author's literary corpus, and many of the texts I shall be discussing are viewed as part of the literary canon: Nerval's *Les Illuminés*, Marcel Schwob's *Vies imaginaires*, and Pierre Michon's *Vies minuscules*, to mention but a few. Indeed, a great deal of contemporary

---

[9] Alexandre de Saint-Chéron, 'Philosophie de l'art: la vie poétique et la vie privée', *L'Artiste*, 4/24 (1832), pp. 269–71. See Part III below for further discussion of this.

[10] As castigated by Wimsatt and Beardsley in their famous essay of 1954, 'The Intentional Fallacy', in W. K. Wimsatt, Jr., and Monroe C. Beardsley, *The Verbal Icon: Studies in the Meaning of Poetry* (Lexington: University of Kentucky Press, 1954).

[11] Jorge Luis Borges, 'Pierre Menard, Author of the *Quixote*', in id., *Labyrinths: Selected Stories and Other Writings*, ed. Donald A. Yates and James E. Irby (Harmondsworth: Penguin, 1970), pp. 62–71.

[12] Gérard Genette, *Fiction et diction* (Paris: Éditions du Seuil, 1991). I shall discuss this in more detail below.

writing in France and elsewhere takes the form of the so-called *récit de vie*, biographical or autobiographical, such as W. G. Sebald's mix of personal memoir and biographical portrait or the teasing semi-fictional biographical texts of Javier Marías. Without including the many straightforwardly fictional versions of such 'lives',[13] one could mention amongst such biographical writing in France: Gérard Macé's *Le Dernier des Égyptiens* (1988), which retells the life of Champollion who first deciphered the hieroglyphs on the Rosetta stone, or François Bon's *C'était toute une vie* (1995), in which the author tries to reconstruct the life of a young woman he knew from one of his writing workshops who died of a drug overdose. In France the field of autobiography is a significant component of contemporary life-writing, since many autobiographical texts in the twentieth century, beginning with Gide's *Si le grain ne meurt*, have acquired full literary status in the modern canon. Further examples might include Michel Leiris's *L'Âge d'homme* and *La Règle du jeu*, or Sartre's *Les Mots* (all of which I shall be discussing); and, from the last three decades of the century, one could also cite Nathalie Sarraute's *Enfance* (1983), Marguerite Duras's *L'Amant* (1984), and Claude Simon's *Le Jardin des Plantes* (1997). It is a feature of many such contemporary *récits de vie* to blur generic boundaries, blending biography with autobiography, or fiction with reportage and the essay, and much of the value of biography in contemporary French literature can be seen in the context of this productive and sometimes provocative mixing of generic modes. In the case of writers such as Roger Laporte or Jacques Roubaud (whom I shall also be considering), life-writing has taken the form of texts that dispense entirely with existing forms of generic classification.

The critical response to literature posed by such generic confusions has hitherto been confined largely to the issue of fiction and the undecidable effects created by its presence in a text. Meanwhile, ideas about literature viewed in terms other than those of fiction have remained relatively unquestioned. If 'Literature' is the label used to designate the work of a particular biographical subject (in the Literary biography), or the object of a critical interpretation based on the material events and emotional states of the writer's life (my mimetic and expressive functions of biography), the question of what defines its Literariness does not normally arise as an object of critical enquiry. At best this happens obliquely in the implied assumption that the chief purpose of any search for biographical origins is to identify the creative qualities of the writer. It does this either by showing up the inventiveness of the poet's treatment of his material, or else by distinguishing his novelty in relation to the poetry of his time: 'grasping more precisely where the true novelty of the poetry lies'.[14] Discrepancies between the source (lived or read) and the text are viewed as a sign of originality and invention, implicitly locating the literary in this surplus

---

[13] Throughout this book I shall use the terms 'life' and 'lives' in inverted commas to refer to written versions of a life, as distinct from the lived counterpart.

[14] Gustave Lanson, 'Avertissement', in Alphonse de Lamartine, *Méditations poétiques*, ed. Gustave Lanson (1915; repr. Geneva: Slatkine, 2000), pp. i–iv (p. iii).

for which mimesis provides the benchmark. However, an explicit concern with the literary as an object is rare in all the biographical approaches I have outlined, but this does not mean that biography might not have a capacity to concern itself with the contested issue of the very definition of literature, and, as I have already indicated, it is precisely with this possibility that my own study is concerned.

LITERATURE AS A QUESTION

The question 'What is Literature?' is the *raison d'être* of much twentieth-century literary theory, and is, of course, the title of an important theoretical essay by Sartre. Moreover, it is one of the stranger features of literature in its modern sense that it should entail such a question. So much so that the very question could be said to be the major defining characteristic not just of literary theory but of literature itself: literature has come to be seen as a form of writing that poses a question about the nature of the literariness it supposedly exemplifies. As the field of what is called literature has shrunk and ceased to refer to writing in general (the *litteratura* of the classical world inherited by the Renaissance), this restriction has had the effect of turning the concept of 'literature' into a question rather than simply refining its application.

In order to pursue this line of thought, it would be helpful to have a sense of the way the term 'literature' emerged and developed in the eighteenth century, since that emergence could be seen as a response to a newly perceived need for such a concept. In French, as in English, the word is used in the early modern period predominantly to refer to a knowledge of books rather than to their production. English has the expression 'a man of literature' and French 'un homme de littérature', both languages assuming that it is men rather than women who 'possess' literature; and this usage remained current until well into the nineteenth century. The term more commonly employed to refer to written works was 'lettres', or, more specifically, 'bonnes lettres' and 'belles lettres', a specification that distinguished writing with no immediate utilitarian intent from its more strictly practical applications. It did, however, include writings that we would now call scientific, since the justification for the appellation 'belles' was that such writing instructed as well as pleased, the two qualities being mutually implicated in the classical view of art as both 'dulce et utile'. When 'littérature' began to be used as a synonym for 'belles lettres' in the seventeenth century, it retained this broader sense. During the course of the eighteenth century the word acquired new applications, initially to refer to the emergent profession of literature through which writers were beginning to earn their living, and latterly also to the body of writing produced by a single nation—'la littérature française', for example.

Only very gradually did 'littérature' enter linguistic use in its more restricted, modern sense, exemplified by its presence in the title of a number of works discussing the literary canon, such as the revised edition of Batteux's *Cours de belles-lettres*, to which he added the subtitle '*Principes de la littérature*' (1763), Marmontel's *Eléments de littérature* (1787), La Harpe's *Le Lycée ou Cours de littérature* (1799–1805), and Madame de Staël's *De la littérature* (1800), all of which I shall be discussing in Part I below. The pedagogical function of these texts, especially marked in those that precede Madame de Staël's, nevertheless keeps the word within the ambit of its pre-modern sense of a knowledge of letters.

There are no doubt many explanations that one could adduce for the redesignation of the term 'literature' to refer to works of an aesthetic character (and, as we shall see in Chapter 1, it should be noted that the word 'aesthetic' itself dates only from 1735) but I would suggest that there are four principal ones to be retained in the context of the argument of this book. The first is a developing interest in the aesthetic quality of all the arts, not just literature. Though the term 'aesthetic' is coined with reference to literature in Baumgarten's *Reflections on Poetry*, it achieved its full consecration in the work of Kant, who affirmed its autonomous character in his conception of art in general as exemplifying 'purposiveness without purpose'.[15] Secondly, the increasing specificity of literature was part of a more widespread tendency within the broader domain of letters: the same phenomenon can be observed in the establishment of philosophy and the various natural sciences instituting them as distinct practices and disciplines.[16] Thirdly, and no doubt concomitantly, the professionalization of writers and the identification of a separate class of such people led to the creation of a separate sphere and its recognition under the term 'literature'.[17] Finally, the development of forms of writing, and most particularly of the novel, that did not figure within an inherited model of classical poetics—as represented, for example, by Boileau's *Art poétique*—required a new category or categories within which they might be placed. Moreover, written in prose, rather than the poetry that classical poetics presupposes, these texts prompted the introduction of a term other than 'poetry' to encompass varieties of writing not acknowledged or anticipated by Boileau.

The result of these developments was not just the refinement and redeployment of the term 'literature', but a profound shift in the fundamental conception of literature and in the nature of the language used to talk about literary texts: it did not lead to a revised poetics, but to a completely different framework and a different set of concepts for thinking about the writing that we now call literature.

---

[15] Immanuel Kant, *The Critique of Judgement* [1790], trans. Werner S. Pluhar (Indianapolis: Hackett, 1987), esp. pp. 73–5.

[16] On the developing distinctiveness of philosophy see Dinah Ribard, *Raconter, vivre, penser: histoire(s) de philosophes, 1650–1766* (Paris: Vrin-EHESS, 2003).

[17] On this see Alain Viala, *Naissance de l'écrivain: sociologie de la littérature à l'âge classique* (Paris: Éditions de Minuit, 1985).

The genre-based approach (that of poetics) and the literary perspective became increasingly independent of each other,[18] and this resulted in an overlapping but often uneasy coexistence of poetics, literary history, and, I would contend, a notion of 'literariness' whose essence is much less easily defined than, say, the conventions of tragedy. Literary history and poetics are to be found in slightly awkward combination in various late eighteenth-century undertakings which will be explored in more detail in Chapters 1 and 2 in the context of their reference to one or other of these frameworks (poetics, literary history, and a prototypical literarity), and in some cases to more than one at a time. At this stage, however, I wish simply to indicate that the history of literature is *inter alia* a history of the concepts and discourses through which, and by means of which, literature is thought. But it is time, after this brief historical excursus, to return to my argument about the self-contesting character of the literary.

From the moment that the idea of literature began to be defined in terms of a constitutive literarity, its ensuing history may be read as a sequence of sometimes conflicting definitions of its nature, all having polemical force, and each designed to oust a preceding one. In proposing that literature be seen primarily as a question, I do not wish to imply that it is inherently unknowable or at best an object of some quasi-mystical contemplation, but that the question 'What is literature?' makes of literature a site of repeated contestations from within. So that when Flaubert opposes the instincts of the pen to the instincts of the heart, he is implicitly contesting the underlying principle of Romanticism, according to which, in the words of the poet André Chénier in his *Élégies*, 'Art only makes verses, the heart alone is a poet'. The potential violence of such contestation is made explicit in the extended metaphor used some seventy years later by the Russian Formalist critic Roman Jakobson to justify his programme for a 'science of literature' based on the apparently neutral presupposition that 'poetry [as the most 'literary' form of literature] is language in its aesthetic function'.[19] Neutral it may be, but the attempt to define the literarity of literature as specifically as possible immediately gives rise to a vigorous denunciation of existing approaches to literary texts which Jakobson characterizes as an indiscriminate round-up on the part of the forces of law and order:

The subject of literary science is not literature, but literariness, i.e. that which makes a given work a literary work. Up till now, however, historians of literature have mostly behaved like the police who when they want to arrest someone take in everyone and everything found in the apartment and even chance passers-by. Historians of literature have in

---

[18] As Marielle Macé says, 'Généricité et littérarité se sont [. . .] progressivement découplées'; see her introduction to ead. (ed.), *Le Genre littéraire* (Paris: Flammarion, 2004), p. 39.

[19] 'La Nouvelle Poésie russe' [1921], in Roman Jakobson, *Questions de poétique*, ed. Tzvetan Todorov (Paris: Éditions du Seuil, 1973), pp. 11–24 (p. 15); Eng. trans. of this statement in Ann Shukman and L. M. O'Toole, 'A Contextual Glossary of Formalist Terminology', in L. M. O'Toole and Ann Shukman (eds. and trans.), *Russian Poetics in Translation*, vol. iv: *Formalist Theory* (Oxford: Holdan Books, 1977), pp. 13–48 (p. 22).

the same way felt the need to take in everything—everyday life, psychology, politics, philosophy. Instead of a science of literature we have fetched up with a conglomeration of cottage industries.[20]

The language of Jakobson's extended metaphor is decidedly peculiar, especially in the context of a projected 'science', but its own polemical thrust and the violence it denounces exemplify perfectly the way in which the specificity of literature is not a given, and remains (as it always does) to be established. The contestatory mode and the emphatic exclusion of extraneous factors, including the private life and the psychology associated with biography, both appear to be necessary to Jakobson's project.

The discussion of literature in what follows will, in consequence, take as its general working principle the fact that literature's specificity is inseparable from the question 'What is literature?', and that its history is therefore characterized by a series of differentiations and often polemical contestations. These are directed in part at the neighbouring disciplines with which literature was once subsumed in the broader category of letters—philosophy, theology, history, and the natural sciences—and with which it continues to be periodically associated—psychology, language, and biography—but they are directed more particularly at itself. The question 'What is literature?' may raise the issue of external limits: literature versus philosophy, for example, but it also raises the issue of internal boundaries: definitions of literature are very often definitions that oppose previous versions of what is called literature.[21] This question and the resulting proclivity to auto-contestation are major factors in the evolution of literature, and they significantly determine its history. Or, put the other way round, the history of literature is in substantial measure the history of the question which literature has repeatedly addressed to itself, and of the internal contentions to which that question gives rise.

This does not, of course, preclude the existence of other versions of literary history, most notably the history of its institutions, rather than of its problematic essence. The history of a self-questioning literary absolute[22] is not necessarily the same as its institutional history, whether one conceives of that history as

---

[20] Jakobson, 'La Nouvelle Poésie russe'; Eng. trans. of this passage in Shukman and O'Toole, 'Contextual Glossary', p. 17. For further discussion of Jakobson's rhetoric of contestation in the context of his theory of literature see my 'Literature, Dominance and Violence in Formalist Aesthetics', in Peter Collier and Helga Geyer-Ryan (eds.), *Literary Theory Today* (Cambridge: Polity Press, 1990), pp. 125–41.

[21] Derek Attridge makes the question of literature's relation to its outside the basis for an interesting discussion in his book *The Singularity of Literature* (London: Routledge, 2004). His interest in the specificity of literature parallels my own, but the book does not deal with literature's polemic with itself, or with literature's historical mode of existence which forms the core of my own argument.

[22] To use the expression in the title of the book by Philippe Lacoue-Labarthe and Jean-Luc Nancy, *L'Absolu littéraire* (Paris: Éditions du Seuil, 1987), which presents the writings of the German Romantics in terms of this self-questioning conception of literature. I am proposing that this self-questioning is coextensive with the very idea of literature as it emerges over the course of the

consisting of its generic practices and its canon composed of movements, schools, and authors—as recounted in most works claiming to be histories of literature; its professional organizations, such as the emergence of the academies in the seventeenth century, described by Alain Viala in *Naissance de l'écrivain*; its socio-economic conditions, such as those described by Pierre Bourdieu in *Les Règles de l'art*; its transmission by the educational system, outlined by Antoine Compagnon in *La Troisième République des lettres*; or of the signs by which it flags its status as literature—the history sketched by Barthes in *Le Degré zéro de l'écriture*.[23]

It is noticeable, however, that these other forms of literary history are also often couched in terms of contestations, albeit of a more localized kind than those produced by the intrinsic questioning of literature itself. Romanticism was, amongst other things, a revolt against the generic prescriptions of neo-classical poetics, and is exemplified in Hugo's rejection in the *Préface de Cromwell* of the generic categories of tragedy and comedy and their associated diction. Schools and movements are almost always constituted in opposition to a literary status quo, whether it be Théophile Gautier promoting 'l'art pour l'art' against a reigning literary ideology of utilitarianism, or the *nouveau roman* protesting against the outmoded realism of post-war fiction. Similarly, the establishment of the academies was the result of an opposition between the *lettrés* who incarnated an encyclopedic humanist erudition and the *littérateurs* laying claim to a more circumscribed disciplinary domain. The socio-economic conditions of literature in the second part of the nineteenth century were determined by the ambivalent opposition to bourgeois society on the part of writers and other artists. And the teaching of literature in universities was the result both of a rejection of rhetoric as the prime framework for the study of literary texts, and of a more parochial opposition on the part of Gustave Lanson to preceding conceptions of literary history. Indeed, the history of French literature could be written in terms of the many manifestos, pamphlets, and prefaces that take issue with what has gone before and announce a new departure: from Stendhal's *Racine et Shakespeare*, to Rimbaud's 'Lettres du voyant', Proust's posthumously entitled *Contre Sainte-Beuve*, Breton's *Manifeste du surréalisme*, or Robbe-Grillet's *Pour un nouveau roman*. The history of literature is at one level a history of such internecine disputes.

Even those accounts of literature by 'non-practitioners' who take a less partisan approach suggest that in institutional terms literature is a concept that does not quite 'add up', and that there is something constitutively incoherent about it. To cite just two examples, Nathalie Heinich in her sociological analysis of the

---

eighteenth century in France, and that it is to be found elsewhere than in Germany and not just at the turn of the nineteenth century.

[23] Pierre Bourdieu, *Les Règles de l'art: genèse et structure du champ littéraire*, rev. edn. (Paris: Éditions du Seuil, 1998); Antoine Compagnon, *La Troisième République des lettres, de Flaubert à Proust* (Paris: Éditions du Seuil, 1983); and Roland Barthes, *Le Degré zéro de l'écriture; suivi de Nouveaux essais critiques* (Collection Points; Paris: Éditions du Seuil, 1972).

literary field concludes that this field is different from others that the sociologist might examine, in that it is uniquely characterized by its indeterminacy. And, in a somewhat different perspective, Gérard Genette's attempt to define the features of literarity generates an approach that is split between a literature that exists both constitutively and conditionally, as 'fiction' and as 'diction', as imaginative content and as a special use of language.[24] In other words, there seems to be something in literature that is irremediably lacking in internal consistency and thus prone to outright conflict, regardless of whether it is viewed as a field, an essence, or a history.

LITERATURE AGAINST ITSELF

From whichever perspective one views it, literature appears to have a peculiar mode of existence that may be most broadly characterized as being 'against itself', whether this be in the internal inconsistency identified by its commentators, the localized controversies of its institutional history, or the history of its literarity. Such inveterate contradictoriness also entails a multiple form of existence, because, however much literature may be against itself, its self-directed opposition neither erases its previous history, nor makes it impossible to talk about a literature that one can choose to see as going back as far as Homer, even if the attributes of a Homeric poem appeared very different in the context of early Greek culture from those that characterize its reading as literature in the modern sense.[25] In other words, literature has as great a capacity for self-consolidation as for self-questioning. Derrida has described literature as 'an institution which tends to overflow the institution';[26] but it could equally well be described as an overflow that tends to institutionalize itself, if only subsequently to provoke further overflow. Although, at one level, the term literature is inseparable from the question 'What is literature?', this does not make it impossible to talk meaningfully of literature, its history, its modes, and, broadly speaking, its canon. Nevertheless, it is a self-questioning literarity that, perhaps more than anything else, marks out literature in its modern, post-1750 sense from what preceded it. So that while it may be possible to trace the history of 'the idea of literature' from antiquity onwards, as Adrian Marino does in his book *The Biography of 'The Idea of Literature' from Antiquity to the Baroque*, or, for example,

---

[24] See Nathalie Heinich, *Être écrivain: création et identité* (Paris: La Découverte, 2000); and Genette, *Fiction et diction*.

[25] See Florence Dupont, *L'Invention de la littérature: de l'ivresse grecque au livre latin* (Paris: La Découverte, 1994).

[26] '"This Strange Institution Called Literature": An Interview with Jacques Derrida', trans. Geoffrey Bennington and Rachel Bowlby, in Jacques Derrida, *Acts of Literature*, ed. Derek Attridge (London and New York: Routledge, 1992), pp. 33–75 (p. 36).

to identify the specificities of a literary field in the sixteenth century,[27] the absence of any sign of literature being 'against itself' distinguishes its existence in the pre-modern period from the modern sense of the term as it began to take form in the mid-eighteenth century.

Furthermore, the establishment of the term 'literature' in this modern sense seems very quickly—and apparently paradoxically—to generate a series of terminological alternatives, a phenomenon in which one might—less paradoxically—see a partial index of the tendency of literature to proceed by a series of moves against itself. It is with such intentions that Hugo uses the term 'poésie' in the *Préface de Cromwell*, and that Gautier invokes 'art' in his defence of 'l'art pour l'art' against the utilitarian aesthetic that he denounces in his 'Préface' to *Mademoiselle de Maupin*.[28] The phenomenon has been even more marked in the twentieth century, particularly in the domain of theory. The very term 'literarity' or 'literariness', which was coined by the Russian Formalists (*literaturnost'*) and which I have been using freely, is itself an attempt to distinguish a defining essence of literature from an institutionalized version of literary existence supposedly under the jurisdiction of an indiscriminate police (to hark back for a moment to Jakobson's metaphor). In his *Degré zéro de l'écriture* Roland Barthes differentiates between an established 'Littérature' (with a capital 'L') and what he calls 'écriture', or, alternatively, as in his later *Leçon*, 'Texte', terms that produce further variants, as when Derrida writes of 'the limitless field of a generalized *textuality*'.[29] A more radically anti-institutional opposition may be seen in the way that Maurice Blanchot (and subsequently Derrida) sets up the individual work (œuvre) against an overarching literature: 'All that matters is the work, the affirmation which is in the work [. . .]. We must not, therefore, say that every book pertains to literature alone, but rather that each book determines it absolutely.'[30] Incapable, by definition, of being turned into an exemplary precedent, each individual work reinvents literature afresh.

The internal differentiation of literature, attested by this terminological diversity is not, as these examples might lead one to suppose, incrementally rarefied or intrinsically avant-gardist. In so far as Sartre answers the question 'Qu'est-ce que la littérature?', it is to propound a 'littérature engagée' detached

---

[27] See Adrian Marino, *The Biography of 'The Idea of Literature' from Antiquity to the Baroque* (SUNY Series in the Margins of Literature; Albany: State University of New York Press, 1996).

[28] On the use of these terms see José-Luis Diaz, 'L'Autonomisation de la littérature (1760–1860)', in Goulet, *Le Littéraire*, pp. 59–77, esp. pp. 69ff. I shall return to Hugo's *Préface de Cromwell* and Gautier's 'Préface' to *Mademoiselle de Maupin* in Chs. 3 and 4, respectively.

[29] See Barthes, *Le Degré zéro de l'écriture*, and id., *Leçon: leçon inaugurale de la chaire de sémiologie littéraire du Collège de France, prononcée le 7 janvier 1977* (Paris: Éditions du Seuil, 1978), p. 34 and *passim*. See also the interview in Roland Barthes and Maurice Nadeau, *Sur la littérature* (Grenoble: Presses universitaires de Grenoble, 1980), p. 7; and Jacques Derrida, 'La Loi du genre', in id., *Parages* (Paris: Éditions Galilée, 1986), pp. 249–87 (p. 262).

[30] Maurice Blanchot, *Le Livre à venir* (Collection Idées; Paris: Gallimard, 1971), pp. 293–4 [pp. 141–2]. Page numbers in square brackets refer to the published English translation listed in the Bibliography.

from pretensions to literary purism and distinct from literature as poetry with its foregrounding of linguistic signs as objects.[31] Equally, one could cite Jean Paulhan's *Les Fleurs de Tarbes*, which is a powerful critique of the paradoxical recognition of literature as entailing the rejection of rhetorical and poetic institutions. 'Our literary arts are the products of refusal', complains Paulhan,[32] and he describes this equating of literary authenticity with a rejection of literary convention as a form of culturally sanctioned Terror. But, in arguing against a conception of literature based on refusal, and in defence of a return to rhetoric, Paulhan is nonetheless doing so in opposition to an established notion of the literary. In short, it would seem that even when it is not identified with its avant-garde, literature is almost invariably conceived as being in one way or another 'against itself'.

BIOGRAPHY AND LITERARINESS

One effect of this view is that literature is treated as the agent and origin of its own definitions. The 'being' of the question 'What is literature?' is transformed into a 'doing' as literature turns against itself and becomes the agent of its own unstoppable evolution. In this apparently autonomous process the author appears to drop out of the picture. As Yury Tynyanov claimed in one of the more provocative formulations of Russian Formalism, *Yevgeny Onegin* would still have been written even if Pushkin had never existed; by this he meant that the forces of literary development were such that a given work, like *Yevgeny Onegin*, was bound, inevitably, to be produced at a given moment, regardless of any input from the author who provided the means of its material realization. Against this view, I am suggesting that biography—so often taken to be the antithesis of literariness—has regularly and repeatedly had a defining role in the internal contestation through which literature is constituted as an idea. Such a move retrieves from an impersonal literariness some of the agency through which literature is cast as a question. This is not primarily an argument in defence of authorship, which would take a different form and has already been convincingly undertaken.[33] Neither is it intended as an argument in defence of biography as necessary to a proper understanding of literature; this too is a separate concern, although at times, like the defence of the author, the issue will surface in my own discussion. Nor, finally, am I arguing that biography deserves to be considered as a form of literature, although some of the texts I shall be discussing are conventionally

[31] All this will be discussed more fully in Ch. 15 below.

[32] Jean Paulhan, *Les Fleurs de Tarbes ou la Terreur dans les lettres* (Paris: Gallimard, 1941), p. 29.

[33] Notably by Seán Burke, for example, in his *The Death and Return of the Author: Criticism and Subjectivity in Barthes, Foucault and Derrida*, 2nd edn. (Edinburgh: Edinburgh University Press, 1998).

read as 'literature'. Rather, I am proposing that biographical writings have—at times, though certainly not always and not inevitably—played a demonstrable part in the self-contestation by which literature has come to be defined since its emergence in the mid-eighteenth century. In a word, this book is not only the history of a question ('What is literature?'), but also the history of a relation that informs this question, namely the relation between literature and biography.

There is, admittedly, a certain spirit of contradiction at work in this project which has been fuelled as much as anything by the question: what if 'it ain't necessarily so'? What if, when we consider the issue of literariness, it might not be the case that 'art has no truck with the artist', or that 'biographical facts are nothing'? It would take a lot to hang an entire argument on sheer defiance, and, as it happens, there are a number of substantive factors that can be marshalled to provide a starting point for this line of attack. The first of these—and we shall see many cases discussed in this book—is that it very frequently turns out that a condemnation of biography (such as the ones I cited at the beginning of this Introduction) is a condemnation of a particular version or application of biography. Authors who appear to be 'against' biography prove on closer scrutiny to have recourse to other conceptions of the practice, which they invoke precisely in order to engage with questions of literariness. This in itself should serve as a renewed reminder that biography is not a single and self-identical phenomenon, as the relative novelty of the word should suggest, and that it has its own history in which it has appeared in a variety of different forms and functions. Unlike the history of 'literature', however, the development of biography is characterized less by contestation than by a variety born of different cultural needs and conventions. In other words, despite or because of the diversity of its manifestations, biography is a more adaptable and more accommodating entity than that of the literature with which it has recurrently been bound up.

Secondly, one of the most fundamental ways in which literature and biography are connected and mutually implicated is in the use of authorship as a marker of literariness itself. The association of authorship with a written text is one of the conditions that make it possible to read that text as literature at all; and, for one reason or another, biography seems to follow as a consequence of such authorial signatures. This is how Ernst Kris and Otto Kurz describe the phenomenon in their book, published in 1934, about the lives of artists from Antiquity onwards: 'the perception of art as art, as an independent area of creative achievement—a perception caricatured in the extreme as "art for art's sake"—declares itself in the articulation of the growing wish to attach the name of a master to his work.'[34] The function of biographies was to endorse the magisterial status of the artist as creative origin of the work of art, and these narratives tended to consist of

---

[34] Ernst Kris and Otto Kurz, *Legend, Myth and Magic in the Image of the Artist: A Historical Experiment* [1934], trans. Alastair Laing, rev. Lottie M. Newman (New Haven and London: Yale University Press, 1979), p. 4.

recurrent biographical topoi designed to illustrate the special character of the artist. The 'artist anecdote', as Kris and Kurz call it,[35] appears in the lives of many different figures and serves to establish the artist's creative credentials. Although their study is concerned chiefly with visual artists (painters, sculptors, and architects), and although the parallels between painters and writers have not always been absolutely in step historically speaking, the principle Kris and Kurz adduce applies equally to writers. Mary Lefkowitz has demonstrated the fictional nature of most of the events described in the 'lives' of the Greek poets,[36] but the evidence she provides could more plausibly be read as the index of a culturally sanctioned form of literary accreditation than as a repeated falsification.

More recently Michel Foucault has argued, in answer to the question 'What is an author?' (another question, almost as far-reaching as the question about literature), that since 'the seventeenth or eighteenth century' (a dating one could nevertheless query) the presence of a named author in a text has served as a major means of marking a text as literary:

> literary discourses came to be accepted only when endowed with the author function. We now ask of each poetic or fictional text: From where does it come, who wrote it, when, under what circumstances, or beginning with what design? The meaning ascribed to it and the status or value accorded it depend on the manner in which we answer these questions.[37]

Foucault argues further that a biographical dimension is presupposed by the attribution of authorship to writing, in that it allows a number of different texts to be gathered together under a single signature and into a single corpus in which variation, and even inconsistency, may be explained as an effect of the author's evolution or maturation. These accounts (Foucault's and that of Kris and Kurz) put forward rather different explanations for the relation between literature and authorship with its attendant biography: the special character of the events in an artist's life serving to confirm the special character of art (Kris and Kurz); biographical sequence validating the single signature to a body of work (Foucault). But in both cases we have an argument for the inseparability—in Western culture at least—of the aesthetic quality of the work of art from an authorial origin that invites biographical representation.

A third element of support for the association of biography with literature, and which follows in part from the second, concerns the way in which, at least since the seventeenth century, authorial biography has been seen as a necessary form not merely of recognition, but of legitimation, of the literary text. The emergence of the category 'literature' in conjunction with that of the author had as its counterpart the emergence of a life-narrative as a 'historical by-product of new conceptions

---

[35] Ibid., p. 11.

[36] See Mary R. Lefkowitz, *The Lives of the Greek Poets* (London: Duckworth, 1981).

[37] Michel Foucault, 'Qu'est-ce qu'un auteur?' [1969], in id., *Dits et écrits*, ed. Daniel Defert, François Ewald, and Jacques Legrange, 4 vols. (Paris: Gallimard, 1994), vol. i, pp. 789–821 (p. 800) [p. 109].

of poetic authority', which 'circulates as a necessary pendant to the poetic œuvre'. These are the terms in which Kevin Pask describes the phenomenon as it occurred in England during the early modern period; and his study seeks to account for the way in which, between the time of Shakespeare, when such life-narratives were largely irrelevant to literary reception, and Johnson's *Lives of the Poets* (first published 1779–81), they became an indispensable requirement for poetic prestige.[38] The factors on which this prestige was dependent evolved over the course of time, and produced different kinds of biographical image for writers from one century to the next. As far as France is concerned, this process of legitimation also gave rise to a huge variety of forms of life-writing, and the century beginning in the 1670s is marked by a proliferation of academic *éloges*, *anas*, prefaces, dictionary entries, and memoirs (these will be discussed more fully in Chapter 1 below).

It is this sudden expansion in forms of life-writing that led, indirectly, to the introduction of the term *biographie*/biography. The word *biographe* is attested almost thirty years before the appearance of its derivative *biographie*, and is defined in the *Dictionnaire de Trévoux* of 1721 as follows: 'Author who writes lives, either of Saints, or of others.'[39] The entry further notes that 'M. l'Abbé Chastelain employed this word to avoid using a periphrasis too often, but it is not in common usage'. (Châtelain's *Martyrologe* was published in 1709.) The Supplement to the 1752 edition of the same dictionary observes that the word has acquired much wider currency since the earlier definition, but there is still no record of 'biographie'.[40] The earliest entry I have found for 'biographie' dates from 1750, when it is included in a dictionary of rare words, *Manuel lexique, ou Dictionnaire portatif des mots françois dont la signification n'est pas familière à tout le monde*, edited by Abbé Prévost, where the entry reads: 'Composite Greek word, meaning History of the life of an individual, just as *Biographer* means the Historian who writes it.'[41] Such life-stories were by no means confined to writers; and what is significant about these biographies in the literary context is not their challenge to the notion of the literary, but their role in defining and legitimating

---

[38] Kevin Pask, *The Emergence of the English Author: Scripting the Life of the Poet in Early Modern England* (Cambridge: Cambridge University Press, 1996), pp. 3, 1. As far as I know, there exists no equivalent study of this phenomenon in France, but the principles of Pask's analysis would apply with equal force to French literature in the same period.

[39] *Dictionnaire universel françois et latin* [*Dictionnaire de Trévoux*], rev. edn., 5 vols. (Paris and Trevoux: 1721).

[40] The *Trésor de la langue française* reports that the word 'biographie' supposedly appears in the 1721 edition of the *Dictionnaire de Trévoux*, but in fact this dictionary records only 'biographe'. See Centre de recherche pour un trésor de la langue française, *Trésor de la langue française: dictionnaire de la langue du XIXe et du XXe siècle (1789–1960)*, ed. Paul Imbs, iv (Paris: Éditions du CNRS | Klincksieck, 1975).

[41] 'Mot grec composé, qui signifie l'Histoire de la vie des particuliers, comme *Biographe* signifie l'Historien qui l'écrit': Abbé Prévost, *Manuel lexique, ou Dictionnaire portatif des mots françois dont la signification n'est pas familière à tout le monde* (Paris: Didot, 1750) (Prévost's italics). Joanne Mosley, however, records an early use of the word in the title *La Biographie, et Prosopographie des roys de France*, dating from 1583: see ead., 'A New Dating of "biographie": An Early Example', *French Studies Bulletin*, 37 (1990–1), pp. 3–5. The Greek word is indeed briefly attested in late antiquity.

the writer. Nonetheless, whether legitimation or contestation, it is the function of such texts that needs to be considered as much as any purely formal aspect, and it is to this question that I now turn.

THE PRAGMATICS OF BIOGRAPHY

The entire history of 'lives', a term that long predates that of biography,[42] is one in which function has appeared as their overriding feature: briefly put, 'lives', in both their classical and their Christian guise, were designed to teach their readers how to live. Their purpose is edification, as the *Dictionnaire de Trévoux* makes clear in the comment figuring in the 1752 definition of 'biographe' (biographer): '*Nothing*, however, is more praiseworthy in a pious *Biographer* than interesting the Reader in edifying facts' (italics in original). The subjects of 'lives' are held up as examples from which the reader is intended to profit, whether through direct imitation of moral or spiritual qualities, or by means of reflection on errors and vices. The principle of exemplarity in these writings means that they are to be understood primarily in terms of their effects, whether secular or sacred. During the Middle Ages the most widespread form of life-writing was the saint's life. Jacobus de Voragine's *Legenda aurea*, dating from about 1260, was a compilation of the lives of the saints, in which the saints were depicted, first, as modelling their own lives on that of Christ, and, secondly, as exemplary figures whose qualities should in turn inspire imitation in the life of the reader. Saints' lives were regularly used as sources for medieval *exempla* whose explicit function was edification: 'those brief narratives presented as being true and aimed at persuading an audience by means of a salutary lesson'.[43] The life of a saint was regarded as a means to spiritual salvation, and to read or listen to such narratives was above all an act of spiritual piety. The rediscovery of classical literature in the Renaissance renewed this tradition of exemplarity, particularly through the 'lives' of Plutarch and Suetonius. Example was perceived to be more efficacious than precept as a basis for action and in the formation of virtue for the Renaissance reader 'to "practise those great souls of the best ages" [as Montaigne expressed it] was to define the self in relation to ideal images of the past'.[44] Plutarch had a special place in this use of writing as a source of moral example, since his

---

[42] On these two terms see Marc Fumaroli, 'Des "Vies" à la biographie: le crépuscule du Parnasse', *Diogène*, 139 (1987), pp. 31–52.

[43] See Marie-Anne Polo de Beaulieu, 'L'Anecdote biographique dans les exempla médiévaux', in *Problèmes et méthodes de la biographie: actes du colloque Sorbonne, 3–4 mai 1985* (Sources: travaux historiques, 3–4; Paris: Publications de la Sorbonne/Histoire au présent, 1985), pp. 13–22 (p. 13). For a fuller discussion of this and other features of saints' lives see Ch. 17 below.

[44] Timothy Hampton, *Writing from History: The Rhetoric of Exemplarity in Renaissance Literature* (Ithaca, NY, and London: Cornell University Press, 1990), p. 3, and *passim*. I shall return to the issue of exemplarity in Ch. 1 below.

Parallel Lives are explicitly presented as having this purpose, as we shall see in Chapter 1. Historically speaking, then, the representation of lives has never been a disinterested affair, but a practice in which the depiction of a self or a subject has been inseparable from the formation of the self of their subject-reader. In a word, the history of the biographical form reveals it to be endowed with a deeply ingrained pragmatic character.

The moral pragmatics of biographical writing has, it is true, been in gradual decline since the end of the eighteenth century, and in his history of biography Daniel Madelénat writes of the consequent 'literarization' of the genre.[45] However, I would argue that it retains its fundamentally performative dimension and not least in its relation to literature. We have already seen that the pragmatic element of biography gives it a significant role in the emergence of the field of 'literature' itself, both in the construction of the literary character of a written text, and in its strategic legitimation of the author as its necessary origin. Similarly, the interventions of biography in the debates around the question of literature are possible only because of these performative qualities. (I use the terms 'performative' and 'pragmatic' in the sense that speech-act theorists ascribe to them in order to refer to the capacity of language to perform as well as simply to describe an action.[46]) Exemplarity continues to inform biography, if only as the reason for selecting a given biographical subject or in the relation between narrator and protagonist, which is implicitly one of admiration or celebration.

To this I would add a further feature of biography that contributes to its pragmatic capacity, and that is its liminality. Biography is traditionally a liminal genre: it is, in the broadest sense, a textual coda to a lived existence; and, as I have just said, it has also operated traditionally as a device preparing its readers for improvement in their own lives. Within the more limited domain of biography in the context of literature, the 'life' frequently takes the form of a preface to the collected works of an author; or else it serves as a supplement to support the reading and interpretation of the literary text. In the literary context, biography exists primarily in relation to the form of writing that is literature. It may well be that this relational position, on the edge, is one of the factors, along with the pragmatic function of exemplarity, that give biography the capacity to intervene in the manner I am ascribing to it. In so far as it is external, a biography is grounded in an authority which is not that of the text; and in so far as it is

---

[45] Daniel Madelénat, *La Biographie* (Paris: Presses universitaires de France, 1984), p. 35. This book is one of the first attempts to propose a historical, geographical, and generic survey of the practice of biography, and I am indebted to Madelénat's mapping of the terrain.

[46] See J. L. Austin, *How to Do Things with Words* (William James Lectures), 2nd edn., ed. J. O. Urmson and Marina Sbisà (Oxford and New York: Oxford University Press, 1975), and Mary Louise Pratt, *Toward a Speech Act Theory of Literary Discourse* (Bloomington, Indiana: Indiana University Press, 1977).

internal, it could be said to have a stake in the literary character of the text it accompanies.[47]

There is something similarly protean about the term 'biography' itself when applied to literature. It refers predominantly, of course, to a free-standing narrative account of an author's life. But the notion of 'biography' also functions for readers of literature as a working hypothesis whereby the life is assumed to be inscribed in the work without necessarily existing as a text in its own right. The term designates at one and the same time a generically distinct form of writing that exists independently of, if in relation to, the literary text, and also a dimension of the literary text itself that gestures outwards to some referential origin in the lived, but not necessarily written, life of its author. In sum, biography is at once a generically distinct form of writing and an enabling construct in the mind of readers.

It retains this ambivalent posture—inside *and* outside the field of literature, explicitly free-standing *and* implicitly inscribed—throughout the period under consideration in this book, between the mid-eighteenth century, when the terms 'literature' and 'biography' began to acquire currency, and the present. It was during this time too that the notion of overt exemplarity was replaced by that of lived experience, which has become the prime validating principle of the genre in a way that serves to perpetuate its performative character. Rémy de Gourmont acknowledges 'the shivers which disturb us in the face of figures who once lived'.[48] Regardless of any moral or spiritual lesson, real 'lives' continue to function as a kind of testimony, producing in their readers a response that might best be described as awe. Despite the existence of many fictional biographies,[49] the performative character of biography and its capacity to intervene either in the lives of its readers or within the field of literature would seem to depend to a significant degree on its status as the record of the life of someone who actually lived (and died), and of which the 'frisson' mentioned by Rémy de Gourmont is a symptom. Fictional biography appears, consequently, as no more than an imitation of biography, its procedures and its principles, and, however faithfully they comply with the formal conventions of the genre, such fictional versions of biography nevertheless fail—necessarily—to satisfy biography's central presumption of veracity and strip it of the pragmatic qualities associated with biography proper.

[47] For a similar discussion of the position of autobiography in relation to the other literary texts within a single authorial corpus, see my 'Autobiography as Intertext: Barthes, Sarraute, Robbe-Grillet', in Michael Worton and Judith Still (eds.), *Intertextuality: Theories and Practice* (Manchester: Manchester University Press, 1990), pp. 108–29.

[48] Rémy de Gourmont, 'Marcel Schwob', in id., *Le Livre des masques: portraits symbolistes, gloses et documents sur les écrivains d'hier et d'aujourd'hui*, 3rd edn., 2 vols. (Paris: Mercure de France, 1896–8), vol. ii, pp. 151–61 (p. 153).

[49] For a history and survey of this form see Alexandre Gefen, 'Vies imaginaires: le récit biographique comme genre littéraire aux XIX*e* et XX*e* siècles', doctoral thesis (Université de Paris IV-Sorbonne, 2003).

Veracity is not, of course, a recent consideration, even if ideas change about what it is and where it might be found. It applies as much to the lives of the saints in Voragine's *Golden Legend* or to the rulers of Suetonius's *Lives of the Caesars* and the Greek and Roman subjects of Plutarch's *Parallel Lives* as it does to the carefully researched biographies of the modern era. The existence of the saints and the Caesars is not in doubt, and the supposedly unadorned nature of the truth offered by biography has regularly been contrasted with the embroidered truths of poetry. And, while biography is not in and of itself enough to serve as proof of an existence (as a photograph conventionally might), where its subjects are authenticated, biography shares with photography the capacity to move its readers to the kind of astonishment or melancholy that Barthes describes in his book on photography, *La Chambre claire*. It is for this reason that, with two exceptions, all the biographical writings discussed in this book portray figures who really lived. The exceptions—Proust's *À la recherche du temps perdu* and Sartre's *La Nausée*—nevertheless treat the biographical subjects who appear within the fictional world of their novels (Bergotte, Vinteuil, and Elstir for Proust; the Marquis de Rollebon and the anonymous songwriter for Sartre) as having, within that world, the status of figures who really lived and so continue each author's non-fictional engagement with the issue of biography. In order to appreciate the pragmatic dimension of biography, it is necessary to restrict the definition of the genre to its referential applications, while accepting, of course, that the criteria for referentiality change over the course of history. If biography is to be understood as 'a singular, strategic and emotionally affecting object' (in Daniel Madelénat's definition), then this requires that its basis be 'strictly and intimately referential'.[50] In discussing the relations between literature and biography I shall not, therefore, be concerned with imaginary versions of biography.

PRINCIPLES, PARAMETERS, AND PROCEDURES

The approach that I am outlining in this book will presuppose that the terms 'biography' and 'literature' are understood broadly as I have set them out in this Introduction: literature as an inherently self-contesting entity, and biography a constitutively performative form of writing. It is this performative quality that enables biography to function as an intervention: the story of a life is always in a sense a demonstration of something. As I have already suggested, that demonstration may, on occasion, concern the nature of literature and so contribute to literature's mode of existence as a question to itself. This view of literature as a self-questioning entity presents literature as formally self-consistent by virtue of this self-contestation yet also as intrinsically susceptible to

---

[50] Madelénat, *La Biographie*, p. 11.

divergence from itself in a perpetual historical development, instigated amongst others by literature's encounters with biography. In this sense, while the two terms, literature and biography, are harnessed to each other in the broad history I am recounting, their respective positions within that history are not entirely symmetrical: biography being neither a self-consistent nor a self-questioning practice but functionally relational and pragmatic, more adaptively responsive to history than literature but without literature's self-contesting propulsion.

Over and above the view of literature as inherently self-questioning, I should make it clear that while it matters that the biographical texts considered should narrate the lives of people who really lived, the literary status of the written biography is largely irrelevant to my concerns: the question of literature here will not primarily be a question about the literary character of any given biographical text. Neither is there any need for the biographical subject to be a writer. Although several of the cases I shall discuss are generally regarded as being part of the literary canon, and although I shall be looking at a number of texts in which the biographical subject is indeed a writer, these factors might best be considered as contributing to a focus on the issue of literariness, without, however, being necessary to that project. In fact the majority of the texts I have chosen to explore could be said to exist on the margins of literature, just 'inside' or just 'outside', if one accepts for a moment that such lines can be drawn. These, then are the broad principles that inform the discussion that follows.

As regards parameters, I have taken the appearance of the terms 'literature' (in its modern sense) and 'biography' as my starting point, on the grounds, first, that the very emergence of 'literature' is bound up with a strategic use of biography, and secondly, that the notion of literature is open to contestation from the outset. My discussion is largely confined to French literature, although the argument could, I imagine, be applied to other literatures. This restriction is a way of containing what might otherwise be an unmanageably large or arbitrary corpus, and in any case French literature is the field I know best. Moreover, I suspect that the driving question 'What is literature?' is one that has been posed more urgently and crucially in France than elsewhere.[51] Finally, if I am to demonstrate that the self-contesting notion of literarity necessarily confers on literature a historical mode of existence, then it makes most sense to see that history unfold in a series of claims and counterclaims within a single national series. On the few occasions where I have momentarily strayed from French territory, this has been because the author in question holds an 'honorary' place within French literature (as the Russian Formalists or Rilke do), or because, as

---

[51] David Carroll certainly suggests that French theory is haunted by this question and that it 'might even constitute the principal characteristic that makes it "French" and distinguishes it from other national theoretical tendencies': id., 'The Post-Literary Condition: Sartre, Camus and the Question(s) of Literature', in Elizabeth Beaumont Bissell (ed.), *The Question of Literature: The Place of the Literary in Contemporary Theory* (Manchester: Manchester University Press, 2002), pp. 66–90 (pp. 71–2).

in the case of Baumgarten, the issues lie at the origin of the questions I am addressing.

The history I am presenting gets under way with Rousseau and continues to the present. The eighteenth century serves as a kind of prelude to the main body of the discussion, which is divided more or less equally between the nineteenth and the twentieth centuries. Broadly speaking, the nineteenth century appears as a century of biography, both in the wider culture and as the basis for thinking about literature. In the twentieth century, by contrast, the dominant issue seems to have been the literary itself, with biography functioning as a means of positive or negative engagement with that question. I have also allowed myself to ignore what has become a cardinal rule of modern criticism by largely disregarding the distinction between biography and autobiography. This might shock some readers, but I do so on the grounds, first, that the notion of 'lives' itself ignored that distinction, as does much contemporary 'life-writing'; secondly, because the pragmatic features of biographical writing that I have identified apply equally to autobiography; and thirdly, because the question of literature seems to me to shift—for reasons that I shall explore when the time comes—from a broadly biographical frame in the nineteenth century to a significantly autobiographical one in the twentieth. Within the overarching project and within each of the two (and a bit) centuries, I have tried to identify a series of different 'moments', corresponding to the parts into which the chapters are grouped, so as to highlight the huge variety of configurations that exist between biography and literature at different times during the two centuries. The relation between literature and biography takes many forms and cannot be reduced to a single presupposition or formula. To a certain extent, the writers and texts I shall be discussing were self-selecting, although the perspective I am adopting might have a wider application. The result is a version of almost three hundred years of French literary history, in which the relation between the idea of literature and the role of biography (understood in the broadest terms) constitutes the central thread.

It was, however, something of a surprise to find that, when I had reached the end of this literary history, there was only one woman writer who figured in the story—Madame de Staël. This circumstance calls for some reflection, and one could advance a number of explanations. The first is that the relative invisibility of women writers in the history of French literature made the prime concern for women that of their right of entry into the field, relegating any question about its definition to secondary importance. (Simone de Beauvoir is eloquent on this matter in *Le Deuxième Sexe*.) Secondly, in so far as women writers have posed a challenge to literature, it has tended to be by means of the canon, and through their choice of allegedly marginal forms: one could cite George Sand's use of the idealist novel, or Marguerite Duras's blurring of generic boundaries between fiction and autobiography. And finally, it could also be that women writers have simply not been sufficiently empowered by the dominant culture to take on the contestatory role which is the one that drives the particular history I am narrating, even supposing that women were drawn to the element of machismo and heroics celebrated, for instance, by Thomas Carlyle, who includes Dante and Shakespeare—but no woman—amongst his poet heroes, and Johnson, Rousseau, and Burns as sole examples of the hero as *man* of letters.[52]

This book, then, is a literary history whose impetus comes from the question 'What is literature?', and which is traced through the relations between literature and biography. It can be read as a single, continuous narrative, with each of the historical snapshots and each of the authors discussed constituting its principal moments. At the same time, I should like to think that the question and the relation open up an approach that leads to fresh insights into the texts and authors I shall be discussing. In that sense the book may also be treated as a collection of essays, each of which could be read on its own as a contribution to the critical discussion of the writer or text in question. Ultimately, however, it is the historical frame that has determined the whole and provided the basis for an exploration of the role of biography in the construction of the idea of literature in France. And for this reason it is with the prehistory of the two key terms that I shall begin in Chapter 1.

[52] Thomas Carlyle, *On Heroes, Hero-Worship and the Heroic in History* (London: Chapman and Hall, 1840).

PART I

'LIVES' AND THE INVENTION OF 'LITERATURE'

Literature; the word is one of those vague terms that are so common in all languages [. . .] like all general terms, whose precise definition is not determined in any language except by the objects to which they are applied.

(Voltaire, *Dictionnaire philosophique*)

THE French word 'biographie' (biography) is a neologism that emerges over the course of the first half of the eighteenth century in the wake of its cognate 'biographe' (biographer), an English equivalent having been used somewhat earlier by Dryden in 1683. The etymological derivatives 'autobiographie' and 'autobiography' do not enter their respective languages until the nineteenth century (1809 for English and 1838 for French). And although the words 'littérature' and 'literature' are attested from the fifteenth century onwards, they do not begin to acquire the restricted sense of 'usage esthétique du langage écrit', as the *Trésor de la langue française* defines it, at least until the 1750s in France. The *Oxford English Dictionary*, in fact, gives no dates prior to the nineteenth century for the use of the term literature in the sense of 'writing which has claim to consideration on the ground of beauty of form or emotional effect'.[1] However, if the terms 'literature' and 'biography' share a common birthdate in the mid-eighteenth century, they also collide significantly for the first time very soon afterwards when Rousseau tells the story of his own life in the *Confessions*. Consequently, it is this text that marks the historical point at which my argument begins in earnest. Nevertheless, this collision would not have been possible without what went before, and I shall therefore prepare the ground by briefly mapping out the parallel paths that literature and biography took prior to this point, and outline the pre-history of their relations. As I have already indicated, the distinctiveness of the literary field was achieved partly as a result of authorial biography, and in what follows I shall be looking at the particular forms that these biographies took in the two centuries that preceded the invention of the term biography itself. I shall then go on to trace the increasingly urgent desire amongst literary commentators, from the end of the seventeenth century onwards, to identify a literary or poetic essence that transcends the variety of different forms and genres described by the poeticians. If Rousseau uses the story of his life in order to stage a contestatory encounter with the idea of literature,

---

[1] See *Shorter Oxford English Dictionary* 3rd rev. edn., ed. C.T. Onions et al. (Oxford: Clarendon Press, 1968). On the history of the term 'literature' see Robert Escarpit, 'La Définition du terme "Littérature": projet d'article pour un dictionnaire international des termes littéraires', in Robert Escarpit and Charles Bouazis (eds.), *Le Littéraire et le social* (Paris: Flammarion, 1970), pp. 259–72; Claude Cristin, *Aux origines de l'histoire littéraire* (Grenoble: Presses universitaires de Grenoble, 1973); René Wellek, *Discriminations: Further Concepts of Criticism* (New Haven: Yale University Press, 1970); Raymond Williams, *Keywords: A Vocabulary of Culture and Society* (London: Fontana, 1976); and Chantal Liatoutzos and Claudine Poulouin, 'La Lecture des "vieux romans" selon Chapelain, fondatrice de l'espace littéraire moderne?', in Alain Goulet (ed.), *Le Littéraire, qu'est-ce que c'est?* (Caen: Presses universitaires de Caen, 2002), pp. 29–43.

the introduction of a developmental conception of literature towards the end of the eighteenth century made it possible to see literature as having a life of its own, analogous to the life of the individual portrayed in biography. The three chapters that follow will therefore set out these different tactics as they emerged in the mutually defining relations between biography and literature before their full-scale manifestations in the nineteenth century.

1

Literature and the Use of 'Lives': A Prehistory

'LIVES'

Until the latter part of the eighteenth century the field of what is now called literature continued to be largely dominated by the conceptual apparatus associated
with the various established and consecrated genres. Before Rousseau's *Confessions*
'literature' remains too embryonic a notion to invite contestation. Nevertheless,
it is in this earlier period of French literature that written 'lives' exemplify most
explicitly the pragmatic quality that gives such writing the potential capacity
to engage subsequently in contestation and redefinition. Renaissance (secular)
culture was concerned with exemplarity in ways that extended well beyond the
particular instances of 'lives', since history and poetry were also seen as sources
of moral example. But whatever the source, the effects of a given example
were always to be measured in the life of the individual reader. As Timothy
Hampton argues, selfhood in the French Renaissance was constructed largely
through exemplarity: 'In setting forth the deeds of the exemplar the Renaissance
text provides the reader with an image of the self, a model of an ideal soul
or personality which mediates between ideals of public virtue and the reader's
self-understanding.'[1] 'Lives' were nevertheless a principal fund of moral example,
and Plutarch, being the chronicler of public virtue in the lives of great men, was
a recurrent point of reference in discussions of exemplarity.

In his introduction to the life of Aemilius, Plutarch claims that his original
motive in writing them was to be useful to others. But, he says, he had
subsequently discovered that he himself was deriving his own moral benefit from
the exercise, 'by looking into these histories, as if I looked into a glass, to frame
and fashion my life to the mould & pattern of these vertuous noble men'.[2] In

---

[1] Hampton, *Writing from History*, p. 19. For further discussion of exemplarity see also John D.
Lyons, *Exemplum: The Rhetoric of Example in Early Modern France and Italy* (Princeton: Princeton
University Press, 1989); and Karlheinz Stierle, 'L'Histoire comme exemple, l'exemple comme
histoire: contribution à la pragmatique et à la poétique des textes narratifs', *Poétique*, 10 (1972),
pp. 176–98.

[2] Plutarque, 'Vie de Paul-Émile', in id., *Les Vies des hommes illustres*, trans. Jacques Amyot
[1559], ed. Gérard Walter, 2 vols. (1951; Bibliothèque de la Pléiade; Paris: Gallimard, 1985), vol. i,
pp. 566–7 [p. 245].

the 'Life of Pericles' he explains how, by a process of spontaneous imitation, the portrayal of virtue necessarily transmits its moral qualities to readers:

For vertue is of this power, that she allureth a mans mind presently to use her; that wisely considereth of her, and maketh him very desirous in his heart to follow her: and doth not frame his manners that beholdeth her by any imitation, but by the only understanding and knowledge of virtuous deeds, which suddenly bringeth unto him a resolute desire to do the like.[3]

Both Cruserius, the Latin translator of Plutarch (whose translation appeared in 1561), and Jacques Amyot, the French translator (whose first edition was published in 1559), mention the principle of 'doing the like' as a distinguishing feature of the lived example. This is how Amyot puts it in the preface to his translation: 'because [examples] do not onely declare what is to be done, but also worke a desire to do it, as well in respect of a certaine naturall inclination which all men have to follow examples, as also for the beautie of vertue, which is of such power, that wheresoever she is seene, she maketh her selfe to be loved and liked.'[4] This tendency towards imitation, which the example of a life inspires, is enhanced by two further characteristics of the 'life', on which Amyot also comments. The first is the particularity of the individual circumstances portrayed: 'examples are of more force to move and instruct, then are the arguments and proofes of reason, or their precise precepts; because examples be the very formes of our deedes, and accompanied with all circumstances.' And the second derives from the fact that the events that the 'life' recounts are true: 'it doth things with greater weight and gravitie, then the inventions and devices of the Poets: because it helpeth not it selfe with any other thing then with the plaine truth.' This primacy of 'plaine truth' distinguishes biographical example from poetry, which, because it aims above all to please, 'doth commonly enrich things by commending them above the starres and their deserving, because the chief intent thereof is to delight'. The moral efficacy of these 'lives' can be attributed to their basis in fact and to the uniqueness of each individual whose life is narrated. For these reasons biographical narratives are implicitly opposed to the inventions of poetry, and the force of their example depends here on the active exclusion of literature.

Writing about Amyot's translation, Montaigne testifies to the moral effects of Plutarch's *Lives* and describes them in one of his essays as 'our breviary'. As we shall see, Rousseau attributes his republican spirit, his love of freedom, and his impatience with all forms of servitude, to the effects of reading Plutarch as

---

[3] Plutarque, 'Vie de Paul-Émile', vol. i, p. 334 [p. 158].

[4] Jacques Amyot, 'Dedication and Preface to Plutarch's *Lives*, 1559', in Bernard Weinberg (ed.), *Critical Prefaces of the French Renaissance* (Evanston, Ill.: Northwestern University Press, 1950), pp. 161–78 (p. 167, and for the quotations that follow). On the Latin translation see Katherine M. MacDonald, 'The Presence of Plutarch in the Preface to the Reader of Cruserius' Latin Translation of the *Lives* (1561)', *Bibliothèque d'humanisme et renaissance*, 62 (2000), pp. 129–34.

a child.[5] By the early nineteenth century, no doubt under the influence of the novel, which had its own claims to moral efficacy, it becomes possible to conceive of such effects as being the positive result of literary talent. Michelet's short thesis on Plutarch's *Lives* (written in 1819) singled out the author's ability to convey moral lessons through his narrative skill: 'Most of the great moral lessons that he gives us are also contained in the simple narrative of events; explanations would be of very little use to anyone who could not grasp the philosophical instruction in the facts which are so well presented.'[6] This comment endows Plutarch's moral lessons with something of the character of Richardson's novels as praised by Diderot in his 'Éloge de Richardson' (not that Michelet himself mentions the connection): readers are supposedly inspired to virtue by the pathos of his depiction of private life and the details of human character. For Michelet morality is the result produced when literary talent is brought to bear on readers' sensibility, and is not the automatic consequence of the representation of virtue; but, either way, biographical portraiture is still understood as being primarily a pragmatic affair.

The same is true for a certain autobiographical tradition that begins, most notably, with Augustine's *Confessions*. The story of Augustine's life is not conceived simply as a narrative of the self, but as an illustration and glorification of God's work. The 'confession' has the triple sense of a confession of sins (*confessio peccati*), a confession of faith (*confession fidei*), and a confession of praise (*confessio laudis*). As Augustine says in Book V:

A man who makes confession to Thee does not thereby give Thee any information as to what is happening within him. The closed heart does not close out Thy eye, nor the heart's hardness resist Thy hand. For Thou dost open it at Thy pleasure whether for mercy or for justice, and there is nothing that can hide itself from Thy heat. But let my soul praise Thee that it may love Thee, and let it tell Thee Thy mercies that it may praise Thee.[7]

The *Confessions*, addressed in part to a God who already knows their content, narrates a sinful past with the avowed purpose of revealing God's mercy and singing his praise. (It is for this reason that the last four books of the *Confessions* abandon past events in order to concentrate on the general issues, such as

[5] 'Nous autres ignorans estions perdus, si ce livre ne nous eust relevez du bourbier: sa mercy, nous osons à cett'heure et parler et escrire; les dames en regentent les maistres d'escole; c'est nostre *breviaire*' ('Ignorant people like us would have been lost if that book had not brought us up out of the mire: thanks to it, we now dare to speak and write—and the ladies teach the dominies; it is our breviary'): Montaigne, 'À demain les affaires', in id., *Les Essais*, ed. Verdun L. Saulnier and Pierre Villey, 3 vols. (Paris: Quadrige/Presses universitaires de France, 1988), vol. ii/4, pp. 363–4 [p. 408]. I shall discuss Rousseau's comment more fully in Ch. 2 below.

[6] Jules Michelet, 'Examen des *Vies des hommes illustres*', in Plutarque, *Vies parallèles*, trans. Robert Flacelière and Émile Chambry, ed. Jean Sirinelli (Bouquins; Paris: Robert Laffont, 2001), vol. i, pp. lxix–lxxxiv (p. lxxiii).

[7] Saint Augustine, *The Confessions of St. Augustine*, trans. F. J. Sheed (1943; Spiritual Masters; London: Sheed & Ward, 1984), p. 63.

memory and time, that preoccupy Augustine in the present.) Moreover, his concerns about the way he writes involve a desire to distinguish between the use of rhetoric for false praise, or fiction, and the 'good' eloquence he observed in Ambrose, for instance. He condemns the pleasure that spectators derive from the false compassion elicited by the representation of suffering in the theatre, and repudiates his former willingness to earn money by teaching the art of rhetoric, which he dismisses, in retrospect, as 'skill in speech to overcome others by' (p. 45). The language of fiction and free-floating eloquence constantly threaten to undermine his spiritual quest, and it is vital for him to distinguish his own enterprise from these quasi-literary components. Augustine's autobiographical narrative requires the exclusion of the literary in order to pursue its overriding purpose, which is the demonstration of divine creation and mercy, whose end result will be felt in the reader's own life. 'Men are a race curious to know of other men's lives, but slothful to correct their own', he acknowledges (p. 167). For Augustine, the decisive factor in his recounting of his own life is that others should be transformed by his confession: 'I, O Lord, confess to You that men may hear, for though I cannot prove to them that my confession is true, yet those will believe me whose ears charity has opened to me' (p. 167). In short, biographical narrative, of which Plutarch and Augustine were prime instances in the culture inherited by the early modern period, placed its value principally on the moral effect produced in the reader. Although a condition of this effect is the exclusion of literature, the subsequent history of lives prior to the invention of the terms 'biographie' and 'littérature' suggests that 'lives' retain this pragmatic efficacity as a means, precisely, of contributing to the creation of a distinctive literary field.

The seventeenth century witnessed both a shift and an expansion in the writing of the 'lives' of figures from many different domains. The two main models inherited from the past—saints and heroes—were both substantially inflected by new approaches. Saints ceased to appear in quite their former guise, and, starting in 1643 with the publication of the first volume of the *Acta sanctorum*, the Bollandists began the huge task of vetting the life of every saint and thoroughly reviewing their documentary sources, with a view to placing saints' lives on a new, historically corroborated footing.[8] At about the same time, the humanist rediscovery of the *vies des hommes illustres* from the ancient world led to the production of modern versions, such as that of Perrault in 1696, *Les Hommes illustres qui ont paru en France pendant ce siecle*.[9] In fact many of these practices had already been established during the Italian Renaissance. Petrarch

---

[8] See René Aigrain, *L'Hagiographie: ses sources, ses méthodes, son histoire* (Paris: Bloud et Gay, 1953), pt. 3, ch. 3.

[9] For a full account of the different forms of life-writing in the early modern period in Europe see Thomas F. Mayer and D. R. Woolf (eds.), *The Rhetorics of Life-Writing in Early Modern Europe: Forms of Biography from Cassandra Fedele to Louis XIV* (Ann Arbor: University of Michigan Press, 1995), which also contains a convenient survey (pp. 12–17).

wrote his own *De viris illustribus*, begun in about 1338, and was himself the subject of one of the earliest literary biographies, *De vita et moribus Francisci Petracchi de Florentia* (1348–9) written by Boccaccio, who followed it up a few years later with a life of Dante.[10] Petrarch's self-laureation was supported by his strategic construction of a 'life' for himself in his 'Letter to Posterity', for which Suetonius's 'Life of Augustus' was an implicit model.[11] Edgar Zilsel suggests in his history of the idea of 'genius' that the superior character of the poet hailed in the Renaissance, and the consequent proliferation of literary biography, were an offshoot of the necessity felt by patrons to acquire *fama*, or the sort of reputation that would justify their status as *viri illustres*: if the poet is to earn his keep by celebrating his patron's *fama*, then that *fama* will be further enhanced if the poet can be seen to have his own exemplary status and claim to his own literary fame, be it in the form of cultural reputation or written biography.[12]

As far as France is concerned, a similar phenomenon of 'lives' of men of letters began to emerge in the course of the sixteenth century. The Plutarchan model of a 'life' was used for the new class of man of letters who acquired professional recognition chiefly on the basis of his moral worth, since, as Katherine MacDonald observes in her discussion of the subject, it was believed that 'only men of good character wrote books'.[13] Not only did this serve to raise the man of letters to the rank of 'king within his own domain',[14] but it also made the 'life' into an integral part of the work: as I mentioned in the Introduction above, many lives were published as prefaces, either to individual works, or to collected works. The first posthumous edition of Ronsard's *Œuvre*, for example, carried a *Vie de Pierre Ronsard* written by its editor, Claude Binet, and this practice continued into the seventeenth century and beyond. Racine's complete works appeared in several editions prefaced by a biographical account written by his son, Louis Racine. And Pascal's *Pensées* were first published in a posthumous edition in 1670 with a biographical preface by his sister Gilberte, who also edited the material; this preface has continued to appear in subsequent re-editions of the text, as if the author's biography were to be regarded as an indispensable component of it.

It was around this time, towards the end of the seventeenth century, that the *homme de lettres* had been replaced by the more professional figure of the *écrivain*, the writer whose existence was beginning to define a distinctively literary field,

---

[10] For a discussion of biographical writing in the Italian Renaissance see Martin McLaughlin, 'Biography and Autobiography in the Italian Renaissance', in Peter France and William St Clair (eds.), *Mapping Lives: The Uses of Biography* (Oxford: Oxford University Press, 2002), pp. 37–65.

[11] See ibid., pp. 59–61.

[12] Edgar Zilsel, *Le Génie: histoire d'une notion, de l'antiquité à la renaissance* [1926], trans. Michel Thévenaz, with a preface by Nathalie Heinich (Paris: Éditions de Minuit, 1993); see esp. pt. 2, ch. 1.

[13] Katherine M. MacDonald, 'Literary Biography in Renaissance France: 1524–1619', D.Phil. thesis (University of Oxford, 2000), p. 9.

[14] Ibid., p. 37.

and whose activities were acquiring the status of a recognized profession. It was also at this point that biographical writing developed a number of new and diverse forms as a means of acknowledging and legitimating this new figure. In addition to the biographical preface there was the academic *éloge*, the *ana*, the dictionary with its biographical and bibliographical entries, and, eventually, the autobiography, although it was commonly known by the term 'memoirs'. This practice was not specifically confined to literary authors: the *éloge* was composed after the death of an academician, and since the *académies* consisted of 'savants' as well as of writers, its legitimating effects extended to domains other than literature (in the narrow, modern sense).[15] Nevertheless, the consecratory value of the *éloge* was sufficiently powerful that after the death of Malherbe in 1628, prior to the constitution of the Académie française (in 1634), his disciple the Marquis de Racan subsequently took it upon himself, as a member of the Académie, to write a 'life' that could serve in place of the *éloge* that Malherbe would have received, had he lived long enough to be elected one of the 'Immortels'. The consecrating effect of these *Mémoires pour la vie M. de Malherbe* (1672), in which Racan presents Malherbe as the founder of French poetry, was ratified by Boileau's *Art poétique* with its celebrated canonizing line: 'Enfin Malherbe vint'.[16]

The same period also saw the development of the so-called *ana*, which were attributed to well-known figures from the newly emerging 'republic of letters'. Although, in fact, this practice was rather more frequently associated with 'savants' than with literary authors, their consecrating effect was similar to that of the *éloge*. The *ana* were a kind of anthology of 'table-talk', collected by a disciple and published posthumously, but under the name of the writer in question. One of the earliest and best-known examples of the genre were the *Menagiana* (1693), being the collected wit and wisdom of Gilles Ménage, scholar and occasional satirist. (One of these utterances contains the first recorded use of the word *biographe*, mentioned in connection with Bayle's projected *Dictionnaire historique et critique*.[17]) The *-ana* suffix, which gave the form its name, testifies to the individual imprint of an authorial cast of mind on his productions, however ephemeral in appearance they might be: the examples of the wit and wisdom of Ménage, for instance, are all implicitly presented as being typical of Ménage, bearing his stamp, as Spoonerisms are typical of William Spooner, one-time Warden of New College, Oxford. In this way, by consolidating the notion of

---

[15] The principal academies in this connection were the Académie française, the Académie des inscriptions et belles-lettres, and the Académie des sciences. On the academic *éloge* see Peter France, 'The French Academic *Éloge*', in France and St Clair, *Mapping Lives*, pp. 83–101.

[16] 'Finally Malherbe appeared.' Racan's life of Malherbe was first published under the title *Mémoire sur la vie de Malherbe* in 1651, but this edition did not survive. See also Marc Fumaroli's account of this episode in 'Des "vies" à la biographie', p. 20.

[17] Quoted and discussed by Jean Sgard in 'Problèmes théoriques de la biographie', in *L'Histoire au dix-huitième siècle: colloque d'Aix-en-Provence 1ᵉʳ, 2 et 3 mai 1975* (Aix-en-Provence: Edisund, 1980), pp. 187–99 (p. 187). This article contains a valuable survey of the forms of biography in the period under discussion.

individual authorship in place of a classical *auctoritas*, the *ana* may be seen to represent a significant moment in the constitution of a modern literary field.[18] One of the last examples of the genre, though not bearing the title *ana*, are the *Propos de table* attributed to that authorial giant Victor Hugo and published in 1885, the year of Hugo's death, by his secretary Richard Lesclide.

A more serious and substantial form of authorial imprint than the *ana* is the collected works, to which the *ana* might be regarded as a sort of appendage. Author and works appear in a mutually confirming relation, further reinforced by the use of the biographical preface, which constitutes their author as a writer and provides a coherent framework for the different individual works. This practice had already existed for the major classical authors throughout the Renaissance, and, as we have already observed, was revived and extended in the latter part of the sixteenth century in France. Racan's life of Malherbe was not only a substitute for an absent *éloge*, but was originally solicited as a preface to an edition of the works projected by Gilles Ménage.[19] Such prefaces were not confined to literary authors, and neither were they necessarily an integral part of the published works: but even as a free-standing publication, Ramsay's *Histoire de la vie de Messr. François de Salignac de la Motte-Fénelon, Archevêque Duc de Cambray* (published in 1723) was complementary to the publication of Fénelon's complete works begun in 1718 under the partial editorship of Ramsay himself. One of the first of such biographical monographs, Adrien Baillet's *La Vie de Monsieur Descartes* (1691), contributed to defining the field of philosophy as a distinct discipline within the larger field of letters.[20] Literary authors also benefited from the practice, which continued into the eighteenth century: Voltaire's complete works, published between 1783 and 1790, were prefaced by a biographical *Vie de Voltaire* by Condorcet, which Voltaire himself anticipated and to which he also contributed indirectly through the offices of his secretary Wagnière.[21]

At the same time, reference works were beginning to appear under the title of 'dictionaries', fostering a growing sense of authorship by providing brief biographical details to accompany bibliographical information about the publications of writers. Bayle's *Dictionnaire historique et critique* (first published in 1697) included figures of all kinds and from all periods. Charles Perrault's *Les hommes illustres qui ont paru en France pendant ce siècle* (1696) included

---

[18] Cf. Antoine Compagnon: 'l'auteur se substitue à l'*auctoritas* comme garant de l'écriture', from *La Seconde Main* [1979], pp. 320 ff.; quoted in Bernard Beugnot, 'Forme et histoire: le statut des *ana*', in id., *La Mémoire du texte: essais de poétique classique* (Paris: H. Champion, 1994), pp. 67–87 (p. 78). Beugnot's article contains an excellent account of the *ana*. For a fuller history and analysis see also Francine Wild, *Naissance du genre des ana 1574–1712* (Paris: Champion, 2001).

[19] Which, however, he subsequently abandoned. See Marie-Françoise Quignard, 'Note sur l'établissment du texte', in Racan, *Vie de Monsieur de Malherbe* [1672], ed. Marie-Françoise Quignard (Paris: Le Promeneur, 1991), pp. 67–8 (p. 67).

[20] For a full discussion of these two texts see Ribard, *Raconter, vivre, penser*, pp. 182–231.

[21] See Jean-Claude Bonnet, *Naissance du Panthéon: essai sur le culte des grands hommes* (Paris: Fayard, 1998), pp. 223–41, 248–51.

writers such as Corneille, La Fontaine, and Racine, as well as bishops, generals, statesmen, mathematicians, sculptors, and so on, each entry being illustrated with a portrait of the biographical subject. In 1727 Jean-Pierre Nicéron published the first volume of his *Mémoires pour servir à l'histoire des hommes illustres dans la république des lettres avec un catalogue raisonné de leurs ouvrages.*[22] The biographical information about writers recorded by Nicéron was intended to provide 'a faithful account of their employment, their actions, and their literary disputes', specifically in so far as these could contribute to a better understanding of the works:

As it is principally knowledge of the Works that I have in view, I shall record only those elements of the life of each Author that reveal him in his capacity as a Man of learning [*Sçavant*], leaving aside all that is foreign to that capacity, excepting nevertheless a number of things which might provide better understanding of his character, and put readers in a better position to make a correct judgement of his Works.[23]

Nicéron's dictionary entries included writers of all kinds, ancient and modern, from Livy to Racine, and Petrarch to Spinoza. Moreover, the principle of bibliographical coverage, in conjunction with supporting biographical evidence, is used as a means of providing coherence for the works as well as a basis for reading, and this is true for all writers, whether literary, philosophical, historical, or other. In short, the writer's life was treated as a necessary adjunct for a proper evaluation of the work, regardless of its discursive nature.

   This integration of the life and the work is taken much further in Rousseau's autobiography, which has a unique status in the eighteenth century, but which inaugurates a form of life-writing whose consequences are very closely bound up with literature (as we shall see in Chapter 2). This is not just because such autobiographical texts have increasingly been read as literature, but because their narratives very often propose a particular vision—if not always the same one—of the relation between the author's life and the production of literature. A major motive behind Rousseau's autobiography was his desire to correct the biographical image that readers had constructed of him on the basis of his writing, and to present a different relation between himself and his work:

Amongst my contemporaries there are few men whose name is better known in Europe and whose person is less known. My books circulated in the towns while their Author wandered only in the forests. I was read by all, criticized by all, spoken of by all, but in my absence; I was as far away from discussion as from men; I knew nothing of what was said. Everyone could picture me as their fancy took them, without fear that the original might appear and refute the image. There was one Rousseau society, and another who lived away from the world and who bore no resemblance to him.[24]

---

[22] (Paris: 1727; repr. Geneva: Slatkine, 1971).   [23] Ibid., vol. i, pp. 7, 9.

[24] Jean-Jacques Rousseau, 'Ébauches des *Confessions*', in id., *Œuvres complètes*, ed. Bernard Gagnebin and Marcel Raymond, vol. i (Bibliothèque de la Pléiade; Paris: Gallimard, 1959), pp. 1148–64 (p. 1151).

Rousseau is insisting that the authorial figure who circulates under the name attached to his books needs to be dismantled so as to reveal the solitary wanderer who, he claims, is their true author. This is a novel form of self-presentation, designed to enable his readers to judge his work in the terms he thought were the ones that mattered: and these were not necessarily the ones that a biographically based *catalogue raisonné*, such as Nicéron's, would have endorsed. Nevertheless, even in asserting the right to choose the terms of its author's recognition, Rousseau's *Confessions* share with the other biographical forms of the late seventeenth century and the first part of the eighteenth century the function of a legitimation of the writer in connection with the circumscription of a distinctive type of writing subsequently identified as literature.

The last of the factors contributing to the association of literature with biography is the rise of what Paul Bénichou has called 'le sacre de l'écrivain' (the consecration of the writer) in his book of that title.[25] Bénichou argues that the increasing secularization of culture and thought led to the creation of a new 'priesthood' in the form of writers, beginning most notably with the *philosophes* of the Enlightenment, who, in turn, became the 'mages et prophètes' of Romanticism.[26] In Bénichou's account the writer is defined first and foremost in terms of a capacity for ideas, rather than with any specific aesthetic practice. But, with the gradual consolidation of a field eventually known as 'literature', and the concomitant decline of genre and poetics as its framework, it is possible to see the consecration of the writer described by Bénichou as a vital counterpart to this process.

In these various ways, then, the growth of literary 'lives' contributed to the establishment of a distinct domain of literature. They did this both through their construction of the category of the writer and through the modes of reading that they promoted. But, for the most part, the phenomena I have described pre-date the emergence of any explicit and overarching idea of literature—as opposed to a genre-based poetics—and it is this issue that will occupy our attention for the remainder of this chapter.

'LITERATURE'

When Voltaire tries to get to grips with the term 'littérature' for the entry written in 1765 as a supplement to his *Dictionnaire philosophique*, it is clear that he is confronted with a proliferating set of definitions. The use of the word, which dates back to the fourteenth century, to refer to a knowledge of writing, rather

---

[25] Paul Bénichou, *Le Sacre de l'écrivain, 1750–1830: essai sur l'avènement d'un pouvoir spirituel laïque dans la France moderne* (Paris: J. Corti, 1973). See also id., *Les Mages romantiques* (Paris: Gallimard, 1988).

[26] Bénichou, *Les Mages romantiques*, p. 25.

than to a written corpus, is evidently still widespread, and was to remain so until well into the nineteenth century. Voltaire defines it as follows: 'Literature [. . .] refers throughout Europe to a knowledge of works of taste, a smattering of history, poetry, eloquence, and criticism.'[27] It is described as a possession: 'One can have literature without being what is called a *man of learning* [*savant*]. Anyone who has read with profit the principal Latin authors in his mother tongue has literature' (p. 591, Voltaire's italics). But the meaning is also shifting from familiarity with a certain corpus of writing to the corpus itself, as Voltaire acknowledges in his definition of the slightly pleonastic (to modern ears, at least) term 'la belle littérature': ' "La belle littérature" designates literature that is devoted to objects endowed with *beauty*, to poetry, eloquence, and to well-written history' (p. 592, Voltaire's emphasis). As I suggested in my Introduction, this potential circumscription of literature as a distinct field is seen more readily in the use of the term that emerged in the late seventeenth century and became widespread in the eighteenth, namely, the professional. Often applied disparagingly, it referred collectively to writers, as when Voltaire (elsewhere) refers to 'la basse littérature' (the lower ranks of literature), a formulation echoed by d'Alembert when he writes, 'All the lower ranks of literature are under the rule of hypocrites'.[28] Finally, although Voltaire does not mention this use in his philosophical dictionary, a different kind of specificity emerges for the term in the course of the eighteenth century, that of nationality. It is associated with the idea of national literary histories, such as 'French literature' or 'English literature', and I shall have more to say about this in Chapter 3. In the meantime, this proliferation of the term 'literature' may be read as a sign of the energies associated with it, expressed in Voltaire's slightly rueful acknowledgement of its semantic diversity quoted in the epigraph to Part I of this study. This diversity may also, paradoxically, be an index of a growing desire for specificity, however varied its manifestations, in which one can discern attempts to identify a qualitative element that sets literary writing apart from other uses of language. It would be convenient to call this quality 'aesthetic', were it not for the fact that, as I have already mentioned, the word 'aesthetic' was coined only in 1735, and thus is itself bound up with the development of the category of literature. But, for the time being, 'aesthetic' will have to do and I shall return to it below.

It would be a mistake to become too fixated on the single term 'literature', since the development of the idea of the 'literary' goes via other words such as

[27] Supplementary entry, 'Littérature', first published in 1819: Voltaire, *Dictionnaire philosophique*, in *Œuvres complètes*, ed. A. J. Q. Beuchot, rev. edn., vol. xix (Paris: Garnier, 1879), pp. 590–2 (p. 591). The epigraph to Part I of the present study appears on p. 590.

[28] In *Mélanges littéraires*, quoted by Escarpit ('La Définition du terme "Littérature"'), p. 260. See also Gerhard Goebel-Schilling, *La Littérature entre l'engagement et le jeu: pour une histoire de la notion de littérature* (Marburg: Hitzeroth, 1988), and the invaluable study by Cristin, *Aux origines de l'histoire littéraire*, esp. pp. 86–109. The comment by d'Alembert is cited in *Dictionnaire alphabétique et analogique de la langue française*, ed. Paul Robert (Paris: Société du nouveau littré, 1963) as an example of this meaning of the word, which it dates from 1680.

'poésie' (poetry) and 'lettres' (letters) and 'belles-lettres', and even 'genius'. In this connection it is interesting to compare Boileau's use of the term 'poetry' with that of 'genius' in his *Art poétique* (1669–74). As far as 'poetry' is concerned, the *Art poétique* treats it as a sort of compendium of verse genres that included everything from tragedy to the epigram, each having its own conventions and characteristics, whether the 'naïveté' of the Gaulish *rondeau*, the role of rhyme in the ballad, or the 'noble simplicity' of the madrigal, which conveys its characteristic 'sweetness', 'tenderness', and 'love'.[29] In other words, 'poetry', according to this view, simply referred to everything that met the existing range of recognized generic requirements. If there is any underlying unity in the various instances of poetic form that Boileau describes, it lies primarily in the skill with which the poet links form with content, thought with expression, and which exemplifes his famous maxim that 'Ce que l'on conçoit bien s'énonce clairement'.[30] It is not poetry itself that possesses a distinctive quality over and above the features of its separate manifestations, so much as the genius of the poet. And this genius, Boileau suggests in his preface, 'consists principally in never presenting to the reader anything but true thoughts and exact expressions'.[31] Although what passes for poetry is, in the first instance, simply a matter of the canon of verse forms, it is important for Boileau to distinguish between genius and mediocrity, between 'the author touched by the divine' and the 'vile writer', the 'vulgar wits and the 'sublime writer'.[32] Genius, the divine and the sublime, which for Boileau are attributes of the poet, are here doing much of the work that the next century will transfer to the domain of 'literature' as a distinct and distinctive category of writing.

Boileau's other major legacy to the eighteenth century was his translation of Longinus's treatise on the sublime, published in the same volume as *L'Art poétique* in 1674, and regarded at the time as the more innovative of the two works.[33] The idea of the 'sublime' operated rather like the idea of genius in the *Art poétique* in that it offered a means of identifying 'that which forms the excellence and the sovereign perfection of discourse'.[34] Longinus had advanced a notion of sublimity, which he also described as 'greatness' or literary excellence, whose characteristic is to transcend specific forms, genres, or techniques, and is 'the echo of a noble mind'.[35] This noble mind is characterized first and

---

[29] Nicolas Boileau Despréaux, *Art poétique*, in id., *Œuvres complètes*, ed. Françoise Escal (Bibliothèque de la Pléiade; Paris: Gallimard, 1966), p. 166.

[30] 'That which is well conceived is expressed clearly', ibid., p. 160.

[31] Boileau, 'Préface', *Œuvres complètes*, pp. 1–6 (p. 1).

[32] *Art poétique*, pp. 160, 182.

[33] On this see Nicholas Cronk, *The Classical Sublime: French Neoclassicism and the Language of Literature* (Charlottesville, Va.: Rookwood Press, 2003).

[34] Quoted by Cronk, ibid., p. 93; my translation.

[35] Longinus, 'On Sublimity', in D. A. Russell and Michael Winterbottom (eds.), *Ancient Literary Criticism: The Principal Texts in New Translations* (Oxford: Clarendon Press, 1972), pp. 460–503 (p. 468).

foremost by 'the power to conceive great thoughts', and secondly by 'strong and inspired emotion'; the writer's skill with figures, diction, and what Longinus calls 'dignified and elevated word arrangement' can follow only from these initial requirements.[36] All this argues very strongly, if only implicitly, for a notion that distinguishes 'beautiful writing' from the run-of-the-mill conception of letters that prevailed at the time. As Nicholas Cronk says in his discussion of the *Traité du sublime*, Boileau follows Longinus and 'invents' *le sublime* as a critical term in an attempt to outline a theory of poetic language.[37] The enthusiasm with which the eighteenth century embraced the sublime could therefore be seen as a further symptom of the growing desire to identify that quality which, eventually, will give rise to the category of the 'literary'.

The preoccupation with genius and the sublime, along with the insistence on the beautiful as the defining feature of a certain kind of writing (*les belles-lettres*) within the broader field of letters, indicates that there was something more at stake in the concept of literature, even before the word had acquired the security of its modern position in the dictionary. The mapping out of an autonomous sphere that we now call literature seems to have been accompanied by the beginnings of a desire to formulate a quality which twentieth-century theorists subsequently called 'literarity'. This crucial, if elusive, essence has also been labelled 'the literary absolute' in connection with the German Romantics, but as I have already indicated the term seems to me to be applicable to all attempts to define literature in more than purely canonical terms.[38]

One of the earliest explicit signs of this desire can be seen in the work of the Abbé Batteux, professor of Greek and Latin at the Collège de France. In 1747 he published the first of several volumes entitled *Cours de belles-lettres*, a revised and enlarged edition of which appeared in 1753 under the title *Principes de littérature*. What is significant here is not so much the use of the term 'littérature' as its association with that of 'principle'. The impetus behind Batteux's project is his wish to identify the general principle that constitutes poetry over and above the variety of its different generic manifestations and the proliferation of rules governing its production. In his case the motive for such an undertaking comes less from any metaphysical preoccupation than from a simple, pedagogical wish to clarify and better organize a confusing mass of poetic rules: 'All the rules are branches that are derived from the same stem. If one went back to its source, one would find a principle that is simple enough to be grasped immediately, and broad enough to include all the smaller rules concerning detail.'[39] His first move, then, is to ask himself an apparently simple question: 'in order to start with a clear idea, I asked myself what Poetry is, and in what it differs from Prose?' (p. iii). He

---

[36] Longinus, 'On Sublimity', p. 467.   [37] Cronk, *Classical Sublime*, p. ii.

[38] See Lacoue-Labarthe and Nancy, *L'Absolu littéraire*.

[39] Charles Batteux, 'Avant-propos', in id., *Cours de belles-lettres, ou, Principes de la litterature*, rev. edn., 4 vols. (Paris: Desaint et Saillant; Durand, 1753), vol. i, p. ii.

initially assumes that the answer will be quickly found because the distinction between the two forms of writing is so easily felt. But when he goes in search of a definition of this palpable difference, he discovers that none of the volumes of poetics that he consults contains such a thing. He is astonished that something he thought he must have overlooked in all the treatises he had read was simply never addressed. The books contain discussions of the origins and purpose of poetry, but nowhere does he discover '[the] definition that I was seeking' (p. iv). In the event, a return to Aristotle provides the basis for an answer which Batteux then finds confirmed, at least by implication, in Horace and Boileau: 'Poetry turned out to be in every regard an imitation, like Painting' (p. vi). This definition of poetry as an imitation of 'la belle nature' endorses the earlier findings in his study of the fine arts, *Les Beaux-arts réduits à un même principe* (1746), which were inspired by the same determination to find a common, underlying principle behind apparent diversity. The importance of Batteux's discussion lies in the sheer fact of asking 'What is Poetry?'; and what is new is that thinking about poetry should begin with a question about its definition. The consequences of this approach are not immediately felt in his own work, since the principle of imitation does little more than provide him with the means for organizing largely familiar material, which he duly does over the course of several volumes.

However, the gradual move towards the notion of the literary as a kind of conceptual absolute does not entail an increasing precision of definition. If Boileau opened his *Art poétique* by acknowledging the difficulty of defining poetic achievement and admitting that the quality of 'un bon ouvrage' is 'un certain je ne sais quoi qu'on peut beaucoup mieux sentir que dire',[40] uncertainty and elusiveness have remained a central feature of all attempts to circumscribe the literary. It is partly because of this that literature comes into being in the form of a question as much as in the form of a claim. The urge to define and distinguish becomes inseparable from contestation and doubt. This is already evident in the earliest use of the term 'aesthetic', which appears in Alexander Gottlieb Baumgarten's treatise *Reflections on Poetry*, published in Latin in 1735. This book is significant not because of its influence, which was initially confined largely to Germany, but because it is one of the earliest sustained attempts to define the poetic as a quality abstracted out from particular forms and figures, and does so in a manner that entails both conceptual precision and implied contestation.

Baumgarten's main concern in this treatise is with what he calls 'sensate discourse', that is to say, with language that speaks to the senses. Such language

---

[40] Boileau, 'Préface', p. 1. See Richard Scholar's discussion of the 'je ne sais quoi' in which he argues that the distinction that Boileau is seeking to establish is primarily a social one, great writing being equated with the social superiority of the 'honnête homme': in id., *The Je-ne-sais-quoi in Early Modern Europe: Encounters with a Certain Something* (Oxford: Oxford University Press, 2005). This does not, however, preclude the possibility of Boileau's successors having shifted the sphere of its application from the social to the literary.

arouses the affects and creates sense impressions through the use of image or the representation of the marvellous; it also exploits the auditory effects of words. Sensate discourse, says Baumgarten, deals with 'things perceived' rather than 'things known', and it belongs therefore not to logic but to the 'science of perception', or what he calls 'aesthetic'.[41] Thus the aesthetic emerges as a concept through its opposition to other kinds of discourse, and specifically the discourse of 'things known'. The term refers here to the general domain of the sensate, as distinct from the intelligible, and it is not proposed with its modern emphasis which makes it a near synonym for the 'beautiful'. Baumgarten's reflections on poetry define it as a 'perfect sensate discourse' whose perfection correlates only with the degree to which it 'awaken[s] sensate representations'.[42] This leads him to create the term 'poetic' to designate the quality of the sensate; and although he refers throughout the treatise to Horace's *Ars poetica* and cites numerous examples from it, like Batteux's *Principes de littérature*, which also takes its examples from Horace, the intention seems to be to shift poetics away from rhetoric and its catalogues of figures in order to establish a general category of the 'poetic' that transcends individual rhetorical features by making poetry synonymous with the quality of the sensate.

In this, Baumgarten's notion of the 'poetic' seems much closer to the 'sublime' or 'genius' in its free-floating essence than to the collection of individual forms and genres that Horace, Boileau, and Batteux list and comment upon. But it differs importantly from those concepts whose opposites in the 'bassesse' and 'le médiocre' serve simply to establish a hierarchy of values: genius is better than the mere talent of the mediocre poet; the sublime is at the other end of the spectrum from the base. For while sensate discourse can be evaluated in terms of degree—poetry is more sensate than other forms of sensate discourse—the 'aesthetic', or science of sensation, is defined in active opposition to logic and the science of the intelligible, the poet in contrast to the philosopher. Baumgarten's concept of the aesthetic presupposes a boundary that marks off from each other two qualitatively different forms of discourse, while simultaneously insisting on the indefinable nature of the aesthetic. The sensate—and poetry as its most perfect incarnation—deals with what we do not know, with what cannot be articulated in intelligible forms. It remains the domain of the 'je ne sais quoi', and yet demands demarcation.

This need for demarcation is further invoked by Baumgarten when he asserts the importance of distinguishing between ordinary language and the language of poetry. For he concludes his brief discussion (it is only forty pages long) by

---

[41] Alexander Gottlieb Baumgarten, *Reflections on Poetry: Alexander Gottlieb Baumgarten's Meditationes philosophicae de nonnullis ad poema pertinentibus*, trans. Karl Aschenbrenner and William B. Holther (Berkeley: University of California Press, 1954), p. 78.

[42] Ibid., p. 39.

asserting that it is the urgent task of philosophers to identify boundaries as a means of arriving at a definition of these concepts:

The philosophers should be busy in general in drawing boundary lines and especially in defining accurate limits between poetry and ordinary eloquence. The difference is, to be sure, only a matter of degree; but in the relegation of things to one side or the other it requires, we think, no less capable a geometer than did the frontiers of the Phrygians and Mysians. (p. 79)

To define the poetic requires carving out a kind of absolute within the continuum that goes from eloquence to poetry. And the reference to the disputed border between the Phrygians and the Mysians also implies a kind of mutual hostility between the domain of the perceptible, which is that of the poetic, and the discursive domain of the intelligible, which is that of philosophy. There are, in other words, the beginnings of the idea of a contestation of established orders of discourse in this demand for the recognition of the distinctiveness of the world of the sensate, even while the sensate itself is characterized by its opacity. Equally, Baumgarten's concept of sensate discourse has the potential to open up a path towards new ways of understanding the relation between writing and the lived life. Although Baumgarten himself does not anticipate any such thing, it becomes possible to envisage some form of connection between the writer's own sensate experience and the literature he produces, and this in turn creates the possibility of a new kind of relation between literature and the life. It is my contention here that this possibility is realized in Rousseau's *Confessions*, written between 1764 and 1770, some thirty years after the publication of Baumgarten's treatise on poetry as sensate discourse, and this book will be the subject of the next chapter.

2

Rousseau's Life-Story and the Experience of Literature

make literature the site of original experience.

(Maurice Blanchot, *Le Livre à venir*)

There are no grounds for suggesting that Baumgarten's treatise had any direct impact on the emergence of the literary in France, but his argument is uncannily prescient of a text in which critics have seen the first appearance of literature in the modern sense of the word, namely, Rousseau's *Confessions*.[1] Put another way, Rousseau's autobiography could be seen to enact Baumgarten's arguments in the very terms—those of the sensate—that Baumgarten's own philosophical mode of exposition inevitably contradicts and certainly could not directly inspire. It is extremely doubtful that Rousseau ever heard of his German contemporary, born in Berlin in 1714. He never visited Germany, and in any case he claims to have had a lifelong difficulty with Latin, the language in which Baumgarten's *Reflections* were written, being, he says, incapable of learning anything that entailed the arts of memory. Indeed, the reasons why Rousseau is unlikely to have been drawn to Baumgarten's book take us to the heart of the question of the literary in his work. For his writing sets itself up in opposition to literature understood both as the social and professional community of writers, and as the sum total of rules and conventions associated with works designated under that heading. He regards his deficiency in Latin as having disqualified him from the world of literature: his attempts to overcome his ignorance of the language with the help of the Port-Royal method merely left him feeling sick, and his inability to speak or write Latin was a shortcoming that, he says, 'has often caused me embarrassment when I have found myself, I do not know how, involved with

---

[1] Perhaps the most compelling case for this point of view is that made by Maurice Blanchot in his essay on Rousseau in *Le Livre à venir*. Claiming of Rousseau's sense of persecution that 'J'ai toujours soupçonné ce vice profond et insaisissable d'être celui auquel nous devons la littérature', he goes on to say that '[Rousseau] aide la littérature à prendre conscience d'elle-même en se dégageant des conventions anciennes et à se former, dans la contestation et les contradictions, une rectitude nouvelle': *Le Livre à venir*, pp. 62–74 (pp. 63 and 64). The epigraph to this chapter is taken from the same essay (p. 69).

men of letters'.[2] It is a problem that is also closely linked to his congenital lack of aptitude for poetry, since the rules of versification require to be learned like the rules of Latin grammar: 'Another disadvantage of this method of learning Latin is that I have never understood prosody, still less the rules of versification' (ibid.). In other words, the ostensible subject matter of Baumgarten's book (poetry) would itself have appealed as little to Rousseau as its language (Latin).

SENSATE DISCOURSE AND UNWRITTEN WORKS

Rousseau's remarks on this score are just one example of the numerous ways in which he too seeks to draw boundary lines around the literary, since in his own fashion he desires to be as precise a geometer as those that Baumgarten called for at the end of his *Reflections*. The difference is that Rousseau's frontiers were designed to exclude rather than to embrace a large part of what constituted poetry and letters for his contemporaries. The *Confessions* recount his hostility to literature as a professional activity, while at the same time elaborating a form of writing (autobiography) that no contemporary poetics would have recognized as belonging within its compass. In short, Rousseau's text is the first to invoke a new version of literature in order to challenge the received idea of the literary, and thus explicitly to open up the entire field of literature to question and contestation.

This is not brought about by a conscious, theorized intention on Rousseau's part, but it is the direct consequence of his making himself and his life the subject matter of his writing. Literature in the modern sense comes into being as a result of being harnessed to Rousseau's quasi-biographical project. In the first instance, this may be seen—despite the reasons that would have disinclined Rousseau from any interest in Baumgarten—as an effect of his writing of sensation. By a nice coincidence, the year in which Baumgarten published his *Reflections* was the one in which Rousseau and Mme de Warens moved to Les Charmettes; and in recalling the start of this happy interlude, Rousseau powerfully invokes the need for what Baumgarten was calling sensate discourse: 'but how can I speak what never was spoken, nor done, nor even thought, but only *tasted*, only *felt*, without my being able to point to any other object of my happiness but this feeling itself?'(p. 265 [p. 220]).[3] In fact Rousseau does indicate the existence of a kind of language of sensation when, some eighty pages earlier, he describes the 'works' he created on the journeys he made on foot in his early youth, works which, however, dispensed with pen, paper, and even words. He refers to the

---

[2] Jean-Jacques Rousseau, *Les Confessions* [1782], ed. Jacques Voisine (Classiques Garnier; Paris: Garnier, 1968), p. 278 [p. 233]. All page references are to these editions.

[3] My emphasis. In quoted material throughout this volume, italics are my own unless otherwise indicated.

mental activity induced by the physical experience of walking as 'thought', but it is an activity that is clearly grounded in the body: 'There is something about walking that animates and activates my ideas; I can scarcely think at all when I am still; my body must be on the move if my mind is to do the same' (p. 183 [p.158*]). The physicality of this experience is not just in the bodily movement, without which Rousseau cannot 'think'; it is also in his engagement with the physical world around him:

The pleasant sights of the countryside, the unfolding scene, the good air, a good appetite, the sense of well-being that returns as I walk [. . .], all of this releases my soul, encourages more daring flights of thought, impels me, as it were, into the immensity of beings, which I can *choose* from, appropriate, and *combine* exactly as I wish without fear or constraint. All nature is at my disposal and my command; my heart, straying from object to object, *identifies* and unites with those it finds beguiling, surrounds itself with *images* that charm, drinks deep of delicious sentiment. (ibid.)

It is a very particular form of 'thinking' that Rousseau outlines here, and one of its most striking features is the parallel with the language of literary creation. Like a writer, he selects and combines the elements of physical objects around him. The world appears to him in the form of 'images', prompting 'identification' and the sort of emotional response ('drink[ing] deep of delicious sentiment') that Rousseau recalls as his own experience of reading in childhood, as we shall see presently.

At this point he begins to describe his experience in terms that echo more directly the language of artistic, if not strictly literary, expression: 'If, to fix these in my mind, I play at describing them in my head, what *vigorous brushwork*, what *freshness of palette*, what *energy of expression* I use!' (p. 184 [p. 158]). It is a language of inward response rather than outward linguistic expression, which, significantly for a modern understanding of the literary, equates art with experience rather than with verbal language. To readers who claimed that his published works actually succeeded in conveying this experience, Rousseau counters that the written and published texts are nothing in comparison with these lived 'works' of his youth: 'if only they could have seen the works of my first youth, those I conceived during my journeys, those I composed and never wrote down' (ibid.). To have written down these wordless works would have changed them by introducing consideration of the reading public; and in any case, had he been already equipped with pen and paper on his travels, the experience that he is equating with literature here could never have taken place: 'If I had thought of all that, nothing would have come to me' (ibid.). There are, then, forms of expression and composition that exist independently of language, particularly of written language, and occupy the domain of sensation and feeling. They amount to a form of sensate discourse, which, unlike Baumgarten's conception, could no longer be mapped back on to the principles of Horace's *Ars poetica*. The language here is informed and justified entirely by Rousseau's own experience, his personality, and his history. Of course, as he says, this language cannot, by definition, be shared with a wider public; but it represents an ideal of expression that the written language of the text implicitly invokes and endorses.

This new language, which only subsequently and in retrospect acquired the status of literature, takes shape as the means whereby Rousseau records his life in the *Confessions*. His justification of what, after Baumgarten, I am calling 'sensate discourse', is not based in an appeal to the philosopher's science of perception to be set against the logic that deals with things known; instead, it is grounded in his own individual make-up. And unlike Baumgarten's opposition, which is used to define a boundary between knowledge and sensation, Rousseau's own nature actually contains this opposition within itself: 'It is as though my heart and my mind belonged to different people. Feelings burst upon me like lightning and fill my soul; but instead of illuminating, they burn and dazzle me. I feel everything but see nothing' (p. 125 [p. 110]). The division between the sensible and the intelligible is one that Rousseau lives as an aspect of his own nature, and the presence of the sensate inside him divides him from the part of himself that sees and knows.

The mismatch between thought and feeling in his own being makes written expression extraordinarily difficult, with the result that writing itself becomes a part of this sensate experience, and not just a record of it:

This slowness of thought allied to impetuosity of feeling is something that affects me not only in conversation, but also when I am on my own and working. It is with unbelievable difficulty that my ideas arrange themselves into any sort of order in my head. They circle there obscurely, they ferment to the point where they stir me, fire me, cause my heart to palpitate; and in the midst of all this emotion I see nothing clearly; I cannot write a word, I must wait. Imperceptibly, the great movement subsides, order succeeds chaos, everything finds its proper place; but slowly, and only after a long and confused agitation. (p. 126 [p. 111])

The language in which Rousseau composes the *Confessions* is described in the terms of sensate experience—heat, palpitation, agitation—rather than in those of rhetorical procedure. It is required to accommodate his own internal contradiction and is thus a direct consequence of the way he is. In a word, the experience with which literature is implicitly equated by Rousseau in the *un*written works of his youth here extends to the language in which the written ones exist.

TIME AND DISCONTINUITY

This new writing also needs to accommodate the temporal evolution of the human subject, and it is here that the biographical element of his project begins to emerge as a necessary dimension of sensate discourse. If sensory experience is integral to Rousseau's sense of human identity, he has a remarkably sophisticated and subtle view of its workings, which includes an awareness of the effects of time. This temporal dimension is further complicated by Rousseau's use of autobiography, whose constantly evolving authorial viewpoint contrasts with the implicitly fixed narrative viewpoint of biography. Human beings, in his account, are not machines, passively registering sense-impressions that are subsequently translated into ideas (to summarize the basic principle of sensualist philosophy). As sensate beings, human subjects are contradictory and inconsistent entities whose lack of self-identity is the consequence of a dialectical to-and-fro of sensation and experience. In his attempt to establish the causes of these inconsistencies Rousseau infers from his own experience that 'they depend in large part on some earlier impression made upon us by external objects, and that, modified continually by our senses and our organs, without our noticing it, we carry the effect of these modifications with us in our ideas, our feelings, and even in our actions' (p. 485 [p. 399*]). To portray sensation fully requires Rousseau to include the dimension of time which is responsible for these transformations. This in turn requires him to have a language that will match the dialectic of the relation between sensation, object, and experience, and convey the way that time regularly makes us unlike ourselves. More than merely a discourse of the sensate, Rousseau's language needs to be a language that encompasses both internal contradiction—a heart divided from the head—and the temporal discontinuity of successive modification.

That 'literature' might offer the possibility of such a language is not an idea that Rousseau ever explicitly proposes, but his earliest experience of books as a child does hint at such a possibility. First of all, his earliest memories, he claims, are memories of reading, and reading is inextricably bound up with his self-awareness: 'all I remember is what I first read and its effect on me; this is the moment from which I date the uninterrupted consciousness of myself' (p. 7 [p. 8*]). The books he read were novels inherited from his mother, many of them heroic novels from the seventeenth century, and to these he attributes a precocious experience of the passions, and 'some bizarre and romantic notions about human life' which experience has never succeeded in 'curing' him of (p. 8 [p. 8]). In short, these books formed both his nature and his outlook on life. From novels he moved on to more serious stuff, including Plutarch's *Lives*, which were his favourite reading and produced a different side to his nature, described by Rousseau as 'that free, republican spirit, that proud and indomitable character, that impatience with servitude and constraint, which it has been my torment to possess all my life in circumstances not at all favourable to its development' (p. 9 [p. 9]). Neither novels nor the more sober 'lives' seem to have fitted him for his own life; instead, the encounter with books created the conditions both for his self-contradiction and for the discontinuities in his own identity: 'bizarre and romantic', but also 'proud and indomitable'. Moreover, reading Plutarch fails to produce an exemplary moral subject, and his readerly identifications serve instead to make him other than himself: 'I became the person whose life I was reading' (ibid.). The sum total of Rousseau's disparate reading experiences is a fundamentally disparate and divided self: 'thus there began to take shape or to manifest themselves within me this heart, at once so proud and so tender, and this effeminate and yet indomitable character, which, continually fluctuating between weakness and courage, indolence and virtue, has to the end placed me in contradiction with myself' (p. 12 [p. 11*]). The kind of literature that Rousseau seems to have read, consisting largely of stories of the lives of others, whether fictional heroes or exemplary Greek and Roman citizens, may have given him the experience of being other than himself. But they also implicitly defined literature for Rousseau as stories of lives, and opened up the possibility of his writing his own life (in the *Confessions*) in ways that might accommodate the inconsistencies that these life-stories had been responsible for producing in their young reader. In other words, it becomes possible to conceive of a writing (not yet called literature) that has the potential for containing contradiction.

LITERATURE REPUDIATED

Nevertheless, if this 'literature' proposes some kind of solution, Rousseau's autobiography is unlike almost all other literary autobiographies in that it is resolutely not the story of a writer, or of an apprenticeship in literature. On the contrary, it seems positively to be written against all literary ambitions. When Rousseau finds himself sleeping in a room once occupied by his seventeenth-century namesake, the poet Jean-Baptiste Rousseau, his host jokingly suggests that Jean-Jacques might one day become Rousseau the Second. Rousseau's response to this quip conveys more than his characteristic disdain for poetry when he insists that his ambition to be 'un grand homme' can never be equated with being a great poet:

Homer and Virgil were never called great men although they were very great poets. Some authors sought very hard to call the poet Rousseau the great Rousseau during my lifetime. When I am dead the poet Rousseau will be a great poet. But he will no longer be the great Rousseau. For while it is not impossible for an author to be a great man, it is not by writing books either in verse or in prose that he will become such a thing.[4]

Rousseau's story could never be summed up in the formula that Gérard Genette proposes as a synopsis of Proust's *À la recherche du temps perdu*: 'Marcel becomes a writer'.[5] Instead, the overt relation to literature that the *Confessions* seeks to establish is a negative one; and on this score the book is first and foremost an

---

[4] Quoted on pp. 175–6, note 1. From a fragment collected and published under the title *Mon portrait*.

[5] Gérard Genette, *Figures III* (Paris: Éditions du Seuil, 1972).

account of Rousseau's rejection of authorship and literature: 'for some time I had been forming a plan to abandon literature altogether, and especially the profession of writer' (p. 605).

The literature that Rousseau repudiates is one marked principally by its social aspect, that is, literature as a type of social accomplishment exemplified by 'the man of literature'. But it is also the literature of the professional world of letters. Literature in both these senses entails varieties of social commerce, which Rousseau mostly abhors and claims as the main reason for his withdrawal from the world and the literary profession. The most sympathetic portrayal that Rousseau gives of literature in its social guise comes in his description of the lawyer M. Simon, a misshapen dwarf, barely 2 foot high, who compensates for his physical deformity by using his intelligence and cultivating social graces in the form of a thorough acquaintance with literature: 'he had, and with success, taken up belles-lettres [*la belle littérature*], where he had acquired, in particular, that veneer of brilliance, that flair, which makes social intercourse, even with women, more enjoyable' (p. 157 [p. 138]). M. Simon's knowledge of 'good books' and of various *ana* forms the basis of his social existence; although it may make him a wonderful conversationalist, such knowledge still remains above all a social attribute.

A rather more negative version of this literary sociability appears in Rousseau's portrait of his patroness, Mme d'Épinay, who decides at one point to take up literature as a form of social amusement by becoming a writer herself: 'she had begun to dabble in literature and had taken it into her head to write, come what may, novels, letters, plays, stories and other such trifles' (p. 488 [p. 402]). According to Rousseau, her main aim in writing all these books is to get herself an audience that will flatter her *amour-propre*: 'But what she enjoyed was not so much writing them as reading them aloud; and just in case she happened to scribble down two or three consecutive pages, she wants to be sure of having, at the end of this immense labour, an audience of at least two or three well-disposed listeners' (ibid.). When she has no other visitors to call upon, Rousseau is summoned to fulfil the role that she requires of these readers, but he lacks the talent for the *galanterie* and literary talk that made M. Simon such good company: 'I did not know what demeanour to affect, not daring to talk about literature, about which it was not my place to pass judgment, nor about gallantry being too timid' (ibid.); and he presents himself as constitutionally incapable of participating in the literary quid pro quo that Mme d'Épinay's writing initiates and requires. The examples of M. Simon and Mme d'Épinay suggest that Rousseau regards literary accomplishment primarily as a pretext for social exchange, an activity for which he claims repeatedly to have no aptitude, but which, more fundamentally, also presupposes a form of social organization whose ills Rousseau discusses at some length, most notably in his *Discours sur l'origine et les fondements de l'inégalité parmi les hommes* of 1755, and has significant implications for his understanding of literature.

The writers portrayed by Rousseau in the *Confessions* are almost all presented as being embroiled in the social world, which, while he never says so in so many words, may explain why they all ultimately turn against him. As he asserts in the *Discours*, '[one makes] man wicked by making him sociable'.[6] So far as the *Confessions* are concerned, 'men of letters' are people one meets at dinner in the houses of aristocrats, as Rousseau did when he first arrived in Paris *chez* Mme de Créqui (*Confessions*, p. 440); and his one-time friends, the writers Grimm, Diderot, and d'Holbach, are described as living in a social whirlwind, 'appearing in the highest society, and sharing all its spheres between them' (p. 581). It is only a small step from these apparently anodyne forms of sociability to the emergence of 'cabals of men of letters', with the resulting 'quarrels' (p. 461) and jealousies (p. 457), plots (pp. 441, 460), and insults (p. 456) on the part of people who are all pretension and sham, 'adopting the jargon about books rather than any knowledge of their content' (p. 251). In other words, the forms that literature takes in its social guise—deception, secrecy, and pretence—exemplify precisely those qualities that result from living in society, which Rousseau describes in the *Discours sur l'inegalité* as follows: 'It was necessary in one's own interest to seem to be other than one was in reality. Being and appearance became two entirely different things, and from this distinction arose insolent ostentation, deceitful cunning and all the vices that follow in their train.'[7] In a word, the social world in which literature flourishes depends entirely on appearances.

This mismatch between appearance and reality means that Rousseau can no longer trust his fellow writers, who, he becomes increasingly convinced, are plotting secretly to do him down. But there is another, more serious reason why a literature based on social premises is anathema to his project, and particularly to the project of the *Confessions*; for in Rousseau's scheme of things sociability is profoundly incompatible with self-knowledge: 'Social man lives always outside himself; he knows how to live only in the opinion of others, it is, so to speak, from their judgment alone that he derives the sense of his own existence' (p. 126 [p. 136]). In the social world we are driven to turn to others to find out who we are, 'never daring to put the question to ourselves' (ibid.). It follows from this that if Rousseau wishes to say 'who he is', he is bound to reject all forms of expression that presuppose or invite the opinions of others. This is one of the principal reasons why the *Confessions*, in which Rousseau is bent on saying 'who he is', are based on a repudiation of a literature so contaminated by social involvements.[8]

---

[6] Jean-Jacques Rousseau, *Discours sur l'origine et les fondements de l'inégalité parmi les hommes*, ed. Bertrand de Jouvenal (Collection Idées; Paris: Gallimard, 1965), p. 85 [p. 107*].

[7] Ibid., p. 101 [p. 119].

[8] Nevertheless, see Robert Elbaz, *The Changing Nature of the Self: A Critical Study of the Autobiographic Discourse* (London: Croom Helm, 1988) for an account of the ultimate impossibility of the exclusion of the other from Rousseau's scheme of things.

WRITING WITHOUT EXAMPLE

The result of this move against literature is in part the creation of the writing which has retrospectively come to be viewed as literary. Rousseau's claim to be doing something without precedent—'I am resolved on an undertaking that has no model' (*Confessions*, p. 3 [p. 5])—later becomes the model for the principle of originality or innovation that is one of the central features of a modern understanding of literature. It has as its basis the unique self, which Rousseau's account sets out to portray: 'I am not made like any that I have seen; I venture to believe that I was not made like any that exist' (ibid.). Equally, his recognition that his project requires the invention of an entirely new language—'To say what I have to say would require me to invent a language as new as my project'—anticipates the call of Rimbaud over a century later, 'Trouver une langue!'[9] When he claims that his style carries its own message and tells its own story over and above the content of what he narrates, he is articulating a view that has subsequently become one of the basic assumptions that modern readers make about the language of literature in general: 'my style, uneven and natural, now rapid and now diffuse, now sober and now extravagant, now grave and now gay, will itself be part of my story' (p. 1154 [p. 648]). Less specifically, the idea that literature can be read autobiographically, as an indirect account of the author's life and feelings, receives enormous impetus from the *Confessions*, and serves to encourage a tendency that contemporary women readers of *La Nouvelle Héloïse* were apparently only too willing to indulge when they believed that Rousseau had painted himself in Saint-Preux, an assumption that prompted one of them to try and obtain a portrait of Julie through the good offices of a mutual friend (*Confessions*, pp. 646–7). It would be possible to go on adding to this list of the characteristics of Rousseau's writing, which are now regarded as part of the repertoire of modern literature, but there is something more fundamental at stake than a modern consensus about what features might constitute such a repertoire.

First of all, there is a question to be asked about the opposition that Rousseau sets up between social forms of literature and a new and supposedly authentic writing based in self-knowledge. Rousseau may be drawing the sort of boundary that Baumgarten demanded from philosophy, but, as Derrida has shown with reference to other oppositions that Rousseau tries to establish (between speech and writing, masturbation and conjugal sexual relations), the terms that are used to define the excluded element invariably apply equally to its contrary, and a difference between inevitably becomes a difference within.[10] As far as Rousseau's

---

[9] Rousseau, 'Ébauches des *Confessions*', p. 1153 [p. 647].

[10] See Derrida's discussion of Rousseau in pt. 2 of *De la Grammatologie* (Paris: Éditions de Minuit, 1967).

characterization of literature is concerned, this would mean recognizing that, to the extent that his claim to unprecedented example requires acknowledgement on the part of his readers, his writing remains embroiled in the social world. Posthumous publication (the case of the *Confessions*) does not avoid this problem, it merely defers it. Furthermore, as Jean Starobinski has shown, there is nothing that guarantees the transparency of Rousseau's writing, nothing that ensures that *être* and *paraître* will coincide, nothing that prevents the style that is supposedly a direct expression of his self-narrative from appearing as a form of the literary 'jargon' he denounced in the writing of others. Rousseau's project of self-disclosure merely condemns him to endlessly renewed attempts at setting the record straight against the implications of appearances.[11] In other words, the differences between 'good' and 'bad' literatures, old and new forms of writing, which the *Confessions* work so hard to affirm, will not ultimately hold. The kind of boundary that Baumgarten sought to establish in order to divide poetry from ordinary eloquence as categorically as the Phrygians wanted to be separated from the Mysians moves inwards in Rousseau's *Confessions*, creating internal contradictions within the self and within what we now call literature. These contradictions, importantly, are at once constitutive and profoundly unstable.

The conclusion to be drawn from the impossibility of maintaining the distinctions that Rousseau is seeking to affirm is not that the attempt was misconceived, since its repercussions determined the course both of Rousseau's life and of all future thinking about literature. Just as it was his life that launched the search for a new language in opposition to the rhetorics of poetry and sociability, so the collapse of the opposition between a social literature and a literature of authentic selfhood is lived as part of Rousseau's own experience and as a series of events in his own existence. Thus he finds himself at the beginning of Book 7 embarking on the second part of a project that he thought he had completed at the end of Part I. And the book ends with an account of his reading of an extract from it to a select gathering of some half-dozen listeners whose utter silence in response prompts further continuations of the project in *Rousseau juge de Jean-Jacques* and the *Rêveries du promeneur solitaire*. The writing of the life can never be rounded off, and instead becomes its own subject matter, a part of the experience that it narrates.

At the other end of the spectrum, the issue is not so much that of differences that do not hold, as of differences that invariably emerge. By which I mean that even at the moments of the most intense, solitary, and sensate experiences, such as the ones in which Rousseau composed his unwritten works and which represent the ideal of 'good' literature, something is opened up that makes it impossible to fix that experience under a single rubric or within a single definition. For these are all moments of movement: Rousseau is quite literally on the move, walking

---

[11] On all this see Jean Starobinski, *Jean-Jacques Rousseau: la transparence et l'obstacle; suivi de, Sept essais sur Rousseau*, rev. edn. (Bibliothèque des idées; Paris: Gallimard, 1971), esp. chs. 3 and 6.

from Paris to Lyon, or wandering in the forest of Montmorency and dreaming of Julie and Saint-Preux. The social world may have disappeared ('What did I care for readers, a public, or all the world?'), to be replaced by a kind of sublime ('I was soaring up high') and an intense self-presence ('I have never [. . .] been so much myself', pp. 183–4 [p. 158*]); but the purity of this experience is inseparable from the 'motion' of his body and the 'succession' of different landscapes, all of which implies the opening up of a space to difference and variety, rather than concentration on a single entity. The word Rousseau regularly uses to describe his state in these moments is 'extase' (e.g. pp. 191, 647, and *passim*), a term that conveys the sense of being carried outside or beyond oneself. The word 'rêverie' occurs even more frequently (e.g. p. 191) and appears in the title that Rousseau chooses for his last autobiographical work, the *Rêveries du promeneur solitaire*. According to Marcel Raymond, 'rêverie' is etymologically derived from *re-extravagare*, meaning 'to wander', which makes the title of Rousseau's last work a kind of pleonasm that doubly opens up a space for movement, since a *rêverie* is already a form of *promenade*.[12] It also gives a name to a type of writing and a conception of literature that present literature as a space in which it may—and sometimes *must*—wander from its own definition.

Rousseau's attempt to write the story of his life inaugurates a kind of language that, on the one hand, has come to acquire institutional recognition as 'literature': being an expression of feeling, pointing beyond what it is able explicitly to convey, mimicking in its form the experience it claims to recount. Moreover, the *Confessions* are often seen as the origin of the 'new' literary genre of autobiography. On the other hand, in establishing a new literary territory that demands comment in terms other than those that Boileau, Batteux, or even Baumgarten would have been able to countenance, Rousseau's autobiography also creates a field that is irrevocably destabilized by internal contradiction when oppositions designed to circumscribe it fail to hold, and when the changes brought by time and forward movement open up that field to the possibility for endless revision. The life has entered the work in an attempt to lay claim to a new kind of literary authority; but in the process of asserting its distinctiveness, it contributes to making literature irremediably susceptible to permanent revision.

---

[12] Marcel Raymond, *Jean-Jacques Rousseau: la quête de soi et la rêverie* (Paris: J. Corti, 1962), pp. 214ff.

3

Literary History and the Biography of Literature: Madame de Staël and Victor Hugo

As the eighteenth century went on, questions of genre and rhetoric did not vanish, but, partly because of the existence of such texts as Rousseau's *Confessions*, they progressively ceased to be the sole or prime criteria for thinking about a 'literature' that was coming to be understood as a distinctive kind of writing within the larger field of letters. This distinctiveness was also increasingly presented in terms of literature's historical development, whose progressive character reinforced the idea of literature as an autonomous entity endowed with its own particular quasi-biographical trajectory. The backward look of literary history, which revealed an array of models from the past, was counterpointed by a forward-looking perspective that envisaged literature's full realization in some more or less imminent future. Biographies of individual writers may have helped to construct a literary field in the first place, but with the gradual consolidation of that field literature acquired a quasi-biographical narrative of its own, albeit one that took different forms with different commentators, as we shall see in what follows. A number of factors are at work in this phenomenon. The first of these is continuing interest in genius, which offered the possibility of understanding literature in terms other than those of neo-classical poetics. The second is the eighteenth-century habit of equating the individual and the collective, which allows the history of mankind or the history of the human mind to be told as if it were the story of a single individual. And the third factor is the way in which the historical cast of mind that emerged in the eighteenth century began to tip over into a developmental outlook, turned towards the future, and for which individual development again provided a powerful model. I shall be discussing each of these in more detail below.

But first let me return to the term 'literature' itself. The shift from the subjective to the objective meaning of the word—from literature understood as the 'cultural capital' of readers, to a notion of literature as the creative production of writers—was accompanied by an ever more widespread use of the term in the latter part of the century, which saw a variety of attempts to provide it with a coherent and principled definition. The polemicist and playwright Louis-Sébastien Mercier published an essay in 1778 entitled *De la littérature et des littérateurs*, where he argued that literature and 'belles lettres' had the power to promote virtue and elevate the mind. 'Universal literature is acquiring a character of political and moral philosophy', he asserts;[1] and he attributes this quality primarily to the moral sensibility of writers, rather than to any formal features of the poetry, drama, and novels whose effects he is defending. The critic Marmontel published his collected articles on literary topics in 1787 under the title *Éléments de littérature*, a compendium that covered many more topics than Boileau, or even Batteux; going from 'Abondance' to 'Vraisemblance', it included a discussion of Memoirs as well as Tragedy, and the whole was introduced by a long historical essay on taste.[2] The term 'littérature' was put into even wider currency by the Revolution, not least because of the huge increase in the variety of written formats that went beyond established literary forms.[3] Jean-François de La Harpe's seventeen-volume *Lycée, ou, Cours de littérature*, which appeared between 1799 and 1805, took the form of a history of literature from its origins in Greece to the present.[4]

The most significant contribution to these discussions, however, is Madame de Staël's *De la littérature* published in 1800, in which she defines literature in the broadest possible terms to include poetry, eloquence, history, and philosophy.[5] However, despite the breadth of this definition, she treats the notion of literature as a single entity, which she examines through its relations with its broader social context. The subtitle to the book spells this out by indicating that literature is to be '*considered in its relations to social institutions*'. Like Marmontel and La Harpe, Madame de Staël compiles a broadly historical account of her subject from the Greeks to the present day, including on the way a variety of other national literatures in addition to French—Latin, Italian, Spanish, English, and German. Indeed, as I have already mentioned, nationality itself increasingly provided a basis for interpreting the coherence of 'literature', and Madame de Staël's own *De l'Allemagne* (1813) amply demonstrates the point (this text will be discussed later in the chapter). In short, the expanded term 'literature' which emerged in the latter part of the eighteenth century associates the concept either with a mission (Mercier) or with a history (Marmontel's essay on taste, La Harpe's *Lycée*), or, most importantly, with both (Madame de Staël). Furthermore, turned towards the past (its history) or to the future (its mission), literature now seems inextricably bound up with a dynamic temporality in which literary history eventually acquires the developmental character of a biographical narrative.

---

[1] Louis-Sébastien Mercier, *De la littérature et des littérateurs: suivi d'un nouvel examen de la tragédie françoise* (Yverdon, 1778), p. 10.

[2] Jean François Marmontel, *Eléments de littérature* [1787], 3 vols. (Paris: Firmin-Didot, 1879).

[3] On this see Michel Delon, 'La Révolution et le passage des belles-lettres à la littérature', *Revue d'histoire littéraire de la France*, 90 (1990), pp. 557–88.

[4] Jean-François de La Harpe, *Lycée, ou, Cours de littérature ancienne et moderne* (Paris: Depelafol, 1825).

[5] Mme de Staël, *De la littérature considérée dans ses rapports avec les institutions sociales*, ed. Axel Blaeschke (Classiques Garnier; Paris: Garnier, 1998). All page references are to this edition.

GENIUS

As I suggested in Chapter 1, it is through a discussion of genius that some of the foundations for thinking about literature as a whole are laid, and such discussion provides that thinking with a broader set of terms than poetics alone could offer. The invocation of genius in the context of hierarchical oppositions such as the ones between genius and talent, or genius and wit (*esprit*), paved the way for thinking about what we might call the transcendental qualities of literature—its literariness. Over the course of the century, it was the creative aspect of genius that came to dominate discussion of the topic. In his *Réflexions critiques sur la poésie et sur la peinture* (1719) the Abbé Dubos had already anticipated this kind of approach through his emphasis on the ability of genius to bypass the rules and produce original work independent of either precept or example: 'That which a man born with genius does best is what no one has ever shown him how to do.'[6] In his *De l'esprit* (1758) Helvétius mentions the inventiveness of genius as one of its prime features: 'genius always presupposes invention'.[7] This point is rather more colourfully made by Mercier in his narrative poem published two years previously, which recounts the battle between *génie* and *esprit* over the course of many centuries of literary history, and in which he describes how Genius originally appeared to his imagination in the form of 'a Creator God'.[8] (Mercier's reference to his imagination as the source of the work's genesis adds its own weight to his account.) Interest in genius was not confined to literature and the arts, but this broader conception served only to underscore the independence of genius from poetics. Helvétius, for example, discusses genius in science, and Charles Bonnet in his *Essai analytique sur les facultés de l'âme* goes so far as to explore what might be regarded as the neurophysiological basis of the phenomenon, suggesting that genius is related to the strength of the fibres in the brain.[9]

The emphasis on the creativity and the originality of genius, however broadly applied, nevertheless had particular value for the way in which literature might be understood. In his *Essai sur l'origine des connaissances humaines* published in 1746, Condillac characterized genius in terms of its originality. Developing the

---

[6] Jean-Baptiste Dubos, *Réflexions critiques sur la poésie et sur la peinture*, 2 vols. (Paris: Jean Mariette, 1719), vol. ii, p. 20.

[7] Helvétius, *De l'esprit*, quoted in Rémy G. Saisselin, 'Genius', in id., *The Rule of Reason and the Ruses of the Heart: A Philosophical Dictionary of Classical French Criticism, Critics, and Aesthetic Issues* (Cleveland: Press of Case Western Reserve University, 1970), pp. 89–95 (p. 93). I am indebted to Saisselin's discussion of the topic of genius.

[8] Louis-Sébastien Mercier, *Le Génie, le goût et l'esprit: poëme, en quatre chants, dédié à M. le Duc de* **** (The Hague: 1756), p. ii.

[9] 'La force du *Génie* dépend donc de la force de l'Attention: celle-ci dépend de la force des *Fibres* sur lesquelles l'Attention se déploye': Charles Bonnet, *Essai analytique sur les facultés de l'âme*, 2nd edn., 2 vols. (Copenhagen and Geneva: Philibert, 1769), vol. ii, p. 45.

established opposition between talent and genius, he emphasizes the creative qualities of genius, which allow it to dispense with existing models of art to the extent that it can invent new genres and even new art forms:

Talent combines ideas of an art or science already known in the right manner to produce effects one would naturally expect. [. . .] Genius adds to talent the idea of the intellect as being somehow *creative*. It invents new arts, or within the same art, new genres of equal validity. [. . .] The quality of a man of talent can be shared by others who may be his equal or even surpass him. The quality of a man of genius is *original*; it is inimitable.[10]

Marmontel picks up this issue of creativity in his entry on genius in the *Éléments de littérature*, where he reiterates the opposition between talent and genius and ascribes industry to the former and 'invention' to the latter. The major attribute of genius, he says, is 'a gift for creating'; and the works of the writer of genius are characterized by originality in both structure and content: 'If it is a plan that he has conceived, its arrangement is *surprising* and resembles nothing that had been done before him.' The originality of content is evident in the writer's treatment of characters, and in particular 'their striking *singularity*, their astonishing *novelty*, the *force* with which he expresses all their traits'.[11] Originality is not just a mark of difference but an index of positive dynamism.

The entry 'Génie' in the *Encyclopédie*, dating from 1757, and an article for which Diderot himself is assumed to be largely responsible, make the case for genius in terms of an active creative power. Genius is constrained by rules of any kind, and is endowed with an energy that allows it simply to break them in order to move beyond and above them: 'Rules and the laws of taste would hamper *genius*; it breaks these in order to soar to sublimity, pathos, and grandeur.'[12] This energy is translated by an idea of movement ('Movement [. . .] is its natural state') which is powerfully orientated towards the future: 'it is ahead of its time, which can only follow it' (p. 13). In the fragment entitled 'Sur le génie', Diderot describes it as 'That sort of *prophetic* mind'.[13] 'Genius' in these discussions veers between a general, abstract force and an attribute of the individual that marks him to such an extent that the term 'genius' sometimes refers to the individual and not to the abstract quality. The forward movement of genius is, at times,

---

[10] Étienne Bonnot de Condillac, *Essai sur l'origine des connoissances humaines*, quoted in G. Matoré and A.-J. Greimas, 'La Naissance du "génie" au xviiie siècle: étude lexicologique', *Le Français moderne*, 25 (1957), pp. 256–72 (p. 268). Matoré and Greimas's article contains an extremely valuable survey of the characteristics of genius in the eighteenth-century literature on the subject. See also Kineret S. Jaffe, 'The Concept of Genius: Its Changing Role in Eighteenth-Century French Aesthetics', *Journal of the History of Ideas*, 41 (1980), pp. 579–99.

[11] Marmontel, *Éléments de littérature*, vol. ii, pp. 196–7.

[12] 'Article Génie', in Denis Diderot, *Œuvres esthétiques*, ed. Paul Vernière (Classiques Garnier; Paris: Garnier, 1959), pp. 9–17 (p. 12). ('*Génie*' is italicized throughout.) On Diderot's thinking about genius see also Herbert Dieckmann, 'Diderot's Conception of Genius', *Journal of the History of Ideas*, 2 (1941), pp. 151–82.

[13] Diderot, 'Sur le génie', in *Œuvres esthétiques*, pp. 19–20 (p. 20).

the effect of a dynamism inherent in the arts themselves; at others, it is the result of the individual's capacity to break the rules of the collective. But either way, the effects—propelling literature and the other arts into the future—are the same.

What all these arguments, from Dubos to Diderot, suggest is that existing literary and critical frameworks can neither contain nor explain the phenomenon of genius. Ultimately, this shift of frame will give rise to a conception of literature that seeks to do justice to it in the form of Sainte-Beuve's biographical studies of individual geniuses and in the self-mythologizing postures of the Romantics. In the meantime, the emergent notion of literature begins to acquire the characteristics of creativity, originality, and novelty that are associated with genius. Or put another way, literature comes to be that which differs from itself as a result of the effects of genius: it is constituted by the works of literary geniuses, and the work of genius is, by definition, unlike all the works of literature that precede it. By introducing the possibility of conceiving of literature from a perspective that differs entirely from that of poetics or rhetoric, genius builds into literature the differential factor that axiomatically opposes it to a previous definition. Even without this somewhat paradoxical factor, the constant references to the force of genius propelling literature forwards into an as yet unrealized future make of literature an entity whose essence always lies ahead. This anticipatory dimension will remain central to the idea of literature as it is traced throughout this book.

COLLECTIVITIES AND INDIVIDUALS

The connection between genius and literature is also made possible by the traffic between the individual and the collective in eighteenth-century thought. This is particularly evident in the historical thinking which determines the approach to so many issues in the period and which habitually presents phenomena in terms of their origins and births. To return briefly to Rousseau, one can see this traffic going in both directions, as he transfers the notion of the four ages of man derived from Hesiod and Ovid (the ages of gold, silver, bronze, and iron) from the collective history of mankind to the account of his own childhood and youth.[14] In the *Discours sur l'inégalité* the history of the human race is both the context for the experience of individuals, such as the first man to lay claim to property, and the story of a metaphorical figure, sometimes called 'the human race', sometimes 'the human Mind', and sometimes simply 'man', but which is almost always portrayed as possessing characteristics normally

[14] This is argued very persuasively by Philippe Lejeune in his discussion of bk. 1 of the *Confessions*: see id., *Le Pacte autobiographique* (Paris: Éditions du Seuil, 1975), pp. 94–9.

associated with individual human personalities. For example, speaking of the end of the state of nature in the development of mankind, Rousseau writes: 'In becoming sociable and a Slave, [man] grows feeble, timid, servile, and his soft and effeminate way of life completes the enervation both of his strength and his courage.'[15] When the boundaries between the collective and the individual are blurred in this way, the distinctions between history and biography also become less clear.

This blurring is even more marked in connection with the topic of 'perfectibility', a term coined by Rousseau in the *Discours* and used again in his pedagogical treatise *Émile*. A defining characteristic of human beings that distinguishes them from animals, perfectibility is as applicable to the development of the human race as a whole as to that of an individual child:

a faculty which, with the help of circumstance, progressively develops all our other faculties, and which in man is inherent in the species as much as in the individual. On the other hand an animal at the end of several months is already what it will remain for the rest of its life, and its species will still be at the end of a thousand years what it was in the first of those thousand years.[16]

This capacity for development and improvement constructs human history and individual biographies in exactly the same way, contributing to the ease with which one may be seen in terms of the other.

The propensity to see history in terms of development, as opposed to simple retrospect or chronology, seems to have promoted the conflating of individual and collective histories throughout the eighteenth century; the German philosopher Johann Gottfried Herder offers perhaps the most consistent and striking example of this phenomenon. The idea of perfectibility was central to his thinking in a number of areas from language to the history of mankind. His interest in language acquisition as set out in his *Treatise on the Origin of Language* (1771) resulted in a theory of parallel developments in the individual and the human race in general; and the ideas in his *Reflections on the Philosophy of the History of Mankind* (1784–91) about the great chain of being, in which individual entities collectively comprise a larger whole, had its counterpart in his contention that each human embryo replicates the developmental stages of all living creatures on earth in its own individual development. It is this conflation that led Foucault to comment that with Herder history takes the form of biography.[17]

---

[15] Rousseau, *Discours sur l'inégalité*, p. 54 [p. 86].

[16] Ibid., p. 58 [p. 88]; see also pp. 60, 63, and 68. Jean Starobinski's discussion of the term and its use in the *Discours* is very informative; see his note to the text in Jean-Jacques Rousseau, *Œuvres complètes*, ed. Bernard Gagnebin and Marcel Raymond, vol. iii (Bibliothèque de la Pléiade; Paris: Gallimard, 1964), pp. 1317–19.

[17] For a full account of Herder's thought see Wulf Köpke, *Johann Gottfried Herder* (Boston: Twayne Publishers, 1987).

This developmental view of history was also part of the emergence of a broadly organicist form of thinking towards the end of the eighteenth century. As Judith Schlanger has argued, the metaphor of the organism replaced that of the machine in the thinking of the period, and promoted a tendency to see phenomena as collective organisms endowed with an internal *élan vital* and subject to a temporality of organic development.[18] Humanity at large comes increasingly to be conceived as a single living entity whose development is discussed in terms borrowed from the psychology of childhood and from pedagogy, and placed in the frame of the different ages of man. In short, 'Humanity constitutes a great and unique living being whose universal history is biography'.[19] When it comes to thinking about literature as a collective entity with its own specific history, this organicist thinking will be deployed in ways very similar to those associated with ideas about humanity at large, endowing it with its own internal lines of development and an implicitly biographical profile.

LITERARY HISTORY: RETROSPECT AND PROSPECT

The shift towards thinking about literature as a coherent and evolving entity was, however, slower to emerge than in other spheres of enquiry. This is partly because the notion that literature might be conceived of historically was itself at odds with the broadly ahistorical principles of poetics, and with the assumption that the great writers of the past, particularly the ancients, constituted models which all their successors should aspire to emulate. Looked at on this basis, literature appears only as an accumulating body of writing offering diminishing possibilities of return for the would-be writer. This position is articulated by La Bruyère when he opens his essay 'On the Works of the Human Mind' of 1688 (in *Les Caractères*) with the statement: 'After above seven thousand years, during which there have been men who have thought we come too late to say anything that has not been said already, nothing is left for us to do but to glean after the ancients and the ablest amongst the moderns.'[20] Over a hundred years later, in writing what he claims is the first history of literature, the *Lycée, ou, Cours de littérature ancienne et moderne*, La Harpe works with the same presumption, although it is seen here from the point of view of the critic rather than that of the prospective writer. On the one hand, works of literature are the result of a cumulative acquisition of insight derived from pre-existing works: 'This art,

---

[18] See Judith E. Schlanger, *Les Métaphores de l'organisme* (Paris: J. Vrin, 1971), p. 121 and *passim*. It is impossible in a footnote to do justice to this important study, which deserves to be much more widely read (no English translation has so far appeared).
[19] Ibid., p. 145.　　[20] La Bruyère, *Les Caractères*, p. 77.

like all the others, was formed by a succession of ideas that could be compared by experience, imitation, and emulation.'[21] And, on the other, the best writers are those who are not lured into artificial innovations, because they have a sure sense of the immutability of the principles of great art: 'A number of superior beings, who are wise enough to sense that beauty is the same in all ages, are still wrestling with the first great masters, and, drawing on the same wellspring, are seeking to derive new riches from it.'[22] This makes literary history little more than an account of accreted wisdom that confirms the unchanging nature of the beautiful.

Marmontel's essay on the history of taste in his *Éléments de littérature* had already made a similar point when he suggests that while taste may take a variety of contingent and ephemeral forms, the qualities of great literature are immutable and not subject to change. This means that a history of literature becomes the history of the conditions created by taste, which can work either to the advantage or to the detriment of literature, just as a plant will thrive to a greater or lesser extent depending on the climate in which it is placed. In this pre-Darwinian argument, the plant is always and everywhere the same, and only its material circumstances alter. For Marmontel, if literature has a history it can only be a history of taste and consequently of transient error and aberration: 'The art of astonishing the imagination, elevating the mind, moving the soul, exciting and soothing the passions of the human heart is almost the same today as at the time of Sophocles or Demosthenes; whereas the frivolous wit of society is subject to all the whims of capricious and ephemeral *taste*.'[23] It would seem that the underlying assumptions of literary history, which treat art and the beautiful as constants, are not able to accommodate the full implications of the creative workings of genius, which both Marmontel and, to a lesser extent, La Harpe invoke in their accounts.

Chateaubriand's *Génie du christianisme*, published in 1802, two years after Madame de Staël's *De la littérature*, is ostensibly a historical account of the relations between poetry and Christianity, in which Christian texts are consistently presented as improvements on their classical counterparts. (Chateaubriand refers throughout to 'poetry' rather than to 'literature', but the term covers all literary genres, including, for example, Rousseau's *Nouvelle Héloïse*.) In this light Milton's portrayal of love between husband and wife in the figures of Adam and Eve in *Paradise Lost* is praised for being both more tender and more sublime than Homer's treatment of Ulysses and Penelope; and Chateaubriand sees Rousseau's Julie and Racine's Phèdre as decidedly more moving figures than Virgil's Dido. But although Chateaubriand distinguishes clearly between the literature of the Ancients and works written after the advent of Christianity, he does so largely on the basis of a straightforward opposition between a before and an after, not on

---

[21] La Harpe, *Lycée*, vol. i, p. xiv.   [22] Ibid., pp. xx–xxi.
[23] Marmontel, *Éléments de littérature*, vol. i, p. 18 (Marmontel's emphasis).

the principle of any continuous development. The advantage of Christianity in Chateaubriand's eyes is that it offers a more complete understanding of human experience than the pre-Christian world view, an advantage that has significant repercussions for literature and the arts: 'Religion is the true philosophy of the fine arts, because, like human wisdom, it does not separate poetry from morality, compassion from virtue.'[24] Once the Christian viewpoint has been acquired there is, however, nowhere further to go. This is why, in his remarks on Madame de Staël's *De la littérature*, Chateaubriand condemns her notion of perfectibility with such vigour, accusing her of fabricating an illusion which, he claims, her own evidence contradicts:

Alas! it would be most agreeable to believe that we improve [nous nous perfectionnons] from age to age, and that the son is always better than his father. If anything were capable of proving this excellent quality of the human heart it would be to see that Mme de Staël has discovered the principle of this illusion within her own heart. However, I fear that this lady who complains so often about mankind, is, in lauding human perfectibility, like those priests who do not believe in the idol on whose altar they burn their incense.[25]

The vehemence of Chateaubriand's condemnation only serves to underscore the divergence between his broadly ahistorical cultural relativism and the anticipatory thrust of Madame de Staël's approach that others had already adumbrated.

One of the first adumbrations of this approach is Mercier's *De la littérature et des littérateurs* published in 1778, some ten years before the Revolution. This is not so much a history of literature as a programme for action by means of literature, and the temporality that Mercier is working with is almost entirely one of project rather than of retrospect. He defines literature primarily as the manifestation of an avant-garde (though not in so many words, since the term did not acquire currency until the mid-nineteenth century), spearheading the spread of 'sound ideas', and he cites the previous thirty years in France as proof of this claim.[26] He singles out the innovatory force of literature, and castigates those whose approach to it is based on the backward glance of the latecomer: 'The rage for saying that *there is nothing new to be said* is [. . .] no more than a form of injustice and malice which aspires to belittle the man of invention' (p. 27). It is this inventiveness which explains the fact that 'Belles Lettres have always preceded the deeper sciences' (p. 5), and which leads to Mercier's view of the development of literature as a progressive enlightenment exactly analogous to the development of an individual writer. The following comment illustrates this analogy very graphically:

---

[24] François-René Chateaubriand, *Essai sur les révolutions; Génie du christianisme* [1797; 1802], ed. Maurice Regard (Bibliothèque de la Pléiade; Paris: Gallimard, 1978), p. 700.
[25] Chateaubriand, 'Lettre à M. de Fontanes sur la seconde édition de l'ouvrage de Mme de Staël', in *Essais sur les révolutions*, pp. 1265–80 (p. 1265).
[26] Mercier, *De la littérature*, p. 7.

I urgently wish that every writer, in examining himself in good faith, as he examines and judges others, would once in his life construct an exact catalogue of all the ideas he has had since his childhood; he would be more surprised than anyone by the singular contradictions he would find in them; he would see that in order to arrive at the truth, one must begin by being the plaything of many a phantom, and that stubbornness is the ultimate form of human folly; the individual resembles the human race only too closely; and ignorance, error, superstition, and moral weakness have, at different times, made of the human mind a creature that is quite unlike itself. (p. 31)

The only valid backward look is the one which shows how far the human race has come since the superstition and ignorance of its infancy, revealing how literature has contributed to making mankind other—and better—than itself as it progresses towards maturity.

A similar conception of the progress of reason and enlightenment informs Condorcet's *Esquisse d'un tableau historique des progrès de l'esprit humain* (1793), except that the underlying principle of progress in this account is not the innovatory force of literature, but the cumulative knowledge that comes from scientific and technological advancement where every new development builds on the results of a previous one. The notion of perfectibility underpins the argument which is presented as a history of scientific and philosophical thought in ten chapters, the tenth and final one being devoted to a future in which 'the sun will shine only on free men who know no other master but their reason'.[27] Once again, it is the developmental associations of the notion of perfectibility that allow Condorcet to set up a parallel between collective and individual progression: 'progress is subject to the same general laws that can be observed in the development of the faculties of the individual, and it is indeed no more than the sum of that development realized in a large number of individuals joined together in society.'[28] Although Condorcet's concern is chiefly with improvements in the material conditions of existence and with the natural sciences that contribute to this, Madame de Staël's *De la littérature* has much more in common with the *Esquisse* than with the assumptions of La Harpe and Chateaubriand. The legitimation of a new conception of literature is far more cogent in the developmental guise of her version of literary history in which literature is constituted as a quasi-organic entity rather than as a series of monuments (La Harpe's term),[29] and where full definition remains a project for the future instead of residing in the achievements of the past. Literary transcendence here is defined not so much by any strictly aesthetic qualities as by this perspective that opens on to the future.

[27] Jean-Antoine-Nicolas de Caritat Condorcet, *Esquisse d'un tableau historique des progrès de l'esprit humain*, ed. Monique and François Hincker (Paris: Éditions sociales, 1966), p. 259 [p. 179].
[28] Ibid., p. 76 [p. 4].
[29] '[L]'imagination créatrice élev[a] ses premiers monuments': La Harpe, *Lycée*, vol. i, p. xi.

MADAME DE STAËL'S *DE LA LITTÉRATURE*: PERFECTIBILITY AND THE DEVELOPMENT OF LITERATURE

It is this forward-looking emphasis that informs Madame de Staël's *De la littérature*, in which she draws heavily on the notion of 'perfectibilité', inherited from Rousseau and Condorcet, in order to apply it to the sphere of literature. This sphere, as I have already mentioned, contains a much broader swathe of writing than a modern use of the term 'littérature' implies; as well as 'works of the imagination', it includes history, philosophy, and what Madame de Staël calls 'the study of moral man'.[30] But it derives its overall coherence from two main factors. The first of these is literature's status as an institution in its own right having reciprocal relations with other social institutions—religion, 'les mœurs', and the law. The institution of literature acquires autonomous agency in part through the reciprocity of the mutual influence that, according to Madame de Staël, operates between these different institutional entities: religion, social behaviour, and the law all influence literature, but literature has equally important effects on them (p. 15). The second factor that contributes to its coherence is literature's powerfully developmental character. Madame de Staël presents her history of literature from Homer to the present day as a history of 'the progress of thought' (p. 3). She argues, furthermore, that the study of the past should never be allowed to hinder 'anything that might lead to a new genre, open up new avenues for the human mind, and, in sum, offer a future to thought' (p. 6). The underlying hope that sustains the book is that the road opened up by literature should offer a pathway out of the violence of the Terror, and put French society back on the track of the Enlightenment ideals that had inspired the Revolution in the first place.

According to Madame de Staël the primary element in the progress of literature is thought, as distinct from its more narrowly poetic qualities. In discussing the Greeks she distinguishes sharply between the imaginative achievements of their poetry, which, she says, have never been surpassed, and the domain of philosophy, to which they contributed very little. The notion of perfectibility can be applied only to the progress of ideas and not to 'the marvels of the imagination' (p. 46). Freedom, most notably, is the goal of thought: 'Progress in literature, that is to say, continuous development [*le perfectionnement*] in the art of thought and expression, is necessary to the establishment and preservation of liberty' (p. 28). It is through the exercise of rational thought that tyranny and injustice can be countered. However, literature as thought is presented as being equally

[30] Mme de Staël, *De la littérature*, pp. 16, 45.

powerful in producing effects of an intensely felt moral elevation in individuals. Ideas generate personal and emotional response as well as social and political consequences. In this way literature acquires a sort of dual transcendence, one element of which lies in a shared future, and the other in this elevation associated with the reader's affective response to moral argument. This duality contributes to the implied continuity between the collective and the individual associated with the developmental model of perfectibility.

Perfectibility for Madame de Staël is in part a moral imperative, so that, for example, the study of past literature ought not to lead to the tyranny of inherited models over the writers of the present: 'In the current situation in Europe, progress in literature *must* serve the development of noble ideas of all kinds' (p. 23). It is in any case an undeniable fact that existence itself is marked by 'the immutable law of progression' (p. 85). The *élan vital* is both an integral aspect of time itself ('the universal progress of ideas through the simple effect of temporal succession', p. 40), and a quality of the human mind ('it is in the nature of the human mind to march ever onwards', p. 158). The vocabulary of successivity in Madame de Staël is repeatedly galvanized by associations of connection and directionality so that succession tends to be recast as progress. There is continuity of thought as generation succeeds generation: 'philosophical thinkers form a *chain of ideas* across the ages, which death never breaks' (p. 48). But equally, the existence of the human mind guarantees such thought a forward movement through time: 'the general *march* of the human mind has never been stopped' (p. 41).

In addition to the growth of the faculty of reason there is also, it would seem, an innate drive in human history towards ever greater understanding of the human heart and an ever-growing sensibility within society. It is this inward preoccupation that characterizes what Madame de Staël calls the 'literature of the North'; associated with an increasing capacity for love (pp. 57–8), it goes hand in hand with an improvement in the position of women in society (pp. 150–1) and generally promotes the qualities of compassion, generosity, and virtue. The dynamism of forward movement is built into Madame de Staël's entire conception of human nature, as she makes clear in the following remark near the end of the book: 'I have sought in this work to assemble all the elements on whose basis one could inspire a love of *progress* in ideas, a conviction about the necessary action of this progress, and thus incite generous minds to direct this *irresistible force* whose cause lies in our moral nature, just as physical nature contains the *principle of movement*' (p. 419). Whether expressed in terms of thought or of sensibility, progress inheres in the collective human spirit, just as the irresistible force of movement inhabits the natural world.

Although the principle of perfectibility makes individual and collective development more or less identical, there seem to be two different axes in play in the case of Madame de Staël, a horizontal one and a vertical one. Perfectibility in the domain of the collective tends to imply forward movement, whereas it is expressed more frequently as elevation in the context of individual experience. This is in part a result of an implicit association of the collective with the domain of thought, and of the individual with sensibility. But as the following assertion makes clear, the soul is elevated as much by contact with ideas as by emotional response: 'literature [and] the art of thought [. . .] cause tears to flow in all situations in life; they elevate the soul to general meditation which diverts thought away from individual sorrows' (p. 37). Where the soul is involved, the intrinsic dynamism of human existence always takes the form of an upward movement: 'as soon as you give the soul a powerful thrust nothing can stop its *ascent* [*essor*]' (p. 414). This is because 'The soul requires *exaltation*' (p. 404). And the study of literature is a powerful source of such elevation: 'by perfecting [men's] taste in literature, one is acting on the elevation of their character' (p. 20). Once again, the model is one of a dynamism that is treated as an integral part of human nature. Although it connotes pedagogy more readily than natural biological growth,[31] the drive towards education and moral improvement is itself viewed as a natural condition of human existence, whether individual or collective, and so makes of Madame de Staël's history of literature something very like a narrative of individual education.

MADAME DE STAËL'S *DE L'ALLEMAGNE*: LITERATURE AND NATION

If the central focus on perfectibility in Madame de Staël's *De la littérature* tends to emphasize thought at the expense of creative imagination, her developmental account nevertheless ascribes to literature an extraordinarily powerful coherence by treating it as the sole agent of its own progression. Although the goals of literature, in the form of freedom and virtue, extend beyond its institutional confines, Madame de Staël consistently endows it with a transcendental function.[32] Taken together, these two factors imply both the possibility of a coherent identity for literature, and a projection of its definition forwards, or upwards, into the future. Madame de Staël's other great innovation in the view of literature is her notion of national literatures where the collective subject of a nation finds collective expression in its literature. As I have already indicated, the eighteenth century saw an increasingly frequent use of the term 'literature' to refer to the writings of a single nation. This created the potential for yet another basis on

---

[31] Such references, however, do appear in the text in the use of phrases such as 'la curiosité de l'enfance' or 'le charme et l'avantage de la jeunesse' to describe the Greeks (pp. 53, 64); or in remarks such as 'le genre humain n'avoit pas encore atteint [. . .] l'âge de la mélancolie' (p. 87).

[32] For a discussion of Madame de Staël's conception of literature see Jean Starobinski, 'Mme de Staël et la définition de la littérature', *Nouvelle Revue française*, 28 (1966), pp. 1045–59. This excellent account nevertheless understates the qualities of coherence and transcendence that Mme de Staël attributes to literature.

which to construct parallels between collective and individual subjects, as is nicely conveyed in Bonald's formula of 1806: 'Style is the expression of the man of intellect, of his thought, his mind, and his character, and so literature will be the expression of the moral part of society; that is to say, of its constitution, which is its soul, its mind, and its character.'[33] Style is to the individual what literature is to the nation.

The nation is one of the most favoured instances of organicist thinking in the period; it is regularly conceived of as a single body endowed with its own life and character, and its literature is regarded as the most spontaneous manifestation of a distinctive national identity.[34] The consequence of this view is not only that literature acquires coherence as the expression of a nation-subject, but more particularly that the criteria for understanding a given national literature lie within the character of the national culture in which it emerges, not in some universal or ahistorical norm. National character presupposes the same degree of uniqueness as that found in individual persons. All this is very powerfully articulated by Frédéric Ancillon in an essay entitled 'Analyse de l'idée de littérature nationale', published in 1817, where this parallel is made explicit in remarks such as the following: 'The ideas, habits, and dominant affections of a nation determine its manner of seeing, feeling, and judging.'[35] This individual national character, according to Ancillon, must provide the basis for any appreciation of a given national literature: 'Each literature must be judged for itself, and not in terms of laws that are foreign to it.'[36] This is a very far cry from Boileau, and even from Marmontel and La Harpe, for whom the defining criteria of poetry and literature were always and everywhere the same. Ancillon's claim is considerably indebted to the work of Madame de Staël in *De la littérature* but particularly in *De l'Allemagne*.

Much of the argument of *De la littérature* rests on the distinction that Madame de Staël proposes between the literatures of the North and those of the South: 'there are two quite distinct literatures, the one that comes from the South and the one that comes down from the North, the one whose main source is Homer, and the one whose origin is Ossian'.[37] A development of this notion of national literatures as expressions of geographical character provides the basis of *De l'Allemagne*. Madame de Staël compares nations to individuals ('those great individuals that we call nations') for whom a distinctive individual character is a crowning national glory: 'The glory and even the charm of each country always

[33] Louis Gabriel Bonald, *Du style et de la littérature*; quoted in Axel's Blaeschke's extremely informative introduction to *De la littérature*, p. cii. No doubt Bonald's claim owes a good deal to Mme de Staël.

[34] On this see Schlanger, *Métaphores de l'organisme*, pp. 152–9.

[35] In Frédéric Ancillon, *Essais philosophiques, ou, Nouveaux mélanges de littérature et de philosophie*, 2 vols. (Paris: J.-J. Paschoud, 1817), vol. i, pp. 39–81 (p. 62).

[36] Ibid., p. 68.

[37] *De la littérature*, pp. 176–7.

consist in the national character and way of thinking.'[38] In the case of Germany, this character is defined in terms of a taste for abstract ideas (i, p. 45), a love of beauty (i, p. 53), an inclination towards literature and philosophy, a preference for imagination over wit (i, p. 57), and a proclivity towards the inner life, which Madame de Staël calls the 'poetry of the soul' (i, p. 58). The atomization of Germany into different regions and states, along with the near absence of any public life encourage a sort of anarchy that of itself promotes the development of the individual characters of its citizens, and particularly of its writers. The German language, which like all languages is intimate manifestation of national identity, discourages the kind of rapid thought that is articulated in the form of the conversation and repartee favoured by French. Instead, it encourages the direct expression of thoughts, and lends itself better to poetry than to the prose of spoken language (i, pp. 111–12). In other words, as well as having national attributes of their own, German culture and society foster precisely those factors that promote the individual expression that is literature.

Moral elevation remains the chief value of literature for Madame de Staël, but in *De l'Allemagne* she is less inclined to associate it exclusively with philosophical ideas than she did in *De la littérature*, and she gives a greater role to imagination and the individual sensibility of the author. Writing here is more the expression of feeling than of thought: 'The prime condition for writing is a keen and powerful manner of feeling' (i, p. 160); and poetry is above all 'the apotheosis of feeling' (i, p. 206). In Madame de Staël's account, this makes German literature less the collective expression of an individual national character, than the collected expressions (in the plural) of a huge variety of individual writers, each with their own unique character and sensibility. Germany is not so much the homeland of German literature as the breeding ground for the individual creativity that is the condition for all literature of any kind. This is what justifies Madame de Staël's presentation of German literature through a series of separate accounts of the different writers. Because each German writer constitutes a literary phenomenon of his own—women scarcely figure in this world—, the temperament and personality of each of them is offered as the means to an understanding of their work: 'since every man of genius forms, so to speak, a separate school in Germany, it seems to me necessary to begin by revealing the principal traits that distinguish each writer as an individual and by personally describing the most renowned men of letters, before analysing their works' (i, pp. 171–2 [p. 241]). Literary worth may be gauged by the extent to which it correlates with the least nuance of the writer's mind and feelings.

However, it is, paradoxically, this degree of individuality amongst German writers that makes it possible after all to construct a coherent national literary

---

[38] Madame de Staël, *De l'Allemagne*, ed. Simone Balayé, 2 vols. (Paris: Garnier-Flammarion, 1968), vol. i, p. 94. All further references are to this edition. Banned by Napoleon just before it was due to be published in 1810, *De l'Allemagne* eventually appeared in 1813.

history. Although the individual has a distinct temperament and a unique sensibility, Madame de Staël does not discuss these in terms of personal development
or biography. Such development happens at a national, collective level both as
the sum total of individual expressions and as the necessary condition for that
expression. The implied contrast here is with France, where the originality of
genius is said to be constantly thwarted by the tyranny of pre-existing literary
models, which results in the impossibility of any literary development in that
country:

Some declare that language was fixed on a given day of a given month, and that since
that moment, the introduction of a new word would be a barbarism. Others assert that
the rules of drama were definitively drawn up in a given year, and that the genius who
wished to change anything now is wrong not to have been born before that irrevocable
year, when all literary discussion, past, present, and future, was concluded. Finally, in
metaphysics in particular it was decided that after Condillac it is impossible to take a
single step further without going astray. Progress is still permitted in the physical sciences
because it cannot be denied to them; but in the philosophical and literary sphere, there
is a desire to oblige the human mind to chase the ring of vanity forever around the same
circle. (ii, pp. 144–5)

The natural progression of language, literature, and thought has been artificially
halted in France in a way that is compounded both by a failure to recognize the
northern dimension to the national character, and by a correspondingly misplaced
insistence on applying models derived from southern antiquity, instead of drawing
on those that originate in the romantic and chivalric traditions of the North:
'Romantic literature alone is still capable of improvement [*d'être perfectionnée*]
because, having its roots in our own soil, it alone can grow and revitalize itself'
(i, pp. 213–14 [p. 248]). National literary development presupposes an organic
entity with roots (a past) and equally the potential for future growth. Because
these conditions have been met in Germany, it is possible for Madame de Staël
to describe what she calls 'the march of German literature through history'
(i, p. 216).

   Change and movement are the essential features of any properly functioning
literature. This puts it somewhat at odds with the society of which it is also
said to be the expression, because disruption is inimical to the social order: 'if
the important thing in the social state is tranquillity, the important thing in
literature is interest, *movement*, emotion' (i, p. 248). It would seem to be in
the nature of literature to be recorded as history, and, equally, the possibility of
literary history depends on literature's self-realization as movement: 'Nothing in
life is stationary, and art becomes petrified when it ceases to change' (i, p. 258).
Literature dies and is turned to stone when it is forced to remain identical to its
own past. The example of Germany demonstrates that it is only when literature
is allowed to function as a collective entity with its own internal dynamic, its
own past, and its own future—in short when it becomes the subject of its own
history—that it can exist as literature at all.

VICTOR HUGO'S *PRÉFACE DE CROMWELL*: POETRY AND THE LIFE CYCLE

With Victor Hugo's *Préface de Cromwell* (1827) the calquing of the development of literature from the model of an individual existence takes a more extreme and more explicit form than that found in previous writing; for literary history here goes not just from birth to maturity, but right the way through to old age and death. The emphasis is shifted from the pedagogical implications of perfectibility, where progress is indefinite and open-ended, to a more overtly biological version of quasi-biography that includes an acknowledgement of the decline implicit in organic life. One of the reasons for Hugo's adoption of a more thoroughly organicist model of development than Madame de Staël's is that the topos of a biological history of mankind or of society had become much more common during the early part of the nineteenth century. The Saint-Simonian view of humanity, as expressed by his disciples in their *Exposition de la doctrine de Saint-Simon* in 1829, is of 'a collective being that develops; this being has grown from one generation to the other, just as an individual man grows as the years succeed each other'. Fourier states quite explicitly that 'Human society or the human race viewed *en masse*, is a body that, like any other, has its four ages of *childhood, growth, apogee, decline*, and *twilight years*.'[39] This decline is different from that implied in the falling away from a golden age or an original paradise as narrated by Hesiod and Ovid, and which can also be read in Rousseau's *Discours sur linégalité* in counterpoint to the progressive implications of perfectibility. In contrast to these there is no pessimism associated with the inclusion of decay in Hugo's model, and he retains from Madame de Staël the notion that poetry develops in parallel with society and that its course is one of progress. The assumption that the movement of literature is inherently forwards and upwards underpins all his remarks on the subject, and this view is very forcefully expressed in a letter to Baudelaire written in 1859: 'Onwards! this is the word favoured by progress; it is also the cry uttered by art. It sums up the language of poetry.'[40] It is this progressive thrust that leads Hugo to use the term 'poésie' in place of 'littérature', the implication being that poetry is an improvement on mere literature: 'The art which for the past hundred years in France had been nothing more than literature has once again become poetry.'[41] The term 'poetry' here carries its widest sense

---

[39] Quoted by Schlanger, *Métaphores de l'organisme*, pp. 149 and 146 (Fourier's italics). Her whole discussion of this issue is well worth consulting (see pp. 144–52).

[40] Victor Hugo, *Correspondance*, vol. ii (Paris: Calmann Lévy, 1898), p. 226. Letter dated 6 Oct. 1859.

[41] Victor Hugo, 'But de cette publication', in *Littérature et philosophie mêlées*, in Victor Hugo, *Œuvres complètes*, vol. xiii: *Critique*, ed. Anne Ubersfeld et al. (Bouquins; Paris: R. Laffont, 1985), p. 54.

without implying any generic specificity; and to that extent it may be understood as a sort of 'super-literature' that exemplifies the progressive impetus contained within all literature.

This impetus, as I have already suggested, is expressed more as innate biological growth than as a developmental quality of the human mind realized by means of education. The latter was the prime manifestation of Madame de Staël's notion of perfectibility in literature, and its grounding in physiology was limited to her preference for those forms of education that took fullest account of the natural evolution and outlook of the mind of the child. In *De l'Allemagne* she claims that children 'understand everything in gradual stages: it is vital to measure progress against the development [*marche*] of reason in childhood. This slow but steady development goes as far as is possible, as long as one refrains from ever trying to hasten it.' It is for this reason that, when it comes to theories of education, she promotes Pestalozzi over Rousseau: 'Pestalozzi has a genius and an instinct for the internal development of intelligence in children; he can see what path their thoughts follow to arrive at their goal'.[42] For Hugo, by contrast, development is recast entirely as physiological or organic process, and carries no trace of pedagogy.

This is due in part to the fact that, in his view, the individual genius realizes the potential of his art to a degree that cannot be bettered or improved by successors, and consequently, the history of literature can no longer be understood in terms of an accumulation of wisdom or technical know-how. As Hugo says in the letter to Baudelaire, 'Art is not perfectible [. . .]. No one will ever surpass Aeschylus, and no one will ever surpass Phidias.' Just as it is impossible to learn from genius, so genius is itself incapable of learning: 'genius [. . .] surmises rather than learns'.[43] Hugo's view of genius continues in the same vein as that of Madame de Staël, but he develops it to the point where the genius is defined exclusively by his truth to his own nature (Hugo's geniuses are all men): 'If true talent could give up [. . .] its own nature, and put its individual originality to one side in order to become someone else, it would lose everything by playing this role of Copycat.'[44] In Hugo's account, progress is construed as a creative force that far exceeds the energies and scope of any individual, however great that individual: 'It is the same sap, spread through the ground, that produces all the trees in the forest, which are so different in their bearing, their fruit, and their leaves. It is one and the same nature that produces and nurtures the most diverse geniuses.'

---

[42] *De l'Allemagne*, vol. i, pp. 145–6.

[43] Victor Hugo, *Préface de Cromwell*, in Hugo, *Critique*, p. 24. All further references are to this edition. Hugo's book on Shakespeare, first published in 1864, includes a chapter entitled 'Les Génies', where he discusses in turn the 'géants de l'esprit humain': Homer, Job, Isaiah, Ezekiel, Lucretius, Juvenal, St John, St Paul, Tacitus, Dante, Rabelais, Cervantes, and Shakespeare; see *William Shakespeare*, in Hugo, *Critique*, pp. 261–89. In the same volume are two further essays on genius dating from the same period. For more discussion of Hugo's ideas about genius see Ch. 7 below.

[44] *Préface de Cromwell*, p. 24.

The fertilizing agent is not the human mind, whether single or collective, but something altogether larger which Hugo here calls nature and which elsewhere in the *Préface* he calls poetry. Poetry exists as much more than the sum of its individual parts, and this is precisely what is conveyed by Hugo's account of the three ages of poetry that parallel the three ages of man.

Poetry is driven by the dynamic of a quasi-biological development that takes it from youth, to virility, to old age. Just as mankind has three ages ('He has been child, and then man; we are now witnessing his impressive old age', p. 4), so too does the poetry that develops in parallel with it, each phase having its own corresponding literary form: 'poetry has three ages, each of which corresponds to a period in [the development of] society: the ode, the epic, and the drama. The primitive era was lyric, the era of the ancients was epic, and the modern era is dramatic' (p. 14). The force of this internal dynamic is such that poetry itself is described as giving birth to the poets who supposedly create it, just as nature fertilizes and nourishes individual geniuses. For example, as the lyric age of the infancy of humanity progresses, poetry acquires new concerns, engendering the epic poet in the process: 'from ideas [poetry] passes to things. It sings of aeons, peoples, and empires. It becomes epic, it gives birth to Homer' (p. 5). Becoming epic and giving birth to Homer jointly testify to a developmental and creative energy that is properly that of poetry and serves to characterize it very powerfully as an autonomous agent in its own right.

More precisely, poetry shares these developmental energies with the rest of the natural world: 'everything in nature passes through these three phases, the lyric, the epic, and the dramatic, because everything encounters birth, action, and death' (p. 15). If the universal structure of this life cycle applies as much to poetry as to the history of mankind, it also provides the model for much smaller units of time, such as each of the three phases of Hugo's history within which there is birth, growth, decline, and ultimately, death. Pushed to a somewhat fanciful extreme, it can apply even to a single day where dawn is a hymn, noon a spectacular epic, and sunset 'a sombre drama where day wrestles with night, and life with death' (p. 15). This recurrence has the advantage of avoiding the negative implication of senescence, which can be read in Hugo's largest-scale version of the life-story, because each phase, while ending in decay and death, gives birth to the next. Taken serially, the life cycles that ground Hugo's history produce a narrative of perpetual regeneration rather than one of an inevitable and final demise.

The beginning of the epic phase is presented, as we have seen, as a development from the lyric phase ('[poetry] *becomes* epic'), but also as a birth (that of Homer). In other words, the epic era is both the next stage in the life of poetry and a new life in its own right. This organic autonomy is even more evident in Hugo's account of its end which he describes quite starkly as a gradual death: 'However, the epic era *was coming to an end*. Like the society which it depicted, this type of poetry was *becoming exhausted* by spinning round on the same spot. Rome was calquing Greece, Virgil copied Homer; and, as if to *end* with dignity, epic poetry finally *expired* in childbirth' (p. 6). The end of antiquity is portrayed as 'the final convulsions of a world in its death throes'; and once it has finally died it becomes '[a] huge corpse', 'a nest of putrefaction' picked over by swarms of rhetoricians, grammarians, and Sophists—an image that extends the life cycle of the epic period beyond death into physical decay and decomposition (p. 8). It is out of all of this that the next phase (the drama) is born: 'This period [contained] the seeds of everything that has subsequently borne fruit.' On the one hand, the poetic form of the era of Christianity—the drama—is said to be a more complete form of poetry than its precursors which nevertheless anticipated it and are contained within it, thus suggesting an unbroken continuity in the development of poetry. But, on the other hand, Hugo emphasizes very strongly the inaugural quality of this moment: 'here was a *new* religion and a *new* society: it is on this dual ground that we must see a *new* poetry begin to *grow*' (p. 9). The newness of this era is every bit as great as the newness of the original birth of mankind and the poetry of the ode.

One might be tempted to accuse Hugo of a flawed logic here, but it would make more sense to read these alternative models of historical development as testimony to the strength of the life force everywhere manifest as life cycle. It is telling in this connection that Hugo presents the end of the epic era not just as a natural decaying, but as a misguided attempt on the part of the Roman poets to copy their precursors, instead of tapping into the forces of nature and following its generative dynamism. The imagery associated with the failure—or refusal—to accept this natural dynamism often expresses oppression and violence (cages containing skeletons, scissors clipping wings, mutilation, and so on); but a most evocative set of images in this context is that of parasitical life forms, such as the polyp and the fungus, which do not subscribe to the natural pattern of a life cycle. The polyp is a false form of growth (p. 27), and parasitical beings do not live in the full and active sense of the word; they merely vegetate: 'it is better to be a bramble or a thistle, nourished by the same earth as a cedar or a palm, than to be the fungus or the lichen on these great trees. A bramble lives, but a fungus vegetates' (p. 24). It is better to live and die as an autonomous organism in one's own right than to perpetuate such parasitical forms of existence.

Autonomy is one of the most convincing signs of life for Hugo, and this is why poetry is treated as an independent entity that develops in parallel to society without being dependent on it, either as its direct expression or as its reflection. Poetry has full agency, as do the constituent elements that Hugo singles out within it. From this perspective, there is far more energy and activity ascribed to the grotesque and to verse form (*le vers*) than to individual writers, at least in the *Préface de Cromwell*. The grotesque has a life of its own in which it both grows and engenders further life: 'the grotesque, which contains the seeds of comedy, was embraced by the modern Muse, and was bound to *develop* and *grow* once it was transported to more favourable terrain' (p. 12). From the moment of its birth in Latin literature ('From *birth* it runs through the dying moments of Latin literature'), the grotesque has all the capacity for action of a human subject. It is capable of movement ('It *spreads through* the imagination of the new peoples of Europe. It *abounds* amongst the storytellers'); it has palpable influence on the world around it ('Above all it *imprints* its character on the marvellous architecture of the Middle Ages [. . .]. It *affixes* its stigmata on the face of cathedrals, *frames* their infernos'); and it has a powerful creative force of its own ('It *cavorts* in the dreams of the Germanic nations, while at the same time it *revives* those admirable Romanceros with *its breath*', p. 13). Just as Homer was born of poetry in antiquity, so the grotesque is credited with producing the comic geniuses of the Renaissance: 'To sum up [the grotesque] in a single image, its verve, its vigour, and its *creative* sap are such in this dawn of letters, that with a single gesture it throws up three comic Homers on the threshold of modern poetry: Ariosto, Cervantes, and Rabelais' (p. 13). The creative powers of the grotesque are such that it creates the creators.

The same sort of creative agency is ascribed to verse poetry. Hugo's apparently retrograde insistence on verse, as opposed to prose, in drama is in fact a profoundly anti-Aristotelian move. It is grounded in his rejection of the mimetic principles of Aristotelian poetics in favour of a view of literature as an autonomous agent with its own creative momentum: 'The truth of art can never be, as many have said, *absolute* reality. Art cannot provide the thing itself' (p. 25, Hugo's emphasis). Poetry for him is the supreme manifestation of this creative autonomy: 'the goal of art is almost divine; to restore to life if it is making history, *to create, if it is making poetry*' (p. 26). All the qualities that might elsewhere be ascribed to the poet are attributed by Hugo directly to verse form as it should ideally exist in the drama. It should have the quasi-human characteristics of ease and openness: 'a free, open, loyal verse, daring to say all without prudishness and express everything without contrivance; moving from the natural pace of comedy to tragedy, from the sublime to the grotesque' (p. 29); and it is poetry rather than the poet that is described as being the artist in this enterprise; 'positive and poetic by turns, at once artistic and inspired, profound and abrupt, broad and true'. It is poetry, too, that displays the technical mastery that one might otherwise expect to find ascribed to the writer: 'knowing the right moment to introduce a break and displace the caesura so as to disguise the monotony of the alexandrine [. . .]. Having the ability to run the whole poetic gamut' (p. 29). In short, poetry may be compared to a man who has the good fortune to have been blessed with the qualities that make for great literature: 'in a word, as it would be made by a man whom a good fairy had endowed with the soul of Corneille and the brain of Molière' (ibid.). This is a strange tautology, which invites us to see poetry itself as if it were a kind of super-poet (Corneille and Molière rolled into one), but which, nevertheless, once again precedes, produces, and upstages any individual poet.

Given his reverence for genius, Hugo is surprisingly uninterested here in the role of the individual poet, although, as we shall see in Chapter 7 in connection with *Les Contemplations*, the poet's personal existence can provide the basis for large-scale enterprises. In the *Préface de Cromwell*, however, it is the life of literature that is the focus of his attention. Right at the outset, he dismisses private individual concerns as irrelevant to the kind of appreciation of art that readers have: 'They want to know about the talent of a writer rather than about the way he sees the world; and whether a work is good or bad, they care little about the ideas in which it is rooted, or what kind of mind it took shape in' (p. 3). The origins of the work in the personal background of the writer are of as little import, he says, as the cellars of a building whose rooms one has just admired. This is very different from the approach of his contemporary Sainte-Beuve (as we shall see in Chapter 6), but it derives from Hugo's view of biography as life cycle, and from his preoccupation with literature itself as the incarnation of an unstoppable life force. Individual human biography has ceased to be the model for collective social and cultural development. The individual is too small to accommodate the scale on which the natural phenomenon of poetry and its various attributes—eras, genres, forms, language—exist, and has become just one version of the generalized organic process that constitutes the natural world.

The endless renewal of the life cycle is the mode in which Hugo conceives of literature's capacity for transformation which ensures that it necessarily and repeatedly becomes different from the former versions of itself. But in all the accounts of literature I have been discussing, from Rousseau via Madame de Staël to the Hugo of the *Préface de Cromwell*, the internal self-differentiation by means of which literature comes into being in its modern guise is opened up by the developmental temporality of the biographical mode: personal and autobiographical in the case of Rousseau, institutional and pedagogical in the case of Madame de Staël, organic and transindividual in the case of Hugo.

PART II

THE NINETEENTH CENTURY
AND THE CULTURE
OF BIOGRAPHY

THE significance of biography for the developing idea of literature in the eighteenth century lay more in a certain quasi-biographical mode of thinking than in the specific biographical practices of the time. This thinking is characterized by a strong developmental slant, and biography acquired a progressive temporality that profoundly determines the conception of literature informed by it. The effects of this remain palpable in the nineteenth century, as the instance of Hugo's *Préface de Cromwell* has already demonstrated; but they are accompanied by an extraordinary proliferation of biography as a wider cultural practice. Biography appeared in a number of new generic forms, most notably in biographical dictionaries, journalism, and literary criticism, all of which I shall be discussing in the next three chapters. The impact of these forms on literature was, first of all, in their role as mediators of certain images of writers and their achievements; writers appeared as subjects of numerous biographical entries and articles not just posthumously, but with increasing frequency during their own lifetime. Additionally however, these new biographical practices had equally significant consequences in the generic potential they offered to literature as material for its own evolution: to such an extent that by the end of the century biography was perceived, at least by Marcel Schwob, as the locus of a quintessential literarity. The idea of the literary as it appears in the various examples under review in the course of the chapters devoted to the nineteenth century therefore derives as much from literature's engagements with these contemporary biographical practices as with its own self-contesting history.

4

Biographical Business in the Century of Biography: Dictionaries and the Press

those skilful hands vied with each other in their devotion to cutting and carving the stones which each brought to the edifice of all.

(Charlies Nodier)

BIOGRAPHICAL MONUMENTS

The nineteenth century was, in many ways, the century in which modern biographical writing came into its own as a widespread and often monumental cultural phenomenon. Individual figures in the nineteenth century frequently acquired—or aspired to—monumental proportions (Napoleon, Hugo), and its great men were commemorated for posterity in paint, stone, and bronze. But whereas the monumentality of English biography in the nineteenth century appears in the form of the multi-volume life and letters of a single individual, the biographical monument that emerges in France is the biographical dictionary, published in huge numbers throughout the century. The focus on a single individual is not the most characteristic form taken by biography in the period, and the generic prestige of biography is predominantly a collective phenomenon. The English have George Henry Lewes's two-volume *Life and Works of Goethe* (1855), John Forster's three-volume *Life of Charles Dickens* (1872–4), and Froude's four volumes on *Thomas Carlyle* (1882–4), and it is these examples that have been emulated in the modern period and have considerably determined our current working assumptions about the forms of biography.

However, in France, Louis-Gabriel Michaud's fifty-two-volume *Biographie universelle ancienne et moderne*, published between 1811 and 1828, is nothing less than awe-inspiring. This dictionary appeared much earlier than the aforementioned English titles, and some seventy-five years earlier than Leslie Stephen's *Dictionary of National Biography*, whose sixty-six volumes were originally published between 1885 and 1901.[1] Each of the original fifty-two volumes

---

[1] In the preface to his new edition of *The General Biographical Dictionary: Containing an Historical and Critical Account of the Lives and Writings of the Most Eminent Persons in Every Nation,*

of the *Biographie universelle* contained some 500 or so entries, making a total of approximately 260,000 for the complete series; and the ambition of its universalist scope is spelled out in its subtitle, which announces it as an '*histoire par ordre alphabétique de la vie publique et privée de tous les hommes qui se sont fait remarquer par leurs écrits, leurs actions, leurs talents, leurs vertus ou leurs crimes*'.[2] Michaud's *Biographie* provided the model for numerous subsequent biographical enterprises over the course of two centuries: these include its own second, revised edition of 1843, Hoefer's *Nouvelle biographie générale* (1852–66), and Balteau's *Dictionnaire de biographie française* (1933–   ), all of which are still present in reference sections of serious libraries.[3] The term 'biographie' here is a collective noun, whose ambition is perceptible in the claim to universality spelled out in Michaud's original undertaking. This is repeated in Hoefer's rival revision (*Nouvelle biographie générale*), but more modestly expressed eighty years later as a national project in Balteau's *Dictionnaire de biographie nationale*, which also abandons the use of 'biographie' as a collective noun, styling itself a biographical dictionary. Whereas the English model of individual biography regularly took literary figures as their subjects, the collective dictionary did not give literature any privileged status as against other kinds of human activity. The significance of the collective *biographie* for literature is more oblique, lying in the manner in which it counters emerging objections to biography and contributes to defining the form as writers subsequently confront it. Dictionaries were not the only, nor probably the most influential, form of biography for writers, but they contributed enormously to what became the somewhat ambiguous prestige of the genre as writers themselves exploited it.

   The collective format was also adopted for the numerous biographical records of contemporary figures, such as Louis-Gabriel Michaud's *Biographie des hommes vivants* (1816), or Gustave Vapereau's *Dictionnaire universel des contemporains: contenant toutes les personnes notables de la France et des pays étrangers* (1858), a wordier version of a modern British *Who's Who?*, which went through several

---

Particularly the British and Irish, from the Earliest Accounts to the Present Time, which was first published in 1761, Alexander Chalmers hails the example of Michaud's *Biographie* (published a year before Chalmers's 1812 edn.) and acknowledges that the original version of the *General Biographical Dictionary* was itself indebted to Bayle's *Dictionnaire historique et critique*. Michaud is regularly cited as one of the 'authorities' from which the entries are drawn.

   [2] 'A history in alphabetical order of the public and private lives of all the men who have distinguished themselves by their writings, their actions, their talents, their virtues or their crimes': Joseph-François Michaud and Louis-Gabriel Michaud (eds.), *Biographie universelle, ancienne et moderne, ou, Histoire, par ordre alphabétique, de la vie publique et privée de tous les hommes qui se sont fait remarquer par leurs écrits, leurs actions, leurs talents, leurs vertus ou leurs crimes: ouvrage entièrement neuf, rédigé par une société de gens de lettres et de savants*, 52 vols. (Paris: Michaud, 1811–28); 3 extra vols. (1832–3) covered the 'Partie mythologique' of the biographical repertoire, and a further 30 vols. (1834–62) appeared in the form of supplements, bringing the total to some 85 volumes. A revised edition in 45 vols. was published between 1843 and 1865.

   [3] e.g. in the Taylorian Library in Oxford and the Bibliothèque nationale de France, where most of the reading and research for this book have been done.

revisions and expansions and is also still available on library shelves. These titles are the few survivors of what was a very extensive phenomenon: Theodore Zeldin records that dictionaries of contemporary biography alone accounted for over two hundred published titles in the nineteenth century (with a further eighty-one projects remaining incomplete). He also notes that the model of the biographical dictionary was used to bolster the identity of lesser geographical entities, with works such as the *Biographie bretonne* (1852–7), which presents itself as a '*recueil de notices sur tous les Bretons qui se sont fait un nom depuis le commencement de l'ère chrétienne jusqu'à nos jours*', or the *Biographie de la Dauphiné* (1856–60), which similarly claims to contain '*l'histoire des hommes nés dans cette province qui se sont fait remarquer dans les lettres, les sciences, les arts, avec le catalogue de leurs ouvrages et la description de leurs portraits*'.[4] Biographical compendia were furthermore a way of marking off different cultural fields, such as that of music in François-Joseph Fétis's eight-volume *Biographie universelle des musiciens* (1835–44), or of professions as in Mullié's *Biographie des célébrités militaires des armées de terre et de mer de 1789 à 1850* (1851). Whether historical or contemporary, universal, national, regional, cultural, or professional, the goal of the enterprise was broadly the same: the creation of totalities out of a collection of individual entries. It was this spirit that prompted Charles Nodier, in his capacity as member of the Académie française and Librarian of the Bibliothèque de l'Arsenal, rather than as the author of works such as *Jean Sbogar*, *Trilby*, or *Inès de las Sierras*, to describe the *Biographie universelle* as 'this fine historic monument' when he wrote the 'Discours préliminaire' to the revised edition of 1843.[5]

Biographies existed in another, less prestigious but equally collective and widely recognized form: they were a regular feature in the press where they constituted a journalistic subgenre on a par with the *chronique* or the *roman-feuilleton* which became established with the growth of the press from the 1830s onwards. They were almost always devoted to living figures and, more often than not, were produced in series. In the case of Eugène de Mirecourt, the format gave rise to an entire weekly publication entitled *Les Contemporains*, whose first number is dated 6 January 1857, and whose editor styled himself 'Le biographe' (The Biographer). These journalistic contributions often generated additional spin-off series, such as that of Eugène de Mirecourt's own, also entitled *Les Contemporains*, published in the form of little 'plaquettes', whose readers were invited to subscribe to a planned annual output of fifty short biographies, mainly of living writers. It is in the field of journalism that the question of literature becomes most actively engaged with the practice of biography during

---

[4] Theodore Zeldin, *France, 1848–1945: Anxiety and Hypocrisy* (Oxford: Oxford University Press, 1981), p. 2.

[5] Charles Nodier, 'Discours préliminaire', in Louis-Gabriel Michaud, *Biographie universelle*, rev. edn. (Paris: Mme C. Desplaces, 1843), vol. i, pp. v–x (p. vi). The epigraph to the present chapter is taken from the same page.

the nineteenth century, since writers so often featured as its subjects. Mirecourt's own 'plaquette' series began with a biography of Musset (published in 1854), and included Hugo, Nerval, Dumas, Vigny, Balzac, Sue, Sand, Lamartine, amongst other literary figures. Elsewhere, the journalistic biography would appear subsequently in a collected volume, whether in Mirecourt's *Histoire contemporaine: Portraits et silhouettes au XIXe siècle* (1867), which collected the individual *plaquettes* in four alphabetically arranged volumes,[6] or in Théophile Gautier's *Les Grotesques* (1844), which brought together in a single publication the separate pieces devoted to French writers that first appeared in *La France littéraire* from 1834 onwards. Sainte-Beuve's various book publications, including the *Critiques et portraits littéraires* (1832–9), *Portraits contemporains* (1846), the *Causeries du lundi* (1851–62), and the *Nouveaux lundis* (1863–8), all of which ran to several volumes, and some of which were recycled in different collected versions (such as the *Portraits littéraires*, 1844, and the *Portraits de femmes*, 1844), are prime examples of this practice, and may indeed have been a major instigator of it. In short, whether as dictionary, as newspaper or publisher's series, or as collected volume, biography made its most powerful impact in collective form, and each of these manifestations will be discussed in what follows.

BIOGRAPHY VERSUS HISTORY: VICTOR COUSIN AND ERNEST RENAN

Despite the new-found popularity of biography, its standing was mixed. Recent history was a major justification for biographies of the contemporary figures who had contributed to events, or who played an influential role in a society no longer based on the social principles of the *ancien régime*. There was a widely felt need in Restoration France for what Loïc Chotard calls a 'historical, social, and moral physiology' modelled on the grand schemes of Buffon, Cuvier, or Geoffroy Saint-Hilaire in order to explain the workings of post-Revolutionary society and also to provide examples of behaviour for its citizens to emulate.[7] Biography helped to meet both these needs. On the issue of exemplarity, Chotard cites Balzac's tale *La Grenadière* in which Lady Brandon gives her son biographies—'interesting but accurate books' about 'great men and famous captains'—and urges the boy to note in particular 'the means used by those of lowly origins, but who are in fact great men, and set out without protectors, from the lowest rungs of society

---

6 Eugène de Mirecourt, *Histoire contemporaine: portraits et silhouettes au XIXe siècle*, 4 vols. (Paris: Dentu, 1867).

7 Cited by Loïc Chotard, 'La Biographie contemporaine en France au dix-neuvième siècle: autour du Panthéon-Nadar', doctoral thesis (Université de Paris IV-Sorbonne, 1987), p. 25. This study, regrettably never published, is one of the most thorough accounts of French biography in the nineteenth century that I have encountered.

to achieve noble destinies'.[8] Biography offered a means of establishing a secular morality and a new social order: 'great men are to the nation what a map is to its territories'.[9] At the same time, precisely because the forces of political as well as natural history were being conceived on a larger scale than any single individual could match, individual biography carried relatively little weight in the overall scheme of things. It was regularly compared with history and very frequently found wanting. By the same token, its self-justification was almost always couched in terms that sought to give it some kind of historical significance.

The clearest case against biography and in favour of larger histories is made by Victor Cousin in the tenth of the lectures (the *Cours de philosophie*) that he gave between 1828 and 1829 at the Collège de France, under the title *Introduction à l'histoire de la philosophie*. The lecture is devoted to the question of 'Great Men', and in it Cousin discusses 'eminent individuals' principally in relation to nations. A nation, he asserts, is a body that consists of more than the sum of the individuals of which it is made up, since it is above all the expression of an idea, that is, of a national idea. This claim develops the thinking that informed the notion of national identity in the work of Madame de Staël, as we saw in Chapter 3. For Cousin, the historical life of a nation is determined by its relation to the national idea; and each individual within the nation is, to a greater or lesser extent, a bearer of this 'idea'. It is impossible, he says, to conceive of an individual without this larger dimension: 'An individual who in his own times and in his own country should be simply an individual, would be a monster.'[10] Equally, an individual who was nothing more than the expression of the national idea would be without significance. What distinguishes a 'great man' is a particular balance of idea and individuality: 'The great man is only great [. . .] upon the double condition of being imbued with the general spirit of the nation, and at the same time of representing this generality, in a deeply individual form; and all with that measure which is the mark of true human greatness' (p. 204 [i, p. 166]). This balance is nevertheless not to the credit of the individual, for the great man is first and foremost a representative of the national idea; he appears when he is needed and vanishes when that need has passed. He is the instrument of a power that is not his, being merely the repository, not the master, of such power. Without the idea, the greatest are as nothing. If you separate the individual from the 'spirit of his people', and consider only the man in the 'great man', then even the greatest will seem petty:

Every individuality, when it is detached from the general spirit which it expresses, is full of wretched adversities. When we read the secret memoirs which we have of some great

---

[8] Loïc Chotard, 'Les "biographies contemporaines" au xixe siècle', in id., *Approches du XIXe siècle* (Paris: Presses de l'Université de Paris-Sorbonne, 2000), pp. 7–20 (p. 17).

[9] Ibid., p. 15.

[10] Victor Cousin, 'Dixième leçon: les grands hommes', in id., *Introduction à l'histoire de la philosophie*, 4th edn. (Paris: Didier, 1861), pp. 201–25 (p. 203) [vol. i, p. 166*]. All further page references are to these editions.

men, and when we follow them into the details of their life and conduct, we are always quite confounded to find them on many points very similar to the commonest of men. (pp. 213–14 [i, p. 173*])

The philosophy of history is concerned exclusively with what is great in such individuals, and the miserable details of their everyday existence belong entirely to the sphere of 'memoirs and biography' (p. 216). For Cousin, biography, with its focus on the life of the individual, is incapable of encompassing the greatness of the subjects it might be drawn to, and its methods reduce every human existence to the same common denominator of undistinguished trivia.

The upshot of this argument is that the criterion of 'greatness' depends to a considerable extent on factors that are independent of individual merit; and there is, moreover, a limited number of spheres in which that 'greatness' can exist. Cousin dismisses industry and commerce as fields that do not lend themselves to such a thing, and claims that 'It is in the arts, in the government of Nations, that all the power of some privileged individuals is revealed' (p. 220 [i, p. 176*]). However, even here, there are hierarchies: if there are great artists, great legislators, and great politicians, they are nevertheless eclipsed by philosophers and warriors, since, for Cousin, war and philosophy are the fields that best promote greatness. This is because they incarnate the two principal ways of serving humanity, expressed very broadly as 'action and thought' (p. 222 [i, p. 178]); but it is also because they entail a combination of the most extreme degrees of generality with individuality. In the case of thought, the individual is required to separate himself off from the rest of humanity in order to engage in reflection, and, at the same time, 'the object of philosophical reflection is what is most general in thought' (p. 221 [i, p. 178]). In a word, says Cousin, the object of philosophical thought is generality, though its form is individuality.

The individual is of interest primarily for his relation to a transcendent generality, whether it be the national 'idea' or the abstraction of philosophical thought. This makes history preferable to biography, and ideas preferable to individuals, a view that determines much of the discussion of biography in the nineteenth century and will largely dictate the terms of its self-justification. So, for example, when Renan comes to write his *Vie de Jésus* in 1863, he is careful to emphasize that it is the first volume of what is to be a seven-part history, the *Histoire des origines du christianisme*, and, furthermore, that the need for a biographical account of Jesus emerged only gradually from his general historical project. He seems to feel bound to produce an apology for the presence of biography in the work, and he acknowledges that 'Many will regret, perhaps, the biographical form which my work has [. . .] taken'.[11] His original plan, he says, was a history of Christian doctrine in which individuals would play almost no role: 'Jesus would scarcely have been named; I should have endeavoured to

---

[11] Ernest Renan, *Vie de Jésus* (1863; Histoire des origines du christianisme, 1; Paris: Arléa, 1992), p. 50 [p. 24]. All further page references are to these editions.

show how the ideas which have grown under his name took root and covered the world' (p. 235 [p. 219]). However, these Cousinian precepts were turned on their head when Renan came to see that individuals counted for more than ideas, and people for more than theories: 'I have learned since that history is not a simple game of abstractions; that men are more than doctrines. It was not a certain theory on justification and redemption which brought about the Reformation; it was Luther and Calvin' (ibid.). In the case of Jesus, this primacy of the human over the abstract is doubly justified in that, according to Renan, his influence did not operate through ideas and doctrines but through his capacity for inspiring love: 'To have made himself beloved [. . .] was the great work of Jesus' (ibid.). It is above all his personal qualities that determined the success of early Christianity: 'The faith, the enthusiasm, the constancy of the first Christian generation is not explicable, except by supposing, at the origin of the whole movement, a man of surpassing greatness' (p. 237 [p. 221]). For Renan, the greatness of the great man lies in the character of the individual, and this only biography can convey.

Although Renan seems to be reversing the priorities that Victor Cousin had defended, history nonetheless remains his ultimate horizon, and in the end the life is justified by an idea. He argues for the importance of a *Vie de Jésus* on the grounds that history in its entirety cannot be understood without taking this individual figure into account, and that the life is a necessary preliminary to any historical understanding: 'His glory does not consist in being relegated out of history; we render him a truer worship in showing that all history is incomprehensible without him' (p. 53 [p. 26]). Biography is necessary as an adjunct to the larger history, and the *Vie de Jésus* is followed by the six further volumes of the *Histoire des origines du christianisme*, for which it serves as the prelude. Even within the frame of the individual life, there needs to be a founding principle, since the life of a great man is more than a collection of discrete biographical facts: 'A great life is an organic whole which cannot be rendered by the simple agglomeration of small facts. It requires a profound sentiment to embrace them all, moulding them into perfect unity' (p. 51 [p. 24]). Biography is justified in terms of some kind of transcendence, whether this be its necessary relation to history or the principle of organic unity that informs it; and the individual is redeemed principally in relation to some more general 'idea'.

BIOGRAPHICAL DICTIONARIES AND COLLECTIVE TRANSCENDENCE

The particular question of literature's transcendent relation to biography will be discussed later, within the context of journalistic biography, but we first need to consider the way in which the various dictionaries of biography in the nineteenth century sought more generally to construct a transcendence. And they did this primarily through the sheer impact of their collective character. It is true, of course, that the majority of biographical writings prior to the nineteenth century existed in collective form, the most notable examples being Plutarch's *Lives*, of which two new translations were published in a huge number of different editions and selections throughout the nineteenth century, the first by Ricard in 1798 and the second by Alexis Pierron in 1843; Jacobus de Voragine's *Golden Legend*, which appeared in a new French translation, also in 1843, to be reprinted several times over the course of the century; Vasari's *Lives of the Artists*; and Perrault's *Les Hommes illustres qui ont paru en France pendant ce siècle*. But in each of these cases the collected lives are those of a specific group: great men of Greece and Rome, saints, artists, or individuals from a specific time and place, such as seventeenth-century France. Where the so-called universal dictionaries of Michaud or Hoefer are concerned, there is no such specificity: the Michaud *Biographie universelle* explicitly covers both the ancient and the modern worlds, even if the bias is towards France in the modern period; and, as the subtitle states, the criterion for inclusion is distinction across a whole variety of fields—writing, action, talent, virtue, and crime.

What this dictionary might have lost in coherence through the ambition of its coverage it professed to have gained through the very enormity of its enterprise. Charles Nodier, in his preface to the revised edition of 1843, emphasizes this grandeur of conception, asserting that the *Biographie universelle* is one of the 'largest and most useful conceptions of the century'; and he goes so far as to claim that the strategy of comprehensiveness constituted 'such a fertile idea that it is almost terrifying in its immensity'.[12] The project amounts to much more than the sum of its parts precisely because it has so many parts; and a quasi-sublime transcendence is achieved through sheer quantity. Nonetheless, size is not the only issue, and Nodier stresses both the presence of underlying principles and 'the unity of its conception and of its aim', so as to counter any view of the dictionary as a mere compilation of discrete biographical facts. It is a collectivity informed by conceptual coherence.

Here the comparison between biography and history seems to be unavoidable, and is made on the grounds that the two practices are inextricably bound up with each other: the biographer's expertise and scholarly research, says Nodier, are every bit as great as the historian's; the model for his narrative relation to his material is that of the great Roman historians; and the moral lessons that readers may derive from biography are no less than those of history—'The history of events being inseparable from that of men, the biographer should explore his subject just as thoroughly as the historian, be naturally equal to the greatness of his types, descend effortlessly to individual characteristics, and distribute teachings and thought through the tissue of his narratives' (ibid.). Adherence to

[12] Nodier, 'Discours préliminaire', p. v.

these methods, says Nodier, will ensure that biography contains as much 'moral sanction' and 'philosophical authority' as those more readily ascribed to history (p. vi). One can hear in this an echo of a Plutarchan principle of exemplarity and an implicit riposte to Cousin's dismissal of biography. But it is a riposte that still relies heavily on the terms of Cousin's argument, and it comes very close to defending biography on the grounds that biography makes better history than history itself. History is obliged to paint with a broad brush and leave out much of the detail of the life of the individuals who participated in it; and for Nodier this becomes an argument for seeing biography as more complete—as well as more exemplary—than its competitor (p. vii).

Overall, however, it is the collective presentation of the biographies in Michaud's dictionary that makes biography a serious rival to history. Michaud's own 'Discours préliminaire' of 1811 opens with a comparison between biography and history, and makes much of the comprehensive and systematic nature of the biographical dictionary, which he claims no history could hope to match: 'Precisely because Biography portrays historical personages of all kinds in isolation, it alone has the power to include them all in a single work, arranging them in a systematic order that History does not possess.'[13] Every person of historical note can be contained within the *Biographie*. Each entry is designed to shed useful light on a given period of political or literary history; there is a system of cross-referencing; and tables at the end allow readers to recompose historical coherence out of the elements contained within the separate entries. Moreover, as Balzac was to argue in his 1842 'Avant-propos' to the *Comédie humaine*, traditional history in any case fails to supply what Michaud here calls 'the details of behaviour and private habits', claiming that they are the special province of biography (p. viii)—just as Balzac will claim that they are the prerogative of the novel. In short, the collective biography supposedly constitutes a far fuller historical resource than any conventional history.

This emphasis on the collective does not apply simply to the biographical subjects, and much is also made of the collective nature of the dictionary's authorship. The strong card of the whole project is its scholarly reliability—presumably a major reason for its continuing survival—and here the combination of multiple authorship and collective vetting is crucial. The title page of the *Biographie* attributes authorship to 'a society of men of letters and learning', but in fact each entry was commissioned from a particular author, chosen for his or her expertise, and is signed with initials that can be decoded at the end of each volume. (Victor Cousin, Madame de Staël, Cuvier, and Benjamin Constant are amongst these authors, before becoming subjects of biographical entries of their own in later volumes or in the revised edition.) The insistence on the factual content of each entry, and the necessity of 'precision in content and concision in style' mean that collective norms restrict individual authors in their normal manner of

---

[13] L.-G. Michaud, 'Discours préliminaire', in id., *Biographie universelle*, vol. i, pp. v–x (p. vii).

expression and guarantee consistency throughout the fifty-two volumes (p. xiv). Nodier describes this as 'the sacrifice of individual reason to a collective one'.[14] All entries were double-checked by a further group consisting—in Michaud's words—of 'several persons filled with zeal and learning who devoted themselves to immeasurable and difficult enquiry' in order that the bibliographies, which constituted a vital component of each entry, should be accurate and complete.[15] Furthermore, these bibliographies recorded sources as well as listing the published works of each figure, where applicable. The scholarly ambition of the *Biographie* could be realized only by extending the collective criterion to include authorship and editing as well.

The principles of Michaud's *Biographie universelle* were adopted by all subsequent dictionaries of biography, and established a model of biographical practice whose scale and ambition contributed in a major way to its importance in the nineteenth century. Furthermore, the collective form and the scholarly procedures later provided a model for certain literary uses of biography, as we shall see in the cases of Nerval and Schwob. And, as we shall also see, its entries were trawled for biographical fact by writers such as Gautier, in his account of Théophile de Viau in *Les Grotesques*, for example, or Nerval, who drew on it freely for his 'Histoire de l'abbé de Bucquoy' in *Les Illuminés*. The biographical dictionary had become a national institution and was an inescapable part of national life. But in the process it created an ambiguous justification for biography by stressing its value primarily as a collective monument and serving indirectly to undermine the singular elements with which the form is so often associated.

BIOGRAPHY AND THE PRESS

At the same time, as I have already mentioned, the biographical essay was emerging as one of the major genres in the press as it developed from the 1830s onwards. Sainte-Beuve's literary portraits (which I shall be discussing in Chapter 6) appeared during the 1830s in the *Revue de Paris*, *Le Globe*, the *Revue des deux mondes*, and *Le National*, and, from 1849 until the year of his death in 1869, in alternation between *Le Constitutionnel* and *Le Moniteur*. But the phenomenon was everywhere, and under the Second Empire the genre achieved particularly widespread currency. It was more often devoted to the living than to the dead, and the term 'biographie' was regularly employed as a synonym for the newly minted 'biographie contemporaine'. In June 1866, to take a random example, *Le Nain jaune* ran a piece on Charles Blondin, the acrobat who had

14 Nodier, 'Discours préliminaire', p. vi.
15 Michaud, 'Discours préliminaire', p. xvi.

crossed the Niagara Falls on a tightrope, and it commented that the moment had come to provide a brief biography for him. As the author of the article notes, 'this type of publication is very much in vogue', and so, he continues, 'I do not see why Blondin should not have his biographical note, alongside other acrobats whose personalities fill the gazettes'.[16] The journalistic biography developed in conjunction with the visual portrait and the caricature, as can be seen, for example, in the various series to which Nadar contributed, both as writer and as caricaturist during the decade 1852–62, in such publications as *Le Journal pour rire*, *Le Tintamarre*, and the *Journal amusant*.[17] The chief rationale for the phenomenon was a combination of financial opportunism and the promotion of celebrity. As Loïc Chotard says, 'the biographer is above all a producer who transforms the raw material provided by celebrities in the media into an easily assimilated product in which text and image are arranged according to the tried and tested recipes of booksellers: the biographical volume or collection'.[18] One of the major representatives of this kind of celebrity was the writer.

In the context of the press, the notion of the collective acquired a problematic ambiguity wherein the idea of a cultural monument coexisted with the principle of mass culture for which celebrity complicated the tradition of exemplarity. Biography became a phenomenon of spectacle, as can be inferred from the titles given to the collective publications, many of which included the word 'Galerie', 'Musée', 'Panorama', and so on.[19] The writer in particular was seen as an incarnation of visible success in ways that seemed applicable to all other spheres. When the publicist Eugène de Mirecourt started his series *Les Contemporains* in 1854, it was explicitly for this reason that he chose writers as his genus, and he presents his project in the following terms:

If there is anything in France that excites the curiosity of the mass of readers who devour our modern publications, it is clearly the private and personal history of famous writers. Witnessing their beginnings, following them in their career, discovering how they obtained the favours of that inconstant fairy godmother we call Fame, catching them when they are off-duty like mere mortals, all this is incontestably a powerful and irresistible incitement, and an attraction that none of us can resist.[20]

---

[16] 'Une biographie d'acrobate', *Le Nain jaune*, 6 June 1866, pp. 4–5.

[17] On this see Chotard, 'La Biographie contemporaine'. The springboard for Chotard's study is the collection of figures Nadar assembled for his famous '*Panthéon*', which was originally destined to appear in four vast collective portraits of the major figures of the nineteenth century. In the event he produced only one series, which depicts some three hundred figures from the contemporary literary and intellectual world, with Victor Hugo at their head. On the wider phenomenon of the literary portrait see the excellent study by Hélène Dufour, *Portraits, en phrases: les recueils de portraits littéraires au XIXe siècle* (Paris: Presses universitaires de France, 1997).

[18] Chotard, 'La Biographie contemporaine', p. 405.

[19] See Chotard, 'Les "biographies contemporaines" au xixe siècle', p. 16.

[20] Eugène de Mirecourt, *Méry* (Les Contemporains; Paris: F. Sartorius and J.-P. Roret, 1854), p. 1.

Cousin's idea of the history of great men may have disdained personal detail, but the private life of writers who have achieved fame is the substance of a genre that sold in mass to a mass readership. As I have already mentioned, readers of the first number of *Les Contemporains* were encouraged to subscribe to the little biographies, at 25 centimes a number; those who did received a biographical narrative of a famous figure, many of whom were writers, illustrated with a lithograph portrait and a facsimile of an autograph work, such as a poem or a letter.

Mirecourt's biographical *plaquettes* were far from being an isolated phenomenon. Baudelaire's *Théophile Gautier* was published in this form by Poulet-Massis in 1859. Léon Vanier, who published many of the Symbolist poets, ran a series of four-page fascicules entitled *Les Hommes d'aujourd'hui* in the 1880s, to which Verlaine contributed a number of biographical portraits, including one of Mallarmé (which I shall be discussing in Chapter 5). These journalistic portraits became one of the major forms in which writers figured in the general cultural imagination over the course of the nineteenth century. As Hélène Dufour says, 'Literary portraits are a new way of promoting the figure of the writer; they create a new type of exchange for ideas and reflections about contemporary literary life, and in particular a new form of critical relation.'[21] The exchange of ideas prompted by these literary portraits took both negative and positive forms, and I shall look at three separate moments—the 1830s, 1860s, and 1890s—through the eyes of three separate literary figures—Gautier, Barbey d'Aurevilly, and Mallarmé—in order to explore the ways in which an idea of literature emerges from the negotiations of writers with the press through the medium of the biographical genre.

On the negative side, writers were obliged to reckon with the existence of a form of writing—journalism—and a popular or mass culture from which they wished to distinguish their own literary concerns. Amongst other reactions, this produced outright condemnations of biography. One of the earliest of these came from Gautier in his preface to *Mademoiselle de Maupin* (written in 1834), where he defends art against the utilitarian values of contemporary society, which he accuses the press of supporting: 'Reading papers prevents the existence of real scholars and real artists. It is a daily excess which leaves you enervated and exhausted when you reach the bed of the Muses. Those hard and difficult women want fresh and vigorous lovers. *The newspaper is killing the book.*'[22]

The press is emasculating artists and destroying literature, for which Gautier blames the critics who write for the newspapers. In particular he accuses these critics of neglecting the text for the author. They assume that an author must always be describing his own experience and is therefore a drunkard if he depicts

[21] Dufour, *Portraits, en phrases*, p. vi.
[22] Théophile Gautier, *Mademoiselle de Maupin* [1835], ed. Michel Crouzet (Collection Folio; Paris: Gallimard, 1973), p. 68 [p. 52*].

an orgy, a lecher if his novel portrays debauchery, or a virtuous man if he writes morally improving prose. The critics fail to see that 'it is the character who speaks and not the author', and their accounts are wilful misrepresentations based in their own envy and mediocrity: 'It is one of the manias of these little scribblers with tiny minds, always to substitute the author for the work and to turn to the personality, to give some poor scandalous interest to their wretched rhapsodies. They know quite well that nobody would read them if they just contained their personal opinion.'[23] The journalist's simplistic recourse to the author's personality and experience is a disguise for his own lack of talent. But it has more serious effects in that it contributes to undermining the aesthetic value of literature, which Gautier characterizes here in terms of freedom from all moral and utilitarian purpose. As the preferred medium of the press, biography is allied with journalism and opposed to the more rigorous demands of literature. In sum, biography for Gautier is the index of a culturally enfeebled attitude of mind to which literature is opposed by virtue of its superior demands; biography is associated with the article rather than the book (a leitmotif of discussion throughout the century), with the journalist rather than the writer, and with the self-interest of utilitarianism rather than the altruism of high aesthetic purpose.

BARBEY D'AUREVILLY AND THE CULTURE OF BIOGRAPHY

One of the most furious attacks on biography came some thirty years or so later from Barbey d'Aurevilly who saw it as a symptom of a society devoted to vanity and self-interest. Writing during the Second Empire, he describes the age as one of 'egoism and affectation', 'boredom' and 'priggishness', where ridicule has replaced vice and mediocrity is universal.[24] Biography is one of the most overt symptoms of this cultural decline, which it will be the task of literature to resist. In an essay written in 1867, 'Les Photographies et les biographies', Barbey jointly condemns biography and photography as 'the siamese twins of a single vanity'.[25] His objection is directed less at the journalists and the press condemned by Gautier, than at the culture of an entire society of individuals preoccupied with

---

[23] Ibid., p. 48 [pp. 34–5].

[24] J. Barbey d'Aurevilly, 'Alfred de Vigny, *le Journal d'un poète*', in id., *Le XIXᵉ siècle: des œuvres et des hommes*, ed. Jacques Petit, 2 vols. (Paris: Mercure de France, 1964–6), vol. ii, pp. 94–6 (p. 94); and Barbey d'Aurevilly, 'Préface', in id., *Les Ridicules du temps* (Paris: Rouveyre et G. Blond, 1883), pp. i–iv.

[25] In *Les Ridicules du temps*, pp. 15–26. This essay first appeared as an article in *Le Nain jaune* on 3 Jan. 1867, pp. 3–4, at a time when Mirecourt was embarking on the collected republication of *Les Contemporains* under the title *Portraits et silhouettes du XIXᵉ siècle*.

their own image: 'an entire people [has], in its decline, become enamoured of itself, and inveterately occupied with contemplating its own beloved image'.[26]

There is a further dimension to Barbey's imprecations, and he blames the democratization of nineteenth-century society for having led to a debasement of both portraiture and history in the forms of photography and biography, respectively. He laments the passing of the *ancien régime* and the values of the nobility, both as a class system and as a set of moral norms. The nineteenth-century society of spectacle that has replaced the society of the *ancien régime* sees the statesman lining up with the porter, and the third-rate actress alongside the duchess to place themselves in front of the camera in quest of 'shop-window celebrity' (p. 18). Photography creates a 'democracy of the portrait' and has replaced the glories of the painted representation—'the images of our elders and the sumptuous portraits of the *ancien régime*, and all those imposing, rare, and finely made things' (p. 17). However, the effects of the 'cheapening of history', for which biography is responsible, are even worse than those of 'the cheapening of the human figure and the portrait' perpetrated by photography: 'the absurd phenomenon [*le ridicule*] of biography has had a deeper influence bordering on vice, for it falsifies history' (p. 22). The biographies that are written by the living about the living who are still in the mid-course of their lives are bound to lack the impartiality and the objectivity of history, with the result that 'the proliferation of biographies and superficial biographers [. . .] are debasing the history of the future in advance while appearing to be preparing it'. Barbey regards biography as the antithesis of true history and as little more than a form of thinly disguised publicity. It is a form cobbled together to suit the immediate requirements of both its subjects and its authors, and lacks the dignity of history, which 'imposed the most difficult obligations on those who sought to write it' (p. 23). The collective is now a negative value, and is condemned as the consequence of bourgeois democracy and the mass culture it has spawned.

Barbey's cultural pessimism is more than a simple desire for a vanished political order based on strict social hierarchies.[27] What he seems to regret most is the passing of an age in which, according to him, individuals were ready to subordinate themselves to ideals that transcended personal existence, and he evaluates literature according to the degree to which it aligns itself with these values. The heroes and heroines of his own tales in *Les Diaboliques* are all willing to sacrifice their lives to something they regard as having greater worth, whether it is the soldier resolved to lose his life on the battlefield, the lovers in thrall to passions 'which ruin a whole career', the duchess devoting her life

---

[26] 'Les Photographies et les biographies', in *Los Ridicules des temps*, p. 17. (Subsequent references appear in text.)

[27] 'Barbey est toujours resté un homme d'Ancien Régime attaché aux traditions': Marie-Christine Natta, 'Introduction', in J. Barbey d'Aurevilly, *Du Dandysme et de George Brummel* [*sic*], ed. Marie-Christine Natta (Bassac: Plein chant, 1989), p. 16.

to revenge on her husband by becoming a prostitute and dying of venereal disease, or the duke who sustains an ancient family tradition of fearlessness in the face of death—'He was not afraid of death. Every generation of Sierra Leones has faced it unflinchingly'.[28] Barbey's condemnation of biography and of the culture in which it flourishes is based primarily on what he sees as the absence among his contemporaries of any such principle of individual courage and moral transcendence.

Much of Barbey's journalistic writing was devoted to a literary criticism in which he is chiefly concerned with charting literature's decline.[29] He seems to have considered the literature of the period to be largely responsible for promoting the climate in which the personal and the biographical flourished to the detriment of the larger concerns he thinks it should be supporting. The social foibles that he attacks in *Les Ridicules du temps* are almost all found in the world of letters, because, says Barbey, the democratic basis of literature in the nineteenth century has offered all comers the chance to satisfy their vanity through writing: 'In a country without titles or distinctions, where each wants to be the equal of all, and where people boast only of their personal worth, there is only one form of pretension and one form of vanity, and that is literary pretension and vanity.'[30] The results are not, however, literature but a journalism which seeks to pass for literature, and which, in addition to condoning authorial vanity, encourages a squalid and intrusive search for biographical material by the 'ogress' of biography:

Biography is an ogress who wants her plate of fodder every morning, and when she does not get it, she chews on air. She chews on inventions and silly hearsay [. . .]. She would willingly listen at doors in order to peep into the life of someone whose only due to the world is his thought! She would corrupt chambermaids. She would write at the dictation of lackeys who had been thrown out of their jobs. [. . .] She is a beggar hungry for facts—the trivial facts beloved of fools.[31]

Barbey accuses Sainte-Beuve of having contributed to the replacement of literature by journalism, and when he died Barbey had little to say in defence of a critic whom he accused of lacking grand literary principles. Nevertheless, he vigorously condemned the newspapers who sent their journalists to Sainte-Beuve's home to report on his death by photographing the deceased man, describing his apartment and his furnishings, and discussing his birds and his cats in the minutest detail, simply in order to satisfy 'public Curiosity, that frightful portress, to whom we

---

[28] J. Barbey d'Aurevilly, *Les Diaboliques*, ed. Jean-Pierre Seguin (Paris: Garnier-Flammarion, 1967), 'Le Rideau cramoisi', 'Le Dessous de cartes' (p. 176 [p. 117]), 'La Vengeance d'une femme' (p. 305 [p. 237]).

[29] For an account of Barbey's criticism see Jacques Petit, *Barbey d'Aurevilly, critique* (Paris: Les Belles Lettres, 1963).

[30] Barbey d'Aurevilly, *Les Ridicules du temps*, p. iv.

[31] 'Les Photographies et les biographies', pp. 24–5.

all pay court'.[32] He portrays Sainte-Beuve as a posthumous victim of the culture that he had helped to foster through his supposed betrayal of literary values.

A mere 'articler' in Barbey's view, Sainte-Beuve had contributed to the trivialization of literature whereby—in words that echo Gautier—'the newspaper article has replaced the book'.[33] But, says Barbey, he also undermined it through his personalization of critical discussion at the cost of higher literary absolutes: 'From then on he was nothing more than an [. . .] anecdotist writing as an individual; since he does not believe in any Absolute or any Truth!'[34] Judged by his own practice, the literary 'absolutes' that Barbey accuses Sainte-Beuve of lacking would seem to amount to a willingness to treat criticism as a matter of fearless and impartial justice, and to make literary evaluations independently of journalistic popularity. In fact, it appears to be principally the readiness to ignore such popularity that determines Barbey's stance; his own literary judgements are ostentatiously ethical—not aesthetic—and are based on an assessment that is itself ultimately biographical. Where that assessment differs from those of the popular press condemned by Barbey is in the criteria he adopts, which ignore the popular preference for celebrity in favour of the metaphysical and moral worth of the author. As he says in his preface to the first volume of *Les Œuvres et les hommes*: 'A book is the man who wrote it, head, heart, liver, and guts. Criticism should therefore reach through the book to the man or through the man to the book, and always nail one to the other!'[35] Barbey's critical vocabulary is one that favours stoical nails and guts over what he regards as the trivia of domestic arrangements, pets, and personal vanity. In the case of Hugo, the man who is ruthlessly nailed to his poetry by Barbey's criticism is one who exhibits nothing but an empty facility with poetic form, and a readiness to satisfy the Ogress of Biography by filling his poetry with a self-indulgent and indiscriminate revelation of the details of his private life.[36] In contrast, Barbey praises both Vigny and Baudelaire for their self-denying 'Roman' attributes, which produce a poetry that merely hints at a personal merit it refrains from flaunting. Vigny's posthumously published *Journal d'un poète* reveals that his poetry amounted to much more than a mere 'masquerade' of formal features, and confirms that behind it was a life of suffering nobly endured: 'despite the stoicism with which he confronted inevitable fate, one sensed that in his *Destinées* the poet was bleeding beneath the polished steel of his armoury, that he was drinking his own blood from his helmet, like Beaumanoir in the Battle of the Thirty, and

---

[32] Barbey d'Aurevilly, 'Sainte-Beuve', in *Le XIXᵉ siècle*, vol. ii, pp. 149–55 (p. 149).

[33] Barbey d'Aurevilly, 'Sainte-Beuve', p. 153.

[34] Barbey d'Aurevilly, 'M. Sainte-Beuve', in *Le XIXᵉ siècle*, vol. ii, pp. 36–8 (p. 38).

[35] J. Barbey d'Aurevilly, 'Préface', in id., *Les Œuvres et les hommes*, 1st ser., i: *Les Philosophes et les écrivains religieux* (1860; repr. Geneva: Slatkine, 1968), pp. i–vii (p. iv).

[36] J. Barbey d'Aurevilly, 'M. Victor Hugo', in id., *Les Œuvres et les hommes*, 1st ser., iii: *Les Poètes* (1862; repr. Geneva: Slatkine, 1968), pp. 1–48 (p. 10).

found it bitter.'[37] Baudelaire is credited with showing similar stoical virtues in his *Fleurs du mal* whose acknowledgements of the inevitability of retribution for every excess are, says Barbey, the fruit of Baudelaire's own experience: 'His Muse sought them out through the chinks in his own heart, and dragged them into the light of day with a hand as pitiless and as ruthless as that of the Roman who tore out his own entrails.'[38] Literary worth is sealed in Barbey's scheme of things by figures whose virtues are rather more military than literary, since it would seem to be soldiers who provide the most compelling examples of a self-denying, but uniquely individual, heroism.

Barbey's literary aesthetic, which pins the poet to his work and the work to the poet, turns out to be, more than anything else, an ethic designed to test the author's moral qualities. In their positive guise these qualities are the reverse of what Barbey sees as the culture of the age: an aristocratic restraint, which he defends against the democratic exhibition of personality promoted by biography, impartial judgement against self-indulgence, and high principle against the squalor of personal data. If he opposes literature to journalism, and the book to the article, it is primarily because the qualities he is defending are associated with books and literature, and those he is condemning with journalism and the newspaper article. Literature is treated as the repository of a kind of moral transcendence to which the life of the individual poet is discreet testimony; journalism is castigated as the vehicle for the self-advertising biographies produced en masse for mass consumption. In Barbey's eyes, the collective in this sphere appears as nothing more than the mediocrity that is bred by a democratic society, and it is the stoical loner who instantiates the moral ideal. This emphasis is more a characteristic of his own defiantly anachronistic values than the expression of a concern about the future of literature. But his presentation of literature as the polar opposite of journalism continues the opposition established by Gautier in his preface to *Mademoiselle de Maupin*, and taken up by others such as Balzac, whose *Illusions perdues* had elaborated on it at length. Barbey's particular concern with biography as the focus of this opposition does, however, touch on a nerve, and the question of literature's relation to the press continues to surface in association with biography for the rest of the century, as we shall see in the next chapter.

[37] Barbey d'Aurevilly, 'Alfred de Vigny', p. 96.
[38] Barbey d'Aurevilly, 'M. Charles Baudelaire', in *Les Poètes*, pp. 371–82 (p. 373).

5

Biography Reclaimed: Gautier, Verlaine, and Mallarmé and the Biographical *recueil*

The opposition between literature and journalism that becomes established with the rise of the press in the nineteenth century is nonetheless complicated by the considerable involvement of literature in journalism from the 1830s onwards, not least in the form of the literary portrait or biography. As well as being the subjects of this hugely popular journalistic genre, offering exemplary instances of those favoured by the 'inconstant fairy godmother of fame' invoked by Mirecourt, writers were also very often the authors of such portraits. Economic necessity meant that many had to write for the press simply in order to survive. As Gautier records in the self-portrait he produced towards the end of his life, journalism took its revenge on him for his attack in the preface to *Mademoiselle de Maupin* by condemning him to a lifetime's enslavement to its practice.[1] He goes on to list the titles of the journals for which he has been obliged to write during the many decades of his career—*La Presse, Le Figaro, La Caricature, Le Musée des familles, La Revue de Paris, La Revue des deux mondes*—and this is a mere sample of the numerous reviews in which his articles appeared. Nerval paints a similar picture of the drudgery of journalistic writing, and he contrasts it even more starkly with his real literary vocation. Writing to his father in 1839 in an attempt to inveigle him into providing some financial support, Nerval spells out the implications of its lack:

Literary work consists in two things: newspaper jobs, which provide a comfortable living and a secure position to anyone who works hard at them, but which unfortunately lead no higher and no further; and work on books, the theatre, or the study of poetics, which are slow and demanding and always require lengthy preparatory work and long periods of contemplation and fruitless effort—but that is also where the future, expanded horizons, and a happy and honourable old age lie.[2]

He compares himself unfavourably with those of his contemporaries who have private means, such as Lamartine, Chateaubriand, Vigny, and Hugo. Journalism

---

[1] Théophile Gautier, 'Théophile Gautier', in id., *Portraits contemporains: littérateurs, peintres, sculpteurs, artistes dramatiques* (Paris: Charpentier, 1874), pp. 1–13 (p. 11).
[2] Letter to his father, Nov. 1839, in Gérard de Nerval, *Œuvres complètes*, ed. Jean Guillaume and Claude Pichois, 3 vols. (Bibliothèque de la Pléiade; Paris: Gallimard, 1984–93), vol. i, p. 1325.

is mere chore, whereas books are associated with something higher, grander, and altogether more demanding of both time and work—a claim that echoes Gautier's remarks in the preface to *Mademoiselle de Maupin* and anticipates Barbey in the same vein. The challenge for writers with serious literary aspirations was how to salvage their literary ideals while at the same time earning their living from journalism, and this dilemma is often particularly evident in the practice of biography as one of the major journalistic genres of the day.

Despite the qualitative and much-repeated opposition between literature as book and journalism as newspaper article, it was nevertheless quite common for writers to republish their journalistic writings in book form. This transition in itself creates the basis for an idea of literature as book in opposition to the journalistic article. Gautier notes that his total output comes to some three hundred volumes, including the collected versions of many of the articles written for the press. I have already mentioned the quasi-systematic collection of Sainte-Beuve's portraits in book form; and Barbey d'Aurevilly's practice was much the same, whether in his series entitled *Les Hommes et les œuvres*, or in the single volume *Les Ridicules du temps*, which collected his denunciations of contemporary cultural tendencies (including the one on biography) that were first published in the weekly journal *Le Nain jaune*. And again, as I have already suggested, it was perhaps because of Sainte-Beuve's example that the literary portrait was one of the most common forms by which to make this transition from newspaper to book publication. Collections of literary portraits are amongst both the first and the last of Gautier's various book publications: *Les Grotesques*, published in 1844, was a 'gallery' of the portraits of French poets that Gautier had contributed to *La France littéraire* from 1833 onwards; and the *Portraits contemporains*, published in 1874, gathered together his sketches of the various '*littérateurs, peintres, sculpteurs, artistes dramatiques*' that had previously appeared in the press, and included the prefatory self-portrait to which I referred earlier. One of his subjects here is Baudelaire, who had himself written two essay-portraits of Gautier, the first appearing in *L'Artiste* in 1859, followed by publication in *plaquette* form, and the second in the *Revue fantaisiste*; this second portrait was also destined to be included in a projected volume under the title *Réflexions sur quelques-uns de mes contemporains*, although the book never appeared in Baudelaire's lifetime.[3] Similarly, Verlaine's account of Mallarmé in *Les Hommes d'aujourd'hui* was subsequently included in his volume *Les Poètes maudits* (1884), and Mallarmé included a portrait of Verlaine in his *Médaillons et portraits en pieds* (1897).

But over and above the material status of such writings—book as opposed to article—there was also a need to confront the terms in which the biographical portrait habitually appeared in a press whose dominant concern was celebrity.

---

[3] Charles Baudelaire, *Œuvres complètes*, ed. Claude Pichois and Jean Ziegler, 2 vols., rev. edn. (Bibliothèque de la Pléiade; Paris: Gallimard, 1975–6), vol. ii, notes on pp. 1128 and 1148. (*Œuvres complètes* is hereafter abbreviated to *OC*; *OC* ii, for example, is used for *OC*, vol. ii.)

In what follows I shall examine the various ways in which writers reclaimed the journalistic biography for literary goals. The formula for the literary portrait was to a greater or lesser degree biographical, portrait and biography—particularly the so-called contemporary biography—being overlapping practices.[4]

LITERARY PORTRAITS AND LITERARY AUTHORSHIP: GAUTIER AND OTHERS

The biographical assumptions behind the portrait had to be negotiated even if they were then rejected, as Baudelaire rejects them in the case of the first Gautier essay. Here he claims that the easy task of compiling facts and dates, appropriate for those whose lives are filled with action and adventure, would be irrelevant to a figure like Gautier whom he describes as 'Nothing but greatness of spirit!' He presents the poet as a different kind of being from those whose lives justify biography: 'The biography of a man whose most dramatic adventures are played out silently under the cupola of his brain is a literary labour of quite another order.'[5] To write the biography of someone whose life takes place in his head, who has devoted himself to an *idée fixe*, and whose qualities are spiritual rather than physical would be like trying to write the life of the sun: 'Who could conceive a biography of the sun? It is a story which, since that star first gave signs of life, is full of monotony, light and grandeur' (ibid.). The poet is not subject to the conditions that govern other lives, for he exists on a different plane, and his preoccupations lie outside the usual material for biographical anecdote. Baudelaire goes so far as to claim that Gautier himself has no memory of the childhood and the schooldays whose record the biographer must conventionally enumerate. In brief, Baudelaire's Gautier refutes the assumptions of popular biography and transcends his own material existence as pure spiritual immensity.

The form of transcendence more commonly offered by these portraits was that made possible by their very existence as a collection within a single volume. Collectively, a series of portraits could make a literary point that piecemeal might be lost; and such points could be further underscored by the choice of title and the argument of a preface. Gautier's *Grotesques* and Verlaine's *Poètes maudits* do just this, turning a series of articles on past or contemporary poets into something more like a literary manifesto and an attack on contemporary literary and critical orthodoxies. In the case of Gautier, the commission for a series in *La France littéraire* offering 'the life and portrait of our old poets' collectively became the basis for a view of poetry that both opposed the classical account of Boileau's *Art poétique*, and illustrated the freedoms of a poetic practice more

---

[4] On this see Dufour, *Portraits*, pp. 75–80.

[5] Baudelaire, *Théophile Gautier [1]*, in id., *OC* ii, pp. 103–28 (p. 104 [p. 256*]). I shall discuss Baudelaire's use of biography more fully in Ch. 8 below.

in tune with that of the poets of Romanticism.[6] By choosing to write about Villon, Scarron, Théophile de Viau, or Saint-Amant, Gautier is providing an alternative to Boileau's account of French poetry and the decisive turning point when 'Enfin Malherbe vint'. In the neglected poets of the fifteenth, sixteenth, and seventeenth centuries, Gautier hears fore-echoes of the battle between the Ancients and the Moderns still being fought by the Romantics opposed to the same 'routine that seeks to govern inspiration with its oppressive rule'.[7] It would seem from Gautier's portraits that 'eunuchs' have always sought to curb the energy and the freedom of the 'stallions', and that this is not a new phenomenon. More specifically, he finds in Théophile de Viau evidence of 'a progressive spirit who was ahead of his own time' and discerns accents of elevation and melancholy that might have come from Lamartine. In short, he discovers in the past a precedent with which to defend and justify the present, and a view of poetry that upholds 'mad audacity' (attributed to Cyrano de Bergerac) against the restrictive precepts of Malherbe, described here as 'sworn faultfinder in the matter of diphthongs'.[8] Thanks to Gautier's 'gallery', Romantic poetry acquires a prehistory and a pre-existing poetics that take the individual presuppositions of biography as the basis for promoting a literary aesthetic whose most vital feature is a daring that contests the mediocrity of social and cultural consensus.

Collectively, Gautier's poets all appear to subscribe to the same poetic values of freedom and innovation, and he suggests that it is their individuality that makes this possible. The advantage of the so-called minor poets is that they are less constrained by socially and culturally consecrated norms, and as a result orthodoxy gives way to innovation and originality in their work:

it is in the poets of the second rank—and I believe I can argue this without paradox—that the most originality and eccentricity is to be found. It is even for this reason that they are poets of the second rank; to be a great poet, at least in the way the word is commonly taken, one has to speak to the masses and influence them; and it is mostly only general ideas that make an impression on the crowd. (p. 45)

But in collectively promoting individuality, Gautier is careful to limit the number of his examples for fear that his critical enterprise take on the character of a catalogue. The collective principles of criticism do not work on the grand scale of the dictionary: 'we sought to remain as far as possible within the confines of criticism, without encroaching on catalogues and dictionaries' (p. 449). To this critical end Gautier also seeks to minimize the emphasis on the strictly biographical aspect of his subjects in order to foreground their poetry. He cribs Michaud's *Biographie universelle* for the facts of Théophile de Viau's brief existence; and, distinguishing between what he calls the 'material life' and the 'intellectual life', he devotes the major part of the essay to an account

---

[6] Théophile Gautier, *Les Grotesques* [1844], ed. Cecilia Rizza (Fasano: Schena, 1985); see also Rizza's excellent introduction to this edn.
[7] Ibid., p. 144.   [8] Ibid., pp. 161, 242, 116.

of Théophile de Viau's 'poetic system', his 'versificatory procedures', and his strengths and weaknesses as a poet. He quotes the poetry at length, and suggests in his conclusion that any reader wanting to know more should get hold of the complete works and read more of the author's œuvre for himself. Biography, while it underpins the anthology, is nevertheless subordinated to it here, and Gautier cannot be said to be guilty of the charge he made in the preface to *Mademoiselle de Maupin*, when he accused his fellow critics of preferring the author to the work. The literary portrait does not necessarily have to subscribe to the ideology attributed to the press in which it appears.

In sum, as well as attracting the anathema of literature, the biographical portrait of journalism seems repeatedly to have been reclaimed and redeemed for literary purposes. On the one hand, literature is asserted against the popular forms of a mass culture preoccupied with personal fame or moral notoriety (Barbey, Gautier); and, on the other, writers assert their own image of the literary author as poet (Gautier), as a morally superior being (Barbey), and as spiritual entity (Baudelaire). These literary writers turn journalistic ephemera into the more durable form of the book; and they use the formula of collected biography to announce more general literary principles (Gautier, Verlaine).

BIOGRAPHY AT THE *FIN DE SIÈCLE*: VERLAINE AND RÉMY DE GOURMONT

The last years of the nineteenth century were marked by a sudden intensification of biographical writing, both by and about writers. Gautier's *Portraits contemporains* appeared posthumously in 1874, with its entries grouped under the headings of 'Litterateurs', 'Painters', 'Sculptors', and 'Dramatic artists'. The genial self-portrait (written in 1867) that serves as its introduction, incidentally gives the lie to Baudelaire's claim that the 'biography of the sun' cannot be written, and contradicts the assertion that Gautier himself has no memory of his early years and his schooling in Tarbes. The tenor of the volume is largely that of reminiscence, as Gautier recalls, through the republication of a variety of journalistic articles, the figures who populated the literary and artistic world that he himself moved in, in addition to many figures from the past. However, it was in the last decade and a half of the nineteenth century that the literary portrait, both in its journalistic guise and in its collected version, saw a particular and often polemical renewal. Between 1885 and 1893 Verlaine contributed some twenty-seven items to *Les Hommes d'aujourd'hui*, the weekly series published by Léon Vanier, whom Mallarmé's biographer Jean-Luc Steinmetz described as 'for better and for worse, the publisher of the future Symbolists'.[9] The series

---

[9] Jean-Luc Steinmetz, *Mallarmé: l'absolu au jour le jour* (Paris: Fayard, 1998), p. 244.

began in 1878 with a number devoted to Victor Hugo, and although it included generals and professors as well as writers, its centre of gravity lay in the literary world. Each four-page publication consisted of a caricature on the first page, followed by three pages of brief biographical portraiture. Verlaine contributed the items on, amongst others, himself, Rimbaud, Villiers de l'Isle-Adam, Barbey d'Aurevilly, Anatole France, and Mallarmé. It was for the Mallarmé number,[10] and in response to Verlaine's request for information about his life, that Mallarmé wrote the piece now commonly known under the title *Autobiographie*; but he was nonetheless appalled, when the number appeared, to see himself portrayed in the caricature on the frontispiece as a daft-looking faun waving a set of pan-pipes.[11] The series made much of the notion of biography, its descriptive rubric being 'Colour caricatures and anecdotal biographies', and this was echoed when Verlaine published his own contributions in a single volume under the title *Vingt-sept biographies de poètes et de littérateurs*.[12] It was also in his contribution on Villiers that Gautier coined the verb 'biographier' (biographize), when he writes: 'Mais biographions un peu'.[13]

Vanier's series seems to have been primarily a money-spinner; the bottom of the last page of each edition almost always advertised previous volumes, and followed the contemporary practice of encouraging readers to sign up for a year's subscription (6 francs). Broadly speaking, it perpetuated, albeit in a slightly more respectable form, the journalistic tradition of contemporary portraiture exemplified in the Second Empire by Eugène de Mirecourt's series. However, as its title provocatively implies, there is clear polemical intent behind Verlaine's other collection of portraits, *Les Poètes maudits*, the first series of which was published in 1884 and the revised and expanded version in 1888. This polemic is more fully articulated in the two prefaces that he wrote for the respective editions, describing and defending his poets as '[des] Poètes Absolus', and proposing this poetic absolute in defiant opposition to the framework of a society which, invoking a darker version of celebrity, constructs these figures as 'maudits' (accursed).[14]

Rémy de Gourmont's *Livre des masques*, which appeared in 1896 and was followed by a second volume in 1898, is less overtly defiant, its subtitle being

---

[10] No. 296 in the series.   [11] On this episode see also Steinmetz, *Mallarmé*, pp. 244, 255.

[12] The collection was published under this title in vol. v of the *Œuvres complètes de Paul Verlaine* (Paris: Léon Vanier, 1904) but it appears as *Les Hommes d'aujourd'hui*, in id. *Œuvres en prose complètes*, ed. Jacques Borel (Bibliothèque de la Pléiade, Paris: Gallimard, 1972), pp. 759–897. All further references will be to the latter edition.

[13] 'Let us biographize a little.' Verlaine, 'Jules Barbey d'Aurevilly', in *Les Hommes d'aujourd'hui*, pp. 781–4 (p. 782) [p. 326]. The *Trésor de la langue française* records the use of the verb *biographier* transitively from slightly earlier in the century ('Chaque nouveau venu se trouva biographié dès son arrivée', in Ponson du Terrail's *Rocambole*, 1859), and attests the use of the expression '*biographier l'histoire*', meaning to simplify history, in an entry in Michelet's *Journal* dating from 1834. The connotations in these two earlier cases are clearly disparaging.

[14] Verlaine, 'Avant-propos' to the 1888 edn., in *Œuvres en prose complètes*, p. 637.

'*gloses et documents sur les écrivains d'hier et d'aujourd'hui*'; but it includes many of the same figures as Verlaine's *Poètes maudits*, along with a number of younger writers of prose such as Rachilde, Lautréamont, Henri de Régnier, André Gide, and Marcel Schwob. Despite the apparent neutrality of the subtitle, the preface to the first series amounts to a manifesto for Symbolism, and sets out a view of literature designed to inflect all the portraits that follow:

> Conformism, imitativeness, submission to rules and to teaching is the writer's capital crime. The work of a writer must be not merely a reflection, but an enlarged reflection of his personality. The only excuse that a man has for writing is to write about himself, to reveal to others the sort of world that is mirrored in his own glass; his only excuse is to be original; he must speak of things not yet spoken of and do so in a form not yet formulated. He must create his own aesthetic—and we must admit as many aesthetics as there are original spirits and judge them for what they are, not for what they are not.[15]

The justification for a literary portrait evidently lies in this supposition that a literary work is the reflection of the writer's individual personality. Individuality and originality are the criteria of a work's literary worth, and a new literary aesthetic is created with each new writer and will therefore be reflected in each new portrait. The uniqueness of the aesthetic that underpins each writer's work makes the biographical portrait an indispensable means of constructing an idea of literature against the assumptions of a society for whom biography functions as the channel for a rather different kind of currency.

MALLARMÉ'S *MÉDAILLONS* AND LITERARY APOTHEOSIS

The issue of a literary aesthetic is certainly central to Mallarmé's collection of biographical portraits, *Quelques médaillons et portraits en pied*, published in 1897 as part of his *Divagations*. Although he had himself been the subject of the literary portraits devised by Verlaine and Rémy de Gourmont, it may appear surprising nonetheless that Mallarmé should also have adopted the biographical format for himself, when one considers that for him poetry entailed 'the elocutory disappearance of the poet', and that in his own work 'the Text speaks of itself and without an author's voice'.[16] Moreover, Mallarmé explicitly condemns all biographical enterprise as 'impertinent' when he writes that: 'Ordering the life of another, in intelligible and probable fragments, is quite precisely impertinent.'[17] He is equally derogatory about the association of literature with the press,

---

[15] Rémy de Gourmont, 'Préface', in *Le Livre des masques*, vol. i, pp. 7–16 (p. 13 [p. 14*]).

[16] Stéphane Mallarmé, *Œuvres complètes*, ed. Bertrand Marchal, 2 vols. (Bibliothèque de la Pléiade; Paris: Gallimard, 1998–2003): 'Crise de vers', vol. ii, pp. 204–13 (p. 211); 'À Paul Verlaine (Autobiographie)', vol. i, pp. 786–90 (p. 789). (*Œuvres complètes* is hereafter abbreviated to *OC*.)

[17] Mallarmé, 'Arthur Rimbaud', in *Quelques médaillons et portraits en pied*, in OC ii, pp. 120–8 (p. 126).

which, as we have seen, was a major forum for biography in general, and literary biography in particular. In his piece on Maupassant, Mallarmé describes the recent promotion of literature by the press as increasing the danger 'that mediocrity will abound'.[18] All these reservations notwithstanding, Mallarmé's strategy as a practitioner of the literary portrait follows the standard pattern of article publication in the press, followed by the collected volume: for example, the portrait of Villiers de l'Isle-Adam appeared both in the Belgian review *L'Art moderne* (February–March 1890) and in *L'Art indépendant*, which also published it as a separate *plaquette*.[19] Similarly, the Verlaine portrait appeared in both *La Revue encyclopédique* and *La Plume* (January 1896); the Rimbaud biography was commissioned by an American review, *The Chap Book* (also 1896); and the pieces on Tennyson and Banville appeared in the British weekly *The National Observer* and the *Mercure de France* (1892 and 1893, respectively). The collected volume was clearly not conceived as a means of making a publishing virtue of journalistic necessity, since Mallarmé seems at one stage to have had plans for a volume provisionally entitled *Les Miens*, which would have included the Villiers biography, and two further pieces on Banville and Manet, although these last were never written. In short, Mallarmé's engagement with biography would in no sense appear to be an accident.

The biographical format that Mallarmé uses is that of the obituary, rather than the contemporary biography more commonly found in the press.[20] The portrait of Villiers was devised for a lecture tour in Belgium in 1890, a few months after Villiers's death, and was based on an itinerary that Villiers himself had planned but was unable to undertake because of the consequences of his final illness.[21] The Verlaine text is that of the oration Mallarmé gave at his funeral; and the one devoted to Banville is that of the speech Mallarmé delivered at the unveiling of the poet's memorial in the Jardin du Luxembourg in 1892. This obituarizing or commemorative function of the portraits means that in every case Mallarmé is writing about poets (or, in three instances, painters) who have, quite literally and very physically, disappeared—a point underscored by the French verb *disparaître*, which means 'to die' as well as 'to disappear'.

Over and above this particularity, and of Mallarmé's own sense of personal loss, his individual portraits are written in the context of a very strongly developed awareness of the relation of the individual artist to a larger and collective artistic endeavour. This approach goes much further, though is much less buoyantly

---

[18] *Quelques médaillons*, p. 320.   [19] See the Notices to the individual texts in *OC* ii.

[20] The obituary, of course, was not in itself an unprecedented basis for the genre, as witness the example of the *éloge*. See also Dufour, *Portraits*, pp. 235–51 for a discussion of its place in the nineteenth-century literary portrait.

[21] For a full account of the circumstances of the composition of the text and of the relationship between Villiers and Mallarmé, see A.W. Raitt's Introduction to Stéphane Mallarmé, *Villiers de l'Isle-Adam*, ed. id. (Exeter: University of Exeter Press, 1991), pp. vii–xxxvii. On Mallarmé's biographies see also Lloyd J. Austin, 'Mallarmé et la critique biographique', *Comparative Literature Studies*, 4 (1967), pp. 27–34.

positive, than that of Rémy de Gourmont, and it treats the emphasis on the individuality of the poet as a by-product of the loss of a coherent collective literary life. In response to a question about 'literary evolution' posed as part of a series of enquiries undertaken for publication in the press in 1891, a year after the Villiers lecture and a year before the texts on Banville and Tennyson, Mallarmé states: 'We are now witnessing a spectacle [. . .] which is truly extraordinary, unique in the history of poetry: every poet is going off by himself with his own flute, and playing the songs he pleases. For the first time since the beginning of poetry, poets have stopped singing from the lectern.'[22] He attributes this multiplication of poetic individualism, so energetically defended by Gautier and Rémy de Gourmont, to a lack of unity in social organization: 'in a society without stability, without unity, there can be no stable or definitive art'. And he concludes: 'From that incompletely organized society—which also explains the restlessness of certain minds—the unexplained need for individuality was born. The literary manifestations of today are a direct reflection of that need.'[23] To that extent, Mallarmé's portraits, which take individuals as their subject, are themselves a fully conscious symptom of a wider social and aesthetic problem, and not merely a protest against it.

But they are, equally, gestures towards a different account of literature, and an attempt to recreate a common, collective language for the literary. This is to say that the individual poets and painters are not the only subjects of Mallarmé's narratives, which from time to time invoke much larger and more impersonal agents whose histories are also being worked out: 'Poetry', 'Language', 'Letters', or 'old French metrics [which] are undergoing, at this very moment, an extraordinary crisis, unknown in any era'.[24] From the outset, the whole of Villiers's 'life' is placed in the context of a much larger issue concerning the nature of literature itself. The question that lies at the heart of the discussion in 'La Musique et les lettres'—'Does something like Letters exist?'[25]—is anticipated in advance of its purely theoretical formulation (in 1894) and elaborated in the context of the actual life of an individual poet: 'Do we know what writing is? an ancient and very indistinct but jealous practice, whose meaning lies in the mystery of the heart.'[26] Biography is explicitly being placed under the aegis of a meditation on the nature of the literary, and provides a forum for engaging with

[22] The author of these questions was one Jules Huret, 'Sur l'évolution littéraire [enquête de Jules Huret]', in Mallarmé, *OC* ii, pp. 697–702 (p. 697 [p. 18*]). For further discussion of this 'interregnum' see Bertrand Marchal, 'Villiers relu par Mallarmé: le poète et la divinité', in *Villiers de l'Isle-Adam: cent ans après (1889–1989): actes du colloque international organisé en Sorbonne les 26 et 27 mai 1989*, ed. Michel Crouzet and A.W. Raitt (Paris: SEDES, 1990), pp. 41–9.

[23] Huret, 'Sur l'évolution littéraire', pp. 697–8 [p. 19].

[24] Mallarmé, *Quelques médaillons*, pp. 143, 144, 115–16.

[25] Mallarmé, 'La Musique et les lettres', in *OC* ii, p. 65.

[26] Mallarmé, 'Villiers de l'Isle-Adam', in *OC* ii, pp. 21–51 (p. 23); the full text of Mallarmé's memorial lecture on Villiers is given separately from the *Quelques médaillons*.

the question that is only later formulated in the critical terms of the theoretical essay.

This mystery—that of literature—is more than just a conceptual framework for the consideration of an individual existence, and Mallarmé presents it as determining both actively and very powerfully the nature of the writer's life: 'Anyone who carries it out, cuts himself off, entirely' (p. 24). The demands of literature are such that the writer is bound to withdraw from the world; and so much so that Mallarmé finds himself asking, in terms that are rather more extreme than those invoked by Baudelaire on the subject of Gautier, whether it makes any sense to speak of Villiers having had a life: 'His life—and I am seeking nothing which corresponds to this term: in actuality, and in the ordinary sense, did he live?' (p. 25). Villiers's only passion was 'Literature', with a capital 'L'; and his only real existence was in the world of dreams: 'the man who was not, except in his dreams' (p. 38).Towards the end of his thirty-page portrait, Mallarmé finds himself acknowledging to his audience that 'the person whom I thought I was recounting had lived so little' (p. 48). Similarly, although in a different register, Rimbaud is presented by Mallarmé as having had a life that was brutally and radically determined by literature. The small and insignificant facts of his youth are appropriate for someone who was 'violently ravaged by literature', whose abandonment of literature is that of someone 'who [. . .] had surgically severed poetry from his living self', and whose existence, all in all, is that of 'a child too prematurely, and impetuously, touched by literature's wing who, almost before he had time to exist, exhausted stormy and magisterial fates, without recourse to any future'.[27] The extreme character of Rimbaud's life as a poet is as much an effect of the mystery of the practice of literature as is the absence of biographical event in that of Villiers.

The presence of literature in the life of the poet does more than simply subject that life to its force. Mallarmé takes Barbey's ethic of the subordination of the individual to higher principles much further than Barbey could ever have imagined. The poet becomes actively caught up in the process of what Mallarmé calls 'divine transposition': '*Divine transposition, for whose realization man exists, goes from facts to the ideal.*'[28] This involvement turns the poet as man into a hero: Villiers, for instance, is 'a pure hero of letters', Verlaine 'remains a hero', and Mallarmé echoes Baudelaire in calling Edgar Allan Poe '*one of the greatest literary heroes*'.[29] Divine transposition further metamorphoses the individual figure into a literary universal: Villiers has the character of 'the authentic writer', Poe is 'the absolute instance of literature', and Banville 'is not someone, but the very sound of the lyre'.[30] The poet is transformed into the Poet, and, as Mallarmé

---

[27] *Quelques médaillons*, pp. 123, 125, 127.   [28] Ibid., pp. 144–5 (Mallarmé's italics).

[29] 'Villiers de l'Isle-Adam', p. 49; *Quelques médaillons*, p. 129; Mallarmé, *Les Poèmes d'Edgar Poe*, in OC ii, pp. 727–87 (p. 767).

[30] 'Villiers de l'Isle-Adam', p. 24; *Quelques médaillons*, pp. 145, 142.

writes of Banville: 'No one now represents the Poet better, the invincible, classic Poet, subordinated to the goddess.'[31] The vague and jealous practice of literature recasts the individualist as the universal figure that the state of modern society seemed initially to preclude.

Indeed the 'Tombeaux' sequence of sonnets in Mallarmé's *Poésies*, some of which date from the same period as the *Médaillons* and are devoted to the same poets, say nothing else—witness 'Le Tombeau d'Edgar Poe':

> Tel qu'en lui-même enfin l'éternité le change,
> Le Poëte suscite avec un glaive nu.[32]

The same idea is present in the 'Toast funèbre' written for Gautier's funeral, which did not, therefore, elicit a prose 'medallion' or portrait: while insisting on the impossibility of any 'magic corridor' that might allow the dead to return, the poem nevertheless asserts that 'Le splendide génie éternel n'a pas d'ombre' ['The splendid, the eternal genius has no shade'], and conjures up the survival of Gautier's poetry as 'Une agitation solennelle par l'air | De paroles' ['A solemn agitation of language by the air'].[33] Death completes the process of transformation that is begun by the individual poet's life, and this is why Mallarmé's biographies can only be obituaries. The poet becomes the Poet only after his death, and emerges from the tomb that both inters and immortalizes him. In the *Poésies* this tomb is Mallarmé's poem (a generic 'tombeau' in the sense of a lyric memorial to someone who has died); but in the *Médaillons* it is often treated as synonymous with the poet's own work. From this perspective, the poet's life can be seen as having been dedicated to constructing the edifice for his own posterity, where he appears in the guise not of the capricious individualist, but of the hero, 'the Poet', 'the very sound of the lyre', or simply his own name. Mallarmé describes Villiers as having built his own sepulchre out of his imaginative creations: 'His imaginings were unprecedented and the sepulchre that he made for himself with them to lay claim loftily to his place is worth the total sacrifice';[34] and this sepulchre-work becomes posthumously interchangeable with its author's name: 'the Work to which the name of Villiers de l'Isle-Adam refers' (p. 48). In the case of Tennyson, Mallarmé suggests that the name is actually the product of the work: 'The poet's name is mysteriously remade with the entire text, which, from the union of words with each other, succeeds in forming just one, which is significant and sums up the whole soul' (p. 140). The poet becomes the work, and is no longer its biographical origin or the person whose individuality is the source of the work's distinctiveness. Mallarmé has a much loftier mission than did the biographers of the press, both for his poets and for his own function in writing about them.

---

[31] 'Villiers de l'Isle-Adam', p. 24; *Quelques médaillons*, pp. 142–3.

[32] *OC* i, p. 38. 'As into himself at last eternity changes him, | The Poet arises with a naked sword.'

[33] See *OC* i, pp. 27–8 [p. 41].   [34] *Quelques médaillons*, p. 43.

What this account leaves out is the precariousness of Mallarmé's project. As Bertrand Marchal has argued, Mallarmé's literary mission is ultimately a fiction, and the potential triumphalism of these aesthetic apotheoses is muted by his awareness of their lack of any real foundation.[35] Seen in this light, Mallarmé's biographies are an attempt to provide an answer to the question about the existence of 'something like Letters', by bringing into some kind of being a Literature which does not yet exist, and which nothing guarantees or underpins. What is also left out of this account is the incidental personal and biographical baggage that Mallarmé's portraits include. There is loss as well as triumph in his narratives: not only was Villiers a friend, but he was also an emblem of many of Mallarmé's own literary aspirations; in narrating his life and his limitations, therefore, Mallarmé is brought face to face with a version of his own pretensions.[36] In celebrating Banville, he is repeating a gesture of admiration that goes back to his youth: 'I exhume, with no pity for myself, one of the first pages which, as a schoolboy, I wrote in solitude, in praise of a god, of whom, to celebrate him today, I would choose to say the same thing better.'[37] And he is certainly aware of the grief of others, when, in hailing the monument to Banville, he acknowledges that there is also a real tomb containing the man's physical remains which are mourned by those who have been left behind: 'The genuine tomb guards his remains and presents a hard stone to the knees of a widow in pain or close relative' (p. 141). For most readers, too, there is the sobering knowledge that Mallarmé himself died less than two years after the book publication of these meditations on the lives of dead poets.

Less soberly, but still as a counterweight to the high literary mission, there is an undeniable zest on Mallarmé's part for the incidentals of biography. And his stern remark in the portrait of Rimbaud about its impertinence is immediately followed by a comic logic of in-for-a-penny-in-for-a-pound when he adds: 'it remains only to push this type of misdeed to its limits', albeit on the basis of proper information, rather than the hearsay or popular myth recycled by many popular biographies—'But I inform myself' (p. 126). So it is that Mallarmé reports the story of Rimbaud stripping off all his clothes and throwing them out of the window of the attic room that Banville had lent him, because he found it too clean and virginal for his flea-ridden wardrobe; he also recounts the escapade with Verlaine, speculates about Rimbaud's time in Africa, and recalls his own memory, from his one encounter with Rimbaud, of the boy's huge hands, red with chilblains, which made him look like a washerwoman. These are not part of Mallarmé's main biographical purpose, but the red hands caught the imagination of Pierre Michon nearly a hundred years later,[38] and constitute exactly the kind of particularity on which Marcel Schwob's biographical practice is based and

---

[35] See Marchal, 'Villiers relu par Mallarmé'.   [36] On this see Raitt, 'Introduction'.
[37] *Quelques médaillons*, p. 142.
[38] See his *Rimbaud le fils* (Paris: Gallimard, 1991) discussed in Ch. 17 below.

which informs a complementary aesthetic to that of Mallarmé, as we shall see in Chapter 10 below.

In Mallarmé's 'medallions' the collective biographical monument was reinvented as the tomb of the individual poet, whose reality was an index of inescapable mortality, but out of which a form of literary transcendence might hypothetically emerge. In apparently subscribing to the conventions of biographical writing as it existed in the nineteenth century by collecting piecemeal journalistic portraits for the more serious enterprise of book publication, Mallarmé is nevertheless shifting the terms of the genre. He re-evaluates the individual basis of biography, which historians condemned, and which the biographical dictionaries, series, and collections sought to defend by adding biographies up to make wholes that were larger than the sum of their separate parts. Mallarmé's version of the biographical portrait is at once a telling comment on the status of literature in the late nineteenth century when it had ceased to have a recognized social function, as well as being an acknowledgement of human loss, which does not figure in biographies of the long-since dead and does not yet apply to those still living. More importantly, the Mallarmean biography gestures towards an idea of literature as an entity that is not a given (as the dangerous mediocrity condoned by the press was a given); instead, this reinvented literariness must be deciphered by the biographer in the lives and legacies of the departed, either as that to which an individual existence has been sacrificed (or by which it has been ravaged), or as the work that remains. 'Literature' is both celebrated and precariously invented out of the lives that Mallarmé records; and biography, with its twin poles of the individual and the general, the incidental and the ideal, allows him to confront the uncertain transition from one to the other, in a manner that is very different from the polemics of earlier manifestos, or from the confident implications of most other collected biographical writings.

6

Sainte-Beuve: Biography and the Invention
of Literary Criticism

The work of modern criticism is to put Art back on its pedestal.

(Gustave Flaubert)

In addition to the biographical dictionary, the journalistic 'biographie', and the biographical *recueil*, the nineteenth century also saw the birth of biographical criticism. Its best-known practitioner, who presided over this birth, was Sainte-Beuve. For him biographical criticism was not just one form of criticism amongst others, but the pretext for a thoroughgoing transformation of literary commentary in general into its modern form. Whereas the proliferation of biography in the realm of the dictionary and the press gave rise to considerable ambivalence about the status and value of the form, Sainte-Beuve, without qualm, places biography at the centre of a new vision of literature. It is only subsequently, and most notoriously since Proust, that the biographical basis of his criticism has become the target of opprobrium. In his own time he was considered by most of his contemporaries to be one of literary criticism's finest practitioners. Barbey may have disparaged him as a mere 'articler', but others thought much more highly of him. Even Flaubert, despite his belief that art 'has no truck with the artist', keenly regretted that the critic died shortly before the publication of *L'Éducation sentimentale* and was therefore never able to read it. Sainte-Beuve was much admired, too, outside France: Matthew Arnold called him 'the most notable critic of our time', and for Henry James (no mean critic himself) he was 'the acutest critic the world has ever seen', and 'a man of extraordinary genius'.[1] More particularly, he was seen not just as a fine critic, but as the inventor of the very practice of criticism. In an appraisal of Sainte-Beuve delivered as a lecture in 1904, Gustave Lanson, whose own work dominated critical habits for many decades, described Sainte-Beuve as 'the patron-saint of literary critics and literary

---

[1] Matthew Arnold, 'Sainte-Beuve', in id., *Five Uncollected Essays of Matthew Arnold*, ed. Kenneth Allott (Liverpool: University Press of Liverpool, 1953), pp. 66–78 (p. 66); Henry James, *Literary Reviews and Essays: On American, English, and French Literature*, ed. Albert Mordell (New York: Grove Press, 1957), pp. 79–83 (pp. 79, 83).

historians'. [2] And Lytton Strachey goes even further when he remarks that it was with Sainte-Beuve that 'one might almost say that criticism as we know it came into existence for the first time'.[3]

For all these people it seems that, although the critical genre developed by Sainte-Beuve appeared in the press as a version of the new and sometimes disreputable form of 'biographie', he was regarded as a serious literary critic. However, he largely avoided using the term 'biographie' for his own contributions, preferring that of 'portrait'. In line with the contemporary practice of transition from press to book, his review articles were subsequently and almost invariably published in book form and ran to many volumes, most of which were re-edited and republished several times both during and after his lifetime.[4] Moreover, the portraits conformed to contemporary journalistic practice, for which they were also an exemplary instance, in that they tended to deal with individual authors rather than individual works, and to discuss them in a broadly biographical frame. The *Causeries du lundi*, which Sainte-Beuve began in 1851 and continued until his death, were less biographically orientated, but were nevertheless grounded in the same general principles as the earlier portraits. Sainte-Beuve claimed that his particular brand of criticism and its format in the portrait were directly attributable to the nature of the literary journals for which he wrote.[5] The portrait also formed the basis of the university lecture courses that he gave during his tenure of a series of university teaching posts,[6] almost all of which led to the publication of a major book: *Port-Royal* (1840–59), *Chateaubriand et son groupe littéraire* (1860), and *Virgile* (1857). In addition to his critical work Sainte-Beuve published four collections of poetry: *Vie, poésies et pensées de Joseph Delorme* (1829), *Les Consolations* (1830), *Pensées d'août* (1837), *Livre d'amour* (1843); and a single novel, *Volupté* (1834). I shall be returning to his creative writings below.

What emerges first from this brief survey of Sainte-Beuve's critical output is that the institutional forms of his writing were all current at the time: journalistic articles and essays, books, and university lecture courses. But in seeking to understand what has given Sainte-Beuve's criticism its status as origin and, to

---

[2] Gustave Lanson, 'Sainte-Beuve', in id., *Essais de méthode, de critique et d'histoire littéraires*, ed. Henri Peyre (Paris: Hachette, 1965), pp. 427–41 (p. 427). It should be said that Lanson, who had his own critical and methodological battles to fight, was not always so generous towards his patron saint. For a fuller account of 'lansonisme' see Compagnon, *La Troisième République des lettres*.

[3] Lytton Strachey, *Landmarks in French Literature* (London: Chatto & Windus, 1948), p. 143.

[4] See Ch. 5 above for a list of some of these titles.

[5] 'Ce genre de *Portraits* que l'occasion m'a suggéré et dont je n'aurais pas eu l'idée probablement sans le voisinage des *Revues*, m'est devenu une forme commode, suffisamment consistante et qui prête à une infinité d'aperçus de littérature et de morale': quoted by Gérald Antoine in his Introduction to Charles-Augustin Sainte-Beuve, *Portraits littéraires*, ed. Gérald Antoine (Bouquins; Paris: R. Laffont, 1993), p. lxiii. See Ch. 5 above for a list of the titles of the journals for which Sainte-Beuve wrote.

[6] At the Académie de Lausanne (1837–8), the Université de Liège (1848–9), the Collège de France (where, as Professor of Latin Poetry, he actually lectured only between 1854 and 1855), and the École normale supérieure (1857–61).

some extent, model for later literary criticism, we need to look beyond the familiarity of its institutional forms. One might, as a first gesture, consider Sainte-Beuve's own individual critical virtues: his huge appetite for reading, his prodigious capacity for hard work—the *lundis* were produced week in week out for almost thirty years—and his own experience as a writer, which, according to him, had given him '[a] keener sense of beauty'.[7] This would, however, require us to overlook what were also his evident shortcomings as a critic. Proust, of course, provides a pretty damning catalogue in his *Contre Sainte-Beuve*: not only the misjudgement of Stendhal, but also Sainte-Beuve's preference for Feydeau and Béranger over Flaubert and Baudelaire, his inability to recognize, or at least to acknowledge publicly, the great figures of his day (Balzac, for example), his destructive jealousy of Hugo (whose wife was for a while Sainte-Beuve's mistress), and so on. And while he wrote perfectly decent prose, he is not normally praised as a stylist, and Proust went so far as to condemn him as someone who merely 'cobbles sentences together'.[8] Yet, just as his individual merits do not necessarily explain the importance of his criticism, his demerits may not disqualify it either.

The issue, in other words, is not whether his literary judgements have been vindicated by posterity, or even whether he worked hard enough to earn serious professional status for a new breed of literary critics. Rather, Sainte-Beuve's critical enterprise owes both its strength and its importance to the fact that it is, in all its complexity, a response to the radical transformation in the conception of literature and of the literary that took place at the turn of the nineteenth century. This change may be summarized by the words of the poet André Chénier, which Sainte-Beuve quotes on a number of occasions: 'art only makes verses, the heart alone is the poet'.[9] Taken at is simplest, Chénier's formula anticipates the impetus for the renewal of literature that came with Romanticism. What is distinctive about Sainte-Beuve is that instead of confining his critical enterprise to a simple defence of the literature that emerged from this view,[10] he recast the fundamental procedures and presuppositions of criticism itself so as to reflect the implications of Chénier's claim and to take account of the new conception of literature that it articulated. In the process he completely redefined the scope and function of literary criticism in ways that in turn transformed the terms in which literature itself was conceived.

For as long as literature was viewed as the expression of an eternal beauty inseparable from truth and reason (the classical view), and as long as literary

---

[7] Quoted in Antoine, Introduction to *Portraits littéraires*, p. xli.

[8] Quoted by Antoine Compagnon, in id., *Proust entre deux siècles* (Paris: Éditions du Seuil, 1989), p. 190 (from Proust, 'Préface' to *Tendres Stocks*, in Marcel Proust, *Contre Sainte-Beuve*, p. 610). Although it was not published until 1954, the work now known as *Contre-Sainte Beuve* (a title that Proust never gave it) was written in 1909, some forty years after the critic's death.

[9] e.g. Sainte-Beuve, 'Mathurin Régnier et André Chénier', in *Portraits littéraires*, pp. 110–22 (p. 118).

[10] Although for a while he also did exactly that through his association with *Le Globe*, which began in 1827 with his article on Hugo's *Odes et ballades*.

expression was evaluated primarily in terms of rhetorical precept, there was little for criticism to do except to measure individual works against the aesthetic blueprint of a universally accepted and pre-established *art poétique*. One of the last proponents of this kind of criticism in France was La Harpe, who in his *Cours de littérature ancienne et moderne* claims quite simply that 'the beautiful is the same at all times, because nature and reason do not change'.[11] The consequence of this view is that between them, Quintilian, Cicero, Horace, and Boileau provide the student of literature with 'a perfect legislation which may be justly applied in all cases, an imprescriptible code whose verdicts will serve forever to tell us what should be condemned and what applauded'.[12] In contrast, the implications of Chénier's claim meant that art for Sainte-Beuve was the product neither of the rhetorical rules of verse, nor of some abstract and universal beauty, but of an individual genius. What made a literary work literary was not its conformity to aesthetic or rhetorical precept, but the fact that it was the product of a genius whose influence may be felt in every aspect of its construction, right down to particular images and linguistic formulations.

The notion of genius was not itself new (as we saw in Chapters 2 and 3 above), and Diderot and Mercier had already made a powerful case for the imaginative and creative powers of genius. Diderot also ascribes genius to individual feeling as part of its inherent disruptiveness of the laws of taste which La Harpe was still defending nearly fifty years later.[13] What Sainte-Beuve brings to the concept of genius is a radical and fully elaborated sense of the uniqueness of each of its manifestations. For him there is no language that could describe genius outside the particular forms that it takes, and these forms are always associated with a particular individual. Invoking the traditional opposition between genius and talent, he categorically associates genius with the uniqueness of the individual: 'I call genius what comes from the person: the rest is talent.'[14] Because genius always has its source in the individual, its characteristics cannot be known in advance, and it therefore becomes the function of criticism to identify what Sainte-Beuve calls the writer's 'dominant quality' or the 'general formula [of his] mind'.[15] In contrast to La Harpe's 'imprescriptible code', which equipped the student of literature with an unvarying and prior notion of the aesthetic, Sainte-Beuvian criticism has always to start from scratch in its search for the defining characteristic of a given writer: 'Let us try to find [the] characteristic name of each

---

[11] La Harpe, 'Introduction', *Le Lycée*, vol. v, p. 20. On this discussion see Ch. 3 above.

[12] La Harpe, 'De Boileau', *Le Lycée*, vol. vi, p. 484.

[13] Diderot, 'Article Génie' and 'Sur le génie', in *Œuvres esthétiques*, pp. 9–20.

[14] Quoted in Antoine, Introduction to *Portraits littéraires*, p. lix.

[15] See Sainte-Beuve, 'M. Ampère', in *Portraits littéraires*, pp. 223–50 (p. 223); and Gérald Antoine, Introduction to Charles-Augustin Sainte-Beuve, *Vie, poésies et pensées de Joseph Delorme*, ed. Gérald Antoine (Paris: Nouvelles Éditions latines, 1957), p. lx.

individual which he bears engraved partly on his brow and partly in his heart.'[16] Literarity becomes something to be discovered afresh with each new critical engagement.

Furthermore, it would seem that it is constitutionally easier for the critic than for the writer to identify the literary, and indeed that literariness comes fully into focus only when it is the object of critical discourse. Criticism thus becomes the guardian of the distinctiveness of literature (the literarity of each genius) by separating itself off from its object and constituting literature as its 'other'. This is in significant contrast to the rhetorically based approach to literature that, alongside the legislative function promulgated by La Harpe, had made the study of literary rhetoric an extension of its practice. When the heart—or the individual genius—came to be seen as the source of literary art, the notion that literary texts could be studied as examples of rhetorical skill that the student might emulate began to go into decline, and with it the sense of continuity between the study of literature and its production.[17] As commentary replaced emulation, the relation between a newly constituted critical discourse and its object made literature simultaneously more elusive (its defining quality always has to be discovered anew) and more elevated (literature and criticism are different orders of discourse). Criticism becomes a kind of necessary supplement to literature, with all the ambiguity that supplementarity entails: both surplus to, and constitutive of the literary.[18]

None of this is presented systematically by Sainte-Beuve, but in what follows I shall attempt to draw together various elements of Sainte-Beuve's thinking about criticism and literature; these elements, in the form of passing comments scattered throughout his critical accounts of individual writers, will be used in support of my contention that the strength of Sainte-Beuve's criticism lies not so much in the accounts of individual writers as in the fact that the criticism was a very fully elaborated response to the shift in the conception of the literary from

---

[16] Sainte-Beuve, 'Chateaubriand jugé par un ami intime en 1803', in *Nouveaux lundis*, 4th edn., 13 vols. (Paris: Calmann Lévy, 1883–6), vol. iii, pp. 1–33 (p. 30).

[17] This shift was not applied across the board, and rhetoric remained the basis of the teaching of literature in schools and universities for a good part of the nineteenth century before a sudden and rapid decline. See Genette, 'Rhétorique et enseignement', in *Figures II*, pp. 23–42; and Compagnon, *La Troisème République des lettres*. For a fuller discussion of the role of rhetoric in nineteenth-century French education see Françoise Douay-Soublin, 'La Rhétorique en France au xixe siècle: restauration, renaissance, remise en cause', in Marc Fumaroli (ed.), *Histoire de la rhétorique dans l'Europe moderne, 1450–1950* (Paris: Presses universitaires de France, 1999), pp. 1071–214; and Antoine Compagnon, 'La Rhétorique à la fin du xixe siècle (1875–1900)', ibid., pp. 1215–50.

[18] This ambiguity of the supplement is the one exemplarily described by Jacques Derrida in *De la Grammatologie*. For an illuminating discussion of the role of criticism and literary self-consciousness see Lacoue-Labarthe and Nancy, *L'Absolu littéraire*. They specifically exclude the French tradition from their discussion, but while there are many differences between the theoretical concerns of German Romanticism and the biographically based criticism of Sainte-Beuve, the function of criticism in relation to literature seems to be broadly and significantly similar in each.

rhetoric and poetics to genius and the heart.[19] In seeking to establish the elements of Sainte-Beuve's critical principles, I shall concentrate primarily on the *Portraits littéraires* and his first collection of poetry, the *Vie, poésies et pensées de Joseph Delorme*, since I wish to suggest that between them they constitute the framework of Sainte-Beuve's literary aesthetic. For one of the consequences of Sainte-Beuve's critical position and of its construction of the literary is that the creative and the critical, despite their separate status, prove to be so mutually, if paradoxically, implicated that it becomes impossible to maintain a clear distinction between the two. Their common denominator is not rhetoric, however, but biography. Commentators on Sainte-Beuve have tended to present the relation between these two aspects of his work—creative and critical—as broadly consecutive and compensatory: his youthful attempts at poetry being not much more than that, culminating in the *Pensées d'août* in 1837, after which Sainte-Beuve supposedly resigned himself, in recognition of the limitations of his own poetic talents, to a career dedicated entirely to criticism.[20] Nevertheless, if one looks more closely at the beginnings of Sainte-Beuve's career as a writer, the critical project and the creative project seem to have been developed alongside each other, or even as versions of each other. His earliest critical work, the articles that appeared in 1828 under the rather long-winded title *Tableau historique et critique de la poésie française et du théâtre français au XVIe siècle*, were written at the same time as the first poems of the *Joseph Delorme* collection.[21] And *Joseph Delorme* itself was published just one day before the first of Sainte-Beuve's literary portraits (on Boileau), which appeared in the newly founded *Revue de Paris* on 5 April 1829. Aside from this chronological overlap, the most striking feature that Sainte-Beuve's critical portraits share with *Joseph Delorme* is the biographical format that they both adopt.

The Boileau portrait constitutes a very bold, if somewhat understated, move on Sainte-Beuve's part precisely through its use of biography. More than any other, Boileau's name had been associated with the rhetorical precepts that had dominated literary thinking and practice since the publication of his *Art poétique* in 1674. To treat Boileau as the object of a biographically conceived critical study is to set the precepts of Boileau's own poetics on one side, and to evaluate his work in quite other terms than those he himself had promoted. In his introduction to the portrait Sainte-Beuve promises to study Boileau

in his private life [. . .] examining him in detail from our perspective and the ideas of our time, moving in turn from the man to the author, from the *bourgeois* of Auteuil to

---

[19] The selection of Sainte-Beuve's writings in Charles-Augustin Sainte-Beuve, *Pour la critique*, ed. José-Luis Diaz and Annie Prassoloff (Collection Folio/Essais; Paris: Gallimard, 1992) is very suggestive in this regard.

[20] See e.g. A. G. Lehmann, *Sainte-Beuve: A Portrait of the Critic, 1804–1842* (Oxford: Clarendon Press, 1962).

[21] For more details on this see Antoine, Introduction to Sainte-Beuve, *Vie, poésies et pensées de Joseph Delorme* (hereafter shortened to *Joseph Delorme*).

the poet of Louis le Grand, not evading the serious questions of art and style when we encounter them, and perhaps occasionally shedding some light on them without ever claiming to settle them.[22]

Sainte-Beuve makes no bones here about his historically relativist *parti pris*, or about the biographical basis of his discussion. The result is a perspective that reveals his approach to be just as radical as, and perhaps ultimately even more effective than, the full-scale attack on the rules of classical dramaturgy that Hugo had mounted just over a year previously in his *Préface de Cromwell* (although, as we saw in Chapter 3, this text had its own investments in a certain conception of biography).

THE LIFE OF THE POET AND THE READING OF POETRY

On its publication in 1829 the *Vie, poésies et pensées de Joseph Delorme* were presented as precisely that—the life, poems, and thoughts of one Joseph Delorme, whose fictional status is nowhere made explicit. Sainte-Beuve's name did not appear as author, and an anonymous 'éditeur' introduces the collection ascribed to Joseph Delorme with a brief biographical sketch of the poet, inviting readers to see the poems themselves as based on episodes in the hitherto unknown life of Delorme. The *pensées* that conclude the volume are also ascribed to Delorme, and are presented as a kind of personal metaphysic recorded by him in a series of private notes and musings. Although lives of poets were by no means an unknown phenomenon at the time, none had quite the same role as that of the fictional Joseph Delorme. Alfred de Vigny's *Stello* (1832) recounts the lives of three poets, Gilbert, Chatterton, and Marie-Joseph Chénier (brother of the more famous André). Gilbert and Chatterton had both died young, and the effect of their biographies is to create an aura of pathos around a vanished or unrealized body of poetic writing, as well as to plead for the protection of poetry from the abuses of political power. Sainte-Beuve knew Robert Southey's account of the life of the English poet Henry Kirke White, the macabrely titled *Remains of Henry Kirke White* (1807). He was also familiar with Johnson's *Lives of the Poets*, claiming to admire them for the quality of their critical commentary. For Sainte-Beuve this critical element of biography was its most vital component, and in his view lives of writers had to be much more than stories in which literary creations appear simply as biographical events like any others. Because of the need to take account of the special features of genius as Sainte-Beuve understood it, biographies of poets could not simply replicate the procedures of the biographies of heroes and the great men whose social role the poets were usurping.[23] According to him, if biographer-critics omit

---

[22] Sainte-Beuve, 'Boileau', in *Portraits littéraires*, pp. 5–22 (pp. 6–7).
[23] As Bénichou argues in *Le Sacre de l'écrivain*.

to grasp the unique character of a poet's genius, they will end up merely 'keeping the registers of the temple, and will not be priests of the god'. In short, their books will be 'useful, accurate, undoubtedly worthy, but not works of high criticism and art'.[24] Evidently, when it came to the issue of literary biography, Sainte-Beuve had something other in mind than either pathos or mere historical accuracy.

These comments, which appear in Sainte-Beuve's essay on Corneille, were written in the same year as he conceived of the tripartite structure of his *Joseph Delorme* and wrote the introductory life for it. Admittedly, this life does have its share of Romantic pathos: Delorme dies young of a characteristically Romantic combination of tuberculosis and 'an affection of the heart',[25] and is revealed to have lived out his poverty-stricken existence in an equally Romantic state of melancholy and suffering. However, there is much more to this biography than the construction of a statutorily dolorous poet, since the life is presented as essential for a proper understanding of the poems: 'the poems on their own, without the history of the feelings to which they relate, would have been no more than a half-understood enigma' (p. 2). Equally, though, the poetry is presented as a straightforward record of the (inner) life, which would otherwise have remained unknown: 'his poems suffice to enable us to understand the active feelings that were sapping him at that time' (pp. 18–19). The life explains the poetry, but at the same time the poetry provides the only complete history of the life, creating a circularity in which each is necessarily presupposed by the other.

The implicitly critical dimension of the biographical introduction is further enhanced by its concluding remarks, where the anonymous editor places Delorme's work in the poetic tradition founded by André Chénier, and also tries to identify the distinctive qualities of Delorme's poetry—its subject matter, its lexis, and the 'individuality [. . .] of its conceptions' (p. 26). The occasional footnote in the poems serves as a continuing reminder of an editorial presence and a critico-biographical context. Sainte-Beuve is not alone in exploiting the fiction of the editorial frame, but whereas Chateaubriand and Constant use this device in *René* and *Adolphe*, respectively, to head off autobiographical readings of their texts and encourage readers to focus on the moral problems raised in each of them, Sainte-Beuve's biographizing strategies seem designed above all to create a (literary-)critical perspective on his work. He takes this editorial topos far further than other writers of the time, and in subsequent editions he actually duplicates the critical frame that the *éditeur* creates, by including samples of the book's real critical reception on its publication in 1829.[26] For Sainte-Beuve the editorial frame is first and foremost a critical frame.

---

[24] Sainte-Beuve, 'Pierre Corneille', in *Portraits littéraires*, pp. 22–37 (p. 25).

[25] Sainte-Beuve, *Joseph Delorme*, p. 21. All page references are to this text.

[26] The 1840 edition of Sainte-Beuve's *Poésies complètes* contains a bibliographical note with references to *Joseph Delorme*'s critical reception; and an 1861 edition of *Joseph Delorme* includes a selection of critical articles written about it. Sainte-Beuve used the same strategy with subsequent editions of his novel *Volupté*, whose second edition he himself reviewed in *Le Globe* in Nov. 1830.

This is made very evident in the first of the 'Pensées', which points the reader firmly towards a critical and biographical approach to the text in implied contradistinction to an autobiographical one. In other words, it is not merely inviting readers to refer the poetry back to a simple autobiographical origin, but confronts them with the issue of the limitations of language and its consequences for all literary expression:

Truth in all things, if it is taken in its purest and most absolute sense, is ineffable and ungraspable; in other words, a truth is always less true when expressed than when conceived. In order to get it to the state of clarity and precision that language requires, one has more or less, but necessarily and invariably, to add to it and to subtract from it, to heighten the colours, remove the shadows, sharpen up the outlines; it is for this reason that there are so many *expressed* truths which resemble *conceived* truths as much as clouds made of marble resemble real clouds. (p. 130, Sainte-Beuve's italics)

Instead of developing this thought into a typical Romantic topos that would focus on the poet's suffering at his inability to articulate an ineffable experience, Sainte-Beuve presents the problem as one that concerns the reader even more than the writer, and requires a particular form of critical response on the reader's part:

whatever the idea is that one is expressing, one cannot be too mindful of what one is leaving out and what one is including, and one must add, mentally at least, all the qualifications which the trenchant speed of language removes, and have constantly in one's mind's eye the vast and amorphous model out of which it was carved. If the writer-philosopher and -critic has to proceed in this way to gain a proper understanding of himself, and avoid becoming the dupe of his own formulae, *how much more must the well-intentioned reader acquire the habit of seeing the things that lie beneath the words, of taking into account as he reads a thousand unspoken circumstances, of following the broad middle way with his author, rather than clinging, like a rebellious child to the brambles in the ditch.* (pp. 130–1)

The limitations and crudeness of language impose on the poet a need for critical vigilance (he is 'the writer-philosopher and -critic'), requiring him, in effect, to act as his own reader-critic. But, as Sainte-Beuve quite clearly states, they also require the reader to supplement the inevitably partial forms of literary expression with a picture of the circumstances in which a work takes shape, and to keep in mind a sense of the larger authorial project. It is precisely these elements that Sainte-Beuve's own critical portraits seek to provide. Moreover, if the poet is isolated, misunderstood, and mocked by his public, this does not make him a victim of political philistinism, as Chatterton is for Vigny, or of straightforward poetic philistinism, as illustrated in Baudelaire's 'Albatros'. Rather, it is a sign that his readers have failed to supply the critical context that will make proper sense of the poet's work. So, for instance, in the poem 'L'Enfant rêveur', the poet addresses the dreaming child and future poet with these words of warning about his future readers:

Personne sous tes chants ne suivra ta pensée,

Et de loin on rira de ta plainte insensée.[27]

The word *suivre* ('follow'), used here to describe the ideal relation of the public to the poet's thought, also occurs as a key element of critical response, as we saw in Sainte-Beuve's comments about the well-intentioned reader who was to 'follow the broad middle way with his author'. The word is used again in the portraits to describe how Sainte-Beuve sees his own role as critic: 'to follow [the writer] in his origins, in his active development, his range, digressions, diversions, the way he mixes things together, present his various phases, his intellectual vicissitudes, and the riches of his soul'.[28] In this regard, the poem 'L'Enfant rêveur' could itself be seen as providing its own tracking, critico-biographical commentary as it addresses the child with knowledge that he does not yet possess, either about himself or about his future experience as a poet. At any rate, the poem implies that the poet will remain highly vulnerable if he does not have a critical counterpart. Such is the importance of this critical or quasi-biographical perspective that its absence is often presented in the poetry as potentially disastrous, even where it is not deliberately rejected by the outside world. So, when the poet turns in on himself in a movement of introspection that excludes the outer world, this merely reveals chaos and frightening confusion. As the child in 'L'Enfant rêveur' plunges into his own inner world, what he sees are

> [. . .] précipices sans fond,
> Arêtes de rocher, sable mouvant qui fond,
> Monstres de toute forme entrelacés en groupe,
> Serpents des mers, dragons à tortueuse croupe,
> Crocodiles vomis du rivage africain,
> Et, plus affreux que tous, le vorace requin.[29]

Delorme's own internal world is described in very similar terms (p. 17), and these images of chaos suggest that without a context or a response the inner self is bound to lack coherence and to collapse in this terrifying manner. As Paul Bénichou remarks of Sainte-Beuve, 'His *moi* is certainly not that of all-conquering Romanticism that we are familiar with'.[30]

Equally, however, a simple, straightforward ardour that rushes headlong towards the world is almost always presented as no less disastrous. The poet who is too avid will inevitably destroy the object that he reaches out for, as in 'Rêverie', where he shatters the image of the stars reflected in the lake's surface

---

[27] *Joseph Delorme*, p. 99. 'No one will follow your thoughts beneath your songs, | And from afar people will laugh at your absurd lament.'

[28] Sainte-Beuve, 'M. Ampère', in *Portraits littéraires*, p. 225.

[29] *Joseph Delorme*, p. 99. '[. . .] bottomless chasms, | Rocky mountain ridges, moving sands which dissolve, | Monsters of every shape entwined in groups, | Sea serpents, dragons with twisted rumps, | Crocodiles vomited up from the shores of Africa, | And, most horrible of them all, the voracious shark.'

[30] Bénichou, 'Sainte-Beuve', in *Les Mages romantiques*, pp. 13–36 (p. 17).

by attempting to seize hold of them. And if poetic inspiration is evoked as the upward thrust of a creative *essor* in the poem 'À mon ami V[ictor] H[ugo]' ('Ton essor souverain'), the speaker is nevertheless troubled by the thought that the thrusting, soaring poet might be deaf to the very crowd that grants him critical recognition:

> Entends-tu ce long bruit doux comme une harmonie,
> Ce cri qu'à l'univers arrache le génie
>   Trop longtemps combattu,
> Cri tout d'un coup sorti de la foule muette,
> Et qui porte à la gloire un nom de grand poète,
>   Noble ami, l'entends-tu? [. . .]
>
> Poussant ton vol sublime et planant, solitare,
> Entre les voix d'en haut et l'écho de la terre,
>   Dis-moi, jeune vainqueur,
> Dis-moi, nous entends-tu? la clameur solennelle
> Va-t-elle dans la nue enfler d'orgueil ton aile
>   Et remuer ton cœur?[31]

The anxiety here is that the crowd's recognition will go unacknowledged by the poet, and his heart remain unmoved—the heart, of course, having now become the source of poetic creativity. In a later, unpublished essay on Hugo this anxiety becomes outright denunciation as the poet's *essor* has evolved into the blind self-assertion of a 'cyclops'. Rather than listening and responding to the world around him, Hugo merely projects himself into it. 'Making and seeing the world in his own image', he has become incapable of reading any poet other than himself: 'He no longer hears Virgil any more than Petrarch; he sees all things and all people in himself.'[32] In *Mes poisons* this crude creative assertiveness is described quite simply as 'the *priapism* of amour-propre' which is the mark of 'our poets [who] are in a perpetual state of useless personal exaltation, and an infatuation that they cannot conceal'.[33] In these images of an over-assertive creativity, the poet is castigated for his blindness to his own (critical) context: the world in which he lives, the literary tradition in which he writes, and the reader-critics who receive him. In short, it would seem that, without a critical component, poetry will find itself fatally undermined.

---

[31] *Joseph Delorme*, p. 49. 'Do you hear the long sound, sweet as harmony, | The shout wrung from the universe by genius | Too long opposed, | A shout suddenly erupting from the silent crowd, | And which sings in praise of the name of a great poet, | Noble friend, do you hear it? [. . .] || Pursuing your sublime, soaring, solitary flight, | Between the voices from on high and the earth's echo, | Tell me, young victor, | Do you hear us? Will the solemn clamour | Make your wing swell with pride among the clouds | And move your heart?'

[32] Sainte-Beuve, 'Des gladiateurs en littérature', in *Pour la critique*, pp. 223–42 (pp. 233–4).

[33] Charles-Augustin Sainte-Beuve, *Mes poisons: cahiers intimes inédits*, ed. Victor Giraud (Paris: Plon-Nourrit, 1926), pp. 130–1 (Sainte-Beuve's italics).

A second image of poetic creativity in *Joseph Delorme* presents it as not only more reflective (like the poet contemplating the lake at the end of 'Rêverie'), but as actively calling for an interpretative response. In its last stanza 'Retour à la poésie' sums up this second version of creativity:

> Tel est le destin du poète;
> Errer ici-bas égaré;
> Invoquer le grand interprète;
> Écouter la harpe secrète,
> Et se mirer au lac sacré![34]

The poet is always lost (*égaré*), because even if he resists the blind thrust of Hugolian inspiration, his picture of himself in his own context can never be complete; his poetry is based on listening ('Écouter la harpe secrète') and reflection ('se mirer au lac sacré'); and it is dependent on the completing response of a third-party 'interpreter'. In other words, the poet relies on the critical attitude both for the construction and for the reception of his work, which gives the mention of 'la harpe' its own echo in the name of Sainte-Beuve's precursor critic, the author of *Le Lycée*.

It seems axiomatic in Sainte-Beuve that the subject can never achieve full self-knowledge, and that every speaker needs a listener or interpreter to make sense of what he himself cannot. So the address to Victor Hugo in 'À mon ami V. H.' ends with the fantasy that the purely assertive poet might eventually prove capable of giving ear to the lesser mortal that the speaker figures himself as being ('I, poor fallen being'):

> [. . .] mais si, comme un bon frère,
> Du sein de ta splendeur à mon destin contraire
>   Tu veux bien compatir;
> Si tu lis en mon cœur ce que je n'y puis lire,
> Et si ton amitié devine sur ma lyre
>   Ce qui n'en peut sortir;
> C'est assez, c'est assez: jusqu'à l'heure où mon ame,
> Secouant son limon et rallumant sa flamme
>   À la nuit des tombeaux,
> Je viendrai, le dernier et l'un des plus indignes,

---

[34] *Joseph Delorme*, p. 55. 'This is the destiny of the poet; | To lose his way and wander here below; | To invoke the great interpreter; | To listen to the secret harp, | And see his reflection in the sacred lake!'

Te rejoindre, au milieu des aigles et des cygnes,
O toi l'un des plus beaux!³⁵

In order to become a poet in his turn the speaker needs the established poet to become a critic-interpreter as well, and to lend an ear to the secrets of the heart that the speaker himself cannot fully decipher or articulate.

Indeed, poetry itself is repeatedly presented in *Joseph Delorme* as a form of listening, and listening seems to be integral to the very substance and content of the poems. The world that the poet inhabits in *Joseph Delorme* is to a quite extraordinary degree a world of sound. Situations are repeatedly portrayed in terms of the noises they contain. Consider, for example, the autumn scene in 'La Plaine' where

> [. . .] de loin l'on entend la charrette crier
> Sous le fumier infect, le fouet du voiturier,
> De plus près les grillons sous l'herbe sans rosée,
> Ou l'abeille qui meurt sur la ronce épuisée,
> Ou craquer dans le foin un insecte sans nom.³⁶

Sainte-Beuve's repetition of fricative 'f's and plosive 'c's ensure that the reader's ear is attuned to this insistence on sonority.

Or again, in 'Les Rayons jaunes', the world from which the poet feels so radically cut off is as much as anything a world of sounds:

> Ce ne sont que chansons, clameurs, rixes d'ivrogne;
> Ou qu'amours en plein air, et baisers sans vergogne,
>   Et publiques faveurs;
> Je rentre; sur ma route on se presse, on se rue;
> Toute la nuit j'entends se traîner dans ma rue
>   Et hurler les buveurs.³⁷

Above all, the poet is described in terms of his relations to those sounds, aware of the noises made by the drunks in the street below or by the unseen crickets hidden in the grass, and alert to the voice of his own inner turmoil. It often seems that the poet's internal world is available to him only when it takes the

---

³⁵ Ibid., pp. 50–1. '[. . .] but if, like a good brother, | From the heart of your splendour so different from my own destiny | You are willing to sympathize; | If you read in my heart what I cannot read in it, | And if your friendship divines on my lyre | What cannot emerge from it; || It is enough, enough; until the hour when my soul, | Shaking off its yoke and rekindling its flame | At the darkening of the tomb, | I shall come, the last and one of the most unworthy, | To join you, amidst the eagles and the swans, | O thou, one of the finest!' Sainte-Beuve always spells 'âme' [soul] without a circumflex on the 'a'.

³⁶ Ibid., p. 126. '[. . .] from afar one can hear the cart cry out | Beneath the foul manure, the driver's whip, | Closer by the crickets beneath the dewless grass, | Or the bee dying on the exhausted briar, | Or a nameless insect crackling in the hay.'

³⁷ Ibid., p. 71. 'It is all songs, clamour, drunken brawls; | Or love in the open air, and shameless kisses, | And public favours; | I set off home; on my path people hurry and hurtle along; | All night long I hear drinkers in my street | Dragging themselves along and bellowing.'

form of something that can be heard. In a comment on himself in *Mes poisons* Sainte-Beuve writes: 'Grand sentiments and the sublime are not my style; but I have a tolerable ear for the din made by the heart.'[38] Similarly, in *Joseph Delorme*, the poet is portrayed as someone for whom thinking is not so much a verb of which he is the subject, as the object of an act of hearing:

> Ainsi parlait la voix dans mon âme oppressée;
> Et moi, silencieux, écoutant ma pensée,
> Par degrés je sentais la tristesse arriver.[39]

So important is the poet's willingness to register an audible world that it ends up being one of his defining characteristics. The *éditeur* of *Joseph Delorme* claims at the end of the 'life' that '[Delorme] always listened to himself before singing' (p. 26), as if to suggest that this is one of his major qualities as a poet. For Sainte-Beuve, then, the function of poetry is to interpret and relay the voices and noises of both the world within and the world without.

As if to concretize this conception of poetry within its very form, 'À la rime' depicts rhyme as poetry's inherent capacity to respond to its own voice. Rhyme is an echo (a familiar enough idea), but it is also (somewhat less conventionally) an answering friend:

> Dernier adieu d'un ami
>   Qu'à demi
> L'autre ami de loin répète.[40]

This slightly bizarre image of rhyme as friend recalls the fact that it was Hugo's 'friendship' that the poet imagined as the quality that would enable him (Hugo) to divine the sounds that could not be played on the speaker's lyre. Poetry, it would seem, is materially constituted by its ability to echo or answer its own voice. But equally, hearing is an essential form of response for the critic whom Sainte-Beuve describes precisely in terms of his willingness to listen: 'always with bated breath, and *keeping his ears open*', as he says of Bayle in his essay 'Du génie critique et de Bayle'.[41] Listening, as a particular manifestation of the critical stance, is both an internal and an external necessity for the very existence of poetry.

The critical perspective associated with *Joseph Delorme* is also powerfully suggested within the poems themselves as a repeatedly fantasized biography scenario, or, to be more accurate, obituary scenario. It would seem that the poet can imagine the self only within the frame of a biography narrated by a third party. In a number of poems he anticipates his own death and pictures himself

---

[38] *Mes poisons*, p. 4.
[39] *Joseph Delorme*, p. 109. 'So spoke the voice in my oppressed heart; | And listening in silence to my thoughts, | By degrees I felt sadness arriving.'
[40] Ibid., p. 29. 'Last farewell from a friend | Which | The other friend half repeats from afar.'
[41] In *Portraits littéraires*, pp. 250–66 (p. 251).

as the object of another's biographizing speculation. In fact, he repeatedly figures himself as a corpse, only to make the painful discovery that there is no 'other' there to write his obituary. In 'Adieux à la poésie' he recognizes that when he dies there will be no 'distraught lover' to weep over his dead body and lay his head in his coffin. And in 'Les Rayons jaunes', a poem inspired by the death of Sainte-Beuve's aunt, who had helped to bring him up, he constructs a similar non-scene, acknowledging the impossibility of there ever being a 'young fiancée' to mourn him after his own death. More elaborately, in 'Le Creux de la vallée' he narrates the poet's suicide and the subsequent discovery by strangers, months later, of his unrecognizable body. These figures—as unknown to him as he is to them—speculate fleetingly and vainly about the poet's life as they trundle his remains to an unmarked grave in the local cemetery and abandon him to anonymity:

> De grand matin venus, quelques gens de l'endroit,
> Tirant par les cheveux ce corps méconnaissable,
> Cette chair en lambeaux, ces os chargés de sable,
> Mêlant des quolibets à quelques sots récits,
> Deviseront long-temps sur mes restes noircis,
> Et les brouetteront enfin au cimetière;
> Vite on clouera le tout dans quelque vieille bière,
> Qu'un prêtre aspergera d'eau bénite trois fois;
>
> Et je serai laissé sans nom, sans croix de bois![42]

These poems all suggest that Sainte-Beuve conceives of identity not so much as something based in self-presence, but as an object dependent on a biographical gaze. This notion is paradoxically reinforced rather than undermined by the non-existence of the gazer (distraught lover or young fiancée) and by the lack of relation between the obituarist and his subject. In any case, such obituarizing fantasies are in sharp contrast to the priapic self-assertion of the cyclops-poet who constructs the world and his others simply as projections of himself.

This brief glance at *Joseph Delorme* appears to confirm the idea that the critical stance and the biographical perspective are integral to the construction and presuppositions of the poems. It would, of course, be perfectly possible to attribute this to Sainte-Beuve's own particular mindset and emotional proclivities, and to see it simply as heralding his ultimate choice of an exclusively critical career—in other words, to interpret the phenomenon purely biographically. But there does seem to be something more at stake, which returns us to the idea

[42] *Joseph Delorme*, p. 104. 'Arriving in the early morning, a few people from thereabouts, | Dragging the unrecognizable body by the hair, | The flesh in tatters, the bones burdened with sand, | Mixing jeers with some foolish tales, | Will converse for a long while about my blackened remains, | And will cart them finally in a barrow to the cemetery; | It will all be quickly nailed into some old bier, | Which a priest will sprinkle with holy water thrice over; || And I shall be left without a name or a wooden cross.'

that at this juncture in the history of literature the critical perspective becomes inseparable from the construction and conception of literature itself. In the remaining pages of this chapter I shall explore this claim from the angle of the more overtly critical 'portraits'.

LITERATURE AND THE NECESSITY OF CRITICISM

The genre of the 'portrait' that Sainte-Beuve adopted for his own purposes did not originally have a literary-critical function. Widely practised in the seventeenth century, portraits were primarily a social pastime, although some of the most striking instances have survived as 'literature', for example in La Bruyère's *Caractères*, Saint-Simon's *Mémoires*, and in the comical 'scène des portraits' in Molière's *Misanthrope*. In Sainte-Beuve's hands the portrait was recast and adapted to the new critical task of defining the genius of the writer. If he chose the term 'portrait' in preference to 'biography', this may in part be to distinguish his own concerns from the growing cult of celebrity, and perhaps from the vulgarity of the kind of biographical writing later denounced by Barbey. There is a small hint of something of this kind in Sainte-Beuve's remark that 'women should never have a biography, a nasty word for use by men'.[43] He also regarded the biographies of poets and artists as different in essence from the records of the lives of other great men, and may therefore have wanted to use a distinctive term for literary figures. It might be for this reason, too, that he claims that his portraits are a 'transformation of the academic *Éloge*' as practised in the eighteenth century, since these were dedicated to 'great men' and not specifically to writers.[44] According to Sainte-Beuve, the poet differs from 'statesmen, conquerors, theologians, and philosophers' in that he does not simply enter a wider stage into which his own contribution will be absorbed. For in the realm of literature 'human initiative has primacy and is less subject to general causes; individual energy modifies and, so to speak, assimilates things'.[45] The individual genius of the writer is as much determining as it is determined, and

---

[43] Quoted (though without source) by Chantal Thomas in 'L'Allée Marcel-Proust', in *Le Biographique = Poétique*, 63 (1985) [special issue], pp. 301–11 (p. 305). The appropriateness of the portrait for women is attested by Sainte-Beuve's *Portraits de femmes* consisting of some eighteen portraits, including one of Madame de Staël.

[44] Preface to *Critiques et portraits littéraires, II*, in Sainte-Beuve, *Œuvres*, ed. Maxime Leroy, vol. i (Bibliothèque de la Pléiade; Paris: Gallimard, 1949), pp. 649–52 (pp. 651–2). The remark is also quoted by Dufour (*Portraits*, p. 13) as part of her broader discussion of Sainte-Beuve's reinvention of the portrait form (ch. 1). She comments on the overlap of the 'biography' and the 'portrait' (ch. 5) and cites the example of a collection entitled *Portraits biographiques contemporains* (p. 78). Sainte-Beuve's portraits are intended to be less dry than the entries in Nicéron's collection of 'hommes illustres', but more insistently realistic in their treatment of their subject than the avowedly celebratory *éloge*. On the *éloge* see Ch. 1 above.

[45] Sainte-Beuve, 'Boileau', p. 7.

this makes the great writer fundamentally different from all other figures. The unpredictable nature of individual genius also makes any causative biographical account problematic. As Sainte-Beuve says in his review of Taine's *Histoire de la littérature anglaise*: 'there is nothing [. . .] more unpredictable than talent, and it would not be talent if it were not unpredictable'.[46] This is the basis of his criticism of Taine's 'method', whose broad-brush determinism is incapable of capturing the unique qualities that constitute genius: 'there is only one soul, one particular cast of mind capable of creating this or that masterpiece. [. . .] There is only one version of each poet' (ibid.).

Moreover, the particular cast of mind identified by the literary portrait is something that the poet-genius himself is unlikely to be able to identify, so that it becomes the critic's task to reveal it to the poet. Sainte-Beuve states this quite categorically in the same essay on Taine, in which he describes criticism as a kind of dialogue or 'causerie' where the critic actually—or at least in imagination—addresses his comments directly to their subject as if he were physically present and listening to what the critic has to say about him:

[O]ne would start to discourse on the great writer, speaking freely and boldly, imagining sometimes that one is even surprising him a little and that he is astonished, but one should try immediately to convince him and win him over to one's view. One would be invigorated by a flattering notion and a powerful motive, the thought that one is teaching him [the writer] as well, that one is taking him a step further in his knowledge of himself and of the place he occupies in literary renown; one would delight in thinking that one is developing an aspect of his reputation and that one is lifting a veil which had hidden a part of it from him.[47]

He makes a similar point in a letter to George Sand, when he praises her for qualities that he assumes she is no better able to explain than he is: 'There is a side of you that I do not properly know or understand [. . .], an area that remains mysterious; it is related to your genius, to your secret, to something that you would undoubtedly not be able to explain yourself.'[48] If he is modest about his own capacities to define the author's genius here, the presupposition of the portraits is nevertheless that this is precisely what the critic can do. The critical portrait contains knowledge that neither the political historian, who writes biographies of statesmen and conquerors, nor the literary historian, who, like Taine, describes the characteristics of a period rather than those of an individual, nor even the writer himself can possess. In the case of the living poet,

---

[46] Sainte-Beuve, ' "Histoire de la littérature anglaise" par M. Taine', in *Nouveaux lundis*, vol. viii, pp. 66–137 (pp. 86–7).

[47] Quoted by Gérald Antoine in 'Sainte-Beuve et l'esprit de la critique dite "universitaire"', in *Sainte-Beuve et la critique littéraire contemporaine: actes du colloque tenu à Liège du 6 au 8 octobre 1969*, ed. Claudette Delhez-Sarlet and André Vandegans (Paris: Société d'édition 'Les Belles Lettres', 1972), pp. 105–23 (pp. 112–13).

[48] Letter dated 21 July 1833, in Charles-Augustin Sainte-Beuve, *Correspondance générale*, ed. Jean Bonnerot and Alain Bonnerot, 19 vols. (Paris: Stock, 1935), vol. i, p. 374.

the insights provided by the critic may be absorbed by the writer as a form of new self-knowledge and feed back into his literary practice. All of which suggests yet another way in which critical activity becomes integral to the creative process itself.

The critical portrait is, however, necessarily biographical, since for Sainte-Beuve genius is always produced, and can only ever be grasped, as a temporal phenomenon. That is to say, despite its occasional appearance as Hugolian *essor*, genius can never be purely spontaneous self-affirmation. Genius is the effect of a conjunction of circumstances with which it interacts, and also has its own evolving dynamic. Amaury, the hero of Sainte-Beuve's *Volupté*, speaks of the 'individual interconnection with things in the world around' that even the humblest existence reveals.[49] For Sainte-Beuve the most important part of this 'interconnection' as regards the poet lies in his origins: 'In order to know an eminent character, the study of his origins and education is essential.'[50] Writing about Chateaubriand, he spells out more fully which aspects of these origins are the most important. First, there are the poet's ancestors and his geographical roots; then his parents (and in particular his mother); then his siblings and even his children.[51] Sainte-Beuve's portraits always begin with the writer's family background, and then go on, as he recommends here, to consider the writer's education and to examine his circle of friends (his 'generation') at the time his talent first appears in adult form. The critic's goal in this exploration of the writer's emergence is, however, not some explanatory model that would reveal the determining causes of his genius; for, if Sainte-Beuve's understanding of genius is temporal, it is not in any real sense of the word determinist.[52] Rather, the aim of what he calls 'the biographical critic' is to identify the particular moment when the poet's genius comes into its own; this is the key to the broader contextual picture, which it is the critic's business is to provide:

If you understand the poet at this critical moment, if you unravel the node to which everything will be connected from that moment on, if you find what you might call the key to this mysterious link made half of iron and half of diamonds joining his second, radiant, dazzling, and solemn existence to his first, obscure, repressed, and solitary one (the memory of which he would more than once like to swallow up), then one could say of you that you thoroughly possess and know your poet.[53]

Nonetheless, it is not enough simply to pinpoint this moment, because the full picture requires that moment to be related to other, subsequent moments: the

---

[49] Sainte-Beuve, *Volupté*, ed. André Guyaux (Paris: Gallimard, 1986), p. 290.
[50] Sainte-Beuve, 'M. de Rémusat', in *Portraits littéraires*, pp. 915–51 (p. 923).
[51] 'Chateaubriand jugé', *passim*.
[52] As Jean-Pierre Richard puts it, in his remarkable essay on Sainte-Beuve, the life is as much an expression of the writer's genius as his work: id., 'Sainte-Beuve et l'objet littéraire', in id., *Études sur le romantisme* (Paris: Éditions du Seuil, 1970), pp. 227–83.
[53] Sainte-Beuve, 'Pierre Corneille', p. 24.

established poet and the unknown poet need to be set alongside each other from a prospective as well as a retrospective standpoint.[54] The time when youthful genius makes its decisive appearance has to be related to the time when it begins to decline:

It is not only important to understand properly a talent at the moment it makes its first attempts and in its first flush, when it appears fully formed and more than merely adolescent, when it becomes adult; there is a second moment which it is no less decisive to note, if one wishes to view it as a whole: it is the moment when it begins to spoil, when it becomes corrupted, when it falls off and loses its way.[55]

Sainte-Beuve sometimes writes as if the task of criticism were to discern the defining moment or the unique distinguishing feature of a writer right down to the single, characteristic 'favourite word' or 'the expression [that] sums up his nature',[56] but he insists equally on the importance both of maintaining the larger picture and of tracking poetic talent as it unfolds. In a letter of 9 June 1861 he speaks of the poet's distinguishing feature as an 'integral molecule',[57] a metaphor that nicely combines a notion of uniqueness and configuration, individual feature, and broader relation. For him, as he says in his review of Hugo's *Feuilles d'automne*, the single work or the singular feature have always to be placed in a broader context, which is pre-eminently a chronological or temporal one:

after the uncontested and universal triumph of the genius to which it devoted itself from the outset, and whose glorious monopoly it sees slipping from its grasp, criticism still retains an honourable task, an attentive and religious concern: to embrace all the different parts of the development of the poetry, to point out the connections with the earlier phases, to place the evolving work as a whole back in its true light, where its more recent admirers see the latest manifestations too prominently.[58]

The poet's work always emerges in a given temporal context and has its own temporal vicissitudes, and this is why biography is the most suitable format for critical commentary. Sainte-Beuve's poet acquires his identity as what one might call a 'subject in process' (to borrow Julia Kristeva's term); but it is the critic's larger view and his biographical frame that enable him to capture that sense of process, and to see beyond the immediate circumstances in which the poet makes his personal choices and develops his characteristic forms. Time and again Sainte-Beuve reminds his readers that the biographer-critic has a longer

---

[54] See Sainte-Beuve, 'Quelques verités sur la situation en littérature', in *Pour la critique*, pp. 141–4 (pp. 141–2).

[55] 'Chateaubriand jugé', p. 26.

[56] Sainte-Beuve, 'M. de Sénancour', in Charles-Augustin Sainte-Beuve, *Portraits contemporains*, rev. edn. (Paris: Didier, 1855), pp. 101–24 (pp. 115–16).

[57] Quoted by Antoine in Introduction to *Joseph Delorme*, p. lx.

[58] Sainte-Beuve, 'Victor Hugo, *Les Feuilles d'automne*', extract in *Pour la critique*, pp. 123–7 (p. 126).

perspective than the poet; caught up in the immediate, liable inevitably to lose sight of his past self, the creative writer is necessarily ignorant of his own future, and at best has only a partial view of the tradition in which his work is created.

THE CRITICAL PERSPECTIVE

If the view that the critic has of his subject embraces a temporal dimension that the subject himself can never fully grasp, and if the critic ends up with insights into the author-subject's work that the author cannot match, criticism itself also turns out to have its own temporality. In an extended metaphor for the role of the critic, Sainte-Beuve describes literature as a kind of landscape whose separate and mutually isolated features can be linked by a critical trajectory that is figured as a journey down a river:

Art which meditates and edifies, art which lives in itself and in its work may be visualized as some venerable and ancient castle washed by a river, as a monastery on a river bank, as an immobile and majestic rock; but from each of these rocks or castles the view—though immense—does not reach the other points, and many of these monuments and marvellous landscapes are not, as it were, aware of each other; so criticism, whose principle is mobility and sequence, moves from place to place like the river below, surrounding them, washing them, reflecting them in its waters, and effortlessly transporting the traveller who wishes to get to know them, from one to the other.[59]

Although criticism is credited here with the ability to relate the individual literary monuments to each other, it is nevertheless portrayed as a river that meanders through space and through time, and not as a single vantage point that takes in the whole landscape. The diversity of literature is such that no single perspective can encompass it in its entirety. For this reason criticism is condemned to perpetual mobility and transformation as its responds to its often very different objects:

And let no one say that if criticism had a central viewpoint, if it judged according to an absolute principle or truth, it would spare itself a large part of the tiring effort of this movement and these forced shifts, and that, from the top of the hill where it might sit like a king in an epic poem or like the judge Minos, it would enumerate with ease and pronounce its oracles with true unity. To my knowledge there is, at present, no viewpoint that, if adopted, would be sufficiently central to allow one to embrace the infinite variety unfolding in the plain below.[60]

The critic is in a paradoxical position whereby, on the one hand, the validity of his enterprise requires him to have a greater knowledge of the literary than literature itself, and, on the other, that validity would be lost if criticism sought to turn its

---

[59] Sainte-Beuve, 'Adam Mickiewicz', in *Œuvres*, vol. i, pp. 536–42 (p. 537).
[60] Ibid., pp. 536–7.

greater insight into universal principle and theoretical precept. To do so would be to revert instantaneously to the position, exemplified by La Harpe, where the critic judged all works by external rather than intrinsic criteria. This was the nub of the objections that Sainte-Beuve made to Taine, for whom criticism was also no more than 'different applications and different aspects of the same thought [. . .] the fragments of the same whole that he keeps redistributing'.[61] As soon as criticism formulates its knowledge of literature as system or as theory, it will lose all connection with the object it claims to illuminate, and its knowledge will become void.

By putting Sainte-Beuve's ideas about criticism and literature together, and by suggesting that they constitute a coherent project, I am, paradoxically, running the risk of removing Sainte-Beuve from the meandering river and transporting him to the mountain top—in short, of turning him from traveller to judge. One of the chief merits of biography or the portrait as practised by Sainte-Beuve is that each one deals successively with the singularity of a given genius whose own evolutionary temporality works against the tendency of critical knowledge to become theoretical system. Moreover, each portrait is itself composed over a period of time, however brief that period may be, in a process that Sainte-Beuve conveys very vividly in the account of his working method that he includes in the introduction to his portrait of Diderot. The biographical portrait is presented as something to be painstakingly produced, rather than as a preformed repository for a set of facts and information:

You shut yourself away for two weeks with the writings of a famous dead philosopher or poet; you study him, you turn him round and round, you question him at leisure; you get him to pose for you; it is almost as if you were spending a fortnight in the country creating the bust of Byron, Schiller, or Goethe [. . .]. Each feature is added in its turn and finds its place in the physiognomy that you are trying to reproduce; it is like each star appearing in succession before one's eyes and beginning to shine at its allotted point in the texture of a beautiful night sky.[62]

Abstraction and generality—the currency of theory and system—are gradually replaced by 'an individual, precise reality, with its own increasing accentuation and sparkle; you sense a likeness emerging and developing'. By submitting to this compositional process, the critic will eventually capture 'the familiar tic, the revealing smile, the indefinable crack in the skin, the intimate and painful wrinkle concealed in vain beneath the already thinning hair' which sum up and reveal the writer. In the same instant, however, criticism and creation merge: 'analysis disappears in creation, the portrait speaks and lives, and one has found the man'. The moment when the biographer-critic reaches his goal and identifies the

---

[61] '"Histoire de la littérature anglaise" par M. Taine', p. 78.
[62] Sainte-Beuve, 'Diderot', in *Portraits littéraires*, pp. 166–83 (p. 166 for this and subsequent quotations in the text).

characteristic that constitutes literary genius is also the moment when criticism itself could be said to become a form of literature.

Just as poetry seemed repeatedly to presuppose criticism in Sainte-Beuve's conception, so the critical portrait comes close to merging with the literature it comments on. Biography as practised in these portraits steers a complex path between, on one side, the theoretical abstractions towards which its own knowledge tempts it, and, on the other, the literary creativity that brings that knowledge to life but within which it would eventually be lost. The middle course is where criticism's greatest value lies: the distinctiveness of critical commentary consists in constructing literature as its object so as to reveal what literature and the writers who create it do not know and cannot themselves fully articulate. Literature is redefined with each critical encounter, and its difference from itself is guaranteed by criticism's basis in the uniqueness of each individual biographical portrait. So that if Sainte-Beuve's criticism can be seen to be restoring art to its pedestal (as Flaubert, in the comment quoted in the epigraph to this chapter, demands that it should),[63] it does so by consistently working against the possibility of any self-identical literariness.

---

[63] Flaubert, letter dated 17 May 1853, in *Préface à la vie d'écrivain*, p. 118.

PART III

POETRY AND THE LIFE
OF THE POET

THE discussion so far has largely skirted round the edge of works conventionally marked as 'literature'; and it has been from the marginal perspectives of auto-biography, literary history, criticism, and the journalistic essay or portrait that biography has confronted and tested the idea of literature. At mid-nineteenth century, however, with Hugo and Baudelaire, the issue of biography moves decisively to the literary high ground of poetry. Hugo's eighth collection, *Les Contemplations*, and Baudelaire's first, *Les Fleurs du mal*, were published just over a year apart, in April 1856 and June 1857 respectively. In each case biography is incorporated into the very fabric of the work, engaging with the conception of poetry at stake, no longer from the periphery but from the inside. The widespread cultural practices of biography, whose principal forms had been established over the first half of the century (see Part II of this study), were here actively co-opted and transformed by the literature on which biography had so commonly commented. In the context of the biographical concerns of this book and its argument about the literary, there are two significant elements that these two collections have in common. First, in each of them a staged biography of the poet-figure is used not as a simple backdrop, preface, or critical vantage point, but as an active structuring principle for the collection as a whole. Secondly, this biographical framework is used as the means of redefining and promoting the idea of poetry itself. Poetry is being reinvented by means of a biographical perspective that is integral to the entire conception of the work. In the case of *Les Contemplations*, Hugo is attempting to bring about this reinvention by means of a strategy of expansion, whereby the remit of poetry is stretched as far as the human mind can imagine (and beyond). For Baudelaire, the principle seems, rather, to be one of intensification, albeit complicated by a certain anxiety about how poetry is to be produced. But whether as expansion or as intensification, euphoria or anxiety, the supremacy of poetry is being passionately affirmed by each of these two poets through their constuction of an exemplary representation of the poet's life within the work.

It is particularly striking to find this near-simultaneous use of a single biographical framework for such high aesthetic ambition in the 1850s. Perhaps more than any other in the nineteenth century, this decade was marked by the publication of huge numbers of biographical collections, in which, as we saw in Chapters 4 and 5, the value of the whole, whether dictionary, *recueil*, or series, was more than the sum of its individual biographical parts. The first volumes of Hoefer's *Nouvelle biographie générale* appeared in 1852, and the first edition of Gustave Vapereau's *Dictionnaire universel des contemporains* in 1858. Sainte-Beuve's *Causeries du lundi* were published in several volumes over the course of the decade, which additionally saw the appearance of his *Derniers portraits littéraires* and a revised edition of *Portraits de femmes*, both in 1852. Furthermore, this was the year in which Nerval's *Illuminés* and Champfleury's *Excentriques* were published and Nadar embarked on his monumental Panthéon project. Finally, Eugène de Mirecourt's biographical series *Les Contemporains* was launched in 1854, with one of the first numbers being devoted to Hugo himself. In other words, if biography was in the air during the 1850s, it was predominantly in this collective guise, and mostly for mass consumption.

Nevertheless, it was also around this moment in the nineteenth century that writers were beginning to publish their memoirs, such as those of Stendhal or Constant, written a few decades earlier, having remained in manuscript form. Chateaubriand's *Mémoires d'outre-tombe* were published posthumously between 1848 and 1850, Lamartine's *Les Confidences* appeared in 1849, Dumas's *Mes mémoires* in 1852, and George Sand's *Histoire de ma vie* was serialized in *La Presse*, starting in October 1854. These literary memoirs took the form of a single autobiographical narrative, often running to several volumes (twenty-two in the case of Dumas), and the effect was to create a preface or a postscript to the works, much as biography had done more literally in the past, and more recently in the prefatory 'life' to Sainte-Beuve's *Joseph Delorme*. It was quite likely as a result of the vogue for such memoirs that Adèle Hugo conceived of the idea of writing the anonymous quasi-biography *Victor Hugo raconté par un témoin de sa vie*, which was eventually published in 1863. Hugo himself refrained from following the example of his contemporaries, despite having set his sights on 'being' Chateaubriand ('Être Chateaubriand ou rien'). By abstaining from any overtly autobiographical enterprise, he was able, as Lejeune says in his illuminating essay on the *Victor Hugo raconté*, to let his work be a witness for his life.[1]

This role was a variant of one of the central tenets of the Romantic aesthetic, according to which the artist was understood to pour himself, heart and soul, into his work. It harks back to the 1820s and 1830s and to what José-Luiz Diaz has called 'the heroic age of biography', when Byron was seen as the archetypal model of the poet whose life and work were entirely consubstantial, who lived his poetry, and wrote his life: 'he felt, lived and acted as a poet', his passions 'transported [him] to the heavens or to hell', and his Childe Harold was taken to be the thinnest of disguises for the poet himself.[2] Art was viewed as the function of a certain kind of life, and the artist was constituted more by a distinctive ('artistic') way of living than by his actual creative output: 'making of one's life a work of art, and if possible a tumultuous work of art, a sort of adventurous, chaotic, and disjointed romance'.[3] The philosopher Pierre Leroux,

---

[1] Philippe Lejeune, 'Biographie, témoignage, autobiographie: le cas de *Victor Hugo raconté*', in *Je est un autre: l'autobiographie de la littérature aux médias* (Paris: Éditions du Seuil, 1980), pp. 60–102 (p. 67); see also his discussion of the new vogue for literary memoirs, pp. 69–70.

[2] Louise Swanton-Belloc, *Lord Byron* (1824), quoted in José-Luis Diaz, 'Écrire la vie du poète: la biographie d'écrivain entre Lumières et Romantisme', in *Le Biographique* [colloque de Cerisy 1990], ed. Alain Buisine and Norbert Dodille = *Revue des sciences humaines*, 224 (1991) [special issue], pp. 215–33 (p. 232).

[3] José-Luis Diaz, 'L'*Artiste* romantique en perspective', *Romantisme*, 54 (1986), pp. 5–23 (p. 10). This article and 'Écrire la vie du poète' contain valuable discussions of this topic.

Hugo's fellow exile in Jersey, summarized this conception when he defined poetry as the direct expression of the author's immediate (emotional) circumstances: 'the life of the poet as it is expressed at the moment when he sings'.[4] So integral was this notion to the conception of art more generally that the writer and critic Alexandre de Saint-Chéron, writing in *L'Artiste* in 1832, condemned the majority of his contemporaries—writers and painters alike—for the absence of any such continuity between their lives and their work:

> In my view, a work of art can be original and true [. . .] only when it intimately resembles the man who created it and bears the imprint of his personality; but never has art had less of this character than the art of our own times, never has the individuality of the author been less represented by the work; never has he put less of his secret emotions, his tears, and his soul into his creations.[5]

This does more than describe the aesthetic assumptions of the connoisseur, since it treats the continuity between the work and the life and personality of the artist as the basic criterion of 'true' (as distinct from 'false') art, whether painting or literature.[6] Originality and aesthetic worth are said to depend upon 'that intense and profound similarity between [the] sublime nature [of the artist] and [his] creations', where the artist's passion, suffering, and loves—in short, 'all of [his] life'—are transferred directly into the work. When this happens, says Saint-Chéron, not only will the work be an authentic and living entity, but it will contain the secret of the artist's existence, 'the mystery of his destiny'. Such works consequently become the artist's true biography: 'it is to his works that one must look for [his] biography'.[7] Even though he rejects the idea of the work being 'a calque of his mundane private life', Saint-Chéron is proposing a theory of creativity that views all authentic art as a form of biography. Here biography is not a mere preface to the work, but is implicit as its very substance, as the subtitle of Berlioz's *Symphonie fantastique* (1830) explicitly states: 'Episodes in the Life of an Artist'.

There were, then, three main biographical models available to writers in the mid-nineteenth century: the collective volume, be it dictionary or *recueil*, the authorial memoir, and the presumed autobiographical basis, inherited from Romanticism, of all literary creation. But for those actively involved in the development of poetry, its biographical basis was beginning to lose validity. The confessional mode implied in the Romantic lyric came under overt attack from Leconte de Lisle in the preface to his *Poèmes antiques* published in 1852, and

---

[4] 'De la poésie de notre époque', in *Revue encyclopédique*, Nov. 1831, quoted in Diaz, 'Écrire la vie du poète', p. 227.

[5] Alexandre de Saint-Chéron, 'Philosophie de l'art: la vie poétique et la vie privée', *L'Artiste*, 4/24 (1832), pp. 269–71 (p. 269).

[6] On the relations between the terms 'artiste' and 'poète' see Diaz, 'L'*Artiste* romantique en perspective'.

[7] Saint-Chéron, 'Philosophie de l'art', p. 270.

his call for a poetry of impersonality and formal purity was a direct response to what he presents here as an exhausted vein of personal expression. The Romantic tradition has become no more than 'a secondhand art', its creators are 'powerless [. . .] to express anything other than their own inanity', and the public has grown impatient with 'that clamorous comedy put on for the benefit of a borrowed autolatry'.[8] The strong poets (the masters) 'have fallen silent or are about to do so, weary of themselves' (pp. xii–xiii); and a younger generation has become aware that the literary climate has changed and is in need of renewal: 'We are a bookish generation; the instinctive, spontaneous life that is blindly fecund with youth has withdrawn from us; this is an irreparable fact' (p. vii). Leconte de Lisle's solution to this impasse is a recourse to objectivity and an exclusive focus on the formal component of literary expression. He prides himself on expunging all trace of personal emotion from his own collection, a strategy that he is proposing as a means of curing poetry of its current ills. This antidote does not preclude an eventual reconnection with the impulses of the soul and the heart: 'Once these ordeals of expiation have been undergone, once poetic language has been cleansed, will the speculations of the mind, the emotions of the soul, and the passions of the heart lose any of their truth and their energy when they have at their disposal clearer, better defined forms?' (p. xiv). But at this juncture, a Parnassian return to classical antiquity is presented as the only possible recourse in face of the overworked personalism of contemporary poetry.

What is distinctive about both Hugo and Baudelaire is that they seem to be responding to the crisis outlined by Leconte de Lisle, not by pursuing the option of his impersonal formalism but by reworking the biographical model. The emphasis is shifted from implied autobiography to staged biography, adapting the current proliferation of the biographical form in the wider social and cultural world to meet the crisis confronting a new generation of poets. Although Hugo in particular makes no active attempt to exclude the autobiographical inference that readers had been schooled to make, he nevertheless foregrounds biography as the structuring principle of *Les Contemplations*, just as Baudelaire does for *Les Fleurs du mal*. Significantly the poetic 'I' in each case does not simply point back to the authorial figure deemed to be its origin: Hugo's first person is explicitly multiplied to include that of the reader in the preface to *Les Contemplations*; and Baudelaire not only implicates the reader in his existential narrative ('Hypocrite lecteur,—mon semblable,—mon frère!'),[9] but goes on to introduce his central figure as a third-person, emblematic 'Poet'. The 'individuality of the author' prized by Saint-Chéron cannot be unproblematically read off these two constructs, since the staging of the life of the poet is biographical (the life-story of another) rather than directly autobiographical (the life-story of the author). The model of the authorial memoir is radically recast by being

---

[8] Charles-Marie Leconte de Lisle, *Poèmes antiques* (Paris: M. Ducloux, 1852), pp. xii, ix.
[9] 'Hypocritical reader—my likeness—my brother!' ('Au lecteur', *Les Fleurs du mal*).

extended to the lives of third parties, and, as I have already said, by being given an active and integral function within the work for which the memoir would otherwise merely be the preface or postscript.

As regards the collective principle of the biographical dictionary or *recueil*, Hugo and Baudelaire neatly invert this, so that a single biography encompasses a whole range of separate constitutive elements. Neither *Les Contemplations* nor *Les Fleurs du mal* takes the form of a continuous narrative in the manner of Byron's *Childe Harold*, or of Lamartine's *Jocelyn* (published in 1836). And although the sonnet has, of course, been used as the basis for poetic sequences ever since its paradigmatic origin in Petrarch, Hugo does not use the form at all in *Les Contemplations*, and Baudelaire alternates it with a considerable variety of other verse forms. In this way each collection is composed of individual poems that vary in form, length, and prosodic pattern, and in a manner that highlights the disparate nature of the component parts for which a biographical principle nonetheless provides a single unifying thread.

In both cases, as I have suggested, these shifts in perspective and approach to the biographical habits of the day go hand in hand with a changed relation between biography and poetry. If poetry was widely accepted as the supreme incarnation of literature, it was because the widespread perception of art as having its source in the emotional events of the poet's life made lyric its quintessential mode. It is precisely this perspective that Hugo and Baudelaire are attempting to revise when they use the biographical model to advance definitions of poetry as something more, or something other, than straightforward lyric expression. The manner in which a revised use of biography is harnessed to this redefinition by each poet will be explored in the next two chapters.

7

Hugo's *Les Contemplations*: Life, Death, and the Expansion of Poetry

Earthly existence is nothing other than the slow growth of a human being towards that flowering of the soul that we call death. It is in the tomb that the flower of life opens.

(Hugo, 'Préface de mes œuvres et post-scriptum de ma vie')

Much has been written about Hugo's ego. Borges claimed that it was empty, Sartre that it was a sham, and Ionesco that it was pure inflation.[1] As we saw in the last chapter, Sainte-Beuve regarded Hugo as unremittingly megalomaniac, a view that the opening poem of *Les Feuilles d'automne* (1831) does little to contradict: 'Ce siècle avait deux ans! [. . .] | Alors dans Besançon [. . .] | Naquit d'un sang breton et lorrain à la fois | Un enfant [. . .]. | C'est moi.'[2] Hugo was also a much photographed poet, and he had his son Charles portray him in poses that frequently matched the postures described in the poetry: alone in contemplation on a rocky outcrop or 'listening to God'.[3] In other words, it is not hard to see in Hugo a man who devoted considerable energy to cultivating his poetic persona for public consumption; consequently, it would appear plausible to read the poetry as one of the many means whereby Hugo sought to promote his self-image. However, when Mallarmé wrote of him that 'he was poetry in person',[4] he was saying something of much greater interest and importance than that Hugo appropriated poetry for the purposes of his own self-aggrandizement. When he calls Hugo a 'giant', or a 'monument' in a desert that he created

---

[1] See Borges, *Labryrinths*; Sartre, *Les Mots*; and Eugène Ionesco, *Hugoliade*, trans. Dragomir Costineanu (Paris: Gallimard, 1982).

[2] Victor Hugo, *Les Feuilles d'automne* [1831], in Victor Hugo, *Œuvres poétiques*, ed. Pierre Albouy, 3 vols. (Bibliothèque de la Pléiade; Paris: Gallimard, 1964–74), vol. i, p. 717. 'This century was two years old [. . .] | In Besançon [. . .] | Was born a child | This child [. . .] | Was myself.' [p. 33].

[3] For this latter depiction see Graham Robb, *Victor Hugo*, 2nd edn. (London: Picador, 1998), pl. 20.

[4] Mallarmé, 'Crise de vers', in id., *OC* ii, pp. 204–23 (p. 205). Mallarmé is writing almost a decade on from Hugo's death. His comments about Hugo (including the following quotations in text) are all on p. 205.

through his silencing of other voices ('he all but confiscated from those who think, discourse, or narrate, the right to speak'), and when he comments on Hugo's identification of poetry with himself ('the giant who identified it with his tenacious and ever firmer blacksmith's hand'), it is to make a point about the radical and thoroughgoing transformation that Hugo brought about within poetry itself. This transformation was nothing less than a massive expansion of its remit. According to Mallarmé, 'Hugo, in his mysterious task, reduced all prose, philosophy, eloquence, and history to verse'; he equated poetry with literature in general—'a majestic, unconscious idea, namely, that the form we call verse is itself simply literature'; and he created the potential for seeing poetry in its traditional antonym—prose. In other words, Hugo's personal gigantism was paralleled by the vast extension of poetry realized in his work. It is this idea that I shall pursue in my discussion of *Les Contemplations*, beginning with a consideration of the expanded biographical subject that he constructs for his volume, and focusing on the poet as the agent of his expansion of poetry, not as the megalomaniac origin of a self-mythologizing personal expression that so many others condemned.

The individual subject, which at the time of the *Préface de Cromwell* was subordinated to the all-encompassing development of the life of a larger literary history, is now scaled up to match such proportions. This shift in scale takes several forms, the chief ones being: proliferation, where the individual subject becomes a multiple subject; and the scope offered by the span of a human life 'emerging from the enigma of the cradle and concluding with the enigma of the coffin'.[5] All this is made very clear in Hugo's preface to *Les Contemplations*. Presenting the book as 'the life of a man', he adds that it is 'the life of other men too', including that of the reader: 'My life is your life, and your life is mine, you live what I live' (p. 4). Such mutuality is due in part to the fact that we all share the same human destiny ('destiny is one'). This extension of the poet's individual identity beyond its own limits was an essential part of Hugo's original conception of *Les Contemplations*, which he outlined in the 1840s under a working title of *Les Contemplations d'Olympio*: 'There comes a certain time in life when, with horizons continuously expanding, a man feels too small to go on speaking in his own name. He then creates a poet, a philosopher, or a thinker, a figure in whom he is personified and incarnated. It is still the man, but it is no longer the self [*le moi*].'[6] The process of multiplication does not stop with the creation of an alter ego (here, Olympio). Genius, which for Hugo is the mark of the true poet, is demonstrated not only by its transcendence of the egoism that corrodes the self, but also by its capacity for multiple existences: 'The self of great souls always

---

[5] Victor Hugo, 'Préface', in *Les Contemplations*, ed. Léon Cellier (Classiques Garnier; Paris: Garnier, 1969), p. 3. All page references are to this edition.

[6] Quoted in Bénichou, *Les Mages romantiques*, pp. 313–14.

tends to become collective. Men of genius are Legion.'[7] I shall return later to this collectivization of the poet's soul as it is realized in *Les Contemplations*.

The preface also insists, as I have already said, on the status of the text as the story of a life, and life, moreover, mostly described in the third person, for example as '*les Mémoires d'une âme*'. Hugo repeatedly mentions the compendious scope of such an enterprise: it goes from birth to death, from the Crowd to Solitude, and moves through all the intervening stages—'youth, love, illusion, struggle, despair'—finally bringing the soul 'to the edge of the infinite', the title of the last of the collection's six 'books'.[8] The emphasis on the temporal dimension of a human existence shows the poet's progression through many different stages and moods, which the narrative duly records: 'all the impressions, all the memories, all the realities, all the dimly outlined ghosts, whether laughing or mournful, that a consciousness can contain' (p. 3). As well as stressing this capacity of a single life for sheer variety of content, Hugo is invoking two different kinds of biographical narrative: the memoir and the day-to-day chronicle. On the one hand, the narrating consciousness is portrayed as recollecting in retrospect all the impressions of a lifetime, 'as they are recalled and return to mind, ray by ray, sigh by sigh'; but, on the other, the narrative is also the result of a gradual accumulation of the experiences of a life as they have been registered over the course of time: 'a destiny is written day by day' (p. 4). Twenty-five years are reflected in a book that records the inner and outer events of the poet's life during that time: 'Life, filtered drop by drop through events and suffering, has placed [the book] in [the poet's] heart' (p. 3). As we shall see later on, Hugo exploits his habit of dating individual poems in *Les Contemplations* to support this effect, while at the same time pursuing the model of the retrospective memoir. It is as if the idea of a life-story is itself being expanded, first by simultaneously including a first- and a third-person dimension, and, just as importantly, by being constructed according to these two different narrative modes, the logbook and the memoir. This, in turn, is made to imply two different origins for the writing: the poet and life itself. The poet is presented both as the active source of his poetry ('it is a soul telling its own story'), and as the passive receptacle for the book that life writes in his heart: 'The author has, as it were, allowed the book to form inside him' (p. 3). The creative source of the poetry turns out to be as varied and as multiple as every other aspect of it: its genius-subject, the content of its life, and the narrative framework of the biographical format. The critic Pierre Albouy has referred to the 'exploded I' of Hugo's poetry,[9] and it would seem that this explosiveness

---

[7] Hugo, 'Les Génies appartiennent au peuple', in *Proses philosophiques de 1860–1865*, in id., *Critique*, pp. 587–96 (p. 590).

[8] Hugo, 'Préface', in *Les Contemplations*, p. 3.

[9] Pierre Albouy, 'Hugo, ou le Je éclaté', *Romantisme*, 1/1–2 (1971), pp. 53–64.

characterizes every aspect of his work as the effect of a sustained strategy of expansion.

It is a remarkable feature of *Les Contemplations* that the dynamism ascribed by Hugo in the *Préface de Cromwell* to Nature and to Poetry in general should now be shifted on to the framework of a single life. For this individual life remains the basic ground of *Les Contemplations*, however expanded or exploded its components prove to be. The biographical principle is no empty formula, and it constitutes the basis of the structural design of the collection of which Hugo made so much. In the preface he alludes to the division of the book into two parts, 'Autrefois' ('Past times') and 'Aujourd'hui' ('Today'), alluding to the before and after in Hugo's own life occasioned by the death of his daughter Léopoldine. In other words, the book's structure is grounded in a unique event in the life of an individual, and the twenty-five years mentioned by Hugo in the preface are neatly split in half by the year, 1843, in which that event occurred. Hugo's correspondence repeatedly attests to these twin concerns with personal memoir and poetic structure. He wrote to the critic Jules Janin on 2 September 1855 that the book's title could equally well have been 'Memoirs', and that: 'It is my whole life, twenty-five years [. . .] recounted and expressed in its innermost parts.' This life-story was the basis for the architectural principle of the collection by which Hugo set great store: 'the components of this wretched collection are like the stones in a vault. It is impossible to shift them about.' Elsewhere he compared the book's structure to a pyramid, adding that 'in buildings of this kind, such as vaults or pyramids, all the stones hold together'. This meant that it was only in the context of the whole that any part would be fully meaningful: 'The first line acquires its full meaning only after the last one has been read',[10] and the issue of structural coherence is echoed once more when Hugo writes to his publisher, Hetzel, to say that he wanted *Les Contemplations* to be 'the most complete' of his poetic works.[11] It is the structuring principle of the life that offered him the means to achieve the compendiousness, or potential for expansion, that informs *Les Contemplations*.

THE MULTIPLE FORMS OF BIOGRAPHICAL NARRATIVE

In order to see this principle at work in the full text of *Les Contemplations*, it will be helpful to explore in more detail the various types of biographical narrative that the volume deploys. As we have just seen, the preface has recourse to two

[10] Letter to Jules Janin, quoted in René Journet and Guy Robert, *Notes sur 'Les Contemplations', suivies d'un index* (Paris: Belles Lettres, 1958), p. 37; others (dated 31 May, 12 July, and 5 Nov. 1855) quoted on p. 4.

[11] '[M]on œuvre de poésie la plus complète' (31 May 1855), quoted by Pierre Albouy in his Introduction to *Les Contemplations*, in *Œuvres poétiques*, vol. ii (1967), p. lvi.

contrasting models—the retrospective and the cumulative—though without any hint of a possible contradiction between the two. In the text itself the dominant form is a staged version of the cumulative model; autobiographical retrospection of the kind that George Sand or Chateaubriand had used in their memoirs is barely deployed by Hugo. Only one poem attempts to tell the story of his life as a single continuous narrative, the 418 lines of 'Écrit en 1846' (Book V, III), which are designed to counter the accusation of political and ideological inconsistency. Hugo here defends the abandonment of his youthful royalism and his conversion to what he calls his current 'Jacobinism' in the form of a narrative of progressive enlightenment:

> J'ai vécu; j'ai songé.
> La vie en larmes m'a doucement corrigé.[12]

Beginning with memories of his childhood and continuing to the (fictitious) present of 1846, the poet stresses the consistency of his identity and the continuity of his fundamental beliefs:

> Rien, au fond de mon cœur, puisqu'il faut le redire,
> Non, rien n'a varié; je suis toujours celui
> Qui va droit au devoir.[13]

He deflects any charge of apostasy by portraying change as a necessary and integral part of the natural order:

> L'immense renégat d'Hier, marquis, se nomme
> Demain; mai tourne bride et plante là l'hiver;
> Qu'est-ce qu'un papillon? le déserteur du ver.[14]

However, such affirmation of retrospective continuity is not a general feature of the collection, where the past is more frequently presented in discrete scenes and episodes. Hugo's childhood and youth are evoked in just a handful of poems, and mainly in Book I (*Aurore*): 'Lise' (XI, which begins 'J'avais douze ans. . .'), 'À propos d'Horace' (XIII), 'La Coccinelle' (XV), 'Vers 1820' (XVI), and 'Vieille chanson du vieux temps' (XIX). The only other poem that deals directly with childhood memories is in Book V, 'Aux Feuillantines' (X). Otherwise, the main source of explicit recall is the childhood of Léopoldine, which is portrayed both before and after the moment of her death (at the beginning of Book IV): 'Mes deux filles' (I, III), 'Magnitudo parvi' (III, XXX), 'Elle avait pris ce pli. . .' (IV, V), 'Quand nous habitions tous ensemble. . .' (IV, VI), 'Elle était pâle et pourtant rose. . .' (IV, VII), and 'Ô souvenirs! printemps! aurore!' (IV, IX).

[12] V, III, ll. 167–8: 'I have lived; I have reflected. | Life's tears have gently corrected me.'
[13] Ibid., ll. 358–60: 'Nothing in the depths of my heart, since I must repeat this, | No, nothing has varied; I am still he | Who goes straight to my duty.'
[14] Ibid., ll. 346–8: 'Yesterday's huge renegade, Marquis, is called | Tomorrow; May does an about-turn and abandons Winter; | What is a butterfly? the deserter of the grub.'

Elsewhere, the recollected past tends to appear more obliquely and is signalled through the dates given at the end of each of the poems, many of these being anniversaries of the events depicted, so that a given poem is not so much a memory of a particular event, as its commemoration, whether explicit or implied. The most obviously commemorative poems are those that deal with the death of Léopoldine, and through them is elaborated the account of a gradually evolving response to that loss. Over and above the repeated return to this central event, retrospect provides the stance for many other individual poems. This recurrent backward look is built into *Les Contemplations* from the outset, and several of the poems with the earliest dates are themselves recollections of earlier times. For instance, 'La Coccinelle' (I, xv) is dated 1830; 'À propos d'Horace' (I, xiii) and 'Vieille chanson du jeune temps' (I, xix), both 1831; 'Elle était déchaussée' (I, xxi), a slightly vaguer June 183—; and 'Réponse à un acte d'accusation' (I, vii), January 1834; yet all were written between 1853 and 1855, the dates principally associated with Books V and VI. In other words, rather than simply offering the memories of a man of 50 in accordance with the model of the literary memoirs of his Romantic contemporaries, Hugo projects himself back in time, into a younger, 33-year-old version of himself, whom he presents as remembering, in turn, a still more distant past. The logbook model of biography is thus conflated with the model of the retrospective memoir, so that a part of what is recorded day by day over a lifetime is the poet already remembering the events of that life: 'Écrit au bas d'un crucifix' (III, iv) is dated March 1842 and (according to Léon Cellier) implicitly commemorates the death of Hugo's brother Eugène in February 1832; 'Claire P.' (V, xiv), dated June 1854, memorializes the death of Juliette Drouet's daughter in June 1846, as does 'Claire' (VI, viii), antedated to December 1846, half a year on from her death. Hugo does not defer recollection until his old age, but presents his life as an ongoing series of commemorations of past events. The result of this continuing preoccupation with the past is, paradoxically, to make the standard narrative form of the memoir largely inappropriate for his project.

Instead, the dominant mode for the biographical narrative in *Les Contemplations* is the cumulative record. It is produced chiefly through the ascription of dates to the poems, as if to demonstrate the way that life deposits the poems in the poet's heart by filtering them, 'drop by drop' (to cite the preface), through the events and suffering that he undergoes. Seen as the index of a straightforwardly lyric mode, Hugo's long-standing habit of dating his poems, most often to the day, might support the view of art as the expression of the moment in which the poet chooses to sing ('the life of the poet as it is expressed at the moment when he sings', as Pierre Leroux had it). But in *Les Contemplations* it is also used to create a basis for the implied biography of its poet-narrator. As the notes to any edition of the text indicate, a good many of these dates are false. 'Écrit en 1846', a poem whose supposed date of composition forms its title, was actually written on 7 November 1854, and the attribution to June 1846 is generally seen as a retrospective attempt on Hugo's part to restore his reputation after his disastrous maiden speech in Chambre des Pairs earlier that year.[15]

Ionesco has a field day with instances like this, and it is on such sleights of hand that he bases his accusation against Hugo of fakery.[16] But, taken together, these datings, whether true or false, add up to tell a story, and, as I have said, it is a predominantly biographical one. Although the poems are not organized according to a strict chronology, each of the six books that make up *Les Contemplations* follows on, broadly speaking, from the previous one. The poems of Book I, *Aurore*, are ascribed largely to the 1830s. Book II, *L'Âme en fleur*, gives the date of composition for every one of its twenty-eight poems (mainly on the theme of love) as a month rather than a precise year (e.g. May 18—). The majority of the poems in Book III, *Les Luttes et les rêves*, are dated 1843, but in the months prior to the fateful day—4 September—when Léopoldine drowned. This date itself is given as the title of an unwritten poem (a blank page with a line of dots) in Book IV, *Pauca meae*, many of whose poems directly commemorate 4 September in subsequent years: 1844 in 'Quand nous habitions. . .' (VI), 1845 in 'À qui donc sommes nous?. . .' (VIII), 1846 in 'Ô souvenirs! printemps!. . .' (IX), 1847 in XIV and XV, and 1852 in XVII. Others do so more indirectly, either by dating a poem 'jour des morts'(V), or by locating its composition 'en revenant du cimetière' (XI). Book V, *En marche*, begins with two poems supposedly written in 1852, but consists mostly of poems dating from 1854 and 1855, with, of course, the notable exception of 'Écrit en 1846'. Lastly, Book VI, *Au bord de l'infini*, covers more or less the same period and includes a final commemorative poem for 4 September 1855, 'En frappant à une porte' (XXIV), as well as two postdated poems, 'Spes' (XXI) and 'Les Mages' (XXIII), attributed to January 1856, which serve to end the poet's trajectory on a broadly optimistic note.[17] As I have already mentioned, this chronological arrangement of the six books also places 4 September 1843 at the midway point of the twenty-five-year span that goes from 1830 to 1855/6, structuring the collection as the two equal halves that correspond to 'Autrefois' and 'Aujourd'hui'.

The effect of this chronological construct is to suggest a transformation of the poet's outlook: from the optimism of the first two books, grounded in his personal experience of nature and of love; to the more sober outlook of Book III, which opens out on to the reality of a society in which the poor suffer and injustice is a commonplace; to the personal grief of Book IV; and to the increasingly visionary picture that emerges from Books V and VI, where the poet confronts death, darkness, and doubt, before being reconciled by the

---

[15] See Robb, *Victor Hugo*, pp. 252, 262–3.

[16] Ionesco, *Hugoliade*; see esp. pp. 56–61 on the dating of the poems commemorating the death of Léopoldine.

[17] I have relied extensively on Léon Cellier's notes in his edition of *Les Contemplations* for information about the real datings of the poems and for interpretations of the significance of the published date. Cellier offers a judicious summary of the existing discussions on these issues.

wisdom of 'la bouche d'ombre' ('the mouth of shadows'), which asserts that there is light beyond the darkness and that 'Le mal expirera, les larmes | Tariront'.[18] The course of the poet's life as it is staged in *Les Contemplations* through the ordering and dating of the poems is an initiation that progressively takes him from naturalism to metaphysics (as Suzanne Nash has put it), from a personal to a universal horizon.[19]

Within that overall structure Hugo achieves other more localized effects through the device of dating his poems. Individual events in his life are recalled through the attribution of dates: 'L'Amour' (III, x), dated July 1843, evokes Hugo's departure for Spain with Juliette Drouet; 'Magnitudo parvi' (III, xxx) is dated to coincide with Léopoldine's fifteenth birthday; 'O gouffre! l'âme plonge. . .' (VI, xiv) is given the fictitious date of September 1853, which is that of the discovery of the turning-tables introduced to the Hugo family by Mme de Girardin; the date ascribed to 'Pure innocence' (IV, i), January 1843, places the poem poignantly one month before Léopoldine's wedding, and it is followed by a poem whose title is the actual date of Léopoldine's wedding day, 15 February 1843. These are, of course, private events in Hugo's life, and not all readers may have been expected to catch the personal references; but public events are alluded to also, so that the private solution of prayer outlined in 'Le Pont' (VI, i) is given an added dimension through the attribution of the date December 1852, referring thereby to the re-establishment of the Empire. In several instances the force of the date is further enhanced by the citing of the place of composition, particularly in the last book, where the solemnity of the visions is underscored through the mention of Hugo's place of exile, for example Jersey for 'Ce que dit la bouche d'ombre' (VI, xxvi), and Guernsey for 'À celle qui est restée en France' (the final poem of the collection), as well as several mentions of his current home, Marine-Terrace; and, even more awe-inspiringly, through the naming of a series of dolmens: '[le] dolmen de Rozel' for 'Ibo' and 'Un spectre m'attendait' (VI, ii and iii), '[le] dolmen de la tour Blanche' (on All-Hallows Day) for 'Ce que c'est que la mort' (VI, xxii), and '[le] cimetière de Saint-Jean' for 'Pleurs dans la nuit' (VI, v). The moment when the poet sings gains a huge quantum of extra resonance from these attributed locations.

Dates that imply a sequence are also used to significant effect. 'À Aug. V.', which opens Book V, is given the same date (4 September 1852) as 'Charles Vacquerie', which closes Book IV (xvii), in order to emphasize the parallel that Hugo creates between the way that Charles followed Léopoldine to her death and the way that Charles's brother, Auguste, followed Hugo into exile. 'Le Pont' is followed by 'Ibo' (VI, i and ii), antedated to January 1853 as if to suggest

---

[18] 'Ce qui dit la bouche d'ombre' (VI, xxvi), ll. 781–2: 'Evil will expire, tears | Will cease to flow.'

[19] See Suzanne Nash, *Les Contemplations of Victor Hugo: An Allegory of the Creative Process* (Princeton: Princeton University Press, 1976), which contains a detailed account of the narrative progression of *Les Contemplations*.

that its dynamism was a product of the poet's discovery of prayer; and it is followed in turn by 'Un spectre m'attendait. . .' which has the effect of implying that the 'portes visionnaires | Du ciel sacré'[20] at the end of 'Ibo' had opened to reveal the spectre awaiting the poet in the following poem. There is a similarly incremental effect achieved by the reversing of the dates of the actual composition of 'Horror' and 'Dolor' (VI, xvi and xvii) to make the latter follow on from the darker mood of the former. It is in the context of these effects and their contribution to the overall narrative of *Les Contemplations* that the sequence of poems recording Hugo's reactions to his daughter's death should be viewed. Hugo has often been accused of faking or misrepresenting his emotional responses. The testimony of his correspondence reveals that the resignation that he achieves at the conclusion of the narrative presented by *Les Contemplations* was actually his first response;[21] and readers have found it difficult to explain how the evocation of nature's euphoric welcoming of the dreamer-poet in 'Le poète s'en va'. . . (I, ii) could have been written only two months after Léopoldine's death. Ionesco finds some of his most incriminating ammunition against Hugo here. But such a view presupposes that the poems are to be read as implied autobiographical confession in accordance with the assumption expressed by Pierre Leroux that art is the transmission of the moment when the poet sings. Leroux himself was shocked by the discrepancy on the matter of belief between 'Relligio' and 'Paroles sur la dune' (VI, xx and V, xiii), which Hugo read to him in a single sitting, and he could not reconcile them as the expression of a single, coherent spiritual outlook.[22] This is, however, to ignore the biographical narrative potential that Hugo derives from his use of these dates. It is this strategy that contributes so much to staging the biography of the Poet, who is, as Hugo originally intended for his Olympio, 'still the man but no longer the self'. Cumulatively, and by grounding the individual poems in dates (and sometimes in places) that form an integral part of their composition, the poems in this volume tell the story of a life as outlined in the preface—that of 'a mind which progresses from glimmering to glimmering, leaving behind it youth, love, illusion, struggle, despair, and which stops, distraught "on the edge of the infinite" '.[23]

This, then, is not a poetic life in the manner of Byron, which Saint-Chéron accused the over-sober artists of his generation of failing to live, and which Leconte de Lisle condemned as weary inanity. Contemplation rather than passion is the mode in which the poet conducts the '*vie intime*' that is the subject matter of his narrative. (And it should be said that all nineteenth-century narratives of this kind claim to concern themselves with the intimate life of the emotions, rather than the sexual and domestic 'private life', which has become a major concern of

[20] VI, ii, ll. 129–30: 'the visionary gates | Of the sacred heavens'.
[21] On this see Cellier's comments on 'À Villequier', in *Les Contemplations*, pp. 63–8.
[22] See Cellier's note on this in *Les Contemplations*, p. 667.
[23] Hugo, 'Préface', in *Les Contemplations*, p. 3.

present-day biography.) It is the story of a life whose preface asks that it be read 'as one would read a book by a dead man'. But at the same time, the progression of a mind that goes from one revelation to the next leaves the book doubly opened up to the future at its close, and the Spectre in 'Ce que dit la bouche d'ombre' (VI, XXVI) predicts a moment when 'un ange | Criera: Commencement!'[24] The book 'which contains the spectre [of] his life' acquires life of its own as the poet hands it to his daughter, summoned by his own words to rise from her grave: 'ce livre | Se mit à palpiter, à respirer, à vivre'.[25] The narrative moves towards a metaphysical vision in which an individual life is subsumed into much wider horizons and a much vaster picture of the universe; but it then veers back to its original anchor in the individual framework of a single existence, as is demonstrated in the movement contained in the last two poems of the collection just cited. The individual existence is not discarded as the book's central concern. Rather, it is opened up and expanded by these ambiguities, which the narrative progressively turns into something much more than private and purely individual testimony.

THE EXPANDED SELF

This expansion of the biographical horizons of *Les Contemplations* and the way in which its subject becomes 'Legion'—as Hugo has it—are brought about by a number of strategies in the text. In the first of these the poet's experience is replicated in that of other figures, and is not unique to him. In particular, the death of Léopoldine is echoed in the two poems that deal with the death of Claire Pradier, the daughter of Juliette Drouet, who died of tuberculosis at the age of 20.[26] The death of children and the grief of parents is treated in several other poems: 'À la mère de l'enfant mort' (III, XIV) and 'Épitaphe' (III, XV) are both addressed to the sister of Auguste Vacquerie, who had lost two children; 'Le Revenant' (III, XXIII) recalls the death of Hugo's own firstborn son in infancy; 'Au fils d'un poète' (V, II) is addressed to the Belgian poet André van Hasselt, whose son had died in childhood; 'À Mademoiselle Louise B.' (V, v) inverts the pattern by addressing the adult daughter of a deceased father, but rehearses the same basic motif of loss; and 'Les Malheureux' (V, XXVI) presents both the 'Mater dolorosa' on Golgotha, and Adam and Eve grieving over their dead son and the misfortune of the one who was responsible for that death. Hugo's own experience is central to the biographical narrative of *Les Contemplations*, but it is scaled up beyond the dimensions of a single existence by being echoed in these multiple parallels.

---

[24] 'an angel | Will cry out: It is the beginning!'
[25] 'À celle qui est restée en France', ll. 5, 13–14: 'the finished book | Began to flutter and breathe and live'.
[26] 'On vit, on parle' (IV, XI), 'Claire P.' (V, XIV).

A second form of expansion is achieved through the range of Hugo's literary references in the collection, so that continuities are established with a whole variety of figures, from Job, to Dante, to Pascal, to Virgil, and so on. As Georges Poulet notes, Hugo is incapable of conceiving of himself as a pure subjectivity and 'a self-thinking consciousness'. In short, 'he does not belong exclusively to himself';[27] and through his association with all these other literary personae the poet acquires a cosmic existence. This continuity is particularly marked when it comes to the depiction of the poet-subject of the narrative, whose poetic identity is constituted through its connection with other poets, rather than by means of any Oedipal demarcation from his precursors. One of the first poems in *Les Contemplations* is addressed to André Chénier (I, v), whose patronage is appealed to in Hugo's stated aim to couple Rabelais with Dante, as if poetry were being defined as a supremely collective or communal enterprise that conjoins apparent opposites (high and low) as well as different points in time (Dante and Chénier). Indeed, in 'Les Mages' (VI, xxiii), this is exactly how artistic endeavour is presented, when, after the invocation of a whole panoply of literary, musical, and artistic 'mages' from all periods of human history, we read:

> Chacun d'eux écrit un chapitre
> Du rituel universel;
> Les uns sculptent le saint pupitre,
> Les autres dorent le missel;
> Chacun fait son verset du psaume;
> Lysippe, debout sur l'Ithome,
> Fait sa strophe en marbre serein,
> Rembrandt à l'ardente paupière,
> En toile, Primatice en pierre,
> Job en fumier, Dante en airain.[28]

A single, universal rite is the collective product of artists working in marble, paint, words, and even 'dung', each contributing to a single, universal 'psalm' whose poetry can be expressed in any medium.

As a result, the poet-subject of the book can be addressed without fear of potential rivalry by Dante (III, i), can allude to Pascal in the title of 'Magnitudo parvi' (III, xxx), and assert an unbroken link with Virgil in 'Mugitusque boum' (V, xvii): 'Mugissement des bœufs, au temps du doux Virgile | Comme

---

[27] Georges Poulet, 'Hugo', in id., *La Distance intérieure* (Paris: Plon, 1952), pp. 194–230 (pp. 209–10 [p. 165]). I have learned much from an unpublished discussion of Hugo's aesthetic of continuity in which these relations with precursors might figure, by Katherine Lunn-Rockliffe, 'Death and the Aesthetic of Continuity: Reading Victor Hugo's *Les Contemplations*', paper given at 'Birth and Death': 3rd Annual Conference of the Society of Dix-Neuviémistes, Queen's University, Belfast, March–April 2005.

[28] VI, xxiii, ll. 191–200: 'Each of them | Writes a chapter of the universal ritual; | Some sculpt the holy lectern; | Others gild the missal; | Each makes his own verse in the psalm; | Lysippe, standing on Mount Ithome, | Makes her stanza in serene marble, | Rembrandt of the burning eyes, | On canvas, Primaticcio in stone, | Job in dung, Dante in bronze.'

aujourd'hui [. . .] vous disiez. . .'.[29] The generic 'poet' whose life and being have gone into the making of the poem in 'Le poème éploré se lamente. . .' (I, IX) is not just an implicit reference to Hugo himself, but turns out, as the poem progresses, to be a compound figure whose creative practice is validated by the instances of numerous individual poets and writers, including Shakespeare, Molière, Corneille, Cato, Homer, St John the Divine, Aeschylus, and Prometheus. This series again expands the notion of a 'poet' well beyond those whose creative medium is poetry in the conventional sense of the word. In other words, it is by aligning himself with a legion of other artists and poets that the poet-genius—genius being the ultimate horizon of poetic identity for Hugo—himself becomes Legion.

In the process of that alignment, the many are simultaneously absorbed into a single, compendious creative entity—the Poet—who is defined precisely by his capacity to contain entire worlds and populations. This is, for example, how Shakespeare is portrayed in the emblematically entitled 'Le Poète' (III, XXVIII):

> Son crâne transparent est plein d'âmes, de corps,
> De rêves, dont on voit la lueur du dehors;
> Le monde tout entier passe à travers son crible.[30]

By being in continuous dialogue with other creative minds, the poet's own mind acquires the ability to accommodate worlds that contain figures from all of human history. Or, as Hugo puts it in the introduction to his life of Shakespeare:

There are indeed oceanic men [*hommes océans*]. Those waves, that ebb and flow, that terrifying to and fro, the sound of every gust of wind [. . .] all that contained in one [. . .] that infinite, unfathomable entity, all this can exist in a single mind, and when it does, that mind is called a genius [. . .] and contemplating such souls is the same as contemplating the Ocean.[31]

The capacious mind, which can contain 'all in one', is the one that is capable of producing poetry; and it is the history of such a mind that is narrated in *Les Contemplations*.

The expansion of the individual to accommodate the many of 'le tout' is also brought about by a third strategy, which treats the poet as the receptacle for the wisdom of others.[32] Hugo's poet is a strangely passive figure, far more inclined to record the words spoken to him by others than to project his own voice into the world (*pace* Sainte-Beuve). If the first poem of the collection is uttered as a

---

[29] V, XVII, ll. 1–2, 4: 'Lowing cattle, in the days of gentle Virgil | As today [. . .] you would say'.

[30] III, XXVIII, ll. 9–11: 'His transparent skull is full of souls, bodies, | And dreams, whose light can be seen from without; | The entire world is filtered through its attention.'

[31] Victor Hugo, *William Shakespeare*, in *Critique*, pp. 245–463 (pp. 247–8).

[32] For a full and very interesting discussion of Hugo's engagement with other voices in his lyric poetry see Ludmila Charles-Wurtz, *Poétique du sujet lyrique dans l'œuvre de Victor Hugo* (Paris: H. Champion, 1998). Her contention is that 'la poésie lyrique de Hugo, que l'on a longtemps lue comme une poésie personnelle, donne à entendre une multitude de voix' (p. 7).

direct address to Léopoldine, the second, 'Le poète s'en va. . .', goes on to present the poet in the guise of listener—'il écoute en lui-même une lyre' ('he listens to a lyre within himself')—and as one who, rather than speak in his own name, causes nature to speak in his place. When the flowers and the trees murmur 'C'est lui! c'est le rêveur!' ('It is he! it is the dreamer!'), it is nature that has recourse to language in order to acknowledge the poet, and not, as poetic convention would more commonly have it, the poet who takes nature as the object of his linguistic utterance. In the fifth poem of Book I, 'À André Chénier', the poet presents his aesthetic credo as the fruit of the wisdom spoken to him by a bullfinch in a garden, and it is the bird who argues for the coupling of Dante with Rabelais. This scenario is repeated throughout *Les Contemplations*, but is particularly firmly established in Book I, with a black holly tree addressing the poet in 'Les Oiseaux' (XVIII), and with the poet in 'Oui, je suis le rêveur. . .' (XXVII) placing himself on the receiving end of a permanent dialogue with nature:

> Oui, je suis le rêveur; je suis le camarade
> Des petites fleurs d'or du mur qui se dégrade,
> Et l'interlocuteur des arbres et du vent.
> Tout cela me connaît, voyez-vous. J'ai souvent
>   [· ·]
> Des conversations avec les giroflées;
> Je reçois des conseils du lierre et du bleuet.
>   [· ·]
> Tous ces doux instruments, m'adressent la parole.[33]

As the horizons open out over the course of *Les Contemplations*, other figures, including Dante (as mentioned above), come forward to speak, and it is their words that form the substance of much of the poetry. In 'Les Malheureux' (V, XXVI) the poet is presented not as the primary source of the poem's message, but as the recipient and faithful transmitter of words addressed to him by a whole parade of unfortunates: the destitute occupant of the hovel he sees in the forest (ll. 38–56), Socrates (l. 105), Jan Hus (l. 106), St Thraseas (ll. 107–11), Christopher Columbus (l. 115), Saint-Just (l. 116), Phocion (l. 118), Savonarola (ll. 122–38), the Virgin Mary (l. 169), the anonymous crowd (ll. 175–260), God (l. 274), those who do harm to others (ll. 314–15), the beggar (l. 327), the innocent (l. 328), and Zeno (l. 331). This continues with even greater intensity in the last book of the collection, where the poet is addressed in turn by St John the Divine in 'Écoutez. Je suis Jean. . .' (VI, IV), and by the spectres who speak in 'Un spectre m'attendait. . .' (VI, III), and, with the ultimate vision on which the whole volume closes, in 'Ce que dit la bouche d'ombre'. It is the voices

---

[33] I, XXVII, ll. 1–4, 6–7, 18: 'Yes, I am the dreamer; I am the comrade | Of the little gold flowers on the crumbling wall, | And the one to whom trees and wind speak. | They all know me, you see. I often have [. . .] | Conversations with gillyflowers; | I take advice from ivy and the cornflower. [. . .] | All these sweet instruments speak directly to me.'

of these other figures who occupy a good part, though not all, of the notional speaking position of the poet in *Les Contemplations*, contributing powerfully to the sense of a multiplied subjectivity in the book.

POETIC EXPANSION

This phenomenon, which casts the poet in a passive, listening role, is, furthermore, the basis of the overall poetic attitude as adumbrated in the volume and articulated in the title: that of contemplation. Contemplation is an openness to the world that allows the poet to hear the language spoken by it, since in that world 'les choses et l'être ont un grand dialogue. | Tout parle'.[34] What distinguishes the poet is not so much an ability to write as his capacity to listen to 'the eternal murmur' of nature and the universe (ibid., l. 20). Nature is repeatedly depicted as a speaking entity: 'Tout conjugue le verbe aimer',[35] and

> Le moindre arbrisseau parle, et l'herbe est en extase;
> Le saule pleureur chante en achevant sa phrase.[36]

Moreover, the language of nature is already constituted as poetry, and the poet's task is to read the language that is nature rather than produce words of his own that might describe or reflect the natural world:

> Je lisais. Que lisais-je? Oh! le vieux livre austère,
> Le poème éternel!—La Bible?—Non, la terre.
> [. . . . .]
> Et je n'ai pas besoin d'emporter dans mes courses
> Mon livre sous mon bras, car je l'ai sous mes pieds.
> [. . . . .]
> Il est sain de toujours feuilleter la nature,
> Car c'est la grande lettre et la grande écriture;
> Car la terre, cantique où nous nous abîmons,
> A pour versets les bois et pour strophes les monts![37]

The earth beneath your feet is a book, the pages of nature can be turned like those one reads, woods are verses, and mountains are stanzas. Even God is an author, whose work is nature, and can be compared to that of Homer:

---

[34] 'Ce que dit la bouche d'ombre' (VI, xxvi), ll. 11–12: 'things and being have a grand dialogue. | Everything speaks'.
[35] 'Premier mai' (II, i), l. 1: 'Everything conjugates the verb to love'.
[36] 'Les oiseaux' (I, xviii), ll. 47–8: 'The least little shrub speaks, and the grass is in ecstasy; | The weeping willow sings as it finishes its sentence.'
[37] 'Je lisais. . .' (III, viii), ll, 1–2, 6–7, 21–4: 'I was reading. What was I reading? Oh! that ancient, austere book, | The eternal poem!—The Bible?—No, the earth. [. . .] | And when I go on my tramps I have no need to take | My book with me under my arm, for I have it beneath my feet. [. . .] | It is wholesome to be always leafing through nature, | For it is the great letter and the great writing; | For the earth, a great hymn in which we are plunged, | Has the woods for verses, and the mountains for stanzas!'

Car Dieu fait un poème avec des variantes;
Comme le vieil Homère, il rabâche parfois,
Mais c'est avec les fleurs, les monts, l'onde et les bois![38]

By adopting a posture of contemplation, the poet acts as a kind of medium for
the poetry written in the natural world, just as he was the conduit for the wisdom
of the various 'mages' and others whose words he records.

Nature may be a poem that the poet reads, but it is also the hand that moves
the poet's pen:

L'être mystérieux, que vous croyez muet,
Sur moi se penche, et vient avec ma plume écrire.[39]

If poetry exists first and foremost in the world outside the poet, it also requires
effort on his part to bring it into being. In 'Le poème éploré se lamente. . .' (I,
IX) poetry is the fruit of his own anguish and experience:

[. . .] le penseur
Souffre de sa pensée et se brûle à sa flamme.
Le poète a saigné le sang qui sort du drame.[40]

On other occasions that effort is a response to an external imperative. In 'Insomnie'
(III, XX) an 'implacable idea' arrives with a line of verse and commands the poet
to leave his bed and write. She calls him '[un] horrible esclave' and '[un] forçat' ('a
horrible slave, a convict'), and the poet eventually complies with her summons,
recognizing that:

Il faut dans ces labeurs rentrer la tête ardente;
Dans ces grands horizons subitement rouverts,
Il faut de strophe en strophe, il faut de vers en vers,
S'en aller devant soi, pensif, ivre de l'ombre.[41]

It is not quite clear what the nature of the poet's production is, since the poem
is already constituted as 'un vers' before he begins his work, but he is clearly
subordinated to a phenomenon whose origin lies outside himself.

Elsewhere he goes in pursuit of a pre-existing 'Strophe', Pluto to poetry's
Proserpine, whom he makes captive and queen in the depths of his soul and 'Sous
son crâne à la fois céleste et souterrain'.[42] In 'Réponse à un acte d'accusation'

[38] 'Pasteurs et troupeaux' (V, XXIII), ll. 12–14: 'For God makes poems with variants; | Like
ancient Homer, he repeats himself sometimes, | But it is with flowers, hills, water, and woods.'

[39] 'Oui, je suis le rêveur. . .' (I, XXVII), ll. 8–9: 'The mysterious being, which you think is
mute, | Bends over me, and writes with my pen.'

[40] I, IX, ll. 9–11: '[. . .] the thinker | Suffers from his thought and burns himself on his own
fire. | The poet has shed the blood which emerges from the drama'.

[41] III, XX, ll. 61–5 [p. 103]: 'To these chores, head burning you | Have to return; stanza by
stanza, bit by bit, | You have to plod ahead with infinite | Horizons spreading out before you; drunk
with gloom'.

[42] 'Ô strophe du poète. . .' (V, XXV), l. 25: 'Beneath his skull, both celestial and subterranean'.

(I, vii), the poet's righteous anger and considerable energies are entirely devoted to freeing a language that has its own independent and autonomous existence. Poetry is not made, but liberated as a result of his intervention, and the poet becomes a passive witness to the activity of the language whose freedom he has merely restored:

> Car le mot, qu'on le sache, est un être vivant.
> La main du songeur vibre et tremble en l'écrivant;
> La plume, qui d'une aile allongeait l'envergure,
> Frémit sur le papier quand sort cette figure,
> Le mot, le terme, type on ne sait d'où venu,
> Face de l'invisible, aspect de l'inconnu;
> Créé, par qui? forgé, par qui? jailli de l'ombre;
> Montant et descendant dans notre tête sombre,
> Trouvant toujours le sens comme l'eau le niveau;
> Formule des lueurs flottantes du cerveau.[43]

Language is a living entity, and it is words rather than their speakers that determine meaning. The poet's hand follows the dictates of a power whose source lies elsewhere and remains a mystery.

This is beginning to sound as if Hugo might be anticipating the impersonal stance of Mallarmé, for whom the poet 'cedes the initiative to words'. But the ambition of Hugo's poet is to take up his own place in a universe where 'everything speaks', as a voice in his own right. In 'Ibo' (VI, ii) he asserts: 'Je suis le poète farouche, | [. . .] la bouche | Du clairon noir.'[44] And in 'À celle qui est restée en France', the final poem, he claims:

> J'ai le droit aujourd'hui d'être, quand la nuit tombe,
> Un de ceux qui se font écouter de la tombe,
> [· ·]
> Et dont la parole, âpre ou tendre, émeut les pierres,
> Les grains dans les sillons, les ombres dans les bières,
> La vague et la nuée, et devient une voix
> De la nature, ainsi que la rumeur des bois.[45]

---

[43] 'Réponse à un acte d'accusation. Suite' (I, viii), ll. 1–10: 'For words, let it be known, are living things. | The dreamer's hand vibrates, trembles to write them; | His very pen, shed from a wingspan, quakes | On the page, when these characters come out— | Words, figures, terms of doubtful origin, | Visage of the invisible, shown by the unknown; | Made by whom? shaped by whom? sprung from the shadows; | Rising and falling in our sombre heads; | Finding the sense as water finds the level; | Formulae of the brain's fluctuating light' [p. 177].

[44] VI, ii, ll. 101, 103–4: 'I am the untamed poet | [. . .] the mouth | Of the black bugle'.

[45] 'À celle qui est restée en France', ll. 169–76: 'And if, nowadays, as the night is falling, | I am the kind of person who speaks to the dead | Pale and alone, who has tombs for his audience | Who raises the dark folds of the grave clothes very slowly, | Whose words, bitter or tender, move the stones, | The furrowed grain, the coffined shades, | The waves and the clouds—till they become a voice | Of nature, like the murmur of the woods' [p. 177].

The poet has here acquired a voice that is on a par with those he merely listened to in his earlier guise as the dreamer hailed by nature and as the attentive reader of its book. He now speaks as a part of the natural universe, for which he is also the conduit. The right to a voice of his own is the outcome of the life narrated in the book; and he hands the completed work to the child whom he is hoping to raise from the grave with its power. The poet's voice nevertheless remains just one amongst many, and the book itself is certainly not the direct product of that voice: 'Dieu dictait, j'écrivais' (ibid., l. 11). The poet goes on to describe both the universe ('ces strophes qu'au fond de vos cieux je cueillais') and himself as a book of poems ('vous tourniez les pages de mon âme'), while at the same time claiming that he has himself written such a book ('j'ai, dans ce livre, enregistré mes jours').[46] All this gives poetry a multiple origin, according to which it exists variously as ready-made stanzas in the heavens, the already written pages of the poet's soul, and the work that he produces through his own creative labour.

The poet's voice cannot be the sole origin of the poetry that records his life, because poetry is now coextensive with a universe that contains many voices. Poetry, too, is scaled up and made as eternal and as infinite as that universe, its verses interchangeable with suns:

> Nous irions tous un jour, dans l'espace vermeil,
> Lire l'œuvre infinie et l'éternel poème,
> Vers à vers, soleil à soleil![47]

The poet nevertheless remains an indispensable figure in all of this, because it is the function of genius, which for Hugo always operates on an epic scale, to reveal existence to humanity as comprising 'humanity, nature, and supernaturalism', and yet to make this 'cosmic synthesis' intelligible. As Hugo says in the 'Préface de mes œuvres et post-scriptum de ma vie': 'The greatest geniuses, the encyclopedic intelligence as well as the epic mind [. . .] spell out the detail of the whole in order to make it comprehensible.'[48] The poet is necessary to this revelation because of the encyclopedic and epic quality of his mind, and because without him the vision would remain unintelligible. It is for this reason that, as Hugo says at the end of *William Shakespeare*, the genius, and not the man of action, must become the leader of humanity: 'It is time that men of action took their place behind, and that men of ideas step out in front. The summit is the head. Where thought is, there lies strength. It is time for geniuses to move ahead of heroes.'[49] The poet is the emblematic form of genius,[50] and the poetry that is coextensive with the

---

[46] Ibid., ll. 144–7: 'those stanzas which I plucked from the depths of your skies, | [. . .] you turned the pages of my soul, | [. . .] in this book I have kept a record of my days'.

[47] 'Saturne' (III, III), ll. 46–8: 'One day we might all go, into the rosy expanse, | To read the infinite work and the eternal poem, | Line by line, sun by sun!'

[48] In 'Préface de mes œuvres et post-scriptum de ma vie', in *Proses philosophiques de 1860–65*, in *Critique*, pp. 698–712 (p. 699). (The epigraph to the present chapter is on p. 708.)

[49] Hugo, *William Shakespeare*, p. 450.

universe is synonymous with all types of thought. It is in this sense that the scope of poetry is expanded beyond the record of the poet's personal experience, but also for this reason that the individual biography remains a necessity. A single life is the form corresponding to the reality of earthly existence that moves from birth to death, but it is also one of the vehicles through which the confusion of the cosmos can be made intelligible: 'being successive, our understanding requires division. Everything at once is not possible for us'.[51] The individual human mind and the temporality of the individual human span are the linchpin for the rest.

All this is brought about through the way in which Hugo constructs and deploys the biography of the poet in *Les Contemplations*. Instead of taking readers back to his '*vie intime*' and producing a purely lyric poetry based on direct emotional expression, Hugo makes a staged version of that life the basis of both the revelation of a world on a cosmic scale and an upgrading of poetry to dimensions that exceed those of all other human activities. It was by transforming personal biography in this way, and by recasting poetry in these terms, that Hugo made it possible for Mallarmé subsequently to say of him that 'he was poetry in person'.

[50] See Bénichou, *Les Mages romantiques*, p. 492.   [51] 'Préface de mes œuvres', p. 699.

8

Baudelaire: Life and the Production of Poetry

It is a very great and a very useful pleasure to compare the features of a great
man with his works.

(Baudelaire, *Edgar Allan Poe, sa vie et ses ouvrages*)

When Barbey d'Aurevilly reviewed *Les Fleurs du mal* in July 1857, he singled
out the structural coherence of the volume as its most striking feature, and spoke
of 'a *secret architecture*, a plan calculated by the contemplative and witting poet'.
The book, he says, is not a collection of individual poems, but 'a poetic work
of the most powerful unity' in which each individual poem has '*a very important
value as an entity and for its position*'.[1] The whole is more than the sum of its
individual poetic parts, and this has consequences for both the moral and the
aesthetic reading of the text: 'From the point of view of art and of aesthetic
sensation, they [the poems] would lose much by not being read *in the order* in
which the poet, who knows very well what he is doing, has arranged them' (ibid.).
Baudelaire included Barbey's article in the dossier he prepared for M[e] Gustave
Chaix d'Est-Ange, the lawyer defending him against the charges of offence to
public morality occasioned by *Les Fleurs du mal*; and in the notes he appended to
the dossier he instructs his lawyer that 'the book must be judged *as a whole*, and a
fearful moral will then emerge from it'.[2] Moral issues were clearly of the essence
at the trial, and in any case Barbey was rather more inclined to attend to moral
matters than to aesthetic ones,[3] but the volume's coherence is essentially a poetic
consideration. Ultimately, and despite the verdict condemning the volume for its
moral offences, the literary effects of Baudelaire's organization of his book could
be said to have been more significant—and certainly more innovative—than
the moral issues that preoccupied the lawyers.

Barbey speaks of unity and architecture, but, in the comments that Baudelaire
himself made on the subject of the book's organization, the issue of sequence is

---

[1] Barbey d'Aurevilly, '*Les Fleurs du mal* par M. Charles Baudelaire', in Baudelaire, *OC* i, pp.
1191–6 (p. 1196, original emphasis).
[2] Baudelaire, 'Notes pour mon avocat', in *Le Procès des 'Fleurs du mal'*, in *OC* i, pp. 193–6 (p.
193). For a full discussion of the trial see the account by Claude Pichois in *OC* i, pp. 1176–83.
[3] As we saw in Ch. 4 above. Indeed, Barbey's article continues: 'Mais elles [the poems] perdraient
bien davantage *au point de vue de l'effet moral*', '*Les Fleurs du mal*', *OC* i, p. 1196 (Barbey's italics).

the one that he particularly chooses to emphasize. In a letter to the editor of the *Revue des deux mondes*, which published eighteen poems under the title *Les Fleurs du mal* in June 1855, Baudelaire insists on having a hand in selecting the order in which the poems will appear: 'Whichever pieces you choose, I am very anxious to put them in order *with you* [Baudelaire's italics], *in order that they follow on from each other, so to speak.'*4* And in the note accompanying the copy of the 1861 edition of *Les Fleurs du mal* that he sent to Vigny, Baudelaire emphasizes the importance of the beginning and the end of the sequential arrangement of the poems: 'The only praise that I would ask for this book is that people recognize that it is not a simple album and that it has *a beginning and an end.'*5* What he does not spell out here is that the beginning is a birth ('Bénédiction') and the end death, death being the subject matter of the last poem, 'Le Voyage', as well as the title of the closing section of the volume, thus turning the sequence as a whole into the story of the life of the poet. In short, the order and consistency of the collection stressed by Baudelaire would seem to be those of biography.

The poet who, as Barbey sees, 'knows what he is doing' is, however, using the form for rather different ends from those of Hugo in *Les Contemplations*. The issue of poetry is just as much at stake in Baudelaire's biographical account of his poet-protagonist as it was for Hugo. But Baudelaire unhitches poetry from the Hugolian nexus of nature, history, and the cosmos that is propelled by the forward momentum that Hugo liked to describe as progress. Instead, he sets poetry up in opposition to those elements, and presents it as being itself the prime focus of the spiritual aspirations of his poet-hero. Poetry is both distinguished from and elevated above the world in which it exists. At the same time Baudelaire also uncouples poetry from any autobiographical basis, explicitly making the life-story he presents that of the volume's poet-hero and not that of its poet-author. Barbey comments on this shift in his essay, and he celebrates the novelty of *Les Fleurs du mal* precisely for its difference from 'la poésie personnelle':

contrary to the majority of contemporary lyrics, which are so caught up in their egoism and their petty little impressions, the poetry of M. Baudelaire is less the outpouring of personal sentiment, than the robust conception of his mind. Although he is highly lyrical in his expression and his verve, the poet of *Les Fleurs du mal* is at bottom a dramatic poet.*6*

It is in the context of a staged biographical drama and not that of an implied autobiography that poetry is postulated as a transcendental value.*7*

---

    4 Quoted in the notes to *Les Fleurs du mal, OC* i, p. 984.
    5 Quoted by Pichois in his 'Notice' to *Les Fleurs du mal, OC* i, p. 799.
    6 Barbey, '*Les Fleurs du mal*', *OC* i, pp. 1192–3.
    7 This emphasis on the third person and on the drama is the basis of D. J. Mossop's *Baudelaire's Tragic Hero: A Study of the Architecture of 'Les Fleurs du mal'* (Oxford: Clarendon Press, 1961), which, to my knowledge, is the only full-length study of Baudelaire to develop this point. He does so, however, not in the context of biography but of tragedy, and he focuses principally on the poet's moral flaws at the expense of aesthetic considerations.

Poetry in *Les Fleurs du mal* is not, then, as Saint-Chéron had it, the expression of the poet's emotions and the implicit record of the events of his life. Rather, poetry itself becomes the supreme passion of the poet in the form of 'a thirst for the infinite', 'a love of beauty'; the only sensibility that counts in this conception is the sensibility of the imagination, not that of the heart; and the entire course of the poet's life is bound up with the creation of his poetry. The life becomes witness to the poet's art, not the art to the life; and the life is significant not as the source of the material for that art, but as the means of its production. Hugo can allow his book to write itself ('The author has, as it were, allowed the book to form inside him') because the book is the record of a 'destiny', which, filtered through the poet's heart, leaves a sediment of poetry behind it. But in the case of Baudelaire the poet's life becomes a testament primarily to the active construction of his art, for which the poet is uniquely, if problematically, responsible.

BAUDELAIRE'S BIOGRAPHIES

Les Fleurs du mal is by no means the only instance of biography in Baudelaire's work, and his critical writings include some major biographical essays: *Edgar Allan Poe, sa vie et ses ouvrages*, first published in 1852 and revised in 1855 as *Edgar Poe, sa vie et ses œuvres*; *Théophile Gautier* (1859); *Un mangeur d'opium* devoted to Thomas de Quincey (1860); and *L'Œuvre et la vie d'Eugène Delacroix* (1863). Nevertheless, as we saw in Chapter 5, Baudelaire disparages the conventions of biography that require accounts of a poet's early schooldays and suchlike, when he suggests that biography is largely irrelevant to a figure like Gautier who lived for an *idée fixe*. In a similar vein, he questions the validity of standard biographical information, when he asks in a draft of his own biographical notice produced in response to the demands of his publishers: 'How do you expect people to write biographical notes? Do you want me to say that I was born in Paris in 1821, and that when I was young I made a number of journeys to the Indian Ocean? I do not believe that one should put that kind of thing.'[8] In the same draft he is, however, quite happy to present himself as an author of biographies (amongst other things): 'CHARLES BAUDELAIRE [. . .] published a curious biographical apologia [for Edgar Allan Poe] in the *Revue de Paris*.' Indeed, according to his friend and fellow writer Charles Asselineau, Baudelaire was so committed to Poe's biography that he could not imagine living 'without a detailed knowledge of Poe, both his life and his works', and sought to ensure that his friends would not remain ignorant of 'the smallest circumstance in the biography of his hero'.[9] For Baudelaire, Poe was 'one of the greatest literary

---

[8] Baudelaire, *Notices bio-bibliographiques*, in *OC* i, pp. 783–6 (p. 783).
[9] Quoted by Henri Lemaitre in his Introduction to Charles Baudelaire, *Curiosités esthétiques; l'art romantique; et autres œuvres critiques*, ed. Henri Lemaitre (Classiques Garnier; Paris: Garnier, 1962), pp. lix–lx.

heroes', and in writing about Poe he claims that he is adding 'a new saint to the martyrology'.[10] Not withstanding his occasional misgivings about biography, the subjects of Baudelaire's essays are mostly heroes and saints in his eyes. And they are so because they exemplify the miracle of artistic production.

I shall have more to say about this in due course, but, as I have already indicated, despite Baudelaire's enthusiasm for the genre, his approach attributes to biography a rather different function from the one it had for his contemporaries, and this gives his biographical practice a somewhat different set of presuppositions from those that were current at the time. He is careful in his own biography of Poe to distinguish his account from the standard biographies in which social norms would be invoked to claim that Poe, if he had only exercised more self-discipline and applied his gifts in a less wanton manner, could have been '*a money making author*'.[11] Poe's first biographer, Rufus Griswold, is dismissed as 'that vampire-pedagogue', and the American biographical dictionary that Baudelaire consulted for its entry on Poe disappoints him by offering nothing more insightful as a description of his hero's work than the term 'strange'. Baudelaire is explicitly writing against the grain of the kind of social consensus ordinarily upheld by both the dictionary and the press through the medium of biography.

Neither are Baudelaire's biographical subjects the representative figures and the 'great men' of the biographical dictionary. His various heroes do not incarnate the spirit of the nation or the society in which they live, but tend to stand out in antagonistic opposition to it. 'Nations have great men only despite themselves', Baudelaire writes in *Fusées*.[12] His poet-heroes live in an 'anti-poetic' world, and he shares the view exemplified by Vigny's *Stello* whereby 'the poet could not find his proper place in either a democratic or an aristocratic society, and no more in a republic than in an absolute or constitutional monarchy'.[13] The artist-hero is neither prepared for, nor received by, people whose qualities he might share; and what marks him out even among other artists is an absolute distinctiveness: 'In the orders of poetry and art, revelations rarely have precursors. Any flowering is spontaneous and individual. [. . .] The artist derives only from himself.'[14] The individuality that both justifies and threatens biography is not redeemed in Baudelaire by being collectivized or made in some way representative of an established social or even literary phenomenon, and the uniqueness of the artist sets him resolutely at odds with the world in which he lives.

Baudelaire's biographies also demonstrate an absence of the developmental principles implied in the genre, whereby progress, time, and nature, whether collectively or individually, guarantee for any biographical narrative an upward

---

[10] Baudelaire, *Edgar Poe, sa vie et ses œuvres*, in *OC* ii, pp. 296–318 (pp. 305, 297).

[11] Ibid., p. 298 (Baudelaire's italics; the italicized phrase is given in English in the original).

[12] Baudelaire, *Fusées*, in *OC* i, p. 654 [Cameron, p.160]. On this see Bernard Howells, *Baudelaire: Individualism, Dandyism and the Philosophy of History* (Oxford: Legenda, 1996), ch. 5.

[13] *Edgar Poe*, *OC* ii, p. 297.

[14] Baudelaire, *Exposition universelle (1855)*, in *OC* ii, pp. 575–97 (p. 581).

path towards a glorious and exemplary culmination. Hugo's faith in Progress, which he repeated in his letter to Baudelaire, published as the preface to the *Théophile Gautier* essay,[15] is one that Baudelaire emphatically does not share and repeatedly condemns. The 'doctrine of progress' is, according to him, nothing more than a form of moral laziness: 'It is the individual counting on his neighbours to perform his task for him', as he says in *Mon cœur mis à nu*.[16] Time never brings change for the better, and humanity is depressingly self-consistent: 'What could be more absurd than progress, since men, as is proved daily by events, are always alike and true to themselves, that is to say, always like savages.'[17] These savages live in the state of nature, and for Baudelaire art is nothing less than a systematic transformation of nature and the natural state: 'I am incapable of being moved by vegetation.' Nature is devoid of the spirituality that is one of the attributes Baudelaire associates with art: 'I shall never believe that the souls of the Gods inhabit plants—sanctified vegetables.'[18] Whereas for Hugo the organic element of nature bestowed the certainty of dynamism and development on all aspects of life, Baudelaire's world lacks temporal continuity altogether. Not only does humankind seem incapable of change, but time itself regularly becomes fragmented or stalled. Proust noted that 'Time is peculiarly chopped up in Baudelaire'; and Walter Benjamin, who quotes this remark, goes on to comment that with Baudelaire the continuity of experience (*Erlebnis*) is broken up into a series of disjointed psychic events (*Erfahrungen*).[19] When time does become perceptible as something other than an isolated instant, it can do so only as the unending stagnation of ennui. Such an understanding does not accord well with the usual principles of biography as they had existed since the eighteenth century, which present lives in terms of sustained development and a narrative of meaningful progression.

The title of Baudelaire's *Mon cœur mis à nu* might, nevertheless, lead one to expect a confessional or autobiographical record. But the rhetoric of these so-called *Journaux intimes* is only very sporadically that of the autobiographical narrative, and much of the personal material is expressed in curiously impersonal style: 'A sense of *solitude* since my childhood. Despite my family, and especially amidst companions—a sense of an eternally lonely destiny'.[20] Or else it takes the forms of moral directives addressed to himself: 'The main thing is to be a "great man" and "a Saint" to oneself.'[21] The self is not a given, but has to

---

[15] In his letter Hugo writes, 'Je n'ai jamais dit: l'Art pour l'Art; j'ai toujours dit: l'Art pour le Progrès. [. . .] En avant! c'est le mot du Progrès; c'est aussi le cri de l'Art.' See notes to Baudelaire, *Theophile Gautier [1]*, in *OC* ii (pp. 103–28), p. 1129.

[16] Baudelaire, *Mon cœur mis à nu*, in *OC* i, pp. 676–708 (p. 681 [Cameron, p. 180]).

[17] *Fusées*, *OC* i, p. 663. [18] Letter to Fernand Desnoyers, quoted in *OC* i, p. 1024.

[19] Walter Benjamin, *Charles Baudelaire: A Lyric Poet in the Era of High Capitalism*, trans. Harry Zohn (London: NLB, 1973), p. 154. The remark made by Proust in 'À propos de Baudelaire' is quoted on p. 139.

[20] Baudelaire, *Mon cœur mis à nu*, *OC* i, p. 680 [Cameron, p. 179] (Baudelaire's emphasis).

[21] Ibid., p. 691 [p. 190].

be actively constructed, and he asserts that unity is a state that only the genius can hope to acquire: unlike his duplicitous fellows, and also unlike the Legion character of Hugo's 'hommes-océans', 'the man of genius wants to be *one*'.[22] Baudelaire's various aphorisms and injunctions seem designed to create the self-consistent subject that biographical convention otherwise takes as the given on which to ground its narrative. These intimate diaries contain the outline of what Baudelaire calls '[a] Hygiene' designed to produce a certain way of living at some point in the future, rather than offering a record of past emotion and event that might amount to the narrative of a life, as they do in Hugo's *Contemplations*.[23]

In all these ways Baudelaire's biographical writings cut across the contemporary assumptions associated with the genre: their subjects have an antagonistic and not a representative relation to their world; they exist in a universe devoid of any potential for development, be it temporal or organic; and their very subjectivity has to be constructed through the efforts of the artist-hero, rather than simply requiring space to express itself through the hero's existence. And yet, as I have said, Baudelaire repeatedly had recourse to biography, and perhaps most intensively between 1856, the year in which the definitive version of the life of Edgar Allan Poe appeared, and 1863, the year of the Delacroix essay, conceived as an obituary after Delacroix's death in August 1863. These, of course, were the years during which the two editions of *Les Fleurs du mal* were published (1857 and 1861, respectively), and I think it would not be unreasonable to assume that the poetry and the essays were mutually informing on this topic, even if the results are not exactly the same in the two genres. That said, what all these biographies—poetic and critical—have in common is Baudelaire's preoccupation with the production of art and poetry. His literary heroes acquire their status through their work rather than their life, and the poetry lies in the poems, not in the lived circumstances that are nevertheless responsible for their creation. Samuel Cramer is a failed poet because the poetry of his life is greater than the poetry of his books. Baudelaire describes him as '[a] sickly and fantastic creature whose poetry shines much more in his person than in his works'.[24] If Baudelaire talks of a desire to see the whole of the *Comédie humaine* in Balzac's features, it is because he views the work as the product of a life that is subordinated to its creation.[25] And if Poe's life can be described as '[a] lamentable tragedy', whose hero 'bore above his eyes the label attached to his life, like the title of a book [. . .] *No Luck!*',[26] this is because Poe's life was entirely subservient to the production of his art. Even the drinking that killed him was, in Baudelaire's account, a calculated creative strategy, 'a mnemonic device, a

[22] Baudelaire, *Mon cœur mis à nu*, *OC* i, p. 700 [p. 197] (Baudelaire's emphasis).
[23] For further discussion of the role of 'hygiene' in the artist's life see Ch. 18 below.
[24] Baudelaire, *La Fanfarlo*, in *OC* i, pp. 553–80 (p. 553).
[25] Baudelaire, *Edgar Allan Poe, sa vie et ses ouvrages*, in *OC* ii, p. 267.
[26] Ibid., pp. 297, 296.

working method'.[27] Where other writers keep a notebook for such purposes, Poe taught himself to drink as the quickest means of recovering the visions and ideas that he wished to use for his work. In this sense man and poet were of a piece, and Baudelaire praises what he calls the 'sincerity' of the work. But it is a sincerity which exactly reverses the one whose absence Saint-Chéron bemoaned in his contemporaries. For Baudelaire, everything in the poet's life is to be harnessed to the creation of his poetry: it is not the life that informs poetry, for the work is the product of a life geared entirely to its production. The biographical studies are all grounded on this principle, and their subjects evaluated on its basis.

Poetry is, however, more than the outcome of a purely mechanical productivity. It is intensely and intimately experiential in its own right, not just the receptacle for other experiences. Poetry as described by Baudelaire is an aspiration, an instinct, an excitement, a sense, a love, a feeling, and thus an integral part of the lived experience of the poet: 'the principle of poetry is strictly and simply the human *aspiration* towards a higher beauty, and the manifestation of this principle is in an *enthusiasm* and an *excitement* of the soul—an enthusiasm entirely independent of the passion that is an intoxication of the heart, and of the truth on which reason feeds'.[28] Lyric refers to a manner of feeling and not just to a poetic form. As Baudelaire says in his essay on Banville: 'there is indeed a lyric manner of feeling', and it engages the entire person:

The men whom nature has least favoured, those to whom fortune has granted the least ease, have sometimes had those impressions that are so rich that the soul is as if illuminated by them, and so keen that it is as if raised up by them. All one's inner being, in these marvellous moments, leaps into the air from an excess of lightness and expansion, as if to arrive at a more elevated region.[29]

The artist is driven by a love of beauty that is itself the source of further emotional effects: 'An artist is an artist only thanks to his exquisite sense of beauty—a sense which procures him intoxicating delight, but which at the same time entails and contains an equally exquisite sense of all deformity and all disproportion.'[30] Art is a profoundly affective experience in both its nature and its consequences, albeit one that is quite distinct from the passions of the heart. Its supreme quality is a transcendence that raises the spirit above the sphere of all other experiences. It is an elevation in which the entire being of the poet is implicated, and this makes it possible to imagine a record of the poet's life as a narrative of his poetic aspirations and of the 'jouissances' that the exercise of his poetic faculty affords him.

This poetic faculty is, of course, the imagination, which Baudelaire describes in the *Salon de 1859* as 'the queen of the faculties' to which all others are

---

[27] Ibid., p. 315.   [28] Baudelaire, *Notes nouvelles sur Edgar Poe*, in *OC* ii, pp. 319–37 (p. 334).
[29] Baudelaire, 'Théodore de Banville', in *Réflexions sur quelques-uns de mes contemporains*, in *OC* i, pp. 162–9 (p. 164).
[30] *Notes nouvelles sur Edgar Poe*, p. 330.

subordinated. It may be the only faculty that 'contains poetry', as he puts it in an essay on Gautier,[31] but the imagination is also the locus of the poet's originality and individuality: 'The artist, the true artist, or the true poet, should paint only on the basis of what he sees and feels. He must be *truly* faithful to his own nature.'[32] Every artist has his own special character that places its stamp on the workings of his imagination: Diderot is 'a red-blooded author; Poe is a writer of the nerves'.[33] For Sainte-Beuve, the writer's individuality was the source of his genius; for Baudelaire it lies in the imagination and, moreover, has its origins in the artist's childhood. The unique character of the artist, to which his work requires him to be faithful, offers another justification for biography as the means of capturing the unique quality of his work. In particular Baudelaire sees in biography the chance to explore the poet's essential characteristics as they emerge in his childhood: 'All biographers have understood, in a more or less complete manner, the importance of anecdotes relating to the childhood of a writer or an artist.'[34] Here Baudelaire is working against the forward chronological direction of a life in order to arrive at the ultimate revelation of a unique aesthetic principle to be found in the artist's earliest years:

Often, when I have been contemplating works of art, not in their easily graspable *materiality*, in the overly clear hieroglyphs of their outlines or in the obvious meaning of their subject matter, but in the soul with which they are endowed, in the atmospheric impression that they contain, in the spiritual light or darkness that they cast on our souls, I have felt something like a vision of the childhood of their authors enter me. Some little sorrow or some small joy experienced by the child, disproportionately enlarged by an exquisite sensibility, later become *the principle of a work of art* in the adult man, even without his being aware of it.[35]

The creative character of the artist exists from his earliest beginnings rather than culminating in his maturity.

Nonetheless, art is neither a natural nor a reliable consequence of this creative origin. Fidelity to one's own nature is an obligation, not an inevitability, and Baudelaire makes much of *volonté* or will-power as an indispensable requirement for the poet. The dandy exemplifies a supreme form of the application of this quality, actively working at the creation of his own originality, and consciously cultivating the ideal of beauty in his person in a manner that endows him with the last remnants of heroism in an era of decadence.[36] *Volonté* is equally a requirement for the creative activity of the artist, and it is because drugs sap the poet's will-power that Baudelaire speaks of 'the immoral character of

---

[31] *Théophile Gautier [1]*, *OC* ii, p. 115.
[32] Baudelaire, *Salon de 1859*, in *OC* ii, pp. 608–82 (p. 620, Baudelaire's emphasis).
[33] *Edgar Poe*, p. 316 [*Works of Edgar Allan Poe*, p. 20*].
[34] Baudelaire, *Un mangeur d'opium*, in *OC* i, pp. 442–517 (pp. 497–8).
[35] Ibid. (Baudelaire's emphasis).
[36] See Baudelaire, *Le Peintre de la vie moderne*, in *OC* ii, pp. 709–12.

hashish'. When will-power is not undermined, it is capable of producing of its own accord the elevation that is poetry: 'enthusiasm and will-power are enough to raise one up to a supranatural existence. The great poets, philosophers, and prophets are beings who, through the free and unadulterated exercise of their will-power, arrive at a state where they are at once cause and effect, subject and object, hypnotist and somnambulist.'[37] It is will-power, too, that is responsible for making the poet's experience available as material to be used for his art. Citing Poe, Baudelaire claims that 'only the man who is the master of his memory, the sovereign of words, the register of his own feelings that can always be consulted is a poet'.[38] Poe himself was, apparently, capable of such efforts, which enabled him to 'subject to his will the fleeting demon of happy moments', to recall former states of 'poetic health', as well as to subject inspiration to rigorous methodological analysis.[39]

Baudelaire treats all his biographical subjects as heroes of *volonté*, and singles out in particular the discipline that gives them control of their technical medium. Delacroix is celebrated for his 'formidable will-power', which he exercised so as to acquire the skill that would enable him to follow the whims of 'the great despotic faculty' that is the creative imagination.[40] Baudelaire reports that Delacroix used to assert that an artist should have the technical ability to sketch a man falling from a window before he hits the ground. And he sees in Delacroix's hyperbolic requirement 'the preoccupation of a lifetime'.[41] The exercise of will-power in the form of this technical discipline determines the course of the artist's life, which means, in turn, that a life may be contemplated—as Baudelaire contemplates that of Delacroix—as an example of this capacity. He admires the equivalent capacity in Gautier, whose maxim was 'The inexpressible does not exist', and who himself acquired such an immense knowledge of the French language that he was never at a loss for the right word, and could place every attribute and capture every nuance in what he wanted to say.[42] Baudelaire adopted Gautier's precept for himself, announcing in one of the 'Projets de préface' to *Les Fleurs du mal*: 'any poet who does not know exactly how many rhymes a word has is incapable of expressing any idea whatsoever'.[43] Such mastery makes demands on the poet's life, but for Baudelaire it also feeds back into it. The rules of prosody are neither a restriction nor an imposition, but, unlike the formalism of Leconte de Lisle's cult of impersonality, they answer an inner spiritual need and promote the expression of the individual imagination: 'rhetorics and prosodies are not tyrannies that have been invented arbitrarily, but a collection of rules required by the very organization of spiritual existence; and prosodies and rhetorics have

[37] Baudelaire, *Le Poème du hachisch*, in *OC* i, pp. 401–41 (p. 439).
[38] *Notes nouvelles sur Edgar Poe*, p. 331.   [39] Ibid.
[40] Baudelaire, *L'Œuvre et la vie d'Eugène Delacroix*, in *OC* ii, pp. 742–70 (pp. 746–7).
[41] Ibid.   [42] *Théophile Gautier Gautier [1]*, *OC* ii, p. 118.
[43] Baudelaire, *Projets de préface*, in *OC* i, pp. 181–6 (p. 183).

never prevented originality from appearing quite distinctly'.[44] A life devoted to the exercise of the will and to the determined acquisition of a technical apparatus produces an art that also nourishes the artist's spiritual life and enhances his individuality. It would seem, in sum, that all aspects of the work of art call on the artist in ways which make his life the necessary context and condition for its production, and which in turn determine the further course of his existence.

At the same time, the work of art transcends the life that produces it, and so makes it possible to speak of art and poetry as absolutes. The function of poetry is not principally to benefit the existence of its practitioners. As Poe says in the *Poetic Principle* (a remark that Baudelaire quotes): 'the aim of poetry is of the same nature as its principle—that it ought never to have anything in view but itself'.[45] This means that any goal in poetry other than itself becomes a form of heresy, the most prevalent being the 'the heresy of teaching' (Baudelaire accuses Hugo of this), whereby poetry is used to teach some (moral) lesson. A little surprisingly, perhaps, in view of this, Baudelaire also treats aesthetic systems as a form of heresy. In his essay on the *Exposition universelle* of 1855 he condemns 'those modern *professors with diplomas* in aesthetics' and the 'insane doctrinaires of Beauty [. . .] locked inside the blinding fortress of their system'.[46] He claims to have discovered from his own experience that 'a system is a form of damnation that forces us into perpetual abjuration'. Art, even absolute art, which has itself as its goal and its principle, is ill-served by its own artistic systems: 'It is easy for everyone to imagine that if the men charged with expressing beauty complied with the rules of the professors with diplomas, beauty itself would vanish from the earth, because all characters, all ideas, and all sensations would merge into one vast, monotonous, and impersonal conglomerate, as immense as ennui and nothingness.'[47] The variety and the surprise essential to art are therefore best achieved by forms of writing that respect those qualities, namely, the individuality of the artist and the bizarreness of beauty ('*Beauty is always bizarre*').[48] The autotelic nature of poetry calls for forms of writing that promote the unique and the individual against the systematic.

Baudelaire's conception of criticism as necessarily 'partial, passionate, and political'[49] meets this requirement without necessarily imposing biography as the means of defending aesthetic variety. However, biography is also a means to this end, and here Baudelaire is echoing some of the assumptions of Sainte-Beuve's criticism, although it was principally as a poet that Baudelaire revered his elder, whom he placed in importance alongside Hugo and Vigny.[50] A poem that Baudelaire wrote and dedicated to Sainte-Beuve in 1844 alludes to the hero of

---

[44] Baudelaire is quoting his own remarks from the *Salon de 1859* in his essay on Delacroix, as part of his discussion of Delacroix's technical mastery (*OC* ii, pp. 749–50).

[45] *Edgar Poe*, *OC* ii, p. 305 [*Works of Edgar Allan Poe*, p. 9].

[46] Baudelaire, *Exposition universelle (1855)*, in *OC* ii, p. 577 (Baudelaire's emphasis).

[47] Ibid., p. 578.   [48] Ibid. (Baudelaire's italics).

[49] Baudelaire, *Salon de 1846*, in *OC* ii, p. 418.   [50] *Théophile Gautier [1]*, *OC* ii, p. 110.

the latter's *Volupté* ('I bore the story of Amaury on my heart'),[51] and in his later years he returns once again to the poetry, and to *Joseph Delorme* in particular. In a letter of 15 January 1866 he mentions Delorme as a model for what he is attempting in *Le Spleen de Paris*. At this time he was also planning an essay (which in the event was never written) on *Sainte-Beuve ou 'Joseph Delorme' jugé par l'auteur des 'Fleurs du mal'*, a project that associates two collections structured around the life of their poet-protagonists. Indeed, in March of the previous year Baudelaire had written to Sainte-Beuve drawing an explicit analogy between the two works: '*Joseph Delorme* is the *Fleurs du mal* of the previous generation'; and in his reply Sainte-Beuve endorsed the comparison: '[my poetry] was close to yours. I had tasted the same bitter fruit.'[52] On rereading Sainte-Beuve's poetry in 1866, Baudelaire found he still knew much of it by heart; and there are occasional echoes of *Joseph Delorme* in some of the poems of *Les Fleurs du mal*, amongst them 'Le Beau Navire', 'Chant d'automne', and 'La Servante au grand cœur'.[53] It is, however, the use of the biographical framework in conjunction with a conscious poetic principle that seems to me to be the most significant common feature of the two books. Sainte-Beuve attributes his collection to the fictitious poet Joseph Delorme, whose death concludes the collection. Similarly, Baudelaire stages the life of his *Poëte* from birth to death, though without including a biographical preface or an appendix of the poet's 'Thoughts', as Sainte-Beuve does. This difference in organization relates to the way that each conceives of poetry's relation to the life. For Sainte-Beuve the life is a necessary critical presupposition; for Baudelaire it is, as we have seen, the necessary condition for the production of the poetry, and is inescapably marked by its consequences.

LES FLEURS DU MAL AS THE LIFE OF THE POET

Before the publication of the revised and expanded version of *Les Fleurs du mal* in 1861, Baudelaire toyed with the idea of writing a preface to the work, in which his aim would have been to 'explain a few very simple questions that have been obscured by the light of modern learning: what is Poetry? what is its aim? the difference between the Good and the Beautiful; Beauty in Evil', and so on. He was stopped in his intention when he became aware of 'the appalling futility of explaining anything to anybody'. There was no need for any such explanation,

---

[51] Baudelaire, 'À Sainte-Beuve', in *Poésies de jeunesse*, in *OC* i, pp. 206–8 [Scarfe, p. 33]).

[52] Quoted in Norman H. Barlow, *Sainte-Beuve to Baudelaire: A Poetic Legacy* (Durham, NC: Duke University Press, 1964), p. 3.

[53] See Pichois's editorial notes in *OC* i, *passim*. For further discussion of the relations between Sainte-Beuve and Baudelaire see also Jean Prévost, *Baudelaire: essai sur la création et l'inspiration poétiques* (Paris: Mercure de France, 1964), pp. 16 ff.; and Graham Robb, *La Poésie de Baudelaire et la poésie française, 1838–1852* (Paris: Aubier, 1993), pp. 54–8. None of these studies mentions the shared feature of the biographical structure of *Joseph Delorme* and *Les Fleurs du mal*.

he realized, because: 'Those who know will understand me, and for those who do not or cannot understand, I would be pointlessly piling up explanations.'[54] At the same time, he was adding poems to the collection and partially rearranging the order by which he set such great store. He created a new section, the TABLEAUX PARISIENS, and repositioned the section entitled LE VIN, so that it no longer preceded LA MORT, as a temporary reprieve in what was now starkly revealed as a trajectory of inexorable decline. He also added the last three poems of that section ('La Fin de la journée', 'Le Rêve d'un curieux', and 'Le Voyage'), as if to boost the impact of the volume's finale in death. It might therefore be supposed that the ordering of the poems is doing the job of answering questions concerning the definition and aims of Poetry, for which the abandoned preface was originally designed, and, moreover, that the biographical sequence is better suited to that purpose than any theorizing preface.

This is in part because Baudelaire's concern with poetry is not strictly theoretical. In the words of Henri Lemaitre, 'Baudelaire did not have a theory but a morality of art'.[55] We have already seen from the critical essays that questions about the nature and function of poetry are posed for the poet under all the varying circumstances of his life as questions about its creation.[56] It is this issue that Baudelaire dramatizes through his arrangement of *Les Fleurs du mal* as a biographical sequence whose subject is the poet-protagonist: 'an anonymous "Poëte" who cannot properly be called Baudelaire however much he may resemble his creator and who is designed to have a universal, as well as an individual, significance'.[57] The existential circumstances in which poetry must be produced are established from the outset in the poem 'Au lecteur', although these are rather less propitious than those of the subjects of Baudelaire's biographical essays. 'Le canevas banal de nos piteux destins'[58] is subject to forces that severely compromise the human agency that is responsible for the creation of art. Life is a downward and not an upward path: 'Chaque jour vers l'Enfer nous descendons d'un pas'.[59] 'L'ennui' threatens to paralyse all initiative; and will-power, celebrated in the critical essays as the key to artistic production, is here said to be at the mercy of an all-powerful 'Satan Trismégiste': 'Et le riche métal de notre volonté | Est tout vaporisé par ce savant chimiste'.[60] The

---

[54] Baudelaire, *Projets de préface*, *OC* i, p. 182.

[55] Lemaitre, 'Introduction', p. xxxi. In a similar vein Graham Robb remarks: 'Ce sont les vers de Baudelaire qui contiennent sa poétique' (*La Poésie de Baudelaire*, p. 13).

[56] On this see Pichois's 'Notice' to *Les Fleurs du mal*, *OC* i, p. 803; and Claude Pichois, *Baudelaire: études et témoignages*, rev. edn. (Neuchâtel: Éditions de la Baconnière, 1976), esp. 'Baudelaire ou la difficulté créatrice', pp. 242–61.

[57] Mossop, *Baudelaire's Tragic Hero*, p. 7.

[58] 'the dull canvas of our lamentable destinies' ('Au lecteur'). With two exceptions (and minor alterations in two instances), all translations of *Les Fleurs du mal* are taken from Francis Scarfe, *Baudelaire* (Harmondsworth: Penguin, 1961). These are prose translations of the original poems.

[59] 'each day we take a further step to Hell' (ibid.).

[60] 'this expert alchemist dissolves our will's precious metal into vapour' (ibid.).

heroism of Baudelaire's critical portraits is denied to his poet-protagonist, and the image of artistic creation is considerably less triumphalist than it is in the case of Poe or Delacroix. The picture of the human condition in which the poet moves from birth to death is, throughout the volume, repeatedly coloured by an image of time as essentially destructive and as holding no promise of any kind: 'Le Temps mange la vie'; it is the 'Noir Assassin de la Vie et de l'Art'; and in the final poem it is 'l'ennemi vigilant et funeste'.[61] Time devours the poet: 'le Temps m'engloutit minute par minute',[62] sapping him of his creative energies; and the personified 'Maintenant' ('Now') in 'L'Horloge' announces: 'Je suis Autrefois, | Et j'ai pompé ta vie avec ma trompe immonde!'[63] As a context for poetry, this relentlessly negative presentation of the temporal complexion of human existence makes poetry all the more necessary as its antidote, yet at the same time all the more difficult to achieve.

This, then, is the world into which the Poet is born and introduced in 'Bénédiction': 'Lorsque, par un décret des puissances suprêmes, | Le Poète apparaît en ce monde ennuyé'.[64] He finds himself in a hostile world where his mother curses him, his fellow humans treat him with fear or aggression, and his woman exploits his devotion before preparing to rip out his heart. This theme is continued in 'L'Albatros', but at this stage, despite the opposition that the poet encounters in the world, poetry is still possible in a relatively unproblematic way. He speaks to God of his certainty about his ultimate salvation despite all; in 'Élévation' poetry is the preserve of '[celui] | Qui plane sur la vie et comprend sans effort | Le langage des fleurs et des choses muettes'.[65] However, as the vertical axis established in these first poems gives way to the horizontal axis in the second part of 'Correspondances', it becomes increasingly clear that poetry is not—or not only—part of an elevated sphere above the human world, but that it has to be made within that world. The Muse has become sick ('La Muse malade'), and in 'Le Mauvais Moine' the poet compares his soul to a tomb and wonders how he can fashion this sorry material into its happy obverse: 'quand saurai-je donc faire | Du spectacle vivant de ma triste misère | Le travail de mes mains et l'amour de mes yeux?'[66] The poet is the source of an art that is rooted not in a symbolic transcendence, but in analogies that can be perceived and established only by the poet himself. As a consequence, the conditions under which he produces poetry also become its subject matter; and the only transcendence to be hoped for is the one he can manufacture by means of his own skill and imagination, these being,

---

[61] 'Time eats away all life' ('L'Ennemi'); 'the black Assassin of Life and Art' ('Le Balcon'); 'that watchful, baneful enemy' ('Le Voyage').

[62] 'Time is engulfing me, minute by minute' ('Le Goût du Néant').

[63] 'I am already your Past and have drained your life with my loathsome suckers' ('L'Horloge').

[64] 'When, by decree of the supreme Powers the Poet enters this weary world' ('Bénédiction').

[65] 'who rides high above life, swift to interpret the speech of flowers and inarticulate things' ('Élévation).

[66] 'When shall I learn to turn the daily scene of my sad misery into my hands' labour and my eyes' love?' ('Le Mauvais Moine').

as we have seen, the key components of poetic composition. The poems of *Les Fleurs du mal* frequently foreground their origin in the creative skill of the poet, who is portrayed, directly and indirectly, as playing a far more active role in their fabrication than that of Hugo's poet, who so often figures as the mouthpiece or the channel for a poetry that has its source in elements that exceed him. Baudelaire repeatedly draws attention to the poet's constructive role, and does so by three main means: the uncoded associations generated by his analogies; the explicit assertion of the poet's creative power; and the virtuoso use of prosody.

The principle of analogy is asserted early on in 'Correspondances', and the model for unconventional links is established in a synaesthesia that not only creates an equivalence between smell, touch, sound, and sight, but also between the quite disparate images that are the cool skin of children, the sound of oboes, and green meadows: 'Il est des parfums frais comme des chairs d'enfants, | Doux comme les hautbois, verts comme les prairies'.[67] The impersonal formulation of 'Il est' does not point directly back at the poet as the creator of these conjunctions, but, as the poems unfold in sequence, the poet's subjectivity is increasingly implied through the metaphors in the poetry. The largely impersonal and third-person figure of 'Le Poète' gives way to a more consistent use of the first person, which emerges quite naturally in the love poems. By the twenty-third poem of the series, 'La Chevelure', the metaphors are proliferating with an insistence and an idiosyncrasy that powerfully indicate the poet's own individual imagination. This idiosyncrasy is palpable from the first stanza of the poem, as the organic perfume is laden with an immaterial 'nonchaloir' ('languidness'), and the poet expresses his wish to shake the woman's hair 'comme un mouchoir' ('as one waves a handkerchief'). The hair becomes a forest, and then a sea, simply by virtue of the poet's say-so: 'Fortes tresses, soyez la houle qui m'enlève!'[68] Apostrophe underscores the transformation: 'Tu contiens, mer d'ébène, un éblouissant rêve'.[69] These transformations continue as the hair is by turns 'Un port retentissant' ('an echoing port'), '[un] pavillon de ténèbres tendues' ('a tent hung with shadows'), and the woman herself in the conclusion, simultaneously an oasis and a gourd, and memory a wine.[70] At the same time the metaphors expand inwardly, so to speak, generating scenes that call up further metaphors, so

---

[67] 'There are perfumes fresh and cool as the bodies of children, mellow as oboes, green as fields; and others that are perverse, rich and triumphant' ('Correspondances').

[68] 'dense tresses, be the swell that carries me away' ('La Chevelure').

[69] 'you contain, O sea of ebony, a dazzling dream' (ibid.).

[70] In this discussion I cannot avoid making some familiar points about the mechanics of Baudelaire's poetry. In the context of these two poems I must at least acknowledge the commentaries of Paul de Man and Jonathan Culler on 'Les Correspondances': see Paul de Man, *The Rhetoric of Romanticism* (New York: Columbia University Press, 1984), pp. 243–52; Jonathan Culler, 'Intertextuality and Interpretation: Baudelaire's "Correspondances"', in Christopher Prendergast (ed.), *Nineteenth-Century French Poetry: Introductions to Close Reading* (Cambridge: Cambridge University Press, 1990), pp. 118–37; and Barbara Johnson on 'La Chevelure', in ead., *Défigurations du langage poétique: la seconde révolution baudelairienne* (Paris: Flammarion, 1979), ch. 2.

that the resonant port becomes a place where the poet's soul can drink perfume, sound, and colour, and where ships acquire arms that can embrace the glory of a sky. The force of the metaphorical invention is such that it moves both forwards as a sequence, and inwards as elaboration, but either way it invites readers to place its origin in the poet's imaginative vision.

This origin is even more emphatically suggested on those occasions—and they are frequent—where idiosyncrasy upstages sheer proliferation, and typically with a touch of provocation. In 'Le Serpent qui danse' the poet's mistress is compared to a young elephant: 'Sous le fardeau de ta paresse | Ta tête d'enfant | Se balance avec la mollesse | D'un jeune éléphant'.[71] More defiantly, perhaps, 'Le Beau Navire' turns the breast of another mistress into the sculpted panels of a cupboard, which in turn are likened to shields described in terms of the breasts that were the original point of departure:

> Ta gorge qui s'avance et qui pousse la moire
> Ta gorge triomphante est une belle armoire
>   Dont les panneaux bombés et claires
>   Commes les boucliers accrochent les éclairs;
>
> Boucliers provocants, armés de pointes roses![72]

The implicit goading in these somewhat bizarre connections suggests an intentionality that defines the images as being of the poet's own making.

There is an even more apparent desire to shock the mistress who is the addressee of 'Une charogne', where the decaying carcass is outrageously compared to a lubricious woman, a cooking dish, a flower in bloom, living rags, the rise and fall of waves, a half-finished painting, and so on. But here, the poet explicitly relates his provocations to his creative ability when, having invited his mistress to see her own corpse in the rotting flesh of the carcass, he underscores the contrast between her future death and decomposition, and the survival of his own poetic rendering:

> Alors, ô ma beauté! dites à la vermine
>   Qui vous mangera de baisers,
> Que j'ai gardé la forme et l'essence divine
>   De mes amours décomposés![73]

The sadism of this twist to a Petrarchan tradition is an act of bravado that draws attention to the poet's deployment of his skill. The invocations of this skill are made in more benign form, as in 'Le Balcon' when the poet states: 'Je sais l'art

---

[71] 'Under the burden of your indolence, your childish head sways to and fro, with the gentle rhythm of a baby elephant's' ('Le Serpent qui danse').

[72] 'Your jutting breast which curves the watered-silk, your triumphant breast is [like] some beautiful press, whose rounded, bright panels catch the light like shields: provoking shields, armed with rosy tips' ('Le Beau Navire').

[73] 'Then, O my beauty, tell the vermin which will devour you with kisses how I have immortalized the form and divine essence of my decayed loves' ('Une charogne').

d'évoquer les minutes heureuses'.[74] In 'À une Madone' he reverts to sadism when he describes the altar within himself that he intends to build for his mistress out of poetry; he portrays it as a highly crafted construct of his own making, designed to preserve her: 'Avec mes Vers polis, treillis d'un pur métal | Savamment constellé de rimes de cristal',[75] before he finally completes his plan by plunging knives into her heart.

It is in the context of these affirmations of poetic skill that Baudelaire's virtuoso use of technique may be read.[76] The presence of the sonnet form and its variants, used for a significant proportion of the poems, already signals an intention to exploit rather than to subvert the rules of prosody. Baudelaire builds on this preference to deploy specific devices like the pantoum in 'Harmonie du soir'; the choice of the '-avane' rhyme, for which there are only four examples in the French language (*havane, savane, pavane, caravane*) in 'Sed non satiata'; and the frequent use of repetition in the form of framed stanzas (e.g. 'Le Balcon', 'Réversibilité', 'L'Irréparable', etc.). There was nothing particularly novel in Baudelaire's use of these techniques, which are all attested in other poets at the time. What is different in his case, however, is that he deploys them in the context of a representation of the poet's life, where his creativity is a recurrent and often very anxious preoccupation, since its availability cannot be counted on.

This preoccupation is made evident by the way in which Baudelaire repeatedly stages his poet in the circumstances in which he is to create. This is an aspect that is particularly foregrounded in the poems added for the 1861 edition. In 'Paysage', for example, he portrays the poet distancing himself from the reality of the city in order to create his own alternative reality through the exercise of his will:

> L'Émeute, tempêtant vainement à ma vitre,
> Ne fera pas lever mon front de mon pupitre;
> Car je serai plongé dans cette volupté
> D'évoquer le Printemps avec ma volonté,
> De tirer un soleil de mon cœur et de faire
> De mes pensers brûlants une tiède atmosphère.[77]

Baudelaire includes in the poem what the poet himself excludes, such as the riots outside his window, thus filling out the picture of the poet's place in the world in which he exists. But most of all, he stresses the way that poetic creation as *volonté* generates a delight (*cette volupté*) that itself becomes a component of the

---

[74] 'I know the art of evoking happy moments' ('Le Balcon').

[75] 'With my polished Verses, a trellis of pure metal skilfully constellated with crystal rhymes' ('À une Madone').

[76] For a full discussion of these techniques see Graham Chesters, *Baudelaire and the Poetics of Craft* (Cambridge: Cambridge University Press, 1988).

[77] 'The clamour of the mob, vainly beating on my window-pane, will not make me lift my head from my desk; for I'll be deep in the sensuous pleasure of evoking spring-time with my will, drawing a sun out of my own heart, making a genial atmosphere with my burning thoughts' ('Paysage').

poet's existence here. Aesthetic pleasure evolves into an existential need, and the search for it may determine the outcome of the poet's ultimate destiny:

> De Satan ou de Dieu, qu'importe? Ange ou Sirène,
> Qu'importe, si tu rends,—fée aux yeux de velours,
> Rythme, parfum, lueur, ô mon unique reine!—
> L'univers moins hideux et les instants moins lourds?[78]

Ecstasy is not just the trigger for art, like Banville's lyric manner of feeling, but is also its ideal consequence; poetry feeds back into the conditions of the poet's life as the cause of its joys or the goal of its strivings.

This affects not just the creation of poetry, but its obverse—the failure to create. Poetic sterility is not just a neutral absence of poetry, but an experience that the poet lives as 'spleen' and pain. When the poet's vision and eloquence fail, the metaphorical process goes into reverse:

> Hermès inconnu qui m'assistes
> Et qui toujours m'intimidas,
> Tu me rends l'égal de Midas,
> Le plus triste des alchimistes.
>
> Par toi je change l'or en fer
> Et le paradis en enfer.[79]

Since he is the source of poetry, the poet's creative collapse turns his whole being into an actively an-aesthetic entity: 'Ne suis-je pas un faux accord | Dans la divine symphonie?'[80] The poet is responsible for his poetry but lacks the power for its realization.

It is this condition that is portrayed in the series of poems that conclude the SPLEEN ET IDÉAL section. Whereas 'Alchimie de la Douleur' is a relatively schematic piece, whose limited metaphoric and prosodic elaboration matches its stated contents, several of the poems, beginning with 'La Cloche fêlée' and including in particular the 'Spleen' sequence, are amongst the richest in the whole collection. The affirmation of failure is couched in some of Baudelaire's most remarkable metaphorical language, so that overt statement is strikingly at odds with its formal expression which produces images as elaborated and original as any of those in the poems of creative euphoria:

> Moi, mon âme est fêlée, et lorsqu'en ses ennuis
> Elle veut de ses chants peupler l'air froid des nuits,

[78] 'What does it matter whether you come from Satan or from God? Angel or Siren, velvet-eyed fairy, all rhythm, perfume, and light, as long as you make the world less hideous and lighten the leaden hours?' ('Hymne à la Beauté').

[79] 'Unknown Hermes who are my helper, but of whom I ever went in fear, you make me the peer of Midas, the unhappiest of alchemists. Through you I transmute gold into iron, and Paradise into Hell' ('Alchimie de la Douleur').

[80] 'Am I not a dissonant chord in the divine symphony?' ('L'Héautontimorouménos').

Il arrive souvent que sa voix affaiblie
Semble le râle épais d'un blessé qu'on oublie
Au bord d'un lac de sang, sous un grand tas de morts,
Et qui meurt, sans bouger, dans d'immenses efforts.[81]

The discordant note in the divine symphony is recast here as the cracked bell of
the poet's soul, which is then remetaphorized as the death rattle of a dying soldier
in a scene that is vividly enough evoked to recall Balzac's novella *Le Colonel
Chabert*. In prosodic terms the rhyme scheme displays considerable density, with
the use of rich rhyme (*ennuis/des nuits*, *affaiblie/oublie*); a particularly intense
sequence of internal rhyme in a chiasmic structure (*bord, lac, sang—grand, tas,
mort*); and a dense cluster of assonance ('f's and 'v's) in the first tercet culminating
in the last line of the stanza: 'Il arrive souvent que sa voix affaiblie'. In the context
of this technical proficiency it becomes possible to read the few prosodic 'cracks'
in the poem, such as the enjambement between the two tercets, or the weak
rhyme of *d'hiver/s'élever* in the first stanza of the poem, as a conscious contrivance
designed to support the image of the poet's soul as a cracked bell, and not as a
failure of poetic mastery. In this, such features differ in no way from the effect of
inertia that is generated by the density of rhyme and assonance, and the sense of
claustrophobia produced by the chiasmus. In other words, the poem is making
two quite contradictory claims about the poet's creative capacity: nil at the level
of represented content, assured and complex at the level of form and language.

To understand this contradiction it is important to remain within the
biographical frame of *Les Fleurs du mal* and to avoid simply having recourse to
autobiographical interpretations. Baudelaire is doing something much more than
describing his own experience of creative impotence. Through his dramatization
of the poet's predicament and his equal dramatization of technique, he is inviting
his readers to consider the question of where poetry comes from—experience or
form, skill or sensibility?—without endorsing either over the other. The poet's
experience is not redeemed by prosody, and neither is technical skill negated by
the picture of failure. Instead, the poet is portrayed as being existentially bound
up in an art that nevertheless resists his ability to command it at will. Under
this pressure it becomes clear that the poet himself, given his status as an agent
of poetic creation and as the subject of his own biography, lacks the consistency
that he might otherwise be assumed to have. Over and above its splitting of
poetry between experience and form, 'La Cloche fêlée' is typical of many of the
poems in the collection in a splitting of the poetic subject between the soul and
a poetic 'I' (*Moi/mon âme*). Even in the first, optimistic poems in the series,
this division is already present, as the poet addresses his spirit (*mon esprit*) in

---

[81] 'But, as for me, my soul is flawed, and when, with all its cares, it would fain fill the night's
chill air with its hymns, most often its faded voice sounds like the thick death-rattle of a wounded
soldier, who lies there forgotten near a pool of blood, beneath a great pile of the dead, and who dies,
without stirring, despite tremendous efforts' ('La Cloche fêlée').

'Élévation': 'Mon esprit, tu te meus avec agilité, | [. . .] Envole-toi bien loin de ces miasmes morbides'.[82] It recurs throughout the collection, with the poet addressing his soul in 'Crépuscule du soir': 'Recueille-toi, mon âme, en ce grave moment, | Et ferme ton oreille à ce rugissement';[83] and asserting in 'Le Voyage' that 'Notre âme est un trois-mâts cherchant son Icarie'.[84] The triumphalism of Baudelaire's voluntarist accounts of the lives of other artists is not a feature of the life of his divided poet-protagonist in *Les Fleurs du mal*.

Where Hugo's 'je' can contain diversity, that of Baudelaire is positioned as witness to the fragmentation of a self that is nevertheless always implicated in the creation of the poetic ideal. Indeed, for Baudelaire, there seems to be a kind of equation whereby the purer the art, the greater this implication, and the more weakly constituted the identity of the poet: 'What is *pure art* according to the modern understanding? It is the creation of a suggestive magic containing both object and subject, the world outside the artist and the artist himself.'[85] What *Les Fleurs du mal* dramatizes is everything that is at stake in this equation: the emphasis on the act of creation and its cost to the poet in existential terms. Or, as he puts it in 'Le Confiteor de l'Artiste' in *Le Spleen de Paris*, which can be read as a kind of summary of *Les Fleurs du mal*: 'L'étude du beau est un duel où l'artiste crie de frayeur avant d'être vaincu'.[86]

If the poet in *Les Fleurs du mal* is not ultimately defeated, he is nonetheless a significantly problematized version of the unified and exemplary genius figures celebrated in Baudelaire's critical biographies. By dramatizing the existential conditions of the production of art, by making emotion the product and not the source of poetic creation, by splitting the poet off from his own faculties (the mind, the soul), and by further placing these in sometimes contradictory relation to the formal elements of prosody, Baudelaire is hugely complicating the issue of poetry and its origins. The result is that poetry is pushed to a kind of crisis. Where Hugo internalized and transformed contemporary cultural assumptions about the biographical basis of poetry in order to recast the scale and function of poetry itself, Baudelaire proceeds by rather more complex and fragmented means. His critical biographies already challenge the basis of many contemporary literary portraits; but *Les Fleurs du mal* takes things a stage further by internalizing and transforming the assumptions of Baudelaire's own biographical writings so as to turn the very idea of poetry into a radical question about its nature and origins. Where Leconte de Lisle sought to renew poetry by temporarily repudiating its supposed origins in the life of the poet in favour of a poetry of technical

---

[82] 'agile you move, O my mind, [. . .] Fly far away from this deadly slough' ('Élévation').

[83] 'O my soul, withdraw into yourself at this grave hour, and stop your ears against this roaring din' ('Crépuscule du soir').

[84] 'Our soul is a three-master in quest of its Icaria' ('Le Voyage').

[85] Baudelaire, *L'Art philosophique*, in *OC* ii, pp. 598–605 (p. 598).

[86] 'The study of beauty is a duel in which the artist cries out in fright before being defeated' ('Le Confiteor de l'Artiste').

perfection, Baudelaire dramatized the palpable effects that such a programme might have on a poet's life. The life becomes the condition under which prosodic mastery may be achieved and enjoyed, though often at a price. It is precisely this tension between the two dimensions of poetry—existential and prosodic—that gives Baudelaire's poetry its peculiar and quite novel intensity. It also inaugurates a radically new understanding of the relations between biography and literature, which, as we have already seen, is developed by Mallarmé, and continued in a number of twentieth-century writers, beginning with Proust or Leiris, and culminating in the life-writing of figures such as Roger Laporte and Jacques Roubaud.

Whatever the differences in their responses, Hugo and Baudelaire are actively appropriating the biographical frame through which poetry was so readily viewed in the nineteenth century, and they integrate it into the very substance of their work. By emphasizing a biographical—and not simply an *auto*biographical—framework, they are able to exploit the generic potential of biography for a new vision of poetry that is a genuine alternative to the hygienic impersonality adopted by the Parnassians. In the next section I shall explore the way in which two prose writers responded to the development of biography, again from a perspective that is rooted within the field of literature, even while it questions the boundaries and the essence of what constitutes its literarity.

PART IV

BIOGRAPHY INTO LITERATURE

THE biographical *recueil* so characteristic of the nineteenth century confronted the issue of literature principally through its choice of subject (*grotesques, poètes maudits*) and the collective impact of those chosen types. These were supported by the critical arguments advanced by the volume, the polemic of its prefaces, or, in the case of Sainte-Beuve, by means of his developmental notion of individual genius that informed each critical account. In other words, despite the occasional complexity of the relation—again, one could cite Sainte-Beuve—the *recueil*'s positioning and construing of the idea of literature was primarily by means of commentary. Very few of such collections are read as literature, and when they are, this tends to be in the context of the œuvre of a single author—Baudelaire or Mallarmé, for example—where the critical commentary is viewed in the light of the general thematic and stylistic features of the author in question. The *Bildungsroman* or the poetry collection may borrow the format of the individual life as a basis for its structure, but for the most part the formal generic features of the biography go unexamined, where they are not simply dismissed, as Baudelaire does when he ostentatiously repudiates the conventional account of the poet's school years in his portrait of Gautier.

Indeed, the cultural uses of the short biography tended to promote the formulaic, whether this was in the imposition of a single house style, as in the case of Michaud's *Biographie universelle*, or in the conventions of the journalistic piece and the biographical series.[1] A Mirecourt *biographie* typically followed a single, repeated narrative that went from early promise to recognition and fame, and it entailed certain key topoi—the childhood in which the early signs of the future writer are writ large (the young Balzac abandoning games to spend his days reading), or which sets up a series of obstacles to a destiny known in advance to the reader (Vigny's misplaced belief in a military vocation), or the recognition of the writer's talent by contemporaries (Goethe telling Eckermann on reading Nerval's translation of *Faust* that this unknown young man will become one of the greatest writers of his generation)—each one being recounted in the mode of the irresistible rise to the 'glory' that is a given before the story begins.[2] The conventions of biography are so predictable that Loïc Chotard concludes that these narratives are best described as 'fairy tales for adults';[3] and, as we shall see in Chapter 15, one of the reasons for Sartre's condemnation of biography in *Les Mots* was his dislike of the ritual deployment of these knowing winks directed at the reader over the head of an innocent biographical subject.

It seems to have been rare for writers to engage directly with the formal elements of a genre that served to construct an idea of literature either through its depiction of literary figures, or by presenting biography itself as a foil against

---

[1] See Chotard, 'La Biographie contemporaine', p. 386.
[2] For the specific examples cited see the following works by Eugène de Mirecourt: *Balzac* (Les Contemporains; Paris: J.-P. Roret, 1854), pp. 9–10; *Alfred de Vigny* (Paris: Gustave Havard, 1855), pp. 32–3; and *Gérard de Nerval* (Les Contemporains; Paris: J.-P. Roret, 1854), p. 19.
[3] Chotard, 'La Biographie contemporaine', p. 392.

which a transcendent 'literariness' could be constituted. I have already explored the responses that Hugo and Baudelaire elaborate by biographical means in their respective revisions of poetry, but these are principally concerned with the broader assumptions implicit in biography, rather than with its constitutive generic components. Two exceptions to this rule that I shall explore in the domain of prose are Nerval's *Les Illuminés* (1852) and Marcel Schwob's *Vies imaginaires* (1896), each published during one of the two decades that, as we saw in Chapters 4 and 5, witnessed some of the most intensive biographical writing of the century. Critics nowadays seem suspicious of the sort of comparisons between Nerval and Schwob that used to be made routinely, and there may be good reasons for their caution. However, it is specifically their respective confronting, within the biographical *recueil*, of the conventions of biographical writing in the context of explicitly literary concerns that has prompted my juxtaposition of the two writers in what follows. Where Schwob turns arguments about biography on their head and makes contingent biographical detail into a central aesthetic principle, Nerval comes at the issue more obliquely, identifying the very procedures of biography and foregrounding them in his narratives in order to address questions about the potential of literature itself. If Schwob's *Vies imaginaires* lend themselves to being read relatively unproblematically as literature, Nerval's *Illuminés* are placed more ambiguously somewhere amongst the domains of the critical portrait, the historical biography, and considerations of his own literary project in a manner that might, or might not, justify reading these biographical narratives as 'literature'.

9

The Virtues of Marginality in Nerval's
Illuminés

In its origins and presentation Nerval's *Illuminés* (1852) conforms very closely to standard nineteenth-century practice whereby separate journalistic biographies were collected and published in a single volume with an omnium gatherum title (*Les Illuminés ou les précurseurs du socialisme*) and an introductory comment ('La Bibliothèque de mon oncle'). It resembles Gautier's *Grotesques* or Arsène Houssaye's *Galerie de portraits du XVIIIᵉ siècle*,[1] in that it portrays figures from the past—the sixteenth, seventeenth, and, especially, eighteenth centuries. Its concern with eccentric figures harks back to Charles Nodier's *Bibliographie des fous*, and chimes with Champfleury's collection of portraits *Les Excentriques*, which was published in the same year as *Les Illuminés*.[2] The original versions of the individual texts by Nerval advertise their biographical nature with more or less uniform explicitness. 'Le Roi de Bicêtre' was published in *La Presse* in September 1839 under the title 'Biographie singulière de Raoul de Spifame, Seigneur des Granges'. 'Les Confidences de Nicolas' originated in three articles in *La Revue des deux mondes* (August–September 1850) with the subtitle 'Histoire d'une vie littéraire du XVIIIᵉ siècle', and is described within the text itself as 'the personal biography of this singular mind'.[3] 'Jacques Cazotte' was originally the preface to an edition of Cazotte's *Le Diable amoureux, précédé de sa vie, de son procès et de ses prophéties et révélations par Gérard de Nerval* (1845), part of which also appeared in *L'Artiste* and a couple of other journals; 'Quintus Aucler' was published in *La Revue de Paris* in November 1851, under the rubric *Curiosités littéraires*

---

[1] 4th edn. (Paris: Charpentier, 1848). Houssaye was also the founder of the review *L'Artiste*, which published the series of articles by Alexandre de Saint-Chéron, one of which I quoted from in the introduction to Part III above.

[2] Charles Nodier, *Bibliographie des fous: de quelques livres excentriques* (Paris: Techener, 1835). Champfleury, *Les Excentriques* [1852], rev. edn. (Paris: Michel Lévy, 1877); Nerval himself is described as 'un excentrique' in the portrait of him in Champfleury, *Grandes figures d'hier et d'aujourd'hui: Balzac, Gérard de Nerval, Wagner, Courbet* (Paris: Poulet-Malassis et de Broise, 1861), pp. 161–228 (p. 172). On the nineteenth-century interest in eccentrics see Miranda Gill, 'Eccentricity and Cultural Imagination in Nineteenth-Century France', D.Phil. thesis (University of Oxford, 2004).

[3] Gérard de Nerval, *Les Illuminés*, ed. Max Milner, in Gérard de Nerval, *Œuvres complètes*, vol. ii (1984), p. 956. All further references are to this edition (and hereafter *Œuvres complètes* will be abbreviated to *OC*).

and the title 'Les Païens de la République: Quintus Aucler'.[4] In donating to the Bibliothèque nationale a copy of the *Histoire de l'abbé de Bucquoy,* whose pursuit is the subject of the first part of *Les Faux Saulniers* (later published as 'Angélique' in *Les Filles du feu*), and on which his own 'history' of the same title in *Les Illuminés* is based, Nerval refers to the book in his accompanying letter as 'the work [. . .] that I used in order to write a *biography* that will appear next month'.[5] When *Les Illuminés* eventually appeared in May of 1852, it was with the subtitle '*récits et portraits*'. In short, the publication history of the volume and of these individual texts, as well as the repertoire of terms used to refer to them, all place Nerval's enterprise squarely within the biographical practices of the day, a point underscored in the preface when Nerval writes: 'In these times, where literary portraits are enjoying some success, I wanted to portray a number of philosophical *eccentrics*.'[6]

Biography, moreover, is the framework within which these 'portraits' were read by their first critics. Paulin Limayrac, writing in *La Presse,* describes the book as 'a collection of biographies made into a novel in a most agreeable fashion'. And in a review where he takes Nerval to task for not addressing the issue of Illuminism seriously enough, Barbey d'Aurevilly refers repeatedly to the biographical character of the collection (though not as pejoratively as one might expect given his subsequent pronouncements on the subject discussed above in Chapter 4). He wishes that Nerval had entitled his work *Les Excentriques,* since the volume simply assembles 'articles produced for newspapers or reviews, those *biographies* that are at best witty, and have only the abbreviated interest of anecdotes'. In Barbey's view, Nerval has wasted on unworthy subjects '*the biographical* form, which we do, moreover, like, because it makes ideas more personal and more human'.[7]

I may appear to be labouring a point in insisting on the biographical character of the collection, but this aspect of it has been consistently sidelined in recent critical discussion. The mention of biography seems almost always to lead modern critics directly to the issue of *auto*biography, and to the assertion that Nerval's biographies were largely rehearsals for the autobiography which was supposedly his ultimate goal, and which he finally brought to fruition in his last work, *Aurélia.* And, of course, Nerval's madness can always be used to explain his interest in characters who themselves are marked by a certain lunacy, further justifying a view of biography as an indirect form of authorial autobiography.

---

[4] The generic affiliation of this last is less overtly biographical than the rest of the six texts which comprise *Les Illuminés*. These details are given in the notes to *Les Illuminés* in the edition cited.

[5] Nerval, letter dated 9 Dec. 1851 addressed to the 'Conservateurs de la Bibliothèque nationale', in *OC* ii, p. 1295.

[6] 'La Bibliothèque de mon oncle', in *Les Illuminés*, p. 887 (Nerval's emphasis).

[7] See Paulin Limayrac, 'Gérard de Nerval', *La Presse*, 31 July 1853, pp. 1–2 (p. 2); and J. Barbey d'Aurevilly, 'Gérard de Nerval', in id., *Les Œuvres et les hommes*, 4th ser., xxvi: *Critiques diverses* (1909; repr. Geneva: Slatkine, 1968), pp. 1–6 (pp. 1, 2).

From this perspective biography appears as a symptom of creative and emotional reticence on the part of the writer, not as a positive generic choice.[8] The other critical move is to place the biographical texts in the context of a preoccupation with a different literary genre: thus, Daniel Sangsue's fine study of the *Récit excentrique* has Nerval tackling the conventions of the *roman-feuilleton*—but not those of biography—in *Les Faux Saulniers*; Ross Chambers treats 'Angélique' (the first part of the Abbé de Bucquoy story) as a characteristic instance of Nerval's digressive travel narratives.[9] I have learned much from all these critics, but am struck by their recurrent sidelining of the question of biography, which, as we shall see in a moment, was a form of writing that Nerval, for a variety of reasons, was repeatedly obliged to reckon with during the course of his career.

LIVING WITH BIOGRAPHY AND THE QUESTION OF GENRE

There were good reasons why Nerval should have been drawn to biography as a form in its own right. The first is that, as we saw in Part II above, it was one of the major journalistic genres of the period, and Nerval was one of the many writers who was obliged to earn his living by writing for the press. In other words, economic necessity placed biography in his way as a means of making money. Two further possible reasons for this choice are personal and aesthetic, respectively. As regards the personal, Nerval had the unusual experience within his own lifetime of being the subject of biographies that were virtually obituaries, their authors having assumed that his madness had taken him outside the realms of normal existence. The first of these was written by the critic Jules Janin and was published in the *Journal des débats* on 1 March 1841, a few days after the event that could be described as Nerval's first psychotic episode.[10] The piece had a strong necrological bias, which meant that Nerval, unlike the subjects of most other portraits of contemporary writers, found himself reading a biographical account that treated him as if he were already dead. He discusses this experience in the preface to *Lorely*, which he addressed to Jules Janin, quoting at length

[8] See e.g. Milner, 'Notice' to *Les Illuminés*, p. 1696. This approach is, of course, not without justification, but it repeatedly sidesteps the issue of biographical writing as a part of Nerval's own corpus. Jacques Bony's discussion of *Les Illuminés* appears in the section of his study of Nerval's narratives that is entitled 'La Conquête du "je" ': see id., *Le Récit nervalien: une recherche des formes* (Paris: J. Corti, 1990). Similarly, Michel Jeanneret claims that 'la biographie infaisable, c'est en définitive, la sienne propre': in id., 'Nerval et la biographie impossible', *French Studies*, 24 (1970), pp. 127–44 (p. 141).

[9] See Daniel Sangsue, *Le Récit excentrique: Gautier—de Maistre—Nerval—Nodier* (Paris: J. Corti, 1987); and Ross Chambers, *Gérard de Nerval et la poétique du voyage* (Paris: J. Corti, 1969).

[10] Nerval's condition was described by his doctor (Dr Blanche) as '[une] manie aiguë'. For fuller discussion see Claude Pichois and Michel Brix, *Gérard de Nerval* (Paris: Fayard, 1995), ch. 14.

from Janin's original article. These *Souvenirs d'Allemagne* were published in June 1852, just one month after the appearance of *Les Illuminés*, and biography was clearly very much on Nerval's mind. He describes Janin's piece as an 'advance biography' in which 'I was thought to have died in the shipwreck [his illness], and friendship, in its initial anxiety, conferred on me honours ahead of time, which I cannot recall without blushing, but which, later on, I shall perhaps believe myself more worthy of'.[11] The embarrassment of reading a premature eulogy caused him both 'joy' and 'melancholy', but it had also entailed a number of inconvenient material consequences. In Germany he was accused by those who had read Janin's supposedly posthumous biography of being an impostor and of trying to usurp 'the only thing that he [its subject, Nerval] had left behind, a little fame surrounding a name'. Others who had known him in the past were disturbed to meet him again, convinced he was an apparition of the kind found in 'old Germanic legends about vampires and corpse-bridegrooms'.[12] He was also discomfited in the practical sphere by Janin's characterization of him as an other-worldly creature to whom no decent bourgeois citizen would dream of giving even a one-eyed or hunchback daughter in marriage.

Outliving his biography was evidently not without its problems, and Nerval found himself in this situation on two further occasions. On 10 December 1853 Alexandre Dumas published a biographical portrait of his lifelong friend in *Le Mousquetaire*, following the series of mental crises Nerval suffered in early spring and autumn of that year. Nerval responded as he had in the case of Janin, by directly addressing the perpetrator of the biography in the preface to one of his works, in this case *Les Filles du feu* (published in May 1854):

A few years ago, I was thought to be dead, and [Janin] wrote my biography. A few days ago, I was thought to be mad, and you devoted some of your most charming lines to an epitaph to my mind, which means a good deal of fame has become my lot in advancement. How shall I dare to wear such a brilliant crown on my head during my own lifetime? I shall have to sport a modest air and beg the public to retreat from so many eulogies accorded to my ashes.[13]

One might have expected, under these circumstances, that Nerval would simply denounce the practice of biography; but, despite his discomfiture, he is remarkably tolerant of its examples. When Eugène de Mirecourt's biographical *plaquette* appeared in 1854, Nerval was presented with an image of himself that he viewed as a distortion, since it portrayed him in an excessively flattering light and exaggerated both his poverty and his generosity towards his friends.[14] It was produced along the usual Mirecourt lines, and depicted Nerval as a kind of holy fool who had devoted his life to an impossible love, a view based on

---

11 Nerval, 'À Jules Janin', in *Lorely*, in *OC* iii (1993), pp. 3–12 (p. 4).
12 Ibid., pp. 10, 11.
13 Nerval, 'À Alexandre Dumas', in *Les Filles du feu*, in *OC* iii, pp. 449–58 (p. 449).
14 Nerval, letter to Georges Bell, 1 June 1854, in *OC* iii, p. 858.

Mirecourt's claim that *Sylvie* was a straightforwardly autobiographical text.[15] But whereas George Sand, for example, simply repudiated Mirecourt's biographical portrait of her,[16] Nerval treats such biographical images as an inevitability that justifies a separation between a writer's professional and private lives, even though biographers tend to conflate the two in order to construct a fictional hero:

I am treated as a hero in a novel, and it is full of no doubt well-intentioned exaggerations, and inaccuracies that are of little concern to me, moreover, since the character is entirely conventional. [. . .] One cannot prevent people from talking, and that is how history is written, which proves that I have been right to keep my poetic life separate from my real life.[17]

He even goes so far as to concede that Mirecourt's biography, despite its many exaggerations and errors, is, at bottom, true.[18] True or exaggerated, embarrassing or inconvenient, biography emerges from Nerval's comments as a phenomenon with its own special logic, one that his own experience repeatedly obliged him to confront in full both before and after the publication of *Les Illuminés*.

This brings me to the third reason for Nerval's potential interest in the topic, and this is the aesthetic one. Nerval was not to any degree an aesthetician or a literary theorist, but he had the century's highly developed sense of the special character of artistic endeavour. We have already seen how he endorsed the emerging opposition between literature and journalism in favour of literature (see Chapter 5 above), and his correspondence contains recurrent allusions to the distinction between high art and popular culture: for instance, he complains of the lack of 'literary worth' in the vaudevilles that he is professionally obliged to review, and regrets the rarity of new talent in what he calls 'high literature'.[19] In the introduction to his anthology of Ronsard's poetry in 1830, he presents an emphatically evolutionary view of literature: 'it is impossible to admit of a literature that is not progressive'.[20] But unlike the position adopted by Hugo or Gautier, Nerval's relation to the classical model of the past is not one of opposition. In order to surpass the achievements of the classical precursors, which is what the progressive character of literature requires, writers need, rather, to find alternatives to them. Specifically, they need to shift their ground away from the consecrated genres and go in search of others: 'It is not therefore a question of [. . .] disparaging the merit of all the great writers to which France owes

---

[15] Mirecourt, *Gérard de Nerval*.

[16] Chotard, 'Eugène de Mirecourt, biographe du troisième type', in id., *Approches du XIXe siècle*, pp. 21–33 (p. 27).

[17] Nerval, letter to his father, 12 June 1854, in *OC* iii, p. 864.

[18] 'C'est exagéré et plein d'erreurs, mais vrai au fond, à moins qu'il n'y ait une forte raillerie dans l'éloge absolu qu'il fait de moi, toujours au dépens des autres': letter to Georges Bell, 27 June 1854, in *OC* iii, p. 875.

[19] Nerval, letter to the editor of *Le Corsaire*, 30 (?) Oct. 1850, in *OC* ii, p. 1279; letter to Léopold Amail, 23 June 1851, in *OC* ii, p. 1291.

[20] Nerval, 'Introduction au choix de poésies de Ronsard', in *OC* i, pp. 281–301 (p. 282).

her glory; but, without hoping to do better than them, trying to do something different, and tackling all the literary genres that they did not get their hands on.'[21] In brief, the future of literature depends on changing its generic make-up.

As far as Nerval himself was concerned, this seems to have meant a reluctance to accept conventional generic categories of any kind: 'the absolute division of genres is a purely academic convention that, from the vantage point of our current position, scarcely bears scrutiny'.[22] Jacques Bony, who has much of interest to say on the topic of genre in Nerval, points to his preference for overtly 'formless' modes of literary expression, at least in the domain of prose, and cites Proust's comment that Nerval was a writer who created 'his art form at the same time as his thought'.[23] The biographies of *Les Illuminés* differ from *Les Nuits d'octobre* or the *Promenades et souvenirs* in that they are not strictly an invented form; but they share with these later, digressive, and apparently formless texts a status that falls outside the generic range with which ('high') literature was conventionally associated. Moreover, despite the codification of their usual journalistic guise, and despite the anti-literary character that journalism had for Nerval, biography offers considerable scope for invention and exploration to a writer committed to a 'progressive literature'. Or, to put the matter even more precisely, the position of biography outside a consecrated 'literature' allows Nerval the chance both to exploit its potential as literature and to consider the issue of literature from its biographical margin.

BIOGRAPHICAL ECCENTRICITIES

Over and above their position in relation to literature, there is much that is eccentric about Nerval's biographies, not least the biographical subjects he portrays, who are twice explicitly characterized as 'eccentrics' in the preface to *Les Illuminés*. To the extent that they are eccentric, they are so first and foremost in relation to the themes announced by the title and subtitle of the *recueil*: *Les Illuminés ou les précurseurs du socialisme*. Unlike the subjects of most other biographical collections, Nerval's heroes do not provide a coherent illustration of the idea or the quality under whose heading they are gathered. Neither are they the best examples of the phenomenon, as Barbey d'Aurevilly complained in his review of the book: 'Was it such men as these whose biographies we awaited, when Illuminism has as exponents in the world such powerful minds as those of Raymond Lull, Albertus Magnus, Roger Bacon, Paracelsus, Cardano,

---

[21] Nerval, 'Introduction au choix de poésies de Ronsard', in *OC* i, pp. 281–301 (p. 282).

[22] Nerval, Article in *La Presse*, 23 Sept. 1850, in *OC* ii, p. 1192.

[23] Jacques Bony, *L'Esthétique de Nerval* (Paris: SEDES, 1997), p. 57; and id., *Le Récit nervalien*, p. 22. For Proust's essay on Nerval ('Gérard de Nerval'), see Proust, *Contre Sainte-Beuve*, pp. 233–42.

Van Helmont, Agricola, Cosmopolite, Swedenborg, Boehme, Saint-Martin, etc., etc.?'[24] Barbey is referring here to the grand tradition of Illuminism, indebted to Gnosticism, Neoplatonism, and Swedenborgianism, whose central doctrine conceives of creation as 'an emanation of God through the Sophia (Wisdom), then the Word, with matter resulting from the Fall because of disobedience'. In this scheme, man has responsibility for the redemption of matter and the 'restoration of the lost harmony and unity of the universe'.[25] None of this appears directly in Nerval's volume and it would seem that only the loosest possible interpretation of the phenomenon is applicable to Nerval's cases. Max Milner has wisely concluded that 'the expression "les illuminés" [Illuminists] in fact covers various categories of character, which corresponds to its various meanings in current usage'.[26] This common usage is defined by the *Trésor de la langue française* as 'Person whose ideas and behaviour appear governed by irrational principles'. As little more than such common or garden irrationalists, Nerval's biographical heroes are somewhat to one side of the phenomenon of Illuminism (let alone socialism) that they supposedly incarnate, and, by the same token, his collection diverges from the conventional rationale for its existence. The passage from individual newspaper article to collective book publication is not, then, designed primarily to validate a particular type or to promote a particular authorial programme.

If Nerval's heroes are off-centre as Illuminists—or if they are eccentrics rather than Illuminists—they constitute a decidedly odd set of choices when considered purely as biographical subjects. The story of Raoul Spifame is that of a man who is not the person he thinks he is. The Abbé de Bucquoy is arrested on the grounds of mistaken identity, and his biographer also has difficulty distinguishing between him and a variety of namesakes; the first part of the narrative ('Angélique' in *Les Filles du feu*) is more or less entirely devoted to the search for the source material of the story, and in the process raises some far-reaching questions about the generic distinction between fiction and history. Jacques Cazotte foresees his own future and thus reverses biography's retrospective narration of a life. And if the identity of Restif de la Bretone (in 'Les Confidences de Nicolas') is less problematic, Nerval is nonetheless infringing a major convention of the genre by devoting so much space to the life-story of a writer whom he presents as neither great nor in any other sense exemplary. In short, nothing in these biographies functions quite as one might expect, and each opens up a different facet of the genre in such a way as to produce a revealingly lopsided version of it. It is this

---

[24] Barbey d'Aurevilly, 'Gérard de Nerval', p. 3.

[25] I am quoting from the helpful entry by Frank Bowman in Peter France (ed.), *The New Oxford Companion to Literature in French* (Oxford: Clarendon Press, 1995), p. 399.

[26] Milner, 'Notice' to *Les Illuminés*, p. 1696. On this issue see also Peter Dayan, *Nerval et ses pères: portrait en trois volets avec deux gonds et un cadenas* (Geneva: Droz, 1992), in which he argues, rather appealingly, that Nerval is actively contesting the notion of any coherent truth or doctrine in this text.

generic eccentricity above all that they have in common. Between them, the first three narratives seem to me to illustrate the major forms of Nerval's biographical lopsidedness, and in what follows I shall therefore be devoting most attention to 'Le Roi de Bicêtre', the 'Histoire de l'abbé de Bucquoy', and 'Les Confidences de Nicolas'.

'LE ROI DE BICÊTRE'

'Le Roi de Bicêtre' tells the (true) story of Raoul de Spifame, a man who, happening to have a remarkable likeness to Henri II, came to believe that he actually was the king. Unlike Mark Twain's *The Prince and the Pauper* (written some forty years later), where pauper and prince swap places in mutual awareness of their physical similarity, Spifame and the king live the coincidence of their resemblance quite asymmetrically. The king sees in Spifame the uncanny phenomenon of a portrait in human form: 'To Henri II it seemed that he had come face to face with a portrait that reproduced his entire person, the sole difference being that his splendid raiments had been rendered in black.'[27] Rather like Nerval's German friends, who, having read his obituary, thought he must be a vampire out of a German legend, the king is unsettled by the superstitious belief that to see one's own image dressed in mourning is a sign of imminent death (Spifame as a recently qualified lawyer is dressed in the colours of his new profession).[28] Again unlike Mark Twain's prince, Nerval's king also has no desire to become acquainted with his alter ego. However, after Spifame escapes from the madhouse in which he has been incarcerated and, in his assumed royal persona, seeks to announce his political reforms to the populace, the (real) king intervenes to provide him with living quarters in one of the royal chateaux because he is anxious to protect this human image of himself from insult or physical harm. When it takes living form, a portrait can be a very disquieting phenomenon for its subject.

Spifame, by contrast, believes that he *is* the king whom he resembles. It is suggested that the similarity might have triggered his madness in the first place, and in his delusion he identifies completely with his double:

Identical in appearance to the king, a reflection of his other self, and confounded by this similarity which everyone agreed was astonishing, Spifame had directed his gaze deep into the monarch's eyes and thereby suddenly acquired consciousness of a second personality. Having thus assimilated himself by his gaze, he then identified with the king in his mind; from that moment on, he imagined himself to be the very figure who, on the sixteenth day of June 1549, had made his triumphal entrance into Paris beneath the gorgeous tapestries bedecking the gate of Saint-Denis. (pp. 890–1 [p. 9])

---

[27] Nerval, 'Le Roi de Bicêtre', in *Les Illuminés*, pp. 887–902 (p. 888 [pp. 6–7]).
[28] The tale was originally published two years before Janin's biography of Nerval, and so cannot be read as an implied reference to Nerval's own experience.

Spifame is not just the living portrait of the king, but, because he is convinced that he is the king, the life of the king appears to him as his own life, and is thus the life he could expect any biographer to record as his own. This conviction is reinforced by his fellow madman Claude Vignet, a poet who believes himself to be 'king of the poets' and feels that he has been unjustly slighted by the poets of the Pléiade. He appoints himself *poète royal* to Spifame, with the self-imposed brief of using his talents to make the fame of his monarch known throughout the world. Vignet is the biographer to the king as he exists in the living portrait, or, rather, the chronicler of the life of the king as Spifame imagines himself to be living it. Portraits and biographies proliferate here in ways that thoroughly complicate the stable identity that biographical narrative normally presupposes. (Few biographers of the 'real' Henri II can have paused to wonder whether they are narrating the life of the right man.) 'Bicêtre' is not, then, just the name of the asylum in which Spifame is incarcerated, but a homophone (*bis-être*, 'repeat being') for the splitting and conflating of identities that take place in this biographical tale. By this means Nerval is unsettling a core presumption of biography and exploiting it as the basis for his own writing.

'HISTOIRE DE L'ABBÉ DE BUCQUOY'

The 'Histoire de l'abbé de Bucquoy' also plays on problems of its protagonist's identity, but this is largely the result of the biographer's frustrated search for his sources. The erudition that is the basis of the biographical dictionaries of the period is foregrounded here, and constitutes a major part of the narrative content of the first part of the story of the Abbé de Bucquoy as it appears in 'Angélique'. (The text of *Les Faux Saulniers* was first published in 1850 with the subtitle *Histoire de l'abbé de Bucquoy*, having been subsequently divided into two parts by Nerval, the first appearing as 'Angélique' in *Les Filles du feu*, and the second as the 'Histoire de l'abbé de Bucquoy' in *Les Illuminés*.[29]) At the outset of the story the Abbé is arrested on the basis of a mistaken identity by the militia who take him to be one Abbé de Bourlie, with the consequence that the entire series of imprisonments and escapes that make up his story follow from this original confusion. The issue is further complicated by the fact that the Abbé is also a count, and therefore sometimes known as the Comte de Bucquoy, in line with the entry in Michaud's *Biographie universelle* (which Nerval consulted for his project).

However, long before Nerval gets to the narrative proper of the Abbé-Comte, his search for its source in the elusive volume entitled *Histoire de l'abbé de Bucquoy*,

---

[29] References will be to the more accessible publications in *Les Filles du feu* (*OC* iii, pp. 459–536) and *Les Illuminés* (*OC* ii, pp. 903–45). The original full text of *Les Faux Saulniers* has, however, been published in *OC* ii, ed. Jacques Bony, pp. 1–169.

which takes him to five separate libraries and several booksellers besides, throws up a number of further possible variants on the Abbé's identity. Confident that he will find the book, the narrator-biographer initially writes: 'I felt no qualms about painting a portrait of the man and writing his biography on the basis of impeccable facts.'[30] When, as a result of a cataloguing error, the book cannot be traced in the Bibliothèque nationale, one of the library employees finds what he thinks is a Dutch translation of it. The author has the right name (Jacques de Bucquoy), but the title of this volume begins *Événements remarquables. . .*, whereas the one that Nerval is looking for is *Événements des plus rares. . . .* The Dutch volume turns out to be an account of a sixteen-year-long journey to the Indies, published in 1744, thus confusing matters further: although the first name of the author and the date of publication appear to be right, the Indies do not seem to belong to the known narrative of the Abbé's life: 'That's not it . . . and yet the book dates from the period when the Abbé de Bucquoy was alive, and his first name was indeed Jacques. But what could this fantastic Abbé have been doing in the Indies?' (p. 466 [p. 73*]). The narrator eventually concludes that the book must have been written by a namesake and relative of the Abbé, not by the man himself.

Matters gets worse when another library employee arrives and claims that the Abbé's name is 'du' Bucquoy, and not 'de' Bucquoy, introducing the possibility that he could have been recorded under 'D', and not 'B', as 'Dubucquoy'. Two pages later, a reference has been found in police reports for the year 1709 to an 'alleged comte du Buquoy', who may be a false count, or who may be the 'real' Comte de Bucquoy (despite the 'du' for 'de' and the missing 'c' in his name) operating under a very thin disguise: 'Could it be a false Bucquoy, who was trying to pass himself off as the other [. . .]? Could it be the real one hiding his name behind a pseudonym?' (p. 467 [p. 74*]). Is the alternative spelling a sign of a different person or of a partially concealed identity?

Continuing his search in the Bibliothèque de l'Arsenal, Nerval finds a Latin volume devoted to one COMES.A.BVCQVOY. However, this turns out to be yet another namesake, who lived during the reign of Louis XIII and was most probably an ancestor of the Bucquoy whose biography Nerval is aiming to write. He then discovers from documents held in the Archives de France that the family name of the Bucquoys is Longueval, and this is how he finds himself telling the story of the Abbé's great-aunt, Angélique de Longueval, before going on to unearth two further versions of the name: the first in a biography that claims that 'Bucquoi' is an alternative spelling for Bucquoy; and the second in a reference in a Dutch bibliography to one 'grave van Busquoy', whose 'prodigious military expeditions' are recorded in a book published in 1625. A note by Nerval solemnly records that this is now the sixth orthographical variant of the surname. These might, or might not, be variant spellings for a single name that belongs

---

[30] Nerval, 'Angélique', in *Les Filles du feu*, in *OC* iii, p. 461 [p. 68*].

in one form or another to at least three other people apart from the Abbé, and may possibly have been borrowed by a fraudulent fourth, whether or not he laid claim to the alternative family name of Longueval.

The erudition designed to authenticate the entries in enterprises such as Michaud's *Biographie universelle* here becomes the pretext for undoing the documented certainties conventionally associated with biographical writing. Yet, astonishingly perhaps, Nerval has invented none of his references, and his own considerable scholarly skills have been brought to bear in constructing the labyrinthine (and at times highly comic) narrative that his biography of the Abbé de Bucquoy becomes.[31] The object of Nerval's bibliographical search, the *Événements des plus rares, ou l'Histoire du sieur abbé comte de Bucquoy*, published in 1719, is the first item listed in the carefully vetted bibliography of the Michaud entry, and it is the very diligence with which he appears to have acted on this bibliographical prompt that unravels its subject. Despite Nerval's declared expectations at the outset of the project, his impeccable sources prove in the event to be highly embarrassing in his attempt to paint the portrait of Bucquoy and to write his biography.

The prominence of Nerval's display of erudition, to which he refers repeatedly in the course of the narrative, is a response to the so-called 'Amendement Riancey'. This law of 16 July 1850 introduced a tax on the *roman-feuilleton* by imposing a supplementary charge on each number of any newspaper that published such a thing. The reason behind this was the belief that the *roman-feuilleton*, from Sue's *Mystères de Paris* onwards, had been responsible for fomenting subversive ideas, and was thus assumed to have been a prime cause of the 1848 revolution.[32] In the light of this new prohibition on the serialized novel, Nerval begins his biography with an address to the editor of *Le National*, promising him the story of the Abbé de Bucquoy, which, he says, is written 'in a historical rather than a novelistic fashion', and Nerval guarantees to provide documents in support of this claim.[33] The narrator returns, provocatively, to this issue on a number of occasions in his narrative, insisting 'this is not a *novel*' or 'I have invented nothing'.[34] He claims to suffer more consternation than he otherwise might when it turns out that the missing history of Bucquoy may have been catalogued under 'novels' rather than 'history' in the Bibliothèque nationale. And he pretends to be worried that the appearance of the potentially fake Bucquoy in the Paris police records could lead to a charge of fictional invention:

there is not a single lawyer in existence who could not have found grounds to contest the material existence of this individual!

What reply could one give to a prosecutor who exclaimed to the courtroom that 'The comte de Bucquoy is a fictional character, a figment of the *novelistic* imagination of

---

[31] See Jacques Bony's 'Notice' and notes to *Les Faux Saulniers* in *OC* iii.

[32] See Bony, 'Notice', *OC* iii, pp. 1313–30 (p. 1314).

[33] Nerval, 'Angélique', p. 461 [p. 68].   [34] 'Angélique', pp. 469, 519 (Nerval's emphasis).

the author! . . .', and then went on to ask for the law to be applied, in other words for a fine of a million francs!—a sum which would be increased by the number of copies seized every day, if they were allowed to accumulate? (p. 467 [pp. 74–5*], Nerval's emphasis)

The costs of straying into fiction might turn out to be unaffordable, and the well-documented biography to which Nerval has committed himself is designed to keep him and his editor boss solvent and on the right side of Riancey's law. By appearing to take the legal threat seriously, and proposing biography as a sop to it, Nerval is making a question out of the distinction between fiction and history by which the government authorities set such store. In the process he is also raising a question about the position of biography in relation to literature. The presence of fictional elements in a supposedly biographical text would place that text automatically within the domain of the literary by turning it into a novel. In leaving the issue unresolved, but crucial, Nerval is implicitly challenging his readers to reflect on the terms in which they might wish to consider the potential literarity of the biographical genre.

'LES CONFIDENCES DE NICOLAS'

All of Nerval's biographies are based on documented sources, which he records in the text along with the titles of the works published by his protagonists. In the case of Restif de la Bretonne, Nerval's source is Restif's own (huge) corpus of writing, and especially his autobiographical *Monsieur Nicolas, ou, Le cœur-humain dévoilé*, orginally published between 1794 and 1797. Although Nerval's title is more suggestive of autobiography than is Restif's, his text firmly recasts autobiography as biography, and in so doing introduces a narratorial perspective that has peculiar results for the conventions of biography. As Nerval knew only too well, the default mode of biography is eulogy, and its presumption is exemplarity; but he presents Restif as being odd rather than estimable, and in particular as strangely blind and self-deceiving with regard to his own moral qualities. If he portrays Restif as the hero of a novel—which, as we have seen, is how Nerval said Mirecourt had depicted him—it is after the manner of Balzac: in the first episode he is characterized as the ignorant young *ingénu* totally at sea in the world of French society.[35] His childhood is presented as less than conventionally prophetic, given that Restif mistakes his taste for solitude as a vocation for minding sheep, and that, despite his future communist convictions, he lays claim to a piece of land on which he proceeds to build a large pyramid for himself (pp. 958–61). And rather than being a great love story (the theme of Mirecourt's life of Nerval), the story of Restif's emotional attachments is one of his fetishistic liking for feet (especially when encased in green mules), a lifelong

---

[35] Nerval, 'Les Confidences de Nicolas', in *Les Illuminés*, pp. 946–1074, ch. 1.

proclivity for illicit liaisons, and a preference for underage girls, most of whom nevertheless succeed in deceiving and outwitting him.

As narrator, Nerval adopts a stance that is curiously—and often very comically—neutral. By introducing an external biographical perspective into the self-narration of Restif's autobiography, Nerval undermines his subject's self-justification, but fails to replace it with an alternative moral position of the kind promised by Michaud in the 'Discours préliminaire' to the *Biographie*.[36] The objectivity of Nerval's account quietly reveals the full extent of Restif's self-deception on a number of issues, as, for example, in the depiction of his relentless search for material for his novels and plays, which took him into homes and families whose every secret he would unearth and exhibit in his next production, on the pretext that he was providing a service to society:

He wormed his way into your *hôtels particuliers*, your alcoves, and the secret parts of those little houses so carefully locked against the world, and whose entire story he will have discovered by seducing your chambermaid, or by meeting your doorman [. . .] in the tavern. Such was the man, sustained until the end, it is true, by the strange illusion that showed him only the duty of the moralist in the business of a fanciful and sententious spy. (p. 996)

It would be easy to denounce the flagrant bad faith of such behaviour, but to do so might run the risk of replicating it, and Nerval refrains from using his intimate knowledge of Restif's own life as material either for fiction or for moral sermons. Instead of sententiousness, the tone of Nerval's narration is much closer to that of understated comedy: he records the havoc that Restif repeatedly creates around himself; the fantastic literary schemes he devises, such as having love scenes in the theatre acted by couples on the eve of their wedding for maximum verisimilitude; and his elaborate and unreadable typographical inventions, such as spellings that replace 'c' with 's', 's' with 't', 't' with 'ç', the use of capitals or tiny type to indicate different vowel lengths, and a range of founts for different styles of writing, such as 'Cicero' for passion, 'Galliard' for simple narrative or moral observations, and 'small Roman' for tedious but necessary detail (p. 954).

As biographical narrator, Nerval neither condones nor condemns his subject, but by following him into certain areas, Nerval is able to throw oblique light on practices much closer to his own time and circumstances. For a start, he shares a number of personal similarities with Restif, whether it is in his belief that his family descends from a Roman emperor, his pursuit of the same ideal in a number of interchangeable women, or even his interest in typesetting. Nerval's *Nuits d'octobre* tacitly acknowledges Restif's *Nuits de Paris*, in both title and subject matter, and Restif's writing exemplifies an extreme form of the realism by which Nerval was both intrigued and appalled. The *Nuits d'octobre* explores this issue in the form of an explicit discussion and self-conscious mimicry of

---

[36] See Ch. 4 above.

the realist style. But the 'Confidences de Nicolas' treat the phenomenon as the product of Restif's convictions, allowing Nerval to consider the practice from the perspective of a writer whose delusions were as compelling as those of Nerval himself when in the grip of dreams or psychosis. In this sense Restif's life is narrated in very similar tones to those of Nerval's account in *Aurélia* of his own madness, which is portrayed both as comedy and as revelation.

This is not to suggest that the biography of Restif should, after all, be read as oblique self-portraiture, but rather to draw attention to the question of belief—or illusion—in Nerval's account of literary production. As Peter Dayan has pointed out, Nerval's Illuminists are united above all by their capacity for unwavering belief in the strangest phenomena, including those of their own creations.[37] In his biography of Jacques Cazotte, Nerval seems to suggest at one point that Cazotte's failing as a writer is that 'he allowed himself to succumb to the most terrible danger in literary life, which is to take one's own inventions seriously'.[38] But he goes on to suggest that this susceptibility is the strength as well as the weakness of writers of the eighteenth century (including Restif, therefore):

It was, it is true, the misfortune and the glory of the greatest authors of that time; they wrote with their own blood and with their own tears; they betrayed the mysteries of their minds and hearts without pity and for the benefit of a common public; they played their part seriously, like those actors in ancient times who stained the stage with real blood for the pleasure of a populace that was king. (ibid.)

There is nothing that automatically limits this tendency to the eighteenth century, and Nerval concludes his biography of Restif by musing at some length on the reasons why his subject was not, finally, a great writer. His imaginative energy is not to blame: 'No writer ever possessed the precious qualities of the imagination to the same high degree perhaps as Restif.' However, that energy on its own was not enough:

A warm heart, a colourful pen, and an iron will were not sufficient to make a good writer. He lived with the strength of several men; he wrote with the patience and the resolve of several authors. Did either Diderot who was himself more correct, or Beaumarchais who was more skilful, possess one half of that quivering and heated verve which does not always produce masterpieces, but without which no masterpiece can exist?[39]

The tenacity of Restif's delusions turns out to be a vital ingredient for great literature. However, it is a necessary rather than a sufficient ingredient, and it has its own fragility, as Nerval's remark to Dumas suggests, when, in the preface to *Les Filles du feu*, he says, 'the last vestige of madness that will probably remain with

---

[37] 'Ce qui attire Nerval, chez Aucler, comme chez les autres illuminés qu'il étudie, ce n'est pas leurs théories en elles-mêmes, ce n'est pas ce qu'ils cherchent à nous apprendre; c'est la façon dont ils arrivent à croire à la valeur, à l'importance et à la vérité de ces théories. En un mot: comment un homme intelligent, cultivé, sensible, peut-il s'aveugler au point de prendre au sérieux de telles énormités?' (Dayan, *Nerval et ses pères*, p. 17).

[38] Nerval, 'Jacques Cazotte', in *Les Illuminés*, p. 1083.   [39] 'Les Confidences', p. 1071.

me, will be the belief that I am a poet.'[40] Self-belief is not something necessarily to be condemned in others, even if it can also be the sign of supreme folly and utter delusion. In short, the example of Restif is the means whereby Nerval raises and explores the question of literature's origins in the personal qualities of the writer, but he maintains an ambivalence about his subject that ultimately makes it impossible to derive any moral—or even—creative lesson from it.

Nerval does not present his biographical subjects in a way that allows them to speak for themselves. But neither does he speak for them in his potentially moralizing role as biographer. Instead, he constructs a narratorial frame which seems to promise an evaluation of its biographical figures, but which never settles into a single perspective. He both ironizes his subjects in a manner highly untypical of biography (whose mode is rarely that of irony), and sees himself in their dilemmas. Above all, he shifts the emphasis away from the certainties of the moral discourse associated with biography, in order to confront issues concerning the basic presuppositions of the genre. On this dislocated ground he can pose questions about the characteristics of the great writer, or the distinction between history and fiction, and the place of biography in its relation to literature. He explores some core principles associated with biography—identity, erudition, exemplarity—in order to explore its potential for a 'high' literature whose development may require going via the 'low' genres associated with the journalism against which it so often defines itself. In this way the linearity of literature's evolution as described by Madame de Staël or Hugo's *Préface de Cromwell* is deflected and rerouted through the biographical margins of the literary, but still in the name of literature's ultimate progression as a series of necessary displacements from its own apparent logic.

[40] 'À Alexandre Dumas', *OC* iii, p. 458.

10

Biography and Literary Principle: Marcel Schwob's *Vies imaginaires*

may every life and every death seem strange and new to you.
(Marcel Schwob, *Le Livre de Monelle*)

With Marcel Schwob's *Vies imaginaires* biography achieves a kind of rehabilit-ation, and for the first time becomes explicitly synonymous with a redefining of the literary. All the features that for Victor Cousin constituted its inferiority in relation to history are re-evaluated here and made central to the high literary purpose that Schwob ascribes to biography. Published in 1896, the year in which the first volume of Rémy de Gourmont's *Livre des masques* and Mallarmé's portrait of Rimbaud appeared, *Vies imaginaires* is one of the last works to be published in Schwob's brief literary career. This career was largely confined to the decade of the 1890s and began with the publication of a collection of tales under the title *Cœur double* in 1891. Gourmont makes Schwob an exemplary representative of his aesthetic of the individual, which, in his introduction to *Le Livre des masques*, he equates with Symbolism:

What does *Symbolism* mean? If one stays with the narrow, etymological sense, almost nothing; but if one goes further, it can mean: *individualism in literature*, artistic freedom, rejection of all formulae that have been taught, a tendency towards what is new, strange and even bizarre; it can also mean: idealism, disdain for social anecdote, anti-naturalism, and a tendency to *take from life only the characteristic detail, to focus only on the action by which a man is distinguished from another man*, to pursue only the essential in any results.[1]

Whether or not one agrees with this account of Symbolism, its key features—the assimilation of literature to the individual, the characteristic detail, and the actions that distinguish one person from another—all derive from Schwob's own aesthetic, which he elaborated in terms that make the actual writing of 'lives' far more crucial to the literary than the individual subjects paraded in *Le Livre des masques*. Schwob is a theorist of biography as much as he is a theorist

---

[1] Rémy de Gourmont, 'Préface', in *Le Livre des masques*, vol. i, pp. 7–16 (p. 8). Apart from the emphasis on the word *Symbolisme*, all italics are mine.

of literature, but for him the two are ultimately and inextricably linked. This is because he regards biographical writing as an exemplary literary practice in which, moreover, practice itself becomes indistinguishable from theory.

Although it is Schwob's erudition that provides the focus of my discussion, his career involved him as much in journalism as it did in learning. His father was the proprietor of the republican newspaper *Le Phare de la Loire*; he wrote a regular 'chronique' for *L'Événement* and *L'Écho de Paris*, as well as for his father's paper; the 'contes' that comprise *Cœur double* and *Le Roi au masque d'or* (1892) were all published serially in *L'Écho de Paris* before being collected in book form; and the individual lives of the *Vies imaginaires* appeared in *Le Journal* over the course of the two years that preceded their publication in a single volume in 1896. These associations notwithstanding, and very much in keeping with the hostility of so many writers in the nineteenth century towards the press, Schwob wrote a devastating satire of what he calls the *Mœurs des diurnales*.[2] As vehement in its way as Barbey's denunciation of biographies, the satire nevertheless targets not so much the generic forms of journalism as its rhetoric. Schwob's relation to the biographical practices of the nineteenth century are tacit and oblique, and his radical reworking of the genre is more obviously based in the erudition associated with the dictionary than in its journalistic guise.

THE USES OF ERUDITION

The *Vies imaginaires* consist of some twenty-two brief 'lives', arranged in chronological order, beginning in antiquity with 'Empédocle, dieu supposé', and ending in the early nineteenth century with 'MM. Burke et Hare, Assassins'. The book version is introduced by an important preface, also included under the title 'L'Art de la biographie' in *Spicilège*, a collection of Schwob's essays and prefaces, published in the same year.[3] *Le Journal* had announced the original series as follows: 'Today we are beginning a series of Lives of a number of poets, gods, assassins, and pirates, as well as several princesses and gallant ladies, brought to light and arranged in a new and agreeable order by Marcel Schwob.'[4] Although the title given to the collection is *Vies imaginaires*, it is not the protagonists of the lives who are imaginary. All the texts are based on documentary and archive sources, even though these are not explicitly referred to in the text. Pierre Champion, Schwob's first biographer and editor of his complete works (1927–30), both affirms and downplays this documentary basis of the lives in his 'Notice' to the text:

---

[2] Published in 1903.

[3] *Spicilège*, in Marcel Schwob, *Œuvres*, ed. Alexandre Gefen et al. (Paris: Les Belles Lettres, 2002). Unless otherwise indicated, all further references to Schwob's works will be to this edition.

[4] Cited in the 'Notice' to *Vies imaginaires*, in *Œuvres*, pp. 367–9 (p. 367).

It would be easy for us to provide all the sources of these beautiful tales, as is done nowadays, not without pedantry, in the theses on literary history defended in the Sorbonne. There would be no difficulty in listing the documents that furnished [Schwob] with the elements for the biographies of Empedocles and Herostratus, in giving references for all the words uttered by Lucretius, in naming all the Italian chronicles used to portray Cecco Angiolieri, the Franciscan sources for the life of Frate Dolcino, the use he made of Vasari to sketch the madness of Paolo Uccello in a single stroke, the documents that contributed to the writing of the life of Spenser, Shakespeare's contemporary, and the classic lives of the English pirates by which he brings back to life for us the buccaneers who hoisted their black flag over the seas.[5]

But, continues Champion, this would be to miss the point of Schwob's biographies, which call for a response in the reader's imagination rather than a scholarly confirmation of his sources:

But to what purpose? Those who are curious will find some of them indicated in the catalogue of Marcel Schwob's library. And what more will we know if we learn that the life of Alain le Gentil and every word of the biography of Katherine la dentellière are in letters of remission kept in the national archives; that the life of Nicolas Loyseleur came from reading the written evidence from the trial of Jeanne d'Arc?[6]

'All that is of little interest', concludes Champion. In fact his comment functions as what rhetoricians call *praeteritio*, and serves precisely to underscore the extent of the grounding of Schwob's 'lives' in the sort of erudition that was the basis of the biographical format of Michaud's *Biographie universelle*, or of Hoefer's forty-six-volume *Nouvelle biographie générale*, a copy of which Schwob owned.[7] Schwob himself would have made an ideal contributor to Michaud or Hoefer. Many of his contemporaries commented on the immense breadth of his reading; his knowledge of other languages equipped him for the numerous translations he undertook;[8] he also had considerable philological expertise and wrote on medieval French argot; and a biographical essay he published on the fifteenth-century poet François Villon was the basis for a projected book which remained incomplete

---

[5] Pierre Champion, 'Notice' to *Vies imaginaires*, in *Les Œuvres complètes de Marcel Schwob (1867–1905)*, ed. Pierre Champion, 10 vols. (Paris: François Bernouard, 1927–30), vol. ii, pp. 195–200 (p. 196). On this see also Willem Geertrud Cornelis Byvanck, *Un Hollandais à Paris en 1891: sensations de littérature et d'art* (Paris: Perrin, 1892), *passim*. Byvanck was a young Dutch scholar who recorded his conversations with a number of French writers and poets whom he encountered during a year-long stay in Paris. The discussion with Schwob is particularly valuable.

[6] Champion, 'Notice' to *Vies imaginaires*, p. 196. The catalogue to which he refers is the one he himself edited, *Catalogue de la bibliothèque de Marcel Schwob* (Paris: Éditions Allia, 1993), introduced by Champion's essay 'Marcel Schwob parmi ses livres' which describes the extent of Schwob's learning.

[7] See Champion, *Catalogue*, p. 91.

[8] Including Thomas De Quincey's *Last Days of Immanuel Kant* and Daniel Defoe's *Moll Flanders*.

at the time of Schwob's early death in 1905.[9] In short, his biographical writing can be seen as a sort of transformation of the erudition that underpinned the biographies in the Michaud and Hoefer dictionaries, and these are worth revisiting as a means of understanding the nature of his continuation of the strand of erudite biography in his *Vies imaginaires*.

Schwob's aims are, however, very different, and he makes no claim to the comprehensiveness implied by Michaud's and Hoefer's description of their biographical enterprises as 'universal' or 'general'. Nevertheless, Schwob's subjects fit most of the criteria listed in Michaud's subtitle to his dictionary: '*Histoire, par ordre alphabétique, de la vie publique et privée de tous les hommes qui se sont fait remarquer par leurs écrits, leurs actions, leurs talents, leurs vertus ou leurs crimes*'. I shall return below to the question of order, but, for the rest, Schwob includes four writers—Lucretius, Petronius, Angiolieri, and Tourneur—a great many actions, often violent ones; men of talent, such as Uccello; qualities, which are flagged in the qualifier of each of the tales, for example 'Cratès, cynique', or 'Cecco Angiolieri, poète haineux'; and a large number of crimes, beginning with Herostratus' burning of the temple, and ending with the multiple murders of Messrs Hare and Burke. Hoefer's subtitle stresses the scholarly nature of his enterprise, mentioning in particular '*les renseignements bibliographiques et l'indication des sources à consulter*'; and both he and Michaud, in their respective prefaces, stress the scholarly qualifications of their contributors. If it would have been pedantic to spell such information out for readers, erudition nevertheless underpins every one of Schwob's 'lives', just as it is the basis for each of the entries in the *Biographie universelle*. Moreover, the impersonality of Schwob's narrative voice in the *Vies* is exactly that of the contributors to the biographical dictionaries, who, while signing their contributions, do not speak in them as the individual scholars or writers that many of them were.

Schwob's 'lives' are extremely brief, running to an average of just three or four pages in the more recent edition of the *Œuvres*. In this respect, too, the texts are in conformity with the editorial directives of the biographical dictionaries of Michaud and Hoefer, both of whom stress the value of concision and the importance of discernment in the choice of information selected for each: Michaud propounds 'precision in content and concision in style',[10] and condemns previous dictionaries for 'a lack of attention and discernment in the choice of articles and in the details of which they are comprised'.[11] As we shall see, Schwob makes brevity the essence of the biographer's art, but it is a matter of principle for him, rather than an editorial necessity associated with the

---

[9] The studies on argot were *Études sur l'argot français* (1889), which he wrote with Georges Guieysse, *Le Jargon des Coquillards en 1455* (1890), and the *Glossaire du jargon de la Coquille* (all in the *Œuvres*). The Villon essay is included in *Spicilège* under the title 'François Villon' (pp. 545–77).

[10] J.-F. Michaud and L.-G. Michaud, 'Avis des éditeurs sur cette première livraison', in *Biographie universelle* (1811), vol. i, pp. v–vi (p. vi).

[11] L.-G. Michaud, 'Discours préliminaire', ibid., pp. vii–xviii (p. xiv).

constraints on space in the dictionary. Hoefer introduces an extra factor into
the issue of brevity when he argues—somewhat speciously, perhaps—that his
project is more scientific than Michaud's because there is a direct correlation
between the length of the entries and the importance of the figures they describe.
The less important a person, the shorter the entry, and vice versa. The majority
of Schwob's characters in the *Vies imaginaires* are either quite unknown (Alain
le Gentil or Katherine la dentellière, for example), or else they are minor figures
who in a conventional historical context would be overshadowed by their more
famous contemporaries: this is the case for Cratès in relation to Diogenes, Clodia
in relation to Cicero, Sufrah to Aladdin, Cecco Angiolieri to Dante, Nicolas
Loyseleur to Jeanne d'Arc, and Gabriel Spenser to Ben Jonson or Shakespeare,
where the historically more important figures are mentioned only as allusions in
the 'life' of the lesser-known figure. According to Hoefer's calibration, then, the
brevity of Schwob's 'lives' is the ideal measure for such historically insignificant
characters.

However, despite the chronological ordering of Schwob's 'lives', everything
that justifies Michaud's (or Hoefer's) *Biographies* as works of history is inverted by
Schwob; his *Vies* could be seen as an attempt to sever biography from any larger
historical purpose, and to give it instead a strategic function in the construction
of the literary. Whereas it was Michaud's aim to provide the material on which
to assemble a national history, or a universal history of literature and painting,
Schwob works against such a project in a number of ways. Apart from the fact
that the subjects of his lives are minor figures, only three of them are French
(Nicolas Loyseleur, Katherine la dentellière, and Alain le Gentil), and these rank
amongst the most marginal and least known in the whole collection. There
are five from the ancient world, and, in the latter part of the collection, eight
Anglo-Saxons, of whom the majority, furthermore, are not English, but (more
marginally from a European standpoint) Irish, North American, Barbadian, and
Scottish. Then, there are the distinctly more exotic figures of Sufrah, who hails
from the Tale of Aladdin, and, from more recent times, Pocahontas, the American
Indian princess. And, whereas Michaud sets mythological figures apart in his
biographical dictionary, Schwob includes Herostratus (as, indeed, does Hoefer,
though supported and justified by a list of bibliographical references that include
Plutarch and Cicero), and two candidates for divinity: Empedocles, who opens the
series with the qualifier 'putative god', and—less conventionally, perhaps—the
playwright Cyril Tourneur, born, according to the opening sentence of his 'life',
from the union of an 'unknown god' with a prostitute.

Finally, whereas Michaud proposes moral consensus as the criterion for
recourse to judgement in his biographies, Schwob exploits the impersonality of
scholarly discourse and reports claims, such as the one about Tourneur's origins,
without comment. This is how Michaud states his purpose on the question of
moral judgement: 'in matters of morality and taste, [there are] sure principles,
about which all men of honour and good sense agree, and which above all they

make it a rule to profess in works written in society, and aimed at the public in its entirety'.[12] Not only does Schwob fail to condemn his many criminals, heretics, pirates, and murderers, but he also writes as if the gods directed human actions, as if the dead could be visited and reanimated ('Septima'), and as if geomancy were a perfectly valid principle for explaining events ('Sufrah'). The moral usefulness of history is provocatively ignored in favour of a different set of principles altogether. And these principles, despite Schwob's meticulous use of historical document and archive material, and despite his recourse to all the historically informed strategies associated with the historical biographies of Michaud and Hoefer, are not actually those of history, but represent a new conception of literature built on the elements of biography least associated with claims to historical status.

PRINCIPIA BIOGRAPHICA

Schwob differs from most of his contemporaries and precursors in the nineteenth century in that he does not use the literary portrait as the basis for his redefinition of the literary. The one exception to this in his œuvre is the biographical essay on Villon, where Schwob argues that Villon's talent as a poet comes not from the invention of new forms, but from the personal inflection that he brings from his own lived experience to inherited literary models: 'He transformed the entire legacy of the Middle Ages by animating it with his own despair and his remorse for a wasted life. Everything that other authors had invented as exercises in thought and language, he adapted to fit feelings that were so intense that the poetry of tradition was no longer recognizable.'[13] In short, 'expressions that in other writers were literary modes seemed in Villon to become nuances of the soul' (p. 546). This insight does, however, require a secure scholarly basis for distinguishing between the factual and the fictional in Villon's work, a procedure which, inversely from that of Mirecourt on the subject of Adrienne in the life of Nerval, allows Schwob to interpret a cruel mistress in Villon's narrative as a purely literary topos (p. 567).

Aside from the Villon essay, Schwob's literary interest in biography is not primarily a means of distinguishing accents of sincerity in literature from poetic convention. Rather, he is deeply preoccupied with biographies (of all kinds) as forms of writing that contain elements which can be deployed to support an idea of literature quite independently of their biographical subjects. In this he is much closer to Nerval than to writers such as Gautier, Verlaine, and Rémy de Gourmont, who adopt the literary portrait as a means of making a literary point. As I have already mentioned, it seems to be a commonplace in Schwob studies to

---

[12] L.-G. Michaud, 'Discours préliminaire', p. xiii.
[13] Schwob, 'François Villon', in *Spicilège*, pp. 545–77 (p. 545).

acknowledge the comparison with Nerval, only then to dismiss it as exaggerated and inappropriate. There are, however, a number of connections that suggest that Schwob may well have had a sense that Nerval shared his own angle of approach to biography. One of Schwob's earliest works is a poem in argot about Nerval's death, 'Ballade pour Gérard de Nerval pendu à la fenêtre d'un bouge' (1888);[14] and the catalogue of Schwob's library lists an edition of Nerval's *Bohême galante*. Furthermore, Schwob entitles one of the *contes* in *Le Roi au masque d'or* 'Les Faux-Saulniers' in tacit reference to Nerval, whose anachronistic spelling he retains; and towards the end of his life he was working on a theatrical project based on *Les Filles du feu*, which never saw the light of day.[15] It is hard to know how to evaluate Schwob's use of the word 'illuminé' in 'Cecco Angiolieri', but the enthusiastic reception that the *Vies imaginaires* received on their publication elicited a number of comparisons with Nerval's *Illuminés*.[16] Nevertheless, the most fruitful basis for a return to this comparison lies less in the eccentric or marginal nature of their respective biographical protagonists (although this is by no means irrelevant), than in their common engagement with the biographical form itself.

It is clear that Schwob was acquainted with a wide range of biographical practices dating from different periods. He mentions Plutarch and cites Diogenes Laertius' *Lives of Eminent Philosophers* at some length in his essay on biography (which I shall come to presently); his library contained a number of lives of the saints; his preface to Flaubert's *Légende de Saint Julien l'hospitalier* alludes to Jacques de Voragine's *Golden Legend*; he owned copies of the memoirs of Cardano and Bellini; he refers to Brantôme in his conversations with Byvanck, and the announcement of the *Vies imaginaires* in *Le Journal* implicitly alludes to Brantôme in its mention of 'dames galantes'; according to Champion's *Catalogue*, his library contained a considerable number of biographies and memoirs with such titles as *Mémoires de Madame Manson, explicatifs de sa conduite dans l'assassinat de M. Fualdes* (1818), the *Mémoires de M. de La Porte, premier valet de chambre de Louis XIV* (1756), and the *Testament d'une fille d'Amour mourante* dating from 1769. As we shall see, Schwob has much to say about Aubrey's *Brief Lives* and Boswell's *Doctor Johnson*. He translated Thomas De Quincey's *Last Days of Immanuel Kant*, which is in no sense the standard intellectual biography one might expect of such a man in the nineteenth century. Instead, as Schwob himself comments in his preface to the translation, it tracks the decline of Kant's intellect alongside his physical disintegration, and records 'the hour

---

[14] 'Ballad for Gérard de Nerval hanged at the window of a hovel'. See Sylvain Goudemare, *Marcel Schwob ou les vies imaginaires: biographie* (Paris: Cherche midi, 2000), p. 61.

[15] See the 'Chronologie' by Bernard Gauthier and Alexandre Gefen in the *Œuvres*, pp. 1263–9 (p. 1269).

[16] See Goudemare, *Marcel Schwob*, p. 202. For a fuller discussion of the pros and cons of such a comparison see Hubert Juin, 'Préface' in his edition of Marcel Schwob, *Cœur double, Mimes* (Paris: Union générale d'éditions, 1979), pp. 7–30 (p. 9).

when Kant ceased to be able to produce general ideas and made errors in his ordering of natural phenomena'.[17] The arcana that Schwob encountered in these texts presumably appealed to the scholar and antiquarian that he undoubtedly was, but his familiarity with biographical forms from earlier periods is also an important factor in his own biographical practice. Schwob's erudition is not the kind that marks out modern 'biography' as a learned form of life-writing. Scholarship, rather, provides him with access to historical examples of the largely popular form of 'lives' which his own writing sets out to emulate: these are, after all, imaginary 'lives' and not imaginary biographies.[18] Schwob's learning enabled him to resurrect and reclaim anachronistic forms of life-writing which could then be put in the service of a new kind of (literary) writing.

Indeed it is the exhaustiveness associated with many modern forms of learned biography to which Schwob most objects. He describes his disappointment over a biography of Captain Kidd because it told him too much; and his major criticism of Boswell's *Life of Samuel Johnson* is that it contains an excessive quantity of information.[19] What Schwob asks of biographers is, first, that they have an understanding of their own art, and secondly, that this understanding be expressed in the form of brevity and singularity. In fact, he makes the two synonymous. Brevity requires choice, and the biographer's skill consists above all in his ability to select the singular feature. As Schwob says in his essay on biography, 'The art of the biographer consists precisely in choice. [. . .] The biographer, like a lesser divinity, knows how, amongst all human possibilities, to choose the one that is unique'.[20] The human possibilities that are the biographer's quarry are not the illustrative or revelatory detail that Sainte-Beuve mentions in his description of the portraitist's working practice designed to pinpoint the tic or the wrinkle that will yield the whole man. Schwob's goal is the unique, the isolated or the inconsequential, with deliberate disregard of any whole to which they may theoretically contribute. Such unique features are the very elements that Victor Cousin had condemned as being unworthy and even destructive of proper intellectual endeavour when he asserted that 'individuality on its own is a wretched and petty entity; for the particular, the contingent, and the finite tend unfailingly to division, dissolution, and nothingness'.[21] The examples that Schwob gives of biographical detail as he understands it are precisely these contingent and particular things: the leather pouch of warm oil that Diogenes Laertius reports that Aristotle wore against his stomach, or the collection of clay

---

[17] See Schwob's preface to his translation of De Quincey's *Last Days*, in *Œuvres complètes*, ed. Champion, vol. i, pp. 262–3 (p. 262).

[18] For a discussion of the role of scholarship as a factor distinguishing biography from 'lives', see Fumaroli, 'Des "Vies" à la biographie', p. 3.

[19] Schwob, 'Robert Louis Stevenson', in *Spicilège*, pp. 578–84 (p. 580); and 'L'Art de la biographie', ibid., pp. 629–34 (p. 633).

[20] 'L'Art de la biographie', p. 633.

[21] Victor Cousin, 'Dixième leçon: les grands hommes', p. 203. See Ch. 4 above for discussion of Cousin's argument.

pots that were found in his house after his death. It is the suggestiveness of these
details that counts above all for Schwob, not any explanatory or illustrative force
that they might have: 'We shall never know what Aristotle did with all those
pots. And the mystery is as delightful as the conjectures that Boswell leaves us
with concerning the use that Johnson made of the dried orange peel that he
customarily kept in his pockets.'[22] The singularity of the biographical detail—the
orange peel in Johnson's pockets and Aristotle's collection of pots—is designed
to disrupt any explanatory series, and for this reason is profoundly anti-historical.

History may be a repository of such singular detail, but it is constitutively
unable to incorporate them into its practice. The biographer, by contrast, actively
exploits this resistance to incorporation. History and biography are polarized
in Schwob's perspective, where history appears as an obstacle to the sort of
biography that Schwob is seeking to elaborate. He may use historical materials
('chronicles, memoirs, correspondences, and scholia'), but the biographer should
not take himself to be a historian, as he has so often been in the habit of doing
(p. 633). The historian inevitably marginalizes the singular detail, and records
only those items that may have played a role in determining the course of
history: the length of Cleopatra's nose, the grain of sand in Cromwell's urethra,
the fact that Napoleon was unwell on the day of the battle of Waterloo, or
that Alexander was drunk when he killed Klitos: 'All these individual facts are
valuable only because they altered events or because they could have diverted
their course. They are real or possible causes. And they should be left to scholars'
(p. 629). Anything that smacks of causality or of a series belongs to history and
has no place in Schwob's conception of biography. Besides, the best biographical
subjects are not necessarily the major actors in the events of history, but the
unknown figures whom history is liable to overlook. When biographers take
themselves to be historians and confine themselves to writing the lives of 'great
men', they are depriving readers of some of biography's most promising subjects:
'Any attempt at the art in which Boswell and Aubrey excelled should without
doubt avoid minute descriptions of the greatest man of his day, or notations
of the characteristics of the most famous figures of the past, but record with
equal care the *unique* existences of men, whether they were divine, mediocre, or
criminal' (p. 634, Schwob's emphasis). History repeatedly connects the particular
to the general, treating its protagonists as representatives or as causes of larger
historical realities, whereas Schwob's conception of biography, with its emphasis
on the unique, works against all such generalities and continuities.

This emphasis on the unique becomes the basis of Schwob's equation between
biography and art, whose ultimate manifestation is that of painting: 'The book
that described a man in all his anomalies would be a work of art like a Japanese
print, where for eternity one can see the image of a small caterpillar glimpsed on
a single occasion at a particular hour of the day' (p. 630). And although he cites

22 Schwob, 'L'Art de la biographie', p. 631.

the examples of Johnson's orange peel and Aristotle's pots, Schwob turns for the underlying justification of this procedure not to a biographer, but to Hokusai the painter. Schwob invokes Hokusai's ideal of an art that has freed itself from the general or the typical, and succeeded instead in asserting the individual: 'The painter Hokusai hoped to attain the ideal of his art by the time he was 110 years old. By then, he used to say, every point and every line drawn by his brush would be a living thing. By "living" one should understand individual' (p. 630). This recourse to the model of painting makes it very clear that the issues Schwob associates with biography are aesthetic, not historical. For all its basis in historical document, the writing of lives here is ultimately a literary practice with a literary goal.

LITERARY THEORY

Seen from this perspective, one could note that the brief 'lives' of the *Vies imaginaires* follow on from the short form of the 'conte', which is the basic unit of Schwob's two previous collections, *Cœur double* and *Le Roi au masque d'or*, and that, strictly speaking, the 'life' is no more than a variation or development of the preference for the short form within his own literary repertoire. But this would be to ignore the extraordinarily acute sense that Schwob has of the development of literature as a whole, which means that every piece of writing needs also to be seen as an intervention in that development, not just as part of the personal production of the individual poet or writer. In other words, Schwob's assertion of the unique is made in a context that inevitably transforms assertion into intervention.

His conception of the literary goes much further than the familiar nineteenth-century affirmation of individuality against a general norm, individual freedom against aesthetic prescription or scientific totality, as invoked by Rémy de Gourmont in his defence of Symbolism. Schwob's notion of the unique or singular detail differs from this recurrent sense of individuality amongst nineteenth-century writers; biography for him is not so much the representation of the individual, as a mode of writing that favours the singularities incidentally associated with individual lives. Moreover, the opposition set up by Rémy de Gourmont between the individual and social or literary consensus does not apply to Schwob's thinking, where the singular serves, rather, to destabilize oppositions between contrasting entities in a variety of spheres. For example, in characterizing the human emotions of terror and pity, which are, he claims, the perennial objects of artistic representation, Schwob describes an alternation between a paranoid terror, where the relation between individuals is based on fear, and a pity that enables one person to conceive of another's terror. In short, if 'man's heart is double', this duality entails a transition between the two extremes: 'the soul goes from one extreme to the other', a movement that Schwob characterizes as '[a] slow and painful [. . .] march' where contrast is recast as movement from one term to the other.[23] Similarly, the opposition between the inner life and external existence needs to be seen as variable, each with its own oscillating movement between 'outer extremities and the centre', but which occasionally connect to produce a paroxystic climax: 'Each time the double oscillation of the outer and inner worlds produces an encounter between them, there is an "adventure" or a "crisis". Then the two lives revert to their independence, each fertilized by the other.'[24] The acuity of such crises lends itself to an intensity that Schwob sees as having considerable aesthetic potential.

Art also has its own internal dynamic, and is not exclusively dependent on the objects of its representation, such as pity and terror. It is the product of a will that alternates within each individual between an instinctive fulfilment of desire and an inner censorship.[25] This is mirrored in turn at the collective, national level in the form of a further oscillation between 'a period of instinct' and 'a period of reflection'. All art is thus the product of what Schwob calls 'this rising and falling march forward', which sees its character alternating between the 'sculptural' and the 'picturesque', the 'symbolic' and the 'naive',[26] and, more importantly, between what he terms Realism and Symmetry: 'Like all manifestations of life, such as action, associations, and language, art has passed through analogous periods that are reproduced from one age to the next. The two extremes between which art oscillates seem to be Symmetry and Realism. In Symmetry, life is subordinated to conventional artistic rules; in Realism, life is reproduced with all its most inharmonious inflections.'[27] Literature thus has a history which is that of the movement between these various opposed extremes. This history is, however, a matter of alternation, of rise and fall, rather than the explanatory series of history proper. Moreover, the oscillations that are manifest over the course of time also exist in the present, so that synchrony as well as diachrony proves to be structured in this unstable way. In short, the literary field is already mapped according to a series of such dualisms, rather than being constructed in terms of an oppositional relation between the individual and the institutional. The result of this is that the contingent and unique details that are Schwob's artistic quarry will figure in the larger context of these shifting contrasts.

I am not suggesting that Schwob's views amount to a full-blown theory or definition of literature, not least because his emphasis on alternation and on crisis excludes the possibility of any fixity of concept: 'Life does not seem to me to be a topic for classroom compositions. Everywhere I try to take hold of it, it explodes in my hands.'[28] The urge to define an entity that exists only by virtue of its alternating manifestations will always result in this volatile reaction, a logic that applies a fortiori to literature. As Monique Jutrin says, the literary

---

[23] Schwob, 'La Terreur et la pitié', in *Spicilège*, pp. 608–16 (p. 608).
[24] Ibid., pp. 615, 616.   [25] Byvanck, *Un Hollandais*, p. 237.   [26] Ibid., pp. 237, 238.
[27] Schwob, 'La Terreur et la pitié', p. 612.   [28] Byvanck, *Un Hollandais*, p. 291.

is never a given for Schwob: 'Art in his eyes does not reside in a secure location that is defined in advance, it can only move indefinitely towards a "promised land" and a refuge that is always denied it.'[29] It is for this reason, too, that the symbol Schwob proposes for the contemporary condition of literature is that of the Wandering Jew:

That is another symbol which suits me: the figure of Ahasverus, the Wandering Jew, the unremitting traveller, who encountered the Ideal on his path, but turned his back on it, because he did not recognize it in the form in which it appeared to him; and he set off walking, furious with himself, driven by the madness of vain hope, and he is walking still.[30]

The Ideal or the Absolute cannot be apprehended, and this impossibility makes art the object of a perpetual quest: 'Every poem—and I take the word in its broadest sense—that contains a scrap of true life has as its refrain: "Walk on! walk on!".'[31] This produces a somewhat paradoxical situation whereby the theoretical essay—or even the conversation about aesthetic principles—risks bringing the peregrinations of poetry to a halt. It is only the tiny scrap of life, contained for instance in the free-floating biographical detail, that keeps literature on the move, as can be seen in Schwob's own practice as a biographer.

BIOGRAPHICAL PRACTICE

A good many of Schwob's biographical subjects seem to respond to his injunction to take to the road, and they live as vagabonds until their (often violent) deaths. Cratès leaves home after his 'conversion' and spends his life wandering the streets of Athens; Clodia the Roman matron also leaves home after the death of her brother and takes to the streets of Rome; Petronius gives up literature for a life of adventures with his slave Syrus, and they become 'wandering magicians, country charlatans, and the companions of vagabond soldiers'; after the death of Jeanne d'Arc, Nicolas Loyseleur 'wandered the roads of France'; Katherine la dentellière abandons not only her trade but her lodgings: 'she took to the roads. And thenceforth she was no longer a Parisienne, or a lace-maker, but was like the women who haunt the outskirts of towns in France, seated on tombstones in cemeteries, to give pleasure to passers-by'; Alain le Gentil is kidnapped from his home at the age of 12 and after twenty-three years of soldiering up and down the country falls into a life of trickery and petty crime, much like that of the vagabond poet Villon as described in Schwob's essay;[32] Schwob's four pirates, William Phips, Captain Kid, Walter Kennedy, and Major Stede Bonnet are

---

[29] Monique Jutrin, *Marcel Schwob, 'Cœur double'* (Lausanne: Éditions de l'Aire, 1982), p. 54.
[30] Byvanck, *Un Hollandais*, p. 304.   [31] Ibid.
[32] Schwob, *Vies imaginaires*, pp. 391 [p. 139], 408 [p. 156], 410–11 [p. 159*]. All further page references are to this text.

all, so to speak, professional vagabonds of the ocean. There is movement of a kind, too, in the passage from social integration to the margins of petty crime, prostitution, theft, and murder, which is that of most of the 'lives', whether or not the characters are literally wanderers. To follow the events in the lives of Schwob's protagonists requires a willingness on the part of readers to relinquish the moral centre and move outwards to the margins of the social order, where things tend anyway to become more unpredictable.

What readers do with this situation is partly prepared for by the Preface to the *Vies imaginaires*.[33] In its introductory guise the Preface could be seen as a sort of traveller's guide, rather than as a full-scale theory of biography which the 'lives' would duly illustrate. The reader needs to be nudged into an appropriate reading stance, and for Schwob that stance has everything to do with mobility: 'The true reader constructs almost as much as the author; except that he builds between the lines. Anyone who does not know to read the white part of a page will never be a good *gourmet* of books. The sight of words, like the sound of the notes in a symphony, brings with it a procession of images that bears you along with it.[34] Reading is a matter of being carried along by the procession of images that emerge from the blanks or gaps in the text.

The unpredictable and often violent nature of the episodes narrated in Schwob's 'lives' is one means by which such gaps are produced. But there is much in the writing itself that produces similar effects.[35] At the level of the narrative, the discontinuous temporality repeatedly favours the instantaneous over the predetermined. Érostrate reads the papyri of Heraclitus's poems in what appears to be a single moment: 'By the light of the sacred lamp he read them, and he knew all.'[36] Knowledge here is a matter of complete and immediate acquisition, and its relevance to Érostrate's incendiarism is implied in the paratactic narrative logic that simply goes on to state: 'He at once cried out: "Fire! Fire!" '(ibid.). Cratès' conversion is equally abrupt (p. 377); and the event in 'Nicolas Loyseleur', which another narrative mode might describe as 'remorse', is presented in a similarly unprepared and elliptical way: 'his head suddenly swam before the light from the Rhine' (p. 408). These rapid transitions help to create the white areas on the page, which Schwob invites his readers to galvanize with the dynamism of their own responses.

The counterpart of connection, curiously, has the same effect. Schwob links his stories not in a larger narrative of the history of civilization, for example, but through incidental details whose significance—or otherwise—is never

---

[33] The *Spicilège* version of the essay is described as 'Préface remaniée des *Vies imaginaires*'.

[34] Schwob, *Il libro della mia memoria*, in *Œuvres*, pp. 1255–69 (pp. 1261–2).

[35] Many of these features have been illuminatingly discussed in existing critical studies; see in particular Jutrin, *Marcel Schwob,'Cœur double'*, and the essays by Dominique Rabaté, Alexandre Gefen, and Yves Vadé in Christian Berg and Yves Vadé (eds.), *Marcel Schwob, d'hier et d'aujourd'hui* (Seyssel: Champ Vallon, 2002).

[36] Schwob, *Vies imaginaires*, p. 376 [p. 126].

elucidated. These connections range from the coincidence (or is it?) of the mention of the birth of Alexander the Great on the night that Érostrate burned down the temple, with the comment in the first lines of the succeeding 'life' of Cratès that he knew Alexander. There are also various suggestive parallels between a number of the individual lives, so that Lucretius is murdered by his wife, and Clodia murders her husband, the spouse in each case administering a poisoned beverage to the victim. Or again, Katherine la dentellière has her throat cut by a ruffian wanting money from the (non-existent) purse in her belt; and in the next 'life' Alain le Gentil behaves like Katherine's murderer when he cuts a purse off the belt of a man whose throat he has just slit. Furthermore, in each of these two texts there is incidental mention of a 'surcoat made of green cloth'. Similarly, it is hard to know what to think of the arrangement whereby 'Nicolas Loyseleur' follows on from the life of Uccello, where much is made of the painter's name in light of his love of birds, and where he is regularly referred to as 'L'Oiseau'. And so it could go on. The effect of all these tangential and more or less aleatory links is to rearrange the surface of the texts so that they become as 'uneven' as the existences narrated in them, prompting the reader to move between and around them, instead of proceeding straight on through them in purposeful linear fashion.

A further strategy for discontinuity worth mentioning in this brief survey is the near-absence of any authorial presence. Whereas a number of the 'contes' adopt a first-person narrator, the *Vies imaginaires* are uniformly marked by complete narratorial absence. As Dominique Rabaté comments, 'the biographizing subject is hidden and invisible'.[37] The effect that Schwob derives from this is to make his texts appear as a kind of compilation, in the manner of many of the older narrative forms that he deploys. He does this either by citing sources ('*Some claim that he had the imprint of an extraordinary seal on his right side*'),[38] or, more obliquely, through the strategy of simply replicating frames of reference, such as geomancy, which cannot command assent in the modern world. Another version of this is the invocation of points of reference that carry no useful information for modern readers; so, for instance, the significance of why Petronius during his childhood 'never wore wool from Tyre a second time' is not immediately obvious (p. 389). Flaubert is clearly a model for this kind of writing, and especially, perhaps, the Flaubert of the *Légende de Saint Julien l'Hospitalier*, for which Schwob wrote a preface; but Schwob, unlike Flaubert, cannot be said to have a characteristic style of his own. This absence of a personal style is exceptional at a time when, as Michel Viegnes has argued, most French writers established their own distinctive 'personal *logos*'. Schwob's refusal of a style is therefore to be seen as a 'deliberate choice of polyphonic explosion', where the writing

---

[37] Dominique Rabaté, 'Vies imaginaires et vies minuscules: Marcel Schwob et le romanesque sans roman', in Berg and Vadé, *Marcel Schwob*, pp. 177–91 (p. 188).

[38] Schwob, *Vies imaginaires*, p. 422.

is composed entirely of a patchwork of different sociolects and vocabularies.[39] This is not a version of Bakhtinian dialogism, so much as a thoroughgoing linguistic fragmentation that, in Schwob's own description of the process, sees sentences break free from periods, and words from individual sentences: 'Just as in language, phrases progressively break away from periods, and words liberate themselves from phrases to take on their independence and their own colour, we have gradually become differentiated into a series of *selves* whose value is indeed relative.'[40] The emergence of the 'unique' at the existential level is thus matched by a parallel phenomenon in the linguistic domain, where the autonomy of linguistic entities breaks up the cohesion of discourse in a manner that introduces a large amount of real or metaphorical white space on to the printed page, and so, ideally, mobilizes the reader's imaginative responses.

DES VIES ALLÉGORIQUES D'ELLES-MÊMES

There is much more that one could say about the discontinuities that constitute Schwob's literary project, but I should like to propose one particular way of reading these imaginary lives: namely—to adapt the title of one of Mallarmé's poems—as 'des vies allégoriques d'elles-mêmes' ('lives that are allegories of themselves'). Midway between a theory of biography as literature on the one hand, and the use of biographical writing as a practice of the unique on the other, this characterization seems to me to apply especially to three of the 'lives' in Schwob's *Vies imaginaires*: 'Cratès', the third in the series, 'Paolo Uccello', which is placed exactly in the middle, and 'MM. Burke et Hare', the last in the collection. Between them, and by a variety of means, these texts could all be said to allegorize the very tension between 'theory' and 'practice' which keeps resurfacing in these considerations, and which make biography a part of the quest for an ungraspable literariness.

In the figure of Cratès one can see an emblem not just of the vagabond, but of the promotion of practice over theory. Cratès' 'conversion' to poverty is prompted not by rational and abstract argument, but by the sheer impact made by the image on stage of 'Telephos, king of Mysia, dressed in a beggar's rags and carrying a basket in his hand'.[41] Rags carry more conviction than philosophy,

---

[39] See Michel Viegnes, 'Marcel Schwob: une écriture plurielle', in Berg and Vadé, *Marcel Schwob*, pp. 242–56 (pp. 242, 252). This point has been borne out in illuminating detail by Evanghelia Stead in 'Marcel Schwob et les Élizabéthains', in *Fictions biographiques, XIXᵉ–XXIᵉ siècles, 11–14 May 2004, Université Stendhal, Grenoble 3*, ed. Anne-Geneviève Chignard et al. (Toulouse: Presses universitaires de Toulouse Le Mirail, 2006), where she itemizes the various literary sources that make up the textual patchwork of Schwob's 'Cyril Tourneur'.

[40] Schwob, 'La Différence et la ressemblance', in *Spicilège*, pp. 621–4 (p. 621, Schwob's emphasis).

[41] *Vies imaginaires*, 'Cratès', p. 377 [p. 128].

and Cratès renounces knowing for living, and recasts the maxim 'Know thyself' as 'Live thyself': 'The idea of any sort of knowledge seemed to him absurd. His only study was the relation of his body to that which was necessary to it, which he sought to limit as far as possible' (p. 378 [p.129*]). Diogenes, who is the theorist of the poverty that Cratès actually practises, appears, by contrast, somewhat half-hearted and distinctly misanthropic. Cratès discovers that the barrel in which Diogenes resided is superfluous to the regime that he prescribes. And whereas Diogenes insults his fellow men by describing them as 'excrement', Cratès deliberately takes up residence in the excremental and 'was kindly disposed towards mankind' (p. 377 [p. 128]). In short, Diogenes is a very bad advertisement for theory; and Cratès offers a very compelling case for practice.

Much the same issues apply to Uccello, whose preoccupation with perspective is treated as an indifference towards reality: 'Uccello cared nothing for the reality of things, only for their multiplicity and for the infinite number of their lines' (p. 402). When his wife smiles at him, all he sees in the smile is its geometry:

And when she looked at him, he saw all the little lines of her eyelashes, and the circles of her irises, and the curve of her eyelids, and the subtle interweaving of the hairs on her head, and he mentally pictured the garland she wore in a multitude of different positions [. . .] but he did not paint her portrait, as other painters do when they love a woman. For the Bird did not know the joy of limiting himself to the individual. (pp. 403–4)

This preoccupation with the general at the expense of the particular becomes a form of madness ('his obsession with perspective'), as Uccello, like an alchemist, tries to find the formula that will contain and subsume all others: 'He thought he could transform all lines into a single ideal vision. He sought to configure the created universe as it is reflected in the eye of God' (p. 403). The 'masterpiece' that is the outcome of Uccello's lifetime obsession with the abstractions of geometry and perspective implicitly recalls that of Balzac's Frenhofer in 'Le Chef-d'œuvre inconnu': when Uccello shows the painting to his fellow artist Donatello, all the latter can see in it is 'a jumble of lines'. Vasari, on whose account Schwob draws, acknowledges the excessive nature of Uccello's concern with perspective, but he nevertheless redeems his subject through his appreciation of a number of individual paintings. Schwob refers to none of these works, and mentions only the portrait that Uccello never painted of the woman who loved him, and the indecipherable masterpiece of the painter's old age that so perplexed Donatello. Vasari also makes much of Uccello's work on perspective as a contribution to the development of the art of painting in general.[42] For Schwob, by contrast, Uccello can appear only as the negative incarnation of an art whose true representative is his exact antithesis—Hokusai. Hokusai's art is an anti-geometry, and his ideal is

---

[42] In his library Schwob possessed an English translation of Vasari dating from 1890; see Champion, *Catalogue*, p. 19.

the reverse of Uccello's, in that it aimed to make every point and every line unique and individual. The challenge presented by this ideal derives from the fact that lines and points inevitably invite a geometrical reading: 'There is nothing that looks more alike than points or lines: geometry is based on this postulate. The perfect art envisaged by Hokusai demanded that nothing be more different.'[43] The life of Uccello can thus be read as an allegory of the theory that is the reverse of the biographer's art.

The final implicitly allegorical life is that of Messrs Burke and Hare, in whom one may see a pair of indefatigable would-be biographers. The chief difference between them and Schwob is that whereas Schwob collects his biographical data from books, documents, and archives, Burke and Hare get their subjects to tell their own stories viva voce. Burke selects his subjects amongst passers-by in the streets at dusk, and invites them in, one each night, to describe 'the most surprising incidents of [their] existence'.[44] At a given point the pair interrupt the narrative, physically stopping its flow by stifling and smothering its narrator, whose death is the necessary precondition for their own imaginative completion of his tale: 'The two of them would muse, remaining motionless in this position, about the end of the story, which they never heard. In this manner, Messrs Burke and Hare terminated a large number of stories that the world will never know' (p. 439). In this new version of the *Thousand and One Nights*, rather than being the means of staving off his execution, narrative suspense positively requires the death of the storyteller. More precisely, one can see in the drastic procedure of Burke and Hare an extreme version of the discontinuities that are the basis of Schwob's own biographical practice, and, in the protagonists' imaginative speculations about their victim's unfinished tale, the procession of images that reading elicits from the blanks in the text. But this particular form of narrative suspense degenerates into a kind of mania, as the demands of Mr Burke's imagination cease to be satisfied by the stories he hears, and his focus shifts instead to the deaths by which they are interrupted:

The fertile imagination of Mr Burke had tired of the eternal similarity of the stories of human experience. The results had never lived up to his expectations. He reached a point where he was interested only in the reality and variety of death. He focused all the drama on the *dénouement*. The quality of the actors no longer mattered to him. (p. 440)

When the individual biographies are dispensed with entirely, and the two assassins begin to concentrate exclusively on the destruction of their victims, the practice of discontinuity turns out to carry the same risks as the excesses of theory. If this 'life' is to some degree a fable, Schwob may be warning himself to stop while the going is good, and not to jade his reader's imagination by telling so many biographical tales that they all end up seeming the same. More generally, as allegory, the 'life' seems to be exploring the question of individual variety

---

[43] Schwob, 'L'Art de la biographie', p. 630.   [44] *Vies imaginaires*, p. 439.

against the potential monotony of the procedures for arriving at it, and to be considering the possibility that the demands of the imagination might have their limits. In other words, the allegorical concerns oscillate—in a characteristically Schwobian movement—between the poles of theory and practice, the general and the particular, as they apply to his own version of what he calls 'the art of biography' and an ever mobile literarity.

With Nerval and Schwob biography is subjected to a new scrutiny that explores it with a view to bringing out its intrinsic potential for a literature. The result is that the question of literariness itself is placed under the spotlight. None of the many biographical subjects who appear in the pages of the two collections is treated as a figure whose life-story might simply be drafted into supporting a particular view of literature. Rather, it is the generic features of biography that become the site of an engagement with literature from which a revised conception of the literary emerges in an emphatically open-ended guise, as both writers reveal a keen sense of the evolving character of the literary. In the case of Nerval's *Illuminés* this is manifested in his concern to create the possibility of a future for a literature that requires generic variation if it is to survive. And in the case of Schwob's imaginary lives, the focus on the unique as the emblematic feature of biography becomes the means whereby literature is kept in perpetual motion and prevented from ever fully coinciding with itself.

PART V

INWARDNESS, EXPERIENCE, AND THE TURN TO FICTION

IN the 1920s biography began to acquire for the first time the recognized status of a literary genre in its own right. Hitherto, its literary role had been to intervene in the construction of the idea of literature from a discursive position that never made any literary claims for itself.[1] Marcel Schwob may have made biographical strategies the essence of the literary, but this was not the same as granting biography the status of an established literary genre. From the early 1920s biography was increasingly considered to be a form of literary expression on a par with the novel, a genre with which it also became very closely affiliated as part of this process. The new phenomenon of the so-called *vie romancée* was a prime instance of this affiliation: read positively, the *vie romancée* was seen as placing the narrative techniques of the novel at the service of biography; read negatively, however, it was regarded as a disreputable manufacturing of imaginative fictions out of the lives of real people. Either way, biography and the novel joined forces on terms that opened up the prospect of treating biography as a fully-fledged literary genre in its own right. This shift in the literary standing of biography gave rise to some fairly sustained reflection on the forms and practices of biographical narrative, culminating in André Maurois's *Aspects de la biographie*, published in 1928. The book was the published version of the Clark Lectures, delivered in May of that year under the auspices of Trinity College, Cambridge. Maurois's title deliberately echoed E. M. Forster's *Aspects of the Novel*, which had been the topic of the previous year's Clark Lectures, and under its rubric Maurois addressed, *inter alia*, such questions as whether biography might be an art, whether it constituted a medium for creative authorial expression, and whether, like the novel, it had a modern form. Such issues were given added weight on English territory by the seriousness accorded to the so-called New Biography, whose supporters and exponents included Virginia Woolf and Lytton Strachey. A decade before Maurois's lectures, Strachey himself had asserted in the preface to his *Eminent Victorians* that biography is 'the most delicate and humane of all the branches of the art of writing', and that we would do well 'to reflect that it is perhaps as difficult to write a good life as to live one'.[2]

In considering the ways in which biography came to be viewed as one of the 'branches of the art of writing', I do not, however, intend to alter the course of

---

[1] See Gefen, 'Vies imaginaires', in which he argues that the generic status of biographical narrative within literature can be established retrospectively to encompass much earlier forms of biographical writing.

[2] Lytton Strachey, 'Preface', in *Eminent Victorians: Cardinal Manning, Florence Nightingale, Dr Arnold, General Gordon* (London: Chatto & Windus, 1928), p. viii. His point about the difficulty of writing a good life being as great as that of living a good one recalls the remark by Carlyle that I quoted in my Introduction. On the 'New Biography' see Laura Marcus, 'The Newness of the "New Biography": Biographical Theory and Practice in the Early Twentieth Century', in France and St Clair, *Mapping Lives*, pp. 193–218. Marcus notes (p. 199) that André Maurois knew a number of the members of the Bloomsbury Group, including Harold Nicolson, whose book *The Development of English Biography* was published in 1928 and is much praised by Maurois in *Aspects de la biographie*.

my own argument, which, as should now be clear, is not primarily concerned with biography as literature, but rather with the way in which biography has played a role in debating and determining what literature is, or might be. Even when the two issues overlap, as they do in this instance, the questions remain distinct. Equally, it should be acknowledged that the annexation of biography to literature does not necessarily entail any contestation or revision of the literary on the part of biography. Indeed, it is not from the *vies romancées* that such interventions come, but from the fictional autobiography that is Proust's *À la recherche du temps perdu*, and from the first of the major literary autobiographies in twentieth-century French literature, André Gide's *Si le grain ne meurt*. (I shall be discussing those of Leiris and Sartre in Part VI.) More or less contemporary with the *vies romancées* of the 1920s, *Si le grain ne meurt* was published in 1925 and the publication of *La Recherche* spanned most of the decade, the second part appearing in 1919, and the final part, *Le Temps retrouvé*, in 1927.

A major factor in biography's acquisition of a literary standing was the value increasingly being placed on the inner life in the context of literary concerns. This shift of focus inwards was the factor that made the greatest call on the imaginative and narrative elements of the novel. As a consequence, it was not just the mental and emotional life of biographical subjects that was henceforward to be represented, but, in the case of writers and other artists, specifically their creative experience.[3] It is above all this concern with inwardness and the nature of the experience of artistic creation that links the otherwise perhaps rather different kinds of writing discussed in the next three chapters.

[3] As John Hope Mason has argued, this idea of creativity is a relatively modern conception: see id., *The Value of Creativity: The Origins and Emergence of a Modern Belief* (Aldershot: Ashgate, 2003).

11

Romancing Lives: Literary Creativity
in the 1920s

As I have already suggested, the literarization of biography during the 1920s was a double-edged phenomenon: both a promotion and a vulgarization, the sign of biography's potential to be art, but also the index of what was seen as a drastic dumbing-down of the French reading public, supposedly grown too lazy and intellectually incurious to be bothered with history, philosophical ideas, or even poetry, at least in unadulterated guise. Writing in the *Revue des deux mondes* in 1927, the critic André Chaumeix notes the plethora of biographical series being published under titles such as 'Le Roman des grandes existences' (Plon), 'Les Vies des hommes illustres' (Gallimard), 'Les Grands Cœurs' (Flammarion), or 'Leurs amours' (devoted largely to female subjects from the Empress Joséphine to the poet Marceline Desbordes-Valmore, and also published by Flammarion); and he comments that 'we are in an age dominated by a taste for biography in the pure state'.[1] He goes on to describe biography as 'a facile form' that banalizes and simplifies history in presenting it by means of the picturesque. Biography, he says, is 'the agreeable form in which serious matters reach a public that does not wish to make any effort'; and he concludes that 'curiosity about individual lives is much greater than curiosity about works of art or political history'. In this he is repeating an objection frequently voiced by critics, who attacked biography by targeting the shortcomings of its readers: 'People prefer the story of the life of a poet to reading poetry. They prefer the life of a statesman to a history of the state at that time.'[2] Biography is condemned here as a glib substitute for other, more serious forms of writing, with literary devices (agreeable form, the picturesque) being identified as the means whereby the unambitious tastes of contemporary readers may be satisfied.

Many of these biographies were known as 'vies romancées', which, in their willingness to describe imagined scenes, to include dialogue, and to present the thought-processes and inward responses of their protagonists, departed from previous biographical practice. In its more extreme forms this novelization of

---

[1] André Chaumeix, 'Le Goût des biographies', *Revue des deux mondes*, 42 (1927), pp. 698–708 (p. 700).

[2] Ibid., pp. 701, 703.

biography was apt to produce pastiche in the style of its author-subject, and a near-systematic interpretation of the subject's literary works as completely and unproblematically autobiographical. Nabokov's hero in *The Gift*—who is himself writing a biography of Chernyshevski—wonders how close he dare get to writing a parody of 'those idiotic *"biographies romancées"* where Byron is coolly slipped a dream extracted from one of his own poems'.[3] This practice is amply illustrated in, for example, René Benjamin's *Prodigieuse Vie d'Honoré de Balzac*, published in 1925. Benjamin's biographical protagonist describes his time in the *collège* at Tours as if he were himself the hero of his novel *Louis Lambert*, and when he arrives in Paris he behaves exactly like his own fictional creations Rastignac or Lucien de Rubempré, captivated by the elegant women he sees passing in their carriages on the Champs-Elysées and ashamed of the ordinary and unfashionable sisters he has left at home. Commenting in the *Nouvelle Revue française* (which, coincidentally, was serializing Proust's *Le Temps retrouvé* at the time), another critic deplores the fact that 'the so-called biographies that are flooding the market bring discredit upon the genre'.[4] He singles out in particular the cavalier way in which the 'improvised historians' who are the authors of these works treat material that would once have been filtered through the most fastidious scholarship. Maurois himself laments the way that the 'biographie romancée' has undermined the position of biography in general:

> For some time now, the detestable expression 'romanced biography' has been much in use. If it means 'a biography constructed like a novel', then let people say: a biography constructed like a novel; and then it is simply a question of technique. But if it means a biography whose details are not accurate, a life that is not a life, imaginary scenes, sentences that are completely made up and attributed to a great man, then, frankly, I prefer a traditional historical novel like *The Three Musketeers*, which at least acknowledged that it was a novel.[5]

In sum, whether it is through the use of picturesque detail or the fictionalization of historical fact in the form of imaginary scenes and conversations, the literary dimension of this type of biography contributed to maintaining the lowly status that had been its default position throughout the nineteenth century.

THE LITERARY STRATEGIES OF THE NEW BIOGRAPHY

In his biography of Shelley, *Ariel, ou La Vie de Shelley* published in 1923, which contains its own share of imagined scenes, reported thoughts, and dialogues,

---

[3] Vladimir Vladimirovich Nabokov, *The Gift* [1952], trans. Michael Scammell (London: Panther, 1963), p. 184.

[4] Jean Schlumberger, '*Vie de Disraëli*, par André Maurois', *Nouvelle Revue française*, 166 (1927), pp. 101–3 (p. 101).

[5] André Maurois, '*La Vie de Franz Liszt*, par Guy de Pourtalès', *Nouvelle Revue française*, 154 (1926), pp. 104–5.

Maurois is careful to indicate that everything in the text is derived from verifiable sources: 'the facts are true and not a single sentence or thought was attributed to Shelley that was not recorded in the memoirs of his friends, his letters, or his poetry'. The brief bibliography at the end of the book is there for the benefit of 'the inquiring reader' but will also reassure those who doubt his knowledge of the sources.[6] Erudition is, however, not the main issue, and the terms in which biography is most actively defended in the 1920s are rather different from those used in the previous century, and frequently make explicit appeal to the skills of the writer of fiction. This new association with the novel, as well as being the perceived cause of the discrediting of the biographical genre, also becomes the basis of biography's elevation to the status of literature.

The first major requirement advanced by the new apologists for the form is that biography should bring life to scholarly fact, and create living creatures out of the figures from the past who are its subjects. These biographies are usually not concerned with contemporary figures, and they constitute what André Chaumeix calls 'a sort of Noah's ark of past glories'.[7] Jean Schlumberger declares that 'the desiccated document must be brought back to life'.[8] And François Mauriac, in his *Vie de Jean Racine*, writes that the task of the biographer is to restore the dead to life: 'The greatest act of charity towards the dead is not to kill them off a second time by endowing them with sublime postures. The greatest act of charity is to bring them closer to us, to divest them of their pose.'[9] The function of biography, then, is to recreate rather than to document the life of its subject. This calls on the novelist's skill, but, Mauriac notes, he has drawn the line at treating his subject as if he were a fictional character: 'We were nevertheless careful not to give Jean Racine the appearance of life, as if he were a character in a novel.'[10] It is for this reason that Mauriac claims to have decided against including an imaginary scene in which Racine would have soliloquized as he sat up late in the royal chamber ready to read aloud to the king if he had trouble sleeping.

The second and related requirement of biography is that it depict the inner life of its subject; the recreated life deals rather more with motive, feeling, and mental existence than with the externals of event and circumstance: '[the] life not the way it unfolded, but *the way he* [the subject] *experienced it*', as Louis Martin-Chauffier put it in an article on biographical writing.[11] Martin-Chauffier was a novelist as well as a journalist, and he continues: 'the aim of a biography

---

[6] André Maurois, 'Note pour le lecteur bienveillant', in id., *Ariel, ou la vie de Shelley* (Paris: Calmann-Lévy, 1939).

[7] Chaumeix, '*Goût des biographies*' p. 698.   [8] Schlumberger, '*Vie de Disraëli*', p. 103.

[9] François Mauriac, *La Vie de Jean Racine* (Le Roman des grandes existences; Paris: Plon, 1928), p. 3.

[10] Ibid.

[11] Louis Martin-Chauffier, 'Biographies', *Nouvelle Revue française*, 174 (1928), pp. 393–7 (p. 393).

is to reconstitute and reanimate the inner activity of a mind and a soul, the outward manifestations of that activity featuring only as a sign, and the episodes in the life as external contrasts whose sole interest lies in the reactions that they provoke or in the *subterranean actions* that they reveal.'[12] This emphasis on the inner life is derived in large part from fiction, particularly as it was conceived at the time. In his study of Dostoevsky (published in 1923), Gide presents the work of the novelist in just such terms: 'The inner life is [. . .] more highly prized than relations with one's fellow man [. . .] each of his characters [. . .] lives by virtue of his own personality, and these intimately personal beings, each with his own peculiar secret, are introduced to us in all their puzzling complexity.'[13] The fictional writing of Gide himself is an exploration of just such complexity, which is also the focus of Proust's treatment of his characters in *À la recherche du temps perdu*. This inward move is evident, too, in the novels of François Mauriac, whose *Thérèse Desqueyroux* was published in 1927, one year before his *Vie de Jean Racine*. No doubt it is because the inner life had come to seem the most vital element of human subjects, not least when they were well-known figures from the past whose external lives were already thoroughly documented in previous biographies, that so many novelists were contracted to write for the new biographical series of the day: François Mauriac (Racine), but also Francis Carco (Villon) and René Benjamin (Balzac), all published in Plon's series 'Le Roman des grandes existences'.

This emphasis was closely bound up with the development of a third criterion regularly invoked in connection with biography, namely, the notion of 'poetic truth'. Historical truth is a matter of recorded fact, but, as Ramon Fernandez writes in his review of Maurois's *Aspects de la biographie*, 'the truth of motive, the feelings of the character [. . .] can by and large only be poetic'.[14] Maurois himself defines the poetic truth of biography as the quality that provides the underlying unity of a life, its tone, its musical colour. It is, he says, a deeper truth than factual truths: 'It is a jumble of often contradictory actions, thoughts, and feelings, and yet it has a unity that is like a sort of musical tonality. Your life is written in C minor or G major.'[15] According to Maurois, this poetic unity can be expressed by means of recurrent motifs, such as the water that runs through his biography of Shelley, or the flowers that are woven into his life of Disraeli. A somewhat more mundane version of this 'truth' is conveyed in many of the titles of the 'Roman des grandes existences' series, where the subject's life is implicitly treated as the expression of his or her personality: see, for example, *La Prodigieuse Vie* [prodigious life] *d'Honoré de Balzac*, *La Vie aventureuse* [adventurous life]

---

[12] Louis Martin-Chauffier, 'Biographies', *Nouvelle Revue française*, 174 (1928), pp. 393–4.

[13] André Gide, *Dostoïevski*, in id., *Essais critiques*, ed. Pierre Masson (Bibliothèque de la Pléiade; Paris: Gallimard, 1999), p. 557 [pp. 15–16].

[14] Ramon Fernandez, '*Aspects de la biographie*, par André Maurois', *Nouvelle Revue française*, 184 (1929), pp. 100–2 (p. 100).

[15] André Maurois, *Aspects de la biographie* (Paris: Au Sans Pareil, 1928), p. 95.

de Jean-Arthur Rimbaud, La Vie raisonnable [reasonable life] *de Descartes, La Vie douloureuse* [unhappy life] *de Charles Baudelaire*, and so forth.

This takes us to a fourth aspect of biography, that of its construction. Maurois stresses the importance of rhythm in the composition of a written life,[16] but he also devotes considerable attention to the question of the narrative organization of the biographical text. Once more, he is borrowing from the repertoire of the novel, while insisting that the biographer's choices are more limited than those of the novelist. Picking up E. M. Forster's discussion of 'point of view' in *Aspects of the Novel* (itself redolent of a Jamesian distinction between 'showing' and 'telling'), Maurois recommends that the biographer adopt the sole point of view of his subject (thereby excluding that of other figures), and avoid the perspective of an authorial 'demiurge', which would lead the author, rather than the biographical subject, to dominate the action: 'It is not the business of the biographer to anticipate the discoveries of his hero.'[17] This issue is also treated at some length by Louis Martin-Chauffier, who distinguishes between the narrative perspectives of the novelist and the biographer, respectively. Whereas the novelist is engaged in a gradual discovery of his characters, the biographer needs to deploy the full knowledge that he already possesses of his subject's life so as to include only the significant material within a framework of what must nevertheless be '[a] spiritual investigation'. This makes the composition of a biography 'the progressive construction of pre-existing and total knowledge'.[18] The danger for the biographer is an excessive anticipation of the future, and Martin-Chauffier's comments on the resulting tendency to create 'fake "childhoods"' voice many of Sartre's subsequent objections in *Les Mots* about the 'retrospective illusion' of numerous biographical narratives: 'the biographer has a tendency to see the seeds of the great qualities of the man long before they have borne fruit.'[19] In concluding his analysis, Martin-Chauffier suggests that the boundaries of biography need firm definition in order to outline a distinctive biographical terrain between lifeless historical analysis on the one hand, and the novelistic pastiche (such as René Benjamin's *Balzac*) on the other. The tools of the novelist are an essential prerequisite for biography so long as they do not lead the biographer too far into the domain of imaginative fiction.

The final element of biography that is characteristically adduced by critics in the 1920s is the biographical author himself. (I say 'himself' because biography was still predominantly a male concern and devoted most often to male subjects.)

---

[16] Ibid., p. 69. In this he is again echoing E. M. Forster's *Aspects of the Novel* (ch. 8, 'Pattern and Rhythm').

[17] Ibid., p. 59 [p. 53].   [18] Martin-Chauffier, 'Biographies', p. 394.

[19] Ibid., p. 395. On Sartre's objections see Ch. 15 below. By contrast, René Benjamin takes this predestination to be the biographer's special task, since in real life so few have the skill to see the signs of future genius in the child. In his distinctly romanced life of Balzac he has the child Honoré simply announce to his sister, 'Laure, sais-tu que ton frère sera un grand homme!': René Benjamin, *La Prodigieuse Vie d'Honoré de Balzac* (Le Roman des grandes existences; Paris: Plon-Nourrit, 1925), p. 304.

To speak of an 'author' in connection with biography is not just to refer to a biographical subject (Balzac, Rimbaud, Baudelaire), but to the writer of the biographical text. The authorial status of the biographer in the nineteenth century had been varied: on the one hand, there was the authorial anonymity of the biographical dictionary; and, on the other, there was the professional imprint of a broadly journalistic writer such as Eugène de Mirecourt, or even Sainte-Beuve. As I have already said, the biographical portraits of established literary authors such as Gautier, Baudelaire, Verlaine, or Mallarmé were read largely for their polemical content, and not especially for their literary achievement, that is, as works in their own right. It is only Nerval and Schwob whose biographical writings raise the possibility of being read as literature, but they do so before the recognition of biography as a literary genre. In short, for nineteenth-century biography, the biographical subject counts for much more than the biographical author. With the 1920s this changes, and it is the biographical author who becomes the criterion of biographical achievement. In his survey of the various biographical series that were being published at the time, André Chaumeix notes the eclecticism of the 'heroes' of these books: 'princes jostle with poets, statesmen with royal mistresses, philosophers with great sea-captains, musicians with financiers; they are a ragbag of eccentrics, men of wisdom and revolutionaries; one even comes across a famous vagabond.'[20] He finds it easier to categorize these lives on the basis of their authors, whom he divides into just three kinds, than of their subjects. And if, after his condemnation of most biographical writing, he is nevertheless prepared to identify a redeeming feature, it is in the author, rather than its 'heroes', let alone its readers. He defends Plutarch's *Parallel Lives* on the grounds of the author's particular personal qualities, not on the merits of the Greek and Roman subjects themselves, citing Plutarch's 'taste for lives, and his sense of grandeur, moral beauty, and horror' (p. 707). In any case, he says, the relative precariousness of biography as compared with other literary genres means that its success depends peculiarly on the talent of its authors: 'It is worth as much as its author', and 'the painter counts for more than his subject' (p. 708).

Maurois, too, makes much of the author's stake in biography. On the one hand, there are the specific skills that the biographer requires for the construction of his narrative and for the overall composition of the text. But, in addition, there are some skills that largely belong to the creative artist: for instance, the biographer needs to preserve an aesthetic objectivity towards his material, and to avoid moralizing intrusions. Furthermore, the greatest biographers treat poetic themes in a manner that produces effects of the same order as those of great literary texts: 'A biographer, such as Mr Strachey, who has the power to diffuse through his record of facts the poetic idea of Destiny, of the passage of time, of the fragility of human fortune, brings us in fact a secret comfort.'[21] But perhaps what interests Maurois most of all is the creative experience of the (biographical)

---

[20] Chaumeix, '*Goût des biographies*' p. 698.   [21] Maurois, *Aspects*, p. 126 [p. 127].

author himself. The creative process, he argues, allows creative artists to free themselves from overpowering emotions which can find expression in no other form, and which give the resulting work a unique intensity. It is this thought that prompts him to consider the possibility that the same process might also apply to biography:

Now let us enquire whether biography, like the novel and autobiography, can be a means of expression, whether it can be an opportunity for the expression of strong emotions which the author has felt, whether, like the art-forms of which we have just spoken, it can have the benefit of a passion within itself and, in short, whether this way of looking at it is legitimate and does not endanger truth. (p. 105 [p. 104])

He concludes that he can indeed find no grounds for excluding the biographer from the experience that he attributes to autobiographers and novelists. His claim could be read as a further device to promote biography to full literary status on grounds that keep it on the right side of the divide between 'serious' literature and fictional vulgarization. For, as we have seen, the literarization of biography was an ambivalent strategy, which, in altering the criteria according to which biography functions, opened up the possibility of both an enhancement of its status and a debasement through its vulgarization. However, Maurois himself was happy to subtitle the 1929 edition of *Ariel, ou la vie de Shelley* with the generic marker '*roman*' ('novel', translated as 'A Shelley Romance'), as if to clinch the implication of his prefatory 'Note for the well-disposed reader', where he presents himself as, above all, a novelist: 'In this book, we have sought to emulate the novelist rather than the historian or the critic.' Not only did Maurois attempt to point his own biographies in the direction of an enhanced literary status, but his comments about biographical writing as a form of authorial expression introduce something quite new, with substantial, if very different, implications for the practice of biography. For the issue he is raising is that of the creative experience itself, seen here from the point of view of the author of biography, and not just from that of its artistic subjects.

THE CREATIVE EXPERIENCE

The creative process was a topic that had attracted renewed interest in the early years of the twentieth century, inspired, in part, by the work of Henri Bergson. This preoccupation would have implications for forms of biographical narrative in spheres outside the generic framework of biography as it was conceived at the time. The *élan vital* outlined in Bergson's *L'Évolution créatrice* (1907) reactivates the forward-looking perspective of the organicist thought of the early nineteenth century. In general, biography itself had become subsumed into a model of deterministic explanation, whereby the work was explained by the life and the life by the historical times. Interpretation, whether historical, aesthetic, or scientific, was always the product of this backward look. In contrast, Bergson's emphasis on the creative force in life shifted the focus away from this determinist framework of causative explanation and towards a future that was open and unpredictable: 'The direction of this action is not predetermined; hence the unforeseeable variety of forms which life, in evolving, sows along its path.'[22] Although Bergson himself was not specifically concerned with the phenomenon of artistic or literary creation, his interest in a generalized creativity and the resulting reorientation of perspective towards the future lent themselves to an aesthetic application.

One of the clearest theorizations of this application is to be found in the work of the critic and Nerval specialist Pierre Audiat, whose study *La Biographie de l'œuvre littéraire*, published in 1924, sought to outline the basis for an understanding of the literary work in the light of a broadly Bergsonian perspective. He contrasts his own approach with conventional critical procedures which explained the work in the light of the author's past and gave biography its explanatory function. Instead, Audiat argues, the work should be given its own biography, since it is written over the course of a particular period of time; being the product of the mental life of the author at the moment in which he or she creates it, it evolves during this period in response to the way its human author evolves. The inner life of the author is a continuous process, but within that process, there are privileged moments that give rise to the creation of works of art: 'there are moments of mental activity that are, so to speak, privileged. [. . .] In the mental life of a writer, these privileged acts, these moments of greater contraction are clearly his works. Imagining and writing a literary work correspond to a happy period of mental activity.'[23] It is this happy present of the author's inner life, rather than the past of his biography, that informs the literary work. This in turn makes the work a living entity with its own temporality, which is that of an unfolding present, not a sum-total of past determinations. For this reason the literary critic needs to be as much a psychologist as a historian; and from this perspective he is dealing not with the history of the author's individual psyche, as the conventional biographers of the period do, but with the 'moment of human activity that is the work of literature'.[24] Audiat's aim is to devise a critical strategy that will be adequate to this conception of the literary work as the manifestation of the creative impulse associated with the privileged moments of the author's mental life. In an argument that anticipates the critical principles of Georges Poulet some twenty-five years later, he proposes that reading be seen as the means whereby the author's mental state may be recreated on the basis

---

[22] Henri Bergson, *L'Évolution créatrice* (1907; Paris: Presses universitaires de France, 1948), p. 97 [p. 102].

[23] Pierre Audiat, *La Biographie de l'œuvre littéraire: esquisse d'une méthode critique* (Paris: H. Champion, 1924), p. 38.

[24] Ibid., p. 56.

of the work itself:[25] reading thus reconstitutes what Audiat calls the 'biography of the work', while the author's biography, as more conventionally understood, vanishes altogether from the critic's consideration. This approach might appear as nothing more than a polemical play on the term 'biography', designed to displace its more familiar application. But the intense preoccupation with creativity conceived as a special moment in the author's inner life, in which his entire being is implicated, continues to make the author's existence central to literary (and critical) concerns. By reconceiving the terms in which the question 'Where does the literary work come from?' might be answered, Audiat is inviting a new approach to the author's life, one in which a distinctive creative experience is itself an essential part.

It is precisely this approach to the author's life that writers themselves were exploring at the time, as we shall see over the course of the next two chapters. In an essay written in 1920 Paul Valéry confronts the issue head on when he states:

The so-called lessons of literary history scarcely [. . .] touch on the arcana of a poem's generation. Everything happens inside the artist, as if the observable events of his existence had only a superficial influence on his work. The most important thing—the very act of the Muses—is independent of any adventures, way of life, incidents, and everything that can be included in a biography.[26]

Valéry goes on to attempt a description of this 'arcane generation of a poem' as it is lived by the poet himself. He acknowledges the huge diversity of the elements that can go into a poem, 'the chance events of memory, attention, or sensation', and to the unknown as well as to the known origins of its substance. He despairs of ever arriving at a precise record of these matters, and suggests that it is a reality that is best imagined since it cannot be recorded: 'I imagine the poet, a mind full of ruses and resources, feigning sleep at the imaginary heart of his still uncreated work, so as better to await that moment of his own power which is his prey. In the indistinct depths of his eyes, all the force of his desire and all the resources of his instincts are stretched taut.'[27] The literary work is the product of an inexhaustible and unrecordable number of sources in the author's experience, not all of which he can be aware of himself, and which can at best be captured in imagination. Valéry's recourse to an imagined representation of literary creativity chimes with some of the strategies of the romanced biographies of the period, and certainly shares with them the preoccupation with the inner stage on which the drama of creation is assumed to be acted out.

---

[25] For a summary of Georges Poulet's critical assumptions see his 'Criticism and the Experience of Interiority', in Richard Macksey and Eugenio Donato (eds.), *The Structuralist Controversy: The Languages of Criticism and the Sciences of Man* (Baltimore: Johns Hopkins University Press, 1972), pp. 56–88.

[26] Paul Valéry, 'Au sujet d'*Adonis*', in id., *Variété* (Paris: Gallimard, 1924), pp. 41–90 (p. 69).

[27] Ibid., pp. 70–1.

These various accounts of creativity shift the idea of literature away from issues of form, and come very close to making literariness equivalent to the creative experience that generates the work. As a genre, biography is limited in its capacity to accommodate such experience, even if the literarized variant that emerged in the 1920s may be read as an attempt to respond to it. However, the biographies that writers wrote about themselves— their *auto*biographies—had infinitely more potential to do justice to this experience. The mental life of the author is better conveyed by its subject than by a third-party biographer, if only because the present tense, which is an essential component of autobiography, allows the author's mental life to be enacted while he is also writing about it. In consequence, it could be plausibly claimed that the forms taken by the literarization of autobiography in the 1920s are far more wide-reaching and radical than those developed in the field of biography *tout court*. But this is to run ahead of my argument, and it is time now to turn to Proust, whose apparently autobiographical novel nevertheless places the issue of biography at the core of its exploration of the inwardness of the creative process.

12

Proust and the Lives of the Artists

> Proust is the massive, daring entry of the author, the writing subject as biographologue into literature.
>
> (Roland Barthes)

Unlike the *vies romancées*, which were largely contemporary with the (partly posthumous) publication of *À la recherche du temps perdu* over the course of the 1920s, Proust's monumental work presents itself quite straightforwardly as a novel, not as a biography, romanced or otherwise.[1] It is one of only two fictional texts that I shall be discussing in this book, and I have included it as an exception to my rule because it does far more than tell the story of a fictional life: the very question of biography lies at its heart, and is inextricably bound up with the question of the status and significance of the literature to which the book aspires. It is in this sense that the novel could be said to emerge from Proust's discussion of the biographical method in his *Contre Sainte-Beuve*, where questions of biography are the means whereby he sets out to explore ideas about art in general and to consider the very definition of the aesthetic:

it seems to me that I would have things that have their importance perhaps to say about Sainte-Beuve, and presently much more in connection with him than about him, that by showing where he sinned, in my view, both as writer and as critic, I should perhaps come to say some things about which I have often thought as to what criticism should be and what art is. [. . .] And then, having criticized [his contemporaries] and at the same time letting go of Sainte-Beuve altogether, I shall try to say what art would have been for me.[2]

---

[1] Only the first four of the seven volumes of *La recherche* were published during Proust's lifetime, beginning with *Du côté de chez Swann* in 1913 and *À l'ombre des jeunes filles en fleur* in 1919. The final three volumes appeared after Proust's death in 1922, between 1923 and 1927.

[2] Proust, *Contre Sainte-Beuve*, p. 219 [p. 10]. Pierre Clarac, in the 'Notice' to this edition, vigorously condemns the idea that *Contre Sainte-Beuve* might be regarded as the origin of *La Recherche*: 'aucun des textes ne nous impose cette idée hors de vraisemblance que le grand roman est sorti de l'essai critique et que l'essai critique n'a eu qu'à se développer pour devenir un grand roman' (p. 827). However, Antoine Compagnon, in his preface to *Du côté de chez Swann*, argues—convincingly, to my mind—that the novel does indeed emerge from the combination of essay and fiction of which *Contre Sainte-Beuve* is composed: 'L'originalité du roman proustien tient beaucoup à la réflexion critique qui l'a précédé. La fiction y est inséparable d'une théorie de la littérature, car c'est à la faveur d'une réflexion critique que Proust est passé des ébauches

Contrary to what is frequently claimed, and to what might be inferred from this quotation, these ideas about art are not a simple refusal on Proust's part of Sainte-Beuve's 'method'; they are, rather, a critique of the manner in which Sainte-Beuve connected the life of an author with the work. Put at its simplest, Proust objects—rightly or wrongly—that Sainte-Beuve substitutes the author for the work because he failed to see that 'a book is the product of a self other than that which we display in our habits, in company, in our vices'.[3] What Proust never suggests is that there should be no connection between the two. Indeed, the very subject matter of *La Recherche* presupposes that they are connected, and everything then turns on the issue of how this connection might be understood, both in the case of the various fictional artists depicted in the work, and in that of the narrator himself. I shall return to this issue and these examples below, but first I need to consider the question of the function of fiction in this work, since it is the frame within which these biographical issues appear.

Fiction in the *vies romancées* was the licence that biography borrowed from the novel in order to enhance the inner truth of the biographical representation. Imagined scenes (like the one which Mauriac abandoned, but which others freely deployed), imaginary conversations (which all of them include), imaginative empathy with the writer's inner life, and the technical strategies borrowed from fiction all ultimately aligned the *vie romancée* with the development of the novel proper. In such fictionalized biographies lives may be imagined from beginning to end, but the genre lends itself to the supposition, commonly held by readers and critics alike, that the author has imaginatively transposed his or her own existence into the world of the fiction. *La Recherche* has also frequently been read on this assumption: the fictional 'je' as a transposition of the author's real 'I', Marcel of Proust, Charlus of Robert de Montesquiou, Françoise of Félicité and Céleste in combination, Combray of Illiers, and so on.

It is not, however, in this sense that Proust's recourse to fiction may best be understood, because from this perspective the fictional text would simply refer back to the life that is supposedly its origin, and be no different therefore from the *vies romancées* whose scenes and dreams are borrowed from fiction and coolly slipped to their author-heroes. Instead, one may see the fiction of *La Recherche* as the means whereby the very question of the relation between the life and the work can be introduced as a matter to be contemplated in its own right: fiction here is the ground for a consideration of the place of the life, rather than vice versa. The story is that of a fictional character who tells the story of his (fictional) life in the first person; or, as Proust put it in a letter written in 1913: 'I don't know if I told

---

fragmentées à l'œuvre. La *Recherche du temps perdu* est issue des pages sur Sainte-Beuve que Proust a rédigées au début de 1909': Antoine Compagnon, 'Préface', in Marcel Proust, *Du côté de chez Swann* (Collection Folio; Paris: Gallimard, 1988), pp. vii–xxxv (p. xiii).

[3] *Contre Sainte-Beuve*, pp. 221–2. There are instances in Sainte-Beuve's work where Proust could be said to be right, but, as I have argued in Ch. 6 above, the underlying principles of Sainte-Beuve's criticism would indisputably prove him wrong.

you that the book was a novel. At least, the novel is still what it departs from least. There is a gentleman who narrates and who says I.'[4] It is in the context of the narrative of this gentleman's fictional autobiography that the question of the relation of biography to art is both enacted and explicitly discussed. Moreover, the gentleman who says 'I' is not just the narrator of the novel, but is revealed at the end to be its author. Readers are thus encouraged to place the origins of the text not in any 'real-life' biographical sources associated with Proust, but in the fictional world that describes Marcel's previous life up to the point when he begins to write. This means that there is no need to seek an exit from the fictional world to an external, explanatory source. The fictional world of the novel is presented as a given within which everything else is staged—biography included. Any connection with the real life of Marcel Proust would need to take its cue from the terms in which the novel itself explores the issue.

BIOGRAPHICAL READINGS

There are several biographical subjects contained in the novel: the narrator, whose story is told in the first person, and the various artists whose lives he depicts (in the third person). As Gérard Genette has written, the action of the novel can be summarized in the briefest of formulae: 'Marcel becomes a writer'. This biographical content makes of *La Recherche*, variously, an account of 'the progression of a vocation', the story of 'an unheroic hero of the adventure of writing', and 'the narrative of an apprenticeship',[5] all of which may be considered as providing the framework for a literary biography. While it is undeniable that this narrative is the principal one, it evolves in relation to the lives of other artists, notably Bergotte, Elstir, and Vinteuil. Michel Butor has written of 'the imaginary works of art in Proust', but the novel has far more to say about the lives of the artists than about their work.[6]

Proust himself was an avid consumer of biographical information about the authors and artists whose work interested him,[7] and he portrays many of his

---

[4] Proust, letter to René Blum, 1913, quoted in Jean-Yves Tadié, *Proust et le roman: essai sur les formes et techniques du roman dans 'À la recherche du temps perdu'* (1971; Collection Tel; Paris: Gallimard, 1995), p. 22. See his ch. 1 for an account of the reduction of autobiographical material in *La Recherche* as compared with the unfinished, third-person novel *Jean Santeuil*.

[5] Jean-Yves Tadié, 'Introduction générale', in Marcel Proust, *À la recherche du temps perdu*, ed. Jean-Yves Tadié et al., 4 vols. (Bibliothèque de la Pléiade; Paris: Gallimard, 1987), vol. i, p. ix (all further references to *La Recherche* are to this edition); Roland Barthes, *La Préparation du roman I et II: Cours et séminaires au Collège de France, 1978–1979 et 1979–1980*, ed. Nathalie Léger (Paris: Éditions du Seuil/IMEC, 2003), p. 155; Gilles Deleuze, *Proust et les signes*, 7th edn. (Paris: Presses universitaires de France, 1986), p. 10 [p. 4].

[6] See Michel Butor, 'Les Œuvres d'art imaginaires chez Proust', in id., *Répertoire*, vol. ii: *Études et conférences, 1949–1963* (Paris: Éditions de Minuit, 1964), pp. 252–92.

[7] '[L]ui-même s'est constamment montré curieux de la vie des écrivains et des artistes qu'il aimait, interrogeant sur ceux qui étaient vivants, comme Hardy, ou lisant des biographies, des

characters as having an unshakeably biographical *parti pris* in their assumptions about art and literature. Mme de Villeparisis is commonly regarded as the most inveterate of these, although she represents a largely negative instance of such biographizing habits: not only does she write her own Memoirs, but she defends a biographical perspective very similar to the one that Proust attributes to Sainte-Beuve:

She possessed the autographs of all these great men [Chateaubriand, Balzac, Hugo, et al.], and seemed, presuming on the personal relations which her family had had with them, to think that her judgement of them must be better founded than that of young people who, like myself, had had no opportunity of meeting them. 'I think I have a right to speak about them, since they used to come to my father's house; and as M. Sainte-Beuve, who was a most intelligent man, used to say, in forming an estimate you must take the word of people who saw them close to and were able to judge more exactly their worth.'[8]

In claiming that personal acquaintance with 'great men' gives her a privileged basis for judging them, Mme de Villeparisis is promoting the life of the author over the work. The fact that Chateaubriand, Balzac, and Hugo visited her parents' house supposedly grants her superior insight, and she condones her father's view of Stendhal as 'appallingly vulgar' in light of his behaviour on the occasions when he had met the novelist in society. But her prejudices are qualified and implicitly refuted by the fact that her own literary gifts compromise her social position, and this introduces a tension between her socially based critical *parti pris* and the social reality of her own experience as a writer.

The case of Mme de Villeparisis should nevertheless not be taken as a sign of an outright rejection of biography, as Proust's own fascination with the lives of writers suggests. In his (relatively unromanced) biography of Proust, André Maurois cites a comment contributed by Proust at the age of 13 to the 'album' of a young acquaintance: in reply to the question 'Which faults do you have the most indulgence for?', he wrote—'For the private life of geniuses.'[9] The private life of the genius is precisely what fascinates the two adolescent acquaintances of the novelist 'C.' in Proust's first attempt at fiction, *Jean Santeuil*, where one of the young admirers introduces C.'s novel with a preface describing their encounter

---

correspondances, de Balzac et Ruskin à Musset et à Sainte-Beuve': Jean-Yves Tadié, *Marcel Proust: biographie* (Paris: Gallimard, 1996), p. 12.

[8] *La Recherche*, vol. ii, p. 70 [vol. i, p. 764].

[9] André Maurois, *À la recherche de Marcel Proust* (Geneva: Édito-Service, 1976), p. 13. This biography, first published in 1949, plays on the title of Proust's novel, but relies far more explicitly than did Maurois's biographies of the 1920s on documentary research and oral testimony for its material, and far less on overt imaginative recreation. Maurois describes the underlying principle of his biography as follows: 'L'histoire de Marcel Proust est, comme le décrit son livre, celle d'un homme qui a tendrement aimé le monde magique de son enfance; qui [. . .] a consacré les années qui lui restaient à recréer cette enfance perdue et les désillusions qui l'avaient suivie; qui enfin a fait, du temps ainsi retrouvé, la matière d'une des plus grandes œuvres romanesques de tous les temps' (p. 3). Maurois's scholarly credentials were well enough regarded for him to have been invited to write the general preface to the first Pléiade edition of *La Recherche*, published in 1954.

with the great writer. The pair are witness to the novelist's life during the summer holiday that they spend in his company, and they persuade him to read to them from the novel he is writing at the time. When C. tells them that 'the things that he wrote were strictly true narratives', and claims that 'he had no capacity for invention and could write only what he had personally felt',[10] this awakens in the boys a burning desire to discover for themselves the biographical truths behind C.'s work:

to what extent was he in what he had written, had he known the Duc de Réveillon, could we, by going to the Marne, see the mill he speaks of, and whose wheel was adorned and reduced to immobility by Virginia creeper? And above all, Jean who, with some of C.'s short-comings, and perhaps more qualities, especially of sensitivity and feeling, but also with more fragile health, had, unlike C., experienced so much suffering, and lacked talent for any art? (ibid.)

C. himself discourages any discussion of these issues, and, according to the narrator of the introduction: 'We dared not question him on these points [. . .]. But, he continues, they interested us more than anything else' (ibid.). The reasons that the boys give for this curiosity are not trivial. Far from it, since they consider such questions to be important enough to warrant devoting a lifetime's enquiry to them:

We thought that a lifetime devoted to solving them would be well employed, because it would be given over to the knowledge of matters which we loved above all else, and we should learn what are the secret relations, the necessary metamorphoses, which exist between a writer's life and his work, between reality and art, or, rather, as we then thought, between appearance and the reality which is the solid ground on which they are based and that art alone has revealed. (ibid.*)

Although the adult author of this preface is surprised and a little shamefaced to admit that this grand project for his life could have been so quickly forgotten when he returned to Paris at the end of his holiday, his curiosity about the writer's life and its connection with the work is nevertheless shared by many of the characters in *La Recherche*, and most notably by Marcel himself.

When Swann first hears the Vinteuil sonata, he immediately assumes that the great musician ('a man of genius') and the insignificant music teacher from Combray ('a silly old fool'[11]) could not possibly be the same person, and his first response to the music is a desire to know more, not just about the work but about the life of its composer: 'he asked for information about this Vinteuil: what else he had done, at what period in his life he had composed the sonata, and what meaning the little phrase could have had for him—that was what Swann wanted most to know' (i, p. 209 [i, p. 231]). This is unrestrained biographical curiosity

---

[10] Marcel Proust, *Jean Santeuil; précédé de, Les Plaisirs et les jours*, ed. Pierre Clarac and Yves Sandre (Bibliothèque de la Pléiade; Paris: Gallimard, 1971), p. 190 [p. 18].

[11] *La Recherche*, vol. i, p. 211 [p. 233*].

in combination with an unembarrassed belief in authorial intention. But, unlike Mme de Villeparisis, Swann starts with the work rather than the man, and the biographical urge is a direct consequence of an encounter with Vinteuil's music, not a substitute for it.

Marcel is even more inveterately biographical in his responses than Swann, for he is not merely curious about the lives of the artists whose work he discovers, but cannot make any sense of them independently of a biographical construct. He finds himself unable to take seriously the work of a new writer after learning that he has a strong physical resemblance to his friend Bloch: 'The latter's image thenceforth loomed over the printed pages, and I no longer felt under compulsion to make the effort necessary to understand them' (ii, p. 624 [ii, p. 339]). Reading Bergotte prompts him to construct an image of the author on the basis of the work: 'From his books I had formed an impression of Bergotte as a frail and disappointed old man, who had lost some of his children and had never got over the loss' (i, p. 95 [i, p. 104]). This fantasy is not a gratuitous by-product of Marcel's reading of the texts, but it sets up a circularity that determines the way Marcel continues to read the books that generated this image of their author in the first place: 'And so I would read, or rather sing his sentences in my mind, with rather more *dolce*, rather more *lento* than he himself had perhaps intended, and his simplest phrase would strike my ears with something peculiarly gentle and loving in its intention' (i, pp. 95–6 [i, p. 104]). When he eventually meets Bergotte in person, he discovers that the novelist is not 'the gentle Bard with the snowy locks' of his readerly conjecture, but 'a youngish, uncouth, thickset and myopic little man, with a red nose curled like a snail-shell and a goatee beard' (i, p. 537 [i, p. 589]). The lovingly elaborated biographical image instantly crumbles, and can be of no further use in understanding the work. This abrupt disillusion is similar to Marcel's discovery that the Duchesse de Guermantes in the flesh bears no resemblance to the latter-day Geneviève de Brabant of his imagining. But the case of the writer differs from that of the Duchess in that Marcel's disappointment, rather than curing him of his initial fantasy, has the effect of inciting him to develop and refine his understanding of the relation of the man to the work.

This process leads to far more than a single insight on Marcel's part, and the encounter with each of the artists he meets in the novel incites him, in one way or another, to continue his exploration of this question. As a result, Marcel realizes an infinitely more thoroughgoing version of the project envisioned by the young acquaintances of C. when they plan to devote their lives to mapping the relations between the novelist's life and his art. Not only could Marcel be said to be doing this for the three major artist figures in *La Recherche* but, in addition to his perspective as a reader, listener, or viewer of the works of others, he spends a lifetime meditating on the principles behind the role his own life might play in his vocation to become an author in his own right.

It is in this way that *La Recherche* may be regarded as an advance on *Jean Santeuil*. Proust's thinking about biography and its relations to the literary began in a decade during which, as we have already seen, others were also actively preoccupied with this issue. More precisely, the years during which Proust was working on *Jean Santeuil* (1895–9) coincide with the publication of Schwob's *Vies imaginaires* (1896), Rémy de Gourmont's *Livre des masques* (1896–8), and Mallarmé's *Médaillons et portraits en pied* (1897). His interest in the question of biography was reignited in *Contre Sainte-Beuve* (written in 1909), and culminated finally in the novel (*La Recherche*) which emerged from the *Sainte-Beuve* and which was begun in the latter part of the same year. The presence of Mallarmé, Gourmont, and Schwob in the context of these concerns introduces the possibility of seeing in *La Recherche* a kind of *recueil* containing the biographies of three major artists in the manner of Mallarmé or Rémy de Gourmont. It also leads me to hypothesize that Proust's novel might be viewed as a radical reinterpretation of biography as the basis of literary creation, in the manner of Marcel Schwob. There is, however, more that separates Proust from Schwob—at least as regards the content of their respective 'theories'—than separates Proust from Mallarmé: Vinteuil and Bergotte are both dead at the time of Marcel's writing, a fact that gives their portraits the necrological character of Mallarmé's retrospective portraits; and Proust also shares with Mallarmé the notion that art is the apotheosis of a unique individuality and the basis of the artist's immortality. Nonetheless, both Mallarmé and Schwob remain suggestive points of reference, and I shall come back to them in what follows. In outlining the history of the relations between literature and biography, it is important to plot Proust's position inside this larger picture: that is, poised between the nineteenth-century practices that culminated in Mallarmé and Schwob, respectively (1890s), and with a recourse to fiction whose role he extends far further into new territory than the *vies romancées* of the early part of the twentieth century ever did.

LIVES OF THE ARTISTS

If a major strand in *La Recherche* consists of a reworking of the biographical *recueil*, one of the most important elements of this reworking involves placing the consideration of the artistic lives within a life, making it part of the life-story of the hero-narrator. Unlike many of the nineteenth-century *recueils* in which lives were mobilized to support a literary position that its author had already formulated and often expressed in a preface (e.g. Gautier, Verlaine, Rémy de Gourmont), there is a constant to-and-fro between what Marcel discovers about the lives of his artists and his own understanding of aesthetic issues. This means that biographical information almost always takes on the character of a lesson for him. In this Marcel reactivates the tradition of exemplarity, which treated 'lives' as the pretext for (moral) instruction; in so far as it contributes above all to his developing understanding of life, art, and the relations between them, however, the instruction derived by Marcel is less moral than aesthetic. The lessons that the lives of these artists provide are largely complementary, and tend towards the same ultimate insights. The lives and their associated examples are nevertheless sufficiently varied to warrant an examination of each case by turn.

Bergotte

Although Bergotte is the only one of the three artists to be introduced after Marcel's encounter with the work, very little is said specifically about Bergotte's novels, and the only one of his publications referred to in any detail is a pamphlet on Racine.[12] I have already discussed the shock that Marcel experiences on discovering how different the real and the imaginary versions of Bergotte are; and the first major lesson for which Bergotte is the pretext turns on the discovery of the difference between life and art, man and work. Having begun with the works, rather than with the man, Marcel is encouraged in his belief that artists exist on a quite other, infinitely more elevated plane than that of the everyday world of ordinary mortals: 'upon almost everything in the world his opinion was unknown to me. I had no doubt that it would differ entirely from my own, since his came down from an unknown sphere towards which I was striving to raise myself'(i, p. 94 [i, p. 103]). This other world is the one where Marcel assumes works of art are made, and where artists live their exalted lives, only occasionally deigning to descend to the world of the everyday. When he imagines Bergotte's conversation at the Swanns' dinner table, it is as a form of 'oracle'; and when he pictures the novelist visiting distant cities in the company of Gilberte, the image conjured up of Bergotte is one where 'he would be walking by her side, unrecognized and glorious, like the gods who came down of old to dwell among mortals ' (i, p. 99 [i, p. 108]). It is this (false) view of the separation of the artist from the real world that the meeting with Bergotte decisively and rather disconcertingly destroys.

The artist is suddenly situated in the real world, endowed with all the apparent banality of a socially ambitious and egotistical personality, and with a physical embodiment that, instead of appearing as a 'temple' worthy to house the work, is 'a squat figure, packed tight with blood-vessels, bones, glands, sinews', and 'avid for the coming meal' (i, pp. 537–9 [i, pp. 589–91]). These are the elements of the kind of Sainte-Beuvian biography that Proust disdains, but which Mme de Villeparisis advocates, and they present Marcel with a number of options. Either he can decide, in the manner ascribed to Sainte-Beuve, that the reality of the man provides the final comment on the work, a view that, in this case, would imply that Marcel had largely overestimated Bergotte's writing; or he can decide that the author is entirely irrelevant to the work, which could then be read quite independently of its creator without needing to be house in any biographical. A third option, however, would be to attempt to find another means of reconnecting the two, and this is the one that Marcel chooses to pursue.

12 On this see Michel Butor, 'Les Œuvres d'art imaginaires', p. 252.

He does so on the basis of the disjunction he perceives between the written style of Bergotte's work and his conversational voice: '[His diction] seemed to me to differ entirely from his way of writing, and even the things that he said from those with which he filled his books' (i, p. 540 [i, p. 592]). But, as Marcel listens to '[the] pretentious, turgid and monotonous delivery' of the writer, he comes to realize that it does after all emanate from the same inner source that produces the style: '[it] was a sign of the rare aesthetic value of what he was saying, and an effect, in his conversation, of the same power which, in his books, produced that harmonious flow of imagery' (ibid.). This power, Marcel goes on to see, is, moreover, not the equivalent of a single stamp that is repeatedly placed on the work: what is 'de Bergotte' ('by Bergotte') does not necessarily appear as 'du Bergotte' ('typical of Bergotte'). The writer is engaged in a perpetual attempt to wrest his own 'beauty' from the world, and this makes each discovery a novelty, each sentence inherently unpredictable. In consequence, Marcel not only succeeds in reconnecting man and work, but he also comes to understand that the dynamic of creativity makes a static image like the one in which he had mentally lodged the work quite inappropriate for the reality of the ongoing creative process that unfolds in time. The temporality of the creative life makes biography—or at least a certain kind of biography—an infinitely better frame for the work of art than any temple he could imagine. It also leads to Marcel's realization that Bergotte is more truly himself in his art than in his social life. The argument of *Contre Sainte-Beuve* had already distinguished between 'le moi social' ('the social self') and 'le moi profond' ('the deeper self'). But the opposition is less starkly expressed in *La Recherche*, where it is presented as a question about where the self is more 'real': Bergotte is more fully himself in his books than in the social world, and from the writer's own perspective 'his true life' is in literature, not in 'his own personal life' (i, p. 548 [i, p. 601]). The point, however, remains—that a life is lived, at one level or another, in books as well as in the world.

The final 'lesson' that Marcel learns from the example of Bergotte comes with his death, when Proust takes advantage of the novelist's imaginative licence to grant Marcel access to Bergotte's dying reflections. At the moment of his death, as he stands before Vermeer's *Vue de Delft*, Bergotte is struck down by an attack which he attributes to the undercooked potatoes he had eaten for lunch (a lunch for which his unprepossessing body had perhaps been too greedy), and is simultaneously granted a final artistic insight. This makes Bergotte himself (as well as Marcel) the recipient of a 'lesson' by another artist. He sees the painting as he has never seen it before, and the 'little patch of yellow wall' becomes an emblem of the way he now realizes he should have written: 'That's how I should have written' (iii, p. 692 [iii, p.185*]). This revelation takes the form of an image in which Bergotte sees his own life and Vermeer's patch of yellow wall placed on either side of a set of 'celestial scales': 'He felt that he had rashly sacrificed the former for the latter' (ibid.). But if Bergotte feels that he has sacrificed too much of his art to the demands of his life, he is nevertheless granted the possibility of a

kind of posthumous redemption in the form of a literary afterlife of the kind that
Mallarmé envisaged for the poets he celebrates in his prose portraits and poetic
tombeaux: 'He was dead. Dead forever? Who can say?' (iii, p. 693 [iii, p. 186]).
The question remains undecided, but a final image holds out the promise of
some form of artistic immortality: 'They buried him, but all through that night
of mourning, in the lighted shop-windows, his books, arranged three by three,
kept vigil like angels with outspread wings and seemed, for him who was no
more, the symbol of his resurrection' (ibid.). Bergotte's life ends on a note that
points in two apparently opposed directions: an excessive investment in earthly
things (lunch, or his life in general), and the transcendence of a literary afterlife.
Even if the world has played too much a part in his life, and the redemption is
no more than a hypothesis, the two are nevertheless put in relation with each
other in a manner that goes well beyond a choice between, on the one hand,
the biographical literalism of a 'Sainte-Beuvian' approach, and, on the other,
Marcel's initial image of Bergotte's exclusively Elysian existence.

Elstir

Just as Bergotte's final lesson as a writer comes from the example of Vermeer, so
Marcel, too, learns his next lesson from a painter. His aim is to become a writer,
but the principles of creation transcend the techniques of particular art forms,
and the question of the ways in which the life relates to the work remain the same
in every sphere, whether literature, painting, or music. In the figure of Elstir,
Marcel is once again presented with a disjunction between the man and the artist,
which the painter's own 'lessons' help him to overcome. The man and the work
appear in Marcel's life more or less simultaneously during his stay in Balbec,
but it subsequently transpires that Elstir is none other than the M. Biche who
frequented the Verdurin salon at the time of Swann's love affair with Odette. The
problem posed by this for Marcel is not that of how to match the man with the
image projected by his work (as was the case with Bergotte), but how the jejune
salonnier who uses the word 'caca' ('poo') to describe a painting, and who is
commissioned by Mme Verdurin to produce a portrait of Cottard's smile, should
be matched with the mature artist who paints the *Port de Carquethuit* and is so
impressively articulate about his art: 'Could it possibly be that this man of genius,
this sage, this recluse, this philosopher with his marvellous flow of conversation,
who towered over everyone and everything, was the ridiculous, perverted painter
who had at one time been adopted by the Verdurins?' (ii, p. 218 [i, pp. 922–3]).
When Elstir acknowledges that he is indeed the M. Biche from Mme Verdurin's
salon, it is not in order to have recourse to the argument of *Contre Sainte-Beuve*
about the need to distinguish between a creative and a social self. Neither is it
to subscribe to the philosophy of the discontinuity of the self exemplified by
so many other characters in the novel. On the contrary, Elstir argues that an
artist needs to accept as a part of himself the times in his life that he might

otherwise prefer to forget, because such moments are necessary stages on the way to becoming 'a wise man', and contribute to producing the self who in turn produces the art. Such episodes are, says Elstir, 'a proof that we have really lived, that it is in accordance with the laws of life and of the mind that we have, from the common elements of life, of the life of studios, of artistic groups—assuming one is a painter—extracted something that transcends them' (ii, p. 219 [i, p. 924]). Thus, while M. Biche is not the truth behind the art, he is nevertheless a necessary and inseparable component of the lived realities out of which that art is created.

This grounding of art in everyday existence is also demonstrated by Elstir's painting. Elstir paints what he sees in the world around him—portraits, still lifes, landscapes—but transforms them by means of his unique individual vision that is the product of the life he has lived. In this way all his portraits share a family resemblance; his still lifes may reveal beauty in the most banal objects, but ultimately the subject matter of his paintings is a pretext for his painterly treatment. More particularly, the transcendence he speaks of is produced not by providing a vertical symbolic translation of the physical world, but is an effect of the horizontal equivalences that he creates, on the basis of his personal vision, between different elements of that world: the sea seen in terms of the land, and land in terms of the sea in the *Port de Carquethuit*. Because the vision that metamorphoses the real world is the product of the artist's evolution, the paintings themselves tell the story of the artist's (creative) life. The portraits can be dated not only by the fashions worn by their sitters, but by the development of the artist's own style (ii, p. 218 [i, p. 922]). In sum, the principal lesson that Elstir's life offers to Marcel is this sense of a unique personal vision as the product of a lived life with all its vicissitudes, which is used, within the context of the life that produced it, to create an art that nevertheless transcends it.

Vinteuil

Of the three principal artists in the novel Vinteuil is the most unlikely author of his work. Swann, as we have seen, is quite unable to connect the 'silly old fool' of the local music teacher with the 'man of genius' behind the sonata, except as a possible cousin. Marcel himself well recalls 'the melancholy, respectable little bourgeois whom we used to meet in the Month of Mary at Combray' (iii, p. 765 [iii, p. 263]); but, unlike Swann, he does not allow the memory of this figure to undermine his conviction that '[his] genius is manifested in [his] works' (iv, p. 298 [iii, p. 740]). Marcel's developing acquaintance with the lives and works of other artists makes this instance of incongruity relatively unproblematic, and not shocking (as it was in the case of Bergotte) or implausible (as it appeared to Swann).

The form in which genius manifests itself to Marcel in the case of Vinteuil is twofold, each manifestation contributing to the development of Marcel's aesthetic understanding. The first leads him to the insight that the individuality of the composer amounts to something far greater than a style (which he discerned in Bergotte), or even a vision (which he saw in Elstir), but constitutes a whole world: 'Each artist seems thus to be the native of an unknown country, which he himself has forgotten, and which is different from that whence another great artist, setting sail for the earth, will eventually emerge' (iii, p.761 [iii, p. 258]). The inner world of the artist revealed by his art is where his real individuality lies, and the two are synonymous: 'those worlds which we call individuals and which, without the existence of art, we should never know' (iii, p. 762 [iii, p. 259*]). It is in this valorization of the individual that Proust differs most profoundly from Schwob, for whom the unique could only ever take the form of a single, disruptive detail; for Proust, artistic individuality exists ultimately as an entire universe and constitutes the basis of its coherence.

The second major insight that Marcel acquires from his contemplation of Vinteuil's life in art is his discovery of creation as a certain kind of experience in its own right, and most notably as an experience of joy. Here the contrast between the misery of Vinteuil's domestic life, caused by his daughter, and the rapture of musical composition is most telling, especially when Marcel considers that it is only thanks to the patient deciphering by Mlle Vinteuil's cruel friend of the manuscripts discovered after the composer's death that anyone has access to 'the formula, eternally true and forever fertile, of this unknown joy' conveyed by the music (iii, p. 767 [iii, p. 264]). The creative process is an integral part of the artist's life, an antidote to its sorrows, and a special kind of joy: 'in the sound of these instruments which he had loved, it had been given him to go on living, for an unlimited time, a part at least of his life' (iii, p. 759 [iii, p. 256]). The life lived by Vinteuil in the process of composition brings him more happiness than any other: 'This Vinteuil, whom I had known so timid and sad, had been capable—when he had to choose a timbre and to blend another with it—of an audacity, and in the full sense of the word a felicity, as to which the hearing of any of his works left one in no doubt' (iii, p. 758 [iii, p. 256]). Because of the equivalence that is assumed between the creative experience and the work of art that it produces, this joy is transmitted in turn to its audience: to listen to Vinteuil's music is to share the emotional state in which it was composed, and to be party to the furious energy of the artist in the moment of creation: 'panting, intoxicated, beside himself, giddy, while he painted his great musical fresco' (iii, p. 759 [iii, p. 256*]).

The image of a radical transformation of the individual through the self-fuelling act of creation recalls the privileged moments described by Pierre Audiat in the book which, though written after *Le Temps retrouvé*, was nevertheless published some four years before the appearance of the final volume of *La Recherche* in 1927. The difference, however, is that Marcel's sense of connection with the moment of creation is not the pretext for a redefinition of criticism (as it is for Audiat), but is intimately bound up with the question of his own life, and in particular with the question of his own chances of ever experiencing a similar creative rapture for himself. Proust also differs from Audiat in maintaining a sense of biography that extends beyond the framework of a single composition, and allows for the development of the artist through time. Although both the sonata and the septet belong to the same world (Vinteuil's), the later composition is an advance on the earlier one, and its musicality takes a different form: 'When his vision of the universe is modified, purified, becomes more adapted to his memory of his inner homeland, it is only natural that this should be expressed by a musician in a general alteration of sonorities, as of colours by a painter' (iii, p. 761 [iii, p. 259]). Art may be 'the true life', but it is one that is subject to the temporal laws of development (or of decline, as is suggested in the case of Bergotte). In a word, the artist has a life in time, which means that an overarching biographical perspective still offers the best way of understanding it.

'MARCEL BECOMES A WRITER'

It would be perfectly possible to read the lives of these artists as the vehicle for a theory of art: the emphasis on the independence of art from the social sphere continues a theme that runs throughout literary and artistic manifestos in the nineteenth century (such as Gautier's preface to *Mademoiselle de Maupin*), as do Proust's emphasis on art as transcendence (Mallarmé) and the value he places on individuality as the prerequisite for artistic creation (defended in Gautier's *Les Grotesques*, Sainte-Beuve, *passim*, Verlaine's *Poètes maudits*, or Rémy de Gourmont's *Livre des masques*).[13] However, as I have already suggested, it is not as illustrations of a theory that these lives figure in Proust's text; and, despite the considerable theoretical sophistication of the novel's self-commentary, Marcel's investment in the project of his own personal existence leads him to downgrade theory in favour of the lessons of his own lived experience.

For instance, in recalling Mme de Cambremer's surprise that he could have been so ready to abandon the company of Elstir for that of Albertine, Marcel comments that she has failed to appreciate the nature of 'the lessons through which one serves one's apprenticeship as a man of letters':

In this process the objective value of the arts counts for little; what we have to draw out and bring to light is our feelings, our passions, that is to say the passions and feelings of all mankind. A woman whom we need and who makes us suffer elicits from us a whole gamut of feelings far more profound and more vital than a man of genius who interests us. (iv, pp. 485–6 [iii, p. 944*])

Crudely put, life is a better preparation for art than theory. Indeed, Marcel is frankly hostile to theory: 'Authentic art has no use for proclamations of this kind; it accomplishes its work in silence' (iv, p. 460 [iii, p. 916]). Theory, he says, is indifferent to language and to image, each of which can only be the product of an individual artistic vision, not of any theorizable aesthetic position. And as the example

[13] Anne Henry has shown how thoroughly versed Proust was in nineteenth-century aesthetic theory; see ead., *Marcel Proust: théories pour une esthétique* (Paris: Klincksieck, 1981).

of Elstir himself demonstrates, it is precisely the cultivation of this vision in the day-to-day context of his personal life that makes the artist. These questions are not treated as purely objective problems, but as burning issues that occupy Marcel's own existence. Genette's summary of *La Recherche* is not false, but it excludes the dynamic of the narrative, for Marcel, unlike the various artists he encounters, is not presented as the creator of finished works. The novel is not a demonstration: '*This* is how Marcel became a writer', but a narrative of suspense: '*Will* Marcel become a writer?' It is first and foremost the story of a desire to write,[14] whose realization appears increasingly remote as the novel progresses. Only at the very end does the reader discover that this same narrative has also been the means of its fulfilment: Marcel has written a novel that tells the story of his own desire to write it.

In so far as this second-order narrative does nevertheless allow a retrospective version of a story that finally shows how Marcel becomes a writer, what it demonstrates is that the prerequisite for art is neither a theory, nor even a set of 'lessons', but a life. At the very end of the novel Marcel finds himself shakily perched on top of something that he is surprised to recognize as 'his life'. It is indistinguishable from his own identity, and essential to his literary project:

And I felt [. . .] a sensation of weariness and almost of terror at the thought that all this length of Time had not only, without interruption, been lived, experienced, secreted by me, that it was my life, was in fact me, but also that I was compelled so long as I was alive to keep it attached to me, that it supported me and that, perched on its giddy summit, I could not myself make a movement without displacing it. (iv, p. 624 [iii, p. 1106])

There is no getting away from the fact that he has had a life, or from the fact that this is the life he has had.

If the artist's life is not just an inevitability but a positive necessity for the art, there are two main reasons for this. The first is that Marcel's vision as an artist is the outcome and the product of that life: 'When I considered my past life, I understood also that its slightest episodes had contributed towards giving me the lesson in idealism from which I was going to profit to-day' (iv, p. 489 [iii, p. 948]). This may have been the lesson of Elstir's life, but Marcel has to apply it to his own circumstances for its truth to take effect. The exemplary force of the lives of the artists acquires its true measure through the use that Marcel makes of those examples in his own existence as an artist. The second reason that his life is necessary to his art is that it constitutes the only possible material for this art: 'I understood that all these materials for a work of literature were simply my past life; I understood that they had come to me, in frivolous pleasures, in indolence, in tenderness, in unhappiness, and that I had stored them up without divining the purpose for which they were destined or even their continued existence'

---

[14] Roland Barthes has much to say on the subject of this desire to write, including its relevance to Proust; see id., *La Préparation du roman*, esp. 'Séance du 19 janvier 1980', pp. 275–96 (from which the epigraph to this chapter is taken, p. 278). The issue of the desire to write, and the possibility of separating it from achieved creation will be discussed in Ch. 18 below.

(iv, p. 478 [iii, p. 934]). These two factors combine to constitute a very particular relation between biography and literature. First, the life produces the artist-writer and is the basis of his artistic vision. And secondly, if the author's life becomes the material for his work, then it can no longer be regarded as the explanation of that work. The life is transformed and transcended not by a process of fictionalization or stylization in which it is moved from biographical 'reality' into the created 'work'. Rather, it achieves transcendence only when two of its (lived) elements are unexpectedly placed in analogy with each other through the phenomenon of involuntary memory: the uneven paving stones in the Guermantes courtyard and the flagstones in St Marks, the chink of a spoon against a plate and the sound of a hammer struck against the wheel of a train, etc.; or else, when the subject who is the product of his own life, and still very much within that life, brings his attention to bear on the things in his world that suddenly seem to require it: the flowering hawthorn in Combray, the steeples of Martinville, or, even, it could be said, everything that figures in the world contained in the novel. The spark comes from the association of elements within the lived life of the artist, and on the basis of the vision produced by that life, not from some external or quasi-divine intervention.

Although the moment of revelation in the Hôtel de Guermantes constitutes Marcel as the artist for which his whole life turns out in retrospect to have been a preparation, and although his old life ceases at this point, the future work will nevertheless be created in a context that is still a material life. Moreover, it is one whose organization needs to be actively considered with the writer's literary task in mind: 'For the fundamental fact was that I had a body, and this meant that I was perpetually threatened by a double danger, internal and external' (iv, p. 612 [iii, p. 1092]). Marcel's creative project will depend for its realization on a life that is devoted to nothing else except writing, where the nights are used for work and the days for sleep, precisely in order to preserve the blood vessels, bones, and ganglions that so dismayed him in Bergotte's physique. Without this physiological basis the life that produces writing cannot be sustained, and for this reason does not just precede the art but is the condition for its very production.

Proust's fiction makes the life of the artist an integral part of its aesthetic ambition in a way that manages to raise the stakes for the aesthetic, while simultaneously insisting on the place of the lived experience of the individual. Art which is simply the product of a technique, or which justifies itself on the basis of its representation of a particular content, or even on the grounds of a particular aesthetic theory has nothing to do with the form of Proust's artistic engagement. By making the individual vision the basis of art—all art, and not just literature—Proust is affirming an aesthetic in terms that oppose it to these others, be they formalist, realist, or theoretical. More fundamentally, he is establishing an aesthetic that makes the individual vision the basis for an absolute definition of each art: Vinteuil's music defines all music for as long as one is inside his musical world, and the same goes for Elstir and painting. In Proust's account, Manet replaces Ingres by requiring a total transformation of approach that goes so deep that it is frequently experienced as a move from a masterpiece to 'une horreur' (as happened with Manet's *Olympia*). If time ends up eventually placing the work of both painters on some kind of par, this does nothing to contradict the underlying truth according to which, with the work of each new artist, '[we] imagine ourselves always to be faced with an experience which has no precedents in the past' (ii, p. 713 [ii, p. 436]). In the Proustian scheme there can in a sense be no literary history or any history of music or painting, since each art form is reinvented from the beginning by the unique creation of the individual artist.[15]

The artist's vision is itself the product of an individual existence, and particularly of the inner existence, as Marcel's passionate scrutiny of the lives of the three individual artists reveals. The essence of literature becomes the unique quality that defines the work of each writer as he is encountered, and it is no doubt for this reason that Marcel, as a future writer, is given more to learn from a painter and a musician than from another writer: there is simply nothing that Marcel could inherit from Bergotte as regards the practice of literature. His own work can only be a total and absolute substitution of those that precede it, without any evident process of contestation. All that can be learned from the precursor artist concerns the manner in which he conducts his life in relation to his art. It is this conclusion which Proust's fictional hero arrives at through his insights into the lives of the fictional artists he encounters, and which his own equally fictional life exemplifies in its turn. Proust's novel is much more than a set of fictional biographies, but the portraits of its various artists constitute a sustained meditation on the nature of creativity and its necessary relation to the physical life (Bergotte, Marcel), the social existence (Elstir, Marcel), the inner life (Bergotte, Elstir, Vinteuil), and the experience of creation itself, exemplified above all in the figure of Vinteuil, and consistently aspired to by Marcel. The idea of literature that is contested in all of this is one that treats the absoluteness of literature as a theoretical universal, since for Proust literature is an absolute that exists only as it is constituted by and within the life of the individual writer.

---

[15] On this see Deleuze, *Proust et les signes*: 'Chaque sujet exprime le monde d'un point de vue. Mais le point de vue c'est la différence elle-même, la différence interne absolue' (p. 55).

13

Gide: Autobiography, Fiction, and the Literature of Experience

> literature (where nothing matters but what is personal)
> (André Gide, *Journal*, 24 January 1914)

> It is from the point of view of art that it is most fitting to judge what I write.
> (*Journal*, 13 October 1918)

I have already suggested that the literary turn taken by biography in the 1920s made autobiography a logical development of some of its trends, and it is with Gide's *Si le grain ne meurt* that this logic begins to take form. The question of fiction accompanies Gide's autobiographical writing in various ways: as a threat, as its true potential, and, with regard to Gide's own fictional writing, as a constant point of reference. Similarly, personal experience is presented as the source of authorial creativity, with implications for the very process of writing; and it is through the story of his own life that Gide argues for a view of literature as, in Maurice Blanchot's words, the 'literature of experience'.[1] Like Proust, however, Gide is also an inheritor of the nineteenth-century tradition of biographical writing, and there is much in these 'memoirs'—Gide's preferred term for *Si le grain ne meurt*—to recall the biographical practices of the preceding century. The term 'memoirs' itself shifts the perspective outwards to include a record of others as well as of the self.[2] If, despite the absence of the rubric 'autobiography', Gide inaugurates the tradition of literary autobiography in the twentieth century, he also continues some familiar forms from the nineteenth century in ways that might need to be acknowledged as part of the history I am tracing in this book.

[1] Maurice Blanchot, 'Gide et la littérature d'expérience', in id., *La Part du feu* (Paris: Gallimard, 1949), pp. 208–20. Focused primarily on Gide's *Journal*, Blanchot's discussion goes to the heart of many of the issues I shall be addressing in this chapter and cannot really be bettered.

[2] See Lejeune, *Le Pacte autobiographique*, p. 14 for the distinction between memoirs and autobiography.

GIDE AND THE BIOGRAPHICAL PORTRAIT

In this connection one could mention, for a start, the fact that Gide was a huge admirer of Sainte-Beuve, who is accorded the status of 'unobtrusive but lasting mentor' by one of Gide's recent commentators.[3] He saw in Sainte-Beuve an exemplary interest in the uniqueness of each human drama at work in a text. In the *Interviews imaginaires* of 1942 he writes, for example: 'I am most willingly drawn to those books in which, behind the ramifications of the narrative, and sometimes as if unbeknownst to the author, there is hidden a secret drama which the reader follows with trembling.' Elsewhere he notes in a more conventionally Sainte-Beuvian vein: 'it seems to me that it is through knowledge of the man that one arrives most surely at an understanding of the work.'[4] These remarks do more than merely outline Gide's assumptions as a reader or critic, for, as we shall see later on, they apply equally to his own creative project. Sainte-Beuve is mentioned on a number of occasions in *Si le grain ne meurt* as the author of the *Lundis*, which were amongst Gide's favourite reading from the date when he received them as a birthday present. He also appears in a more comical moment as a female saint, when Gide's tutor, M. Vedel, who lived in the house once occupied by Sainte-Beuve, points out the critic's bust to his pupils: 'This peculiar lady saint was presented to my astonished gaze under the aspect of a paternal old gentleman, wearing a tasselled cap on his head. Monsieur Vedel had indeed told us Sainte-Beuve was "a great critic", but there are limits to a child's credulity.'[5] For the adult, the critic-'saint' nevertheless became, in the words of Pierre Masson, a 'patron saint' of writing.[6]

Sainte-Beuve's legacy is visible in the numerous portraits that make up a substantial part of *Si le grain ne meurt*. Gide includes portraits of members of his family—his uncle Charles Gide, Anna Shackleton as an honorary family member, his cousin Albert Démarest, and so on; of friends such as 'Lionel de R—' (François de Witt) and Armand Bavretel; of the various teachers and tutors responsible for his education—M. Vedel, M. Richard, Mlle de Gœcklin, M. Gueroult, M. Merriman, Marc de la Nux; as well as of the members of the literary world he frequented in his youth. Only the last could be said to constitute literary portraits in the nineteenth-century mode—Gide actually speaks of 'portraits' in this context. And on the whole he has rather more to say about the men—for all the gender ambiguity of 'Sainte-Beuve', the figures in this world are all male

---

[3] Pierre Masson, 'Introduction', in Gide, *Essais critiques*, p. xxxv. On the importance of Sainte-Beuve to Gide, see pp. xxviii–xxxv.

[4] Quoted by Masson, Introduction, pp. xxix, xxxi.

[5] André Gide, *Si le grain ne meurt* (1926; Collection Folio; Paris: Gallimard, 1972), p. 136 [pp. 66–7]).

[6] Masson, 'Introduction', p. xxix.

in Gide's account—than about their work. (I shall return to the issue of the relation between man and work in a moment.) The literary world he describes in these sketches is that of the 1890s, the decade that produced the literary portraits by Mallarmé and Rémy de Gourmont, and the biographical texts of Marcel Schwob's *Vies imaginaires*. Gide mentions all these figures, although he has more to say about Mallarmé in *Si le grain ne meurt* than about the other two writers.[7] His portraits of Henri de Régnier, Viélé-Griffin, and Pierre Louÿs also have their counterparts in Gourmont's *Livre des masques*. The most extensive of these portraits is that of Oscar Wilde, who appears not in the Parisian literary world, but in the context of Gide's North African adventure. The importance that Gide attaches to his account, and in particular to its validity as a likeness of the man, can be inferred from his inclusion of a letter he received from Robert Ross, a friend of Wilde and the executor of his will. In it Ross congratulates Gide on his 'brilliant Souvenirs of Oscar Wilde', and goes on to say that it was 'not only the best account of Oscar Wilde at the different stages of his career, but the only true and accurate impression of him that I have ever read'.[8] In contrast to third-party comments which Gide cites concerning his account of his own life, and which largely provide correctives to Gide's version of events, this one stands out for the author's enthusiastic endorsement of Gide's accuracy.

To describe Gide as a portraitist in the nineteenth-century tradition is to acknowledge that he places more emphasis on portraiture than on biography, in the sense that, even when he knew a particular person over a period of time, he tends, on his own admission, to collapse temporality into a single composite image: 'My readers will understand that in making these portraits, I have collected and put together observations scattered over a period of ten years and more' (p. 256 [p. 207]). This is quite different from the importance that Gide, when he is talking about himself, ascribes to change over time, which, as we shall see, is the basis of the value that he ascribes to experience. The closest Gide could be said to come to innovation in the field of biography proper is in connection with his 'theory' that people with the kind of divided family background that is his own tend to become either artists or arbitrators as a means of accommodating such contradictions. This is more a psychological theory than a strictly biographical one, but he claims to have explored the fifty-two volumes of the *Biographie universelle* (that other great legacy of the nineteenth century) and a number of other biographical works in search of corroboration from other historians of this hypothetical 'law' (p. 90). In short, although biographical portraits make up a

---

[7] He writes at greater length elsewhere about both Rémy de Gourmont and Marcel Schwob; see ' "L'Amateur" de M. Rémy de Gourmont' (written in 1910), in *Essais critiques* (pp. 228–35). He contributed a 'homage' to Schwob after his death (ibid., p. 855), and recalls his visits to Schwob in the 'Feuillets' appended to his *Journal*; see André Gide, *Journal*, new edn., vol. i: *1887–1925*, ed. Éric Marty (Bibliothèque de la Pléiade; Paris: Gallimard, 1996), pp. 1292–3 [vol. ii, pp. 377–8].

[8] *Si le grain ne meurt*, p. 299 (quoted in English in the original).

substantial part of *Si le grain ne meurt*, they have much more in common with those of the 1890s and before than with the forms of biography practised during the decade in which Gide's book appeared.[9]

GIDE AND THE 'NEW' BIOGRAPHY

As well as looking back towards models from the past, Gide's life-writing also looks forward to new forms; but it is much more in the autobiographical dimension of the text than in the biographical one that Gide's preoccupations converge with those of his contemporary biographers. Moreover, it is specifically on the common ground of these preoccupations that the literary aspect of this form of writing emerges as an issue. Biography's new-found concern with the inner life of its subject is, in a sense, a given for autobiography as outlined some fifty years later by Philippe Lejeune, who defines it as the history of a subject where the emphasis is on the development of his personality: '*The retrospective narrative in prose that a real person gives of their own existence when the emphasis is placed on the individual life, and in particular on the history of the personality*'.[10] Gide emphasizes this dimension of what he does not yet call autobiography by stressing something other and more inward than mere 'personality'. This preoccupation recalls the criterion adduced by Louis Martin-Chauffier when he argues that biography should convey '[the] life not the way it unfolded, but *the way he* [the subject] *experienced it*'.[11] This emphasis may well have been partially fostered by Gide's own autobiographical example (Martin-Chauffier was writing in 1928, two years after the publication of *Si le grain ne meurt*), since he repeatedly insists on the primacy of his own vision over factual episode. The narrative of *Si le grain ne meurt* is presented as that of the discovery of his own 'personal morality' (p. 262), or what he later calls 'the tables of my new law' (p. 322 [p. 284*]. For him 'real life' (p. 288 [p. 245]) corresponds to a certain quality of experience, not to external circumstance; so much so that Gide is willing on occasion to allow factual error to stand, on the grounds that the erroneous account is closer to his emotional truth than any more objectively accurate version would be. It is for this reason that the misremembering of a military parade as the entry of the Prussians into Rouen or the misattribution of a ball to his grandmother's lifetime are preferred over his mother's subsequent rectifications of fact. The truth of Gide's distorted memories becomes the basis for his elaboration of the sense of a 'second reality', which each of these misremembered scenes contained for him: 'there is reality and there are dreams; and there is *another reality* as well' (p. 93

---

[9] *Si le grain ne meurt* was published in 1926, although the date of publication is given in the text as 1924.

[10] Lejeune, *Le Pacte autobiographique*, p. 14 (original italics).

[11] See Ch. 11 above.

[p. 17], Gide's italics). This other reality was an integral part of his personal sense of existence ('life as he experienced it'), and its vestiges almost certainly survive in the narrating adult: 'The vague, ill-defined belief that something else exists alongside the acknowledged, above-board reality of everyday life, inhabited me for many years; and I am not sure that even to-day I have not still some remnants of it left' (pp. 93–4 [p. 17]). Gide's inner truth is at times best conveyed by partial fiction in these slightly imaginary versions of reality. Such inward truths are also expressed in the form of the kind of motif which, Maurois suggests, can sum up the quality of a particular existence in the biographer's account of it. The metaphorical motif of water in his own *Ariel* is matched in *Si le grain ne meurt* by the set of motifs related to darkness and light, or by the metaphor of arrested development contained in the image of the 'larva' with which Gide associates his past self. The recurrent metaphors in Gide's text exemplify exactly the kind of poetic truth that was the goal of so many of the biographies of the 1920s.

Furthermore, Gide shares with his contemporary biographers a concern with narrative technique. As a writer of fiction (the various *récits*, the highly self-conscious *'sotie' Les Caves du Vatican*), and with plans for the 'novelist's novel', *Les Faux-monnayeurs*, well under way,[12] Gide was actively aware of the possibilities represented by different forms of narrative organization. In his novels he was keen to explore reality in a variety of narrative modes: not just 'lengthwise', as he has Édouard say in *Les Faux-monnayeurs*, but also 'in breadth', or even 'in depth'.[13] As an autobiographer, he initially refers to these considerations in connection with the principle of veracity, but refuses recourse to any fictionalizing strategies. He repeatedly states that artlessness is the key to the authentic ordering of memory: 'This is not a literary composition; I am just writing down my recollections as they come to me.'[14] When he does acknowledge an ordering principle, using places and people rather than time, it is in response to the particular cast of his own mind, which makes him weak on dates and chronology (p. 91). He repudiates 'artifice' (p. 267), rejects verisimilitude (*le vraisemblable*) in favour of truth (*vérité*, p. 310), and condemns fiction as tantamount to falsification and self-flattery: 'but this is no romance [*roman*] I am writing and I have determined not to flatter myself in these memoirs, either by adding anything agreeable or hiding anything painful' (p. 100 [p. 24]). However, as the narrative progresses, he begins to find that the spontaneity of association produces its own falsifications, and that he needs, as it were, to modify his original account by adding elements that had been inadvertently omitted through such non-methodical method. This is the case, for example, with the two episodes of *Schaudern* (shuddering) in his childhood, and with the supplementary portrait of his mother, which he has to

---

[12] This is how E. M. Forster characterized *Les Faux-monnayeurs*.

[13] André Gide, *Les Faux-monnayeurs*, in id., *Romans, récits et soties*, ed. Yvonne Davet and Jean-Jacques Thierry (Bibliothèque de la Pléiade; Paris: Gallimard, 1958), p. 1081 [p. 168].

[14] *Si le grain ne meurt*, p. 114 [p. 42].

introduce in order to compensate for the excessively negative picture of her that he finds he has unintentionally drawn. He is also increasingly faced with the sheer difficulty of the representation of the experiential quality that he is trying to convey. It is a difficulty that seems to have less to do with his own lack of skill than with the very genre of 'memoirs': 'This is the fatal defect of my story, and indeed of all Memoirs; one sets out the most apparent, but the things that matter most, having no contours, elude one's grasp' (p. 215 [p. 158]). He even goes so far as to speak of the 'duperie' of autobiographical narratives in this regard (p. 223). In short, the elusiveness and complexity of his autobiographical subject matter may make autobiography inadequate as a means of representing it.

This seems to be Gide's conclusion in the note that ends the second part, where he begins by suggesting that, paradoxically, the autobiographical desire to 'say everything' will end up being a source of artifice: 'My intention all along has been to say everything. But in making confidences, there is a limit which cannot be overstepped without artifice, without strain; and what I aim at above all is to be natural' (p. 267 [p. 220*]). In his own case, this is compounded by his natural inclinations, which tend to distort his own account of himself: 'No doubt there is in me some intellectual need that inclines me to simplify everything to excess for the sake of tracing my lines with greater purity.' In any case, all representation imposes the limitation of choice: 'all drawing necessitates choice.' There seems to be no way that autobiography can convey the simultaneity that is the 'truth' of his experience: 'what hampers me most is having to represent states that are really one confused blend of simultaneous happenings as though they were successive.' Finally, the contradictions of his own nature undermine the sincerity that is fundamental to the autobiographical contract: 'I am a creature of dialogue; everything in me is conflicting and contradictory. Memoirs are never more than half sincere, however great one's desire for truth; everything is always more complicated than one makes out' (ibid.). Between them, the forms of autobiographical narrative and the nature of Gide's own temperament work against his attempt to portray his most intimate and essential experience. In consequence, he ends up suggesting that the novel might, after all, provide solutions to the limitations of the autobiographical enterprise: 'It may even be that one gets nearer to truth in the novel [*le roman*]' (ibid.*). His arguments are more subtle and are arrived at more reluctantly than in the case of the practitioners of the *vie romancée*, but their general drift is remarkably similar to the case being made for fiction by his contemporaries in the field of biography.

Gide's defence of fiction here should nevertheless not be overstated. It is only envisaged as a possibility, not outlined as a programme. The remaining quarter of the text continues within the generic frame of autobiography (as it is now understood), and does not become a novel. The issue of fiction is significant in a rather different way, for it allows Gide's actual fiction to acquire a measure of autobiographical validity. There are several occasions in *Si le grain ne meurt* where Gide makes explicit links with his fictional works: La Roque is acknowledged to be the model for La Morinière and its surroundings in *L'Immoraliste* (p. 122); the death of Anna Shackleton is twice mentioned as having contributed to *La Porte étroite* (pp. 229, 244); and the description of the apartment where Gide stayed in Biskra is said to have been used in *L'Immoraliste* (p. 280). In addition, Gide mentions his intention to use certain characters and situations in future works, and the Bavretel family is easily recognizable in the 'Azaïs-Vedel pension' in *Les Faux-monnayeurs* (pp. 197–200). Even without these explicit pointers there are a number of instances where the similarities with the fictional works would be hard for his readers to ignore. This also applies to the episode in the rue Lecat, where Gide's first encounter with his cousin's distress at her mother's infidelity is narrated, and which is almost exactly replicated in *La Porte étroite*; or to the scene of Daniel's brutal seduction of Mohammed (p. 311), which has a near-identical parallel in *L'Immoraliste*. Since the fictional versions precede the autobiographical accounts, the effect as much as anything is to underwrite retrospectively the autobiographical standing of the fiction, rather than to fictionalize the 'memoirs'.[15] However, perhaps more than anything else, the opening of the fictional corpus on to the autobiographical one serves to define Gide as the creative origin of his autobiographical text. Just as in Maurois's account of biography the biographer acquired the status of literary author for the first time and is ascribed creative impulses that may be satisfied in the writing of biographical works, so Gide, as the author of his autobiography, is portrayed as being involved in a similar creative process, of which the text itself may be seen as the record.

EXPERIENCE AND CREATION

Although Gide claims that *Si le grain ne meurt* is not his 'defence' but his 'story' (p. 286), and although he argues that any morality can only be 'particular' (p. 262), the book does have a certain exemplarity as regards the idea of literature. Gide's 'story' is the story of a literary vocation, where the question of literature itself is a vital element. *Si le grain ne meurt* is not in any immediately recognizable sense the story of a literary apprenticeship, as Gide himself acknowledges in a journal entry of 1940: 'I should like to write, if only out of gratitude, in praise of the works that taught me to know myself, that formed me. The great defect of *Si le grain ne meurt* [. . .] is that I do not tell in it who were my initiators. There would be substance in this for another book, on a quite different plane.'[16] Instead, the book offers the narrative of a different kind of literary

---

[15] Lejeune has some interesting things to say about this network, which he characterizes as an 'autobiographical space': see id., 'Gide et l'espace autobiographique', in *Le Pacte autobiographique*, pp. 165–96.

[16] 21 Aug. 1940: André Gide, *Journal*, vol. ii: *1926–1950*, ed. Martine Sagaert (Bibliothèque de la Pléiade; Paris: Gallimard, 1997), p. 725 [vol. iv, p. 42].

initiation, in which recognized versions of literature appear distinctly marginal. The only career mentioned as a future possibility for the young protagonist is that of piano teacher, and this appears at best a casual thought arising out of the two years during which he taught the piano to the illegitimate daughter of his cousin Albert Démarest. There are certainly no signs of literary precocity in the account of Gide's childhood. In fact, a number of episodes would seem to stress the absence of any such signs in his childhood self and to propose a series of decidedly negative images of the future writer. When he is taken by his father to visit the École alsacienne and encouraged to participate in the class, he fails to grasp the concept of a synonym that the teacher is explaining, and, despite having the example spelled out to him, cannot come up with the synonym '*noisetier*' for '*coudrier*' (both meaning 'nut-tree' in French). M. Vedel's pedagogy is not to be faulted, and the only blame lies with Gide's own 'stupidity' (p. 119) in a domain that would seem particularly significant for a future writer.

Similarly, when he and his cousins start a newspaper, the young Gide makes no original contributions to the publication. His cousins produce poems and pieces of prose, but Gide is content to copy out pages from 'great authors' such as Buffon and Boileau (p. 141). Not only is there a failure to create the future writer's 'juvenilia', but his choice is itself the sign of a certain 'stupidity' in neglecting to imagine what would please adults in this kind of venture. This taste for 'great authors' leads Gide astray again when, later on, he and his friend Lionel undertake a rather earnest 'study' of them. Everything is wrong about the way they go about it. The attraction is a 'grandiloquence' that leads to pretentious vapidity and self-congratulation: 'so enamoured were we of grandiloquence that every step that did not take us out of our depths we despised as humdrum; the learned glosses and paraphrases we elaborated would make me blush if I read them again to-day, but they [. . .] were chiefly ridiculous because of the self-satisfaction we found in them' (p. 196 [p. 136]). Even the episode in which Gide is singled out by an escaped canary, which supposedly consecrates his literary destiny, is somewhat burlesque and seems to compound Gide's misdirected literary efforts. The young Gide is shown to have made a whole series of 'errors' that run counter to the kind of vocation implied by his adult writing in the 1920s. The first of these is his assumption that a literary vocation must mean poetry:

a desire for poetry, indeed, never ceased tormenting me, but no muse ever wore heavier shackles than mine. In reality, my whole effort was centred upon 'translating into verse' thoughts to which I attached far too much importance, in the style of Sully Prudhomme about whom I was besotted at the time, and whose example and teaching were the very most pernicious a sentimental schoolboy like myself could follow. I was horribly hampered by the rhymes. Instead of letting them escort, guide, and support me, I exhausted all my emotion searching for them. (p. 227 [p. 173])

Gide presents himself here as having as little insight into the nature of poetry as he did into the nature of language on the occasion of his encounter with synonymy.

Even when his literary career gets under way with the publication of the *Cahiers d'André Walter* in 1891,[17] this narrative of misdirection continues. Gide may finally have abandoned poetry for prose, but he seems in this book to be repeating the same kinds of mistake as those illustrated in his earlier studies of literary example: empty grandiloquence, excessive abstraction, and self-preoccupation:

> When I open my *Cahiers d'André Walter* to-day, their inspired tone exasperates me. I was fond at that time of using words that leave imagination full licence, such as *indefinite, infinite, inexpressible* [. . .]. The fact that words of this kind abound in German made me consider it a particularly poetical language. I did not realize till much later that the distinctive characteristic of the French language is its striving after perfection. (p. 243 [p. 191]).

The literary style of *André Walter* is, according to *Si le grain ne meurt*, a symptom of a continuing lack of insight into the language out of which (French) literature is made. The book is also condemned in retrospect as alarmingly vague at the level of its content:

> I disdained history and considered events important and disruptive intruders. To-day, when there is perhaps nothing that I admire more than a well-constructed narrative, I am filled with irritation as I re-read my *André Walter*; but at that time, far from understanding that art can only live and have its being in the particular, I held that it should be removed from all contingencies, considered any definition of outlines to be contingent and aspired only after the quintessential. (p. 228 [p. 174])

This lack of understanding about the nature of art is due in part to the young writer's self-absorption. The copyist again comes into play, except that here he is copying himself and, more particularly, pages from his own *Journal*: 'The very serious drawback to the state of preoccupation in which I then lived was that all my attentive faculties were absorbed by introspection; I wrote, and wished to write, nothing that was not intimate' (ibid.). This narcissistic enquiry, which forms the basis of his art, here prevents him from becoming the artist he so wishes to be: 'my desire to look exactly what I felt myself to be, what I wanted myself to be—namely an artist—was so great that it prevented me from having any existence of my own and turned me into a *poseur*' (p. 235 [p. 183]). On all these counts, then, the *Cahiers d'André Walter* constitutes a literature that does not succeed in fully being literature. This is not because of a lack of talent or technique on Gide's part, but because of a failure of insight into the nature of the literary.

Much of the narrative of *Si le grain ne meurt* concerns the question of the ways in which art might relate to the life of the artist, and here many of the portraits

---

[17] This work, described on the title page as 'Œuvre posthume', recalls Sainte-Beuve's similarly posthumous *Joseph Delorme*.

contribute as much to the exploration of the question as does the narrative of Gide's own existence. If *Si le grain ne meurt* is the story of a literary apprenticeship that could be summarized as 'André Gide becomes a writer', it constructs this narrative around a series of oppositions between different views of literature, which it constantly invokes in the examples that it cites—and most of which are negative—where everything turns on the place of the art in the life. In a number of cases the mismatch between the two is a consequence of a conception of art as device or technique. Gide repeatedly expresses a horror of art as technique: 'Anything that turns (or even *can turn*) into a device becomes hateful to me.'[18] In *Si le grain ne meurt* this horror tends to be projected on to characters who, in one way or another, do treat art as technique, or at any rate as separate from their own nature and experience. One of the most extreme versions of this preference is Gide's piano teacher, M. Merriman, whose approach to music is entirely mechanical. He divides every piece of music into eight-bar components to be learned, one section at a time, by his pupil. His musicianship is described as being more like accountancy or arithmetic than art: 'when he sat down to the piano, it was like a cashier sitting down to his desk; his fingers added up the notes—the minims and crotchets and quavers—as if they were figures; he would check through the piece as if it were a sum' (p. 182 [p. 121*]). The problem is not so much the emphasis on technique as such, but the way that this emphasis separates art from any kind of experience for the performer.

Gide's implicit objection to the Symbolists appears to be based on what he sees as their tendency towards a similar kind of technical accountancy that serves to maintain this division. When he meets Hérédia, he is surprised to find that the man in no way resembles his idea of a poet. But unlike Proust's Bergotte, who disappoints Marcel for the same reasons, the encounter does not ultimately require Gide substantially to alter his conception of what a poet might be. Hérédia is someone who, despite his generosity and his enthusiasm for literature, deals entirely in externals: 'He was more of an artist than a poet, or rather, more of an artisan than either' (p. 253 [p. 204]). He regards his art as a 'métier', and, lacking any kind of self-awareness ('he was unaware of his deficiencies'), has a mind that is largely closed. Even Mallarmé, for whom Gide had enormous personal admiration, illustrates a tendency—at least in Gide's account—to separate his life from his art by protecting himself from the unexpected. Gide recalls that Mallarmé always prepared his 'mardis', and that his talk was like a spoken version of the written 'Divagations'; however much Mallarmé succeeded in creating an aura of spontaneity in his speech, the concern with elegance and preciosity that 'tormented' him served, in Gide's eyes, to keep his art separate from his life (p. 254). It is for this reason, no doubt, that Gide's association with the Symbolists is not presented as a positive part of his literary apprenticeship.

---

[18] 7 May 1912: *Journal*, vol. i, p. 727 [vol. i, p. 329] (Gide's italics).

The question is raised, from a slightly different angle, in connection with the artistic ambitions of his cousin Albert. Gide claims that Albert was by nature an artist, but he nevertheless presents him as a failure in this regard. The reason is that Albert, in spite of his natural aptitude, confines his painting to a separate sphere in the mistaken belief that he needs to protect it from the flaws he perceives in his own nature: 'With a little more confidence and a little more ingenuity, his very awkwardness might have stood him in good stead; but, out of conscientiousness and modesty, he took the utmost pains to correct them and merely succeeded in making his first charming impulses look commonplace' (p. 231 [pp. 177–8]). It is this failure to connect that condemns Albert's painting to mediocrity. Oscar Wilde, despite his official recognition as a writer, is also presented as a kind of failed artist. This failure is due to the same lack of connection, although in his case it has a different cause. Gide portrays Wilde as having an over-aesthetic perspective on his life, and this, paradoxically, is what introduces the split between that life and his art. It is revealed first in Wilde's dislike of Dickens, an author whom Gide particularly enjoys, and he comments: 'Wilde never forgot to be an artist, and he could not forgive Dickens for being human' (p. 301 [p. 261]). The preoccupation with artistry over humanity is precisely what leads to the error—as Gide sees it, and which Wilde himself acknowledges in his famous comment—whereby he put all his art into his life and only his talent into his works (p. 306). In all these portraits, then, from M. Merriman and Hérédia to Albert Démarest and Oscar Wilde, a certain negative conception of art and literature is explored, where, in one way or another, artistic failure is ascribed to a lack of continuity with the artist's life.

APPETITE VERSUS APPRENTICESHIP

In the light of these largely negative examples some aspects of Gide's account begin to appear as elements of a narrative of what might, after all, be a literary vocation. This version of his initiation into literature is described largely in terms of appetite or passion, and not in those of education or acculturation, let alone the technical aptitude he describes himself as so wretchedly wanting in (for example, his inability to grasp a synonym). Accordingly, when he describes his literary tastes as a child, the apparently unliterary thrills that he derives from George Sand's *Gribouille* or from *Les Dîners de Mademoiselle Justine* by Mme de Ségur may be read as the basis for a different kind of literariness. The tale of Gribouille, who falls in the water and is turned into the branch of an oak tree, gives Gide an erotic frisson; as does the play by Mme de Ségur, in the episode where the servants wreak havoc while their master and mistress are out, and a maid drops a pile of plates when the coachman gives her a pinch: 'Crash! The crockery was smashed all to pieces. This disaster made me swoon with delight' (p.117 [p. 43*]). Despite his suggestion that it does him no credit, sexual appetite and literary appetite are tellingly indistinguishable here, and the basis for a positive account of literature, in contrast to the many negative examples discussed so far, begins to emerge.

There are indeed significant parallels between the sexual and the literary in *Si le grain ne meurt*, which is as much concerned with Gide's sexuality as his literarity. What links the two is the idea of an intrinsic 'nature', which it is imperative to uncover and acknowledge. This has as much polemical force in relation to arguments about homosexuality as to those about literature:[19] homosexuality cannot be 'cured', and literature cannot be acquired. Gide was writing *Si le grain ne meurt* at the same time as *Corydon*, his apologia for homosexuality, which appeared in a private edition in 1920 and in a public one in 1924. The core of Gide's argument is that homosexuality is both natural and normal: it is not a perversion, neither is it subversive of nature, but it represents a perfectly commonplace form of sexuality. In fact, he asserts, it is the only form of sexuality. In defence of his case that homosexuality is innate and not adopted, he claims that the entire culture pressurizes its subjects very strongly into heterosexuality, and that the sexuality of the homosexual exists despite such pressures: 'everything in our society and in our customs directs one sex towards the other. Everything teaches heterosexuality, everything invites and promotes it; the theatre, books, newspapers, the example held up by our elders, the whole parade, whether public or private.'[20]

This is relevant to *Si le grain ne meurt*, not only because of the importance of his own homosexuality to the story that Gide is telling, but also because it is related to his view of the self in general: for Gide the self, however protean and elusive, is something that is discovered as innate and not something that is constructed through accumulated experience and externally imposed education. Just as the homosexual has to unlearn or shake off a heterosexual education, so, in order to become who he is, Gide has to unlearn and shake off the various forms taken by his own education, his literary education included. The underlying principle of *Si le grain ne meurt* is that 'innate qualities are much stronger than acquired ones, and [. . .] in spite of every kind of starching, dressing, pressing, and folding, the natural stuff persists and remains unchanged—stiff or limp, as it was originally woven' (p. 206 [p. 148*]). In short, homosexuality is emblematic of a certain view of the self and of education that would make a nonsense of the conventional notion of a literary apprenticeship. If the concept of education has any sense at all for Gide, it is less as a construct that might be added on to the 'the natural stuff' than as a deliverance.[21] Gide is highly sensitive to the

---

[19] On Gide's homosexuality see Patrick Pollard, *André Gide: Homosexual Moralist* (New Haven and London: Yale University Press, 1991); and Michael Lucey, *Gide's Bent: Sexuality, Politics, Writing, Ideologies of Desire* (New York: Oxford University Press, 1995).

[20] André Gide, *Corydon* (Paris: Gallimard, 1925), p. 50 [p. 42*].

[21] On Gidean pedagogy see Naomi Segal, *André Gide: Pederasty and Pedagogy* (Oxford: Clarendon Press, 1998).

pedagogical skills of his various tutors and teachers, and, in the light of his experience at their hands, formulates his own pedagogical principle, which is that good teachers (who are themselves born and not made), 'far from over-burdening a child's brain, devote themselves instead to delivering it' (p. 216 [p. 160*]). Like homosexuality, art would also have to be something that was discovered within him rather than learned from outside, the fruit of a release and not an external adjunct or imposition.

This is what *Si le grain ne meurt* demonstrates by means of a variety of different strategies in which the notion of appetite is central. It is the young Gide's appetite for books that earns him access to his father's library, and it is one that is only increased by reading, as is demonstrated by his enthusiasm for even the most difficult books on his father's bookshelves: 'I took delight [in these books] and my appetite was so keen, that my preference went to what was most educational, most dense, and most arduous' (p. 211 [p. 154*]). Just as he justifies his homosexuality through repeated examples of his innate lack of desire for women (the female cousin whose bare shoulder he bites as a child, the various prostitutes and the Swiss maid he is not attracted by or who render him impotent), he has a deeply ingrained incapacity for history despite his good will towards the subject: 'Many a time since then have I tried *to force my inclination* and apply myself to the best of my abilities; but *my brain continues to resist*' (p. 212 [p. 154*]). The logic here is that his innate homosexuality is 'proven' by his innate incapacity for heterosexuality, and his innate aptitude for literature by his equally innate inaptitude for history. In both cases his own nature is presented as resisting the force of any attempt (including his own) to make it other than what it constitutively is.

Appetite is an index of nature and is expressed here in terms of an opposition of likes and dislikes, attraction and indifference. However, a further aspect of Gide's nature is its own internal oppositions, an inherent contradictoriness that Gide repeatedly associates with literature. For literature alone, he states, can accommodate such contraries. Gide presents himself constantly as not only a very complex but also a very contradictory being: 'I am a creature of dialogue; everything in me is conflicting and contradictory.' These contradictions are established from the very beginning with his family heritage, divided between Normandy and Provence, Catholicism and Protestantism. Whereas Gide predicates his homosexuality on the necessary separation of love and desire, which is fundamental to his personality, literature is ascribed the capacity positively to accommodate such divisions and to hold out the possibility of some mysterious resolution. For example, while Gide is preparing for his confirmation, his enthusiasm for ancient Greece and for its literature is as great as his religious fervour. It is not just that the two coexist, but that they also interpenetrate:

Strange! This brave pagan fervour flared so brightly in me at the very time I was being prepared for Confirmation in the Christian faith. Today it is a wonder to me that the lengths to which I went with the one interfered so little with the other; there might have been some explanation if I had been luke-warm as a catechumen; but I was not! and presently I shall tell of my zeal and the extremes to which I took it. (p. 220 [p. 165*])

He goes on to say about his enthusiastic reading of the Bible at the time:

I read the Bible *eagerly, greedily* [. . .] the emotion I felt was no doubt not purely religious in its character, just as that with which I read the *Iliad* and the *Oresteia* was not purely literary. Or rather art and religion were devoutly wedded in my heart and I tasted my most perfect ecstasy where they melded mostly closely into one.' (pp. 221–2 [pp. 166–7*])

Although literature is implicitly opposed to religion here, it also has the capacity to forge a marriage with it because of its capacity to contain contradictions: 'I have often been convinced that I was driven to create works of art because it is the only way I could reconcile these excessively disparate elements which would otherwise have led to a state of perpetual warfare or at any rate of dialogue and debate' (p. 89 [p. 13*]). The 'creature of dialogue', whose nature is constituted by apparently irreconcilable opposites, finds in literature not just an echo or reflection of that nature, but a resolution that transcends it. In a first move, literature is defined against what is not literature, including the various versions of itself that are not properly literature (for example, Gide's own *Cahiers d'André Walter*); but, in a second move, it is also defined as that which contains oppositions. For literature to be literature it has to be continuous with Gide's own nature, which is able to survive its own contradictions precisely thanks to that continuity. Literature and the writer's nature are not just mapped on to each other as passive reflections of each other, the one subordinated to the other. Each needs the other in order to be fully itself.

'Being oneself' is, however, never a straightforward business for Gide. Much about Gide's nature escapes his own ability to grasp it. He claims that he will go to the grave without understanding the workings of his own body, and he regularly admits his inability to understand his own motives. For example, he is unable to distinguish between malingering and genuine illness in the case of the presumed neurological problems that followed his smallpox infection; and he denounces his former self-denunciations for their unjustified certainty about his motives (p. 152). Gide's writing is based on the presupposition that, to some extent, it will exceed its author's conscious intentions. As he says in the preface to *Paludes*: 'though we may know what we intended to say, we do not know if that was all we have actually been saying.—One always says more than just THAT.—And what interests me most in my book, is what I have put in without being aware of it—the part that belongs to the unconscious, which I should like to call, the part that belongs to God.'[22] Elsewhere, he attributes this unconscious dimension to the Devil, a further ambiguity that serves only to increase its involuntary character. The upshot is that the reader is always in a better position

---

[22] André Gide, *Paludes* (1895), in *Romans, récits et soties*, p. 89 [p. 13].

than the author to understand what the author has said: 'Before I explain my book to others, I am waiting for others to explain it to me' (ibid.). The self that writes may be completed by writing, but this completion happens in ways that escape that self.

Even if the writing-self had complete self-knowledge, such knowledge would be undone by the very process of writing, since Gide presents writing as interacting with its author in a manner that inevitably makes him other than himself. This is the principle of all his fiction, and it is spelled out in the famous *Journal* entry of 1893, where he postulates a narrator whose relation to his narrative is one of active reciprocity: 'That retroaction of the subject on itself has always tempted me. It is the very model of the psychological novel. An angry man tells a story; there is the subject of a book. A man telling a story is not enough; it must be an angry man and there must be a constant connection between his anger and the story he tells.'[23] Writing reinforces the dynamic process, which constantly displaces the subject that is nevertheless its source and the basis of its validity: 'when one is writing a novel or a play, or telling one's own story, speaking in simple terms about oneself does no harm; it helps one to change; and what else is there to tell about oneself except the ways in which one has changed?'[24] The Gidean self is essentially a changing self, where the self of today differs from the self of tomorrow, and is changed in no small part by the very activity of self-expression. In a variant of the notion of creative experience that preoccupied so many of his contemporaries, Gide discovers that by narrating himself he is changing the very thing he aims to portray; and the veracity of autobiography cannot exempt him from that process.

This dynamism is equally operative for the aesthetic domain. Many of Gide's texts read like notes for a future work. This is the case with *Paludes*, and at a more literal level than the one implied by the idea that it will be complete only in its readerly reception: the story is that of someone preparing to write a book called *Paludes*. The same is true of Édouard in *Les Faux-monnayeurs*, who is planning to write novel called *Les Faux-monnayeurs*; and also of Gide himself in the *Journal des faux-monnayeurs*, which returns the already published work to the status of future project. Something similar is suggested by Gide's account in *Si le grain ne meurt* of Rubinstein's playing at the series of concerts given in the Salle Érard in 1883. What characterizes Rubinstein's performance is the way in which it projects a familiar work into the future as an object that has yet to come into being: 'He seemed to be not so much presenting a piece to them as to be searching for it, discovering or composing it as he went along—not like an improvisation, but as it were in a glowing inward vision, a progressive revelation, which filled even himself with astonishment and rapture' (p. 190 [p. 130]). A well-known piece by Beethoven or Schumann is encountered as a new object, provoking surprise and

---

[23] Sept. 1893: *Journal*, vol. i, p. 172 [vol. i, p. 30].
[24] André Gide, 'Lettres à Angèle', in *Prétextes*, in *Essais critiques*, pp. 8–112 (p. 33).

unexpected delight even in its most practised performer. The role of the artist here is to propel the work into a time that always lies ahead: only here will it become itself, and its essence, as music or as literature, be fully realized. Self-realization, both for self and for work, can therefore never be complete. Each may need the other fully to be itself: literature can properly be literature only when grounded in Gide's own nature; Gide's divided nature can be fully realized only by means of literature. But, in a further move, this reciprocity becomes, as it were, syncopated, where each—the individual nature and literature's literariness—mobilizes the other and directs it towards a fulfilment that will always remain to be achieved.

This is the 'secret drama' (mentioned in the *Interviews imaginaires*) which is acted out in Gide's writing and which makes 'knowledge of the man' necessary for, and inseparable from, the work. The principle of the Sainte-Beuvian portrait is reworked by Gide in this new guise where autobiography, more than biography, serves as the enabling factor. The writing subject is implicated in autobiography much more explicitly than in biography, and his susceptibility to the force of retroaction is much more visible than in other forms of writing. It is this that focuses the question of literature. It serves equally, as I have already said, to open up an autobiographical dimension in all Gide's writing: every text invites the reader to become aware of a secret drama that can never be pinned down to a single moment. The effect of the autobiography is to establish a Gidean corpus whose principle is perpetual self-differentiation, where the opposition between past and present self, or with negative examples of artistic endeavour, is transcended and absorbed within a project whose sense derives not from any relation to the past but from an orientation towards the future. As Gide says in *Si le grain ne meurt*: 'I had rather not succeed than stick to one style. Even if it leads to honour and glory, I detest following a road already laid out. I like chance, adventure, the unknown; I like not to be where people think I am' (p. 247 [p. 195*]). Each work explores different generic possibilities, and with them the writing subject escapes the predictability of his own development. He is moved on by his own writing and at the same time moves that writing on to new versions of itself. This constantly prospective authorial experience galvanizes, and is in turn galvanized by, a literariness that will inevitably also be perpetually differentiating itself from itself. In this way Gide inaugurates a twentieth-century autobiographical practice that, as we shall see in the next two chapters, continues to be deployed so as to engage the very question of literature.

PART VI

ACTS OF LITERATURE: THE SACRED AND THE WRITER'S LIFE

write a book that is an act.
(Michel Leiris)

THE interest in the experience of literary creation continues to be a major preoccupation throughout the course of the twentieth century. But whereas for Proust and Gide the focus is largely on the interiority of that experience, Leiris and Sartre, a decade or two later, envisage creation above all as a form of action with external as well as internal consequences. During a period of some three decades between the late 1930s and the mid-1960s the question of literature is recast as one concerning its value, which can be fully assessed only in relation to this lived action, and only in the context of the writer's life. Biography, and also autobiography, for reasons that Leiris explains, become the frame within which the worth of literature may best be gauged. The notion of authentic action is central to this shared concern, but the two writers differ radically, if not always quite explicitly, in the way they understand the status of literature in this perspective. Put succinctly, Leiris's project is designed to resacralize the literary, while Sartre's goal is a thoroughgoing desacralization of literature's mission. But the writer's engagement remains the key to the process: for Sartre literature constitutes an existential choice made by the writer, which lays him open to the risk of the inauthenticity of *mauvaise foi*; while for Leiris the valorization of literature can take place only if the writer places himself in a position where his activity might require him to pay with his life. Sartre sees danger in an overestimation of the literary; while from Leiris's perspective, danger constitutes the only basis for the consecration on which the very existence of literature depends.

In the discussion that follows in the next two chapters my concern is not principally with the actual relations between the two men.[1] Nevertheless, the friendship that lasted from their first meeting in 1942 into the 1950s, the inclusion of Leiris on the *comité de redaction* during the early years of *Les Temps modernes*, and the publication of several extracts from *La Règle du jeu* in the same journal may all be read as signs of a mutual interest concerned precisely with the interconnected issues of the status of literature, the function of the writer's life, and the forms of his engagement in his literary project (for both men, it should be said, the writer was conceived generically as male). More specifically, Sartre

---

[1] For information and discussion of this relation see Anna Boschetti, *Sartre et 'Les Temps modernes': une entreprise intellectuelle* (Paris: Éditions de Minuit, 1985); Howard Davies, *Sartre and 'Les Temps Modernes'* (Cambridge: Cambridge University Press, 1987); Aliette Armel, *Michel Leiris* (Paris: Fayard, 1997); Catherine Maubon, 'Leiris, Bataille et Sartre: poésie et engagement, 1939–1950', *Europe*, 847–8 (1999), pp. 93–107; and Denis Hollier's commentary in Michel Leiris, *La Règle du jeu*, ed. Denis Hollier et al. (Bibliothèque de la Pléiade; Paris: Gallimard, 2003); see also the preface that Leiris wrote for the book publication of Jean-Paul Sartre's essay *Baudelaire* (Paris: Gallimard, 1947).

records in the *Carnets de la drôle de guerre* that Leiris's *L'Âge d'homme* was one of the factors that had led him to take seriously the idea of writing 'a full-length portrait of myself' and not to condemn introspection, as he previously had on the grounds that 'by poking your nose into such base minutiae one magnified them'.[2] For his part, Leiris was impressed both by *La Nausée*, which he read when it first came out, and by *L'Être et le néant*, which he read in 1943, and whose significance for the writing of *Biffures* he mentions in the text itself.[3] Moreover, whether they were offered or solicited, it is telling that the pieces by Leiris that appeared in *Les Temps modernes* include some of his most important discussions of the writer's relation to the practice of literature.[4]

Mutual interest and shared concerns do not, however, necessarily entail reciprocal understanding. Leiris acknowledged that he and Sartre parted intellectual company on the question of poetry,[5] but the real—if unspoken—difference between them turns on the question of the sacred as the central factor in the literary. This difference is both highlighted and masked (depending on one's point of view) by the similarity of their shared interest in the conception of literature as an (authentic) act, and of their consequent concern with the role of literature in the writer's life. In the case of Leiris—for reasons that I shall be explaining—this was articulated by means of autobiography. For Sartre, while biography is the central plank in these preoccupations, the issue is also explored in the fictional form of *La Nausée* and in the autobiographical instance of *Les Mots*, as well as in his theoretical essay *Qu'est-ce que la littérature?* The cluster of underlying concerns is, however, common to both, albeit with radically contrasting evaluations of the literary.

---

[2] Jean-Paul Sartre, *Carnets de la drôle de guerre: septembre 1939–mars 1940*, ed. Arlette Elkaïm Sartre (Paris: Gallimard, 1995), p. 351.

[3] *Biffures*, in Leiris, *La Règle du jeu*, p. 205. All further references to this edition will be given as *RJ*.

[4] e.g. 'Dimanche' from *Biffures*, published in nos. 5 and 6, Feb. and Mar. 1946, and the last section of *Fibrilles*, which appeared under the title 'Être un poète' in no. 239, Apr. 1966, more than ten years after Leiris had ceased to be part of the editorial board of the journal.

[5] As he recognized from the outset, 'Ce qui différencie Sartre de nous c'est qu'il est, essentiellement, rationaliste. C'est un philosophe et non pas un poète.' Journal entry, 6 July 1943, quoted in Maubon, 'Leiris, Bataille et Sartre', p. 107 n. 40.

14

Michel Leiris: Autobiography and the Sacred

A LITERATURE IN SEARCH OF ITSELF

It is in his retrospective preface to *L'Âge d'homme*, 'De la littérature considérée comme une tauromachie', that Michel Leiris spells out his desire to 'write a book that is an act'.[1] This act, which he imagines as the equivalent of the motions of a matador in a bullfight, would be the means whereby literature could become something other than 'the vain grace of a ballerina', and himself something more than a mere 'littérateur'.[2] Amongst literary genres, autobiography is for Leiris the one that lends itself best to being an act, enabling something like the bull's horn to be introduced into literature and make it other than simply 'aesthetic':

> is not what occurs in the domain of style valueless if it remains 'aesthetic', anodyne, immune to any penalty, if there is nothing in the fact of writing a work that is equivalent (and here supervenes one of the images closest to the author's heart) to the sharp horn of the bull, which alone—by reason of the physical danger it represents—affords the *torrero*'s art a human reality, prevents it from being no more than the vain grace of a ballerina? (ibid.*)

Through this self-exposure the autobiographical writer incurs the element of risk, making the *torero* the model for the writer and bullfighting the model for literature. In other words, Leiris's autobiographical project, as exemplified in *L'Âge d'homme* and in the four books comprising *La Règle du jeu* (*Biffures*, 1948; *Fourbis*, 1955; *Fibrilles*, 1966; and *Frêle bruit*, 1976), is presented as the means whereby literature might become something other, or something more than, itself. The writer puts his life on the line by narrating it in the public domain and by laying himself open to the consequences that his account might have for his future existence.

[1] Michel Leiris, *L'Âge d'homme, précédé de: De la littérature considérée comme une tauromachie* (1946; Paris: Gallimard, 1964), pp. 9–25 (p. 15 [p. 14]). Written between Dec. 1945 and Jan. 1946, the essay was published in the 2nd edition of *L'Âge d'homme* in 1946. The 1st edition appeared in 1939, although the dates of composition given at the end of the text itself are Dec. 1930–Nov. 1935. All further page references are to this edition.

[2] 'De la littérature', pp. 10, 12 [p. 10]. The phrase 'grâces vaines de ballerine' comes from the section of the essay that formed the 'Prière d'insérer' of the 1st edition. The implicit machismo of the ballerina–matador opposition is attenuated through the importance given to the singer Claire Friché in *Fibrilles*. See discussion below.

This reconfiguring of literature is also treated as a search for literature's essence, as if literature, in becoming other than itself, were also becoming more fully itself. In a Journal entry dated 28 June 1942, Leiris writes of the importance of identifying the specificity of the literary: 'doing for literature what Husserl did for philosophy: *define its specific domain*, in order to ensure its existence as an autonomous discipline'.[3] The autobiographical undertaking is proposed in 'De la littérature considérée comme une tauromachie' as an exemplary form of 'literary activity, *in its specific aspect* as a mental discipline'.[4] But it is an undertaking that serves to open it up as a question rather than to provide a simple defining answer. In the final sentence of *Fibrilles* Leiris writes of the inherently elusive essence of literature, which he here calls 'poetry': 'that fascinating thing, which *always remains to be pursued because it is never fully grasped*, and which one might believe is purposely designated by a feminine noun: *la poésie* [poetry]'.[5] Literature, or—in its most exalted guise—poetry, is the elusive goal of Leiris's quest, in which he hopes both to identify the 'specific domain' of literarity, and to push its status beyond the one already ascribed to it. Literature conceived in relation to this twofold goal is always prospective rather than realized, pursued rather than achieved. Although autobiography is the frame in which Leiris carries out his quest, the autobiographical texts are not themselves presented as belonging to the category of 'literature'; they appear instead under the rubric 'Essais' on the list of 'Works by the same author' in the Gallimard editions of Leiris's writings. Literature's difference from itself, which takes the name of 'poetry', is demonstrated less by any generic affiliation than by this projection into the future: it is not a difference between a past and a present, so much as one between a present and future.

It is also a difference that occupies a space between two further conceptions of literature that are, in Leiris's eyes, equally demeaning of its potential: art for art's sake, on the one hand, and politically or socially committed literature, on the other. Art for art's sake is dismissed along with the 'vain grace of a ballerina'; while the problem with politically motivated writing is that 'social commitment [. . .] quickly takes precedence over strictly literary concerns'.[6] Leiris's search is for a literarity that will remain pre-eminent. Moreover, in both the cases that Leiris is rejecting—art for art's sake and committed writing—literature follows a predetermined and pre-existing course, whether in the matter of rhetorical procedure or of ideological determinants. By contrast, the literature he calls 'poetry' has to invent its own rule (*la règle [de son] jeu*), and, for this reason, the writer of such literature must reject all forms of apriorism, both moral and aesthetic.

---

[3] Quoted by Denis Hollier in his 'Notice' to *Biffures*, in *RJ*, p. 1316.
[4] 'De la littérature', p. 23 [p. 21].   [5] Leiris, *Fibrilles*, in *RJ*, p. 797.   [6] Ibid., p. 752.

THE SACRED

It is because such 'poetry' is not a given that it requires to be proven, its worth tested. This creates what Leiris recognizes as a paradox, whereby the unique and distinctive value of all art (not just poetry) can be measured only by seeing it in relation to something that lies beyond it:

> the paradox of art is that, being valuable as an allusion to something that goes beyond its closed world, the highest art turns out to be that which excites us too deeply for us not to regard as powerless to satisfy us the very art which has made us more demanding and given us the desire for something beyond art.[7]

This 'beyond' is not the social world, which, according to Leiris, inevitably downgrades the specifically literary concerns of literature. Instead, it may best be described as the sacred, although it is a very different form of the sacred from that entailed in Paul Bénichou's 'consecration of the writer', whereby the institutional status of the Church passed to the writers who inherited its consecrating function. Leiris's sacred is of its time, and for this reason is also peculiar to him, despite the interest that he shared on the subject with his co-founders of the Collège de sociologie, Georges Bataille and Roger Caillois.[8]

Leiris sets out his own understanding of the sacred in his essay 'Le Sacré dans la vie quotidienne', which is not so much a theoretical exposition as the outline of a personal vision whose individual basis is an integral and indispensable component of Leiris's account of the topic. Accordingly, he begins by asking: 'What is the *sacred*, for me? Or more precisely: what does *my* sacred consist of?'[9] He goes on to gloss the phenomenon as 'that mixture of fear and attraction, that ambiguous attitude produced by proximity to a thing that is both attractive and dangerous, prestigious and refused, that mix of respect, desire and terror that may be taken as the psychological index of the sacred' (ibid.). The terms of this gloss and its emphasis on ambiguity would command wider assent from his contemporaries. But where Leiris differs from them and from most other commentators is in

---

[7] Leiris, *Fourbis*, in *RJ*, p. 406 [pp. 123–4*].

[8] For Bataille's account of the sacred see Georges Bataille, 'Le Sacré', in id., *Œuvres complètes*, vol. i (Paris: Gallimard, 1970), pp. 559–63. For Caillois's discussion, see id., *L'Homme et le sacré* (Collection Folio/Essais; Paris: Gallimard, 1988). The avowed aim of the Collège de sociologie, which was in existence between 1937 and 1939, was the study of a so-called *sociologie sacrée*, focusing in particular on aspects of modern Western culture that can be interpreted from an anthropological perspective as equivalents of certain tribal phenomena. It had no defined doctrine, and, as Denis Hollier notes in his introduction to the anthology of some of its proceedings, 'la sociologie ne serait plus une science, mais quelque chose de l'ordre d'une maladie, une étrange infection du corps social, la maladie sénile d'une société acédieuse, exténuée, atomisée': Denis Hollier, 'À l'en-tête d'acéphale', in id. (ed.), *Le Collège de sociologie* (Paris: Gallimard, 1979), pp. 11–18 (p. 11).

[9] Leiris, 'Le Sacré dans la vie quotidienne', in *RJ*, p. 1110 (Leiris's emphasis). This essay was originally delivered as a lecture to the Collège de sociologie.

his insistence that this mix of terror and attraction can come only from objects, places, sights, and words that are part of his own—individual—experience. He goes on, consequently, to recall such objects as his father's Smith and Wesson revolver, the stove-heater in the family home; places such as his parents' bed-room, the lavatory where he and his brother would sit and recount their invented mythologies, and the nearby racecourse in Auteuil; spectacles such as the jockeys at the races; and words that for him triggered 'the transition from a profane state to a sacred one' (p. 1117). This private world of childhood memories, much of which forms the basis of *L'Âge d'homme* and *La Règle du jeu*, is, however, much more than strictly private or personal. The elements of Leiris's 'sacred' have their special status for him precisely because they entail a crossover to another world. The sacred is both what is unique or special to him, and what exceeds him: 'The "sacred" will be what is *heterogeneous* (or transcendent?) in relation to me, that which is external to myself but to which I adhere in order to go beyond myself.'[10] It is to be understood as another world, as different from ordinary life as fire is from water, and one that, being a world unto itself, forms a totality. Leiris's childhood memories seem to have a dual function here: their distance in time confers on them a sort of exoticism that constitutes them as just such an other, self-enclosed domain. But at the same time they offer 'windows' on to that other world. The sacred is marked by intimacy and strangeness in equal measure: 'It is in the sacred that one is both most oneself and the most beside and outside one-self' (p. 1135). This means neither simply identifying certain elements from his own experience as bearing the marker 'sacred', nor simply moving into an exotic and alternative reality. Rather, it calls for an attention to the occasions when the sacred emerges: 'The need to study the sacred in its "nascent state"', he notes (p. 1136). It is not a condition, but a moment in time; not an institutionalized form, but a spark that creates a crossover from one world to another.

This same combination of being 'oneself' and 'outside oneself' determines the nature of autobiography for Leiris, and makes autobiography the ideal form of writing for anyone wishing to explore the sacred as Leiris understands it. Accordingly, the essay on the sacred concludes with a call for self-knowledge through an examination of personal memories:

If one of the most 'sacred' goals a man can set himself is to acquire a knowledge of himself that is as intense and as accurate as possible, it appears desirable that, scrutinizing our memories with maximum honesty, each of us should consider closely whether we can discover some indication that might allow us to make out what *colour* the notion of the sacred itself has for each of us.[11]

The sacred is, nonetheless, not limited to the content of Leiris's autobiographical project, and while the exploration of personal memory permits the identification

---

[10] Leiris, 'Notes', in *RJ*, p. 1128 (Leiris's emphasis).
[11] 'Le Sacré dans la vie quotidienne', p. 1118 (Leiris's emphasis).

of moments where the everyday opens on to the transcendent, that shift into a beyond is just as much the function of what Leiris calls 'communication'. The very process of transforming self-knowledge into writing, in the movement from the inner self to the world outside the self, can work to open up the self to the sacred: 'Being simultaneously completely "oneself" and completely "outside oneself" is the sacred state *par excellence*. Resolve this apparent contradiction through the idea of the sacred as communication: project outwards, give as hostage what is most intimate; the most secret "self" that is projected "outside the self".'[12]

Indeed, Leiris frequently describes language itself as 'sacred' because of this capacity for communication, as is demonstrated in the passage from the private to the social that the correction of 'Reusement' to 'Heureusement' ('luckily') reveals in the opening scene of *Biffures* (also briefly recounted in 'Le Sacré'). The sacred character of verbal communication is not automatically conferred by language, and in the 'Notes' Leiris speaks of the need to reinvent language so as to make possible such genuine communication. Poetry can become a 'sacred art' only if it succeeds in provoking certain feelings, attitudes, and responses in its reader. The strategy for achieving this is not given in the existing forms of the literary, and one object of Leiris's quest in *La Règle du jeu* is precisely the discovery of the rules for a communication that would embody this sacred character of language. The auto-biographical undertaking is not the demonstration of a rule, but, as the publicity strip on the original edition of *Biffures* put it, 'A game [*un jeu*] in search of its rules'.

Leiris records in the 'Notes' that for him the sacred has the character of 'a game' and of 'poetry' (p. 1143). This makes *La Règle du jeu* and its pursuit of 'poetry' the enactment of an attempt to realize the sacred in the form of communication. The comment also brings us back to the question of poetry and literature, which now appears in two alternative lights: on the one hand, as I said earlier, the sacred provides the measure of literature's worth as its 'beyond'; on the other, literature is the means whereby the sacred can take form. The question of which has priority—literature or the sacred—would be impossible to determine, but it does seem more than plausible to regard Leiris's thinking about the sacred (in 'Le Sacré' and in the 'Notes') as forming the kernel from which *La Règle du jeu* subsequently developed. This is not just a matter of chronology (*Biffures* was begun in the summer of 1940, not long after the lecture to the Collège de sociologie), or of content (in *Biffures* Leiris alludes to the Notes from which he drew some of his material). The autobiographical project as a whole may be seen as Leiris's pursuit of his own sacred through the exploration of his personal memories, and as part of his search for a form that would constitute authentic communication with another. Whichever way round the issue is approached, literature appears to be inseparable from the sacred, even if the word ('le sacré') itself is rarely invoked in *La Règle du jeu*.

[12] 'Notes', *RJ*, p. 1145.

BEING A POET

Leiris's positioning of literature, whose value depends on its implication in the sacred, is suggested by a rather fluid set of terms in his writing: sometimes he speaks of 'literature', sometimes of 'poetry' (which he opposes to 'mere' literature or even *belles-lettres*), and very often, more generally, of 'art'. His aim is not primarily to define an aesthetic object in isolation, but to relate the notion to a certain way of living. This is not a matter of subscribing to a recognizably 'artistic' way of life, with its late nights and excessive drinking, or of following a poetic vocation, both of which Leiris dismisses as misconceptions on the part of his past self.[13] Rather, it is a matter of being 'more—and more truly—alive', to use Leiris's expression in the 'Prière d'insérer' of *Biffures*. The purpose behind *La Règle du jeu*, then, is to find both a way of writing, and—just as importantly—a way of living: 'I propose to define what the "rules of the game" are for me, or, put more pompously: my *ars poetica* and the codes of my own art of living, which I should like to discover melded in a single system, since I see in the literary use of language chiefly a means of heightening consciousness in order to be more—and more truly—alive.'[14] And if poetry is a way of life, it follows that it is not best grasped by means of theoretical discourse:

> To try and expound clearly the truth of poetry is to seek to circumscribe poetry by means of language, to enumerate its elements supposedly to gain a better understanding of it, and, in fact, to let it escape, since it is, in essence, a matter of all or nothing [. . .]. Even if I managed in this way to acquire a poetics and a moral code, I would not have won the game.[15]

A conception of poetry that treated it as an object of analysis or of theoretical definition would ultimately be worthless, since the value of poetry is above all an existential matter, a certain quality of experience: 'I am aiming for a practical goal and what I would need is something that is foreign to all theories, which is to feel that I am firmly planted in the heart of poetry' (p. 761). Ultimately, this position at the heart of poetry is one that even the combined forces of an *art poétique* and a *savoir-vivre* cannot guarantee; and towards the end of *Fibrilles* Leiris abandons his earlier formulation of the ideal 'rule' that would combine these two things, and now recasts his pursuit of poetry as an attempt to 'be a poet': 'there is no question of reverting to my search for a golden rule on a new basis. Rather than elaborating an *ars poetica* and a moral code, is not the most important thing to be, as fully as one can given the available resources, that hybrid of sage and maniac, truth teller and illusionist that we call a poet?' (p. 774). The emphasis

---

[13] e.g. *Fibrilles*, pp. 755–6; *L'Âge d'homme*, p. 182. The question of the writing life will be explored in more detail in Ch. 18 below.
[14] 'Prière d'insérer', in *Biffures*, p. 1286.   [15] *Fibrilles*, pp. 760–1.

has shifted from a preoccupation with the entity he calls poetry to an existential ambition to become a poet, while nevertheless acknowledging the ambivalence and the precariousness of such a figure, part circus performer and part prophet, whose activities engage the question of his very existence.

Writing poetry may require the mastery of prosody and a distinctive vocabulary, the capacity to produce images, or to invent radical new forms of rhetoric. But without a certain existential investment in these strategies, there can, for Leiris, be no poetry of the kind that he envisages. The poet is not just someone who writes poetry, but someone whose life is entirely given over to '*being* a poet', however ambiguous a hybrid this might be (p. 757). For this reason Leiris is much more preoccupied with artist figures than with forms or theories of art. The sacred quality of art derives above all from the artist's relation to that art, and not, ultimately, from any intrinsic feature it might have. This relation is expressed in a variety of ways by Leiris. A Journal entry dating from October 1945 describes it as a form of 'commitment', in a formulation that implicitly distinguishes Leiris's understanding of the concept from the Sartrean one, and which puts the emphasis on the writer's relation to the work, rather than on the work's relation to the world: 'Much more than a "committed literature", I believe in a literature that commits me.'[16] At its most extreme Leiris characterizes such engagement as a willingness to pay with one's life, and it is this extreme version that is incarnated in the figure of the *torero* as the model for the writer. The appeal of the *torero* lies in the fact that the risk to the matador's life involved in bullfighting saves his art from futility (the 'vain grace of the ballerina'). The *torero*'s skills are his only defence against the threat posed by the bull's horn; but they can equally well be viewed as an increased vulnerability to it: 'the rule, far from being a protection, contributes to the danger he is in: to deliver the thrust under the requisite conditions demands, for instance, that he put his body, during an appreciable length of time, within reach of the horns; hence there is an immediate connection between obedience to the rule and the danger incurred.'[17] Either way, the bullfighter's art places him in a life or death situation, which, however hyperbolic it may appear in connection with poetry, Leiris takes as the measure of true artistic commitment.[18]

The *torero* is the first of a series of exemplary models for the artist—none of them, incidentally, a writer or a poet—who are presented and discussed in *L'Âge d'homme* and *La Règle du jeu*: the actors who as a child Leiris imagined were really killed on stage in the opera *I Pagliacci*; circus artistes, including his acrobat

---

[16] Quoted by Catherine Maubon in ead., *Catherine Maubon présente L'Âge d'homme de Michel Leiris* (Foliothèque; Paris: Flammarion, 1997), p. 126. In 'De la littérature' Leiris speaks of 'cet engagement essentiel qu'on est en droit d'exiger de l'écrivain essentiel' (p. 24).

[17] 'De la littérature', p. 19 [pp. 17–18*].

[18] On the place of bullfighting in Leiris's work see Annie Maïllis, *Michel Leiris: l'écrivain matador* (Paris: L'Harmattan, 1998).

uncle; jockeys; and his aunt by marriage, Claire Friché the singer.[19] The 'essential' artist is not necessarily an exponent of 'high art'; and what all these figures have in common is that, being performers of one kind or another, their activity requires a level of physical engagement that inevitably places them in a position of risk. The acrobat uncle tells the young Leiris how the circus artiste needs to devote 'body and soul' to his art, a point underscored by the fact that he is portrayed at a moment when he himself has a broken arm, the possible consequence of his risky occupation. In *Biffures* Leiris describes part of the pleasure of circus performance for its audience as deriving from 'the tremulous anxiety with which one witnesses a *tour de force, at the very moment* it is being performed, and which at any moment may end in failure'.[20] The spectacle is a real event in the life of the performing artist, just as the horse race is for the jockeys participating in it: 'For here nothing is false: however important the stage production may be, and however strong the element of illusion, the sporting event, whose outcome is theoretically unpredictable [. . .] is *a real act* and not a make-believe, all of whose vicissitudes, down to the least important, take place in conformity with what has been arranged in advance.'[21] The demands made by this real event makes confer upon the jockey—at least in the imagination of the young Leiris and his brother—a 'halo of sainthood', consisting of qualities such as 'daring and self-control combined with a perfect simplicity of manners' that, as an adult, he now regards as those of 'authentic' poets and artists (pp. 369–70).

The implicit denigration of all forms of performance, which do little more than merely follow a preordained protocol, would seem to rule out theatre or opera as valid forms of art for Leiris, since everything in them is written and rehearsed in advance. However, the portrait of Claire Friché in *Fibrilles* presents her as having had as much devotion to her operatic art as that required of the circus acrobat, and as being as physically and personally vulnerable to its demands as a jockey, if not a matador. Whereas initially he had seen the way she lived her roles in real life as an inauthentic self-dramatization, Leiris comes to understand Friché's approach as a total investment of herself in her art. Apparent self-love is reinterpreted as the expression of an unconditional devotion to theatre, which is, so to speak, proven by the fact that she eventually ruins her voice as a result of the way she throws herself into her roles. 'The profession of artist was the most important thing in her life', and for this reason Leiris sees in her 'the incarnation of the artist that I hold now to be the most moving'.[22] She is one of a number of figures who come to mind as Leiris recovers from his suicide attempt, and he gradually begins to see that they embody a kind of insight as to what it might mean to 'live one's art':

[19] *L'Âge d'homme*, pp. 47–8; ibid., pp. 82–3; *Biffures*, 141–2; 'Tablettes sportives', in *Fourbis*; pt. II of *Fibrilles*.
[20] *Biffures*, p. 141 [p. 129*] (Leiris's italics).　　　[21] *Fourbis*, p. 360 [p. 76].
[22] *Fibrilles*, pp. 652, 636.

What they bore [. . .] like a smuggler's fortune, was not the artistic life as I may have imagined it when I set my heart on being a poet, but a more archaic chapter of my lived existence: the one [. . .] allowed me to glimpse that world apart which the tiny word 'art' serves to present as a whole, even though it is ill-suited to summing up the fantastic diversity of its glories. (pp. 638–9)

The otherness and the absolute character of the world of art are the markers of its sacred quality, which, it would seem, can be realized only through the unstinting commitment of the individual artist to everything that is entailed and required by the tiny word that refers to it. By opening the field of the literary up to the broader concept of 'art', and by defining art itself in terms that include the performing arts more commonly associated with popular culture, Leiris seems to be suggesting that for literature to become more essentially literary, it needs to align itself with the performance-based principles of these other, non-literary arts.

WRITING AND LIFE

The sacred character of literature to which Leiris aspires is something to be exemplified, rather than theorized; and, as we have seen, it is incarnated in persons much more than in finished works or literary techniques. Leiris's project requires his own implication in it on the lines illustrated by the various performing artists that he portrays. But his autobiographical writing is not the record of a prior understanding acquired through his contemplation of such figures. Instead, he is seeking to match their example by making writing itself as much of a performing art as opera was for Claire Friché, as open to risk as bullfighting is for the matador, and as demanding of the flesh and blood reality of the writer as horse racing is for the jockeys at Auteuil. Autobiographical writing is more amenable to these requirements than either fiction or poetry, and in 'De la littérature considérée comme une tauromachie' Leiris specifically describes *L'Âge d'homme* as the 'negation of a novel' and as the mark of a break with his literary past as a Surrealist.[23] Although it appears as the preface to *L'Âge d'homme*, the essay may be best read as a continuation of the principles contained in 'Le Sacré dans la vie quotidienne' and in the 'Notes pour "Le Sacré dans la vie quotidienne"' (both written after *L'Âge d'homme* itself), since, as if in response to the final injunction in 'Le Sacré dans la vie quotidienne', it shifts the emphasis away from questions of definition to issues of enactment. In this preface Leiris pursues the analogy—which is itself risky—between the risks encountered by the autobiographer and those that confront the *torero* in the bullring. Leiris's rigorous refusal of invention and his 'predilection for realism'[24] turn the writing of autobiography into an act whose tangible consequences will be played out in

---

[23] 'De la littérature', p. 16.   [24] Ibid., p. 17 [p. 16].

his own life. Autobiography may record memories, but in Leiris's case this is primarily with a view to discovering things about himself that he does not already know; its orientation is towards the future as much as, if not more than, towards the past. In *Biffures* he describes this as 'the use of writing as an instrument for achieving heightened awareness and therefore for having an effect on oneself and for fabricating'.[25] The autobiographical undertaking is an act in relation to the self because it is a form of self-fashioning; but it is also presented as being an act in relation to others. This is because Leiris will have to live with the effects that his self-revelation has on the people in the world around him. The final characteristic of autobiography's status as an act, in Leiris's eyes, is its capacity to reveal the underside of his previous literary production: 'a backstage revelation that would expose, in all their unenthralling nakedness, the realities which formed the more or less disguised warp beneath surfaces I had tried to make alluring, of my other writings'.[26] This commitment to truth-telling is proposed by Leiris as a 'rule' whose rigour is equal to that of the protocols of bullfighting, and is designed to make of autobiography the kind of 'real act' that a circus trick or a horse race are for their respective performers. Autobiography is constituted as an act by virtue of its repercussions on himself and others, as well as by the rigour of its obligation to veracity.

There are further unanticipated risks that derive in considerable measure from the nature of autobiographical composition, which, perhaps, more than any other type of writing, is affected by the evolving present in which the autobiographer writes. In the case of *L'Âge d'homme* this is acutely evident in the changed context for the publication of the book between the eve of the 'drôle de guerre' in 1939 (which already considerably postdates the book's completion in 1935) and the devastation that confronts Leiris in Le Havre towards the end of 1945 when he begins to write his preface for the second edition, making 'the personal problems with which [*L'Âge d'homme*] is concerned' appear in comparison as 'obviously insignificant' (p. 11 [p. 11]). The original blurb had already built in an awareness of how passing time had serially altered his understanding of manhood, between the socially sanctioned event as it took place in 1922, the conclusion of the book in 1935, and its publication in 1939 under the threat of imminent war. The notes he adds to the 1945 and 1964 editions underscore these alterations of perspective, many of which are the unforeseeable result of the passage of time, by correcting errors of fact (such as an erroneous reference to Act 3 of Gounod's *Faust* that should be to Act 4); or else by introducing new interpretations, such as the sharpened sense that the ever-present threat of torture under the Occupation had brought in retrospect to the comments about his physical cowardice.[27] The inadvertent anachronisms of *L'Âge d'homme* that are revealed by these revisions could be seen as proof of the susceptibility to risk that Leiris had originally

25 *Biffures*, p. 226 [p. 205*].   26 'De la littérature', p. 15 [p. 14].
27 *L'Âge d'homme*, p. 229.

desired for his text, though in a form that he had not anticipated—that of time. At any rate, the project that succeeded it, *La Règle du jeu*, is no longer organized around the implicitly atemporal thematic principles of the earlier text, but, from the outset, is made to be much more susceptible to the destabilizing effects of an unfolding temporality.

Leiris devotes relatively little commentary to the here and now of the moment of writing, but a notable first exception comes in the 'Perséphone' and 'Dimanche' sections of *Biffures*, where he introduces a number of moments that signal a skip forward in time from a previous paragraph: 'Scarcely two and a half hours ago—the day after I wrote the preceding paragraph'; he records a visit to the square du Vert-Galant, which in a previous paragraph he knew only from the view of it that he had from his new flat; and he shifts from an anticipation of making love the following day to a brief note that the event has taken place in the intervening lines.[28] These jumps serve to remind the reader that the apparently continuous unfolding of the writing emerges from a present that has its own varying and interrupted momentum in the life of the author. Explicit comment reminds readers that the writer's life goes on alongside the writing that is in part a record of it: 'my life, which wends its way through time just as my sentences wend their way from page to page in a time, it is true, that is more limited' (p. 125 [p.114*]). This parallel is presented with increasing frequency as a mismatch: not only does time become increasingly short (as hinted in the last quotation), but it also comes increasingly to undermine his project, as the gap widens between 'the I that I am' and 'the I that I write'.[29] The delayed progress of writing threatens the veracity of the content, as when Leiris records removing his 'fiches' (the notes that constituted the source material for his work) to his house in the country at a time when, as he later reveals, he was on the point of deciding to return them to his flat on the quai des Grands-Augustins.

The project is also threatened by Leiris's uncertain sense of his own ability to pursue it, and at these moments he stresses how much his writing draws on his human capacities for its existence. At the end of *Biffures* he announces a halt in an undertaking that is nevertheless clearly not complete: 'Since the literary work to which I am devoting myself with such difficulty seems less and less uplifting and no longer necessary (because it gives me nothing beyond what I put into it myself with more or less contrivance), it would be better to abandon it and wait for better times. And right now the most serious hope I have for recovery is to let everything lie dormant.'[30] Changes in Leiris's life, or in his attitude, might also threaten the project, as he concedes at the beginning of the subsequent volume, *Fourbis*, when he acknowledges how easily it could be sabotaged by the progressive difficulties caused by the dwindling stock of recorded memories, the loss of mental acuity on his part in bringing them back to life in writing, and

---

[28] *Biffures*, p. 182 [p. 166], p. 73 [p. 68], pp. 234–6 [pp. 212–13]. [29] *Fibrilles*, p. 729.
[30] *Biffures*, p. 271 [p. 245*].

the possibility that he might also lose interest in keeping the notes on which his work depends.[31]

It is not just the fulfilment of the project that is threatened by time: the very nature of Leiris's undertaking is altered by the passage of time in a manner that simultaneously vindicates the strategy of risk, and threatens to invalidate its goals. Towards the end of *Fibrilles* Leiris acknowledges 'how vulnerable this work is to time, since its goal, which alters as it goes along instead of preserving a sort of ideal intemporality, has turned out to be itself the plaything of the passing of the years'.[32] Indeed, Leiris devotes a considerable amount of discussion throughout *La Règle du jeu* to a recognition of these changing goals that are a direct result of the way the project evolves as the years pass. From being an instrument of liberation designed to make its author 'more—and more truly—alive', writing has become a ball and chain.[33] At the beginning of *Fourbis*, where Leiris records the publication of *Biffures*, he concedes that 'the quasi-stellar projection of ourselves by which we might have believed that our fate would be—as though magically—transformed' has resulted in nothing more than another book to add to the thousands that already exist.[34] The transformation of his life that he had hoped for from his writing is reduced to being nothing more than the principal occupation of his existence: 'its purpose is more and more contained within itself and as it gradually eclipses my other preoccupations, it is becoming a reason for living when it was originally intended to be a means of enlightening me for a more coherent conduct of my way of living' (p. 296 [p. 9]). The relation between the book and the life it was meant to illuminate has been altered; and the life-consuming labour of writing means that the chances that Leiris's own life might benefit from the discovery of a 'rule' in the book become ever more remote, until the project, which was originally directed entirely towards the future, looks set to be nothing more than the testament that Leiris will leave behind.[35] In *Frêle bruit* Leiris goes so far as to say that having devoted thirty-five years of his life to his undertaking, he now realizes that his hope for the future can no longer be that it will reveal the answer to his question; the most he can hope for now is that the question itself will finally emerge. The continuous recalibrations of Leiris's goals produce concomitant changes in the nature—and even the possibility—of the relation between writing and living. This has serious implications for the sacred, since it was originally by means of this relation that it was to be enacted.

Leiris comes to realize that the writing that occupies such a large part of his life and calls for so much resource within that life does not necessarily transform it. The sacred power contained within words does not spare him '[the] common lot of mortals'.[36] The publication of *Fourbis*, which was the first of Leiris's books to attract any sizeable critical response, led him to understand how large a gap there was between the mythical version of his life on the page as read by the critics,

---

[31] *Fourbis*, p. 297.   [32] *Fibrilles*, p. 733.   [33] *Biffures*, p. 277.
[34] *Fourbis*, p. 291 [p. 3].   [35] Ibid., p. 515.   [36] *Biffures*, p. 250.

and the lived reality of his own experience: 'I knew only too well as far as I was concerned that, even if I conceded that I have transformed my life into a myth, it has become one only *in writing*, in the past-tense narrative that I made out of it and not in itself, in the present where I live it.'[37] Self-exposure through the self-representation of autobiography, which was one of Leiris's self-imposed risks in 'De la littérature considérée comme une tauromachie', has consequences that he finds unbearable when it makes him the object of other people's commentary. To him the reviews of the book read like obituaries, and once it is in the public domain, the figure of himself that he has 'sculpted' in his writing suddenly seems like nothing so much as a gravestone. He fears that he is 'finished' as a writer, being paralysed by the consequences of his own achievement. The writing retroacts (to use Gide's term) on the life in ways that seem to make more writing impossible, and it is in this situation that Leiris attempts suicide.

Paradoxically, this reintroduces the life and death dimension into the arena of writing, and, according to Leiris's account of the event, does so in a way that once again directly implicates literature. As he fades out of consciousness after taking a drug overdose, he says to his wife: '*All that is literature*'.[38] He glosses this strange assertion in retrospect by explaining how deeply literature had affected his life: 'that literature had contaminated me to the core and that it was all I now was, but that from then on nothing could happen to me which would carry the same weight as what is created out of ink and paper in a world devoid of at least three of the statutory dimensions' (ibid.). The risks entailed by autobiography are less dramatic than the fall to which a jockey or an acrobat is prone, and the means by which the bull's horn enters the autobiographical picture are not as strictly encoded as they are for the matador. Leiris's predicament is neither intended nor foreseen, but, perhaps precisely for that reason, it is as authentic as his uncle's broken arm or Claire Friché's ruined voice. At any rate, Leiris concludes *Fibrilles* by claiming that the risk represented by his failed suicide, an act that was precipitated largely by the deleterious effects of writing on his life, brought him closer than ever before to the poetry that is still his goal: 'it seems to me too that it was at that moment, marrying life and death, intoxication and insight, ardour and negativity, I came closest to embracing that fascinating thing, which *always remains to be pursued because it is never fully grasped*, and which one might believe is purposely designated by a feminine noun: *la poésie* [poetry]' (p. 797). Such an act could never have been produced by design, or by any 'rule', being, almost by definition, unrepeatable and inimitable. Profoundly ambiguous, due as much to drink as to insight, and with as much destructiveness behind it as positive purpose, Leiris's attempted suicide is, by the same token, potentially allied to the profoundly ambiguous character of the sacred. It takes not only the period of Leiris's convalescence, with its parade of artist figures who appear in his delirium, but also the patient, time-consuming business of reflection and writing

---

[37] *Fibrilles*, p. 603 (Leiris's italics).   [38] *Fibrilles*, p. 619 (original italics).

for this quality, which he here calls 'la poésie', to appear as the possible hallmark of his act.

Poetry is both synonymous with this unrepeatable, unplanned, and ambivalent act, and something whose reality can emerge only through the time-consuming process of writing which cannot of itself transform a life, and which will ultimately result in nothing more than another book. In other words, it takes the negative view of literature that in part drove Leiris to run the risk of self-destruction, to reveal the positive literary quality contained in that self-destructive act. The limits of literature's capacity for real effects in the world may become gradually more apparent over the course of Leiris's protracted undertaking; but that very protraction engages the writing in lived time, which in and of itself reintroduces a dimension of risk and uncertainty. It is in this way that Leiris's autobiographical project is once again opened up to the sacred and to a 'beyond' that might still provide the measure of its worth as 'poetry'.

15

Sartre and Biography: Existential Acts and the Desacralization of Literature

> all of Art is engaged in the adventure of a single man.
>
> (Sartre, *Situations, IX*)

'Write a book which is an act': this injunction, which is the guiding thread of Leiris's literary project, could equally well have been devised by Sartre for his own. But where for Leiris the act of literature was a means of opening up literature to the sacred, Sartre's aim is to position literature in a secular world as one form of action amongst others. He conceives of literature primarily as a means of intervention: writing changes the world by naming it; it acts upon its readers by revealing their own freedom to them; it constitutes an existential choice that determines the life of its author; and every piece of writing takes up, explicitly or implicitly, a stance in relation to the notion of 'literature' itself. However, Sartre's notion of 'committed literature' is less prescriptive than it is interrogative: the title of the text most commonly associated with 'littérature engagée' is, after all, a question, *Qu'est-ce que la littérature?*, rather than the announcement of a particular literary programme. And the terms in which literature is presented as a self-contesting act make biography rather than theory the forum in which the notion is most extensively challenged and investigated in his work.

THEORY

In order to understand why biography—so often seen as the antithesis of theory—should have this capacity, it will nonetheless be necessary to begin with the theory. Contestation is written into Sartre's literary-theoretical project from the outset. In addition to the question posed by the book's title—*Qu'est-ce que la littérature?*—the brief preface portrays Sartre as the target of criticism from a variety of quarters, and thereby creates a context that allows him to introduce the idea of literature as a topic of debate in its own right: 'since critics condemn me in the name of literature without ever saying what they mean by it, the best way of answering them is to examine the art of writing without prejudice.'[1] This examination is itself conducted under the head of three further questions, which introduce the first three (out of four) sections of the book: 'What is writing?', 'Why does one write?', and 'For whom does one write?'

Moreover, although the title *What is Literature?* has come to seem characteristically Sartrean,[2] it has contestation written into it by virtue of the fact that the question had already been posed by others, for rather different purposes and under very different circumstances. Charles Du Bos took the question as the title of a series of four lectures delivered to a Catholic audience at Saint Mary's College, Notre Dame, Indiana, in 1938. First published in English in 1940 under the title *What is Literature?*, these lectures subsequently appeared in a French translation in 1945, two years before Sartre's text was serialized in *Les Temps modernes*. Du Bos's perspective is self-avowedly Christian, and literature is presented as the necessary counterpart to life understood as the place where souls are formed until they are recalled by God: 'Literature is [. . .] that very same Life becoming conscious of itself when, in the soul of a man of genius, it joins its plenitude of expression.'[3] Du Bos views art as a vital element in a spiritual quest, and writes with the irenic confidence of a recent convert to Catholicism. By appropriating the title for altogether more profane and earthly purposes, Sartre is turning calm assertion into a topic of energetic controversy. And all the more so since Jean Paulhan had also posed the question 'What is literature?' in his essay *Les Fleurs de Tarbes*, published in 1941. Unlike Du Bos, Paulhan adopts an overtly polemical stance, arguing for a conception of literature based on rhetoric against what he calls the 'terrorism' of original expression.[4] By re-posing the question after both Du Bos and Paulhan, within yet another framework, Sartre is ensuring that the notion of literature remains an object of continuing contention.

In the words of Ronald Hayman, Sartre's English biographer, writing for Sartre is necessarily a 'writing against'.[5] This oppositional perspective emerges in a number of different ways in *Qu'est-ce que la littérature?* A given text's representation of the world is implicitly opposed to the ones that preceded it, and its revelation of the reader's freedom is bound to challenge those who would prefer to keep readers blind to their own possibilities. More importantly for my own argument, it is also a writing against literature itself. In an interview he gave in 1960, Sartre asserts that 'to write is always to put the whole of writing

---

[1] Jean-Paul Sartre, *Qu'est-ce que la littérature? Situations, II* (Paris: Gallimard, 1948), p. 58 [p. xviii].

[2] For a discussion of Sartre's ideas about literature see Christina Howells, *Sartre's Theory of Literature* (London: Modern Humanities Research Association, 1979).

[3] Charles Du Bos, *Qu'est-ce que la littérature?*, trans. Juliette Siry Du Bos (Paris: Plon, 1945), p. 10 [p. 14].

[4] Jean Paulhan, *Les Fleurs de Tarbes, ou la Terreur dans les lettres* (Paris: Gallimard, 1941), p. 26.

[5] Ronald Hayman, *Writing Against: A Biography of Sartre* (London: Weidenfeld & Nicolson, 1986).

in question'.[6] This putting into question of literature is achieved by means of a further series of oppositions. The first of these is that between poetry and prose: contrary to the tendency to regard poetry as the supreme form of literature, as Leiris did, Sartre unequivocally equates literature with prose. The poet treats words as things out of which he makes poems, which are objects. By contrast, the prose writer is a speaker, not a maker, and his every utterance performs some kind of action: 'he designates, demonstrates, orders, refuses, interpolates, begs, insults, persuades, insinuates.'[7] Prose is a fundamentally utilitarian art that serves to reveal the world, and the gratuitousness of 'pure art' is condemned as merely 'empty' (p. 77). Poetry does no more than propose an object for passive contemplation, while prose articulates an appeal to the reader whose active participation is needed for the full realization of the text. In short, Sartre circumscribes the notion of 'literature' by constructing an opposition between two forms of writing—poetry and prose—which he defines as 'incommunicable universes' (p. 70 [p. 13]). His 'literature' is a literature defined against the super-literariness of poetry.

Secondly, literature is also a historically specific phenomenon, taking different forms at different times. The writer's institutional relation to it alters according to social and cultural circumstances, and Sartre charts its history from the twelfth-century clerks who wrote at the behest of the Church, to the France of 1947 where literature was still an alibi for bourgeois hegemony. Each society has its own understanding of what it means to write, but, over and above these large-scale transformations in which one conception of literature replaces another, literature is also the means whereby individual writers break out of the inevitable limitations of a given society's understanding of what the literary is: 'each book proposes a concrete liberation on the basis of a particular alienation' (p. 119 [p. 64]). The writer writes against what literature is deemed to be in his cultural and social circumstances, so that literature is produced in opposition to itself through the way that a given writer rejects these socially institutionalized constraints on its definition.

This idea is subsequently developed in Sartre's thinking to the point where literature can be understood as a complete break with the past and with everything that has gone before under that name. By choosing to write, a writer is effectively reinventing literature from scratch, 'as if no one before him had ever thought of writing', as Sartre puts it in his essay 'De la vocation d'écrivain'.[8] The writer has a choice between a literature that he needs to reinvent, and a continuation of its

---

[6] 'Les Écrivains en personne', interview with Madeleine Chapsal, in Jean-Paul Sartre, *Situations, IX* (Paris: Gallimard, 1972), pp. 9–39 (p. 31). The term 'écriture' was being used as a synonym for 'literature' with increasing frequency at this time, under the impetus, perhaps, of Barthes's *Le Degré zéro de l'écriture*, published in 1953.

[7] *Qu'est-ce que la littérature?*, p. 70 [pp. 13–14]. All further page references are to these editions.

[8] In Michel Contat and Michel Rybalka (eds.), *Les Écrits de Sartre: chronologie, bibliographie commentée, textes retrouvés* (Paris: Gallimard, 1970), pp. 694–8 (p. 698). The essay was first published in 1950.

existing forms. Sartre, like Leiris, calls these existing forms 'les Belles-Lettres' and, again like Leiris, views them as the antithesis of authentic literature. He elaborates this point in the conversations with Simone de Beauvoir recorded in 1974, when he suggests that the essence of literature is created afresh by each new writer. There are as many essences as there are writers, each of them equally valid, so that one cannot say that Chateaubriand, for example, is more or less representative of the essence of literature than Proust.[9] In this case, each writer writes against all the literature that has gone before, as well as against the situation of the literature of his own time.

Literature's existence as these various forms of difference from itself is made possible only through the agency of the individual writer, and it is the choice made by a single individual that determines whether a piece of writing is a (prose) act or a (poetic) object, 'literature' or 'Belles-Lettres'. To be effective, that choice requires the wholesale, active engagement of the writer: 'the writer should engage himself completely in his works [. . .] as a resolute will and as a choice, as this total enterprise of living that each one of us is.'[10] If literature is an act, then it needs to be rooted in the choices and decisions that make up the totality of the life of the writer. Ultimately, the difference between prose and poetry lies less in any formal distinction than in the attitudes and positions of their respective authors. The poet exists at a remove from both language and the world, which he decides to view as a spectacle; the prose writer, on the other hand, is someone who 'knows' that language is action and who opts positively for writing as a means of acting on the world: 'the prose-writer is a man who has chosen a certain method of secondary action which we may call action by disclosure' (p. 73 [p. 17]). To appreciate the force of literature's intervention in the world requires the reader to ground the literary text in the existential project of its author. As Sartre says, with reference to the example of Flaubert, 'If we do not regress continually [. . .] in the process of reading, to *the author's desires and ends*, back to the *total enterprise* of Flaubert, we would quite simply make a fetish of the book [. . .] just like a piece of merchandise, considering it as a thing and not as the reality of a man objectified by his work.'[11] This 'total enterprise' is not just a prior condition for literature, but is palpable in every aspect of the writer's work, right down to the smallest stylistic detail, as Sartre makes clear when he outlines his aims in his study of Genet: 'to discover the choice that a writer makes of himself, of his life and of the meaning of the universe, right down to the formal characteristics of his style and composition, even the structure of his images and of the particularity of his tastes; to review in detail the history of a

---

[9] Simone de Beauvoir, *La Cérémonie des adieux: suivi de Entretiens avec Jean-Paul Sartre, août–septembre 1974* (1981; Collection Folio; Paris: Gallimard, 1987), p. 237. This position is itself an echo of that of Proust (see Ch. 12 above).

[10] *Qu'est-ce que la littérature?*, p. 84 [p. 29].

[11] Jean-Paul Sartre, *Critique de la raison dialectique* (Paris: Gallimard, 1960), p. 100; quoted in Douglas Collins, *Sartre as Biographer* (Cambridge, Mass.: Harvard University Press, 1980), p. 6.

liberation'.[12] Because literature is an act, and writing the implementation of an existential enterprise, biography becomes a necessary perspective, both for the understanding of a given literary text in all its aspects, and for the definition of literature itself.

It is no coincidence, then, that Sartre's prolific biographical writing begins alongside the theoretical *Qu'est-ce que la littérature?* and seems to take off in its wake. His *Baudelaire* was first published in 1946 as an introduction to Baudelaire's *Journaux intimes*, before being published in book form with Leiris's preface in 1947 (the year that also saw the publication of *Qu'est-ce que la littérature?*). It was followed by the 700-odd pages of *Saint Genet, comédien et martyr* (1952), and then by his study of Mallarmé written in 1952 and published in 1979.[13] The essay on the writer's vocation was published in 1950; and it was in 1953 that he first began work on the autobiographical account of his own vocation, which appeared as *Les Mots* in 1963. Sartre was also an avid reader of biographies and an innovative theorist of biography (in his *Question de méthode*, 1960).[14] However, these biographies and the associated discussions of the issue of biography need to be seen above all as the logical continuation of the theoretical arguments of *Qu'est-ce que la littérature?*, and for this reason I shall be concentrating on the issue of literary biography in what follows.

Sartre's theoretical account of literature may presuppose biography, as I am suggesting, but the biographies also considerably complicate the view of literature proposed by the theory. Biography does more than provide the necessary condition for literature to be literature: it also reveals literature's negative and more problematic side. And biography emerges here as something that can prevent literature from being literature, for the image of the writer's biography proves to be the lure that tempts writers away from action and into the evasions and inertia of *mauvaise foi*. The triumphalism of *Qu'est-ce que la littérature?*—according to which it is enough to choose the act of prose over the object that is poetry, or literature against its previous incarnations—is modulated in the biographies to present literature as an altogether more ambivalent entity, and writing as a more dubious existential choice than the theory would have its readers believe. In what follows I shall concentrate primarily on the biographical studies of Baudelaire, Genet, and Mallarmé, before returning to *La Nausée* in order to explore the ways in which, even before the emergence of his 'littérature engagée', Sartre's entry into literature as a writer of fiction placed biography

---

[12] Jean-Paul Sartre, *Saint Genet, comédien et martyr* (Paris: Gallimard, 1952), p. 645 [p. 584].

[13] A substantial part of the original manuscript vanished when explosives planted by the OAS went off in Sartre's apartment in 1961. The published version is the sole surviving fragment of the original.

[14] On Sartre as a writer of biography see Collins, *Sartre as Biographer*; Christina Howells, 'Sartre's Existentialist Biographies: Search for a Method', in France and St Clair, *Mapping Lives*, pp. 267–82; and Michael Scriven, *Sartre's Existential Biographies* (London: Macmillan, 1984). On Sartre as a reader of biography see Beauvoir, *La Cérémonie*, p. 284.

at the heart of his understanding of the literary enterprise. In the last part of the discussion I shall be examining the role of biography in constructing and undoing the sacred in the autobiographical text *Les Mots* where Sartre takes his leave of literature. I shall leave aside the Flaubert study, since it belongs to the period of Sartre's own life when he claimed to have abandoned his personal stake in the question of literature.

BAUDELAIRE, GENET, AND MALLARMÉ: THE AMBIVALENCE OF LITERATURE

In the three figures of Baudelaire, Genet, and Mallarmé, Sartre presents three different ways of using and defining the literary, by focusing on the role that literature played in the lives of the three writers. In each case literature figures as part of an active existential project and is never treated as the mere expression or illustration of an author's vision or personality. If literature is to be an act, it has to have behind it the intentional force of the writer's choice; to read a literary text as the passive expression of a prior existence is, in fact, to misread its potential for action. It is on these grounds that Sartre denounces what he calls the 'culture of subjectivity', and castigates the tendency of a certain kind of biographical approach to literature that limits writing to being the 'involuntary expression' of their writers' souls.[15] This kind of biographical reading, so often adopted in the name of a 'pure' literature by critics who ignore the intervenient thrust of writing, reduces the work of literature to an ephemeral, surface phenomenon that is made to count for less than the revelation of an authorial personality. For these critics, writers may argue, refute, or assert in their work, but 'the cause they are defending must be only the apparent aim of their discourse; the deeper goal is to yield themselves without seeming to do so' (p. 81 [p. 26]). Such a biographizing approach allows critics to sidestep the political arguments of Rousseau on the grounds that he abandoned his children, or to refuse to confront the 'strange revelations' of Nerval's *Sylvie* because its author lost his mind (p. 83 [p. 28]). In short, Sartre makes it clear that his recourse is not to biography in general, but to a particular biographical perspective that, in contrast to the presuppositions of the 'culture of subjectivity', treats the biographical subject as a full agent and his writing as the embodiment of an active project.[16]

---

[15] *Qu'est-ce que la littérature?*, pp. 83, 81.

[16] All Sartre's biographical subjects are men, and the entire discussion of *Qu'est-ce que la littérature?* presupposes that writers are male. Over and above the fact that *écrivain* is a masculine noun, Sartre invariably glosses the writer as 'un homme'. See the epigraph to this chapter and the quotation from *Critique de la raison dialectique*. His emphasis on agency and action presumably contributes to this assumption.

These are the broad principles of the theory. In actual biographical practice, however, Sartre begins by asking why anyone would choose literature as their preferred existential mode. Literature may be a 'total enterprise', but it nevertheless constitutes a somewhat aberrant choice for any individual to make; and far from presenting literature as a mode of intervention in the world, Sartre's biographical writings tend to emphasize its fictional, imaginary status. From this perspective literature negates the reality of the world rather than revealing it. It is 'a hole in being through which beings disappear', and contains something perverse and slightly mad.[17] As Sartre says in an interview in 1970, 'A writer is always a man who has to a greater or lesser degree chosen the imaginary: he requires a certain dose of fiction'.[18] The central question for the Sartrean biographer then becomes: how does someone come to make this strange choice?; and the focal interest of a Sartrean biography is the birth of the bizarre decision to write. Literature retains the status of an active project, but it is a project whose aim is the virtual destruction of the real world, and is undertaken because its subject is unable to live in the situation in which circumstances have placed him. Sartre's approach makes the most of the drama of this moment, which is portrayed as an existential crisis where literature appears as the only option available, with consequences for the writer that can be as disastrous as they are admirable.

The three instances of Baudelaire, Genet, and Mallarmé represent three different uses of this recourse to literature *in extremis*, illustrating between them a range of the existential risks to which that choice exposes the writer. Despite the fact that Mallarmé is a poet, and thus, according to *Qu'est-ce que la littérature?*, a producer of objects rather than the subject of an act, the most positive of these accounts is that of Mallarmé, precisely because his literary enterprise is shown to put the whole issue of 'literature' into question. The 'engagement' mentioned in the title of the surviving piece on Mallarmé is twofold. First, it is a lucid and thoroughgoing response on Mallarmé's part to the condition of literature at a time when a new awareness of the absence of any divine underpinning to poetry had left it without any justification: 'words collapse back on to themselves', and all that remains for poetry is what Sartre calls a 'desperate nominalism'.[19] With no divine transcendence to confirm the position of literature within the established bourgeois order, it became possible for the first time to ask the fundamental question: 'Does something like literature exist?'[20] If literature is to exist in this post-theological age, it can only be in a purely human and thoroughly desacralized mode. Mallarmé, says Sartre, was the first to respond to this situation by questioning the very terms of literature's existence, and he did so in a manner that determined not just the form and content of

---

[17] 'De la vocation de l'écrivain', p. 694.

[18] 'Sartre par Sartre', in *Situations, IX*, pp. 99–134 (p. 123).

[19] Jean-Paul Sartre, 'L'Engagement de Mallarmé [ed. M. Sicard]', *Obliques*, 18–19 (1979), pp. 169–94 (p. 170).

[20] Ibid., p. 193. Sartre slightly misquotes Mallarmé.

his poetry, but his entire personal being. The latter is the second element of Mallarmé's engagement in Sartre's account: 'he creates his own existence through the consciousness he has of his own impossibility' (p. 194). This consciousness is a new mode of human consciousness—reflexive, critical, and tragic—and it determines the entire course of Mallarmé's life as an inevitable downward progression. Existence and poetry become part of the same critical enterprise, which means that 'the poem is the suicide of the man and also of poetry', as Sartre puts it in his introductory essay to the *Poésies*.[21] In spite of the apparent negativity in this account—the poem becomes a kind of enactment of suicide, literature discovers its own impossibility, the poet's life can only appear as tragic—the underlying principle is, nevertheless, a positive one within a Sartrean perspective. For, far from using literature to provide a false solution to an existential dilemma, Mallarmé's engagement with poetry serves to challenge the very validity of his own existence, and his life appears as a lucid, if bleak, working out of that challenge—in short, as a kind of sustained existential undertaking under the shadow of literature's now questionable status.

In the figures of Baudelaire and Genet, Sartre explores the more negative and self-deceiving elements of the choice of literature by the writer. Baudelaire exemplifies the most extreme version of such a choice, and Sartre presents his engagement with literature primarily as a means of evading the reality of existence. The solitude into which the young Baudelaire was thrown by his mother's remarriage is, according to Sartre, the origin of his existential preference for seeing himself in his solitude, from without, as a self-sufficient and autonomous Other. He tries to turn the accident of his own isolation into a situation of his own deliberate choosing, and to create circumstances where this position can appear as desirable. The production of poetry is one means of achieving this: each poem Baudelaire writes represents a kind of assertion of self-possession 'a symbolical satisfaction of a desire for complete autonomy, of a longing for demiurgic creation'.[22] But, Sartre suggests, what Baudelaire chooses in poetry is less the chance to establish his creative independence than an image of himself as a poet. This image is the means by which he seeks to repress the sense of his own existence as an indistinct and murky condition where he is unable to see himself as gloriously 'other', and instead feels himself to be 'a vapid, glassy humour without consistency or resistance, which he could neither judge nor observe' (p. 28 [p. 24*]). As Sartre argues from *La Nausée* onwards, this viscous state is the truth about the way things are for each and every individual. Any choice that fails to acknowledge this truth and pretends that it is possible to 'be' rather than merely 'exist' is a false one; and to take oneself for a 'poet', a

---

[21] 'Mallarmé (1842–1898)', first published in 1966, and included in *Situations, IX*, pp. 191–210 (p. 197).

[22] Jean-Paul Sartre, *Baudelaire* (Paris: Gallimard, 1947), p. 80 [p. 68*]. All further page references are to these editions.

being whose role is preordained, amounts to a classic example of such *mauvaise foi*: 'Every poet pursues in his own way this synthesis of existence and being which, as we have already seen, is an impossibility' (p. 199 [p. 166]). In other words, choosing to be a poet is an (unrealizable) attempt to acquire a ready-made image of personhood, with a ready-made purpose in existence.

The chief culprit in this existential sleight of hand is not poetry as such, despite the fact that its supposed status as object promotes the false idea of a creative demiurge. The fatal conception of the poet that governs his *mauvaise foi* is derived above all from the image of the poet's life purveyed by biography. In Sartre's account, Baudelaire's choice of himself as 'poet' can in large part be attributed to the narrative of the life of Edgar Allan Poe. Sartre's reading makes little use of Baudelaire's own interpretation of the life,[23] but sets up an opposition between Poe's experience as he no doubt lived it in the present and the image conferred on his life by retrospect: 'When he was alive, the author of *Eurêka* would have been no more than indistinct flesh like [*Baudelaire's*] own [. . .]. Dead, however, the figure is completed and its outlines defined, the names poet and martyr can be applied to him quite naturally, his existence is a destiny, his misfortunes appear as the result of predestination' (p. 165 [p. 134]). Baudelaire supposedly seizes upon this figure constructed by the backward look of biography and views it as an existential truth that he seeks to make his own. He treats the narrative of Poe's life as a mirror in which he decides to see himself: 'That is what he *is*' (ibid.). As a consequence, his existence achieves a sacred justification: 'At once his existence was consecrated.' The poet becomes a kind of saint in his own eyes, not by virtue of any act, but by virtue of his self-appointed membership of a class of special beings: 'This means that in Baudelaire's mystic soul the lay community of artists had assumed a deeply religious value. It had become a church' (p. 166 [p. 138]). When Sartre identifies the sacred, it is in the form of the self-aggrandizement of *mauvaise foi* in which the biographical record of past poets functions as the means of a fake consecration. The false exemplarity of biography is based not on the lived experience of its subject, but on the profile created by posthumous retrospection. Baudelaire's error as a poet is to have wanted to live the story of a dead man's life; and it is not so much Poe, as the pastness of his biography that Baudelaire tries to replicate as the solution to his existential predicament: 'the Past offered him the image of that impossible synthesis of being and existence' (p. 196). This imitation of a life (Poe's) transformed by means of biographical retrospect makes Baudelaire's own life a failure: 'Baudelaire was the man who chose to look upon himself as though he were another person; his life is simply the story of the failure of this attempt' (p. 31 [p. 27]). In Sartre's account, Baudelaire's use of the story of Poe's life gives rise to the story of a failed life.

The biography of Genet, *Saint Genet*, recounts a similar existential 'error' on Genet's part, but, unlike Baudelaire, Genet finds a way out of the *mauvaise foi*

---

[23] Discussed in Ch. 8 above.

of his initial choice of himself as 'a writer'. He resembles Baudelaire in seeking a means of appearing to himself as Other. But whereas for Baudelaire this was a response to his experience of solitude, in Genet's case it is a reaction to being defined as a thief: 'Genet is a child who has been convinced that he is, in his very depths, *Another than Self.* His life will henceforth be only the history of his attempts to perceive this Other in himself and to look it in the face—that is, to have an immediate and subjective intuition of his wickedness, to *feel* he is wicked—or to flee it.'[24] By becoming a thief, Genet is attempting to become the person that others claim to see in him; and by then becoming a writer, he is simply pursuing a more visible form of 'glory' than that offered by theft. He opts for poetry as a means of salvation, albeit of a rather perverse kind, viewing it as a strategy for magnifying the abjection of his own self-image: 'The appearance of the word poem is still only one of the secondary aspects of his effort to become the Other that he is in the eyes of others' (p. 337 [p. 302*]). He avoids the failure of Baudelaire's life (at least as narrated by Sartre) because of his indifference to the recognized representatives of literature, and he is impervious to the temptations of biographical imitation. His attempt to 'be' on the basis of literature consists instead in his displacement of theft from the domain of real acts to its manifestation as literature:

Regarded as a thief, he wants to become a thief; but one does not give being to that which is. The stroke of genius, the illumination that finds the way out, is the choice of writing. He will create himself as a thief in another domain by establishing other relationships with the good citizens. He becomes the person who *manifests theft.* (p. 607 [p. 549], Sartre's italics)

Not only is this more subversive of the social order than actual theft, whose broader implications can be ignored by society, but it leads him to a changed awareness of his readers. By becoming a thief in literature, Genet is able not just to be the Other in his own eyes, but to use this role to defy his readership. In the process he turns literature from being a pretext for establishing a false persona for himself into an act of communication, however provocative, with contemporary readers.[25]

Summarizing Genet's trajectory from thief to poet, Sartre suggests that the degree of Genet's commitment to his choices leads him to acknowledge unforeseen dimensions in each successive situation. Genet's engagement with literature allows his literary enterprise to become the means whereby his choice is contested and shifted into a different domain: 'His extraordinary books are their own rebuttal: they contain both the myth and its dissolution' (p. 627 [p. 567]). Genet discovers something unexpected in literature—a readership of human beings—and this leads him then to acknowledge his own status as

---

[24] *Saint Genet*, p. 47 ([p. 35], Sartre's italics). Further page references are to this text.
[25] Or so Sartre claims. For further discussion of Genet's relations with his readers see Ch. 16 below.

a human being over and above that of thief or poet. Sartre describes Genet's development as follows: 'In willing himself, unreservedly, to be a thief, Genet sinks into the dream; in willing his dream to the point of madness, he becomes a poet; in willing poetry unto the final triumph of the word, he becomes a man; and the man has become the truth of the poet as the poet was the truth of the thief' (p. 643 [p. 582]). The unanticipated dimension that Genet encounters in literature ultimately makes literature unnecessary for his own existence, except as the means whereby he may become a man, rather than simply concoct a self-image of the poet as Other. Literature may serve as his 'salvation' as long as salvation is conceived in terms of acts rather than existential images. Once Genet has emerged on the far side of these images, his choice of himself as Other (thief, poet, manifestation of theft) is forgiven by Sartre in what eventually becomes the biography of a man, not the biography of a writer. It is, moreover, the biography of a man who has successfully sidestepped the lure of literary biography within his own existence.

   In these various ways Sartre's biographical writings considerably complicate the picture of literature outlined in *Qu'est-ce que la littérature?* Literature is opened up to question through its engagement with biography in terms that extend well beyond the purely theoretical discussion of the 1947 text. Similarly, biography appears as a double-edged project: in its positive form it is the means whereby the writer's 'total enterprise' can be revealed; while in its negative form, as an image of existence, its emulation leads the writer away from action and into a *mauvaise foi* that passes itself off as a form of consecration. The simple oppositions of the theory give way to a picture of literature as much more ambivalently placed between the authentic (secular) and the inauthentic (falsely sacred), with the use of biography being the key element in tipping the balance one way or the other. Literature's negative incarnation is grounded to a large extent in the misleading effects of biography, transforming existence into the essence that is character and the consecrated course of predestination. In its positive incarnation, where it portrays the writer's total commitment of his life to writing, biography not only validates literature as a project, but also has the effect of actively turning literature into a question to itself (Mallarmé's 'Does something like literature exist?'), or a contestation of its status (Genet's books become their own contestation). In short, literature's difference from itself would seem to be inseparable from such biographical configurations.

LA NAUSÉE: BIOGRAPHY AND THE POSSIBILITY OF LITERATURE

For Sartre everything depends on how the writer makes literature consubstantial with his life: as a misconceived attempt to live out a biographically based 'essence', or as an act with repercussions on the life. This preoccupation with the idea of living literature, and the ambivalence in the conception of literature itself are evident throughout Sartre's own literary career, from his entry into literature with the fictional text *La Nausée* (1938), to his farewell in the form of autobiography with *Les Mots* (1963). From the outset, and long before his espousal of 'engagement', Sartre's thinking about literature is inextricably bound up with biography, and this subject is built into the very fabric of his first novel, thus justifying its exceptional inclusion in my discussion. Sartre's preoccupation with the issue in *La Nausée* extends far beyond the fact that Roquentin abandons his biography of the Marquis de Rollebon as a prelude to his final decision to write a novel, and the problems with biography are only incidentally the problems that Roquentin encounters in his attempt to establish a coherent historical account of Rollebon's life. Rather, Sartre's novel presents biography as posing a permanent threat of distortion to the understanding of existence that Roquentin is gradually acquiring. This threat derives from the way that biography, sanctioned by a certain kind of literature, is allowed to become the model for the way that life is actually lived. Roquentin is not able to make the turn to writing until he has found a new way to position biography in relation to the artistic enterprise. *La Nausée* is far from being a simple condemnation of biography, for it pitches various alternative versions of literary or artistic biography against each other as a basis for its exploration of the issue of art.

Roquentin's biography of Rollebon is not a literary, but a historical, under-taking. Literary issues are not drawn into the frame until Roquentin, having discovered that the historical evidence provides nothing more than a series of disparate and inconsistent facts, considers that the only means of achieving coherence would have to come from fictional imagination. The principles of biographical narrative require an (imaginary) order to be imposed on (historical) facts that do not necessarily fit. The biographer constructs

reasonable hypotheses which take the facts into account: but I am only too well aware that they come from me, that they are simply a way of unifying my own knowledge. Not a single glimmer comes from Rollebon's direction. Slow, lazy, sulky, the facts adapt themselves at a pinch to the order I wish to give them but it remains outside of them. I have the impression of doing a work of pure imagination.[26]

Roquentin is led to abandon his biographical project because of the gap that he perceives between this principle of biographical coherence, which he associates with fiction, and the resistance of the biographical material that derives from history. There is a problematic lack of fit between the man (Rollebon) and any putative biographical representation.

However, the more fundamental criticism of biography to emerge from *La Nausée* arises from instances where a biographical order is integrated into a lived

---

[26] Jean-Paul Sartre, *La Nausée* [1939], in id., *Œuvres romanesques*, ed. Michel Contat and Michel Rybalka (Bibliothèque de la Pléiade; Paris: Gallimard, 1981), p. 80 [p. 26]. All further page references are to this edition.

existence, with the result that the nature of that existence becomes disturbingly distorted. This distortion concerns not only the way a life is represented, but the way it is lived. There are two moments when biographical representation is quite explicitly implicated in the production of false myths of a life. The first of these is through the figure of Gustave Impétraz, commemorated in the form of a bronze statue in the square outside the library, an image that is corroborated by a biographical entry in the *Grande Encyclopédie*. From this entry Roquentin learns that Impétraz flourished in the 1890s (incidentally, as we saw in Chapter 5, a golden decade for biography), was an 'inspector of the academy', a competent watercolourist, the author of two academic works and a 'poetic testament', as well as a person who was much missed by his family and 'people of taste' when he died in 1902 (pp. 35–6). In short, this biographical narrative provides the basis for the bourgeois respectability whose authority and ideological orthodoxy the bronze figure continues to endorse, posthumously exuding 'une sourde puissance' that Roquentin experiences as an actively hostile pressure.

In the case of Olivier Blévigne, the subject of one of the portraits that Roquentin describes on his visit to the Bouville museum, a two-page entry in the nineteenth-century *Petit Dictionnaire des grands hommes de Bouville* contributes to the gross misrepresentation,[27] both physical and moral, that Roquentin eventually discerns in the portrait. A man who, as Roquentin discovers from an old newspaper, was only 1.53 metres tall and spoke in a squeaky voice, is depicted in his portrait as an imposing personage with 'a threatening face, a superb gesture, and the bloodshot eyes of a bull' (p. 111 [p. 136]). On the moral plane, the real-life young man who was terrified by the Commune and subsequently became a furious, diminutive deputy is obscured behind a representation of 'the president of the club of Order' and 'the orator of the Moral Forces'. Biography and portraiture collude in these examples to convey a false record to posterity in the name of a bourgeois social order.

Despite the attempt to conflate them, the gap between the biographical representation and the actual historical fact is clearly visible here:

They had been painted with minute care; and yet, under the brush, their features had been stripped of the mysterious weakness of men's faces. Their faces, even the feeblest, were as clear-cut as porcelain: I looked at them in vain for some link with trees and animals, with the thoughts of earth or water. The need for this had obviously not been felt during their lifetime. But, on the point of passing on to posterity, they had entrusted themselves to a celebrated painter so that he should discreetly carry out on their faces the dredging, drilling, and irrigation by which, all around Bouville, they had transformed the sea and the fields. (p. 107 [p. 131])

Portraiture and biography share the same retrospective strategy of draining the sogginess out of real experience in order to propose a false image of human faces and human lives as having clean lines and necessary purpose.

---

[27] On such local dictionaries see Ch. 4 above.

In a number of the other portraits, however, the distinction between the mysterious weakness of men's faces and their porcelain-like effigies no longer holds, and Roquentin seems to be identifying ways in which biographical narrative has actually informed the experience of the subjects depicted in the paintings. Like Baudelaire, these subjects lived their lives as if they were already biographies. For Jean Pacôme life appears to have been a combination of rights and duties, which, from the start, gave it the necessity that biography and portraiture otherwise bestow in retrospect:

> For sixty years, without a moment's failing, he had made use of his right to live. [. . .] He had always done his duty, all his duty, his duty as a son, a husband, a father, a leader. He had also unhesitatingly demanded his rights: as a child, the right to be well brought up, in a united family, the right to inherit a spotless name, a prosperous business; as a husband, the right to be cared for, to be surrounded with tender affection; as a father, the right to be venerated; as a leader, the right to be obeyed without demur. (p. 101 [p. 124])

Leadership in particular confers a sense of necessity on any existence whose subject, like Pacôme, or General Aubry, or Lucien in Sartre's story 'L'Enfance d'un chef' in *Le Mur*, is defined as 'a boss'. A boss's life is already structured as an anticipation of his own biography, whose course he has simply to act out. The episode in the portrait gallery demonstrates not only how lives can be misrepresented by art, but also how those representations can determine the very substance of experience. This experience is contrasted with Roquentin's sense, after his visit to the gallery, that he has no right to his own existence, which appears to him as a kind of accident. His experience of his own life is quite unlike those of the subjects of portrait and biography: 'My life grew in a haphazard way and in all directions. Sometimes it sent me vague signals; at other times I could feel nothing but an inconsequential buzzing' (p. 101 [p. 124]). Such inconsequentiality could never provide the basis of a life-story of the kind implied by the portraits and confirmed by the biographical dictionary.

What Roquentin also discovers is that these life-stories are not the sole prerogative of the bourgeois citizen, the boss, or the civic dignitary, but are constantly being told in the world around him. While Roquentin is preoccupied with the fact that his own life has acquired '[a] halting, incoherent aspect' (p. 9 [p. 14]), others are narrating their experience in the form of 'clear, plausible stories' (p. 12 [p. 17]). The Autodidacte tries to persuade Roquentin that his life can be portrayed as a series of 'adventures'; Anny's 'moments parfaits' are her attempt to make real time conform to the dramatic structures of leave-takings and departures; Dr Rogé presents himself to the world as the sum total of his own past. These figures all construct their lives within the rhetorical framework of a 'life-story', and constantly seek to map their own experience on to the presuppositions of biographical narrative: 'a man is always a teller of tales, he lives surrounded by his stories and the stories of others, he sees everything that happens to him through them; and *he tries to live his life as if he were recounting it*' (p. 48 [p. 61]). In other words, man is an inveterate biographer. But, says Roquentin, such biographical narratives prevent him from living: 'you have to choose: to live or to recount' (ibid.).

The problem with 'adventures' is that they exist only in retrospect: events occur in one order, but we narrate them in reverse, with the hindsight that makes it possible to speak of the beginnings that never occur in unnarrated experience. The two orders—of narrative and of experience—can never coincide, but people persist in behaving as if they do. As the minutes tick by towards the moment of parting from Anny, Roquentin feels that every gesture has been choreographed, every word scripted by what he calls the 'rituals' of her *moments parfaits*, which are designed to confer on life the character of a staged play. It is not for nothing that Anny is an actress. Dr Rogé stockpiles his own experience in order to produce a construct called 'his past', which is a kind of capital on which he draws for the 'wisdom' that he dispenses in his dealings with others: 'never, not even for a moment, has he misjudged the way to keep and use his past: he has quite simply stuffed it, he has turned it into experience to be used on women and young men' (p. 81 [p. 100]). He turns himself into a living record of his own experience, but the result is like nothing so much as a stuffed animal. Not only does this taxidermy contradict Roquentin's own sense of the past as a gaping void, it also corrupts Dr Rogé's relation both to himself and to others. Accumulated experience has the effect of making people appear as so many 'cases', mere illustrations of a knowledge long since confirmed. The stockpiling of his past is moreover a device for Dr Rogé to conceal from himself his own impending death: 'he would like to shut his eyes to the unbearable reality: that he is alone, without any attainments, without any past, with a mind which is growing duller, a body which is disintegrating' (p. 84 [p. 103]). The principle of accumulation presupposed by the idea of a past does not square with the reality of dissolution: passing time vanishes, and bodies decay in ways that biographies, with their incremental view of lived time, are not constitutively designed to acknowledge.

La Nausée is an attempt to show how life-stories mislead us about the nature of living. Although the false coherence of biography is associated from early on in the novel with forms of fictional narrative, the question of literature is not directly addressed again until the end of the novel. It is only at this point that Roquentin, inspired by the example of the jazz song 'Some of These Days', decides to write a book, one of whose functions would be to throw some light on his own past and to allow him to recall it without revulsion. But what makes this different from the life-stories associated with official biography, civic portraits, adventures, perfect moments, and accumulated wisdom? The answer, if there is one, may be inferred from Roquentin's positioning of biography in relation to the song, which seems to represent the ideal work of art in Sartre's novel. Earlier on, while listening to this music, Roquentin has a fantasy of redemption through an art that would turn his life into a tune: 'what summits I would not reach if my *own life* were the subject of a melody' (p. 48 [p. 60], Sartre's italics). The real breakthrough comes when he is able to perceive the life alongside, but not assimilated to, the art. The relation between the work and the life is different from the one that the narrative constructs of adventure, perfect moments, and a stock-piled past impose on the existence they claim to represent.

As Roquentin listens to the song towards the end of the novel, it is not his own life that appears to him, but those first of the singer, and then of the songwriter. The life of the writer is more extensively pictured than that of the singer:

I am no longer thinking about myself. I am thinking about that fellow out there who composed this tune, one day in July, in the black heat of his room. I try to think about him *through* the melody and the white, acid sounds of the saxophone. He made that. He had troubles, everything wasn't working out for him as it should have: bills to pay—and then there must have been a woman somewhere who wasn't thinking about him the way he would have liked her to—and then there was this terrible heatwave which was turning men into pools of melting fat. There is nothing very pretty or very glorious about all that. (p. 208 [p. 250], Sartre's italics)

The songwriter's life is revealed through the song, with its money worries, its problems with women, and the sweat caused by the heatwave during which the song was composed. It is not, as Sartre concludes, a particularly pretty story, but this makes it all the clearer that its reality is not masked or misrepresented by the song. As Roquentin continues to listen, he finds himself wanting to know more about the writer's life: 'I should like to know something about that fellow. I should be interested to find out what sort of troubles he had, whether he had a woman or whether he lived alone' (p. 209 [p. 251]). Roquentin's desire for such information (which recalls Swann's desire to find out about the composer of the Vinteuil sonata) is so strong that Sartre seems to have invented much of it for the purposes of his novel, attributing its composition to a New York Jew (where Shelton Brooks was in fact of Afro-Canadian origin) and its performance to a black woman (who in reality was a Jewish New Yorker).[28] The biographical information that Roquentin wishes to have is relatively banal, but he seems to require it as a necessary counterpart to the song—'because he made that'. The writer's life is not regarded as the source material for the song, and if the song is imagined by its creator as a solution to the life, it is only on the material level of the money it is likely to make: 'He must have thought: with a little luck, this thing ought to bring in fifty dollars!' (p. 208 [pp. 250–1]). The life is presented above all as the situation in which the song is created, as if it were not possible for the listener to fully appreciate the aesthetic qualities of the music (its rigour, its serenity, its invulnerability) without having some knowledge of

---

[28] See Sartre, *Œuvres romanesques*, p. 1747, note to p. 27. Sartre was not alone in assuming that the singer, Sophie Tucker, was black: she occasionally blacked herself up for performances in accordance with the practices of the time, and was widely believed in Europe to be black. For further discussion of the history of this song see Adrian van den Hoven, ' "Some of These Days" ', *Sartre Studies International*, 6/2 (2000), pp. 1–11; and Deborah Evans, ' "Some of These Days": Roquentin's "American" Adventure', *Sartre Studies International*, 8/1 (2002), pp. 58–72.

the very different and decidedly humdrum circumstances of its creation. The song does not attempt to portray the life, and neither is the life the 'truth' of the song: the two are kept firmly apart, even while each requires and presupposes the other. In this way Roquentin reverts to biography, but here as a necessary element in his understanding of the creative enterprise. The role of biography is quite different from the one he rejects in the case of Rollebon as a false coherence imposed by fiction on the disparateness of material fact. It differs, too, from the misrepresentations of biographical entries and municipal portraits, and even more so from the false understanding of existence that derives from the life-stories that circulate in the everyday world, contaminating the sense that subjects have of their own individual lives.

Roquentin's ambition for himself is to produce a work of literature behind which his own existence would similarly become visible to its readers. There is, nevertheless, a hint of bad faith in this hope: for where it seems to be important that the songwriter has no awareness of the way in which the picture of his life affects the listeners to his song (Roquentin is deeply moved by it), Roquentin himself seems only too conscious of the possibility of this outcome, even before he has begun to write. When he claims that the 'Jew' and the 'Negress' have been 'saved' by the song, and 'washed of the sin of existing' (p. 209), their salvation seems operative only because they do not know it has happened. By contrast, it is precisely the desire for salvation that lies behind Roquentin's decision to write: 'there would be people who would read this novel and who would [. . .] think about my life as I think about the life of that Negress: as about something precious and almost legendary' (p. 210 [p. 250]). Although Roquentin seems to have arrived at a point where he can maintain a distance between art and biography (in the case of 'Some of These Days'), his final projection collapses the two together, albeit inadvertently, with the result that art reverts once again to being a false means of redemption and an inauthentic existential solution for the artist, as Sartre himself ruefully acknowledges in *Les Mots*.

Roquentin—and Sartre with him—is placed in a kind of double bind whereby, despite their realization that that a certain kind of art is made possible through a certain use of biography, the art in question is then permanently vitiated by this knowledge. In *Les Mots* Sartre hesitates between blaming his own self-deception and accusing the institution of literature in general. But the real problem lies elsewhere. The discovery of a different kind of aesthetic practice linked to an alternative biographical situation is valid only as long as it remains that of the reader-listener or the biographer, since the reader or listener seems inevitably to be a would-be biographer. The fatal moment comes when, under the aegis of his new-found knowledge, the reader decides to become a writer. The knowledge he has as a reader about the biographical basis of art, however enlightened in comparison with established views, will fatally undermine his own literary practice as a writer. This, no doubt, is why Sartre's farewell to literature is not a farewell to literary biography, and why *Les Mots* is followed by the biographical enterprise of *L'Idiot de la famille*. If the writer's life is the means whereby literature becomes literature through its difference from itself, it is only in the eyes of the biographer—not the writer—that this can be so.

LES MOTS AND THE 'RETROSPECTIVE ILLUSION'

It is largely for this reason that *Les Mots* is not just a contestation of literature, but an attempted farewell. The autobiographical account of Sartre's childhood takes on literary form in order to underscore the break with literature that the book is designed to mark:

> I wanted it to be more literary than the others because I felt that it was a way of saying goodbye to a certain kind of literature, and that I should produce it, explain it, and take my leave of it. I wanted to be literary in order to show the error of being literary. [. . .] I wanted to show that the literature I'd pursued in my youth and then in my novels and short stories was over and done with, and I wanted to emphasize the fact by writing a very literary book about my childhood.[29]

However, it is not so much a certain type of literature that Sartre is renouncing here, as a certain use of it. Specifically, it is the use of literature as a means of acquiring the kind of life that the biographies of writers create for their subjects. Described here as the 'retrospective illusion',[30] this backward look also informed the kind of life that Roquentin, at the end of *La Nausée*, was hoping to acquire through his decision to write. Sartre himself acknowledges that 'for a long time, writing was asking Death or Religion in disguise to remove my life from chance' (p. 210). *Les Mots* is a sustained attempt actively to desacralize the figure of the writer. Paul Bénichou's 'consecration of the writer' is reinterpreted by Sartre as a fraudulent and anachronistic appropriation of a defunct Christianity; and his break with literature seems to be based on the assumption that literature cannot avoid this sham consecration of its practitioners, even when, as the examples of *La Nausée* and Sartre's own biographical studies suggest, it tries to draw a distinction between 'good' and 'bad' versions of biography. The form that the farewell takes is not that of a simple denunciation, although the book contains some exuberant excoriations, for Sartre includes himself in the self-aggrandizements produced by literary biography through his own autobiographical narration. Furthermore, it is on the basis of autobiography's anchorage in the present that this denunciation is also a personal renunciation, and that the writing of the book seeks to inaugurate a life without literature for its author: Sartre presents himself as 'a man [. . .] who no longer knows what to do with his life' (p. 212 [p. 157*]).

---

[29] Beauvoir, *La Cérémonie*, pp. 305–6 [p. 214*].
[30] Jean-Paul Sartre, *Les Mots* (1960; Collection Folio; Paris: Gallimard, 1972), p. 168 [p. 156*]. All further page references are to this text.

The sacred provides the basis for a large part of the book's metaphorical repertoire: Sartre's family history is one of a series of substitute religions. It begins with his great-grandfather's move from schoolteaching into the grocery business, described by Sartre as a defrocking which the misguided grocer seeks to reverse through the careers of his sons. Charles Schweitzer's decision to become a teacher in his turn is presented as a compromise, an 'attenuated spirituality', the exercise of a kind of 'priesthood' that allows a certain latitude (pp. 11–12). Literature is annexed to this secular priesthood in ways that profoundly affect all its manifestations in Sartre's own childhood: books turned his grandfather's study into 'a tiny shrine' (p. 37), or a 'temple' (p. 53); Charles's German language primer, the *Deutsches Lesebuch*, was a sacred object, and its author 'a craftsman who specialized in the manufacture of holy objects, as respectable as an organ-builder or an ecclesiastical tailor' (p. 39 [p. 29*]); the exact repetitions of stories read from books makes story-time the equivalent of a church liturgy: 'I was at Mass: I was present at the endless round of names and events' (p. 43 [p. 32*]); books are the repositories of an 'incorruptible substance', the text (p. 155); the Holy Spirit shimmers between the lines of Flaubert's writing (p. 52); and Sartre describes himself as being as 'zealous as a catechumen' (p. 42 [p. 32]). Under the priestly tutelage of his grandfather, the young Sartre discovers a sacred calling in literature: 'I had found my religion: nothing seemed more important to me than a book' (p. 52 [p. 39]).

Books themselves may be 'raised stones', but their sacred status derives ultimately from their authors who figure as the saints and prophets of the religion defended by Charles's priesthood and the young Sartre's neophyte zeal: '[My grandfather] taught me the names of famous men; alone, I would recite the list from Hesiod to Hugo, without making a mistake: they were the Saints and the Prophets' (p. 54 [p. 40*]). Books are a kind of transubstantiation of their creators: Corneille, for example, transmigrates into a large red volume with sharp corners, and to become an author is to metamorphose from a chrysalis into 'twenty-five folio butterflies, which would escape, feverishly beating all their pages, and settle on a shelf in the Bibliothèque Nationale' (p. 164 [p. 122*]). The young Sartre looks forward to a future as a writer, when 'my bones are leather and cardboard, my parchment flesh smells of glue and mildew, and I settle comfortably through a hundredweight or so of paper' (ibid.*). The sacred character of literature is demonstrated in the effect that books supposedly have on the lives of their authors. The function of writing in the eyes of Sartre's childhood self is to turn its subject into an 'author', and authorship appears as a way of acquiring a reality that is missing from everyday existence: 'Painting real objects with real words written with a real pen, I was damned if I would not become real myself too' (p. 136 [p. 101*]). Authorial status confers an essence and an identity on its practitioners: 'I was a writer just as Charles Schweitzer was a grandfather: from birth and for ever' (p. 145 [p. 108*]). Writing is a means of transforming one's being into a different, more glorious substance, and of becoming an 'Other' in the eyes of the world:

I could [. . .] replace the sounds of my life by imperishable inscriptions, my flesh by a style, and the languid spirals of Time by eternity. I could appear to the Holy Spirit as a precipitate of language, become an obsession for the human race and at last be *other*, other than myself, other than others, other than everything. I would not write for the pleasure of writing but to carve this glorious body in words. (p. 163 [pp. 121–2], Sartre's emphasis)

Sixty kilos of paper in twenty-five volumes of collected works are the prerequisite for acquiring this consecration, which also takes the form of 'the memory of an exemplary life' that the writer leaves behind him for posterity (p. 152). This was precisely Roquentin's fantasy and the motive for his recourse to literature. It is mediated by biography and reinforced by the 'retrospective illusion'.

The biographies narrated in the *Enfance des hommes illustres* leave their young reader living his life as his own obituary (p. 174). Biography recasts the whole quality of a life, for in biographical representations the passage of time is cancelled, and readers can enter the life at any point they choose. Each moment illustrates the essential truth of its protagonist—'his story becomes a kind of circular essence which is summed up in each of his moments' (p. 169 [p. 126])—and in any case chronology is covertly reversed: 'This was nowhere stated but everything would suggest that the chain of causes conceals an inverse and secret order' (ibid.). The end of a life is written into its beginning, in a mirage that the principle of exemplarity encourages readers to imagine they can enact in their own lives which will then be marked by the secret characteristic of predestination. The example of these narratives encourages the would-be writer to choose literature as the means whereby, as Baudelaire supposedly imagined, he might transform the banality of his existence into the kind of destiny that biographies of writers exhibit:

I came back in secret to this life, which I found tedious and which I had been able to fashion only into the instrument of my death, in order to save it; I looked at it through future eyes and it seemed to me a moving and wonderful story which I had lived on behalf of everyone, which no one, thanks to me, would ever have to relive and which it was enough to recount [. . .] I chose for a future the past of a famous dead man, and I tried to live in reverse. (pp. 167–8 [p. 125*])

Sartre's debunking of literature is carried out by this mockery of his own gullibility, and his sustained metaphorical representation of literature as a form of the sacred is used to expose a wilful misinterpretation on his own part: 'I thought I was giving myself to literature when I was, in fact, taking holy orders' (p. 210 [p. 155]). By identifying a sacred equivalent for every aspect of literature, but particularly by highlighting the myth of the writer as saint, Sartre is seeking to empty it of its power, and he increasingly equates his self-conferred consecration with 'imposture' (*passim*). *Les Mots* is an attempt at a thoroughgoing exorcism of the sacred in literature, which, by the end of the book, Sartre claims to have carried out: 'martyrdom, salvation, immortality have all crumbled, the building is becoming a ruin, I nabbed the Holy Spirit in the cellars and threw him out; atheism is a long drawn out and cruel undertaking: I believe I have seen it through to the end. I see clearly, I am undeceived' (p. 212). The language of the sacred on which literature was founded is systematically voided of its power in these denunciations.

More important in Sartre's strategy is the way that he continues to implicate himself in the myth he is denouncing. There turns out to be no simple opposition between adult and child, narrator and protagonist, even though much of the comedy in the book comes from the adult narrator's portrayal of the child protagonist. The errors of the child reader turn out also to have been those of the adult writer, and Sartre condemns himself for the self-deception of his aims in *La Nausée* and *L'Être et le néant*, where he used his position as author to exempt himself from the very condition he was describing. He has, he says, been disabused for a relatively short time: 'for the past ten years or so I have been a man who is waking up, cured of a long, bitter-sweet madness, who cannot believe it happened, and who cannot recall the folly of his old ways without laughing' (p. 212 [p. 157*]). He does not, however, say what this change was, or how it was brought about. There was a conversion, at some unspecified point, which has prompted this autobiography, but—strangely in the autobiographical tradition—it is not included in the narrative. The effect is to create a somewhat disturbing continuity between the derided past and the present of writing. For a start, Sartre is still writing: 'I have renounced my vocation, but I have not unfrocked myself. I still write. What else can I do?' (ibid.). He attempts to redefine writing as labour rather than as a mark of election, since it is, after all, his profession. In any case, he claims, he lacks any talent for it: 'my books reek of sweat and effort' (p. 139 [p. 103]). As indeed does all writing, since it is, by definition, a foreign language for its practitioners: 'From this I conclude that we are all the same in our calling: all convicts, all branded' (p. 140 [p. 104.]). By choosing to make his farewell to literature as literary as possible in its formal aspects, Sartre makes himself vulnerable to the possibility of continuing self-deception. The careful structure of the book that underpins its air of spontaneity, the density and classicism of its literary allusions, and the style of brilliant paradox,[31] combine to give it the appearance of a sequence of

---

[31] For discussion of these literary features of the text see Philippe Lejeune, 'L'Ordre du récit' dans *les Mots* de Sartre', in id., *Le Pacte autobiographique*, pp. 197–243 (on the structural organization of the text); Geneviève Idt, '*Les Mots*': *une autocritique en bel écrit* (Paris: Belin, 2001); Jacques Deguy, 'Les Références culturelles dans les manuscrits des *Mots*', in Michel Contat (ed.), *Pourquoi et comment Sartre a écrit 'Les Mots': genèse d'une autobiographie* (Paris: Presses universitaires de France, 1996), pp. 293–319; Jacques Lecarme, 'Sartre palimpseste', in Contat, *Pourquoi*, pp. 183–248; Jacques Lecarme, 'Table des allusions et des concordances intertextuelles dans "Les Mots"', in Contat, *Pourquoi*, pp. 249–91; and David Bellos, 'Patchworking in Sartre and Perec', in Hafid

'imperishable inscriptions' whose substance might, according to the myth that the book so elegantly castigates, replace the earthly form of its author. It is partly for this reason that Sartre confronts himself with the fact that 'this old ruined house, my imposture, is also my character: you can get rid of a neurosis but you are never cured of yourself' (p. 213 [p. 157]). The comically repudiated child does not exist in a different world, but lives on in the 50-year-old adult. Sartre has consequently to consider the possibility that his denunciation of the myth of literary salvation could turn out to be a covert perpetuation of it: 'I sometimes wonder if I am not playing at loser takes all and if I am doing my best to trample on the hopes of my past so that everything will be rendered to me a hundredfold' (p. 213 [p. 158]). And indeed nothing can guarantee that this is not the case.

Despite the self-cancelling threat that these autobiographical continuities pose to Sartre's enterprise, they differ in a crucial respect from the false illusion of the sacred generated by biography. For they identify a narrative viewpoint that is located in real time with real connections to the biographical subject that the young Sartre is in *Les Mots*, and this positions the book as an act that is likely to have concrete repercussions in an ongoing existence. Unlike the literary saints and heroes of his childhood, Sartre is not dead; and the story of his life has not reached the mirage of an end point that would confer a unique essence on its every moment. A future lies ahead, and he does not know how to use it ('what else can I do?'), or what form it will take, not least because it is liable to be perceptibly affected by the book he has just written. Leiris hoped that writing his autobiography would retroact upon his real life; but whereas for him this was an attempt to restore an element of the sacred to literature, for Sartre the challenge is, quite on the contrary, to make a break with literature and to explore the possibility of writing beyond and outside its permanent susceptibility to a fake consecration.

The self-containment of biography, whose role is instrumental in such consecrations, is undone by the continuities of autobiography: the continuity of identity between protagonist and narrator, and the temporal continuities between past, present, and future. While it is perfectly possible to write autobiography as a form of biography, using retrospect to narrate a life as destiny and vindicate the retrospective illusion (like *La Nausée*'s Dr Rogé, for example), Sartre chooses to exploit the characteristics of the genre in ways that make autobiography a kind of anti-biography: the story of his life (or at least of his childhood) describing a predicament that turns out still to be current, and intended as an act (in this case of farewell) in a life whose end has not been reached. In this way autobiography, poised here on the frontier between literature and its beyond,

Gafaïti (ed.), *Recyclages culturels/Recycling Culture* (Paris: L'Harmattan, 2003), pp. 95–102 (on literary and other cultural allusions).

takes as its target, once and for all, the biographical presuppositions associated with the notion of literature. The instability of the idea of literature in Sartre is a direct consequence of literature's entanglement with biography which from beginning to end of his career is the source of the contrasting evaluations of the literary as authentic existential project on the one hand, and, on the other, as the promoter of *mauvaise foi*.

PART VII

HEROES, SAINTS, AND GENERIC ANACHRONISMS

FROM the early years of the twentieth century biography was turned in the direction of both fiction and autobiography, and, as we have seen, it was in these arenas that the question of the literary was most fully explored. The emphasis on the inner life, and the concern with lived experience and creativity all contribute to this turn, and the results in the domain of autobiography are considerable, with Gide's *Si le grain ne meurt*, Leiris's *L'Âge d'homme* and *La Règle du jeu*, and Sartre's *Les Mots*. Over and above the tendency towards fiction within biographical writing, the novel also absorbed the interest in the relations between biography and the literary, as instanced, for example, by *La Recherche* and *La Nausée*. What follows suggests a further change of direction, as the biographical perspective reasserts its role in literature, but does so by looking to the distant past for its generic models. Both Genet, writing in the 1940s and 1950s, and Pierre Michon, writing in the 1980s and 1990s, choose to present themselves as writers of 'lives', rather than as 'biographers'. Genet, for all his reputation as an autobiographical writer, assigns himself the function of the celebrant of the lives of his hero-subjects, and he has recourse to medieval models of life-writing as the means whereby he can carry out his self-appointed role. Pierre Michon engages in a similar kind of generic experimentation, where his literary ambitions are realized in a resurrection of the form of the lives of the saints. 'Hagiography' is often used as a term of disparagement in contemporary discussions of biography, but, in adopting the model of the saint's life, Michon radically revises the assumptions of contemporary biographical writing in ways that, like Genet's 'lives' of his heroes, place the literary at the centre of his concerns.

16

Genet's *chant d'amour* and the Lives of the Heroes

our literary delight, our heart [. . .] beats for something that is horrible, for a condemned man in Genet who is going to his death, for soaks who drink like fish and keel over in barns. It is another instance of grand rhetoric clothing worthless matters.

(Pierre Michon, 'Pierre Michon, Arlette Farge, entretien')

Genet's prose writings are presented by means of a first-person narrator, in whom it is tempting to decipher the figure of Genet himself. Life and work appear to connect in ways that mean he is most often read as a broadly autobiographical writer whose prose works in particular, produced between 1942 and 1949, draw freely on his own, often scandalous, experience up to and including the time of writing. Genet is also unusual amongst writers in that his literary activity was limited to a relatively short period of his life lasting little more than twenty years,[1] and this has led many critics to make sense of the work by placing it in the wider context of Genet's overall development. In other words, it is commonly assumed, first, that Genet is writing about himself, and secondly, that the work needs to be seen as a stage in a larger and longer life project.

This is certainly how Sartre, as early as 1952, construed Genet's development, in his existential biography *Saint Genet, comédien et martyr*, which served as the first volume of the collected works of Genet published by Gallimard. As we saw in Chapter 15, Sartre argues that literature is a freely chosen solution

---

[1] For the poems, 1939–47; for the prose, 1942–9; for the plays, 1946–61; see Edmund White, *Genet* (London: Chatto & Windus, 1993). In his interview with Hubert Fichte, Genet gives the year 1939 as the moment when he began to write: 'Entretien avec Hubert Fichte', in Jean Genet, *Œuvres complètes*, vol. vi: *L'Ennemi déclaré: textes et entretiens* (Paris: Gallimard, 1991), pp. 141–76 (p. 165). (Hereafter *Œuvres complètes* will be abbreviated to *OC*.) Genet's last play, *Les Paravents*, was first performed and finally published in 1961. Jean-Bernard Moraly adopts a slightly different perspective by arguing that all of Genet's life was the life of the writer from beginning to end: see id., *Jean Genet: la vie écrite* (Paris: Éditions de la Différence, 1988). Genet's final published work, *Un Captif amoureux*, is not ostensibly a work of literature, although Nathalie Fredette argues for a continuity between it and his earlier prose fiction: see ead., *Figures baroques de Jean Genet* (Montreal: XYZ; Saint-Denis: Presses universitaires de Vincennes, 2001).

to an impossible situation, and that Genet's ultimate achievement was to have moved beyond his strictly literary project: 'The Poet had buried the Saint; and now the man is burying the Poet.'[2] Genet himself lent support to this kind of assumption by repeatedly emphasizing the finite and short-lived nature of his literary activities. When he was signing his first book contract (for three titles) in 1943, Genet was already announcing the end of his writing career;[3] and when talking about it in retrospect, he tended to downplay his writing by stressing the purely instrumental function that his books served in providing him with a means of getting out of prison: 'My own view is that since all my books were written in prison, I wrote them in order to get out of prison. Once I was out of prison, there was no reason to go on writing. My books got me out of clink, but after that what else is there to say?'[4] However, in making this point, he also mentions Rimbaud in a way that suggests a comparison between the poet and himself, and implies a seriousness of literary ambition in the work that he claims to have left behind him.

A sense of that seriousness has led critics to focus on the ways in which Genet complicates, or even undermines, an apparently autobiographical record. Autobiography engages the literary first and foremost around questions concerning the demarcations between fact and fiction in his works. Genet invites his readers to read his 'novels' as the story of his own life. But if it seems reasonable to see his childhood in Alligny-en-Morvan ascribed to Louis Culafroy in *Notre-Dame-des-Fleurs* (1948), his time in the reform school of Mettray depicted in *Miracle de la rose* (1946), and his years as a vagrant in Spain as the subject of *Journal du voleur* (1949)—these being his most overtly 'autobiographical' texts—the rest is largely conjecture. Genet himself did much to foster uncertainty about his own experience, using both his writing and the interviews he gave to blur the line between the imagined and the real as it applied to his own life. Most critics, however, accept these uncertainties, and see the literary interest of Genet's writing precisely in the way a simple autobiographical reading of his work is blocked or made problematic by the very activity of writing, thus raising the stakes involved in connecting the autobiographical and the literary: 'in the final analysis, Genet pursues his project less in order to find himself (or even to go in search of himself) than to renew the adventure which consists of writing, writing himself and rewriting (himself).'[5] Even Derrida, while claiming that neither

---

[2] Sartre, *Saint Genet*, pp. 645, 635.   [3] See White, *Genet*, p. 246.

[4] 'Entretien avec Bertrand Poirot-Delpech' [1982], in Genet, *OC* vi, pp. 227–41 (p. 230).

[5] Fredette, *Figures baroques*, p. 22. Similarly, Mairéad Hanrahan writes of 'cette recherche de soi qu'implique pour Genet l'écriture': in ead., *Lire Genet: une poétique de la différence* (Montreal: Presses de l'Université de Montréal, 1997), p. 21. See also Susan Marson: 'the writer cannot be found at the centre of his images' but instead 'appears in the space between them, in the mosaic formed by their juxtaposition', in ead., 'The Empty Crypt: Autobiographical Identity in Genet's *Journal du voleur*', *Romance Studies*, 19 (2001), pp. 29–39. Serge Meitenger's discussion of the *Journal du voleur* is based on the question as to whether life or fiction is at the origin of Genet's *récit de vie*: see id., 'L'Irréel de la jouissance dans le *Journal du voleur* de Genet', *Littérature*, 62

autobiography nor literature is relevant to Genet's writing, nonetheless proposes a view of that writing as a kind of extended 'signature' on Genet's part,[6] so that, for all his opposition to them, Derrida's approach may still be regarded as a kind of variant of the concepts 'autobiography' and 'literature'. In one way or another, despite their acknowledgement of the complex and problematic nature of these terms and of the relation between them, critics still tend to treat them as the ultimate horizon of their understanding of Genet's writing. Read as autobiography, Genet's texts construct the literary in terms either of fiction, which complicates autobiographical fact, or of writing, which subverts their apparently autobiographical aim.

It would, of course, be absurd to deny the presence of an autobiographical component in Genet's writing, however hard it might be to identify this component with any certainty. And one cannot ignore the autobiographical intentions that his 'fiction'claims for itself,[7] such as the one made in the opening pages of *Notre-Dame-des-Fleurs*: 'I want [. . .] to recreate as I please, and for the enchantment of my cell [. . .] the story of Divine whom I knew so little, the story of Notre-Dame-des-Fleurs, and have no doubt, *my own story.*'[8] But if Genet claims to be writing his own story (the place and date given at the end of the text—'La Prison de Fresnes, 1942'—serve to endorse the reference to his cell in the quotation),[9] he makes it equally clear here that he is writing the lives of others, and that his project is more biographical than autobiographical. His apparent ignorance of Divine's life and the improbability of the name of Notre-Dame-des-Fleurs do not detract from his stated intention. Neither, I would argue, does his occasional, albeit equivocal, assertion that he is ascribing his own experiences to others: 'you will not doubt that ultimately it is my own destiny, whether true or false, that I am placing, sometimes as rags, and sometimes as court robes, on the shoulders of Divine' (*NDF*, pp. 77–8). Over and above the autobiographical intent, and despite the complexity he introduces into it, Genet

(1986) pp. 85–74 (p. 67). In a similar vein Richard N. Coe claims that Genet hesitates between autobiography and fiction: see id., *The Vision of Jean Genet* (London: Owen, 1968), p. 102. Finally, Marie Redonnet argues that: 'la vie passée du narrateur [. . .] se confond avec celle de l'auteur. Mais le projet n'est pas autobiographique, il est légendaire': in ead., *Jean Genet, le poète travesti: portrait d'une œuvre* (Paris: Grasset, 1999), p. 40.

   6 Jacques Derrida, *Glas*, 2 vols. (1974; Paris: Denoël/Gonthier, 1981).

   7 The generic ambiguity of the prose texts that I am discussing makes it hard to know quite how to refer to them. They are too autobiographical and too factual for 'fiction' not to pose problems, and too fictitious for 'autobiography'. As far as possible I shall avoid using any term, but, where some word is inescapable, I shall use 'fiction' and 'novel' to describe Genet's prose texts that have a creative rather than a critical or documentary function. My own discussion will bypass the fictional status of the texts and treat them as biographies, since the core issue is that of the non-fictional status of the biographical subjects, not that of their representation.

   8 Jean Genet, *Notre-Dame-des-Fleurs* (1944; Collection Folio; Paris: Gallimard, 1976), p. 17 (hereafter referred to as *NDF*).

   9 He also talks about 'mon besoin de parler de moi' (*NDF*, p. 225), and welcomes the moment when he claims he can speak openly about himself: 'Maintenant, je pourrais, sans fard, sans transposition, sans truchement, dire ma vie ici' (p. 293).

is presenting himself first and quite simply as a biographer, as a narrator of the lives of others. Curiously, however, this claim has been taken much less seriously by readers and critics than his claim to be an autobiographer. So much so that many have followed the cue, in comments like the one just quoted, as a basis for adopting a perspective that can treat his biographical narratives only as a thinly veiled form of autobiography. Sartre, for example, asserts that 'Divine is Genet himself'; and of the *Journal du voleur* he writes: 'Genet presents a teeming and sprawling crowd which intrigues and transports us, and *changes into Genet before Genet's own eyes.*'[10] Even when he is depicting a mass of others, says Sartre, Genet can only ever write about himself.

However, I propose to take Genet's biographical project as seriously as others have taken the autobiographical one, and to read his writing primarily as a biographical venture. There is certainly much in Genet's writing to support this view, and nowhere more so than in the texts that seem to contain an autobiographical narrative—*Notre-Dame-des-Fleurs*, *Miracle de la rose*, and *Journal du voleur*—and it is these that I shall be exploring in this discussion. Indeed, it is the very self-consciousness of Genet's narrative in these texts that allows him the space to discuss his biographical aims, namely, to tell the story of others (Divine or Notre-Dame-des-Fleurs), and to do so with maximum awareness of his own narratorial role as biographer: 'recreate [the story of Notre-Dame-des-Fleurs] as I please, and for the enchantment of my cell'. In this particular instance Genet may seem to be presenting a rather egocentric view of his storytelling function, underscoring his control of the material and stressing his need to alleviate the boredom of prison, but it is much more common for Genet to present his 'biographies' as a celebration of their subjects.[11] The aim of his writing, it would seem, is principally to glorify the people he portrays. *Notre-Dame-des-Fleurs* opens with Genet recalling three murderers and one traitor: Weidmann, 'Ange Soleil the negro', 'the soldier Maurice Pilorge', and 'a ship's ensign who was still a child'. He goes on to explain his role in relation to these figures: 'it is *in honour of their crimes* that I am writing my book' (pp. 9–10). In other words, the book is introduced as a celebration of the deeds of others. Similarly, he writes in *Miracle de la rose*: 'Harcamone [. . .] when all is said and done, remains [the book's] *sublime and final cause.*'[12] Since the protagonists of Genet's biographies are all criminals, celebration is inextricably entwined with provocation. As a biographer Genet will exploit every strategy at his disposal in order to glorify his unlikely

---

[10] Sartre, *Saint Genet*, p. 500, and Sartre's preface to *Journal du voleur*.

[11] In fact, he never uses the word 'biography', in part perhaps because of its modern connotations; and neither, indeed, does he use the word 'autobiography'. But I shall use both terms in my discussion as the simplest way of referring, respectively, to stories about others, and to stories about himself.

[12] Jean Genet, *Miracle de la rose* [1946], 4th edn. (Décines: M. Barbezat, L'Arbalète, 1993), p. 50 [p. 41] (hereafter referred to as *MDR*). Genet's *Pompes funèbres*, written and published (n.p.) in 1948 after *Miracle de la rose* and before *Journal du voleur*, is dedicated to Jean Decarnin and, as Genet writes, 'il a pour but de *dire la gloire de Jean D.*' (p. 5).

heroes, and it is in this celebration that his engagement with the idea of literature is most radically worked out.

GENET AND THE *GRAND CHANT COURTOIS*

The word Genet most frequently uses to refer to the manner in which he presents his biographical subjects is 'chanter'. As we shall see, this word and the strategy it refers to remain a central and uncontested element of Genet's outlook long after he has ceased to write fiction,[13] but it is there in the very earliest texts. For example, in speaking of Mignon, another of the biographical protagonists of *Notre-Dame-des-Fleurs*, Genet provides what he claims is 'an almost accurate portrait' of him, and continues: 'if I describe him, I cannot stop *hymning* [*chanter*] him' (*NDF*, p. 23). Later on, in a slightly more abstract formulation, he writes: 'I want to *hymn* [*chanter*] murder, since I love murderers. *Hymn* [*chanter*] it without disguise' (p. 107). In *Miracle de la rose* he emphasizes Mettray, the reformatory, as the object of his song: 'Will it be said that I'm singing [*je chante*]? I am. I sing Mettray'; and he contrasts this with the objectless song of the readers whom he so frequently repudiates: 'Your song [*votre chant*] has no object. You sing the void.'[14] Genet's song is not a simple lyrical outburst that begins and ends with the singer; it presupposes and requires an object. In a comment in the *Journal du voleur* Genet specifically uses the notion of song to shift emphasis away from a preoccupation with himself (autobiography) and to focus instead on an Other, a hero and a beloved: 'this report on my inner life [. . .] will be only *a song of love* [*un chant d'amour*]'.[15] The importance of this Other is so great that Genet will go so far as to invent his lover if need be: 'heroism is what seems to me most charged with amorous properties, and since there are no heroes except in our minds, they will therefore have to be created' (*JV*, ibid.). In some cases the focus is so powerfully on the object being celebrated that it is no longer the writer who is said to sing, but the objects he describes: 'Talent is courtesy with respect to matter; it consists in *giving song* [*un chant*] *to what was dumb*' (p. 123 [p. 99]).

---

[13] I am referring here to the texts he wrote in the late 1950s about Abdallah the tightrope walker, and about the work of Giacometti and Rembrandt, which I shall be discussing below.

[14] *MDR*, p. 95 [p. 79]. For a discussion of Genet's relations with his readers see Michael Sheringham, *French Autobiography: Devices and Desires* (Oxford: Clarendon Press, 1993), pp. 146–8; and Colin Davis, *Ethical Issues in Twentieth-Century French Fiction: Killing the Other* (London: Macmillan, 1999), pp. 160–85. I am suggesting here that the relations Genet has with the others he depicts in his texts need to be distinguished from those he has with the others who are his readers. I shall return below to the question of Genet's treatment of his readers.

[15] Jean Genet, *Journal du voleur* (1948; Collection Folio; Paris: Gallimard, 1982), p. 112 [p. 89] (hereafter referred to as *JV*). Genet used the phrase 'chant d'amour' as a title for two of his other works. The first was a poem dedicated to his lover Lucien Sénémaud, written in 1946 and positioned after *Miracle de la rose* in *OC* ii (Paris: Gallimard, 1951), pp. 397–402. The second was for the only film that Genet ever directed; it was made in 1950 and stars Lucien Sénémaud. See White, *Genet*, pp. 328–31.

Elsewhere it is the very words he uses that become the source of his *song of love*: 'So I have recourse to words. Those which I use, even if I attempt an explanation by means of them, will *sing*' (pp. 112–13 [p. 89]). This is borne out in the description he imagines for his lover Lucien: 'I would be overjoyed if I could call him scoundrel, blackguard, riff-raff, guttersnipe, hoodlum, crook, charming names whose function is to evoke what you, derisively call a pretty world. But these words *sing*. They *hum*' (pp. 183–4 [p. 145]). Genet's song creates harmonics in every dimension of his work, from singer to object to medium.

Moreover, in using the term 'chant', Genet is invoking a highly traditional conception of the literary, in which poetry is equated with song, whether it is in Victor Hugo's *Chants du crépuscule*, or the 'cantos' (*chants* in French) that form the basic unit of many poetic works, from Dante's *Divina commedia* to Lautréamont's *Chants de Maldoror*. More specifically, given that Genet's *chants* are presented as *chants d'amour*, designed to celebrate the objects of Genet's love, the term harks back as far as the troubadour tradition developed in the form of the 'grand chant courtois' in some of the earliest poetry to be written in French.[16] In this tradition singing is inseparable from its object. Singing and loving are interchangeable activities, and the function of the poem as song is to 'express *fine amour*'. Or as Paul Zumthor summarizes it: 'if [the beloved] is loved, she is sung'.[17] Except for the fact that Genet's lovers are all male, exactly the same could be said of him.

This is not, however, to suggest that Genet's project is based on a scholarly acquaintance with medieval poetry, but rather that, perhaps through his reading of Ronsard at Mettray,[18] he seems to have had an intuitive sense of the workings of this literary tradition. Added to which, one might mention the affinity he claims to feel with the feudal cast of mind, as in his image of himself as valet or faithful hound to Stilitano's duke (*JV*, pp. 64, 66), or the more general assertion he makes about the way his search for a literary language takes him back in time to the Middle Ages (and beyond):

In order to achieve poetry here [. . .] my words make appeal [. . .] to the beauty of those [epochs] that are dead or dying [. . .]. It is always to these that I have recourse. They proliferate and absorb me. It is their fault that I make my way through genealogical strata, the Renaissance, the Middle Ages, Carolingian, Merovingian, Byzantine and Roman times, epics and invasions, in order to arrive at the Fable where all creation is possible. (*JV*, pp. 189–90 [pp. 149–50*], original italics)

It is this retrospective mindset that contributes to Genet's transformation of the *grand chant courtois* into a narrative of the life of his beloved as hero.

---

[16] The reference is to the work of the 'trouvères' in twelfth-century France. The term 'grand chant courtois' was coined by Roger Dragonetti in 1961 and is discussed by Paul Zumthor in his *Essai de poétique médiévale* (Paris: Éditions du Seuil, 1972), ch. 5, to which I am indebted here. See also Simon Gaunt and Sarah Kay, *The Troubadours: An Introduction* (Cambridge: Cambridge University Press, 1999).

[17] Zumthor, *Essai*, p. 212.   [18] See Genet, 'Entretien avec Hubert Fichte', p. 165.

When looked at from the perspective of biography, Genet is clearly and unambiguously flaunting the literary dimension of his enterprise and making it an integral part of his biographical project conceived as a hymn to the objects of his love or of his admiration. He foregrounds an ancient literary tradition, he highlights his own role as writer, and he explicitly discusses the literary qualities of the language that he uses in singing his beloved. This contrasts with the role that the literary is given when his work is approached from an autobiographical perspective in which it appears either as fiction, which opposes autobiographical fact, or as a writing, which undermines self-representation.

GENET'S HEROES

Genet hymns the objects of his love by treating them as heroes to whom he ascribes a glorious destiny, and this glorious destiny is indispensable to Genet's celebratory intentions. Celebration is always the celebration of a life: 'being crime, and celebrating it by a *magnificent life*', he writes in the script of his radio talk 'L'Enfant criminel'.[19] Genet's heroes acquire both their heroic status and their magnificent lives largely by virtue of the deaths that bring those lives to an end. All his biographical protagonists are dead. *Notre-Dame-des-Fleurs* introduces Divine with an announcement of her death ('Divine died yesterday', *NDF*, p. 17); and *Miracle de la rose* ends with a roll call of deaths: 'Harcamone is dead, Bulkaen is dead', to which he adds 'the death of Pilorge' (*MDR*, p. 346). A comment in the *Journal du voleur* spells out the necessity of this death for the hero's very existence as hero: 'The hero cannot turn his back on a heroic death. He is a hero only because of that death; it is the condition so bitterly sought by creatures without glory; itself is glory [. . .] the crowning of a predisposed life' (*JV*, p. 238 [p. 187*]). It is his death that turns the hero's life into a destiny that can be glorified by the poet, and it is his death, too, that allows glorification to take the form of a narrative of the hero's life.

Death is also the condition of the hero's knowability; the biographer can get to know his subject only once he is dead, because it is only then that he ceases to change, and only then that his secrets can come to light. As Genet says in his interview with Hubert Fichte: 'Death transforms everything, perspectives are changed; as long as a man is alive, as long as he can alter his thoughts [. . .] as long as he can disguise his true personality [. . .] no one really knows what is going on. Once he is dead, all the pretence vanishes. The man is fixed and you see his image differently.'[20] Genet makes the backward look of biography,

[19] Jean Genet, 'L'Enfant criminel', in id., *OC* v (Paris: Gallimard, 1979), pp. 377–93 (p. 388). The text for this radio talk was written in 1948. Although it was published the following year, the broadcast itself was banned. See Albert Dichy's Chronology in White, *Genet*, p. xxi.

[20] Genet, 'Entretien avec Hubert Fichte', p. 154.

repudiated by Sartre, the cornerstone of his own biographical practice. In his version of the *grand chant courtois*, the poet's song to his beloved presupposes the beloved's death much more than any particular qualities that he may have had. 'Since Divine is dead, the poet can hymn [*chanter*] her, recount her legend, the Saga, the *dict* of Divine' (*NDF*, p. 36). The underlying principle of Genet's 'poems', then, is the story of a life: a legend, a saga, a love poem of its hero. Genet's mention of these medieval genres (emphasized by the archaic spelling of '*dit*' as '*dict*'[21]) distinguishes his writing from biography in the modern sense of a factual chronology of a life. Genet's account of Divine is quite unlike Edmund White's biography of Genet or even Sartre's discussion of 'Saint Genet'. Chronology and documentation count for nothing, and Genet has none of the modern biographer's interest in the psychology of his subject: 'my mind was unconcerned with psychological motives' (*JV*, p. 58 [p. 46]). Celebration usurps information, or even explanation, as the goal of his narrative. But to the extent that it is recounting the lives of others, Genet's writing demands to be read as biographical in its very foundation.

In one of his more provocative displays of abjection, Genet writes of Divine that 'I shall bring him to life with my breath and the smell of my farts' (*NDF*, p. 40); but however much he may be breathing his own life into the figure of Divine, he can write about him/her only by treating him/her as other to himself. In contrast, if he remains within the confines of his own being, he can communicate nothing: it is more or less impossible, he says, to translate his experience of himself into terms that readers could make any sense of, or—to continue in the idiom of the previous quotation—'to convey to you what my mouth smells like to me' (*MDR*, p. 213 [p. 178*]). Genet's relation to his subject matter is one of 'outsideness', to borrow the term used by the Russian theorist Mikhail Bakhtin in an essay tellingly entitled 'Author and hero in aesthetic activity'.[22] Genet is 'author' to his 'hero' protagonists, and this relation is entirely dependent on the author's external perspective on his hero: 'A man is great if he has a great destiny; but this greatness belongs to the order of visible, measurable greatness. It is *magnificence seen from without*' (*NDF*, pp. 341–2). One might even say that magnificence exists only in an external perspective, and this certainly is what Genet seems to be suggesting when he continues: 'Squalid perhaps, when seen from within, it becomes poetic, if you are willing to concede that poetry is the break (or rather the encounter at the point of rupture) between the visible

---

[21] The medieval genre of the *dit* is a spoken poem (although sometimes parts are in prose), as opposed to a sung lyric. It is normally enunciated in the first person, has the narrator/poet as the protagonist, and commonly tells the story of its own creation. The subject matter is often love—hence the *dit amoureux*. For further discussion of the form see Sarah Kay, 'The Middle Ages: From The Earliest Texts to 1470', in Sarah Kay, Terence Cave, and Malcolm Bowie, *A Short History of French Literature* (Oxford: Oxford University Press, 2003), esp. pp. 56–7, 75–80.

[22] In M. M. Bakhtin, *Art and Answerability: Early Philosophical Essays*, ed. Michael Holquist and Vadim Liapunov, trans. Vadim Liapunov and Kenneth N. Brostrom (Austin: University of Texas Press, 1990), pp. 4–256.

and the invisible' (p. 342). The author's external perspective turns the abject of internal experience into glory and poetry.

It is a condition of the author's status as author that he have a perspective on his hero-subject that the subject himself does not, and cannot, have. Genet repeatedly portrays his heroes as being unaware of the qualities that he is celebrating in them, particularly when it comes to their physical beauty: '[Albert] was beautiful, as all the males in this book are, strong and supple, *unaware of their grace*' (*NDF*, p. 164). Even when the boundaries between Genet and his characters seem to break down, as when he feels 'penetrated' by Bulkaen's physical beauty, this experience is made possible by Genet's exclusive, external viewpoint on his lover:

I have used the word penetrate. I have done so deliberately: his beauty entered me by the feet, went up my legs, rose to my body, to my head, spread over my face [. . .] that beauty was in me and not in him. *It was outside him* since it was on his face, in his features, on his body. *He could not enjoy the spell it cast on me.* (*MDR*, p. 188 [p. 157*])

Genet is invaded from top to toe by Bulkaen's beauty; but in spite of being so thoroughly taken over by this quality in the other, he remains author to his hero, who has no access to the beauty that only an outsider—in this case Genet—can see on the external surface of his face and body.

Whether one places Genet's writing in the context of the medieval genres of the *grand chant courtois*, the legend, the saga, or the '*dict*' to which he refers, or whether one takes a more general view of the author–hero relation as one based in 'aesthetic activity', as Bakhtin proposes, the biographical viewpoint and the literariness of Genet's undertaking would seem to go hand in hand.

THE POET'S ROLE

In line with the courtly tradition to which Genet appeals, the supposed object of poetic celebration very often turns out to be little more than a pretext for poetic bravura.[23] It is this foregrounding of the writer's intervention in his material that makes it apposite to speak of Genet as a poet, and of his writing as poetry. The underlying principle of Genet's prose writing is not a realism that provides a faithful record of the world; rather, it proposes a continual metamorphosis of that world. It is metaphor and not mimesis that informs his literary enterprise. Indeed, Genet is often at pains to maximize the gap between, on the one hand, the base and undeserving nature of the beings and objects that he celebrates, and, on the other, the magnificence that his writing bestows upon them. The tube of vaseline taken from him by the police in Barcelona is described in all its abjectness as 'this puny and most humble object', and its most repulsive features

---

[23] See Zumthor, *Essai de poétique médiévale*.

are emphasized in Genet's depiction of it: 'by barely squeezing his fingers together the weakest of them could squirt out of it, first with a light, brief and dirty fart, a ribbon of gum which would continue to emerge in a ridiculous silence' (*JV*, p. 23 [p. 18*]). In counterpoint to this, Genet insists on comparing his tube of vaseline to 'a tragic *hero*', and on finding 'the newest words in the French language' with which 'to *hymn* it' (ibid.). The object is redeemed by sheer poetic fiat: 'To say that it is beautiful is to decide that it will be so' (p. 24 [p. 18]). The cause of this transformation lies not in the discovery of a hidden virtue in the object, but solely in Genet's own poetic skill: 'Spain and my life as a beggar familiarized me with the splendours of abjection, for it took a great deal of pride (that is, of love) to embellish those filthy and despised creatures. *It took a great deal of talent*' (p. 20 [p.15*]). And, Genet continues, that talent consists not in masking the squalor of the world he encounters, but in simultaneously affirming the sordid and the splendid: 'Never did I try to make of it [that wretched life] something other than what it was, I did not try to adorn it, to mask it, but, on the contrary, I wanted to affirm it in its exact sordidness, and *the most sordid signs became for me signs of grandeur*' (ibid.). The introduction of poetic grandeur is not designed to obliterate the abject aspect of the real, but precisely to draw attention to the gap between the two.

Genet portrays the lovers whom he is celebrating as also contributing in large measure to the squalor of this world. This squalor is as much moral as it is physical, with the graphically described dribble of excrement on Stilitano's trousers or the flea on his collar receiving less attention overall than the hypocrisy, stupidity, meanness, cruelty, and servility of the man's character. Stilitano is far from being alone in this moral baseness, which is a recurrent feature of Genet's protagonists throughout his work, beginning already with Mignon in *Notre-Dame-des-Fleurs*, who is characterized as being 'splendorously despicable' (*NDF*, p. 100). There is little to admire in the failings of Genet's heroes, for they are markedly lacking in the daring and defiance of those who actively challenge the moral order. A comparison with the dramatis personae of Camus's *L'Homme révolté* dating from the same period (1951) would support this point. None of Genet's heroes has anything like the moral audacity of, for example, Sade, Milton's Satan, Dostoevsky's Ivan Karamazov, Nietzsche, Saint-Just, or Pisarev. Neither do they seek to engage with the problem of evil in the ways explored by Genet's other near contemporary, Georges Bataille.[24] The figures in Genet's world are squalid rather than bad, and their interest for the reader lies less in what they are than in how they are portrayed, or, rather, in the tension that Genet establishes between these two things.

---

[24] This in part explains Bataille's frustration with Genet in the essay devoted to him in Georges Bataille, *La Littérature et le mal: Emily Brontë, Baudelaire, Michelet, Blake, Sade, Proust, Kafka, Genet* (1957; Collection Idées; Paris: Gallimard, 1967), pp. 197–244. I shall return below to Bataille's account of Genet.

The poetic mechanism of the portrayal of this squalor takes two forms, both of which serve to foreground the poet's role in the transformation of his subjects. In the first he simply redefines the qualities he encounters, so that the base is recast as noble, the unlovely as gorgeous. Genet comments quite liberally on this technique, and acknowledges in himself 'a will to rehabilitate persons, objects and feelings that are reputedly vile', renaming them 'with words that usually designate what is noble' (*JV*, p. 122 [p. 97*]). In retrospect, however, this strategy appears to him slightly infantile in its systematic reversal of the values of the established order. More challenging is the other strategy, which, as he says of Stilitano's moral failings, makes of them 'the most obscene triumph'. Genet repeatedly asserts his power to redefine the world as he chooses. A notable example is his stark affirmation in the opening lines of the *Journal du voleur* that the pink and white striped uniform worn by convicts has a connection with flowers. He justifies this unorthodox connection entirely on the basis of his own ability to see as many meanings as he pleases in the world around him: 'I have [. . .] the power of finding in it the many meanings I wish to find', and this power means that '*there is a close relationship between flowers and convicts*' (*JV*, p. 9 [p. 7], Genet's italics). But what might appear as sheer autocratic whim on his part is elsewhere presented by him as a more general characteristic of poetry: 'In a poem, ordinary words are shifted around in such a way that their usual meaning is enriched by another: the poetic meaning' (*MDR*, p. 213 [p. 178*]). As a definition of poetry this seems pretty uncontentious. So that on the quite frequent occasions when Genet seems to suggest that the poetic meaning ends up supplanting its original designation, poetic ambition appears an acceptable motive for the writing: 'The work blazes and its model dies', as he puts it (p. 247 [p. 207*]). The poetic names that he confers on his characters will, he says, be all that survives of them, like light coming from stars that have been dead for a thousand years: 'These names alone will remain in the future, divested of their objects' (p. 347 [p. 291]). Lives, including his own, exist only in order to provide material for the literary object being created by the poet; and speaking of his enterprise in the *Journal du voleur*, he spells out this aesthetic priority in quite unequivocal terms: '[this journal] is not a quest for time past, but a work of art whose pretext-subject is my former life' (*JV*, p. 80 [p. 63*]).

The revelation that the life—whether Genet's or that of his biographical subjects—is merely a pretext for the art that initially seemed devoted to its celebration, is far from unprecedented in literature. It is implicit in the courtly tradition to which Genet subscribes, and its provocatively explicit reworking is a commonplace in Baudelaire (in poems like 'Une charogne', for example). The reason why Genet is interesting lies to one side of this topos. Or, more precisely, he is interesting because of the deeply ambiguous way in which he places a relatively familiar literary move within the wider field of literature.

GENET AND THE LITERARY

The question of what poetry is appears as a recurrent preoccupation in Genet's writing, and explicitly aesthetic concerns continue to be an issue in essays and interviews long after he has ceased to write prose fiction. On the one hand, as we have seen, Genet has recourse to a range of literary markers, all of which fall broadly within the field of possibilities created by existing conceptions of the literary: the use of generic tradition, the foregrounding of the role of the poet, the recourse to metaphor and defamiliarization, and considerable self-reference. But, on the other hand, he also makes assertions about poetry that remove it entirely from a common repertoire of recognizable topoi by declaring that it is an emotion within himself of which he is the sole arbiter. Poetry here is no longer defined in terms of a shared language, or as the product of a set of figural moves on the part of a poet whose activity is sanctioned by a communal sense of the modes of operation within the field of literature. The poetic fiat that transforms the world by renaming it is used to rename poetry itself from without. Poetry is redefined as emotion, and it is the poet alone who determines that this emotion is poetry: 'The very particular emotion *which I have called poetic*' (*JV*, p. 193 [p. 152]). This equation of poetry with emotion rather than with language or poetic tradition allows Genet to claim in his interview with Antoine Bourseiller that his writing career began in Mettray: 'If writing means experiencing emotions or feelings that are so strong that your entire life will be delineated by them, if they are so strong that only their description, recollection, or analysis can truly account for them, then yes, it was at Mettray and at the age of 15 that I began to write.'[25] In *Notre-Dame-des-Fleurs* he describes this poetic emotion as 'the elegant, sudden, luminous, and unambiguous resolution of a conflict in my inner depths'; and its existence is demonstrated by his internal responses: 'I have proof of it in the peace which follows my discovery' (*NDF*, p. 225). Poetry, in other words, has become a feature of Genet's internal world and is no longer part of any currency of exchange.

This, largely, was the basis of Bataille's quarrel with Genet. Initially he saw in Genet's celebration of criminality and the ignoble an index of an attempt to revalorize literature as a form of the sacred, and in his assertion of poetic fiat a sign of the sovereignty that Bataille regards as inseparable from transgression. Viewed in this light, Genet might also appear to be making common cause with Leiris, who also sought to raise the stakes of what passes for the literary.[26] But Genet ultimately disappoints Bataille, who condemns him for the solipsism of his strategies, which turn transgression and subversion into a means of retreat

---

[25] 'Entretien avec Antoine Bourseiller', in Genet, *OC* vi, pp. 225–6.
[26] See the discussion in Ch. 14 above.

rather than the basis for engagement. In short, says Bataille, 'Genet's work [. . .] is [. . .] neither sacred not poetic because the author refuses to allow it to be communicated'.[27] I am not suggesting that Genet should have lent himself to Bataille's programme, but that Bataille's objection is a symptomatic response to the way in which Genet appropriates and internalizes the literary, and does so, moreover, without presenting this as part of a questioning of an inherited concept of the literary. Instead, he simply ignores it.

Genet's position on this topic is therefore strangely ambivalent. There are times when, as we have seen, he flaunts the traditional and conventionally sanctioned literary component of his celebratory project; but he is equally apt to disengage himself, quite contradictorily but very emphatically, from any literary pretensions or associations whatsoever. 'The idea of a work of literature just makes me shrug', he asserts in the *Journal du voleur*, claiming that for him writing had never been anything more than an antidote to the boredom of prison life and a way of making money on his release (*JV*, pp. 121–2). Comments such as these chime with Sartre's ambition to secularize literature and make it simply an existential choice like any other.[28] But Genet is unlike Sartre in that he also elevates beauty to an absolute value, and is more than willing to place poetry on the same plane as the sacred: 'Like beauty—and poetry—with which I confuse it, saintliness is singular. Its expression is original. Nevertheless, it seems to me that its sole basis is renunciation' (*JV*, p. 237). Genet's apparent rejection of literature is a complex and ambivalent thing, and it would be wrong to accept it at face value. Derrida may declare that 'Genet buried literature like no one else',[29] but Genet is not so much dispatching or shrugging off literature, as simultaneously promoting and repudiating it.

Curiously, though, his repudiation of the literary is apt to repeat the very form that constituted literariness for him in the first place. The moves that take Genet out of literature, as we shall see, mime those that also establish it in his work, and this means that neither endorsement nor rejection can be understood as simple options. Moreover, it also means that neither can be seen without reference to the other. In this mode Genet positions himself as both indifferent and actively hostile to the world he attributes to his readers. He marks his difference from that world by asserting his ability to attribute alternative meanings to its objects in a way that sounds remarkably like his definition of the workings of poetic meaning. Addressing his readers directly, as he so often does when he is denouncing them, he says: 'I live in so closed a universe. Each object in your world has a meaning different for me from the one it has for you. I refer everything to my system, in which things have an infernal signification' (*MDR*, p. 93 [p. 78]). Genet's private, infernal meaning is as distinct from the meaning his readers see in a given object, as poetic meaning is from everyday meaning. From the perspective of Genet's closed universe, this displacement of meaning

---

[27] See 'Genet', in Bataille, *La Littérature et le mal*, pp. 197–244 (p. 222).
[28] As we saw in Ch. 15 above.   [29] See Derrida, *Glas*, vol. i, p. 50.

is even practised upon literature itself, which he treats as a part of the world he is rejecting: 'even when I read a novel, the facts, without being distorted, lose the meaning which has been given them by the author and which they have for you, and take on another so as to enter smoothly the otherworldly universe in which I live' (pp. 93–4 [p. 78]). In a similarly non-consensual move, the aesthetic potential of the crime of theft is explicitly formulated in a comment in the *Journal du voleur*, where Genet highlights its disinterestedness and compares it to a work of art: 'theft [. . .] had become a disinterested enterprise, a kind of active and deliberate work of art' (*JV*, p. 128 [p. 102]). Furthermore, it is a work of art to which language is indispensable: 'which could be achieved only with the help of language, my language, and which would be confronted with the laws springing from this same language' (ibid.). The thief's language is distinguished from the language of the established order in a manner that more than anything else resembles the transgressions that are characteristic of poetic writing.

This haunting of Genet's denunciations of the literary by the literature he appears to be condemning can then, after all, be restored to the status of the literary. For these echoes could be read just as convincingly as an effect of the theft and the betrayal which Genet calls 'two fascinating elements' and which, along with homosexuality, constitute, he says, 'the three virtues which I set up as theological' (*JV*, p. 167 [p. 133]). Genet insists repeatedly on the connections between these three virtues, and for him they have in common a guaranteed breaking of the ties that bind him to his fellow men. In considering his theft of the money his friend Pépé had given him for safe-keeping, Genet writes: 'In carrying out [the theft], I had once again—and, I thought to myself, once and for all—destroyed the dear bonds of brotherhood' (p. 91 [p. 73*]). Similarly, he says of betrayal that 'betraying means breaking the laws of love' (p. 167 [p. 133*]); and he views homosexuality as guaranteeing exclusion from the world (ibid.). Genet's theological virtues provide him with a means of positioning himself outside society and in opposition to the world. Literature seems to play a double-edged role in this: sometimes offering him models of the transgressive strategies he is espousing and proposing terms in which to celebrate taboos; and sometimes appearing as part of the world he is denouncing. These are the criteria according to which the literary is both promoted and sidelined. It is made to matter when it is oppositional, and treated as irrelevant when it appears as part of a social consensus. Given this ambivalence, it would seem important not to try and flatten out such contradictions but to build them into an understanding of Genet's project.

LOVE AND AESTHETIC RELATIONS

The nub of Genet's objections to the world's treatment of art in general concerns the nature of its relation to that art. In the first instance he accuses the world of having a hypocritical relation to works of art, condoning things in the aesthetic domain that it condemns in its own reality. In 'L'Enfant criminel' he voices his objection in the form of a direct accusation of his listeners: '*Your* literature, *your* arts, *your* after-dinner entertainments celebrate crime. The talents of *your* poets glorify the criminal whom in real life you hate.'³⁰ This is tantamount to saying that the world's relation to works of art is half-hearted, insufficient, and that people are failing to put their existential money where their aesthetic mouth is. In short, the insufficiency of the relation limits and trivializes the aesthetic, and leads Genet to dismiss all artists who encourage this kind of relation: 'Allow us in our turn to despise your poets and your artists' (ibid.). In the second instance Genet seems to be saying that the world establishes the wrong kind of relations for its works of art. These wrong relations are those that place the work in a network of links with other works of art, with a tradition, and with a set of techniques that do not entail the engagement of the reader or viewer, or even of the artist.

These issues are all drawn together in the scene from the *Journal du voleur* where some French tourists interrupt their cruise to take photographs of a group of beggars, who include Genet and his boyfriend Lucien. The tourists are prompted to pause at the sight of what Genet calls 'these archipelagos of poverty' by their decision to regard them as 'picturesque' (*JV*, p. 185 [p. 146]). In a sense, the tourists behave no differently from Genet in that this is a decision whose rights they simply assert: 'they had inwardly granted themselves the right to find these archipelagos of poverty picturesque' (ibid.*). Where they differ is in seeking to establish a connection not between themselves and the scene, but between the scene and painterly precedent, citing 'something out of Goya' and 'images from Gustave Doré' (ibid.*).³¹ From Genet's point of view, what is missing from this aestheticization of the scene is any investment on the part of the tourists in the transformation of squalor into art. Instead of being the starting point for an aesthetic metamorphosis, such as the one that transmutes the tube of vaseline into a hero, the picturesque beggars are perceived as a form of art from the moment the tourists set eyes on them. One tourist mentions 'the originality of the poses' adopted by the beggars, and others comment that 'there's a perfect harmony between the tonalities of the skies [*ciels*] and the slightly greenish shades of the rags', as if the beggars already constituted a work of art that could be described in terms of its compositional features—as is implied by the use of the word 'ciels', which refers only to painted skies (p. 186 [p. 146*]). All that is then required is a technique for replicating that predetermined image, and this is the tourists' main preoccupation as they deploy their photographic equipment: 'The tourists complained about the light, but they praised the quality of the films'

---

³⁰ Genet, 'L'Enfant criminel', p. 390 (italics original).
³¹ Marie Redonnet makes a similar point about Genet's rejection of any historical relation between his own writing and literary tradition: 'Genet n'est pas poète pour continuer la poésie comme histoire d'un genre. Il s'échappe de l'histoire de la poésie que lui transmet la littérature, comme il s'échappe de l'image du poète qu'elle a façonnée' (*Jean Genet*, p. 12).

(p. 186 [p. 147]). The images they produce are the combined product of Goya's example and the single-lens reflex camera; and the dialogue the tourists engage in is not with the subjects of their photographic representations, but, over the heads of those subjects, with each other: 'Without considering that they might be wounding the beggars, [the tourists] carried on, above their heads, an audible dialogue, the terms of which were exact and rigorous, almost technical' (p. 185 [p. 146]). As far as Genet is concerned, the tourists' aesthetic relation with their subject matter is a non-relation. They rely on technique and tradition to do the job that Genet himself undertakes as sole author to his heroes, and as the singer of the *chant d'amour* ('song of love') that celebrates them.

Against the tourists' perspective here, Genet counterpoints his own relation to Lucien, which is of a quite different order. He presents Lucien, who had a starring role in the tourists' scenario, as suffering for not yet having broken his ties with the world of the tourists, ties that exist because he still retains youth, beauty, elegance, hunger, and a need for earthly glory. Consequently, he is pained by the world's rejection, experiencing his encounter with the photographers as an exclusion and a humiliation that bring him to despair. What Genet offers Lucien in the place of this is an image of himself (Lucien) which makes no pretence of connection with the world that has rejected him, and which is entirely the product of the relation between the two of them. In this particular case the image that Genet gives to his lover is actually an image of himself (Genet), which he invites his lover to adopt: 'He is served by my adventures. I have lived them. Upon my chosen image of Lucien I cruelly impose the same ordeals. Save that it is my body which has suffered them, and my mind. Then, with them as a basis, I shall shape an image of him which he will imitate' (p. 187 [p. 148]). This is a complex exchange in which Genet projects an image of himself for his lover to take on; and at the same time it is an image of himself that he can construct only by visualizing it from Lucien's external perspective and in terms of his lover's reciprocal response: 'I therefore require that he know about my prostitution and that he acknowledge it. That he know every detail of my most despicable felonies, that he *suffer* from them and that he accept them' (p. 188 [p. 148*]). In imagining Lucien's perspective on himself, and emphasizing the reciprocity of their mutual portraiture, he is also imagining it as an affective relation. This is not the neutral, objective, painterly stance exemplified by the tourists' photographs. Unlike them, Genet projects himself figuratively and emotionally into the image he creates of Lucien by making that image one *of* himself but *for* Lucien. It is inspired by love rather than aesthetic tradition, and what counts is not technical skill but emotional reciprocation. Finally, in comparison with the relation between the tourists and the beggars, the most striking thing about the image that Genet creates is that, far from establishing a zone of exclusion between viewer and object, it ends up making the boundaries between Lucien and Genet inextricably blurred: Lucien becomes Genet, and Genet is the Genet who is seen by Lucien.

Genet is establishing a separate sphere beyond the boundary that exists between himself and the world, and between his own activities and the world's conception of the aesthetic. But within that sphere he also establishes a kind of relation to the Other that presupposes a different kind of aesthetic altogether. This relation is more than a celebration of the Other, and more than a simple authorial depiction of a hero, for, as in the case of Lucien I have just mentioned, it is marked by an extraordinary fluidity of the boundary between self and other. This connection is as much a feature of crime as it is of art. If Genet's 'theological' virtues of theft, betrayal, and homosexuality have the merit of breaking bonds and establishing an impenetrable boundary between himself and the world, two of them at least—theft and homosexuality—are presented as also promoting this highly permeable attachment to the other. Exactly such a nexus of relations informs Genet's own preferred conception of aesthetic relations, so that it becomes necessary to see a continuum rather than a set of alternatives between the criminal and the aesthetic in his writing.

It is, however, with the crime of murder (not theft) that Genet launches his enterprise. The first page of *Notre-Dame-des-Fleurs* begins with a glorification of Weidmann, a murderer six times over, and the first sentences simultaneously adopt Genet's characteristically oppositional stance towards the world with the opening words: 'Weidmann appeared to you . . .'. Commenting in an interview on his insistence on his use of the pronoun *vous* as against the *nous* proposed by his publisher's copy-editor, Genet explains that with this *vous*, 'I was already establishing the difference between the you to whom I am speaking and the I who am speaking to you'.[32] Weidmann is the first of the 'enchanting murderers' (*NDF*, p. 9) to whom Genet devotes his fervour, Notre-Dame-des-Fleurs himself being its principal object in the novel that bears his name. When Genet narrates the murder committed by Notre-Dame-des-Fleurs, he ends up describing a relation in which the murderer is taken over by the victim he has just dispatched:

it's the initial physical disgust felt by the murderer for his victim, which many men have spoken to me about. He haunts you, doesn't he? The dead man is full of energy. Your dead man is inside you; mingling with your blood, he flows in your veins, seeps through your pores, and your heart lives off him, like flowers germinating from their corpses in the cemetery. [. . .] He comes out of your eyes, your ears and your mouth. (pp. 106–7)

The act of murder creates an inextricable bond between the two parties involved.

Much the same turns out to be true of theft. Genet's own crimes are those of theft rather than the murder he celebrates in others; but his relation as burglar to the owner of the goods he steals is very similar to that between murderer and murder victim. Burglary is less a matter of acquiring the goods of another than of taking on his identity:

---

[32] Genet, 'Entretien avec Bertrand Poirot-Delpech', p. 231.

I do not think specifically of the owner of the place, but one by one all my gestures conjure him up as they see him. I am steeped in an idea of property while I loot property. *I recreate the absent owner.* He lives, not in front of me, but all around me. *He is a fluid element which I breathe, which enters me and inflates my lungs.* The beginning of the operation goes off without too much fear. The fear starts mounting the moment I have finally decided to leave. The decision is born when the apartment contains no more secrets, when *I have taken the owner's place.* And this is not necessarily when I have discovered the treasure. (*JV*, pp. 174–5 [p. 139*])

The burglar becomes the owner of the property he steals, not in the sense that ownership is transferred along with the goods, but by virtue of a process more akin to osmosis than appropriation. The identity of the owner is a 'fluid element' that enters the body of the thief and becomes the air he breathes, just as the same fluidity enables the victim's blood to circulate in the veins of his murderer.

As we saw in the description of the lover's portrait, love relations in Genet almost always produce the same confusions of identity as those produced by crime. The fact that for Genet these are—scandalously—homosexual relations guarantees the difference between himself and the world so necessary to him, in a manner which is similar to that guaranteed by the criminal acts of theft and murder; but love proves to be even more prone to the sort of fluidity that characterizes criminal relations. The positions of 'worshipper' and 'idol' that Genet so readily adopts for himself and his beloved invariably collapse the distinction that the terms themselves appear to guarantee. The passion of the adorer for his idol moves him to adopt all the qualities of the object of his adoration: 'I was not completely at ease unless I could completely take his place, take on his qualities, his virtues. When I imagined I was he, making his gestures, uttering his words: when I *was* he' (*MDR*, p. 33 [p. 26]). Genet inhabits the body of his other in the same way that the victim takes over the body of his murderer.

The process is not limited to this one-way traffic between lover and beloved. The love relation can also incite the lover to offer his own identity to the beloved, as Genet does to Lucien. Or again, it can move the lover to take on the identity that his beloved seems to ask of him: 'I would strive to be the man Armand saw in me' (*JV*, p. 211 [p. 166*]). This gesture is even more graphically expressed in Genet's description of the way that Lucien plays with the features on Genet's face, rolling up his ear, squeezing his cheek, and wrinkling up his forehead. A gesture of affection between two lovers is recast as an act of creation, and Genet willingly submits to being treated as raw material for his lover's inventions: 'It amused him to invent wrinkles, hollows and bumps, but it seemed to amuse him solemnly. He did not laugh. Under those inventive fingers I felt his kindness. They made it seem such a blessing to be kneaded and moulded, and I knew the love that matter must feel for the person who fashions it with such joy' (pp. 177–8 [p. 141*]). The love relations that Genet depicts in his work present the lovers as mutual celebrants of each other, in roles that resemble that of Genet the biographer of his subject heroes.

PORTRAITURE AS ART

The love relation that is the pretext for Genet's songs of love is, as Lucien's moulding of his lover's face suggests, also a model for artistic creation. In Genet's comments about his experience of being the raw material for Lucien's inventions the love relation is perceived as a form of aesthetic relation: 'I understand what binds the sculptor to his clay, the painter to his paints, each worker to the matter he works with, and the docility and acquiescence of matter to the movements of the person who brings it to life; I know what *love* passes from the fingers into those folds, those holes and those bumps' (*JV*, pp. 178–9 [p. 142*]). The lover is like a sculptor or a painter, and it is precisely to a sculptor and a painter that Genet is drawn in two of the essays that he wrote during the year 1957–8, in which he discusses Giacometti and Rembrandt in terms that echo very precisely those he uses here. Genet stopped writing prose fiction after the *Journal du voleur*, published in 1949, and thereafter his creative energies were largely devoted to theatre, which does not lend itself to exploring the kinds of relation found in the prose fiction. In any case, by 1957–8 Genet was coming to the end of his career as a playwright, and in 1958 was finishing a first version of his last play, *Les Paravents*.[33]

The first of these essays, however, 'Le Funambule' ('The Tightrope Artiste'),[34] is dedicated to his lover Abdallah and deals primarily with the relation between the tightrope walker and his tightrope. At one level it is one of Genet's last *chants d'amour*, celebrating the skill of his lover whom, almost without interruption, he addresses directly as 'tu'. But it is also a portrayal of the mutually constructive bond between the artist and the wire he walks on: 'The love [. . .] that you must show to your wire will be as strong as the one displayed by the iron wire to support you.' The loving skill of the tightrope artiste brings the wire to life: 'The wire was dead—or, if you like, mute, blind—and as soon as you appear it comes alive and starts to speak' (p. 9). The acrobat's performance is not a form of self-expression, let alone of self-glorification, but a celebration of the tightrope on which he performs:

Charge your steel wire with *the most beautiful expression not of yourself but of it.* You will succeed in your leaps and jumps and dances [. . .] not in order for you to shine, but so that an iron wire which was dead and without voice will finally sing. It will be so grateful to you if you are perfect in your poses *not for your glory, but for its glory.* (p. 10)

The tightrope is the acrobat's raw material, which, once animated by the song that the acrobat's skill elicits from it, will reciprocate with its own creative energy and endow Abdallah with special qualities: 'In turn the iron wire will make the

---

[33] See the Chronology by Dichy in White, *Genet*, pp. xiii–xxxv.
[34] Jean Genet, 'Le Funambule', in id., *OC* v, pp. 8–27.

most wonderful dancer of you.'[35] At the end of the essay Genet describes his own role in relation to Abdallah in similar terms. What he has written is a 'poem' in which 'the point was to set you ablaze, not to instruct you.'[36] Genet's essay presents the tightrope walker's art as a mutually creative relation to his material (the tightrope), in which each enhances the other, just as the essay itself is a celebration of his lover's skill designed to animate its dedicatee. The different participants are bound together by a relation that takes the form of the *chant*, whether it is Abdallah's skill in causing the wire to sing, or Genet's in hymning the skill of the performer-lover.

The relation between Genet and Abdallah is, nevertheless, largely a one-way affair, not having the reciprocity that Genet celebrates within the 'poem'. He sees and celebrates the artist-hero of his essay in a largely unilateral perspective, which is also the one adopted for the essays about Rembrandt and Giacometti, informing both the artistic relations described in the essays, and the relation between Genet and his painter-subjects.[37] In this, Genet seems to be reverting to the author-hero model of the *grand chant courtois* mode, but its application is extended to the whole sphere of the aesthetic: Abdallah's acrobatics, the plastic arts of Giacometti and Rembrandt, as well as Genet's own essay-poem. His interest is not limited to the literary but concerns the work of art in general. Whatever medium they use, the arts for Genet derive entirely from the relation between the artist and his subject, and their mode is essentially that of the outsideness of biography and portraiture. The skill of the artist consists in seeing the unique quality of the other, a quality which Genet associates with a wound, and which implies a biographical cause, even if this origin is not directly depicted: 'For the tightrope artiste I am speaking of, [that wound] is visible in his sad look which must allude to images of a wretched, unforgettable childhood in which he knew he had been abandoned.'[38] It is this ability to decipher and portray the distinctive 'wound' in his subjects that Genet singles out for praise in Giacometti: 'The art of Giacometti seems to me to be trying to discover that secret in every being and even in every object, so that they will be illuminated by it.'[39] In other words, Genet equates artistic achievement in general with the biographer's ability to portray another subject by locating the point that grounds his unique identity. One of the effects of establishing the uniqueness of the subject in this way is that it also establishes his solitude, which becomes a guarantee of a non-relation with the world: 'my eye [prevents] that face from

[35] See the original published version of this essay, entitled 'Pour un funambule', in *Preuves*, 79 (1957), pp. 30–7 for a correct reading of a misprint in *OC* v (p. 31).

[36] 'Funambule', p. 27.

[37] The situation is slightly more complicated in the case of Giacometti, who had done a series of portraits of Genet in 1955—three paintings and six drawings; see Dichy's Chronology in White, *Genet*, p. xxiii. However, neither these portraits nor Genet's essay have the mutually constructing effect of the relation between Abdallah and his tightrope.

[38] 'Funambule', p. 13.

[39] Jean Genet, 'L'Atelier d'Alberto Giacometti', in id., *OC* v, pp. 39–73 (p. 42).

becoming merged with the rest of the world [. . .] and [. . .] the result is this solitude, by which my eye cuts it off from the world' (p. 48). Equally, in order for the artist to perceive and portray the unique solitude of his subjects, he too has to disentangle himself from all worldly involvements: 'This capacity to isolate an object and to bring out in it its own meanings, and only those meanings, is possible only through the historical abolition of the person looking. He needs to make an exceptional effort to lose his taste for history of all kinds' (p. 58). The intensity of the artist's gaze on his subject is enough in itself to sever all ties with the world without need for recourse to Genet's theological virtues of theft, betrayal, or homosexuality. Portraiture, in and of itself, establishes this essential exclusion.

In the case of Rembrandt, portraiture becomes a form of full biographical representation: 'All [his subjects] seem to contain an exceptionally weighty and close-packed drama. His characters are almost always, in their compact, gathered postures, like a tornado that has been kept at bay for one instant. They contain a very dense destiny, which has been quite precisely evaluated by them, and which from one moment to the next they will "act" to the very end.'[40] By the same token, Genet's own account of Rembrandt here is itself broadly biographical, chronicling the development he sees in the paintings from Rembrandt's youthful infatuation with luxury to a more evolved sense of painting as a celebration both of the figures he depicts and of the medium of paint by means of which he depicts them (p. 37). Genet's purpose here is to celebrate a celebrant, to provide a portrait of a portraitist, and to sing the life of dramatist of the lives of others.

This is not to say that he sees in Rembrandt, or indeed in Giacometti, a version of himself, but that Genet's aesthetic principles continue to be those that treat art as a glorification of the lives of others. By broadening out the scope of this conception from poetry to art in general, he reinforces this principle as the fundamental criterion of the aesthetic. He also disengages even further from all possibility of negotiation or dialogue with tradition. For Genet portraiture and the celebration of a life preclude any literary- or art-historical dimension, and an implicitly timeless aesthetics takes him out of a history that would create relations other than those between the artist and the object of his celebratory representation. One could say that it is Genet's way of not being one of the tourists who photograph the beggars in Barcelona.

It also makes Genet a rather peculiar figure in the history of the configuration between the biographical and the literary that is the subject of this book. His affirmation of a biographical relation between author and hero as the central feature of his literary enterprise serves simultaneously to promote the literary as 'un chant d'amour' and to short-circuit any interest in it. He pretends not to know where he belongs in history, and feigns total ignorance about the tradition in which his writing nevertheless cannot avoid being placed. He may implicitly

---

[40] Jean Genet, 'Le Secret de Rembrandt', in id., *OC* v, pp. 29–37 (p. 33).

acknowledge the trouvères of the Middle Ages, but he affects a curious blank when it comes to the literature of his own time, whether it be in the specific development of prose fiction, or in the more general conception of the literary that is at stake in the 1940s. Sartre and Bataille (the latter as a representative of a larger group, including, as I have already suggested, Michel Leiris) represent two broadly opposite poles in the debate, the one seeking to secularize the literary, and the other to resacralize the arts at large. Each of them sees in Genet a potential interlocutor concerning these issues, but in each case the dialogue fails to materialize, as Genet refuses to participate in a debate that, whichever side he took, would only end up placing his writing in the 'wrong' relation to the world. In short, Genet's very particular use of the biographical has the perverse effect of both affirming and suspending the literary to which it initially seemed so ostentatiously to subscribe.

17

Pierre Michon's Lives of the Saints

'Anyone who follows me shall not walk in darkness,' says the Lord. These are the words of Christ, and by them we are reminded that we must imitate His life and His ways if we are to be truly enlightened and set free from the darkness of our own hearts. Let it be the most important thing that we do, to reflect on the life of Jesus Christ.

(Thomas à Kempis, *The Imitation of Christ*)

What is striking is that, in literature, deception and mystification are not only inevitable, but constitute the honesty of the writer, the component of truth and hope that there is in him.

(Blanchot, *La Part du feu*)

Between the 1960s and the 1980s the question of literature became a predominantly theoretical concern, but the end of the age of theory in France was quite strikingly signalled by the simultaneous appearance between 1983 and 1984 of a number of biographical and autobiographical texts whose aim seemed to be to ring the changes on the theoretical discourses with which their authors had previously been associated. Nathalie Sarraute's *Enfance* appeared in 1983, and Marguerite Duras's *L'Amant* in the following year, along with the first of Alain Robbe-Grillet's autobiographical 'Romanesques', *Le Miroir qui revient*. For Robbe-Grillet the turn to autobiography is predominantly strategic, a way of deflecting issues away from a now orthodox theoretical discourse and on to a new terrain that is as heterodox as possible in relation to theory. This is, however, not the only way in which biographical and autobiographical writing engages with the question of the literary in the texts of this period. Neither is this writing confined to writers weary of the critical orthodoxies they helped to create. A new generation of younger writers also emerged at this time, whose perspective from the outset was broadly biographical or autobiographical, and whose work prompted the coining of new terms such as *le récit de vie, autofiction, biofiction,* and (in English) 'life-writing', as well as the rehabilitation of 'vies', in order to describe a phenomenon that in the event could not be contained precisely within the established generic categories of biography and autobiography. Annie Ernaux's first book, *La Place*, was published in 1983 (the same year as Sarraute's *Enfance*), and Pierre Michon's *Vies minuscules* appeared in 1984, the same year as Robbe-Grillet's *Le Miroir qui revient* and Duras's *L'Amant*.[1] If Ernaux, by adopting a sociological perspective on her own life and that of her parents, was seeking to expand the repertoire of discourses that might be contained under the rubric 'literature', the work of Pierre Michon returns the question of the literary to centre stage in heightened and intensified form. His chief recourse in this project is to the model of the lives of the saints. Like Genet with his 'chant', Michon resurrects not just the figures whose lives he chronicles, but the more ancient forms and functions associated with biographical narratives of the distant past.

LITERATURE AND THE SACRED

Literature—or rather its possibility—becomes the central criterion around which both Michon's own life as a writer and the lives of others are constructed. The issue of literarity is shifted from the domain of theory to the domain of the biographical, to lives as they are lived and 'lives' as they are written. In the process the literary also changes its status and role, ceasing to be the object of theoretical discourse, and becoming instead what Blanchot once called 'le souci de l'art' (the 'concern of the work'). This comment from 'L'Expérience originelle', an essay originally published in 1952 (before the emergence of theory in the 1960s and 1970s),[2] seems peculiarly apt for a consideration of the move from theory to the literary enterprise as it is formulated in the work of Michon:

Investigations on the subject of art such as those the aesthetician pursues bear no relation to the concern for the work of which we speak. Aesthetics talks about art, makes of it an object of reflection and of knowledge. [. . .] The work is deeply concerned about art. This is to say that, for the work, art is never a given, and that the work can find art only by continuing towards its own completion in radical uncertainty as to whether it can know in advance whether art is and what it is.[3]

In the case of Michon, however, it is not just the work for whom this 'souci' is central. The question of literature and this 'souci de l'art' are directly addressed in all Michon's writings about writers and painters, which, in one way or another, take the form of an examination of the artist's or writer's life rather than his work. The *Vie de Jospeh Roulin* (1988) describes Van Gogh's time in Arles by means of an evocation of Roulin, the postman who befriended Van Gogh and sat for a number of portraits; *Maîtres et serviteurs* (1990) portrays Goya, Watteau, and Lorentino d'Angelo, a pupil of Piero della Francesca; and *Le Roi du bois*

[1] Other writers one might cite in connection with this phenomenon are François Bon and Gérard Macé. I shall be discussing the work of Jacques Roubaud and Roger Laporte in Ch. 19 below.

[2] A revised version was published in 1955 in Maurice Blanchot, *L'Espace littéraire* (1955; Collection Idées; Paris: Gallimard, 1968), pp. 317–38. All quotations will be taken from this edition.

[3] Ibid., p. 317 [p. 235*].

(1996) is an account of Claude Lorrain.[4] In each case the perspective on the painter in question is provided obliquely, by means of an incidental or minor figure in his life. When it comes to writers, however, the engagement is rather more immediate: *Rimbaud le fils* (1991) is a broadly biographical account of its poet-subject—at least on the surface; the *Trois auteurs* (1997) consists of essays on Balzac, Cingria, and Faulkner, all of which confront the writer in the context of his life. *Corps du roi* (2002) contains pieces on Beckett, Flaubert, a fourteenth-century Arab writer called Muhamad Ibn Manglî, Faulkner (again), and Hugo's poem 'Booz endormi', and only in this last essay is the focus more on the life of its reader, Michon, than on that of its author. In short, a very substantial part of Michon's work (six out of a total of eleven titles to date) is devoted to a consideration of the lives of writers and artists.

But it starts with the *Vies minuscules* (1984), which recounts the lives of various figures who populated the world of Michon's childhood (and youth), and whose example, he suggests, was the source of his own literary vocation. It is through these quasi-biographical concerns that Michon formulates what is for him the abiding question of art, which is articulated most explicitly at the end of *Rimbaud le fils*: 'What is it that endlessly relaunches literature? What is it that makes men write?'[5] Painters and writers, that is to say, the 'great' painters and writers (Michon is unashamedly elitist in these matters) are dual figures. Like monarchs in the era of the divine right of kings, they are both the incarnation of something 'eternal' and 'dynastic', and also merely 'mortal', 'functional', 'relative'.[6] It is this conjunction that fascinates Michon, and through it he explores what Jean-Pierre Richard has called 'the enigma of an emergence'.[7] Michon's 'lives of the artists' are not biographical in the sense of providing a chronological and documented account of their existence; neither are they a pretext for criticism of the work.[8] They are far more concerned with the 'when' of the emergence of creative inspiration than with the 'why':

On what day did Balzac see Vautrin pass by? On what day did he know that he would pass by again, that they would all pass by again, that they would *return* [. . .]? What was the weather like? What was the fat man looking at? In what part of Touraine, in which part of Paris? Were the trees in flower or were they dark?[9]

---

[4] Pierre Michon, *Le Roi du bois* (Lagrasse: Verdier, 1996).

[5] Pierre Michon, *Rimbaud le fils* (Paris: Gallimard, 1991), p. 120.

[6] Pierre Michon, *Corps du roi* (Lagrasse: Verdier, 2002), p. 13.

[7] See Jean-Pierre Richard, 'Pour lire "Rimbaud le fils"', in Pierre Bergounioux et al. (eds.), *Compagnies de Pierre Michon* (Lagrasse: Verdier; Orléans: Théodore Balmoral, 1993), pp. 117–40 (p. 119).

[8] Dominique Viart has nevertheless referred to them as 'essais-fictions' and 'fictions-critiques': see id., 'Les "fictions-critiques" de Pierre Michon', in *Pierre Michon, l'écriture absolue: actes du colloque Michon de Saint-Étienne (Musée d'Art Moderne, 8, 9, 10 mars 2001)*, ed. Agnès Castiglione (Saint-Étienne: Publications de l'Université de Saint-Étienne, 2002), pp. 203–19.

[9] Pierre Michon, *Trois auteurs: Balzac, Cingria, Faulkner* (Lagrasse: Verdier, 1997), pp. 13–14 (Michon's italics).

What does the world look like, asks Michon for whom writing is a sort of grace, when that grace descends and takes up residence in the mortal body of the writer?

The very terms of this question already point us towards the Christian saints and their lives as models for this conception of the writer. The saint, says René Aigrain in his account of hagiography, is 'a man who, by corresponding to divine grace, has been constituted in a supernatural state of holiness'.[10] Or, as Peter Brown puts it, he represents a 'joining of Heaven and Earth', which provides an exemplary paradigm for his fellow Christians to emulate.[11] The divine is transmitted through a hierarchy of instantiations: the saint imitates Christ, and in turn the believer seeks to imitate the saint. Each saintly life participates in what one might call a Christian 'meta-biography': 'the deeper sense of Christian biography [is] that it is, in a sense, a continuation of the biography of Christ who is present in the most perfect members of his mystic Body.'[12] This is also the implication of Michon's listing of Dante, Shakespeare, Bruno, Vico, Joyce, and Beckett in his discussion of Beckett in *Corps du roi*, and of Malherbe, Racine, Hugo, Baudelaire, and Banville in *Rimbaud le fils*, who between them form an umbilical cord that ultimately goes as far back as Virgil and Homer.[13] Literary history in Michon's eyes becomes a kind of continuous biography composed of the 'most perfect members' of a mystic literary body. Just as the function of the saint's life, in both lived and written form, is to 'glorify God and edify man',[14] so the writer's life is a kind of glorification of literature, and requires to be glorified in its turn. This secondary glorification, says Michon, is the primary function of culture itself:

If culture has a meaning, it is this brotherly salute to the spirits of the glorious dead—like an impoverished form of what in the days of the Burgundian king Sigismond, the monks of Cluny instituted under the name *laus perennis*, the perpetual praise and unceasing prayer provided by three groups of monks who succeeded each other in a regular daily cycle.[15]

Michon's approach presents individual writers as instances of a mysterious incarnation, and the goal of his biographical writing is primarily to perpetuate a literary *laus perennis*.

The issue of literature as a form of grace has a particular urgency for Michon, but it also drives many of the figures in *Vies minuscules*, though none is a

---

[10] René Aigrain, *L'Hagiographie: ses sources, ses méthodes, son histoire*, p. 8.

[11] Peter Brown, *The Cult of the Saints: Its Rise and Function in Latin Christianity* (London: SCM, 1981), p. 1.

[12] Jacques Fontaine, 'Introduction', in Sulpicius Severus, *Vie de saint Martin*, ed. Jacques Fontaine, 3 vols. (Paris: Éditions du Cerf, 1967), vol. i, p. 68. For further discussion of saints' lives see Michel de Certeau, *L'Écriture de l'histoire* (Paris: Gallimard, 1975), pp. 274–88.

[13] Michon, *Corps du roi*, p. 13; *Rimbaud le fils*, pp. 19–20.

[14] Fontaine, 'Introduction', p. 67.

[15] Michon, *Trois auteurs*, p. 12 (original italics).

writer or artist. Michon portrays himself as the subject of an overwhelming but long-frustrated desire to write, and as being in pursuit of a vocation that is almost religious in its intensity.[16] What constitutes a writer for him is 'nothing but the will to speak'.[17] However, to speak as a writer is to enter a different order of experience and to become 'literature in person'. The writer brings literature into being, and simultaneously becomes the vehicle for another voice, the voice of literature:

for a writer nothing is more personal to him, nothing makes him more what he is than this will to utter [. . .] this violent desire that presides over each sentence, the imperceptible and decisive *putsch* in his inner parliament, which means that suddenly the despotic voice of what is called, and which is, literature begins to speak in his place.[18]

When Michon hears this voice, for example in William Faulkner's *Absalom, Absalom!*, he describes it as 'the inconceivable mouth of Literature which speaks, in person' (p. 87). It is the thing he seeks, but it is also 'inconceivable', a quasi-miraculous event that gives rise only to a series of questions: 'How is it done? [. . .] Where does it come from? Who is speaking? *What happened* to make those sentences come, wrested from a vain little man in Oxford, Mississipi. What *rush of wind*, what *shadow*? It is an understatement to say that I feel intimately close to these questions. They are my very life' (p. 88, Michon's italics). Michon's life as a writer is 'en souci de l'art', as he contemplates the life of this figure who is 'literature in person'. At the same time the literature he desires to write remains a radical uncertainty (to use Blanchot's expression), because it is so closely bound up with questions of belief about its very possibility.

The question 'How does one become a writer?' is, then, the one that presides over Michon's own existence; and his engagement with it has two strands. The first is the implied course of his own life, which he never narrates directly as autobiography but introduces into the margins of his work. The second, more central strand takes the form of a contemplation of the lives of others—writers and non-writers alike. If the story of a frustrated vocation is a familiar one in twentieth-century literature (Proust's *Recherche* is just one such story), Michon's portrayal of the lives of others in the context of this vocation introduces a new version of the relation between the biographical and the literary. He presents his own life-story in the *Vies minuscules* (and in the various interviews he has given) as the story of a vocation which began in childhood and which he pursued over the course of many years by a variety of means, most of which were misguided.[19] On a number of occasions he mentions a misplaced commitment to theory and

---

[16] As reported by Marianne Payot: 'Pierre Michon, une vocation tardive', interview with Marianne Payot, *Lire*, May 1997 <http://www.lire.fr/portrait.asp/idC=32578/idTC=5/idR=201/idG=3>, accessed 1 Mar. 2006.

[17] Pierre Michon, 'Entretien avec Catherine Argand', *Lire*, 271 (1998), pp. 32–40.

[18] Pierre Michon, 'Le Père du texte', in *Trois auteurs*, pp. 77–88 (pp. 82–3).

[19] I shall be returning to the issue of vocation in Ch. 18 below.

formalist experiment as one of these errors: 'literary theory repeated *ad nauseam* that writing exists where the world does not', he records in the *Vies minuscules*; and the result of his application of these theoretical principles in his own writing was work that he describes as 'piously modern', 'Joycean Abracadabras' that creaked under the weight of 'cumbersome formal "researches"'.[20] Like a latter-day Frédéric Moreau, he surrounds himself with the paraphernalia of art: 'the instruments for the ritual were in position, the typewriter by my left hand, and the sheets of paper by my right hand'; he adopts what he takes to be the appropriate pose: 'did I not have the look of a writer, his imperceptible uniform?'; and he waits for the grace of literary genius to descend: 'I was preparing for it with [. . .] so many picaresque Imitations of the lives of the Great Authors, that it could not be long in coming [*elle ne pourrait tarder à venir*]' (p. 136), a phrase that recalls quite precisely the opening scene of Flaubert's *Éducation sentimentale*, where Frédéric, musing ineffectually about a variety of artistic projects, 'found that the happiness merited by the excellence of his soul was too *long in coming* [*tardait à venir*]'.[21] Michon presents his escape from this false avenue as a return to the world and the acceptance of the human, both in himself and in others, the *Vies minuscules* being the material outcome of this change of heart.[22] In other words, what makes him different from Flaubert's failed hero is that at some point 'grace' did finally descend, and Michon's story is informed by the resulting conversion narrative, and a quasi-Christian model is consequently reinscribed in Michon's conception of the literary.

Recounted in these terms, Michon's conversion story is probably too good to be true, and certainly too sentimental to be very interesting. What makes it original is the way Michon undercuts his narrative by questioning the authenticity of his own 'conversion'. Thus he claims to have realized that 'going after Grace through Works [. . .] is the only [way] that allows one to glimpse the harbour', but he then turns back on this claim when he asks: 'But have I really understood this?'[23] The effect is compounded by his sustained use of the same religious metaphors and vocabulary both for his 'new' insights and for the false basis of the writing that he pursued for so long. Belief in Grace is as much a symptom of misjudgement as of enlightenment; or again, the notion of scales falling from one's eyes, which seems to explain how Michon was saved from his erroneous path, is given as an example of the false assumptions that kept him fixed upon that same path: 'What I demanded in vain, with growing fury and despair, was a road to Damascus, there and then' (p. 137). As a further consequence

[20] Pierre Michon, *Vies minuscules* (Paris: Gallimard, 1984), pp. 138–9. All page references are to this edition.

[21] Gustave Flaubert, *L'Éducation sentimentale: histoire d'un jeune homme* [1869], ed. P. M. Wetherill (Classiques Garnier; Paris: Garnier, 1984), p. 4.

[22] See e.g. Pierre Michon, 'Entretien avec Thierry Guichard', *Le Matricule des anges*, 5 (1993).

[23] *Vies minuscules*, p. 137.

of this confusion between error and enlightenment, the ordinary people in *Vies minuscules*, who supposedly represent the humble reality of the world to which Michon returns from the aberration of his theoretical and avant-gardist practices, are all nevertheless presented as being not just victims but very active perpetrators of the misguided beliefs that helped to lead Michon astray. In sum, the belief that sustains literature in Michon's account is a complex and ambivalent thing, and literature itself is the product of the arbitrary fiat of pure assertion: 'what is called, and which is, literature'.[24]

BELIEF AND IMPOSTURE

This brings us back round to the second strand of Michon's engagement with the question 'How does one become a writer?', namely, his depiction of the lives of others, whether in the *Vies minuscules*, *Rimbaud le fils*, or the *Vie de Joseph Roulin*.[25] The term 'lives' already carries with it certain associations of anachronism, particularly by comparison with the term 'biography'. As Marc Fumaroli has put it in his essay contrasting the two terms, biography is a 'serious' enterprise, implying scholarship on the part of its author, and development on the part of its subject; whereas 'lives' are a repository of self-evident example, be they Plutarch's *Lives*, the Lives of the Saints, or Vasari's *Lives of the Artists*. The exemplary qualities of their subjects are such a fundamental given of both the lived and the written life that the subject does not need to be shown to evolve. Time, Fumaroli argues, is not a feature of such writings.[26] Michon chooses to revert to a form (that of the 'life') whose assumptions thus run counter to many of those of modern biography, and indeed autobiography. But it enables him to make the question of (literary) belief and (artistic) example central to his concerns. Or, rather, since the question of belief is so crucial to his conception of literature, it is the 'life' that offers the best means of exploring that conception, and not the painstakingly researched and empirically based demystifications of modern biography.

Before going any further on the question of lives, this issue of belief as the indispensable component of Michon's sense of the literary needs to be examined in more detail. The first thing to be said about it is that it changes the nature of the underlying question from 'What is literature?' to 'What do I—or what does she or he—believe that literature is?', a question that is perhaps better recast as 'What do I need to believe that literature is in order to be able write?' In other words, the issue does not concern the definition or the truth of literature, but

---

[24] This phrase is itself a repetition, with minor variations, of a phrase, 'ce qu'on appelle est qui est la peinture', from Antonin Artaud: see id., *Van Gogh ou le suicidé de la société* (1947; Paris: Gallimard, 2001), p. 46.

[25] Pierre Michon, *Vie de Joseph Roulin* (Lagrasse: Verdier, 1988).

[26] Fumaroli, 'Des "Vies" à la biographie'.

the beliefs about literature that are most effective in bringing it into existence. The problem with theory for Michon is that it produces nothing, or at any rate something so derisory that, as he says of his 'Joycean Abracadabras', it makes the angels laugh. By contrast, the figures whose lives he narrates in *Vies minuscules* all sustain beliefs which in some sense can be seen as naive or absurd from the standpoint of modern literature, but which from a different perspective offer examples that, if correctly emulated, might nonetheless produce results. And the very existence of the *Vies minuscules* constitutes implicit testimony to this.

It is Michon's willingness to embrace belief as a basis for literature that makes him in some senses the mirror image of Sartre, with whom he shares not only the status of fatherless child, but, more importantly, the inheritance of a set of anachronistic, largely nineteenth-century convictions about the sacred character of the literary (as we saw in Chapter 15 above). Unlike Sartre, however, Michon seems to be fascinated by belief, and to be quite happy to restore the traffic between a supposedly secular literature and a sacred Christianity. In a published fragment of his unfinished novel *Les Onze*, Michon describes the moment towards the end of the eighteenth century when this traffic began:

it was at the time when literary belief was beginning to oust that other, great and ancient belief, to relegate it to its limited historical moment and to its limited place, [. . .] and to claim that it was in its own space, the pages of novels and Anacreontic *bouts rimés*, that the universal now deigned to appear. God was, in a sense, changing nest.[27]

This is the shift documented by Paul Bénichou in *Le Sacre de l'écrivain*, but Michon seems to work actively to restore the religious origins of the literary; reversing Sartre's exorcism of the sacred, he positively revels in words like 'God, Meaning, Grace, the Absolute',[28] less with the direct aim of recovering a Christian truth in the literary than in order to exploit the peculiar capacities of such language in an age of unbelief. 'God' is a word without empirical reference, comments Michon, but it has retained a strangely powerful quality, being 'one of those mere words whose referent is unverifiable and yet, precisely because of that, exists only all the more' (ibid.). Such words, he continues with a certain provocation, function like the bumper on a flipper-machine; or, put more seriously: 'It is not the meaning of these words that is important, it is the fact that through their enquiry, through their empty aspiration, they relaunch a sequence of prose' (ibid.). It is their efficacy in producing literature that counts above all: 'It is something that works well.' Despite this emphasis on the simple functionality of the religious for the purposes of the literary, the use of such language still requires something like belief for it to be valid. Michon states quite baldly that belief is an essential prerequisite for his writing: 'Nothing is more

---

27 Pierre Michon, 'Deux chapitres des *Onze*', *Scherzo*, 5 (1998), pp. 13–30.
28 Pierre Michon, 'Entretien avec Pierre Michon: propos recueillis par Anne Sophie Perlat et Franz Johansson', *Scherzo*, 5 (1998), pp. 5–12 (p. 11).

necessary to me [. . .] for writing than to have strong beliefs, in man, in God or in literature.'[29] The question, then, is how one comes by belief, particularly when, to modern eyes, it can so easily seem fraudulent. The solution seems to be precisely to accept 'imposture', or what Michon calls 'bluff', as a necessary component of belief, so that bluff must always be described as 'the bluff that is not a bluff'.[30] This conundrum would seem to suggest that belief, however fraudulent and unfounded, is a necessity—in life perhaps, but in art most definitely: 'It's an imposture, but that's all we have' (ibid.).

If there is an element of nostalgia in Michon's approach to belief, it is as much as anything a nostalgia for a capacity for belief that can encompass imposture or bluff, rather than for a belief that can be guaranteed to be immune from such travesty. He rarely describes contemporary reality head-on, but chooses people and periods for whom and in which belief of this more complex kind appears to have been commonplace. The medieval world is a recurrent element in Michon's work (e.g. *Mythologies d'hiver* and *Abbés*),[31] where saints, monks, nuns, and bishops are shown to found monasteries, drain marshes, acquire the power of eloquence through the sheer force of their belief, knowing all the while that, as Bertran the bishop says to the monk who writes the 'life' of 'Saint' Erminie—itself a means of establishing a fraudulent claim to land—lies are integral to that belief: 'you will have to speak the truth and yet lie.'[32] Although it is not within the bishop's power to absolve him of this falsehood, the monk's own writing might itself have the capacity to do so: 'Only the truth that you will place at the heart of your lie will be able to absolve you' (ibid.). The nineteenth century is also depicted by Michon as an age of powerful belief, offering examples of figures whose convictions verge on what a modern view might dismiss as megalomaniac obsession. Two such figures in *Mythologies d'hiver* are Barthélémy Prunières, doctor and amateur anthropologist, and Édouard Martel, founder of the science known as speleology. Both are semi-madmen whose capacity for belief is an indispensable part of their scientific activities, and this gives them their place alongside the medieval saints in the same volume. In a similar vein, Michon sees in Balzac, another nineteenth-century example, the supreme impostor who 'delighted in demonstrating through his own person that the arts are an imposture', and for whom the writing of the *Comédie humaine* is the product of 'the exhausting drama of *genius* [which] he acts out for himself'.[33]

[29] Pierre Michon, 'Entretien avec Pierre Michon: propos recueillis par Jean-Christophe Millois', *Prétexte*, 9 (1996), pp. 58–62.

[30] 'Entretien avec Pierre Michon: propos recueillis par Anne Sophie Perlat et Franz Johansson', p. 11.

[31] Pierre Michon, *Mythologies d'hiver* (Lagrasse: Verdier, 1997), and id., *Abbés* (Lagrasse: Verdier, 2002). For an interesting discussion of Michon's use of the Middle Ages see Sabine and Patrick Boucheron, 'Pierre Michon écrivain du Moyen Âge', *Scherzo*, 5 (1998), pp. 54–66.

[32] *Mythologies d'hiver*, p. 68.

[33] Pierre Michon, 'Le Temps est un grand maigre', in *Trois auteurs*, pp. 11–46 (pp. 15, 27–8).

For Michon, Balzac offers proof that genius is a farce that can work, and he is hailed as one of the 'glorious dead' whose memory it is the business of culture to honour: he is even styled 'Saint Balzac' at one point, and treated quite seriously as an instance of '*literature in person*'.[34]

In a passage devoted to the contemplation of relics of saints, Michon remarks that the signs that once made them sacred have become illegible to the modern viewer, who, when faced with the remnants of a lost faith, can conceive of belief only in terms of the stark alternatives of cynical fraudulence or foolish gullibility: 'we do not understand it, and only the words cynicism and total naivety come to mind, but most certainly not knowledge and truth.'[35] The desire that informs Michon's own writing is for a belief that cuts across the dualism of these modern alternatives. It is not the content of belief that is at issue, so much as its quality. In other words, Michon is in pursuit of the kind of belief that he finds (or imagines that he finds, which comes to the same) in earlier ages, while nevertheless taking into account the unbelief of the contemporary world that is, of necessity, his starting point.

SAINTS' LIVES

Belief, then, rather than theory, is asserted as the force that generates literature and justifies it as a vocation. In considering the role of 'lives' in Michon's work, it begins to become apparent that saints' 'lives' might logically have a role in the workings of such belief. Michon mentions several examples of pre-modern 'lives' in various places, and saints are certainly not the only protagonists of the 'lives' that he refers to. These include Suetonius' *Lives of the Caesars* and Racan's *Vie de monsieur de Malherbe*, but he also refers on several occasions to Jacobus de Voragine's *Golden Legend* and to the fourth-century *Life of St Martin* by Sulpicius Severus.[36] The 'lives' of saints have a particular role in producing and sustaining belief, which does not apply to other kinds of exemplary 'lives'. First of all, they portray people who are, by definition, believers, and whose belief is tested and proved either by their martyrdom, or by their powers of persuasion in converting others to the faith. Such is the case of St Martin, who converted brigands intending to rob him and pagans attempting to resist him with demonstrations of the power of their own rival faith. But over and above the illustrations of the effects of faith in the life of an individual saint, the written 'lives' of the saints differ from modern biography in that they are designed to nurture faith amongst the believers who hear or read those 'lives'. In this their

---

[34] Ibid., pp. 12, 32, 40 (italics in original).

[35] *Abbés*, p. 57.

[36] The blurb on the cover of the Gallimard edition of *Vies minuscules* compares the book's 'lives' to 'une curieuse *Légende dorée* où les miracles seraient réticents'. The life of St Martin by Sulpicius Severus in the edition by Jacques Fontaine is a key text for him (personal communication, June 2002), and there are a number of allusions to St Martin in his work, e.g. *Abbés* (p. 11).

function is spiritual and liturgical rather than informative; the 'life' of each saint was either read and meditated in private or read aloud as one of the lessons at matins on his or her day in the annual liturgical calendar which determines the order in which the 'lives' appear in the *Golden Legend*. Rather than being a source of factual information, the saint's 'life' is first and foremost a 'legend', a text to be read (*legenda*) on a regular basis, proposing an example of faith intended to be imitated by those to whom it is addressed. Michon speaks in an essay of the contagion of belief,[37] and whether through the liturgy or through private meditation, the 'lives' of saints are devised and compiled precisely with a view to spreading this 'contagion'. In so far as it makes sense to see saints' 'lives' as a model for Michon's work, the modern reader, faced with his texts, is being invited to contemplate a series of examples of belief—religious, literary, and other—which, although they may often seem as alien as the vanished reverence for the holy relics that can no longer speak to us, are nevertheless to be taken seriously as instances of the 'bluff that is not a bluff' on which the continuation of literature depends. In what follows I shall explore Michon's use of this model in his first and best-known work, the *Vies minuscules*.[38]

VIES MINUSCULES

The *Vies minuscules* consists of eight 'lives' of people who figured in one way or another in Michon's own life: ancestors, grandparents, school friends, a fellow patient in a hospital ward, the local *curé*, an old girlfriend, and a sister who died in infancy before he was born. In various ways they illustrate the rural backwater in La Creuse where Michon grew up but which he had repudiated in his quest to become a writer. The writing of the *Vies*, however, is presented as a necessary return to these origins and treated as the final enabling stage in this quest. The book complicates this narrative of return and acceptance by treating the figures as both exemplary and benighted, both as the source of Michon's own errors and as guides to his redemption.[39] Equally, his own story as it is implicitly presented through the lives of these other figures is one of both imposture and achievement, an ambiguity that is heralded in the opening sentence of the book: 'Let us proceed through the genesis of my pretensions.' Nothing, either here or subsequently, determines whether 'prétentions' should be read as meaning a claim based on entitlement, pure demand, or sheer fraudulence. (The dictionary

---

[37] '[L]a conviction est chose contagieuse': 'La Danseuse', in *Trois auteurs*, pp. 49–75 (p. 54).

[38] For an account of *Rimbaud le fils* in this connection see my article 'The Hagiographies of Pierre Michon: *Rimbaud le fils*', *French Studies*, 58 (2004), pp. 205–17.

[39] Jacques Chabot writes that 'les personnages de Pierre Michon sont presque tous des paysans pervertis par la Littérature': in id., '*Vie de Joseph Roulin*: une "vie minuscule"', in *Pierre Michon, l'écriture absolue*, ed. Castiglione, pp. 23–37 (p. 32).

defines the word according to these three main criteria.[40]) At the end of the book, where Michon articulates his hope that his writing has in some sense breathed life into the figures from his past, he acknowledges that there is no way of knowing whether he has succeeded. All he is left with is his own desire to believe that things happened the way he has described them, and that his language has somehow actually called into being the people that he writes about. Belief is as essential as it is unfounded in Michon's literary ambitions.

The protagonists of these 'lives', then, are not saints in the strict sense of the word, but are presented by Michon as having appeared worthy of contemplation for the example they propose, as legends, or 'lives' to be read and emulated. Each of the characters instantiates a virtue or an attitude, and all provide examples of the power and nature of belief, though in this case chiefly concerning the power of language and, in particular, of literature. In a manner very similar to Sulpicius Severus recounting the life of St Martin, Michon writes himself into the text as a witness to much of what he describes, or as the recorder of hearsay about the lives he narrates, and in any case as a follower in the footsteps of quasi-spiritual example. The language of Christianity is woven into the text not just in association with the false pursuit of grace discussed earlier, but to convey the attitudes of the figures he depicts and to provide a framework for interpreting the events he narrates. Religious belief is an integral part of the peasant world that Michon describes, and it spills over into the language he uses to represent it. So that, for example, the 'Vie d'Antoine Peluchet' begins with an account of an object that is, quite literally, a relic that has been kept in the family for generations, and then goes on to characterize the family stories told by Michon's grandmother as 'anecdotes running along the beads of a rosary'.[41] When Michon alludes to his relation to his absent father at the beginning of the 'Vies d'Eugène et de Clara', the language used casts him as a faltering believer in need of divine intercession: 'I am incapable of thinking directly about my father, inaccessible and hidden like a *god*. Like one of the *faithful*—but who perhaps no longer *believes*—I need the succour of intermediaries, *angels*, or *clergy*' (p. 57). There is something in Michon's *Vies* of the Flaubert of 'St Julien l'hospitalier' or 'Un cœur simple' in their depiction of anachronistic forms of belief; but, unlike Flaubert, Michon figures himself as subscribing actively to the idiom and the world view of his protagonists. This idiom is also written into what, for want of a better word, one could call the epistemology of Michon's narrative. Much of this narrative

---

[40] The *Trésor de la langue française*, for example, lists the following definitions: '1. 'Volonté nettement déclarée d'obtenir telle chose comme un dû, revendication d'un droit réel ou supposé, d'un privilège jugé mérité.' 2. Gén. au plur., parfois avec une nuance péj., iron. Volonté marquée de parvenir à tel but, aspiration délibérée à telle qualité (parfois hors d'atteinte). 3. C. Au sing., péj. 1. Trait de caractère qui porte à se flatter de qualités exagérées, à être excessivement satisfait de soi-même et à afficher des airs supérieurs [À propos d'une œuvre hum.] Excessive recherche dans les moyens d'expression; Gén. au plur. Personne ou chose qui manifeste de la prétention.'

[41] *Vies minuscules*, p. 25.

is conveyed in the confident tone of an unproblematic recall: 'It was the start of summer, during the early sixties, in Clermont-Ferrand' (p. 113); or 'I went out into the night, drunk; Marianne was worried, the indifferent gaze of the prostitutes followed us to the end of the dark street; the lights on the central boulevards exasperated me' (p. 114). However, there are also moments that are clearly announced as entirely the product of Michon's desire to subscribe to a certain version of events: 'for a moment I *dare to believe*, knowing there's no truth in it, that what drew him was less the crude bait of a fortune to be made than an unconditional surrender into the hands of intransitive Fortune' (p. 14 [p. 174]). And there are others, such as the occasion at the end of the book when he saw his dead sister in the form of a 10-year-old child, which hover between factual assertion and wishful thinking. On the one hand, Michon writes of the girl, 'she was there, in front of me'; but, on the other, he qualifies this unequivocal assertion with a more problematic comment: 'Our tender years are full of boasts, but this was not entirely a boast' (p. 205). The vision is both true and not totally untrue, in a manner that makes it, as indeed the entire text of the eight 'lives', the fruit of every sense of 'pretension', from justified to totally fraudulent, and undeniably the fruit of the capacity for belief that their protagonists exemplify.

Although at one point Michon refers to a number of the protagonists of his 'lives' as the 'sirens' of his youth (p. 16), they are also implicitly accorded the status of intercessors. Or, rather, they are presented as the cause and origin of his 'errors', but also as versions of himself ('I know, because I am he', p. 102), and, most importantly, as exemplars of the writing self he wishes to become. The sequence of the 'lives' is broadly, if not strictly, chronological, and seems also to follow a kind of progression corresponding to the implied development of Michon himself. This would explain the two hiccups in the chronology, whereby André Dufourneau is positioned before Antoine Peluchet, and the 'dead infant', whose dates should place her second or third in chronological order, is reserved until the very end. What this arrangement does is to make the first 'life' the story of a disastrous entry into language and a fatal misuse of literature, and the last 'life' the story of a life without language that culminates in a sort of miracle with the resurrection of the dead sister in the form of an apparition. This constitutes a powerful narrative frame, but it is constantly complicated, if not directly undercut, by the endorsements of erroneous belief that I have already mentioned, and, even more so, by the sumptuously literary nature of Michon's own prose and its sustained allusion to consecrated literary example. Any discussion of this narrative needs to take account of the implications of the flamboyant literariness of its language, quotations, and references. Unlike the lives in the *Golden Legend*, the relation that the aspirant writer has with his models is not quite the same as the one that his readers have with them.

The opening text, the 'Vie d'André Dufourneau', tells the story of a boy sent from the 'assistance publique' to live with the family of Michon's great-grandparents and to work on their farm. This practice was common in the poorer parts of rural France from the late nineteenth century onwards, and it cannot but recall the case of Genet, although Michon does not explicitly allude to him here.[42] Michon's grandmother, who was a girl at the time, teaches the child to read, and in the process he acquires a different language that reveals to him the existence of a way of life beyond his own: 'Amid all the chatter in dialect, a voice rises in nobler tones, seeks in richer sonorities to mould itself to a language of richer words' (p. 11 [p. 172]). Because this language is not Dufourneau's birthright, it changes his entire relation to the world, cutting him off from the one he knows, but excluding him from the one to which his new language seemed to grant him access:

He does not yet know that for those of his class or his kind, born closer to the soil and more liable to revert back to it, Fine Language does not confer grandeur, but a nostalgia and a desire for grandeur. He ceases to belong to the present moment, the salt of time is diluted, and in the death throes of the past which are always beginning, the future rises up and immediately starts to run. (ibid.)

Michon positions himself alongside Dufourneau as the first of the excluded figures in the book ('in speaking of him, it is myself that I am speaking of', p. 14 [p. 174]), and a member of the class to which Dufourneau belongs. Since one could only describe the language Michon uses as proof that he has himself mastered 'the language of richer words', the sentences in Michon's text simultaneously assert an achievement and record the loss it entailed.

When Dufourneau is called up for military service and goes to the city, he realizes, as he hears 'Fine Language' spoken around him, that his own mastery of it is limited. His place in the social order remains unchanged: 'He discovered that he was a peasant' (p. 13 [p. 173]). The language he has learned has nevertheless infected him with nostalgia and a desire for greatness, inciting him to a series of extravagantly literary gestures that determine the subsequent course of his life. The peasants have already invented a fiction that makes him the illegitimate child of a local landowner, and his acquaintance with 'Fine Language' has convinced him that he is a chosen being with a glorious destiny ahead of him. As an adult Dufourneau opts for a life in Africa, creating for himself a kind of destiny, which he announces with the melodramatic bravado of a 'bon mot', asserting: 'I shall come back rich, or die in Africa' (p. 16 [p. 175]). Michon presents this as a slightly burlesque attempt on Dufourneau's part to rise to the 'nobility' of the occasion. But although its crassness may be a result of his

---

[42] There is a reference to '[les] marlous de Jean Genet' in the 'Vie du père Foucault', p. 121, but none to his status as an 'enfant de l'assistance publique', of which Sartre makes so much in his *Saint Genet, comédien et martyr*. For more on this practice see White, *Genet*, p. 10. In his interview with Arlette Farge (from which the epigraph to the present chapter is taken) Michon briefly mentions Genet as someone who, like Michon in the *Vies minuscules*, makes rhetorical splendour out of the lowly and insignificant: see Pierre Michon, 'Pierre Michon, Arlette Farge, entretien', *Cahiers de la Villa Gillet*, 3 (1995), pp. 151–64 (pp. 156–7).

limited education, it still succeeds in conveying an effect that Michon is willing to characterize as exemplarily 'literary':

no doubt, uttered with a certain complacency by a person wishing to underscore the gravity of the moment, but too poorly educated to know how to make the most of it by pretending to lay it low with a *bon mot*, and thus reduced to drawing on a repertoire which he regarded as 'noble' in order to mark its special character, these words were, to that extent, 'literary'. (ibid.)

This literariness is nonetheless complex. On the negative side, it evokes a certain kind of adventure-story idiom ('poems full of echoes and massacres', p. 16 [p. 175]); and it also attests a dubious desire to turn life into art, which Michon sees reflected in the complicity between himself and his grandmother since they are both equally 'guilty' of trying to make Dufourneau's life into the sort of novel that his parting words seemed to sketch out: 'I said that my grandmother had dug [them] out a hundred times over from the ruins of time [. . .] but it was I who always asked her to do so, I who was always wanting to hear the leave-taker's cliché once more' (ibid.). This novel goes on being elaborated, with Dufourneau in the self-appointed role of hero; and when the family eventually cease to hear tell of their adoptive protégé and are obliged to presume that he is dead, it is Michon's grandmother who comes up with the most seductively literary hypothesis about his death, namely, that he had been murdered by the natives who worked for him. As both child and adult, Michon endorses his grandmother's version of events, precisely on account of its novelistic qualities: the death she imagines for Dufourneau is psychologically consistent, being the (plausible) outcome of the (plausibly) excessive cruelty deployed by someone who could not allow himself to recognize his own humble origins in the people under his command. Furthermore, this inference makes a well-constructed destiny out of Dufourneau's life, providing a fitting response on the part of Fate to the bravado of the young adventurer's parting shot: not only does he die, but he dies at the hands of the very people whose labour was the source of the fortune he had gone to seek. Michon and his grandmother conspire to read the life like a book, in a way that turns out to be as determining of Michon's own life as the grand literary gestures of Dufourneau were for his.

Dufourneau's life is thus also literary in the sense that it clinches Michon's own vocation and provides a metaphor for it. In Dufourneau's grandiloquent phrase, Michon retrospectively sees his own future taking shape: 'for me these words were an Annunciation and a living prophecy' (p. 16 [p. 175]). The dark continent of Africa into which Dufourneau disappears is compared to the world of literature: 'I had not yet discovered that writing is a continent far darker, far more enticing and delusive than Africa, the writer a breed far more eager to lose his way than the explorer' (pp. 16–17 [p. 175]). It is a world whose stakes are as high as those uttered in Dufourneau's rhetorical formula: 'though he explores memory and memorious libraries in place of dunes and forests, to return rolling in words as others roll in gold, or to die amongst them poorer than when you started—to die of them—these are the alternatives that also confront the scribe' (p. 17 [p. 175]). The fall into 'Fine Language', and the ensuing nostalgia and desire for greatness that Michon originally ascribes to Dufourneau are then re-enacted by himself as a consequence of hearing the story of the man (Dufourneau) whose life was so decisively marked by his entry into 'Fine Language'.

The final way in which Dufourneau's life is made the stuff of literature is to be found in the very fact that Michon's retelling of it becomes his own passport to the dark continent of literature (the 'Life of André Dufourneau' is the first text in Michon's first book). Michon recounts it, moreover, in a literary register that goes far beyond any of the references that mapped out the world of either Dufourneau or Élise. Thus, the word 'mémorieuse' ('memorious') in the sentence just quoted, is described by the dictionary as 'dated', the most recent attested instance of it being in the work of the nineteenth-century writer George Sand.[43] More overtly, the text is tagged with a series of quotations, marked and unmarked, from Rimbaud, Faulkner, and others, which permeate the language in which Dufourneau's adventures are narrated. As Dufourneau sets sail for Africa, it is Rimbaud's words from *Une saison en enfer*—'My day is done; I am leaving Europe'—that are summoned to mark the event (p. 17 [p. 175]). A few lines later, when Michon launches into a physical description of his hero, he affects suddenly to concede that Dufourneau looks like a writer, and, quite specifically, like Faulkner. (Both Rimbaud and Faulkner are emblematic figures for Michon: and he attributes to his discovery of the work of Faulkner the catalyst of his own writing.) When, in the following paragraph, Africa finally heaves into view, the literary references thicken. Gide's description of Grand-Bassam is called up as the lens through which the continent's coastline should be seen; and the landscape is described by Michon as filled with 'Mallarmean palm-trees', and 'anabases large and small' implicitly derived from Saint-John Perse.[44] Michon's own literary repertoire is considerably larger, more sophisticated, and inevitably more modern than that of his subject, but the two are overlaid in such a way as to convey a highly ambiguous message. Michon takes his inspiration from Dufourneau's imposture, its reckless acting out, and its attempts at the grandiose, all of which he both replicates and ambiguously redeems in his own literary practice.

Some of the subsequent lives continue to explore the dangers entailed by the acquisition of the very eloquence that Michon's writing self exhibits. In the 'Vie d'André Dufourneau' Michon acknowledges the power of the desire to be a 'Fine Talker' (p. 15 [p. 174]) when he suggests that Dufourneau saw Africa as a place

---

[43] See the entry for this word in the *Trésor de la langue française*.
[44] Or Xenophon, from whose work of the same name the term is originally taken. Saint-John Perse's epic poem *Anabase* was first published in 1924, which places it in the same time span as Dufourneau's departure. *Vies minuscules*, p. 18.

where he might compensate for the linguistic exclusion he suffers in France and acquire status simply by virtue of a contrast with the non-francophone natives. It is a land where the bluff will never be called on rhetorical imposture. In the 'Vie du père Foucault' Michon casts himself in a particularly odious version of the role of rhetorician, when, under the influence of drink, he provokes a verbal duel with a fellow drinker that ends with a physical fight as the rival retaliates to the taunt of words with physical blows. Recovering afterwards in hospital, Michon encounters an old man, *le père* Foucault, who eventually confesses to being illiterate. The old man's acknowledgement of his lack of linguistic mastery comes as a sort of revelation to Michon, and this is repeated in the figure of 'l'abbé Bandy', whose life is told in the following section; the move from triumphant eloquence to near-aphasia takes place here within a single individual—Bandy himself—thus suggesting that rhetorical restraint is a literary virtue to be imitated.

Bandy is the local priest of Michon's childhood, a figure whose personal panache is initially matched by his verbal prowess, whether in the manner in which he utters the Latin liturgy or in the language of his sermons. Michon speculates that the priest's linguistic bravura is in part an arrogant attempt to be equal to the gorgeousness of the world he sees around him: 'the only possible response to [the] riches [of the world] was to set against them, or add to them, an exhausting and total verbal magnificence, in an act of defiance that had always to be repeated, and whose only motor is pride' (p. 153). And, Michon's speculation continues, it is also in part a desire to seduce, whether it be his women parishioners, God, or Bandy himself. However, when Michon comes across Bandy some years later, all panache and all eloquence have vanished, and there is no trace of either pride or seduction about the man. In a sermon delivered in a dilapidated church before a congregation of inmates from the local mental hospital, Michon hears nothing of the verbal glory that he remembered from his childhood: 'the sovereign emphasis in word and gesture had sovereignly collapsed, the mediocrity of his diction was perfect, his weary language reached nothing and nobody; the bloodless words were muffled in the rubble, vanished through the cracks; like Demosthenes, and for the reverse effect, Bandy had in some manner filled his mouth with stones' (pp. 171–2). Michon, who writes himself into the narrative as being at a particularly low ebb in his quest to become a writer, chooses, however, to hear in this linguistic dereliction not defeat, but a kind of wisdom on Bandy's part. His idea is that Bandy, by abandoning rhetorical style and theological ambition, has discovered a kind of ascesis that might have a better chance of leading him to Grace than the other means he had pursued: 'Perhaps, like St Francis of Assisi, the priest wanted to speak only for the birds and the wolves; because if those creatures without language had understood him, then he would have been certain that he had been touched by Grace' (p. 174). In filling out the picture of Bandy's death—drunk, at night, in the forest—Michon allows this hypothesis to triumph in a vision of Bandy as a latter-day St Francis surrounded by all the beasts of the forest, and attended by a legendary stag bearing a crucifix between its antlers. Since the 'moral' of the last 'life', the 'Vie de la petite morte', would seem to be that writing needs to try and do justice to the wordless experience of the infant sister he never knew, Bandy's insight is given further credence.

What complicates the force of these examples of reticence is that Michon's own prose bears many of the characteristics of the eloquence that Bandy abjures. Verbal magnificence is Michon's stock in trade, and the seductive power of his writing is incontrovertible. Unlike Bandy, Michon does not at any point abandon style, and the text is dense with literary allusion, from the dedication to Louis-René des Forêts at the beginning of the 'Vie de Georges Bandy', to references to Flaubert's correspondence and the modern form of writing known as 'écriture blanche' at the end. But even if the narrative content of the 'life' seems to condemn literary learning by associating it with Bandy's negative counterpart in the psychiatrist treating Michon, the text nevertheless makes particularly effective use of one of the rhetorical tricks for which Bandy is implicitly condemned in Michon's account of his early sermons, namely, the orotund use of proper names. Perplexingly, proper names and cultural references that would certainly have been lost on Bandy's last congregation are drafted into Michon's celebration of Bandy's final self-denying mode, with unrestrained mention of Demosthenes and St Francis, supported by imperfect subjunctives and the rhetorical flourish of ternary constructions. Indeed, a considerable part of the charm of Michon's language in the *Vies minuscules* comes from the incantation of a particularly euphonious and suggestive series of proper names, whether it is the litany of the place names of Michon's childhood (Les Cards, Saint-Goussaud, Mourioux, Chatelus), or the names that are recorded in the titles of the 'lives': 'Vie d'André Dufourneau', 'Vie d'Antoine Peluchet', 'Vie des frères Bakroot', 'Vie du père Foucault', and so on. If Bandy's life is being held up by Michon as an example, in the manner of the 'lives' of the saints, the language in which he does so suggests that Michon has failed to learn the lessons that his story contains.

But 'lessons' may not, after all, be the issue. Lessons might be too like the 'theory' to which 'lives' seemed to offer an alternative. Towards the end of his book Michon acknowledges the characteristics of his own style, but it is not with the intention of suggesting that he has betrayed the example proposed by the lives of his humble masters. Instead, the issue is one that places a quite different emphasis on the idea of a life, namely, the rekindling of lives through writing. Michon's ultimate goal is to bring the figures from his past back to life, and its realization is treated as more dependent on miracle than on the moral of his tales: 'Nothing entrances me like a miracle', he writes (p. 206). Michon's only anxiety about his language here is whether it stands in the way of this resurrection: 'this tendency towards archaisms, that sentimental indulgence when style can do no more, that quaint desire for euphony are none of them the way that the dead speak when they have wings, when they return in the pure Word and in light. I tremble at the thought that they have become even more obscured by my writing' (p. 206). Writing has become a pursuit of vanished beings, whose realization depends on the miracle he mentions combined with the force of his own belief, however fraudulent and unfounded: '*I believe* that the gentle lime trees, white with snow, bent down to meet the last gaze of old Foucault, now more than mute, *it is what I believe*, and perhaps he wishes it thus' (pp. 206–7). The closing words of the text are a series of quasi-imperatives (or what grammarians call 'jussives') summoning the dead back to life, and culminating in a final exhortation that calls for the protagonists of the *Vies minuscules* to *be*: 'In the winged conclave held in Les Cards on the ruins of what might have been, *may they be*.' If Michon has succeeded, it is as a result of incorporating the imposture of his biographical models and integrating it into what Blanchot (in the epigraph above) calls the writer's own literary 'truth' and the hopes that impel it. The lives of these literary saints and impostors are the inspiration for the imposture of Michon's own writing, which might or might not achieve the literariness that is the central concern of his life. This uncertainty ultimately turns his language into a kind of prayer in which he prays that his beliefs may be sanctioned by the conferring of literary grace on the words that make up these microscopic lives.[45] And it is perhaps at this point that the readers of Michon's text are finally called upon to share a belief of which they have hitherto been little more than observers in the traffic between Michon and his literary models.

Michon's return to the 'lives' of the saints is much more than a matter of formal or stylistic borrowing. By treating his biographical subjects as models to be meditated and emulated in pursuit of a belief that is necessary for the production of the literature that portrays them, Michon reactivates the pragmatic element that lies at the heart of the biographical tradition. The result is a peculiar and distinctly precarious circularity that is rather more modern than medieval, and on which Michon's writing nevertheless thrives: literariness is both the means whereby the original biographical subjects exist for the would-be believer, and the fruit of the belief that these figures inspire.

[45] Michon explores the relation between poetry and prayer in his essay on Hugo's 'Booz endormi': Pierre Michon, 'Le Ciel est un très grand homme', in *Corps du roi*, pp. 71–102.

PART VIII

THE WRITING LIFE

Nicht, was wohl sonst des Menschen Geschick und Sorg'
　Im Haus und unter offenem Himmel ist,
　　Wenn edler, denn das Wild, der Mann sich
　　　Wehret und nährt! denn es gilt ein anders,

Zu Sorg'und Dienst den Dichtenden anvertraut!
　Der Höchste, der ists, dem wir geeignet sind,
　　Daß näher, immer neu besungen
　　　Ihn die befreundete Brust vernehme.

　　　　　　　　　　(Hölderlin, 'Dichterberuf')[1]

'I am not decrying the life of the true artist. I am exalting it. I say, it is
out of the reach of any but choice organizations—natures framed to love
perfection and to labour for it; ready, like all true lovers, to endure, to wait,
to say, I am not yet worthy, but she—Art, my mistress—is worthy, and I
will live to merit her. An honourable life? Yes. But the honour comes from
the inward vocation and the hard-won achievement; there is no honour in
donning the life as a livery.'

　　　　　　　　　　　　(George Eliot, *Daniel Deronda*)

　　Art too is only a way of Living.

　　　　　　　　　　　　　(Rilke, *Letters to a Young Poet*)

The artist is the origin of the work. The work is the origin of the artist.
　　　　　　　(Heidegger, 'The Origin of the Work of Art')

As all these epigraphs attest, the question of the nature and function of art has
been addressed in the past two hundred years of European literature through the
notion of the writer's vocation. Since the beginning of the nineteenth century it
has become a commonplace to assert that art makes special claims on the lives of
artists. When art becomes a vocation, a calling to the higher things mentioned
by Hölderlin, it creates a special kind of life for the poet, setting him at the same
distance from his fellow men as men are set from animals. And as Klesmer the
musician is telling Gwendolen in the quotation from *Daniel Deronda*, the artist's
life imposes its own exacting requirements on those 'choice organizations' who
are called upon to follow it: a regime of humility, self-denial, and ferocious hard
work. These remarks come at the point in George Eliot's novel when, in her
desire to avoid the equally unwelcome alternatives of a marriage of convenience
or a post as governess, Gwendolen has decided that a career as a singer would
provide her with a solution to her dilemma. However, Klesmer's categorically

---

[1] 'Not that which else is human kind's care and skill | Both in the house and under the open
sky | When nobler than wild beasts, men work to | Fend, to provide for themselves—to poets ||
A different task and calling have been assigned. | The Highest, he it is whom alone we serve, | So
that more closely, ever more newly | Sung he will meet with a friendly echo ('The Poet's Vocation',
trans. Michael Hamburger).

stated view is that it is too late for her to think of such a thing, and that she would need to have acquired the habits of artistic discipline no later than the age of 14 to have any chance of achieving the honourable life of an artist that he extols here. Both the singer, and the actress Gwendolen also imagines becoming, would have had to live according to very specific routines for them to realize their artistic potential.

It is this question of regime that Rilke is also addressing in his *Letters to a Young Poet*, while Heidegger's comment points to the imbrication of the work of art and the life of the artist. The vocation described by Hölderlin and the accompanying regime outlined by George Eliot are the principal markers of the life of the artist as it figures in European literature throughout the nineteenth and twentieth centuries. It is from the perspective of those two terms that the artist's life has come to be seen as the very source of artistic creation. This life is much more than the origin of the material used in the work, more than its explanatory context, and, as Baudelaire was one of the first to recognize, is above all its necessary condition. In these last two chapters I shall be examining the conditions of the 'writing life' as determined both by and for the literary enterprise under the two main, but closely related, headings of vocation and regime: that is to say, literature as a calling or compulsion (vocation), and literature as the product of a certain mode of existence (regime). And although the notion that the writing life is the key to literature may initially seem to belong to high Romanticism and the literature of the nineteenth century, I shall go on to argue that its assumptions inform a number of instances of recent and contemporary life-writing in the French literary context. I shall therefore conclude this study with an exploration of the contemporary incarnation of the issues of vocation and regime, respectively, in the work of two recent French writers, Roger Laporte and Jacques Roubaud.

18

Vocation, Regime, and the Production of Literature: Max Jacob and Roland Barthes

Nulla dies sine linea
(attrib. Apelles;
Pliny, *Historia naturalis*)

VOCATION AS COMPULSION

Unlike the musician, the actor, or the practitioner of the fine arts, the writer does not need to acquire specific technical mastery before embarking on the practice of literature. Instead, the emphasis for writers is chiefly on the wholesale existential involvement of the writer him- or herself in their art. This involvement is conventionally not so much willed as accepted in response to a demand, and it corresponds to a widely held belief that has dominated the conception of literature over the past two hundred years. Its continuing currency is repeatedly confirmed in the interviews with some thirty contemporary French writers conducted by the French literary sociologist Nathalie Heinich for her analysis of the conditions that are perceived to constitute the status of 'writer'; she concludes that being 'a writer' calls for '[a] total investment, as it implicates the entire person'.[1] Writers write because it is impossible for them not to do so: 'it is in virtue of an inner constraint or impulsion that one writes: because one cannot do otherwise, because one is driven to it by a vital need, "in order to exist".'[2] In his *Letters to a Young Poet* written between 1903 and 1908, Rilke makes this compulsion to write the sole and overriding criterion for producing poetry. He instructs the neophyte to ask himself, 'in the stillest hour of the night: *must* I write?',[3] and urges him to consider whether he would actually die if he were to

---

[1] Nathalie Heinich, *Être écrivain: création et identité* (Paris: La Découverte, 2000), p. 95. Heinich's book is based on interviews carried out in 1989 with some 30 writers, and explores the terms in which they perceive this identity. Ch. 3 of her discussion of 'the writer' is devoted to the issue of this 'investment'.

[2] Ibid., p. 103.

[3] Rainer Maria Rilke, *Letters to a Young Poet* [1929], trans. M. D. Herter Norton (New York and London: W. W. Norton, 1993), pp. 18–19.

be prevented from doing so. The basis for this insistence on compulsion is the principle that 'a work of art is good if it has sprung from necessity' (p. 20). In short, aesthetic value is directly correlated with the degree of urgency through which the literary vocation manifests itself.

From this compulsion there also flows the need for the poet to organize his life right down to the smallest details so as to enable its fulfilment: 'build your life according to this necessity; your life even into its most indifferent and slightest hour must be a sign of this urge and a testimony to it' (p. 19). A certain kind of life and a certain way of living become the very condition of the work of art. This has a further consequence, in that the demands of art place the artist in a position of risk: it might kill him not to write, but equally, those demands are such that they might themselves prove fatal. Indeed, as Heinich says, this produces a logic whereby for the writer there is no real life without writing, and no real writing unless the life of the writer itself is at stake.[4] The madness and death of writers such as Hölderlin or Nerval are conventionally read as providing some of the earliest examples of this equation; and, in the twentieth century, as we have already seen, Leiris's autobiographical enterprise is based on his desire to make the writer's art as great a personal risk as that of the bullfighter.

This mutually determining relationship between art and life, the writer and the work, has become an integral part of the way that literature, and the arts more generally, are conceived, to the point that, as Nathalie Heinich admits, it is now one of the major clichés of the literary which made it one of the reasons why the author was banished from the conception of literature in the latter part of the twentieth century. Writing in 1963 as a self-appointed spokesman for the *nouveau roman*, Alain Robbe-Grillet rejects any existential and experiential criterion for authorship, and protests against the persistence of the nineteenth-century 'myth' of the genius in thrall to the very things most likely to cloud the critical and creative intelligence on which writing depends. He argues instead for a conception of authorship defined purely in terms of formal awareness and critical competence: 'Alcoholism, misfortune, drugs, mystical passion, and madness have so encumbered the more or less fictionalized biographies [*biographies . . . romancées*] of artists that it is now quite natural to see these as essential prerequisites for their wretched condition, and in any case to see an opposition between creation and awareness.'[5] Nevertheless, as we shall see in more detail later on, the mutually formative relation between life and work has, despite such objections, been remarkably persistent, and not just as cliché. Philippe Sollers, in an essay tellingly entitled 'L'Écrivain et la vie', has defended an interest in biography by drawing attention precisely to the different nature

---

[4] 'Cette double mise en équivalence de la vie et de l'œuvre (pas de vraie vie sans écriture, pas de véritable écriture sans une mise en jeu de sa vie) rend à la fois possible et, à la limite, banal, le sacrifice de l'écrivain à son œuvre, au point qu'on peut voir dans ce thème un "cliché" du créateur' (Heinich, *Être écrivain*, p. 121).

[5] Alain Robbe-Grillet, *Pour un nouveau roman* (Collection Idées; Paris: Gallimard, 1963), p. 11.

of the writing life: 'Biographical curiosity is fully legitimate, if only in order to demonstrate that it comes up against a way of living differently.'[6] This other way of living is important, he claims, because it has as much subversive potential as that more commonly attributed to writing itself: the singularity of a life primarily devoted to writing is always disturbing and may be seen as a form of revolt in its own right.

For all its familiarity, the notion of literature as an all-consuming demand placed on the life is, however, a relatively modern invention. When Rilke, for example, presents the literary vocation as the solemn acceptance of a destiny whose central condition is solitude, he is treating as a serious existential requirement an idea that for the ancients was little more than a topos in the conventional, quasi-mythological representation of the poet.[7] Even as late as the eighteenth century there is no conception of vocation as this all-consuming demand, or of the writing life as necessitating particular protocols and regimes. On the matter of the former, Diderot's *Neveu de Rameau* raises the question of whether the lives of great writers are different from those of ordinary mortals, but it does so primarily in relation to the morality of the writer's conduct. The question is therefore framed as that of a hypothetical trade-off between the moral flaws of the man Racine in his own lifetime as against the moral benefits that his plays brought to their many audiences over the years.[8] The book's central character, whose manic energies and disrupted life have been seen by later generations as the unquestionable mark of his genius, is presented by Diderot as a distinctly dubious quantity, subject to the moral and rhetorical ambivalence that was frequently associated at the time with the equally ambivalent phenomenon of poetic enthusiasm.[9] In the end, however, what counts most against the nephew is that, despite his many talents and qualities, and despite the seductiveness of many of his antics, he fails to create a single work. In short, notwithstanding its singular and subversive nature, his life cannot be read here as the index of an artistic vocation.

Equally, the organization of the writing life is not a matter of special concern in this period. Although Rousseau, on the basis of his actual experience, talks in the *Confessions* about the difficulty of writing, and although he is clearly interested in the question of how best to order his life, he rarely discusses the one as having a necessary correlation to the other. The organization of his day as he describes it during his stay in Les Charmettes has nothing to do with the needs of writing (in any case, at this stage of his life, Rousseau was not

---

[6] Philippe Sollers, *La Guerre du goût* (Paris: Gallimard, 1994), pp. 323–9 (p. 324).

[7] Rilke, *Letters*, pp. 62–3. On the classical topos of the poetic vocation see Lefkowitz, *Lives of the Greek Poets*, esp. pp. 95–8.

[8] Denis Diderot, *Le Neveu de Rameau: ou, Satire seconde; accompagné de la Satire première*, ed. Roland Desné (orig. pub. in Ger. trans., 1804; Paris: Éditions sociales, 1972), pp. 97 ff.

[9] On this see Timothy Clark, *The Theory of Inspiration: Composition as a Crisis of Subjectivity in Romantic and Post-Romantic Writing* (Manchester: Manchester University Press, 1997), ch. 3.

yet a writer), and he is chiefly concerned with creating the best conditions for learning: mornings devoted to the contemplation of nature and to study, the afternoons to gardening and to reading for pleasure, with breakfast and dinner being the pretext for conversation with Mme de Warens.[10] Rousseau's later withdrawal from the world has much more to do with his general antipathy towards social existence than with the need to create the ideal conditions for his literary activities. In so far as writing itself *is* addressed in the context of his preoccupation with the ordering of his life, it applies to occasional questions of practical detail. He is concerned, for instance, with such issues as how best to ensure that the work he has composed in his head during the night can be physically notated before it fades from his memory in the morning; his solution is to arrange for Thérèse's mother to take dictation before he gets out of bed (pp. 417–18). Despite the developing association during the eighteenth century of writing with genius and with lived experience, the image of the writer's life remained broadly within the two main alternatives of the professional writer, where writing was a job like any other (Diderot's Nephew is a professional), and the pastime of the man of leisure: Rousseau asserts very powerfully the need to write on the basis of his personal freedom and not as a way of earning his keep (pp. 476 ff.).[11]

It is only with the nineteenth century that a different picture begins to emerge, whereby the writer's life is read as being indelibly marked by his writing, and vice versa. Living and writing become coterminous for the writer, and writing is lived as much as it is practised. The extreme symptoms of this inseparable connection are conventionally attributed to the degree of the personal investment that writers brought to their artistic creation. Thus, comparing Goethe and Hölderlin on the place of the contradictions that they both explore in their writing, Michael Hamburger argues that whereas Goethe's instinct for self-preservation kept him to one side of the tensions outlined in his work, Hölderlin was driven to enact his to the point of self-destruction.[12] Aside from madness, other extreme manifestations of the demands exacted by writing as vocation are suicide or premature death, which are frequently read as being indices of the effects of literature on the writer's life. Balzac's death at the age of 51 is commonly regarded, if not as a consequence of his emotional investment in writing, then at least as evidence of the toll that writing had taken on his physical energies. Much of this has become the stuff of the sort of myth that Robbe-Grillet is attacking, not in the sense that it is invented, but that the biographical material encourages the mythologization

---

[10] Rousseau, *Les Confessions*, pp. 271 ff.

[11] See Ch. 2 above for a discussion of Rousseau's hostility to the professionalization of literature.

[12] See Michael Hamburger's Introduction to Friedrich Hölderlin, *Selected Poems and Fragments*, trans. Michael Hamburger (Harmondsworth: Penguin, 1998), p. xlii. Hölderlin is a recurrent point of reference for Roger Laporte, whose work I shall discuss in the next chapter: see e.g. Roger Laporte, 'Hölderlin ou le combat poétique', in id., *Quinze variations sur un thème biographique: essais* (Paris: Flammarion, 1975).

of the writer. Balzac's huge expenditure of energy is celebrated, for example, in books such as René Benjamin's *Prodigieuse Vie d'Honoré de Balzac*. These were no doubt partly inspired by the fates Balzac himself meted out to his fictional characters, such as Louis Lambert, who loses his mind, or Frenhofer, whose commitment to his art is such that it eventually destroys both the art and its creator. In other words, one of the effects of this notion of art as something that has to be lived to be of value—or, as Rilke says, that has to be born of necessity to be good—is to have produced a new kind of interest in the lives of artists and writers, since some of those lives have been determined in very extreme ways by that injunction.

But, as I have already suggested, although this phenomenon can be dated from the beginning of the nineteenth century, it is not just nineteenth-century writers who lend themselves to this sort of perspective; neither is that interest confined to the production of the sort of clichés about the writer condemned by Robbe-Grillet. In the twentieth century the question of the writing life was to become a major concern in France, as we shall see more fully in the discussion of Roger Laporte and Jacques Roubaud in the next chapter. Moreover, these are not isolated figures. Antonin Artaud has been regarded as an exemplary case of the imbrication of life and art, not just by Laporte, but also by Philippe Sollers, whose concerns are very far from those of the *vie romancée* of the tormented genius. The promoter of a theatre that redefines the relations between art and life so as to make theatre itself a part of life, Artaud also refused the separation between writing and his own existence: 'The question for me was not to discover what things might manage to find their way into the framework of written language, but into the texture of my living soul.'[13] Sollers reads this imbrication not as a symptom of Artaud's madness, but as proof that writing has to be thought of as a categorical imperative in the writer's existence, and he proclaims: 'We know now that writing is what requires someone to live *in a certain way* or it is nothing.'[14] Roger Laporte's comment on Artaud makes a similar point—though in the rather different context of Denise Colomb's well-known photographs of Artaud taken during his stay in the asylum at Rodez—when he says that Artaud's face reveals the extent to which writing is imprinted on his very existence: 'The mark of the work of writing, the only concrete mark that there is, is stamped on the face of a person. It is, in a sense, a proof.'[15] And Laporte seeks to place his own writing under the sign of the same all-consuming vocation whose repercussions should be felt in every aspect of his life and his work—and, ideally, also be visible in his face.

[13] Quoted by Philippe Sollers in his essay 'La Pensée émet des signes', in id., *Logiques* (Paris: Éditions du Seuil, 1968), pp. 133–49 (p. 137).

[14] Ibid., p. 141 (Sollers's italics).

[15] Roger Laporte, 'Entretien entre Mathieu Bénézet, Roger Laporte et Jean Ristat', in *Roger Laporte = Digraphe*, 18–19 (1979) [special issue], pp. 121–55 (p. 136).

REGIME

So far I have been concentrating on the aspect of compulsion in the concept of the writer's vocation, with its vision of the writer's life as branded by its demands: Hölderlin's madness, Nerval's suicide, Balzac's premature death, Artaud's face. In this perspective the writer submits to a call that comes from somewhere else. But, as we have also seen, the notion of vocation also entails issues of the writer's regime, the way that day-to-day existence is organized so as to make writing possible. Viewed from this angle, the writer's life appears as something actively constructed, and determined less by some outside fate or inner compulsion than by the conscious will of the writer him- or herself. Again, persistent and powerful as this image appears, it is a relatively recent phenomenon that may be most tangibly dated from Flaubert's conception of writing as work. The question of how writers organize their lives is one that comes up in almost any interview nowadays, and books such as Jean-Louis de Rambures's *Comment travaillent les écrivains*, a collection of interviews with some twenty-five contemporary French writers dealing with exactly this issue, testify to the widespread interest that readers have in this topic.[16] It is Barthes who suggests that this conception of writing as labour begins with Flaubert, and he associates it with a conception of 'the writer-artisan who shuts himself away in a legendary location, like a workman in his workshop', painstakingly honing and polishing according to a regular timetable of solitary endeavour.[17] According to Barthes, this understanding of the writing life as a regular regime of disciplined labour is the source of the image of Flaubert himself, living a hermit-like existence in Croisset and devoting his days and evenings to the production of his sentences; or of Valéry rising in the early hours of every morning and sitting down at his desk to write his *Carnets*. Like the topos of the tormented genius, it has also been questioned and parodied, and not least by Flaubert himself, whose own *Éducation sentimentale* endows its hero Frédéric with the artist's life for a period of his existence, but leaves him with no concrete outcome to show for it.[18] More recently, as we have seen in the case of Pierre Michon's account of his frustrated vocation, the writer's regime can still appear as nothing more than a set of empty and unproductive gestures. However, such parodies do not undermine its continuing importance in the construction of the writing life.

It is Zola who, perhaps more than any other writer, makes one of the strongest cases for the writing life as a matter of regular and daily discipline. He had the

---

[16] Jean-Louis de Rambures, *Comment travaillent les écrivains* (Paris: Flammarion, 1978). The interviews were conducted between 1970 and 1976 and first appeared in *Le Monde des livres*.

[17] Barthes, *Le Degré zéro de l'écriture*, p. 46.

[18] On this see Pierre Bourdieu, 'L'Invention de la vie d'artiste', *Actes de la recherche en sciences sociales*, 2 (1975), pp. 67–93.

motto '*Nulla dies sine linea*'[19] carved into his mantlepiece as a reminder of his creative task, and his daily life was as much dominated by the routine of work as is that of the characters in his novels. More particularly, he seems to have used his depiction of the painter Claude Lantier in *L'Œuvre* as a foil for his alter ego, the writer Sandoz, in order to play off an image of the painter's life as subject to the destructive demands of a vocation based entirely on inspiration, against the model of the regular discipline of the writer's day-to-day existence that was his own. The ideal of a total dedication of the writer's life to his art is articulated by Sandoz when he says: 'it would be so fine to give your entire existence over to a work';[20] and it is his recourse to what Barthes calls the 'work value' as against Lantier's 'genius value' that proves to be the more successful means of realizing his artistic goal.[21] Because of this, Zola's novel seems to me to be doing something more than simply pitching painting against literature. The difference between the two art forms turns precisely on the question of the terms in which the artist's life relates to his vocation in each case: Zola ascribes to the painter the passive version of a life that is ravaged and destroyed by the compulsion of an ultimately unproductive vocation, and to the writer the active model that makes the creative life a matter of discipline and regime. Claude is represented as 'sinking into the depths of the heroic madness of art' (p. 294), and he envies Sandoz the productivity that is the result not of less devotion but specifically of a capacity for regular labour: 'The great work of his life was progressing, the series of novels that he was bringing out, one after the other, with his *persistent and regular hand*, marching towards the goal he had given himself, and defeated by nothing, be it obstacles, insults, or fatigue' (p. 366). In the case of Zola himself, his working regime is evaluated primarily in terms of its productivity, because, when the aesthetic ideal is one of the comprehensive inclusion of 'universal life' and 'the grand totality', the capacity of the creative mechanism has to be able to match it. Measured against these aims, Sandoz the writer is simply more productive than Lantier the painter, who, after the initial visionary moment, remains caught up in an endless but impotent revision of the same work until it is eventually destroyed, and his life with it. Tellingly, it is Sandoz who has the last word in the novel, which offers a guarantee of continued literary production, when he says, 'Let's get down to work' (p. 408).

Although a concern with regimes is nothing new, this association with productivity is another relatively recent phenomenon. As Judith Schlanger has argued in her book on the subject, the whole question of vocation as a basis for production is only a little over two centuries old, and is a feature of a

---

[19] Attributed to the painter Apelles by Pliny in his *Historia naturalis*. Paul Klee's adoption of the same motto is cited by Jacques Roubaud in his *Grand Incendie de Londres*, which I shall be discussing in the next chapter.

[20] Émile Zola, *L'Œuvre* [1886], ed. Henri Mitterand (Collection Folio Classique; Paris: Gallimard, 1983), p. 66.

[21] Barthes, *Le Degré zéro de l'écriture*, p. 47.

distinctly modern understanding of the idea. This modern ethos is characterized by what she calls a productivist principle, whose ideal manifestation is the artistic vocation in which production takes the form of creation. In this perspective, 'doing, acting, and creating count for more than being, experiencing a state, or achieving spiritual transformation'.[22] The modern vocation is conceived of as a self-realization of the individual that is measured in terms of external results and visible output. This, says Schlanger, is in contrast with an older notion of vocation as the basis for spiritual or moral enhancement. Certainly, in the ancient world the concept of what Foucault has called the 'arts of existence' had nothing to do with productivity and everything to do with the self-mastery that guarantees autonomy for its practitioner:

> The accent was placed on the relationship with the self that enabled a person to keep from being carried away by the appetites and pleasures, to maintain a mastery and superiority over them, to keep his senses in a state of tranquillity, to remain free from interior bondage to the passions, and to achieve a mode of being that could be defined by the full enjoyment of oneself, or the perfect supremacy of oneself over oneself.[23]

Attention to the practical conduct of one's life, particularly in relation to one's needs and pleasures, diet, sexual relations, exercise, and the organization of day-to-day existence, was the means whereby a Greek or Roman subject could free himself from dependency of any kind and thus ensure his own freedom. This was a lifelong undertaking whose goal was the transformation of the individual's existence into a permanent exercise of self-control and self-discipline and which, unlike the modern vocation, was not geared to any material outcome.

Under Christianity self-control was recast as self-denial, but the concern with self-discipline and regime remained central, particularly in the context of the monastic life. Again, the focus is on the transformation of the individual, not on any productive benefits that a particular way of living might bring. The monastic life is conceived as an acting out of the precepts of the Gospels, and its prime concern is with the inner spiritual being of the individual: 'it adapts itself to the workings of grace in each individual soul, and gains its end when it has brought that individual soul to the highest perfection of which its natural and supernatural gifts render it capable.'[24] The Benedictine order, for example, was, from its foundation in the early sixth century, devoted to the service of God by means primarily of self-discipline and prayer, and only secondarily of work.

---

[22] Judith E. Schlanger, *La Vocation* (Paris: Éditions du Seuil, 1997), pp. 21, 28.

[23] Michel Foucault, *Histoire de la sexualité*, vol. ii: *L'Usage des plaisirs* (Paris: Gallimard, 1984), p. 38 [p. 31]. See also Michel Foucault, *Histoire de la sexualité*, vol. iii: *Le Souci de soi* (1984; Collection tel; Paris: Gallimard, 1997). The horror of passivity that characterizes Greek culture means that these practices of the self designed to ensure maximum autonomy were the preserve of men, passivity and dependence being regarded as a sign of femininity.

[24] Cardinal Gasquet, *Sketch of a Monastic History*, quoted in Edward Cuthbert Butler, *Benedictine Monachism: Studies in Benedictine Life and Rule*, 2nd edn. (London: Longmans Green, 1924), p. 29. I am indebted to Butler's account of the monastic life.

The organization of daily life ascribed almost twice as much time to church offices, reading, and meditation as it did to work, and thus exemplified the principle that of the two lives, the active and the contemplative, 'the active life is more productive than the contemplative, but the latter is of greater merit and better.'[25]

When it comes to a project like Ignatius Loyola's *Spiritual Exercises* (dating from the first part of the sixteenth century) with their minutely organized daily regime, this principle continues to reign supreme. The underlying rationale behind the careful planning of prayer, examination of conscience, penance, meals, and so on, is the fact that 'Man has been created to praise, reverence and serve our Lord God, thereby saving his soul'.[26] The *Exercises* are more a guide for retreats than a manual for everyday life, and Ignatius advocates solitude as the prerequisite for closeness to God and for receipt of divine goodness, but this aim is very different from the production of poetry that was the goal of the isolation recommended by Rilke: 'The more our soul finds itself in perfect solitude, the fitter does it become to approach and reach up to its Creator and Lord; and the closer it gets to Him, the more disposed does it become to receive favours and gifts from His supreme divine goodness.'[27] Solitude is necessary for this kind of spiritual traffic with the Divine, but leaves no tangible trace in the real world—perhaps not even on the faces of its most fervent practitioners.

The monastic calling has often been taken to be the model for an artistic vocation, not only in the degree of commitment it requires (the artist gives up an ordinary or worldly existence in order to devote himself to the higher calling of his art), but because the day-to-day discipline of the monastic life has also been regarded as a model for the kinds of practice taken to be necessary for writing. The pervasiveness of this association can be seen, for example, when Barthes seeks to establish a parallel between Ignatius's programme of spiritual exercises and the regimes of the writer, arguing that in each case the aim is to overcome an underlying aphasia and to find a language:

It is doubtless for this reason that the organization of the method set up by Ignatius, determining days, times, postures, and regimens, recalls writers' protocols in its extreme minutiae (which, it is true, are generally not well known, and this is a pity): the person who writes, through an ordered preparation of the material conditions of writing (place, time, notebooks, paper, etc.), commonly called the writer's 'work' and which is most often nothing more than a magic rite to overcome his in-born aphasia, seeks to capture the 'idea' (which the rhetorician also helped him to do), just as Ignatius sought to provide the means to grasp the signs of divinity.[28]

[25] Butler, *Benedictine Monachism*, p. 97.
[26] See St Ignatius of Loyola, *The Spiritual Exercises of St. Ignatius*, ed. Thomas Corbishley (London: Burns & Oates, 1963), p. 22 and *passim*.
[27] Ibid., p. 20.
[28] Roland Barthes, *Sade, Fourier, Loyola* (Paris: Éditions du Seuil, 1971), p. 51.

In itself this is an extremely interesting passage, not least for the claim that the regimes and protocols of writing are a neglected topic, but the emphasis on linguistic production ignores the irrelevance of the whole concept of production to the spiritual life that Ignatius is promoting.

MAX JACOB'S 'ÉCOLE DE VIE INTÉRIEURE'

I shall return in a moment to Barthes's personal interest in these protocols of writing, but first it would be worth exploring another attempt to present the writing life as a version of the monastic life. This is Max Jacob's *Conseils à un jeune poète*, published in 1945, the year after his death in the transit camp at Drancy. In a series of fragments, notes, and maxims addressed to a medical student with poetic leanings, Jacob sets out his poetic credo. What is striking from the point of view of my own argument is that Jacob is answering a question about the definition of poetry by outlining a programme for the poet's existence. The father of the would-be poet had invited Jacob to dinner in order to hear his reply to the question: 'What is a lyric poem?' In his written response (the *Conseils*) Jacob repudiates the whole notion of definition, especially with regard to poetry: 'Poetry has nothing to do with definitions, even definitions of the aesthetic.'[29] Poetry, he asserts, is lived and not explained, and he supports this affirmation by adducing Picasso's relation to his painting: 'M. Picasso was never able to "explain" Cubism. He created it, he lived it. [. . .] The key thing is to be a man, and a definer is not a man' (ibid.). For Jacob 'being a man' is the prime requirement for producing poetry: 'People imagine that in order to be a poet you have to string together lines of unequal length with a half-pun at the end. But to be a poet you have to be a man first, and then a Man-Poet.'[30]

To become a man is itself an undertaking that requires considerable spiritual discipline, and Jacob instructs his poet-pupil to work on himself before devoting himself to poetry: 'make something of yourself before you write' (p. 38). He recommends a regime that has many points in common with a monastic one: retreat from the world, silence, abstinence, celibacy, examination of conscience, daily meditation, and even Christian belief. To this end, he imagines founding a 'school of the inner life' on whose door would be written 'school of art'. His school turns out to have many of the features of Ignatius's retreat or even of the monasteries of the Benedictine order, and, compared with the pantheism of Rilke's programme for another young poet in search of literary advice, is rather

---

[29] Quoted in Marcel Béalu's prefatory note to Max Jacob, *Conseils à un jeune poète, suivis de Conseils à un étudiant* (Paris: Gallimard, 1945), pp. 7–11 (p. 11).

[30] Jacob, *Conseils*, p. 31.

more spiritual and Christian (p. 15).[31] Indeed, the whole idea of conceiving of poetry in terms of lived example rather than abstract definition is itself based on the Christian principle of bearing witness through one's life. Jacob seems to be pushing the monastic analogy as far as it will go, but his ultimate criterion is still the modern one of production. The cultivation of the soul and the emphasis on the inner life are a means of fostering the originality and invention that he regards as the prerequisite for poetry. Poetry, according to Jacob, is the effect of an inner 'conflagration', which can be achieved only by cultivating an existential porousness to the outside world and allowing the results to mature: 'True originality can exist only in maturing, because what is original is the innermost self' (pp. 18–19). The conduct of the poet's life is designed to produce this inner self which will in turn produce a poem. In essence, then, Jacob's reply to the father of the would-be poet is what philosophers call an 'ostensive definition' encapsulated in a certain way of life as the necessary condition for the poetry that then results from it. The poet's life is a substitute for—and even a riposte to—theoretical definitions; but it is also the indispensable basis for poetic production.

THE 'VITA NOVA' OF ROLAND BARTHES

When Barthes, in the last two or three years of his life, returned to the issue of the writer's protocols, he expanded his earlier conception of those protocols from the strictly material conditions of writing to one that included a whole way of living, which, borrowing from Dante and Michelet, he called the 'Vita Nova'.[32] The question of the material conditions of writing was one that had interested him for some time, as can be seen not only from the comment about Loyola, but also from his *Roland Barthes*, where he describes the organization of his working space and of his daily routine.[33] In a book that has complex generic links with autobiography, it is telling that the writing life is presented in these strictly practical terms, and not in those of a retrospective narrative of the writer's vocation typical of many autobiographies. As Barthes himself notes in *Sade, Fourier, Loyola*, the etymology of the word 'protocol', which refers to the scribe's gluing of his first page, foregrounds the pure materiality of writing and

[31] The French translation of Rilke's *Letters to a Young Poet* appeared in 1937, and it seems probable that Jacob, writing in 1941, had Rilke's precedent in mind when he presented his own thoughts on poetry in the form of advice to a younger man.

[32] On this see Barthes, *La Préparation du roman*, p. 28; and Louis-Jean Calvet, *Roland Barthes 1915–1980* (Paris: Flammarion, 1990), p. 299 and *passim*.

[33] Roland Barthes, *Roland Barthes* (Paris: Éditions du Seuil, 1975), pp. 42–3 (the space in the form of three photographs) and pp. 84–5 (the routine in the entry 'Emploi du temps').

of the conditions under which it is produced. In the 'Vita Nova', however, these protocols are extended to include a more general existential venture, which he explored in the 'Cours' given at the Collège de France between 1978 and 1980, and published after his death from his lecture notes under the title *La Préparation du roman*.[34]

Specifically, the 'new life' referred to Barthes's wish to construct an 'art of living' which he seems to have intended to set out in a book entitled *Vita Nova* for which he left notes and plans. These included the issue of 'regimes', under a chapter heading 'Imagination d'une V[ita] N[ova]' ('[Imagining a V[ita] N[ova]'), later developed in a section of the *Cours*.[35] The key to the whole project was his presumed desire to write a novel. Chapter 6 of the projected book was to be devoted to the possibility of Barthes's initiation into literature as a writer, and the 'Vita Nova' itself was devised as a necessary precondition of that writing. For Barthes, to write a novel meant something much more fundamental than adding a new genre to his repertoire. As he explained in the lectures at the Collège de France, a new life was not a change in doctrine, theory, philosophy, or even belief, but the discovery of a new practice of writing. This practice entailed a shift of gravity from ideas to affects, from commentary to production, and could be arrived at only by a thoroughgoing change in conduct and outlook. To write meant acting on a desire to write, or what he calls a 'vouloir-écrire'; and living meant living as the writer of the utopian novel imagined as the object of that desire: 'I shall act *as if* I were going to write [a novel] → I shall set myself up in that *as if*.'[36] This existential 'as if' entailed a radical assessment of his positioning in life: 'I place myself in the position of someone who is doing something and not in that of someone who is talking about something; I am not studying a product, I am taking on a production.'[37] The method for writing a novel was to live as the writer of the novel, not just in his mental make-up, but in his day-to-day existence: 'I come back [. . .] to the simple, and ultimately intractable idea, that "literature" is always made with "life".'[38] This included such practical aspects as keeping a notebook in which to make notes as well as questions of timetable, diet, working space, and even dress (to accommodate the notebook and allow for its easy retrieval).

[34] The question of a 'Vita Nova' is also discussed in the lecture series published (also posthumously) under the title *Comment vivre ensemble*, ed. Claude Coste (Paris: Éditions du Seuil/IMEC, 2002), but here it does not specifically concern the writing life.

[35] 'Vita Nova: Projet de livre', in Roland Barthes, *Œuvres complètes*, ed. Jacques Petit and Éric Marty, 3 vols. (Paris: Éditions du Seuil, 1993), vol. iii, pp. 1287–94 (see esp. p. 1288). The *Œuvres complètes* contain Barthes's own notes and drafts on this topic and were published prior to the full text of the *Cours*.

[36] *La Préparation du roman*, p. 48 (Barthes's emphasis).

[37] ' "Longtemps, je me suis couché de bonne heure" ', in Barthes, *Œuvres completes*, vol. iii, pp. 827–36 (p. 835, Barthes's italics). This is the text of a lecture given at the Collège de France in October 1978 before the lecture series proper began, and it addresses a number of the same issues.

[38] *La Préparation du roman*, p. 45.

These concerns rekindle Barthes's interest in biographical considerations as they apply to a number of canonical writers, such as Chateaubriand, Flaubert, Nietzsche, Proust, and Kafka, with a special focus on the biographical context of the literary work. The subtitle of the lectures in which Barthes addressed these issues was 'de la vie à l'œuvre' ('from life to work'), and in them he spells out the principle that the path towards the creation of a literary work would lie in the conduct of his life. An identification with other writers also contributes to producing a mental stance treating the project as a 'sacred' task: 'I present myself as a writer, to the full extent, and in the fully sacred character of the role, *in order* to help myself to become one.'[39] The writer recalls the saint not just in the sacred character he ascribes to his calling, but in the principle of imitation of the lives of his literary models. Barthes may also be reverting to a non-productivist model of a vocation, for, as with the saints, his concern with the writer's way of life seems in the end to have departed from considerations of any concrete literary result. This absence of any material outcome to the existential project might not have been accidental, and, as Diana Knight has suggested, Barthes's untimely death might not have been the reason why the projected novel was never written.[40] By imagining the writing life as a set of necessary preconditions for literary production, Barthes is emphasizing the importance of this dimension of writing. And he does so all the more by framing those conditions in a hypothetical future, rather than as a retrospective narrative of a literary vocation with a vantage point in a completed œuvre. As Barthes himself acknowledges, 'the desire to write [*le vouloir-écrire*] relates only to the language of the person who has written'.[41] The kind of writing that he anticipates on the basis of his *vouloir-écrire* is one that would be coextensive with the life, not the end-product of an existence that it then justifies in retrospect.

This perspective generates a new conception of the writer, which Barthes calls the *Scribens*. This figure is distinct from the writer's other incarnations, namely, the civic *Persona*, the *Scriptor* (the public image), and the *Auctor* whose authorial role is what gives the text its authority. The *Scribens* is the writer in so far as his life is absolutely contemporary and coterminous with his writing: 'the *I* which is involved in the practice of writing, which is in the process of writing, and which lives writing on a daily basis' (p. 280). Barthes's own discussion, in which he proposes this simultaneity of life and writing as what he calls 'une écriture de vie' ('a life writing', pp. 278–9), nevertheless has a peculiar temporal status of its own: the life of the *Scribens* becomes the content of a semi-critical discourse

---

[39] Ibid., p. 296 (Barthes's emphasis). The section devoted to the material practicalities of the writing life is contained in pp. 266–349.

[40] 'Il s'agissait plutôt pour lui de s'impliquer dans un apprentissage imaginaire qui serait partiellement disséqué en public pendant le cours': Diana Knight, 'Vaines pensées: la Vita Nova de Barthes', in Claude Coste (ed.), *Sur Barthes = Revue des sciences humaines*, 268 (2002) [special issue], pp. 93–107 (p. 96).

[41] *La Préparation du roman*, p. 33.

whose mode is hypothesis rather than actual literary achievement, simulation rather than any documented context associated with an existing work. But while the principle of an equation between the writing life and a life-writing remains intentionally hypothetical for Barthes, it becomes the basis for a fully realized writing project in the case of the two contemporary writers Roger Laporte and Jacques Roubaud, whose work is the subject of the next chapter.

19

Life-Writing in Roger Laporte and Jacques Roubaud

> different from biography, *life writing*, the written life (in the strong sense which transforms the word 'writing')
>
> (Roland Barthes)

The 'life-writing' that characterizes so much of contemporary French literature has taken many forms, but the examples I have chosen to examine here seem to me to represent a particularly interesting and relatively unusual version of the phenomenon. Neither Laporte's *biographie* nor Roubaud's *Grand Incendie de Londres* has much to do with the genres of biography or autobiography as they were previously understood, or even as they have more recently been practised by other late twentieth-century writers such as Marguerite Duras, Nathalie Sarraute, Alain Robbe-Grillet, and Annie Ernaux, amongst others. Instead, I would suggest that the term 'life-writing' as it applies to their work can be seen as an elaboration of the issues of the writing life as I have been outlining it, with each of them foregrounding the questions, respectively, of vocation (Laporte) and regime (Roubaud). Neither writer makes any explicit claim in such terms, but each is embarking on a project in which writing is demonstrably produced in the context of a life that becomes its necessary condition, and in which the question of literature itself is in some way at stake.

ROGER LAPORTE'S *BIOGRAPHIE* AS A LIFE IN WRITING

In 1970 Roger Laporte published a work entitled *Fugue* in which he inaugurated a new type of writing that he called '*biographie*'. It was a radical response to a literary vocation, and it had nothing whatsoever to do with biography as it is otherwise and more commonly known. Laporte's '*bio-graphie*' (literally, 'life-writing') is not the story of the life of another person, and he reworks the etymology of the term to make it mean something like a 'life in writing', or even a 'life *as* writing'. This is how he describes his project on the opening page of *Fugue*: 'I am expecting of the work to be written what one usually demands of life.' By which he means, as he goes on to explain, that he takes the events of what he calls 'my life as a man' to be of no interest compared with those that will befall him as he writes, or, more precisely, 'what can happen only to the extent that I shall be writing'.[1]

Fugue was Laporte's fourth published work, the first (*Souvenir de Reims*, first published in 1954) being more conventionally 'literary' in the way it combines elements of fiction and autobiography to provide an account of its own genesis. The three texts published immediately prior to *Fugue* are all explorations of a vocational desire to write.[2] With *Fugue* these various strands are fused and recast to become the basis for a completely new project in which the '*biographe*' ('biographer'/'life-writer') replaces both novelist and autobiographer, and which is not the record of an experience that precedes the writing so much as its realization in the process of writing itself. This led to four further texts,[3] and finally to a single compendium volume containing all eight texts from *La Veille* to *Moriendo*, under the title *Une vie* with the descriptive subtitle '*biographie*'.[4] Its subject is the devotion of a life to writing, but rather than being the narrative of a literary vocation, Laporte's perspective here is all prospect and no retrospect: the language is that of expectancy, and the project is mostly described in the future tense. His *biographie* will not be the written record of his life, and neither is it the product of a prior vocation or a pre-existing writing life:

Biography usually designates the literary genre whose object is the story of a life, but I would not have created a sort of pun on the basis of its etymology had I not thought that it was possible to reverse the long-established relation between living and writing. Whereas ordinary life precedes the narrative that can be made out of it, I am laying a bet that a certain kind of life is neither prior nor external to writing: I could not therefore entrust any substitute with the task of writing my memoirs, or rather at the outset there was nothing to narrate, because one can only tell the story of something that has not yet taken place, the unprecedented life to which only writing can provide access. (*Fugue 3*, p. 423)

Laporte interprets his vocation as a total commitment of his life to writing, but he does so in terms far more thoroughgoing than any that could previously have been imagined, even by Zola's Sandoz when he dreams of 'giving over his entire life to a work'. Writing for Laporte is also more than the act that it represents for Sartre or Leiris, where the measure of any action is to be found

---

[1] Roger Laporte, *Fugue* [1970], in id., *Une vie: biographie* (Paris: P.O.L., 1986), p. 255.

[2] *La Veille* (1963), *Une voix de fin silence* (1966), and *Pourquoi* (1967).

[3] *Supplément* (1973), *Fugue 3* (1976), *Suite* (1979), and *Moriendo* (1983). The ongoing nature of Laporte's project is evident in the choice of titles.

[4] A ninth and previously unpublished text, *Codicille*, is also included in this volume. I shall be quoting from *Une vie: biographie*, but in every case giving the title of the original text from which the quotation appears. The fullest discussion of Laporte's project is to be found in Ian Maclachlan, *Roger Laporte: The Orphic Text* (Oxford: Legenda, 2000).

in its consequences in the external world. Laporte's project severs all connection with everything that lies outside it.

When it comes to the literary dimension of Laporte's *biographie*, this is no longer a question of working with established genres such as the novel or the *récit*. Instead, it is the sphere of literature in general that makes the undertaking viable: 'For physics, geography, or history [. . .] such a project would be aberrant, but I am betting that there is a domain, and only one domain, where that project can be realized: literature' (*Fugue*, p. 257). The oppositions that distinguish between form and content in physics, geography, or history do not hold in literature, where what you say is taken to be an inextricable part of how you say it. Laporte is motivated by the possibility of a writing in which 'what I write cannot be separated from the manner in which I write it: the content cannot be detached from its form, or rather from its mode: writing' (*Supplément*, p. 375). This is a largely uncontentious conception of literature, but Laporte takes the implications of the inseparability of form and content much further, and his literary project is aimed at overcoming the more fundamental opposition that exists between the life and the work, living and writing: '"*biographie*" is living writing', he says, which means, by the same token, that 'one can also say that "*biographie*" is *writing life*'.[5]

Laporte places this living of writing under the sign of the sort of compulsion outlined by Rilke in the letters to the young poet, echoes of which can be heard in the following remark: 'Any true writer [. . .] knows this compulsion to write, this "*es muss sein*".'[6] For Laporte, writing is not just the product of that compulsion, but is constituted as its very manifestation: 'responding to the compulsion to write consists in articulating that experience as such.' The vocation becomes the subject matter of writing as well as its origin. It is a demand whose price in his day-to-day life Laporte hints at but refrains from narrating: 'my job not only diverts me quite unjustifiably from the most pressing obligations in my life as a man, but obliterates the faces that are dearest to me' (*Fugue*, p. 297). The human price exacted by the writing life, which conventionally forms the narrative of biographies of many writers, is not a part of Laporte's *biographie*. His focus, instead, is exclusively on the effects of the compulsion on and in the writing that articulates it, and these are often frustratingly absent or unclear: 'Other human activities no doubt require an investment that is just as great as the one demanded by writing, but its stock is unquestionably the one that gives the worst return of all, because enormous labour results in pure loss' (*Fugue*, p. 288). Even the material and existential conditions imposed by the demands of the writer's vocation, which Jacob and Barthes spell out, do not feature in

---

[5] Roger Laporte, *Lettre à personne*, with foreword by Maurice Blanchot and afterword by Philippe Lacoue-Labarthe (Paris: Plon, 1989), pp. 65–6 (Laporte's emphasis). In this book Laporte is looking back over an experience of writing that had come to an end with *Moriendo* (1983).

[6] *Lettre à personne*, p. 61.

Laporte's project, so rigorously does he apply his rule that writing and experience be exactly coterminous.[7]

Initially Laporte writes as if the outcome of this equation between life and writing would simply be a new literary form—the *biographie*: 'Writing without vainly reproducing what has already been lived: this wish [. . .] would be fulfilled to the extent that this book, escaping the age-old distinction, the almost primeval opposition between saying and doing, language and life, might contribute to establishing a new literary form and—why not?—a virtually unknown genre' (*Fugue*, p. 276). This previously unknown 'genre' might be something like Barthes's '*écriture de vie*', and, as I have already suggested, could constitute a quite specific application of the term 'life-writing' that distinguishes it from forms of writing derived from autobiography and biography (as conventionally understood). But, in addition, such life-writing has a central role in reconfiguring the entire literary field within which it emerges. By constructing a space within literature, Laporte's *biographie* does much more than simply establish a new literary genre. In a review essay of Sollers's *Logiques* written in the same year as *Fugue*, Laporte presents *biographie* as a literary enterprise that opens up the entire idea of 'literature' beyond the purely aesthetic or art for art's sake, so as to make it coextensive with the experience of the writing life: 'literature is not opposed to life, but it is, on the contrary, to the extent that language is our reality, and that only literature exists, that one can rightfully talk about *biographie*.'[8] The writing life is no longer just the condition for the production of literature, but a constitutive element of its overall literarity.

Laporte repeatedly insists on the unique quality of the reality that a life in writing brings, and his desire to write can be seen in part as a desire for the kind of experience that writing alone can offer: 'it is important to assert that in giving himself up to the play of writing, the writer, even as a man, achieves an intensity of joy, torment, terror, distress, freedom, surprise, and zest that would otherwise remain unknown to him' (*Fugue*, p. 329). This intensity of experience in writing, already anticipated by Proust in his portrayal of Vinteuil's experience of musical composition, as well as by Leiris's desire to be 'more—and more truly—alive', is the reward for acceding to its demands, as Laporte goes on to affirm: 'a *biographie* [. . .] is thus uncommon in what it brings, but above all in what it demands by way of work, strength, endurance, implacable tenacity, sharp intelligence, close attention, circumspection, love of precise language, infinite delicacy and extreme cruelty, ambition and detachment, mastery and free-wheeling, unstinting commitment but also abandon' (ibid.).

---

[7] It is only when he has ceased to be a writer in the sense determined by his *biographie* that Laporte is willing to address such issues; e.g. in his *Entre deux mondes* (Montpellier: Gris Banal, 1988), where, amongst other things, he describes and provides accompanying photographs of the room in which he writes.

[8] 'Bio-graphie', in Laporte, *Quinze Variations*, pp. 135–44 (p. 141).

Writing makes unique demands on human resources, and in return constitutes a space in which human experience exceeds the bounds that ordinary life can offer. It does so because it goes in pursuit of something that always lies ahead. The experience that it brings can never be known in advance, so that it cannot be said that Laporte writes in order to feel joys and torments that he is already familiar with and wishes to recapture. By the same token, writing itself is neither known nor given in advance. Just as writing is synonymous with the compulsion which drives it and which it articulates in turn, so it is also synonymous with the question 'What is writing?' Laporte's project is launched as much as anything by his acknowledgement that he does not know what writing is: 'writing is an unknown to me' (*Fugue*, p. 255). The literature that is redefined by this *écriture de vie* is not a self-identical entity, since the relation of the writing to that literature is largely prospective. The writing of *biographie* mobilizes a literarity that it never quite succeeds in capturing.

Writing becomes the pursuit of its own definition, and the text of Laporte's *biographie* is a relentless quest to discover the nature of the writing which comprises it. Every strategy that Laporte adopts is exhaustively probed, worried at, and worked through, until it is discarded for another that seems to promise a better insight. In the early stages Laporte sees his project as a 'mobile' (of the kind produced by Alexander Calder, although he is not mentioned by name), then as 'Chinese portrait' (or a sort of twenty-questions guessing game), then as a pitting of '*écriture*' against a '*contre-écriture*', then as a weave that produces its own loom, then as a writing machine, then, when he begins to mull over some of the earlier parts of his text, as an 'inexact copy', then in terms of a 'divergence' ('*écart*'), then, later again, as an Ariadne's thread, and so on. What propels Laporte forward is the wish not only to get to grips with what writing is, but also, despite the growing sense of the impossibility of ever achieving such a thing, to acquire the measure of his own enterprise: 'in writing a work whose intention was nevertheless to throw light on its own writing, I have discovered the impossibility of any absolute intelligibility' (*Fugue*, p. 308). The project is constantly destabilized not by intrusions from without, but by the forces it contains within: 'not only does what is found, or rather glimpsed in writing, constantly exceed the limits of writing, but also how can I not have a sense that writing brings other elements into play that the text perhaps picks up and reveals, but to which I remain blind?' (ibid.). The implication here is that, whereas the life-writing that is *biographie* holds out the possibility of eroding oppositions such as form/content, language/reality, doing/saying, living/writing, ultimately these terms can never fully coincide: 'I have in fact gradually learned and understood that the play of writing proceeds by multiple spacings and discrepancies' (*Fugue*, p. 318). Laporte can never quite catch up with the insights of his own writing, because of the text's capacity to reveal things to which he himself remains blind; equally, when he returns to earlier moments in his written text, the return itself produces a gap that makes full repetition impossible.

The writing life constitutes writing as a sort of living, and vice versa; but it also makes it impossible for the two to become entirely coterminous at any given point. The goal of an equivalence between living and writing turns out, paradoxically, to mean that part of the experience of writing is an inevitable non-coincidence of experience and writing. The unfolding of the project is a process which sometimes runs ahead of the writer (he cannot properly see what it is that he has written), and which places its previous manifestations beyond his grasp: it lies either in the future or in the past, but never in the form of the immediate coinciding of being and writing that was the original goal of the project.

The result is that the language of the *biographie* becomes increasingly negative, and the euphoria of its initial formulation gives way to a painful sense of writing as an ordeal: 'the "subject" endures an ordeal linked to writing' (*Codicille*, p. 477), or even as outright torment: 'For a long time I thought that writing—a certain modality of writing—led, and would always lead to the threshold of an unknown life, but writing has brought me to an anti-life, against the grain of language, to a silent torment' (*Suite*, p. 542). Worse still, the principle of non-coincidence that haunts the writing obliges Laporte to consider the possibility that even his torment is merely a pale reflection of some truer torment that has somehow escaped him: 'does everything that I have undergone, even the most inhuman things, turn out to have been only a simulacrum of a quite other ordeal that I ultimately succeeded in evading?' (*Suite*, p. 561). The *biographie* comes to feel more and more like a *thanatographie* (*Suite*, p. 542), and 'writing resembles [. . .] interminable death throes' (*Moriendo*, p. 575). However, Laporte is reluctant to interpret this as a sign of the failure of his original enterprise, and he continues to uphold it by persisting until there is nowhere further for the writing to go. That is to say that he stops before he reaches the point when writing degenerates into 'sad autobiographical chatter' (*Moriendo*, p. 613). If Laporte's desire to live his writing and to make his writing a form of living brings him to feel more and more that he is not living, or that writing imposes such a sterile, painful form of living that it becomes a kind of death, he nevertheless takes this to be a consequence of the original imperative; and torment—even a torment that seems a shadow of some more 'real' ordeal—remains preferable to settling for a different relation between living and writing. To this extent Laporte remains faithful to his original aim.

As far as literature goes, Laporte's experiment leads him beyond the bounds where he can still consider what he is doing as part of the literature that first licensed his undertaking. The movement out of literature has both a euphoric and a more agonized guise. In the euphoric mode, Laporte redesignates his project in terms other than the strictly literary. This is partly because it blurs the boundary between philosophy and literature, and partly because the process of writing predominates so powerfully over any possible product that it becomes impossible to conceive of such a thing as a 'literary work':

My ambition as a writer was not only to enlarge literature with a hitherto unknown genre, but to participate in the creation of an order that can be reduced neither to the philosophy nor to the literature from which it nevertheless derives, a new reign that could be called scriptography, [. . .] the play of writings that do not lead to any definitive work, the only adventure that should allow one to work and to wander without any fixed goal. (*Fugue*, p. 310)

The endless working and wandering that Laporte anticipates here are gradually severed from any notion of a 'writer's ambition' as he becomes increasingly subject to the forces and the processes into which his writing draws him. He finds himself becoming caught up in configurations that make the notions of 'writer' and of 'literature' more and more irrelevant, and even the original formulation of the enterprise of the *biographie* has eventually to be discarded:

'That the writer as writer, and consequently as a man, is affected, or even threatened in his life, is doubtless a sufficient condition for the work to be stamped with the seal *Biographie*': even this quotation which I retained for a while as my opening sentence, had to be rejected because the writer, and consequently literature, have ceased to be operative, and have given way to another scene where the 'subject' is brought into play by means of writing. (*Codicille*, p. 477)

Despite its vicissitudes, the logic of Laporte's literary undertaking enables him to realize his central aim of radically reinterpreting the literary vocation as an absolute equation of living and writing. Indeed, he succeeds to such an extent that the field of literature itself is displaced and gives way to something much less specifically defined and which is at best described as a 'scriptography' or as 'bringing the subject into play through writing'.

Laporte's venture in his *biographie* can nonetheless be fully appreciated only when it is seen as having its origins in the notion of a literary vocation. It is the most extreme interpretation of vocation as the 'compulsion' that has been such a notable feature of literary writing for the past two centuries. This extreme character is the effect of Laporte's refusal to treat this compulsion as merely instrumental in the production of writing. As a result, his work is neither the narrative of a vocation, as Proust's could be said to be, nor even a diary of a writer's life, as Leiris's could at times be said to be. It turns the perspective of writing away from the past and towards the future, but without the programmatic element of a Sartrean project. Because it is unremittingly abstract, and because it also communicates to the reader the frustrations and torments that are Laporte's own experience as he writes, his work can be difficult to read. But it radically reworks a notion which can otherwise so easily become cliché, and which, as Robbe-Grillet points out, consequently seems very far removed from the processes of writing itself. On the contrary, Laporte's *biographie* demonstrates by its own (lived) example that the writing life can become the stuff of writing itself, and the basis for a sustained questioning of the literary.

JACQUES ROUBAUD: REGIME AND THE PERPETUATION OF WRITING

With Jacques Roubaud's five-volume *Grand Incendie de Londres*, written between 1985 and 2001, a notion of literature as vocation is discarded in favour of a deliberately more restricted project of writing conceived as the product of a regular daily regime. Although the project is described as 'the prose of my memory',[9] the writer's life is engaged rather more as the means of its production than as the object of its narrative representation. Generically, the narrative is marked by what Roubaud calls its 'absolute gratuitousness', being neither poetry, novel, nor autobiography (p. 309). And if it can be described as 'a historical enquiry into myself', the book makes no attempt to imply any significance for the life in the manner of an 'exemplum', a 'symbol', or an 'allegory' (p. 311). Roubaud is adamant that the writer's life is distinguished by nothing other than the fact that he (or she) is a producer of writing, or, as he says of the genus 'poet', they are 'composers of poetry, makers [*fabricants*] of poems'.[10] At the same time, the notion of what he calls '*l'œuvre-vie*' ('the work-life') is the antithesis or 'negation' of poetry, and he repudiates the tendency to confuse the poet's productions and the documentary evidence of his life, the latter being of interest only in so far as it relates to those productions. The writer—poet or otherwise—is above all, then, a producer of writing, and such a conception lends itself to an entirely pragmatic consideration of the life in terms of its appropriateness to that activity.

The consequences of these assumptions are played out in Roubaud's *Grand Incendie de Londres,* and they radically determine the nature of the writing which is the product of his 'writing life', and which, perhaps more than most others—though differently than Laporte's *biographie*—might justify the use of the term 'life-writing'. Anchored in the present of each daily 'moment of writing', there is no retrospective vantage point from which a continuous autobiographical narrative might be constructed. Moreover, the relation between writing and memory posited here is that of erasure rather than record:

Once it has been put on paper each *fragment of memory* [. . .] becomes *de facto* inaccessible to me. It is doubtless not that the memory trace where it is situated beneath the skull, in the neurones, has disappeared, but it is as if a transfer had been effected [. . .] which means that henceforth the words that compose the black lines of my transcription stand between it (the trace) and me, and end up replacing it entirely. (p. 260, Roubaud's italics)

---

[9] Jacques Roubaud, *Le Grand Incendie de Londres: récit, avec incises et bifurcations, 1985–1987* (Paris: Éditions du Seuil, 1989), p. 31. In what follows I shall refer principally to this first volume, or 'branch', of the series, and all page references will be to this text unless otherwise indicated. The other branches in the series, whose generic title is also *Le Grand Incendie de Londres* (all Paris: Éditions du Seuil) are: *La Boucle* (1993), *Mathématique: récit* (1997), *Poésie: récit* (2000), and *La Bibliothèque de Warburg: version mixte* (2002).

[10] Jacques Roubaud, *Poésie, etcetera: ménage* (Paris: Stock, 1995), p. 133.

The 'prose of memory' (p. 101) is less a restitution of a past as it exists in memory (a conventional aim of autobiography) than it is its destruction. Accordingly, the first of the five 'branches', which correspond to each of the five volumes of which the project is composed, is subtitled '*La destruction*'.

This destruction applies equally to the unrealized, twenty-year-long project—also entitled 'Le Grand Incendie de Londres'—which the new one supersedes. As outlined by Roubaud here, the failed project would seem to have been informed to a very considerable degree by a principle of vocation; and, in describing it, he is also renouncing its implicitly vocational ideals in favour of an attempt at a pragmatism devoid of all illusion. The denunciation of past error has, of course, a long pedigree in confessional writing, but in this case the past illusion is not replaced by any truer ideal, but by a repudiation of all ideals. As Roubaud presents it here, the original 'Grand Incendie de Londres' was the product of a dream he had in 1961 and from which he had awoken with the certainty that he would devote himself to a dual project, one part consisting of a novel called 'Le Grand Incendie de Londres' and the other part consisting of something more vaguely defined as both its source material and its commentary, and which he refers to as the '*Projet*' (in italics with a capital 'P'). Roubaud does not use the word 'vocation' as such, but his dream, at least in its effects, has all the characteristics of a calling. It appears to inaugurate a *vita nova* (the word is there) and to put an end to the despair that had followed the suicide of Roubaud's brother, an event he alludes to indirectly on a number of occasions in the first volume but does not narrate explicitly until later: 'The dream and its cinematic image were charged with a mental and also a moral brilliance [. . .] containing an urgency, an idea of futurity, a joyousness, the joy of another life, a "*vita nova*" ' (p. 168, Roubaud's italics). Thanks to the dream—although this is not directly announced in it—Roubaud becomes the designated author of two future works. In addition, and perhaps even more importantly, he acquires a new way of life that not only offers hope after despair, but demands a rigorous existential discipline designed to prepare him for his literary undertaking:

I was to carry out my preparation for the project elsewhere: in mathematics, in poetry, in a great austerity of existence. [. . .] During those years, I lived under *constraint*: the constraint of an apprenticeship in arithmetic, in poetic forms, and their simultaneous practice. But also constraints in life itself [. . .]. I lived under a system of rules. The rules of poetic writing, the rules of mathematical demonstration, and rules for living, constituting three systems that for me resembled each other, and had parallel paths. Each rule, and each act carried out in accordance with the rules, was thought of as a preparation. (p. 160, Roubaud's emphasis)

For the nineteen years following the dream, Roubaud lived his life as a vocation, which appears to have been every bit as rigorous as the one that Klesmer outlines to Gwendolen in *Daniel Deronda*, and whose outcome—unlike Barthes's voluntarily hypothetical novel—was to have been the original 'Grand Incendie de Londres' with its accompanying '*Projet*'. Moreover, literature was conceived in this scheme as more than the material outcome of a vocation. The rules of Roubaud's existence were also the pursuit of a certain idea of poetry: 'the project was the discovery of poetry; of a new variation on the meaning of "poetry". To carry out the project was to *find* poetry' (p. 199, Roubaud's emphasis). The vocation, then, was a way of life, with rules to live by and rules to write by; and it had as its goal both a literary production and the discovery of a certain conception of literature, the latter specifically focused on poetry, since the projected novel is described as a 'transformation of poetry into fiction', and the '*Projet*' as 'a *Trobar*: a contemporary version of the "trobar" of the troubadours' (ibid.).

With the new *Grand Incendie de Londres* Roubaud is cancelling the unrealized project of the novel and its accompanying '*Projet*', and, as I have suggested, is simultaneously relinquishing the vocation that was to have produced them. What is also discarded is the quest for poetry and with it the question of its idea; the issue now is rather that of 'literature'. Like Sartre in *Qu'est-ce que la littérature?*—though in very different terms—Roubaud distinguishes between poetry and literature as separate entities. He refuses to position poetry as a part of literature, on the grounds that poetry is above all an intangible that is given form in individual poems, whereas literature is coterminous with its material manifestations. All this is discussed at length in the series of essays contained in *Poésie, etcetera*, published during the course of the writing of the *Grand Incendie de Londres* series. If poetry is like the intangible 'soul' of the concrete form of the poem—'a breath of the language of poetry in poems, in the body of letters, words and verses'[11]—narrative prose, which Roubaud equates broadly with 'literature', is its obverse. The new version of *Le Grand Incendie de Londres* is not the work of the 'troubadour' Roubaud, but belongs to the far more mundane domain of 'literature', stripped of any informing, ideal notion of itself. In short, the loss of vocation is accompanied by a scaling down of the conception of the project to which the vocation had been devoted, so that, as vocation is reduced to pure regime, the enterprise becomes one of 'literature' instead of 'poetry'.

Roubaud's 'prose enterprise' (*Grand Incendie*, p. 13) is entirely defined and determined by the daily routine in which it is produced: he rises in the very early morning and writes until daylight reaches his desk, creating units of writing time that will vary according to the seasons. Each day brings 'a single unit of morning time, never going beyond the boundaries of the night hours that precede the morning', and the outcome of which is a sequence of '(almost) daily paragraphs of prose' (p. 30). The structure of a unit of writing is temporal rather than formal or rhetorical, a '*prose moment*' (p. 281, Roubaud's italics). The daily routine to which the writing owes its existence is described in some detail, beginning with the alarm clock, the instant coffee made with hot water from the tap, the material arrangements of the room in which Roubaud writes, including the objects on his

---

[11] *Poésie, etcetera*, p. 185.

desk and the cone of artificial light projected by his lamp before daylight brings the 'moment' to an end. Roubaud describes his writing regime as a 'constraint' (a term redolent of his practice as a member of Oulipo, to which I shall return presently), which, unlike the formal constraints associated with his previous vocation, pretends to no special virtues or qualities: 'It is like that of all other daily actions: getting up, getting dressed, shaving, eating' (p. 31). The writing produced within this constraint is without prior planning or subsequent revision: it is exactly mapped on to the present in which it emerges, 'without any crossing out, change of heart, thought, imagination, impatience, or promise other than of their guaranteed existence, line after line on the page of the exercise book in which I write' (p. 13). The joy, the conviction, and the anticipation associated with the earlier project are absent from the current one, whose mode is one of modesty (the word appears several times in the text) and maximum neutrality. The existential requirements of the new project are an evacuation of any euphoria or ambition, and are geared entirely to the practical routine of writing:

the possibility [of] the '*grand incendie de Londres*', which I am writing, and still do not know whether I shall bring into existence [. . .] is linked to the uncertain conquest of a state that is as close as possible to indifference, renunciation, the absence of hope, belief, or passion, bordering on what I naively imagine to be the *ataraxia* beloved of Sextus Empiricus. (p. 55, Roubaud's italics)

The figure of the hermit, which Roubaud invokes on a number of occasions, is another model for this existential quietism where all that counts is the regularity of routine, albeit, in Roubaud's case, a routine geared exclusively to productivity.

It is also an attempt to make a virtue of the emotional and material circumstances in which Roubaud finds himself, following the death of his wife in 1983. The new *Grand Incendie de Londres* is as much marked by death and grief as the previous project, but this one is, as it were, a thoroughgoing elaboration of the grief that follows loss, not, as the earlier one promised to be, a euphoric resolution to it.[12] The routine of writing is presented as an entirely pragmatic endeavour to fill a life which has become empty and which is lived in the shadow of the question 'what's the point?':

In a project for existence, any project for existence, there is in fact no reply other than a pragmatic one to the generalized 'what's the point': time passes. Any project, and particularly a formal writing project like the one I have now, which has outlived all value (I ascribed value to the Project, and at the time it was set up in opposition to the *what's-the-point*), fills the time, orders it and blanks out its empty moments. Each hour determines the next, pushes it on, swallows it up, and cancels it. (p. 321, Roubaud's italics)

---

[12] For a discussion of these deaths in Roubaud's writing see David Bellos, *The Pact of London* [online text], in Peter Consenstein (ed.), Dalkey Archive: A Casebook on Jacques Roubaud's *The Great Fire of London* (2003) <http://www.centerforbookculture.org/casebooks/index.html>, accessed 1 Mar. 2006.

Writing is synonymous with a day-to-day regime designed to pass time that has become a void, and is informed by no other ambition or purpose beyond its mere production.

There is, however, a danger of reducing Roubaud's enterprise to this auto-biographical dimension and to seeing it as little more than a kind of therapy appropriate to the process of mourning. From the point of view of the writing itself, the existential conditions of its production can perhaps be better evaluated in terms of the way in which they tally with the attempt to make writing coincide with the temporal conditions of its production, rather than being an index of its emotional or psychological context. The advantage of this perspective is that a further aspect of the enterprise then becomes visible. The existence of the 'prose enterprise' is the result of sheer persistence and an adherence to the self-imposed constraints for the writing: absolute regularity of production, no prior scheme to direct it, no crossing out, and absolute truthfulness. Each 'moment of prose' conforms to its present, even when it is recalling a fragment of memory: a hotel room in Fez, the visit to Madrid during which the original dream occurred, the layout of Roubaud's parents' house, making azarole jelly, a stay at the University of Iowa, the croissants he used to buy in Paris, visits to the British Library in London, the photograph of the night taken by his wife Alix, and so on. The insistence on this anchoring in the present, reinforced by the 'constraint' of veridicity, has two important and related consequences. The first is an increasingly complex narrative structure, and the second is an indefinitely deferred conclusion to the project.

Everything in the project is angled towards an unanticipated future, and it is this aspect that *Le Grand Incendie de Londres* shares with the principles of Oulipo, despite the (apparent) absence of formal constraints in its production. Roubaud's own accounts of Oulipo all make the question of potential its essential feature: '*L'Ouvroir de Littérature Potentielle*, OULIPO, has a goal: the Potentiality, inscribed in its very name.'[13] The purpose and value of the constraints—whose invention is Oulipo's central concern—lie precisely in their potential for production, as Roubaud goes on to spell out: 'In order to achieve that goal [Potentiality], Oulipo has several strategies. And of these, the chief one is the constraint.'[14] A constraint is evaluated primarily in terms of its generative capacity: 'the unicity of an Oulipian text actualizing a constraint [. . .] should be envisaged only on condition that the text contain all the *possibilities* of the constraint, all its virtual and potential texts and readings [. . .] its implicit

[13] Jacques Roubaud, 'Notes sur l'Oulipo et les formes poétiques', in Marcel Bénabou et al., *Un art simple et tout d'exécution: cinq leçons de l'Oulipo, cinq leçons sur l'Oulipo* (Belfort: Circé, 2001), pp. 21–32 (p. 21); see also Roubaud, 'De l'Oulipo', in *Poésie, etcetera*, pp. 197–219; and 'La Mathématique dans la méthode de Raymond Queneau', in Oulipo, *Atlas de littérature potentielle* (Collection Folio/Essais; Paris: Gallimard, 1981), pp. 42–72.

[14] 'Notes sur l'Oulipo', p. 21. All underlinings are Roubaud's.

multiplicity.'[15] A constraint is always oriented towards the future: the future manifestations of its productive potential, the future moment of its reading. The bulk of Oulipo's preoccupation is in the domain of poetry (this is certainly the focus of Roubaud's own activities as a member of Oulipo), but there are also formal constraints that operate in the domain of prose, as Perec's novels *La Disparition* and *La Vie mode d'emploi* both attest. Although Roubaud is a self-confessed admirer of Perec's fiction, and although he mentions the concealed presence of formal constraints in *Le Grand Incendie de Londres* designed to appeal to any 'Oulipian nutters' (*Grand Incendie*, p. 40) amongst its future readers, it is the constraints of regime that have the greatest potential for sheer production in this text. In other words, the Oulipian principle of potentiality is shifted from formal devices on to existential practice and the organization of daily life, a factor that Roubaud relates to the book's status as prose, rather than poetry: 'It is true that in none of my other exercise books (of poetry or arithmetic, for example) do I achieve such regularity, clarity, or uniformity in the slow encroachment on the space of their pages' (p. 23). Regime is not a matter of sheer asceticism, but meets the Oulipian requirement of generative potential in the sphere of prose.

What is generated is not just prose as a neutrally measurable entity—so many lines per day—but a prose that has, as I have already suggested, a peculiar and peculiarly complex narrative structure by virtue of its basis in the present. The teleological linearity of the narrative structure of fiction (i.e. the novel) becomes impossible. Each 'moment of prose' is launched by its incipit, which also serves as its title, and which, instead of announcing a recapitulatory summary of the episode about to be narrated, does nothing more than initiate what is to follow. The first three such titles, for example, are: 'This morning of 11 June 1985', 'I should like, in sum', and 'Yesterday evening, before I went to bed'. Each 'moment', grounded in the present tense of the life of the writer ('The present of my life saturates them, will saturate them, like the daylight that ceaselessly enters to combat the yellow circle [of light from the lamp] that surrounds my hand', pp. 30–1), thus constitutes a fresh start. The result of this practice is that the book as a whole is composed of a series of new beginnings, cumulatively establishing a permanent orientation towards the future, but without expectation of any conclusion. This perspective is underscored by the fact that, not being produced by any particular plan and solely by the absolute regularity of a daily routine, the nature of the project can be discovered only further down the line. The character of the 'prose enterprise' will be eventually be revealed when it is finally completed: ' "*le grand incendie de Londres*" will be what it will be only once it is finished [. . .] that is to say if it gets far enough for it to be said to be' (p. 29). For all its concern with memory, *Le Grand Incendie de Londres* is, like Laporte's *biographie*, constitutively *pro*spective, not *retro*spective.

---

[15] Roubaud, 'La Mathématique dans la méthode de Raymond Queneau', p. 69 (Roubaud's emphasis).

As a result of this repeated and regular grounding in the present of the writer's regime with its consequent set towards the future, the text becomes structurally digressive and fails to follow the kind of linear progression that would presuppose a plan or a plot more suggestive of a novel. This is acknowledged in the terms that Roubaud uses to describe the structural organization of his project: each volume is referred to as a 'branch', and within each one the narrative (such as it is) is constantly interrupted by the series of '*incises*' ('interpolations') and 'bifurcations', announced by the subtitle: 'As I advance through the prose I encounter, with almost every step, the impossibility of keeping it on a single line, and pointing it in a single direction', writes Roubaud (p. 33). The constant diversion into parenthesis, or what he calls a 'digressive interpolation' (ibid.), has significant effects on the structural arrangement of the book, whose sequence of 'chapters', each consisting of a series of 'prose moments', is interrupted—or followed, depending on one's reading preferences—by such 'interpolations' and then, finally, by a number of more substantial 'bifurcations'.

In one sense all this is simply the logical consequence of the principle of writing on the basis of a daily routine, with its associated requirement of a fresh starting point in the present moment of each new day. But the resulting complexity is not just a matter of managing such consequences, and neither is it simply a form of narrative experiment: to the extent that its effects militate against the possibility of an ending, the strategy goes to the heart of a tendency that for Roubaud is a perpetual hazard of literary prose, namely, its suicidal tendency to end. It might sound somewhat exaggerated to speak of suicide in this connection, but it is Roubaud himself who uses the term to characterize the way that fictional narratives strive, fatally, to end. In his discussion of the novel in *Poésie, etcetera*, he makes this the chief distinguishing feature of narrative prose as distinct from poetry: 'It is the fate of the novel-form as a non-poetry-form to come to an end.'[16] Poems are not susceptible to this inevitability because, according to Roubaud, they are designed to be retained in the memory, to be repeated and revisited at will. Since a novel, by contrast, is designed to be read only once and is not retained in the memory, its ending is its end, and is lived as such by readers: 'All novels, in finishing, disappoint; because they finish' (ibid., Roubaud's underlining). The end of writing is a kind of loss or defeat, the reverse of the end-less potentiality of an Oulipian constraint. And if it is not a defeat, then it can be no more than a willing suicide (this is where the word appears): 'The ending of a novel is the narrative's *suicide*. (A voluntary end.)' (ibid.).

Roubaud evaluates fiction in terms of the manner and degree to which novels succeed in resisting their inevitable ending. Novelists, he says, are engaged in a struggle against a 'fated ending' (p. 238) and 'the terrible obligation to end' (p. 243), and their choice of narrative strategies is determined by the need to postpone the moment when writing ceases. These options include

---

[16] *Poésie, etcetera*, p. 237.

digression, deferral of solutions to narrative mysteries, protracted conclusions, the introduction of incidental material from other domains (Roubaud, somewhat flippantly, mentions sociology, tourism, palaeontology, and philately, amongst others), or (and here Roubaud sounds more approving), as Sterne does in *Tristram Shandy*, by never even reaching the point where the narrative proper begins. It is, however, the medieval romance, and in particular the *Lancelot en prose* with its characteristic 'interlacings', that for Roubaud best exemplifies the possibility of avoiding or deferring endings. Not only does *Lancelot* employ a systematic structure of 'forking forest paths' (*embranchements*), but it solves the problem of endings by never proposing anything more than 'provisional endings' (p. 245, Roubaud's underlining). These provisional endings conclude what Roubaud describes as each 'branch' of the romance, and have the effect of making possible an infinite number of continuations. They ensure that the text need never 'die', and it remains animated by its own inherent potential for unending continuation.

Roubaud mentions the *Lancelot* on a number of occasions in *Le Grand Incendie de Londres*, both in connection with the unwritten novel of his previous project, and with reference to the current project. This project is, of course, not a novel, and does not therefore immediately appear to require the invention of the kind of narrative strategy that Roubaud discusses in *Poésie, etcetera*. But the issue of endings does nonetheless arise, as, for instance, in the comment that the regularity of his writing routine will produce a 'narration [. . .] in which I hope, by a process of accumulation and perseverance, to reach, if only involuntarily, my end' (p. 15). An ending would have the merit of finally revealing the nature of the prose enterprise to its author, and indeed of justifying his dogged perseverance with the regime by, as it were, providing something to show for it. At the same time, the wording that Roubaud uses here ('*ma fin*') makes a textual ending the equivalent not only of a goal, but also of an existential ending, even if it is, as he says, 'involuntary'. On the one hand, for the book to exist, it needs to end: 'above all there will be an ending (long afterwards or not, it does not matter (that is to say long afterwards as well, if I stick closely enough to the rule of more or less daily progression)); or else the book will not be' (p. 47). But, on the other, endings remain associated with death: the text seems ultimately to be more profoundly haunted by the possibility of its own demise than by the actual deaths of Roubaud's brother and wife.

Ideally, it would seem, any textual ending would be like that of the haiku. At a party in America, Roubaud meets a Japanese writer from whom he discovers that although the end of a haiku is 'a sort of death', the form is, by definition, both infinitely extensible in itself—'a haiku was always [. . .] open, and implicitly expandable into a long poem in a series of linked poems, a "renku"'—and also a continuation of all its previous incarnations. In short, the haiku is 'virtually infinite as regards the future; that is to say [. . .] infinite in both senses: continuing all previous haikus in a new beginning [. . .] but above all, imaginatively and potentially infinite in the writing of it' (p. 75). The end of a haiku is only a 'sort of death', since it is inherently revivable and perpetually extensible. The principle of the haiku also applies to *Le Grand Incendie de Londres* because, as long as Roubaud maintains his daily regime and adds to his stock of 'moments of prose', the book remains revivable and extensible just like the haiku. By harnessing writing to existential regime, and by producing a generically indeterminate 'life-writing' (my term, I should say, not Roubaud's) within the frame of a writing life, Roubaud is keeping the text alive, and defying the 'death' that is immanent in all prose narrative. The 'life-writing' produced by the 'writing life' becomes the means whereby it is kept alive against the pull of its inherent tendency to end. It is a 'life-writing' in the fullest sense of the word.

The modesty of Roubaud's literary enterprise, reflected in the scaling down of his ambition from vocation to regime, and in his restriction of the definition of literature to being the converse of poetry, might seem to have placed his writing outside the scope of my argument concerning the contestation of literature by itself. But *Le Grand Incendie de Londres* can be seen as a sustained attempt to set literature against itself by pitting the obstinate persistence of a writing regime against literature's equally determined bent towards self-destruction. It is by writing against literature that literature can be made to survive. And here it is the grounding of the literary project in the existential routine that is made to be the main bulwark of resistance against the worst prospect that literature has in store for itself: its end.

Afterword

The prospective note on which this history has ended may be heard as a warning against any impulse to conclude. The preparatory nature of the 'writing life' and the anticipatory stance of the 'life-writing' of Roger Laporte and Jacques Roubaud both largely dispense with the retrospective stance that might otherwise seem integral to the practice of biography. Taking my cue from their anticipatory emphasis, I shall therefore not attempt to summarize the long trajectory recorded in this book—hence my choice of 'Afterword' rather than 'Conclusion' as a title for the final leg of my journey through some three centuries of French literature. Instead, I shall use these last few pages to consider the single issue of the temporality of biography since the first appearance of the term in the eighteenth century, which coincided with the emergence of the modern sense of the word 'literature'.

It might have appeared plausible to regard the orientation towards the future in contemporary life-writing as a sign that the era of biography is over. But a backward look over these three centuries reveals a recurrent concern in biographical writing with an evolving rather than a completed temporality. The issue has surfaced time and again in the various instances I have described, repeatedly complicating retrospect with a dynamic of process and prospect. At the point when the concepts of 'literature' and 'biography' begin to take shape in the eighteenth century, the notion of perfectibility and the progressive implications of the organicist model of social and cultural institutions already inflect biography with developmental assumptions. Equally, since literature comes into being as, and on the basis of, a series of differentiations from prior versions of itself, it too exists to a very significant degree as an entity constantly propelled forward in time. In short, the two phenomena—literature and biography—might almost be said to have been made for each other, sharing not just a birthdate in the mid-eighteenth century, but a temporality embroiled in a present that looks as much towards the future as back towards the past.

This phenomenon is already evident in Rousseau's *Confessions*. Rousseau's conception of selfhood contains a temporal dimension that repeatedly introduces a margin of difference between past and present versions of himself. An awareness of this difference between his past and his present is built into the record of Rousseau's life in ways that ground his writing in a present tense that obdurately resists closure and finality. Similarly, Rousseau's equation between the practice of autobiography and the construction of literature introduces an internal differentiation between 'good' and 'bad' versions of literature that is never conclusively resolved and has constantly to be reasserted with the passage of time. The dynamic of Madame de Staël's account of literature as a continuous refinement of civilized sensibility entails less contradiction than that of Rousseau; but her version of literary history nonetheless portrays literature as an essentially open-ended project, committed, like an individual, to an unceasing improvement of life. If Hugo's defence of 'Progress' makes an exception for the longer history of art as a record of equally exceptional geniuses, the energies that drive that Progress forward are manifest in every phase of literature's history as a series of irrepressible renewals and rebirths, and as the inexorably forward march of the individual poet-hero. In a slightly different vein, Sainte-Beuve's invention of literary criticism presupposes the transient nature of the individual genius; moreover, critical writing is subject to its own temporal constraint of a weekly newspaper deadline, and is necessarily written in the context of a perpetually evolving literary landscape. Baudelaire has an even more acute sense of the existential limits within which poetic transcendence has to be produced in a race against diminishing human resources. And although Nerval and Schwob place less emphasis on the ongoing temporality of biography, and (in the case of Schwob at least) actively exploit the instantaneity of events in the lives of the subjects they portray, that characteristic is nevertheless deployed with a view to keeping literature itself in perpetual motion, and preventing it from collapsing into stasis.

With the turn of the twentieth century, biography becomes a means of focusing on the process of artistic creation in the inner life of the artist, whether in Pierre Audiat's idea of the 'biography of the work of art' or in Proust's evocation of the creative experience of the artist-figures. The temporal organization of his novel produces a narrative of sustained suspense out of Marcel's desire to write, angled towards an uncertain future, and defers as long as possible the retrospective revelation of the eventual realization of that desire as art. Literature comes to be equated with the moment of its fabrication rather than with a genesis that preceded its material existence. In Gide's affirmation of literarity as experience, and in his recourse to autobiography as the means of its demonstration, the moving present of the autobiographer's narrative perspective appears as an exacerbation of the unresolved present that is already implicit in the temporal orientation of biography. Leiris makes even more than Gide of the mobility of his position in time, and explicitly assigns to the future the proof of literature's literarity in the form of the sacred: the status of literature as an act can be determined only by its unforeseen consequences in the world. Critics such as André Maurois and Martin-Chauffier were the first to spell out as a major criterion of good biographical writing the biographer's ability to refrain from infusing his retrospective knowledge into a narrative that should ideally be that of the subject's own sense of the forward movement of his life. This principle was made axiomatic by Sartre in his wholesale condemnation of the 'retrospective illusion' as being profoundly antithetical to a proper understanding of human existence. Moreover, in his view, personal authenticity also depends on resisting the temptation to live life as biographical retrospect, an imperative that makes the authenticity of literature equally dependent on a willingness to resist biography's inherent capacity for complicity with that retrospective standpoint. For Sartre both literature and the human subject are required to be of their time, in step with the present tense of their historical situation; and a corresponding temporality offers biography a means whereby this may be achieved.

Genet, nevertheless, provides an exception to this principle of biographical anticipation, and his refusal to engage in any chronological series whatsoever—aesthetic or social—is part of his strategy of resistance to an established literary institution. His recourse to generic anachronism is one way of simply ignoring the issue of time. The same might also be said of Pierre Michon in his use of the lives of the saints. But if Michon's ideal temporality is that of the miracle—a total and transforming instant—he resembles Schwob in placing such miracles at the service of a literature viewed as being perpetually in need of remobilization: 'lives' record and, at their best, also embody the phenomenon of grace that 'endlessly relaunches literature'. Which brings us back to the writing life and the life-writing that were the point of departure for this brief summary of the inveterately prospective character of the dual phenomenon I have been exploring.

This rapid overview has brought the temporal character of biography to the fore through its sheer recurrence in so many of the examples that I have discussed. Not every case is the same: emphasis varies between the present and the future. And the reasons for that emphasis vary too both from one period to the next, and from one writer to the next: from the concern with perfectibility to that of experience, from a focus on genius to that of the sacred, from miracles to the acquisition of the skills of prosody, and so on. It is in the nature of biography, as the record of the lives of individuals, to facilitate such leaps from one topic or terrain to the next alongside acknowledgements of broader historical parameters. This responsiveness on the part of biography to individual circumstance has nevertheless been used by the argument of this book as a means of harnessing biographical practices to the question of literature—and the question of literature to biographical principles. The individual basis of biography is one factor that serves to raise the question of literature with each new authorial encounter, since definitional continuities cannot be taken for granted in the progression through the authors who make up the literary-historical series. Indeed, we have seen how often it has been claimed, and most categorically by Sainte-Beuve, Proust, and Sartre, that literature is reinvented from scratch with each new author.

Literature's constitutive difference from itself, which results from these reinventions, is considerably underscored by its association with the evolving temporality of biography, an element that is notably absent from the so-called philosophical present of the discourse of theory. When literature is mapped on to the openended temporality of biography, it is untethered from the fixity of theoretical definition and taken in directions that make it necessarily as different from itself as any biographical subject might expect to become over the course of a life. This parallel could be taken one stage further, where it might be used to suggest that the idea of literature is therefore better served by biography than by theory; but I shall hold back from such extremes of assertion and content myself (and, I hope, those readers who have lasted the course) with the proposal that we add this temporal element to those I outlined in my Introduction as supporting biography's capacity to intervene in debates concerning the question of literature. As well as the performativity of the genre inherited from its traditional exemplarity, and its liminality in relation to the field of literature, there is now the issue of its prospective temporality as it has emerged from the history of the genre in its dealings with literature. This may give my Afterword something of the character of an afterthought, but it would be nice to make a virtue of the retrospective nature of this insight, since it is a combination of criticism and literary and cultural history, rather than pure theoretical argument, that has given rise to it. I make this point not in order to attack theory, which is all too easily maligned in this supposedly post-theoretical era, but in order to demonstrate that biographical concerns do not preclude conceptual issues, as has often been claimed, whether by philosophers such as Victor Cousin or theorists such as Roman Jakobson. Such conceptual issues are arrived at differently in the domain of biography—deductively as opposed to inductively, perhaps—and biographical practices subject them to a different kind of treatment from that of philosophical or theoretical procedure: by actively exploiting those factors such as lived example, the variables of history and individual circumstance, or the special temporality that has been under the spotlight in these last pages. This is, of course, to comment, by way of a final consideration, on the nature of my own discourse in this book, which is certainly not that of theory: for what I am proposing here is not in any sense a *theory* of the relations between biography and history, but a history that attempts to attend equally to the distinctiveness of individual cases and to the perennial recurrence of the question 'What is literature?' in its encounters with biography.

Bibliography

References to translations are given in square brackets where the translation has been cited in the text. Date of original publication is given, where relevant, either in square brackets after the title, or as the first element within the parentheses containing publication details. Where appropriate, *Œuvres complètes* is abbreviated to *OC*. In footnotes *OC* ii (for example) means vol. ii of *Œuvres complètes*.

AGUETTANT, LOUIS, *Victor Hugo: poète de la nature*, ed. Jeanne Lonchampt and Jacques Lonchampt (Paris: L' Harmattan, 2000).

AIGRAIN, RENÉ, *L'Hagiographie: ses sources, ses méthodes, son histoire* (Paris: Bloud et Gay, 1953).

ALBOUY, PIERRE, 'Hugo, ou le Je éclaté', *Romantisme*, 1/1–2 (1971), pp. 53–64.

AMYOT, JACQUES, 'Dedication and Preface to Plutarch's *Lives*, 1559', in Bernard Weinberg (ed.), *Critical Prefaces of the French Renaissance* (Evanston, Ill.: Northwestern University Press, 1950), pp. 161–78.

ANCILLON, FRÉDÉRIC, *Essais philosophiques, ou, Nouveaux mélanges de littérature et de philosophie*, 2 vols. (Paris: J.-J. Paschoud, 1817).

ANTOINE, GÉRALD, 'Sainte-Beuve et l'esprit de la critique dite "universitaire" ', in *Sainte-Beuve et la critique littéraire contemporaine*, ed. Delhez-Sarlet and Vandegans [1972], pp. 105–23.

ARMEL, ALIETTE, *Michel Leiris* (Paris: Fayard, 1997).

ARNOLD, MATTHEW, *Five Uncollected Essays of Matthew Arnold*, ed. Kenneth Allott (Liverpool: University Press of Liverpool, 1953).

ARTAUD, ANTONIN, *Van Gogh ou le suicidé de la société* (1947; Paris: Gallimard, 2001).

ATTRIDGE, DEREK, *The Singularity of Literature* (London: Routledge, 2004).

AUDIAT, PIERRE, *La Biographie de l'œuvre littéraire: esquisse d'une méthode critique* (Paris: H. Champion, 1924).

AUGUSTINE, SAINT, *The Confessions of St. Augustine*, trans. F. J. Sheed (1943; Spiritual Masters; London: Sheed & Ward, 1984).

AUSTIN, J. L., *How to Do Things with Words* (William James Lectures), 2nd edition, ed. J. O. Urmson and Marina Sbisà (Oxford and New York: Oxford University Press, 1975).

AUSTIN, LLOYD J., 'Mallarmé et la critique biographique', *Comparative Literature Studies*, 4 (1967), pp. 27–34.

L'Auteur: colloque de Cerisy-la-Salle, 4–8 octobre 1995: actes, ed. Gabrielle Chamarat-Malandain and Alain Goulet (Caen: Presses universitaires de Caen, 1996).

AVERINTSEV, SERGEI S., 'From Biography to Hagiography: Some Stable Patterns in the Greek and Latin Tradition of Lives, Including Lives of the Saints', in France and St Clair (eds.), *Mapping Lives* [2002], pp. 19–36.

BAFARO, GEORGES, 'L'Architecture des livres IV et V des *Contemplations*', in Martin (ed.), *Analyses et réflexions sur 'Les Contemplations'* [1982], pp. 29–45.

BAKHTIN, M. M., *Art and Answerability: Early Philosophical Essays*, ed. Michael Holquist and Vadim Liapunov, trans. Vadim Liapunov and Kenneth N. Brostrom (Austin: University of Texas Press, 1990).

BALTEAU, J., et al. (eds.), *Dictionnaire de biographie française* (Paris: Letouzey et Ané, 1933–).

BARBÉRIS, PIERRE, 'Signification de Joseph Delorme en 1830', *Revue des sciences humaines*, 135 (1969), pp. 365–90.

BARBEY D'AUREVILLY, J., *Les Œuvres et les hommes*, 1st ser., i: *Les Philosophes et les écrivains religieux* (1860; repr. Geneva: Slatkine, 1968).

_____ *Du Dandysme et de George Brummel* [*sic*], ed. Marie-Christine Natta (1861; Bassac: Plein chant, 1989).

_____ *Les Œuvres et les hommes*, 1st ser., iii: *Les Poètes* (1862; repr. Geneva: Slatkine, 1968).

_____ *Les Diaboliques* [1874], ed. Jean-Pierre Seguin (Paris: Garnier-Flammarion, 1967). [Trans. Jean Kimber, with introduction by Enid Starkie, *The She-Devils (Les Diaboliques)* (London: Oxford University Press, 1963).]

_____ *Les Ridicules du temps* (Paris: Rouveyre et G. Blond, 1883).

_____ 'Les Photographies et les biographies', in id., *Les Ridicules du temps*, pp. 15–26.

_____ *Les Œuvres et les hommes*, 3rd ser., xxiii: *Poésie et poètes* (1906; repr. Geneva: Slatkine, 1968).

_____ *Les Œuvres et les hommes*, 4th ser., xxvi: *Critiques diverses* (1909; repr. Geneva: Slatkine, 1968).

_____ *Œuvres romanesques complètes*, ed. Jacques Petit (Bibliothèque de la Pléiade; Paris: Gallimard, 1964).

_____ *Le XIXe siècle: des œuvres et des hommes*, ed. Jacques Petit, 2 vols. (Paris: Mercure de France, 1964–6).

BARLOW, NORMAN H., *Sainte-Beuve to Baudelaire: A Poetic Legacy* (Durham, NC: Duke University Press, 1964).

BARTHES, ROLAND, *Sade, Fourier, Loyola* (Paris: Éditions du Seuil, 1971).

_____ *Le Degré zéro de l'écriture: suivi de Nouveaux essais critiques* (Collection Points; Paris: Éditions du Seuil, 1972).

_____ *Roland Barthes* (Paris: Éditions du Seuil, 1975).

_____ *Leçon: leçon inaugurale de la chaire de sémiologie littéraire du Collège de France, prononcée le 7 janvier 1977* (Paris: Éditions du Seuil, 1978).

_____ *Œuvres complètes*, ed. Jacques Petit and Éric Marty, 3 vols. (Paris: Éditions du Seuil, 1993).

_____ *Comment vivre ensemble*, ed. Claude Coste (Paris: Éditions du Seuil/IMEC, 2002).

_____ *La Préparation du roman, I et II: Cours et séminaires au Collège de France, 1978–1979 et 1979–1980*, ed. Nathalie Léger (Paris: Éditions du Seuil/IMEC, 2003).

_____ and NADEAU, MAURICE, *Sur la littérature* (Grenoble: Presses universitaires de Grenoble, 1980).

BATAILLE, GEORGES, *La Littérature et le mal: Emily Bronte, Baudelaire, Michelet, Blake, Sade, Proust, Kafka, Genet* (1957; Collection Idées; Paris: Gallimard, 1967).

_____ 'Genet', in id., *La Littérature et le mal*, pp. 199–244.

_____ 'Le Sacré', in id., *Œuvres complètes*, vol. i (Paris: Gallimard, 1970), pp. 559–63.

BATCHELOR, John (ed.), *The Art of Literary Biography* (Oxford: Clarendon Press, 1995).

BATTEUX, CHARLES, *Cours de belles-lettres, ou, Principes de la litterature*, rev. edn., 4 vols. (Paris: Desaint et Saillant; Durand, 1763).

BAUDELAIRE, CHARLES, *Curiosités esthétiques: l'art romantique; et autres œuvres critiques*, ed. Henri Lemaitre (Classiques Garnier; Paris: Garnier, 1962).

____ *Œuvres complètes*, ed. Claude Pichois and Jean Ziegler, 2 vols., rev. edn. (Bibliothèque de la Pléiade; Paris: Gallimard, 1975–6). [Trans. Norman Cameron, *My Heart Laid Bare and Other Prose Writings*, ed. Peter Quennell (London: Weidenfeld and Nicolson, 1950); trans. with introduction P. E. Charvet, *Selected Writings on Art and Artists* (Cambridge: Cambridge University Press, 1981).]

____ *La Fanfarlo*, in id., *OC* i, ed. Pichois and Ziegler, pp. 553–80.

____ *Les Fleurs du mal*, in id., *OC* i. [Prose trans. Francis Scarfe, *Baudelaire* (Harmondsworth: Penguin, 1961).]

____ *Fusées*, in id., *OC* i, pp. 649–67.

____ *Mon cœur mis à nu*, in id., *OC* i, pp. 676–708.

____ *Réflexions sur quelques-uns de mes contemporains*, in id., *OC* i, pp. 129–81.

____ *Edgar Poe, sa vie et ses œuvres*, in id., *OC* ii, ed. Pichois, pp. 296–318. [Trans. *The Works of Edgar Allan Poe with a Study of his Life and Writings by Charles Baudelaire* (London: Hotter, 1872)].

____ *Notes nouvelles sur Edgar Poe*, in id., *OC* ii, pp. 319–37.

____ *L'Œuvre et la vie d'Eugène Delacroix*, in id., *OC* ii, pp. 742–70.

____ *Salon de 1859*, in id., *OC* ii, pp. 608–82.

____ *Théophile Gautier [1]*, in id., *OC* ii, pp. 103–28.

BAUMGARTEN, ALEXANDER GOTTLIEB, *Reflections on Poetry: Alexander Gottlieb Baumgarten's Meditationes philosophicae de nonnullis ad poema pertinentibus* [1735], trans. Karl Aschenbrenner and William B. Holther (Berkeley: University of California Press, 1954).

BAYLE, PIERRE, *Dictionnaire historique et critique* [1697, 1702], 4th edn., 4 vols. (Amsterdam: P. Brunel et al., 1730).

BEAUJOUR, MICHEL, *Miroirs d'encre: rhétorique de l'autoportrait* (Paris: Éditions du Seuil, 1980).

____ 'Pierre Michon biographe', in Joseph Brami, Madeleine Cottenet-Hage, and Pierre Verdaguer (eds.), *Regards sur la France des années 1980: le roman* (Saratoga, Calif.: Anma Libri, 1994), pp. 179–83.

____ *Terreur et rhétorique: Breton, Bataille, Leiris, Paulhan, & Cie: autour du surréalisme* (Paris: J.-M. Place, 1999).

BEAUVOIR, SIMONE DE, *La Cérémonie des adieux: suivi de Entretiens avec Jean-Paul Sartre, août–septembre 1974* (1981; Collection Folio; Paris: Gallimard, 1987). [Trans. Patrick O'Brian, *Adieux: A Farewell to Sartre* (London: Deutsch, 1984).]

BECQ, ANNIE, 'Politique, esthétique et philosophie de la nature dans le Groupe de Coppet: le concept d'organisme', in *Actes et documents du deuxième colloque de Coppet, 10–13 juillet 1974*, ed. Simone Balayé and Jean-Daniel Candaux (Geneva: Slatkine; Paris: H. Champion, 1974), pp. 83–98.

____ *Genèse de l'esthétique française moderne: de la raison classique à l'imagination créatrice, 1680–1814* (Paris: Albin Michel, 1984).

BELLOS, DAVID, *The Pact of London* [online text], in Peter Consenstein (ed.), Dalkey Archive: A Casebook on Jacques Roubaud's *The Great Fire of London* (2003) <http://www.centerforbookculture.org/casebooks/index.html>, accessed 1 Mar. 2006.

BELLOS, DAVID, 'Patchworking in Sartre and Perec', in Hafid Gafaïti (ed.), *Recyclages culturels/Recycling Culture* (Paris: L'Harmattan, 2003), pp. 95–102.

BELLOUR, RAYMOND, 'Entretien avec Michel Leiris', *Lettres françaises*, 29 Sept.–5 Oct. 1966, pp. 3–4.

BÉNABOU, MARCEL, et al., *Un art simple et tout d'exécution: cinq leçons de l'Oulipo, cinq leçons sur l'Oulipo* (Belfort: Circé, 2001).

BÉNICHOU, PAUL, *Le Sacre de l'écrivain, 1750–1830: essai sur l'avènement d'un pouvoir spirituel laïque dans la France moderne* (Paris: J. Corti, 1973).

——— *Les Mages romantiques* (Paris: Gallimard, 1988).

——— *L'École du désenchantement: Sainte-Beuve, Nodier, Musset, Nerval, Gautier* (Paris: Gallimard, 1992).

BENJAMIN, RENÉ, *La Prodigieuse Vie d'Honoré de Balzac* (Le Roman des grandes existences; Paris: Plon-Nourrit, 1925).

BENJAMIN, WALTER, *Charles Baudelaire: A Lyric Poet in the Era of High Capitalism*, trans. Harry Zohn (London: NLB, 1973).

BERG, CHRISTIAN, and VADÉ, YVES (eds.), *Marcel Schwob, d'hier et d'aujourd'hui* (Seyssel: Champ Vallon, 2002).

BERGOUNIOUX, PIERRE, et al. (eds.), *Compagnies de Pierre Michon* (Lagrasse: Verdier; Orléans: Théodore Balmoral, 1993).

BERGSON, HENRI, *L'Évolution créatrice* (1907; Paris: Presses universitaires de France, 1948). [Trans. Arthur Mitchell, *Creative Evolution* (London: Macmillan, 1911).]

BERSANI, LEO, *The Culture of Redemption* (Cambridge, Mass., Harvard University Press, 1990).

BERTHIER, PHILIPPE, *L'Ensorcelée: 'Les Diaboliques' de Barbey d'Aurevilly* (Paris: H. Champion, 1987).

BEUGNOT, BERNARD, 'Forme et histoire: le statut des *ana*', in id., *La Mémoire du texte: essais de poétique classique* (Paris: H. Champion, 1994), pp. 67–87.

Le Biographique = Poétique, 63 (1985) [special issue].

Le Biographique [colloque de Cerisy 1990], ed. Alain Buisine and Norbert Dodille = *Revue des sciences humaines*, 224 (1991) [special issue].

BISSELL, ELIZABETH BEAUMONT (ed.), *The Question of Literature: The Place of the Literary in Contemporary Theory* (Manchester: Manchester University Press, 2002).

BLANCHOT, MAURICE, *La Part du feu* (Paris: Gallimard, 1949).

——— 'Gide et la littérature d'expérience', in id., *La Part du feu*, pp. 208–20.

——— *L'Espace littéraire* (1955; Collection Idées; Paris: Gallimard, 1968). [Trans. Ann Smock, *The Space of Literature* (Lincoln: University of Nebraska Press, 1982).]

——— *Le Livre à venir* (1959; Collection Idées; Paris: Gallimard, 1971). [Trans. Ian Maclachlan, 'The Disappearance of Literature', in Michael Holland (ed.), *The Blanchot Reader* (Oxford: Blackwell, 1995), pp. 136–42.]

——— 'Combat avec l'ange', in id., *L'Amitié* (Paris: Gallimard, 1971), pp. 150–61.

——— 'Poésie et langage', in id., *Faux Pas* (Paris: Gallimard, 1975), pp. 157–62.

——— *Après coup: précédé par Le Ressassement éternel* (Paris: Éditions de Minuit, 1983).

BLOOM, HAROLD, *The Anxiety of Influence: A Theory of Poetry* (New York: Oxford University Press, 1973).

BOILEAU DESPRÉAUX, NICOLAS, *Œuvres complètes*, ed. Françoise Escal (Bibliothèque de la Pléiade; Paris: Gallimard, 1966).

____ *Art poétique* [1674], in id., *OC*. [Trans. as *The Art of Poetry, Written in French by The Sieur de Boileau. In four Canto's. Made English, By Sir William Soames, Since Revis'd by John Dryden, Esq* (London: H. Hills, 1710).]

____ *Traité du sublime* [1674], in id., *OC*.

BONALD, LOUIS GABRIEL A., *Mélanges littéraires, politiques, et philosophiques*, 2 vols. (Paris: 1819).

BONNEFOY, YVES, *L'Improbable, suivi de Un Rêve fait à Mantoue*, rev. edn. (Paris: Mercure de France, 1980).

____ *Baudelaire: la tentation de l'oubli* (Conférences Del Duca; Paris: Bibliothèque nationale de France, 2000).

BONNET, CHARLES, *Essai analytique sur les facultés de l'âme*, 2nd edn., 2 vols. (Copenhagen and Geneva: Philibert, 1769).

BONNET, JEAN-CLAUDE, 'Le Fantasme de l'écrivain', *Poétique*, 63 (1985), pp. 259–77.

____ *Naissance du Panthéon: essai sur le culte des grands hommes* (Paris: Fayard, 1998).

BONY, JACQUES, *Le Récit nervalien: une recherche des formes* (Paris: J. Corti, 1990).

____ *L'Esthétique de Nerval* (Paris: SEDES, 1997).

BORGES, JORGE LUIS, *Labyrinths: Selected Stories and Other Writings*, ed. and trans. Donald A. Yates and James E. Irby (Harmondsworth: Penguin, 1970).

BORIE, JEAN, *Un siècle démodé: prophètes et réfractaires au XIXe siècle* (Paris: Payot, 1989).

BOSCHETTI, ANNA, *Sartre et 'Les Temps modernes': une entreprise intellectuelle* (Paris: Éditions de Minuit, 1985).

BOUCHERON, SABINE and PATRICK, 'Pierre Michon écrivain du Moyen Âge', *Scherzo*, 5 (1998), pp. 54–66.

BOURDIEU, PIERRE, 'L'Invention de la vie d'artiste', *Actes de la recherche en sciences sociales*, 2 (1975), pp. 67–93.

____ 'L'Illusion biographique', *Actes de la recherche en sciences sociales*, 62–3 (1986), pp. 69–72.

____ *Les Règles de l'art: genèse et structure du champ littéraire*, rev. edn. (Paris: Éditions du Seuil, 1998).

BOWIE, MALCOLM, 'Plutarch to Proust: Exemplary Lives', *New Comparison*, 25 (1998), pp. 9–24.

BRIX, MICHEL, *Sainte-Beuve, ou, La Liberté critique* (Jaignes: Chasse au Snark, 2002).

BROMBERT, VICTOR, 'Sartre et la biographie impossible', *Cahiers de l'Association internationale des études françaises*, 19 (1967), pp. 155–66.

BROWN, PETER, *The Cult of the Saints: Its Rise and Function in Latin Christianity* (London: SCM, 1981).

BUISINE, ALAIN, 'Biofictions', in *Le Biographique*, ed. Buisine and Dodille [1991], pp. 7–13.

BURKE, SEÁN (ed.), *Authorship: From Plato to the Postmodern: A Reader* (Edinburgh: Edinburgh University Press, 1995).

____ *The Death and Return of the Author: Criticism and Subjectivity in Barthes, Foucault and Derrida*, 2nd edn. (Edinburgh: Edinburgh University Press, 1998).

BUTLER, EDWARD CUTHBERT, *Benedictine Monachism: Studies in Benedictine Life and Rule*, 2nd edn. (London: Longmans Green, 1924).

BUTOR, MICHEL, 'Une autobiographie dialectique', in id., *Répertoire*, vol. i: *Études et conférences, 1948–1959* (Paris: Éditions de Minuit, 1960), pp. 262–70.

—— 'Les Œuvres d'art imaginaires chez Proust', in id., *Répertoire*, vol. ii: *Études et conférences, 1949–1963* (Paris: Éditions de Minuit, 1964), pp. 252–92.

BYA, JOSEPH, 'Persistance de la biographie', *Le Discours social*, 1 (1970), pp. 23–32.

BYNUM, CAROLINE WALKER, *Fragmentation and Redemption: Essays on Gender and the Human Body in Medieval Religion* (New York: Zone Books, 1991).

BYVANCK, WILLEM GEERTRUD CORNELIS, *Un Hollandais à Paris en 1891: sensations de littérature et d'art* (Paris: Perrin, 1892).

CAILLOIS, ROGER, *L'Homme et le sacré* (1939; Collection Folio/Essais; Paris: Gallimard, 1988).

CALVET, LOUIS-JEAN, *Roland Barthes, 1915–1980* (Paris: Flammarion, 1990).

CAMUS, ALBERT, *L'Homme révolté* (Paris: Gallimard, 1951).

CARCO, FRANCIS, *Le Roman de François Villon* (Le Roman des grandes existences; Paris: Plon, 1926).

CARLYLE, THOMAS, *On Heroes, Hero-Worship and the Heroic in History* (London: Chapman and Hall, 1840).

—— *Critical and Miscellaneous Essays*, 3rd edn., 4 vols. (London: Chapman and Hall, 1847).

CARON, PHILIPPE, *Des 'Belles lettres' à la 'littérature': une archéologie des signes du savoir profane en langue française (1680–1760)* (Paris: Société pour l'information grammaticale, 1992).

CARROLL, DAVID, 'The Post-Literary Condition: Sartre, Camus and the Question(s) of Literature', in Bissell (ed.), *The Question of Literature* [2002], pp. 66–90.

CASTIGLIONE, AGNÈS, '"Tu connais Pierrot": un autoportrait de l'artiste', in *Pierre Michon, l'écriture absolue*, ed. Castiglione [2002], pp. 45–57.

CASTIGLIONE, AGNÈS (ed.), *Pierre Michon, l'écriture absolue: actes du 1er colloque international pierre Michon (Musée d'Art Moderne de Saint-Étienne, 8, 9, 10 mars 2001)*, (Saint-Étienne: Publications de l'Université de Saint-Étienne, 2002).

CELLIER, LÉON, *Baudelaire et Hugo* (Paris: J. Corti, 1970).

Centre de recherche pour un trésor de la langue française, *Trésor de la langue française: dictionnaire de la langue du XIXᵉ et du XXᵉ siècle (1789–1960)*, ed. Paul Imbs, 16 vols. (Paris: Éditions du CNRS; Klincksieck; Gallimard, 1971–94).

CERTEAU, MICHEL DE, *L'Écriture de l'histoire* (Paris: Gallimard, 1975).

CHABOT, JACQUES, '*Vie de Joseph Roulin*: une "vie minuscule"', in *Pierre Michon, l'écriture absolue*, ed. Castiglione [2002], pp. 23–37.

CHALMERS, ALEXANDER, *The General Biographical Dictionary: Containing an Historical and Critical Account of the Lives and Writings of the Most Eminent Persons in Every Nation, Particularly the British and Irish, from the Earliest Accounts to the Present Time*, rev. edn. (London: Nichols, 1812).

CHAMARAT-MALANDAIN, GABRIELLE, *Nerval, réalisme et invention* (Orléans: Paradigme, 1997).

CHAMBERS, ROSS, *Gérard de Nerval et la poétique du voyage* (Paris: J. Corti, 1969).

CHAMPFLEURY, *Les Excentriques* [1852], rev. edn. (Paris: Michel Lévy, 1877).

—— *Grandes figures d'hier et d'aujourd'hui: Balzac, Gérard de Nerval, Wagner, Courbet* (Paris: Poulet-Malassis et de Broise, 1861).

CHAMPION, PIERRE, *Marcel Schwob et son temps* (Paris: Bernard Grasset, 1927).

_____ (ed.), *Catalogue de la bibliothèque de Marcel Schwob* (Paris: Édtions Allia, 1993).

CHARLES-WURTZ, LUDMILA, *Poétique du sujet lyrique dans l'œuvre de Victor Hugo* (Paris: H. Champion, 1998).

CHARTIER, ROGER, 'L'Homme de lettres', in Michel Vovelle (ed.), *L'Homme des Lumières* (Paris: Éditions du Seuil, 1996), pp. 159–209.

CHATEAUBRIAND, FRANÇOIS-RENÉ, *Essai sur les révolutions; Génie du christianisme* [1797; 1802], ed. Maurice Regard (Bibliothèque de la Pléiade; Paris: Gallimard, 1978).

_____ 'Lettre à M. de Fontanes sur la seconde édition de l'ouvrage de Mme de Staël', in id., *Essai sur les révolutions*, pp. 1265–80.

CHAUMEIX, ANDRÉ, 'Le Goût des biographies', *Revue des deux mondes*, 42 (1927), pp. 698–708.

CHESTERS, GRAHAM, *Baudelaire and the Poetics of Craft* (Cambridge: Cambridge University Press, 1988).

CHOTARD, LOÏC, 'La Biographie contemporaine en France au dix-neuvième siècle: autour du Panthéon-Nadar', doctoral thesis (Université de Paris IV-Sorbonne, 1987).

_____ *Approches du XIXe siècle* (Paris: Presses de l'Université de Paris-Sorbonne, 2000).

CLARK, PRISCILLA, 'Stratégies d'auteur au xixe siècle', *Romantisme*, 17–18 (1977), pp. 92–102.

CLARK, TIMOTHY, *The Theory of Inspiration: Composition as a Crisis of Subjectivity in Romantic and Post-Romantic Writing* (Manchester: Manchester University Press, 1997).

CLIFFORD, JAMES LOWRY (ed.), *Biography as an Art: Selected Criticism, 1560–1960* (London: Oxford University Press, 1962).

COE, RICHARD N., *The Vision of Jean Genet* (London: Owen, 1968).

COGMAN, PETER, *Hugo, Les Contemplations* (London: Grant & Cutler, 1984).

COLLINS, DOUGLAS, *Sartre as Biographer* (Cambridge, Mass.: Harvard University Press, 1980).

COMPAGNON, ANTOINE, *La Troisième République des lettres, de Flaubert à Proust* (Paris: Éditions du Seuil, 1983).

_____ 'Préface', in Marcel Proust, *Du Côté de chez Swann* (Collection Folio; Paris: Gallimard, 1988), pp. vii–xxxv.

_____ *Proust entre deux siècles* (Paris: Éditions du Seuil, 1989).

_____ 'La Rhétorique à la fin du xixe siècle (1875–1900)', in Fumaroli (ed.), *Histoire de la rhétorique* [1999], pp. 1215–50.

_____ *Le Démon de la théorie: littérature et sens commun* (Collection Folio/Essais; Paris: Éditions du Seuil, 2001).

_____ 'Histoire de la littérature ou histoire des auteurs?', in Louichon and Roger (eds.), *L'Auteur entre biographie et mythographie* [2002], pp. 29–36.

CONDILLAC, ÉTIENNE BONNOT DE, *Essai sur l'origine des connoissances humaines* (Amsterdam, 1746). [Trans. Hans Aarsleff, *Essay on the Origin of Human Knowledge* (Cambridge: Cambridge University Press, 2001).]

CONDORCET, JEAN-ANTOINE-NICOLAS DE CARITAT, MARQUIS DE, *Esquisse d'un tableau historique des progrès de l'esprit humain* [1794], ed. Monique and François Hincker (Paris: Éditions sociales, 1966).

CONTAT, MICHEL (ed.), *Pourquoi et comment Sartre a écrit 'Les Mots': genèse d'une autobiographie* (Paris: Presses universitaires de France, 1996).

CONTAT, MICHEL and RYBALKA, MICHEL (eds.), *Les Écrits de Sartre: chronologie, bibliographie commentée, textes retrouvés* (Paris: Gallimard, 1970).

COUSIN, VICTOR, *Introduction à l'histoire de la philosophie* [1828–9], 4th edn. (Paris: Didier, 1861). [Trans. O. W. Wight, *Course of the History of Modern Philosophy*, 2 vols. (Edinburgh: T. & T. Clark, 1852).]

COUTURIER, MAURICE, *La Figure de l'auteur* (Paris: Éditions du Seuil, 1995).

CRISTIN, CLAUDE, *Aux origines de l'histoire littéraire* (Grenoble: Presses universitaires de Grenoble, 1973).

CRONK, NICHOLAS, *The Classical Sublime: French Neoclassicism and the Language of Literature* (Charlottesville, Va.: Rookwood Press, 2003).

CULLER, JONATHAN, 'Intertextuality and Interpretation: Baudelaire's "Correspondances"', in Christopher Prendergast (ed.), *Nineteenth-Century French Poetry: Introductions to Close Reading* (Cambridge: Cambridge University Press, 1990), pp. 118–37.

DAVIES, HOWARD, *Sartre and 'Les Temps modernes'* (Cambridge: Cambridge University Press, 1987).

DAVIS, COLIN, *Ethical Issues in Twentieth-Century French Fiction: Killing the Other* (London: Macmillan, 1999).

DAYAN, PETER, *Nerval et ses pères: portrait en trois volets avec deux gonds et un cadenas* (Geneva: Droz, 1992).

DE MAN, PAUL, 'Madame de Staël et Jean-Jacques Rousseau', *Preuves*, 190 (1966), pp. 35–40.

—— *Allegories of Reading: Figural Language in Rousseau, Nietzsche, Rilke, and Proust* (New Haven and London: Yale University Press, 1979).

—— *The Rhetoric of Romanticism* (New York: Columbia University Press, 1984).

DEGUY, JACQUES, 'Les Références culturelles dans les manuscrits des *Mots*', in Contat (ed.), *Pourquoi et comment Sartre a écrit 'Les Mots'* [1996], pp. 293–319.

DELEUZE, GILLES, *Proust et les signes*, 7th edn. (Paris: Presses universitaires de France, 1986). [Trans. Richard Howard, *Proust and Signs* (London: Allen Lane, 1973).]

—— 'La Vie comme œuvre d'art', in id., *Pourparlers: 1972–1990* (Paris: Éditions de Minuit, 1990), pp. 129–38.

DELON, MICHEL, 'La Révolution et le passage des belles-lettres à la littérature', *Revue d'histoire littéraire de la France*, 90 (1990), pp. 557–88.

DERRIDA, JACQUES, *De la Grammatologie* (Paris: Éditions de Minuit, 1967).

—— *Glas*, 2 vols. (1974; Paris: Denoël/Gonthier, 1981).

—— *Otobiographies: l'enseignement de Nietzsche et la politique du nom propre* (Paris: Éditions Galilée, 1984).

—— *Parages* (Paris: Éditions Galilée, 1986).

—— *Acts of Literature*, ed. Derek Attridge (New York and London: Routledge, 1992).

—— '"This Strange Institution Called Literature": An Interview with Jacques Derrida', trans. Geoffrey Bennington and Rachel Bowlby, in id., *Acts of Literature*, pp. 33–75.

DESCOMBES, VINCENT, *Proust: philosophie du roman* (Paris: Éditions de Minuit, 1987).

DESORMEAUX, DANIEL, *La Figure du bibliomane: histoire du livre et stratégie littéraire au XIXᵉ siècle* (Paris: Nizet, 2001).

DIAZ, JOSÉ-LUIS, 'L'*Artiste* romantique en perspective', *Romantisme*, 54 (1986), pp. 5–23.

—— 'Écrire la vie du poète: la biographie d'écrivain entre Lumières et Romantisme', in *Le Biographique*, ed. Buisine and Dodille [1991], pp. 215–33.

_____ 'L'Autonomisation de la littérature (1760–1860)', in Goulet (ed.), *Le Littéraire, qu'est-ce que c'est?* [2002], pp. 59–77.

Dictionnaire universel françois et latin [*Dictionnaire de Trévoux*], rev. edn., 5 vols. (Paris and Trévoux: 1721).

DIDEROT, DENIS, *Le Neveu de Rameau: ou, Satire seconde; accompagné de La Satire première*, ed. Roland Desné (orig. pub. in Ger. trans., 1804; Paris: Éditions sociales, 1972).

_____ *Œuvres esthétiques*, ed. Paul Vernière (Classiques Garnier; Paris: Garnier, 1959).

DIDIER, BÉATRICE, 'Révolution et identité dans *Les Illuminés*', *Cahiers Gérard de Nerval*, 12 (1989), pp. 2–10.

_____ *Madame de Staël* (Paris: Ellipses, 1999).

DIECKMANN, HERBERT, 'Diderot's Conception of Genius', *Journal of the History of Ideas*, 2 (1941), pp. 151–82.

DOMECQ, JEAN-PHILIPPE, *Artistes sans art?* (Paris: Éditions Esprit, 1994).

DOUAY-SOUBLIN, FRANÇOISE, 'La Rhétorique en France au XIXe siècle: restauration, renaissance, remise en cause', in Fumaroli (ed.), *Histoire de la rhétorique* [1999], pp. 1071–214.

DU BOS, CHARLES, *Qu'est-ce que la littérature?*, trans. Juliette Siry Du Bos (Paris: Plon, 1945). [Orig. pub. as *What is Literature?* (London: Sheed & Ward, 1940).]

_____ 'André Maurois, *Ariel ou Vie de Shelley*', in id., *Approximations* (Paris: A. Fayard, 1965), p. 1549.

DUBOIS, JACQUES, 'Mme de Staël et l'institution littéraire', in *Le Groupe de Coppet et le monde moderne: conceptions—images—débats: actes du 6e Colloque de Coppet, Liège, 10–12 juillet 1997* (Liège: Droz, 1998), pp. 33–46.

DUBOS, JEAN-BAPTISTE, *Réflexions critiques sur la poésie et sur la peinture*, 2 vols. (Paris: Jean Mariette, 1719).

DUFOUR, HÉLÈNE, *Portraits, en phrases: les recueils de portraits littéraires au XIXe siècle* (Paris: Presses universitaires de France, 1997).

DUPONT, FLORENCE, *L'Invention de la littérature: de l'ivresse grecque au livre latin* (Paris: La Découverte, 1994).

EAGLETON, TERRY, *The Ideology of the Aesthetic* (Oxford: Blackwell, 1990).

ELBAZ, ROBERT, *The Changing Nature of the Self: A Critical Study of the Autobiographic Discourse* (London: Croom Helm, 1988).

ELIADE, MIRCEA, *Le Sacré et le profane* (Collection Folio/Essais; Paris: Gallimard, 1987).

ELIOT, GEORGE, *Daniel Deronda* (1876; London: Everyman, 2000).

ELLMANN, RICHARD, *Literary Biography: An Inaugural Lecture Delivered before the University of Oxford on 4 May 1971* (Oxford: Clarendon Press, 1971).

ESCARPIT, ROBERT, 'Histoire de l'histoire de la littérature', in Raymond Queneau (ed.), *Histoire des littératures* (Paris: Gallimard, 1963), pp. 1737–43.

_____ 'La Définition du terme "Littérature": projet d'article pour un dictionnaire international des termes littéraires', in Robert Escarpit and Charles Bouazis (eds.), *Le Littéraire et le social* (Paris: Flammarion, 1970), pp. 259–72.

EVANS, DEBORAH, ' "Some of These Days": Roquentin's "American" Adventure', *Sartre Studies International*, 8/1 (2002), pp. 58–72.

FAYOLLE, ROGER, *La Critique littéraire*, rev. edn. (Collection U; Paris: Armand Colin, 1964).

FAYOLLE, ROGER, 'Les Procédés de la critique beuviennes et leurs implications', *Littérature*, 1 (1971), pp. 82–91.

FERNANDEZ, RAMON, '*Aspects de la biographie*, par André Maurois', *Nouvelle Revue française*, 184 (1929), pp. 100–2.

FLAUBERT, GUSTAVE, *L'Éducation sentimentale: histoire d'un jeune homme* [1869], ed. P. M. Wetherill (Classiques Garnier; Paris: Garnier, 1984).

—— *Trois Contes* [1877], ed. P. M. Wetherill (Paris: Garnier, 1988).

—— *Préface à la vie d'écrivain: extraits de la correspondance*, ed. Geneviève Bollème (Paris: Éditions du Seuil, 1963).

FLEITH, BARBARA, and MORENZONI, FRANCO (eds.), *De la sainteté à l'hagiographie: genèse et usages de la 'Légende dorée'* (Geneva: Droz, 2001).

FORSTER, E. M., *Aspects of the Novel* (London: Edward Arnold, 1927).

FOUCAULT, MICHEL, *Les Mots et les choses: une archéologie des sciences humaines* (Paris: Gallimard, 1966).

—— *Histoire de la sexualité*, vol. ii: *L'Usage des plaisirs* (Paris: Gallimard, 1984). [Trans. Robert Hurley, *The History of Sexuality*, ii: *The Use of Pleasure* (Harmondsworth: Penguin, 1987).]

—— *Histoire de la sexualité*, vol. iii: *Le Souci de soi* (1984; Collection tel; Paris: Gallimard, 1997).

—— *Dits et écrits*, ed. Daniel Defert, François Ewald, and Jacques Legrange, 4 vols. (Paris: Gallimard, 1994).

—— 'Qu'est-ce qu'un auteur?' [1969], in id., *Dits et écrits*, vol. i., pp. 789–821. [Trans. Josué V. Harari, 'What is an Author?', in Paul Rabinow (ed.), *The Foucault Reader* (Harmondsworth: Penguin, 1986), pp. 101–20.]

—— 'L'Écriture de soi' [1983], in id., *Dits et écrits*, vol. iv, pp. 415–30.

FRANCE, PETER, *Rousseau, Confessions* (Cambridge: Cambridge University Press, 1987).

—— 'The French Academic *Éloge*', in France and St Clair (eds.), *Mapping Lives* [2002], pp. 83–101.

—— (ed.), *The New Oxford Companion to Literature in French* (Oxford: Clarendon Press, 1995).

—— and ST CLAIR, WILLIAM (eds.), *Mapping Lives: The Uses of Biography* (Oxford: Oxford University Press, 2002).

FREDETTE, NATHALIE, *Figures baroques de Jean Genet* (Montreal: XYZ; Saint-Denis: Presses universitaires de Vincennes, 2001).

FUMAROLI, MARC, 'Des "Vies" à la biographie: le crépuscule du Parnasse', *Diogène*, 139 (1987), pp. 31–52.

—— (ed.), *Histoire de la rhétorique dans l'Europe moderne, 1450–1950* (Paris: Presses universitaires de France, 1999).

GALETTI, MARINA, 'Secret et sacré chez Leiris et Bataille', in Marmande (ed.), *Bataille–Leiris* [1999], pp. 126–36.

GAUCHER, ÉLISABETH, and DUFOURNET, JEAN (eds.), *L'Hagiographie = Revue des sciences humaines*, 251 (1998) [special issue].

GAUNT, SIMON, and KAY, SARAH, *The Troubadours: An Introduction* (Cambridge: Cambridge University Press, 1999).

GAUTIER, THÉOPHILE, *Mademoiselle de Maupin* [1835], ed. Michel Crouzet (Collection Folio; Paris: Gallimard, 1973). [Trans. with introduction Joanna Richardson, *Mademoiselle de Maupin* (Harmondsworth: Penguin, 1981).]

_____ *Les Grotesques* [1844], ed. Cecilia Rizza (Fasano: Schena, 1985).

_____ *Portraits contemporains: littérateurs, peintres, sculpteurs, artistes dramatiques* (Paris: Charpentier, 1874).

GEFEN, ALEXANDRE, 'Vies imaginaires: le récit biographique comme genre littéraire aux xixe et xxe siècles', doctoral thesis (Université de Paris IV-Sorbonne, 2003).

GENET, JEAN, *Notre-Dame-des-Fleurs* (1944; Collection Folio; Paris: Gallimard, 1976).

_____ *Miracle de la rose* [1946], 4th edn. (Décines: M. Barbezat, L'Arbalète, 1993). [Trans. Bernard Frechtman, *Miracle of The Rose* (London: Blond, 1965).]

_____ *Journal du voleur* (1948; Collection Folio; Paris: Gallimard, 1982). [Trans. Bernard Frechtman, *The Thief's Journal* (London: Blond, 1965).]

_____ *Pompes funèbres* (n.p., 1948).

_____ *Un chant d'amour* [1950], in *Gay Classics: Un chant d'amour; Looking for Langston; Flames of Passion* (VHS videocassette, Connoisseur Video CR 052, London, 1992).

_____ 'Ce qui est resté d'un Rembrandt déchiré en petits carrés bien réguliers et foutu aux chiottes', in id., *OC*, iv (Paris: Gallimard, 1968), pp. 19–31.

_____ 'L'Atelier d'Alberto Giacometti', in id., *OC*, v (Paris: Gallimard, 1979), pp. 39–73.

_____ 'L'Enfant criminel', in id., *OC* v, pp. 377–93.

_____ 'Le Funambule', in id., *OC* v, pp. 8–27.

_____ 'Le Secret de Rembrandt', in id., *OC* v, pp. 29–37.

_____ *L'Ennemi déclaré: textes et entretiens*, in id., *Œuvres complètes*, vol. vi (Paris: Gallimard, 1991).

GENETTE, GÉRARD, *Figures II* (Collection Points; Paris: Éditions du Seuil, 1969).

_____ *Figures III* (Paris: Éditions du Seuil, 1972).

_____ *Fiction et diction* (Paris: Éditions du Seuil, 1991).

GIDE, ANDRÉ, *Corydon* (Paris: Gallimard, 1925). [Trans. P. B., *Corydon: Four Socratic Dialogues* (London: Secker & Warburg, 1952).]

_____ *Si le grain ne meurt* (1926; Collection Folio; Paris: Gallimard, 1972). [Trans. Dorothy Bussy, *If It Die* (London: Vintage, 2002).]

_____ *Journal*, new edn., vol. i: *1887–1925*, ed. Éric Marty; vol. ii: *1926–1950*, ed. Martine Sagaert. [Trans. Justin O'Brien, *The Journals of André Gide*, 4 vols. (London: Secker & Warburg, 1947–51).]

_____ *Romans, récits et soties: œuvres lyriques*, ed. Yvonne Davet and Jean-Jacques Thierry (Bibliothèque de la Pléiade; Paris: Gallimard, 1958).

_____ *Paludes* [1895], in id., *Romans, récits et soties*. [Trans. George D. Painter, *Marshlands*, in *Marshlands; and Prometheous Misbound: Two Satires* (London: Secker & Warburg, 1953).]

_____ *Les Faux-monnayeurs* [1926], in id., *Romans, récits et soties*. [Trans. Dorothy Bussy, *The Counterfeiters* (Harmondsworth: Penguin, 1987)].

_____ *Essais critiques*, ed. Pierre Masson (Bibliothèque de la Pléiade; Paris, Gallimard, 1999).

_____ *Dostoïevski*, in id., *Essais critiques*. [Trans. Arnold Bennett, *Dostoevsky* (Harmondsworth: Penguin, 1967).]

GIDE, ANDRÉ, 'Lettres à Angèle', in *Prétextes*, in id., *Essais critiques*, pp. 8–112.

GILL, MIRANDA, 'Eccentricity and Cultural Imagination in Nineteenth-Century France', D.Phil. thesis (University of Oxford, 2004).

—— 'Sketching Social Marginality in Nineteenth-Century France: Jules Vallès and his Contemporaries', *Modern Language Review*, 101 (2006), pp. 375–87.

GILMAN, MARGARET, *The Idea of Poetry in France: From Houdar de La Motte to Baudelaire* (Cambridge, Mass.: Harvard University Press, 1958).

GOEBEL-SCHILLING, GERHARD, *La Littérature entre l'engagement et le jeu: pour une histoire de la notion de littérature* (Marburg: Hitzeroth, 1988).

GOODDEN, ANGELICA, *The Backward Look: Memory and the Writing Self in France, 1580–1920* (Oxford: Legenda, 2000).

GOUDEMARE, SYLVAIN, *Marcel Schwob ou les vies imaginaires: biographie* (Paris: Cherche midi, 2000).

GOULD, WARWICK, and STALEY, THOMAS F. (eds.), *Writing the Lives of Writers* (Basingstoke: Macmillan/Centre for English Studies, School of Advanced Study, University of London, 1998).

GOULEMOT, JEAN MARIE, and OSTER, DANIEL, *Gens de lettres, écrivains et bohèmes: l'imaginaire littéraire, 1630–1900* (Paris: Minerve, 1992).

GOULET, ALAIN (ed.), *Le Littéraire: qu'est-ce que c'est?* (Caen: Presses universitaires de Caen, 2002).

GOURMONT, RÉMY DE, *Le Livre des masques: portraits symbolistes, gloses et documents sur les écrivains d'hier et d'aujourd'hui*, 3rd edn., 2 vols. (Paris: Mercure de France, 1896–8). [*An Anthology of French Symbolist & Decadent Writing Based upon 'The Book of Masks' by Rémy de Gourmont*, texts selected and trans. Andrew Mangravite, illustrations by Felix Vallotton, additional trans. Iain White et al. (London: Atlas Press, 1994).]

Le Grand Homme = Romantisme, 100 (1998) [special issue].

GREIMAS, A.-J., *Sémantique structurale: recherche de méthode* (Paris: Larousse, 1972).

GUYAUX, ANDRÉ, and MARCHAL, SOPHIE (eds.), *La Vie romantique: hommage à Loïc Chotard: actes du colloque, Paris, Musée de la vie romantique et Université de Paris-Sorbonne, 2 et 3 juin 2000* (Paris: Presses de l'Université de Paris-Sorbonne, 2003).

HALPERN, JOSEPH, *Critical Fictions: The Literary Criticism of Jean-Paul Sartre* (New Haven: Yale University Press, 1976).

HAMPTON, TIMOTHY, *Writing from History: The Rhetoric of Exemplarity in Renaissance Literature* (Ithaca, NY, and London: Cornell University Press, 1990).

HAND, SEÁN, *Alter Ego: The Critical Writings of Michel Leiris* (Oxford: Legenda, 2004).

HANRAHAN, MAIRÉAD, *Lire Genet: une poétique de la différence* (Montreal: Presses de l'Université de Montréal, 1997).

HAYMAN, RONALD, *Writing Against: A Biography of Sartre* (London: Weidenfeld & Nicolson, 1986).

HEIDEGGER, MARTIN 'The Origin of the Work of Art', extract in Singer and Dunn (eds.), *Literary Aesthetics: A Reader* [2000], pp. 122–7.

HEINICH, NATHALIE, *Du peintre à l'artiste: artisans et académiciens à l'âge classique* (Paris: Éditions de Minuit, 1993).

—— *Être écrivain: création et identité* (Paris: La Découverte, 2000).

HENRY, ANNE, *Marcel Proust: théories pour une esthétique* (Paris: Klincksieck, 1981).

HESIOD, *Works and Days*, trans. S. Butler (London: J. H. Mason, 1923).

HIDDLESTON, J. A., *Baudelaire and the Art of Memory* (Oxford: Clarendon Press, 1999).

HOEFER, JOHANN CHRISTIAN FERDINAND (ed.), *Nouvelle Biographie générale: depuis les temps les plus reculés jusqu'à nos jours, avec les renseignements bibliographiques et l'indication des sources à consulter*, 46 vols. (Paris: Firmin-Didot, 1852–66).

HÖLDERLIN, FRIEDRICH, *Selected Poems and Fragments*, trans. Michael Hamburger (Harmondsworth: Penguin, 1998).

HOLLIER, DENIS (ed.), *Le Collège de sociologie* (Paris: Gallimard, 1979).

HOUSSAYE, ARSÈNE, *Galerie de portraits du XVIIIᵉ siècle*, 4th edn. (Paris: Charpentier, 1848).

HOVEN, ADRIAN VAN DEN, ' "Some of These Days" ', *Sartre Studies International*, 6/2 (2000), pp. 1–11.

HOWELLS, BERNARD, *Baudelaire: Individualism, Dandyism and the Philosophy of History* (Oxford: Legenda, 1996).

HOWELLS, CHRISTINA, *Sartre's Theory of Literature* (London: Modern Humanities Research Association, 1979).

—— 'Sartre's Existentialist Biographies: Search for a Method', in France and St Clair (eds.), *Mapping Lives* [2002], pp. 267–82.

HUBERT, MARIE-CLAUDE, *L'Esthétique de Jean Genet* (Liège: SEDES, 1997).

HUGO, VICTOR, *Correspondance*, 2 vols. (Paris: Calmann Lévy, 1896–8).

—— *Les Contemplations* [1856], ed. Léon Cellier (Classiques Garnier; Paris: Garnier 1969). [Trans. E. H. and A. M. Blackmore, *Selected Poems of Victor Hugo: A Bilingual Edition* (London: University of Chicago Press, 2001.]

—— *Œuvres poétiques*, ed. Pierre Albouy, 3 vols. (Bibliothèque de la Pléiade; Paris: Gallimard, 1964–74).

—— *Les Feuilles d'automne* [1831], in id., *Oeuvres poétiques*, vol. i (1964). [Trans. E. H. and A. M. Blackmore, *Selected Poems of Victor Hugo* 2001.]

—— *Œuvres complètes*, vol. xiii: *Critique*, ed. Anne Ubersfeld et al. (Bouquins; Paris: R. Laffont, 1985).

—— *Préface de Cromwell* [1827], in id., *OC* xiii: *Critique*.

—— 'Préface à mes œuvres et post-scriptum de ma vie' [1864], in id., *OC* xiii: *Critique*.

—— *Proses philosophiques de 1860–1865*, in id., *OC* xiii: *Critique*.

—— *William Shakespeare* [1864], in id., *OC* xiii: *Critique*.

HYTIER, JEAN, 'Le Roman de l'individu et la biographie', *Cahiers de l'Association internationale des études françaises*, 19 (1967), pp. 88–100.

IDT, GENEVIÈVE, 'L'Autoparodie dans *Les Mots* de Sartre', *Cahiers du vingtième siècle*, 6 (1976), pp. 53–86.

—— '*Les Mots*': une autocritique en bel écrit* (Paris: Belin, 2001).

Ignatius of Loyola, Saint, *The Spiritual Exercises of St. Ignatius*, ed. Thomas Corbishley (London: Burns & Oates, 1963).

ILLOUZ, JEAN-NICOLAS, *Nerval, le 'rêveur en prose': imaginaire et écriture* (Paris: Presses universitaires de France, 1997).

IONESCO, EUGÈNE, *Hugoliade*, trans. Dragomir Costineanu (Paris: Gallimard, 1982).

IRESON, J. C., *Victor Hugo* (Oxford: Clarendon Press, 1997).

JACOB, MAX, *Conseils à un jeune poète, suivis de Conseils à un étudiant* (Paris: Gallimard, 1945).

JAFFE, KINERET S., 'The Concept of Genius: Its Changing Role in Eighteenth-Century French Aesthetics', *Journal of the History of Ideas*, 41 (1980), pp. 579–99.

JAKOBSON, ROMAN, 'La Nouvelle poésie russe' [1921], in *Questions de poétique*, ed. Tzvetan Todorov (Paris: Éditions du Seuil, 1973), pp. 11–24.

JAMES, HENRY, *Literary Reviews and Essays: On American, English, and French Literature*, ed. Albert Mordell (New York: Grove Press, 1957).

JEANNERET, MICHEL, 'Nerval et la biographie impossible', *French Studies*, 24 (1970), pp. 127–44.

_____ *La Lettre perdue: écriture et folie dans l'œuvre de Nerval* (Paris: Flammarion, 1978).

JEFFERSON, ANN, 'Autobiography as Intertext: Barthes, Sarraute, Robbe-Grillet', in Michael Worton and Judith Still (eds.), *Intertextuality: Theories and Practice* (Manchester: Manchester University Press, 1990), pp. 108–29.

_____ 'Literature, Dominance and Violence in Formalist Aesthetics', in Peter Collier and Helga Geyer-Ryan (eds.), *Literary Theory Today* (Cambridge: Polity Press, 1990), pp. 125–41.

_____ 'The Hagiographies of Pierre Michon: *Rimbaud le fils*', *French Studies*, 58 (2004), pp. 205–17.

JOHNSON, BARBARA, *Défigurations du langage poétique: la seconde révolution baudelairienne* (Paris: Flammarion, 1979).

JONES, DAVID HOUSTON, *The Body Abject: Self and Text in Jean Genet and Samuel Beckett* (Oxford: Peter Lang, 2000).

JOURNET, RENÉ, and ROBERT, GUY, *Notes sur 'Les Contemplations', suivies d'un index* (Paris: Belles Lettres, 1958).

JUTRIN, MONIQUE, *Marcel Schwob, 'Cœur double'* (Lausanne: Éditions de l'Aire, 1982).

KANT, IMMANUEL, *The Critique of Judgement* [1790], trans. Werner S. Pluhar (Indianapolis: Hackett, 1987).

KAY, SARAH, CAVE, TERENCE, and BOWIE, MALCOLM, *A Short History of French Literature* (Oxford: Oxford University Press, 2003).

KEIM, ALBERT, and LUMET, LOUIS, *Victor Hugo* (Les Grands Hommes; Paris: Pierre Lafitte, 1913).

KNIGHT, DIANA, 'Vaines pensées: la Vita Nova de Barthes', in Claude Coste (ed.), *Sur Barthes = Revue des sciences humaines*, 268 (2002) [special issue], pp. 93–107.

KÖPKE, WULF, *Johann Gottfried Herder* (Boston: Twayne, 1987).

KRIS, ERNST, and KURZ, OTTO, *Legend, Myth, and Magic in the Image of the Artist: A Historical Experiment* [1934], trans. Alastair Laing, rev. Lottie M. Newman (New Haven and London: Yale University Press, 1979).

KRISTEVA, JULIA, *Pouvoirs de l'horreur: essai sur l'abjection* (Collection Points; Paris: Éditions du Seuil, 1983).

LA BRUYÈRE, JEAN DE, *Les Caractères*, ed. Gaston Cayrou (La Littérature française illustrée: collection moderne de classiques; Paris: H. Didier, 1926). [Trans. Henri van Laun, with introduction by Denys C. Potts, *Characters* (London: Oxford University Press, 1963).]

LA HARPE, JEAN-FRANÇOIS DE, *Lycée, ou, Cours de littérature ancienne et moderne* [1799–1805], 14 vols. (Paris: Depelafol, 1825).

LACOUE-LABARTHE, PHILIPPE, and NANCY, JEAN-LUC, *L'Absolu littéraire* (Paris: Éditions du Seuil, 1987).

LAMARTINE, ALPHONSE DE, *Méditations poétiques* [1820], ed. Gustave Lanson (1915; repr. Geneva: Slatkine, 2000).

LANSON, GUSTAVE, *Boileau* (Les Grands Écrivains français; Paris: Hachette, 1892).

_____ *Essais de méthode, de critique et d'histoire littéraire*, ed. Henri Peyre (Paris: Hachette, 1965).

LAPORTE, ROGER, 'Bio-graphie', *Critique*, 281 (1970), pp. 813–20.

_____ *Quinze variations sur un thème biographique: essais* (Paris: Flammarion, 1975).

_____ 'Entretien entre Mathieu Bénézet, Roger Laporte et Jean Ristat', in *Roger Laporte = Digraphe*, 18–19 (1979) [special issue], pp. 121–55.

_____ *Une vie: biographie* (Paris: P.O.L., 1986).

_____ *Fugue* [1970], in *Une vie*.

_____ *Supplément* [1973], in *Une vie*.

_____ *Fugue 3* [1976], in *Une vie*.

_____ *Suite* [1979], in *Une vie*.

_____ *Moriendo* [1983], in *Une vie*.

_____ *Codicille* [1986], in *Une vie*.

_____ *Entre deux mondes* (Montpellier: Gris Banal, 1988).

_____ *Lettre à personne*, with foreword by Maurice Blanchot and afterword by Philippe Lacoue-Labarthe (Paris: Plon, 1989).

_____ et al., *Autour de Roger Laporte: textes et entretien* (Nîmes: Terriers, 1980).

LAVIALLE, NATHALIE, and PUECH, JEAN-BENOÎT (eds.), *L'Auteur comme œuvre (l'auteur, ses masques, son personnage, sa légende)* (Orléans: Presses universitaires d'Orléans, 2000).

LECARME, JACQUES, 'Sartre palimpseste', in Contat (ed.), *Pourquoi et comment Sartre a écrit 'Les Mots'* [1996], pp. 183–248.

_____ 'Table des allusions et des concordances intertextuelles dans *Les Mots*', in Contat (ed.), *Pourquoi et comment Sartre a écrit 'Les Mots'* [1996], pp. 249–91.

LECLERC-OLIVE, MICHÈLE, *Le Dire de l'événement (biographique)* (Villeneuve d'Ascq: Presses universitaires du Septentrion, 1997).

LECONTE DE LISLE, CHARLES-MARIE, *Poèmes antiques* (Paris: M. Ducloux, 1852).

LEE, HERMIONE, *Body Parts: Essays in Life-Writing* (London: Chatto & Windus, 2005).

LEFKOWITZ, MARY R., *The Lives of the Greek Poets* (London: Duckworth, 1981).

LEHMANN, A. G., *Sainte-Beuve: A Portrait of the Critic, 1804–1842* (Oxford: Clarendon Press, 1962).

LEIRIS, MICHEL, *L'Âge d'homme, précédé de: De la littérature considérée comme une tauromachie* (1946; Paris: Gallimard, 1964). [Trans. Richard Howard, *Manhood, Preceded by The Autobiographer as Torero* (London: Jonathan Cape, 1968).]

_____ *Brisées* (Paris: Mercure de France, 1966).

_____ *La Règle du jeu*, ed. Denis Hollier et al. (Bibliothèque de la Pléiade; Paris: Gallimard, 2003).

_____ 'Le Sacré dans la vie quotidienne' [1938], in id., *La Règle du jeu*, pp. 1110–18.

_____ *Biffures* [1948], in id., *La Règle du jeu*. [Trans. Lydia Davis, *Scratches* (New York: Paragon House, 1991).]

_____ *Fourbis* [1955], in id., *La Règle du jeu*. [Trans. Lydia Davis, *Scraps* (Baltimore: Johns Hopkins University Press, 1997).]

_____ *Fibrilles* [1966], in id., *La Règle du jeu*.

_____ *Frêle bruit* [1976], in id., *La Règle du jeu*.

LEIRIS, MICHEL, Notes pour 'Le Sacré dans la vie quotidienne' ou 'L'Homme sans honneur' [1994], in id., *La Règle du jeu*, pp. 1119–54.

LEJEUNE, PHILIPPE, *L'Ombre et la lumière dans les 'Contemplations' de Victor Hugo* (Archives des lettres modernes; Paris: Lettres modernes, 1968).

—— *Le Pacte autobiographique* (Paris: Éditions du Seuil, 1975).

—— *Lire Leiris: autobiographie et langage* (Paris: Klincksieck, 1975).

—— 'Biographie, témoignage, autobiographie: le cas de *Victor Hugo raconté*', in id., *Je est un autre: l'autobiographie de la littérature aux médias* (Paris: Éditions du Seuil, 1980), pp. 60–102.

—— 'Où s'arrête la littérature?', *Raison présente*, 134 (2000), pp. 25–40.

LEPENIES, WOLF, *Sainte-Beuve: au seuil de la modernité*, trans. Bernard Lortholary and Jeanne Étoré (Paris: Gallimard, 2002).

LEVI, GIOVANNI, 'Les Usages de la biographie', *Annales ESC*, 9 (1989), pp. 1325–36.

LIATOUTZOS, CHANTAL, and POULOUIN, CLAUDINE, 'La Lecture des "vieux romans" selon Chapelain, fondatrice de l'espace littéraire moderne?', in Goulet (ed.), *Le Littéraire, qu'est-ce que c'est?* [2002], pp. 29–43.

LIMAYRAC, PAULIN, 'Gérard de Nerval', *La Presse*, 31 July 1853, pp. 1–2.

LONGINUS, 'On Sublimity', in Russell and Winterbottom (eds.), *Ancient Literary Criticism* [1972], pp. 460–503.

LOUICHON, BRIGITTE, and ROGER, Jérôme (eds.), *L'Auteur entre biographie et mythographie* (Modernités, 18; Bordeaux: Presses universitaires de Bordeaux, 2002).

LUCEY, MICHAEL, *Gide's Bent: Sexuality, Politics, Writing, Ideologies of Desire* (New York: Oxford University Press, 1995).

LUKÁCS, GEORG, 'The Biographical Form and its "Problematic"', in id., *The Historical Novel*, trans. Hannah and Stanley Mitchell (Harmondsworth: Peregrine, 1981), pp. 362–88.

LUNN-ROCKLIFFE, KATHERINE, 'Death and the Aesthetic of Continuity: Reading Victor Hugo's *Les Contemplations*', paper given at 'Birth and Death': 3rd Annual Conference of the Society of Dix-Neuviémistes, Queen's University, Belfast, March–April 2005.

LYONS, JOHN D., *Exemplum: The Rhetoric of Example in Early Modern France and Italy* (Princeton: Princeton University Press, 1989).

MACDONALD, KATHERINE M., 'Literary Biography in Renaissance France: 1524–1619', D.Phil. thesis (University of Oxford, 2000).

—— 'The Presence of Plutarch in the Preface to the Reader of Cruserius' Latin Translation of the Lives (1561)', *Bibliothèque d'humanisme et renaissance*, 62 (2000), pp. 129–34.

—— 'Selling Lives: Bernado di Giunta (*fl.* 1518–50), Imitation and the Utility of Intellectual Biography', *Renaissance and Reformation/Renaissance et réforme*, 25/3 (2001), pp. 5–24.

MACÉ, MARIELLE (ed.), *Le Genre littéraire* (Paris: Flammarion, 2004).

MACINTYRE, ALASDAIR C., *After Virtue: A Study in Moral Theory*, 2nd edn. (London: Duckworth, 1985).

MACLACHLAN, IAN, *Roger Laporte: The Orphic Text* (Oxford: Legenda, 2000).

MCLAUGHLIN, MARTIN, 'Biography and Autobiography in the Italian Renaissance', in France and St Clair (eds.), *Mapping Lives* [2002], pp. 37–65.

MADELÉNAT, DANIEL, *La Biographie* (Paris: Presses universitaires de France, 1984).

_____ '1918–1998: deux âges d'or de la biographie?' in *La Biographie, modes et méthodes: actes du deuxième colloque international Guy de Pourtalès, Université de Bâle, 12–14 février 1998*, ed. Robert Kopp, Regina Bollhalder Mayer, and Catherine Gautschi-Lanz (Paris: Champion; Etoy: Fondation Guy de Pourtalès, 2001), pp. 89–104.

Maïllis, Annie, *Michel Leiris: l'écrivain matador* (Paris: L'Harmattan, 1998).

Majewski, Henry F., *Paradigm & Parody: Images of Creativity in French Romanticism: Vigny, Hugo, Balzac, Gautier, Musset* (Charlottesville: University Press of Virginia, 1989).

Mallarmé, Stéphane, *Villiers de l'Isle-Adam* [1890], ed. A. W. Raitt (Exeter: University of Exeter Press, 1991). [Trans. with introduction by Bradford Cook, *Selected Prose Poems, Essays, & Letters* (Baltimore: Johns Hopkins University Press, 1956).]

_____ *Œuvres complètes*, ed. Bertrand Marchal, 2 vols. (Bibliothèque de la Pléiade; Paris: Gallimard, 1998–2003).

_____ *Poésies* [1899], in *OC* i. [Trans. with commentary by Henry Weinfield, *Collected Poems* (Berkeley and London: University of California Press, 1994).]

_____ 'Crise de vers', in *OC* ii, pp. 204–23.

_____ *Quelques médaillons et portraits en pied* [1897], in *OC* ii.

_____ *Correspondance, 1862–1871*, ed. Henri Mondor (Bibliothèque de la Pléiade; Paris: Gallimard, 1959).

Marchal, Bertrand, *La Religion de Mallarmé: poésie, mythologie et religion* (Paris: J. Corti, 1988).

_____ 'Villiers relu par Mallarmé: le poète et la divinité', in *Villiers de l'Isle-Adam: cent ans après (1889–1989): actes du colloque international organisé en Sorbonne les 26 et 27 mai 1989*, ed. Michel Crouzet and Alan Raitt (Paris: SEDES, 1990), pp. 41–9.

Marcus, Laura, 'The Newness of the "New Biography": Biographical Theory and Practice in the Early Twentieth Century', in France and St Clair (eds.), *Mapping Lives* [2002], pp. 193–218.

Marino, Adrian, *The Biography of 'The Idea of Literature' from Antiquity to the Baroque* (SUNY Series in the Margins of Literature; Albany: State University of New York Press, 1996).

Marmande, Francis (ed.), *Bataille–Leiris: l'intenable assentiment au monde* (Paris: Belin, 1999).

Marmontel, Jean-François, *Eléments de littérature* [1787], 3 vols. (Paris: Firmin-Didot, 1879).

_____ 'Littérature', in id., *Œuvres* (Paris: Amable Costes, 1819).

Marson, Susan, 'The Empty Crypt: Autobiographical Identity in Genet's *Journal du voleur*', *Romance Studies*, 19 (2001), pp. 29–39.

Martin, Jacques (ed.), *Analyses et réflexions sur 'Les Contemplations' (livres IV et V) de Victor Hugo: la vie et la mort* (Paris: Édition Marketing, 1982).

Martin-Chauffier, Louis, 'Biographies', *Nouvelle Revue française*, 174 (1928), pp. 393–7.

Martinoir, Francine de, 'Vie privée et vie publique dans *Les Contemplations*', in Martin (ed.), *Analyses et réflexions* [1982], pp. 108–18.

Mason, John Hope, *The Value of Creativity: The Origins and Emergence of a Modern Belief* (Aldershot: Ashgate, 2003).

MATORÉ, GEORGES, and GREIMAS, A.-G., 'La Naissance du "génie" au XVIIIᵉ siècle: étude lexicologique', *Le Français moderne*, 25 (1957), pp. 256–72.

MAUBON, CATHERINE, *Michel Leiris: en marge de l'autobiographie* (Paris: J. Corti, 1994).

——— *Catherine Maubon présente L'Âge d'homme de Michel Leiris* (Foliothèque; Paris: Flammarion, 1997).

——— 'Leiris, Bataille et Sartre: poésie et engagement, 1939–1950', *Europe*, 847–8 (1999), pp. 93–107.

MAURIAC, FRANÇOIS, *La Vie de Jean Racine* (Le Roman des grandes existences; Paris: Plon, 1928).

MAUROIS, ANDRÉ, *Ariel, ou la vie de Shelley* (1923; Paris: Calmann-Lévy, 1939).

——— '*La Vie de Franz Liszt*, par Guy de Pourtalès', *Nouvelle Revue française*, 154 (1926), pp. 104–5.

——— *Aspects de la biographie* (Paris: Au Sans Pareil, 1928). [Trans. S. C. Roberts, *Aspects of Biography* (Cambridge: Cambridge University Press, 1929).]

——— *À la recherche de Marcel Proust* (1949; Geneva: Édito-Service, 1976).

MAY, GEORGES, ' "Sa vie, son œuvre": réflexions sur la biographie littéraire', *Diogène*, 139 (1987), pp. 31–52.

MAYER, THOMAS F., and WOOLF, D. R. (eds.), *The Rhetorics of Life-Writing in Early Modern Europe: Forms of Biography from Cassandra Fedele to Louis XIV* (Ann Arbor: University of Michigan Press, 1995).

MEHLMAN, JEFFREY, *A Structural Study of Autobiography: Proust, Leiris, Sartre, Lévi-Strauss* (Ithaca, NY: Cornell University Press, 1974).

MEITENGER, SERGE, 'L'Irréel de la jouissance dans le *Journal du voleur* de Genet', *Littérature*, 62 (1986), pp. 85–74.

MERCIER, LOUIS-SÉBASTIEN, *Le Génie, le goût et l'esprit: poëme, en quatre chants, dédié a M. le Duc de* **** (The Hague, 1756).

——— *De la littérature et des littérateurs: suivi d'un nouvel examen de la tragédie françoise* (Yverdon, 1778).

MICHAUD, JOSEPH-FRANÇOIS, and MICHAUD, LOUIS-GABRIEL (eds.), *Biographie universelle, ancienne et moderne, ou, Histoire, par ordre alphabétique, de la vie publique et privée de tous les hommes qui se sont fait remarquer par leurs écrits, leurs actions, leurs talents, leurs vertus ou leurs crimes: ouvrage entièrement neuf, rédigé par une société de gens de lettres et de savants*, 52 vols. (Paris: Michaud, 1811–28); 'Partie mythologique', 3 vols. (1832–3); suppl., 33 vols. (1834–62).

MICHAUD, LOUIS-GABRIEL (ed.), *Biographie des hommes vivants: ou, Histoire par ordre alphabétique de la vie publique de tous les hommes qui se sont fait remarquer par leurs actions ou leurs écrits* (Paris: L. G. Michaud, 1816).

——— *Biographie universelle*, rev. edn., 45 vols. (Paris: Mme C. Desplaces, 1843–65).

MICHELET, JULES, 'Examen des *Vies des hommes illustres*' [1819], in Plutarque, *Les Vies parallèles*, trans. Robert Flacelière and Émile Chambry, ed. Jean Sirinelli (Bouquins; Paris: Robert Laffont, 2001), pp. lxix–lxxxiv.

MICHON, PIERRE, *Vies minuscules* (Paris: Gallimard, 1984). [Trans. Ann Jefferson, *Microscopic Lives*: 'The Life of André Dufourneau', *Common Knowledge*, 10 (2004), pp. 170–80.]

——— *Vie de Joseph Roulin* (Lagrasse: Verdier, 1988).

——— *Rimbaud le fils* (Paris: Gallimard, 1991).

_____ 'Entretien avec Thierry Guichard', *Le Matricule des anges*, 5 (1993), p. xxx.

_____ 'Pierre Michon, Arlette Farge, entretien', *Cahiers de la Villa Gillet*, 3 (1995), pp. 151–64.

_____ 'Entretien avec Pierre Michon: propos recueillis par Jean-Christophe Millois', *Prétexte*, 9 (1996), pp. 58–62.

_____ *Le Roi du bois* (Lagrasse: Verdier, 1996).

_____ *Mythologies d'hiver* (Lagrasse: Verdier, 1997).

_____ 'Pierre Michon, une vocation tardive', interview with Marianne Payot, *Lire*, May 1997 <http://www.lire.fr/portrait.asp/idC=32578/idTC=5/idR=201/idG=3>, accessed 1 Mar. 2006.

_____ *Trois auteurs: Balzac, Cingria, Faulkner* (Lagrasse: Verdier, 1997).

_____ 'Deux chapitres des *Onze*', *Scherzo*, 5 (1998), pp. 13–30.

_____ 'Entretien avec Catherine Argand', *Lire*, 271 (1998), pp. 32–40.

_____ 'Entretien avec Pierre Michon: propos recueillis par Anne Sophie Perlat et Franz Johansson', *Scherzo*, 5 (1998), pp. 5–12.

_____ *Abbés* (Lagrasse: Verdier, 2002).

_____ *Corps du roi* (Lagrasse: Verdier, 2002).

MILLOT, CATHERINE, *La Vocation de l'écrivain* (Paris: Gallimard, 1991).

MINTZ, ALAN L., *George Eliot and the Novel of Vocation* (Cambridge, Mass.: Harvard University Press, 1978).

MIRECOURT, EUGÈNE DE, *Les Contemporains* (Paris, 1854–   ).

_____ *Balzac* (Les Contemporains; Paris: J.-P. Roret, 1854).

_____ *Gérard de Nerval* (Les Contemporains; Paris: J.-P. Roret, 1854).

_____ *Méry* (Les Contemporains; Paris: F. Sartorius and J.-P. Roret, 1854).

_____ *Alfred de Vigny* (Les Contemporains; Paris: Gustave Havard, 1855).

_____ *Histoire contemporaine: portraits et silhouettes au XIXe siècle*, 4 vols. (Paris: Dentu, 1867).

MOLHO, RAPHAËL (ed.), *La Critique littéraire en France au XIXe siècle* (Paris: Buchet/Chastel, 1963).

MONTAIGNE, MICHEL DE, *Les Essais*, ed. Verdun L. Saulnier and Pierre Villey, 3 vols. (Paris: Quadrige/Presses universitaires de France, 1988). [Trans. with introduction and notes M. A. Screech, *The Complete Essays* (London: Penguin, 2003).]

MORALY, JEAN-BERNARD, *Jean Genet: la vie écrite* (Paris: Éditions de la Différence, 1988).

MOREAU, PIERRE, *Les Contemplations: ou le temps retrouvé* (Paris: Lettres modernes, 1962).

MOSLEY, JOANNE, 'A New Dating of "biographie": An Early Example', *French Studies Bulletin*, 37 (1990–1), pp. 3–5.

MOSSOP, D. J., *Baudelaire's Tragic Hero: A Study of the Architecture of 'Les Fleurs du mal'* (Oxford: Clarendon Press, 1961).

NABOKOV, VLADIMIR VLADIMIROVICH, *The Gift* [1952], trans. Michael Scammell (London: Panther, 1963).

NASH, SUZANNE, *Les Contemplations of Victor Hugo: An Allegory of the Creative Process* (Princeton: Princeton University Press, 1976).

NERVAL, GÉRARD DE, *Œuvres complètes*, ed. Jean Guillaume and Claude Pichois, 3 vols. (Bibliothèque de la Pléiade; Paris: Gallimard, 1984–93).

_____ *Les Faux Saulniers* [1850], in *OC* ii (1984).

_____ *Les Illuminés* [1852], in *OC* ii (1984).

NERVAL, GÉRARD DE, *Les Filles du feu* [1854], in *OC* iii (1993). [Trans. Richard Sieburth, in Gérard de Nerval, *Selected Writings* (London: Penguin, 1999).]

NICÉRON, JEAN-PIERRE, *Mémoires pour servir à l'histoire des hommes illustres dans la république des lettres, avec un catalogue raisonné de leurs ouvrages* (Paris: 1727; repr. Geneva: Slatkine, 1971).

NODIER, CHARLES, *Bibliographie des fous: de quelques livres excentriques* (Paris: Techener, 1835).

——— 'Discours préliminaire', in L.-G. Michaud (ed.) *Biographie universelle*, rev. edn. [1843], pp. v–x.

OSTER, DANIEL, *Passages de Zénon: essai sur l'espace et les croyances littéraires* (Paris: Éditions du Seuil, 1983).

——— *L'Individu littéraire* (Paris: Presses universitaires de France, 1997).

OULIPO, *Atlas de littérature potentielle* (Collection Folio/Essais; Paris: Gallimard, 1981).

PAINTER, GEORGE DUNCAN, *Marcel Proust: A Biography*, 2 vols. (London: Chatto & Windus, 1959).

Paradoxes du biographe, ed. Dominique Viart = *Revue des sciences humaines*, 263 (2001) [special issue].

PARKE, CATHERINE NEAL, *Biography: Writing Lives* (New York and London: Routledge, 2002).

PASK, KEVIN, *The Emergence of the English Author: Scripting the Life of the Poet in Early Modern England* (Cambridge: Cambridge University Press, 1996).

PAULHAN, JEAN, *Les Fleurs de Tarbes, ou la Terreur dans les lettres* (Paris: Gallimard, 1941).

PENEFF, JEAN, *La Méthode biographique* (Paris: Armand Colin, 1990).

PERRAULT, CHARLES, et al., *Les Hommes illustres qui ont paru en France pendant ce siècle: avec leurs portraits au naturel*, 2 vols. (Paris: Antoine Dezallier, 1696–1700).

PETIT, JACQUES, *Barbey d'Aurevilly, critique* (Paris: Les Belles Lettres, 1963).

PICHOIS, CLAUDE, 'Sainte-Beuve ou l'eau critique', *Revue des sciences humaines*, 135 (1969), pp. 419–27.

——— *Baudelaire: études et témoignages*, rev. edn. (Neuchâtel: Éditions de la Baconnière, 1976).

——— and Brix, Michel, *Gérard de Nerval* (Paris: Fayard, 1995).

——— and Ziegler, Jean, *Charles Baudelaire*, rev. edn. (Paris: Fayard, 1996).

Pierre Michon, l'écriture absolue: actes du colloque Michon de Saint-Étienne (Musée d'Art Moderne, 8, 9, 10 mars 2001), ed. Agnès Castiglione (Saint-Étienne: Publications de l'Université de Saint-Étienne, 2002).

PIERSSENS, MICHEL, 'Le Sens de la "vie" et le nouveau *Grand Dictionnaire universel du XIXe siècle* de Pierre Larousse', *Dix-neuf: Journal of the Society of Dix-Neuviémistes*, 1 (2003), pp. 29–42.

PLUTARCH, *Plutarch's Lives*, ed. Bernadotte Perrin, 11 vols. (Loeb Classical Library; London and Cambridge, Mass.: Harvard University Press, 1914).

——— PLUTARQUE, *Les Vies des hommes illustres*, trans. Jacques Amyot [1559], ed. Gérard Walter, 2 vols. (1951; Bibliothèque de la Pléiade; Paris: Gallimard, 1985). [Jacques Amyot, *The Lives of the Noble Grecians and Romains*, trans. Thomas North et al. (London: Printed by George Miller and are to be sold by Robert Allott at the signe of the black Beare in Pauls Churchyard, 1631).]

POLLARD, PATRICK, *André Gide: Homosexual Moralist* (New Haven and London: Yale University Press, 1991).

POLO DE BEAULIEU, MARIE-ANNE, 'L'Anecdote biographique dans les exempla médiévaux', in *Problèmes et méthodes de la biographie*, pp. 13–22.

POULET, GEORGES, *La Distance intérieure* (Paris: Plon, 1952). [Trans. Elliott Coleman, *The Interior Distance* (Baltimore: University of Michigan Press, 1959).]

—— 'La Pensée critique de Mme de Staël', *Preuves*, 196 (1966), pp. 27–35.

—— 'Madame de Staël', in id., *La Conscience critique* (Paris: J. Corti, 1971), pp. 15–25.

—— 'Criticism and the Experience of Interiority', in Richard Macksey and Eugenio Donato (eds.), *The Structuralist Controversy: The Languages of Criticism and the Sciences of Man* (Baltimore: Johns Hopkins University Press, 1972), pp. 56–88.

PRATT, MARY LOUISE, *Toward a Speech Act Theory of Literary Discourse* (Bloomington, Indiana: Indiana University Press, 1977).

PRÉVOST, l'ABBÉ, and DYCHE, THOMAS, *Manuel lexique, ou Dictionnaire portatif des mots françois dont la signification n'est pas familiere a tout le monde: ovrage fort utile a ceux qui ne sont pas versés dans les langues anciennes et modernes, et dans toutes les connoissances qui s'acquierent par l'etude et le travail; pour donner aux mots leur sens juste & exact, dans la lecture, dans le langage & dans le style: recueilli des explications de divers auteurs* (Paris: Chez Didot, 1750).

PRÉVOST, JEAN, *Baudelaire: essai sur la création et l'inspiration poétiques* (Paris: Mercure de France, 1964).

Problèmes et méthodes de la biographie: actes du colloque, Sorbonne, 3–4 mai 1985 (Paris: Publications de la Sorbonne/Histoire au présent, 1985).

PROUST, MARCEL, *À la recherche du temps perdu* [1913–27], ed. Jean-Yves Tadié et al., 4 vols. (Bibliothèque de la Pléiade; Paris: Gallimard, 1987). [Trans. C. K. Scott Moncrieff, Terence Kilmartin, and Andreas Mayor, *Remembrance of Things Past*, 3 vols. (London: Chatto & Windus, 1981).]

—— *Contre Sainte-Beuve; Précédé de, Pastiches et mélanges, et suivi de, Essais et articles*, ed. Pierre Clarac and Yves Sandre (Bibliothèque de la Pléiade; Paris: Gallimard, 1971). [Trans. with introduction and notes John Sturrock, *Against Sainte-Beuve and Other Essays* (London: Penguin, 1988).]

—— *Jean Santeuil; précédé de, Les Plaisirs et les jours* [1952; 1896], ed. Pierre Clarac and Yves Sandre (Bibliothèque de la Pléiade; Paris: Gallimard, 1971). [Trans. Gerard Hopkins with a preface by André Maurois, *Jean Santeuil* (London: Weidenfeld & Nicolson, 1955).]

PUECH, JEAN-BENOÎT, 'Du vivant de l'auteur', in *Le Biographique = Poétique*, 63 (1985) [special issue], pp. 279–300.

—— 'La Création biographique', in Louichon and Roger (eds.), *L'Auteur entre biographie et mythographie* [2002], pp. 45–74.

RABATÉ, DOMINIQUE, 'Vies imaginaires et vies minuscules: Marcel Schwob et le romanesque sans roman', in Berg and Vadé (eds.), *Marcel Schwob, d'hier et d'aujourd'hui* [2002], pp. 177–91.

—— 'Ce qui n'a pas de témoin? Les vies imaginaires dans l'écriture contemporaine', in *Stratégies narratives 2: le roman contemporain: actes du colloque de Gênes 14–15 décembre 2001*, ed. Rosa Galli Pellegrini (Fasano: Schena; Paris: Presses de l'Université de Paris-Sorbonne, 2003), pp. 29–44.

RABATÉ, DOMINIQUE, (ed.), *L'Invention du solitaire* (Modernités, 19; Bordeaux: Presses universitaires de Bordeaux, 2003).

RACAN, HONORAT DE BUEIL, seigneur de, *Vie de Monsieur de Malherbe* [1672], ed. Marie-Françoise Quignard (Paris: Le Promeneur, 1991).

RAMBURES, JEAN-LOUIS DE, *Comment travaillent les écrivains* (Paris: Flammarion, 1978).

RAYMOND, MARCEL, *Jean-Jacques Rousseau: la quête de soi et la rêverie* (Paris: J. Corti, 1962).

Récits d'enfance, ed. Monique Gosselin-Noat = *Revue des sciences humaines*, 222 (1991) [special issue].

REDONNET, MARIE, *Jean Genet, le poète travesti: portrait d'une œuvre* (Paris: Grasset, 1999).

RENAN, ERNEST, *Vie de Jésus* (1863; Histoire des origines du christianisme, 1; Paris: Arléa, 1992). [Trans. as *The Life of Jesus*, (London: Watts & Co., 1935).]

RHODES, S. A., 'Marcel Schwob and the Art of Biography', *Romanic Review*, 25 (1934), pp. 112–17.

RIBARD, DINAH, *Raconter, vivre, penser: histoire(s) de philosophes, 1650–1766* (Paris: Vrin-EHESS, 2003).

RICHARD, JEAN-PIERRE, 'Sainte-Beuve et l'expérience critique', in Georges Poulet (ed.), *Les Chemins actuels de la critique* (Paris: Union génerale d'éditions, 1968), pp. 109–23.

—— 'Sainte-Beuve et l'objet littéraire', in id., *Études sur le romantisme* (Paris: Éditions du Seuil, 1970), pp. 227–83.

—— *L'État des choses: études sur huit écrivains d'aujourd'hui* (Paris: Gallimard, 1990).

—— 'Servitude et grandeur du minuscule', in id., *L'État des choses*, pp. 87–106.

—— 'Pour lire "Rimbaud le fils"', in Bergounioux et al. (eds.), *Compagnies de Pierre Michon* [1993], pp. 117–40.

RIFFATERRE, MICHAEL, 'La Vision hallucinatoire chez Victor Hugo', *Modern Language Notes*, 78 (1963), pp. 225–41.

RILKE, RAINER MARIA, *Letters to a Young Poet* [1929], trans. M. D. Herter Norton (New York and London: W.W. Norton, 1993).

ROBB, GRAHAM, *La Poésie de Baudelaire et la poésie française, 1838–1852* (Paris: Aubier, 1993).

—— *Victor Hugo*, 2nd edn. (London: Picador, 1998).

ROBBE-GRILLET, ALAIN, *Pour un nouveau roman* (Collection Idées; Paris: Gallimard, 1963).

—— *Le Miroir qui revient* (Paris: Éditions de Minuit, 1984).

Roger Laporte = *Digraphe*, 18–19 (1979) [special issue].

ROUBAUD, JACQUES, *Le Grand Incendie de Londres: récit, avec incises et bifurcations, 1985–1987* (Paris: Éditions du Seuil, 1989).

—— *La Boucle* (Paris: Éditions du Seuil, 1993).

—— *Poésie, etcetera: ménage* (Paris: Stock, 1995).

—— *Mathématique: récit* (Paris: Éditions du Seuil, 1997).

—— *Poésie: récit* (Paris: Éditions du Seuil, 2000).

—— *La Bibliothèque de Warburg: version mixte* (Paris: Éditions du Seuil, 2002).

ROUSSEAU, JEAN-JACQUES, *Discours sur l'origine et les fondements de l'inégalité parmi les hommes* [1755], ed. Bertrand de Jouvenal (Collection Idées; Paris: Gallimard, 1965). [Trans. Maurice Cranston, *A Discourse on Inequality* (Harmondsworth: Penguin, 1984).]

—— *Les Confessions* [1782], ed. Jacques Voisine (Classiques Garnier; Paris: Garnier, 1968). [Trans. Angela Scholar, with an introduction by Patrick Coleman, *Confessions* (Oxford: Oxford University Press, 2000).]

_____ *Œuvres complètes*, ed. Bernard Gagnebin and Marcel Raymond, 5 vols. (Bibliothèque de la Pléiade; Paris: Gallimard, 1959–95).

_____ 'Ébauches des *Confessions*', in *OC* i, pp. 1148–64.

RUSSELL, D. A., and Winterbottom, Michael (eds.), *Ancient Literary Criticism: The Principal Texts in New Translations* (Oxford: Clarendon Press, 1972).

SAINT-CHÉRON, ALEXANDRE DE, 'Philosophie de l'art: la vie poétique et la vie privée', *L'Artiste*, 4/24 (1832), pp. 269–71.

SAINTE-BEUVE, CHARLES-AUGUSTIN, *Vie, poésies et pensées de Joseph Delorme* [1829], ed. Gérald Antoine (Paris: Nouvelles Éditions latines, 1957).

_____ *Volupté* [1834], ed. André Guyaux (Collection Folio; Paris: Gallimard, 1986).

_____ *Portraits littéraires* [1836–46], ed. Gérald Antoine (Bouquins; Paris: R. Laffont, 1993).

_____ *Portraits de femmes* [1844], ed. Gérald Antoine (Collection Folio; Paris: Gallimard, 1998).

_____ *Portraits contemporains* [1846], rev. edn. (Paris: Didier, 1855).

_____ 'Chateaubriand jugé par un ami intime en 1803', in id., *Nouveaux lundis*, pp. 1–33.

_____ *Nouveaux lundis*, 4th edn., 13 vols. (Paris: Calmann Lévy, 1883–6).

_____ *Mes poisons: cahiers intimes inédits*, ed. Victor Giraud (Paris: Plon-Nourrit, 1926).

_____ *Correspondance générale*, ed. Jean Bonnerot and Alain Bonnerot, 19 vols. (Paris: Stock, 1935).

_____ *Œuvres*, ed. Maxime Leroy, vol. i (Bibliothèque de la Pléiade; Paris: Gallimard, 1949).

_____ *Pour la critique*, ed. José-Luis Diaz and Annie Prassoloff (Folio/Essais; Paris: Gallimard, 1992).

Sainte-Beuve et la critique littéraire contemporaine: actes du colloque tenu à Liège du 6 au 8 octobre 1969, ed. Claudette Delhez-Sarlet and André Vandegans (Paris: Société d'édition 'Les Belles Lettres', 1972).

SAINT-VICTOR, PIERRE DE, 'Le Concept de littérature dans l'*Encyclopédie*', *French Review*, 44 (1970–1), pp. 1057–66.

SAISSELIN, RÉMY G., 'Genius', in id., *The Rule of Reason and the Ruses of the Heart: A Philosophical Dictionary of Classical French Criticism, Critics, and Aesthetic Issues* (Cleveland: Press of Case Western Reserve University, 1970), pp. 89–95.

SALWAK, DALE (ed.), *The Literary Biography: Problems and Solutions* (Iowa City: University of Iowa Press; Basingstoke: Macmillan, 1996).

SANGSUE, DANIEL, *Le Récit excentrique: Gautier—de Maistre—Nerval—Nodier* (Paris: J. Corti, 1987).

SARTRE, JEAN-PAUL, *La Nausée* [1939], in *Œuvres romanesques*, ed. Michel Contat and Michel Rybalka (Bibliothèque de la Pléiade; Paris: Gallimard, 1981). [Trans. Robert Baldick, *Nausea* (Harmondsworth: Penguin, 1965).]

_____ *Baudelaire* (Essais; Paris: Gallimard, 1947). [Trans. Martin Turnell, *Baudelaire* (London: Horizon, 1949).]

_____ *Qu'est-ce que la littérature? Situations, II* (Paris: Gallimard, 1947). [Trans. Bernard Frechtman, *What is Literature?* (London: Harper & Row, 1965).]

_____ 'De la vocation d'écrivain' [1950], in Contat and Rybalka (eds.), *Les Écrits de Sartre* [1970], pp. 694–8.

SARTRE, JEAN-PAUL, *Saint Genet, comédien et martyr* (Paris: Gallimard, 1952). [Trans. Bernard Frechtman, *Saint Genet* (London: W. H. Allen, 1964).]

—— *Les Mots* (1960; Collection Folio; Paris: Gallimard, 1972). [Trans. Irene Clephane, *Words* (Harmondsworth: Penguin, 1964).]

—— *Situations, IX* (Paris: Gallimard, 1972).

—— *Situations, X* (Paris: Gallimard, 1976).

—— 'L'Engagement de Mallarmé [ed. M. Sicard]', *Obliques*, 18–19 (1979), pp. 169–94.

—— *Carnets de la drôle de guerre: septembre 1939–mars 1940*, ed. Arlette Elkaïm Sartre (Paris: Gallimard, 1995).

SCHAEFFER, GÉRALD, *Une double lecture de Gérard de Nerval: 'Les Illuminés' et Les 'Filles du feu'* (Neuchâtel: Éditions de la Baconnière, 1977).

SCHAEFFER, JEAN-MARIE, *L'Art de l'âge moderne: l'esthétique et la philosophie de l'art du XVIIIe siècle à nos jours* (Paris: Gallimard, 1992).

—— *Les Célibataires de l'art: pour une esthétique sans mythes* (Paris: Gallimard, 1996).

SCHLANGER, JUDITHE, *Les Métaphores de l'organisme* (Paris: J. Vrin, 1971).

—— *La Vocation* (Paris: Éditions du Seuil, 1997).

SCHLUMBERGER, JEAN, '*Vie de Disraëli*, par André Maurois', *Nouvelle Revue française*, 166 (1927), pp. 101–3.

SCHOLAR, RICHARD, *The Je-ne-sais-quoi in Early Modern Europe: Encounters with a Certain Something* (Oxford: Oxford University Press, 2005).

SCHULTE-SASSE, JOCHEN, and HORNE, HAYNES (eds.), *Theory as Practice: A Critical Anthology of Early German Romantic Writings* (Minneapolis: University of Minnesota Press, 1997).

SCHWOB, MARCEL, *Cœur double, Mimes* [1891, 1893], ed. Hubert Juin (Paris: Union générale d'éditions, 1979).

—— *Les Œuvres complètes de Marcel Schwob (1867–1905)*, ed. Pierre Champion, 10 vols. (Paris: François Bernouard, 1927–30).

—— *Œuvres*, ed. Alexandre Gefen et al. (Paris: Les Belles Lettres, 2002).

—— *Livre de Monelle* [1894], in *Œuvres*.

—— *Spicilège* [1896], in *Œuvres*.

—— *Vies imaginaires* [1896], in *Œuvres*. [Trans. Iain White, *The King in the Golden Mask and Other Writings* (Manchester: Carcanet, 1985).]

SCRIVEN, MICHAEL, *Sartre's Existential Biographies* (London: Macmillan, 1984).

SEGAL, NAOMI, *André Gide: Pederasty and Pedagogy* (Oxford: Clarendon Press, 1998).

SEVERUS, SULPICIUS, *Vie de saint Martin*, ed. Jacques Fontaine, 3 vols. (Paris: Éditions du Cerf, 1967).

SGARD, JEAN, 'Problèmes théoriques de la biographie', in *L'Histoire au dix-huitième siècle: colloque d'Aix-en-Provence 1er, 2 et 3 mai 1975* (Aix-en-Provence: Edisud, 1980).

SHERINGHAM, MICHAEL, *French Autobiography: Devices and Desires* (Oxford: Clarendon Press, 1993).

Shorter Oxford English Dictionary 3rd rev. edn., eds. C. T. Onions et al., 2 vols. (Oxford: Clarendon Press, 1968).

SHUKMAN, ANN, and O'TOOLE, L. M., 'A Contextual Glossary of Formalist Terminology', in L. M. O'Toole and Ann Shukman (eds. and trans.), *Russian Poetics in Translation*, vol. iv: *Formalist Theory* (Oxford: Holdan Books, 1977), pp. 13–48.

SIMON, ROLAND H., *Orphée médusé: autobiographies de Michel Leiris* (Lausanne: L'Âge d'Homme, 1984).

SINGER, ALAN, and DUNN, ALLEN (eds.), *Literary Aesthetics: A Reader* (Oxford: Blackwell, 2000).

SMITH, ROBERT, *Derrida and Autobiography: Literature, Culture, Theory* (Cambridge: Cambridge University Press, 1995).

SOLLERS, PHILIPPE, *Logiques* (Paris: Éditions du Seuil, 1968).

_____ *La Guerre du goût* (Paris: Gallimard, 1994).

SOURIAU, ÉTIENNE, 'L'Œuvre d'art en tant que personne', in Ignace Meyerson (ed.), *Problèmes de la personne: exposés et discussions* (Paris: Mouton, 1973), pp. 331–45.

STAËL, MADAME DE, *De la littérature considérée dans ses rapports avec les institutions sociales* [1800], ed. Axel Blaeschke (Classiques Garnier; Paris: Garnier, 1998). [Trans. Morroe Berger, *Madame de Staël on Politics, Literature, and National Character* (London: Sidgwick & Jackson, 1964).]

_____ *De l'Allemagne* [1813], ed. Simone Balayé, 2 vols. (Paris: Garnier-Flammarion, 1968).

_____ 'Lettres sur les ouvrages et le caractère de J.-J. Rousseau (1788)', in id., *Œuvres de jeunesse*, ed. Simone Balayé and John Claiborne Isbell (Paris: Éditions Desjonquières, 1997), pp. 33–99.

STAROBINSKI, JEAN, 'Mme de Staël et la définition de la littérature', *Nouvelle Revue française*, 28 (1966), pp. 1045–59.

_____ *Jean-Jacques Rousseau: la transparence et l'obstacle: suivi de, Sept essais sur Rousseau*, rev. edn. (Bibliothèque des idées; Paris: Gallimard, 1971).

_____ 'Critique et principe d'autorité (Madame de Staël et Rousseau)', in *Mouvements premiers: études critiques offertes à Georges Poulet* (Paris: J. Corti, 1972), pp. 87–106.

STEAD, EVANGHELIA, 'Marcel Schwob et les Élizabéthains', in *Fictions biographiques, XIXᵉ–XXIᵉ siècles, 11–14 May 2004, Université Stendhal, Grenoble 3*, ed. Anne-Geneviève Chignard et al. (Toulouse: Presses universitaires de Toulouse Le Mirail, 2006).

STEINMETZ, JEAN-LUC, *Mallarmé: l'absolu au jour le jour* (Paris: Fayard, 1998).

STIERLE, KARLHEINZ, 'L'Histoire comme exemple, l'exemple comme histoire: contribution à la pragmatique et à la poétique des textes narratifs', *Poétique*, 10 (1972), pp. 176–98.

STRACHEY, LYTTON, *Eminent Victorians: Cardinal Manning, Florence Nightingale, Dr Arnold, General Gordon* (London: Chatto & Windus, 1928).

_____ *Landmarks in French Literature* (London: Chatto & Windus, 1948).

STURROCK, JOHN, *The Language of Autobiography: Studies in the First Person Singular* (Cambridge: Cambridge University Press, 1993).

TADIÉ, JEAN-YVES, *Proust et le roman: essai sur les formes et techniques du roman dans 'À la recherche du temps perdu'* (1971; Collection Tel; Paris: Gallimard, 1995).

_____ *Portrait de l'artiste: de Carlyle à Proust: An Inaugural Lecture Delivered Before the University of Oxford on 22 February 1990* (Oxford: Clarendon Press, 1990).

_____ *Marcel Proust: biographie* (Paris: Gallimard, 1996).

THIBAUDET, ALBERT, 'Au pays de la biographie romancée', in id., *Réflexions sur la littérature, II* (Paris: Gallimard, 1941).

THOMAS, CHANTAL, 'L'Allée Marcel-Proust', in *Le Biographique = Poétique*, 63 (1985) [special issue], pp. 301–11.

Thomas à Kempis, *The Imitation of Christ* [1418], ed. William C. Creasy (Macon, Ga.: Mercer University Press, 1989).

TODOROV, TZVETAN, *La Notion de littérature, et autre essais* (Collection Points; Paris: Éditions du Seuil, 1987).

TREMBLEY, GEORGE, *Marcel Schwob: faussaire de la nature* (Geneva: Droz, 1969).

TROTTEIN, SERGE, et al., *L'Esthétique naît-elle au XVIIIᵉ siècle? Débats philosophiques* (Paris: Presses universitaires de France, 2000).

VALÉRY, PAUL, *Variété* (Paris: Gallimard, 1924).

VAPEREAU, GUSTAVE, *Dictionnaire universel des contemporains contenant toutes les personnes notables de la France et des pays étrangers: ouvrage rédigé et tenu à jour avec le concours d'écrivains de tous les pays* [1858], 6th edn. (Paris: Hachette, 1893).

VASARI, GIORGIO, *The Lives of the Artists*, ed. and trans. Julia Conaway Bondanella and Peter E. Bondanella (Oxford: Oxford University Press, 1998).

VAUVENARGUES, *Introduction à la connaissance de l'esprit humain* (Paris: Flammarion, 1981).

VERLAINE, PAUL, *Œuvres complètes de Paul Verlaine* (Paris: Léon Vanier, 1904).

—— *Œuvres en prose complètes*, ed. Jacques Borel (Bibliothèque de la Pléiade; Paris: Gallimard, 1972).

—— *Les Poètes maudits* [1884–8], in *Œuvres en prose complètes*.

—— *Vingt-sept biographies de poètes et de littérateurs*, in *Œuvres en prose complètes*.

VIALA, ALAIN, *Naissance de l'écrivain: sociologie de la littérature à l'âge classique* (Paris: Éditions de Minuit, 1985).

VIART, DOMINIQUE, 'Les "fictions-critiques" de Pierre Michon', in *Pierre Michon, l'écriture absolue*, ed. Castiglione [2002], pp. 203–19.

—— 'L'Imagination biographique dans la littérature française des années 1980–90', in Michael Bishop and Christopher Elson (eds.), *French Prose in 2000* (Amsterdam: Rodopi, 2002), pp. 15–33.

—— *'Vies minuscules' de Pierre Michon* (Foliothèque; Paris: Gallimard, 2004).

VIEGNES, MICHEL, 'Marcel Schwob: une écriture plurielle', in Berg and Vadé (eds.), *Marcel Schwob, d'hier et d'aujourd'hui* [2002], pp. 242–56.

VIGNY, ALFRED DE, *Stello* (1832; Paris and New York: Nelson, n.d.).

VOLTAIRE, *Œuvres complètes de Voltaire*, ed. Charles Lahure (Paris: Hachette, 1859–62).

—— *Œuvres complètes*, ed. A. J. Q. Beuchot, rev. edn., vol. xix (Paris: Garnier, 1879).

VORAGINE, JACOBUS DE, *The Golden Legend: Readings on the Saints* [1275], ed. William Granger Ryan (Princeton: Princeton University Press, 1993).

—— *La Légende dorée*, ed. Gustave Brunet (Classiques Garnier; Paris: Garnier, 1923).

WARDMAN, ALAN, *Plutarch's Lives* (London: Elek, 1974).

WELLEK, RENÉ, *A History of Modern Criticism: 1750–1950*, vol. ii: *The Romantic Age* (1955; Cambridge: Cambridge University Press, 1983).

—— *Discriminations: Further Concepts of Criticism* (New Haven: Yale University Press, 1970).

WHEELER, KATHLEEN M. (ed.), *German Aesthetic and Literary Criticism* (Cambridge: Cambridge University Press, 1984).

WHITE, EDMUND, *Genet* (London: Chatto & Windus, 1993).

WILD, FRANCINE, *Naissance du genre des ana: 1574–1712* (Paris: H. Champion, 2001).

WILLIAMS, HUNTINGTON, *Rousseau and Romantic Autobiography* (Oxford: Oxford University Press, 1983).

WILLIAMS, RAYMOND, *Keywords: A Vocabulary of Culture and Society* (London: Fontana, 1976).

WIMSATT, W. K., Jr., and BEARDSLEY, MONROE C., *The Verbal Icon: Studies in the Meaning of Poetry* (Lexington: University of Kentucky Press, 1954).

WRIGHT, BARBARA, and SCOTT, DAVID H. T., *Baudelaire: La Fanfarlo and Le Spleen de Paris* (London: Grant & Cutler, 1984).

Writing Lives: Sartre, Beauvoir & (Auto)biography = *L'Esprit créateur*, 29/4 (1989) [special issue].

ZELDIN, THEODORE, *France, 1848–1945: Anxiety and Hypocrisy* (Oxford: Oxford University Press, 1981).

ZEMEK, THEODORA, 'Mme de Staël et l'esprit national', *Dix-huitième siècle*, 14 (1982), pp. 89–103.

ZILSEL, EDGAR, *Le Génie: histoire d'une notion, de l'antiquité à la renaissance* [1926], trans. Michel Thévenaz, with a preface by Nathalie Heinich (Paris: Éditions de Minuit, 1993).

ZOLA, ÉMILE, *L'Œuvre* [1886], ed. Henri Mitterand (Collection Folio; Paris: Gallimard, 1983).

ZUMTHOR, PAUL, *Essai de poétique mediévale* (Paris: Éditions du Seuil, 1972).

Index